ENCYCLOPEDIA OF TRANSITIONAL JUSTICE, VOLUME 2

This comprehensive three-volume reference work collects and summarizes the wealth of information available in the field of transitional justice. Transitional justice is an emerging domain of inquiry that has gained importance with the regime changes in Latin America after the 1970s, the collapse of the European and Soviet communist regimes in 1989 and 1991, and the Arab revolutions of 2011, among others. The *Encyclopedia of Transitional Justice*, which offers 287 entries written by 166 scholars and practitioners drawn from diverse jurisdictions, includes detailed country studies; entries on transitional justice institutions and organizations; descriptions of transitional justice methods, processes, and practices; examinations of key debates and controversies; and a glossary of relevant terms and concepts. The *Encyclopedia*'s accessible style will appeal to a broad audience interested in understanding how different countries have reckoned with post-conflict justice.

Lavinia Stan is an Associate Professor of Political Science at St. Francis Xavier University, Canada. She is regional editor for Europe for the peer-reviewed *Women's Studies International Forum* (since 2010), a member of the Scientific Council of the Institute for the Investigation of Communist Crimes and the Memory of Romania Exile (in Bucharest, since 2010), a member of the Social Science Adjudicating Commission of the Romanian Ministry of Education (in Bucharest, since 2011), and a member of the editorial boards of eleven scholarly journals in Europe. Her books include *Church, State, and Democracy in Expanding Europe* (coauthored with Lucian Turcescu); *1989–2009: Incredibila aventura a democratiei dupa comunism* (coedited with Lucian Turcescu); *Transitional Justice in Eastern Europe and the Former Soviet Union: Reckoning with the Communist Past*; *Religion and Politics in Post-Communist Romania* (coauthored with Lucian Turcescu); *Leaders and Laggards: Governance, Civicness and Ethnicity in Post-Communist Romania*; and *Romania in Transition*.

Nadya Nedelsky is an Associate Professor of International Studies at Macalester College in Saint Paul, Minnesota. She is the author of *Defining the Sovereign Community: National Identity, Individual Rights, and Minority Membership in the Czech and Slovak Republics*; numerous chapters in edited volumes on transitional justice; articles in the journals *Ethnic and Racial Studies, Ethnicities, Nations and Nationalism,* and *Theory and Society*; and the national report on the Czech and Slovak Republics commissioned by the European Commission Directorate General of Justice, Freedom and Security titled *How the Memory of Crimes Committed by Totalitarian Regimes in Europe Is Dealt with in the Member States*.

Encyclopedia of Transitional Justice

VOLUME 2

Edited by

Lavinia Stan
St. Francis Xavier University

Nadya Nedelsky
Macalester College

CAMBRIDGE
UNIVERSITY PRESS

32 Avenue of the Americas, New York NY 10013-2473, USA

Cambridge University Press is part of the University of Cambridge.

It furthers the University's mission by disseminating knowledge in the pursuit of
education, learning and research at the highest international levels of excellence.

www.cambridge.org
Information on this title: www.cambridge.org/9780521196246

© Cambridge University Press 2013

This publication is in copyright. Subject to statutory exception
and to the provisions of relevant collective licensing agreements,
no reproduction of any part may take place without the written
permission of Cambridge University Press.

First published 2013

A catalogue record for this publication is available from the British Library

Library of Congress Cataloguing in Publication data

Stan, Lavinia.
Encyclopedia of transitional justice / Lavinia Stan, Nadya Nedelsky.
   p.   cm.
Includes bibliographical references and index.
ISBN 978-0-521-19617-8 (hardback volume 1 : alk. paper) – ISBN 978-0-521-19624-6 (hardback
volume 2 : alk. paper) – ISBN 978-1-107-02764-0 (hardback volume 3 : alk. paper)
1. Transitional justice.   2. Political crimes and offenses. I. Nedelsky, Nadya.   II. Title.
K5250.S73   2013
340′.115–dc23   2012017960

ISBN 978-0-521-19617-8 Volume 1 Hardback
ISBN 978-0-521-19624-6 Volume 2 Hardback
ISBN 978-1-107-02764-0 Volume 3 Hardback
ISBN 978-0-521-19627-7 Three-Volume Hardback Set

Cambridge University Press has no responsibility for the persistence or accuracy of
URLs for external or third-party internet websites referred to in this publication,
and does not guarantee that any content on such websites is, or will remain, accurate
or appropriate.

Contents

Volume 1

Alphabetical List of Entries .... page vii
Thematic List of Entries xvii
About the Editors xxvii
List of Authors xxix
Preface xli

    Entries on Transitional Justice Methods, Processes, and Practices 1

    Entries on Transitional Justice Debates, Controversies, and Key
    Questions 112

    Entries on Transitional Justice Concepts and Terms 280

Index 293

Volume 2

Alphabetical List of Entries vii
Thematic List of Entries xvii

    Entries on Countries 1
Index 521

Volume 3

Alphabetical List of Entries vii
Thematic List of Entries xvii
List of Transitional Justice Institutions by Country xxvii
Timeline of Transitional Justice Institutions and Organizations xxxv

    Entries on Transitional Justice Institutions and Organizations 1
Index 493

Alphabetical List of Entries

A

Access to Secret Files (Vol. 1)
Accountability (Vol. 1)
Accountability Mechanisms (Vol. 1)
Acknowledgment (Vol. 1)
Administrative Justice (Vol. 1)
Afghanistan (Vol. 2)
Afghanistan Independent Human Rights Commission (Vol. 3)
African Union (Vol. 3)
Albania (Vol. 2)
Algeria (Vol. 2)
All-Inclusive Political Dialogue / Dialogue Inclusif Politique (Central African Republic) (Vol. 3)
Amnesty (Vol. 1)
Amnesty Commission / Comissão de Anistia (Brazil) (Vol. 3)
Apology (Vol. 1)
Archival Records as Evidence (Vol. 1)
Argentina (Vol. 2)
Armed Conflict (Vol. 1)
Art and Transitional Justice (Vol. 1)
Auratic Sites (Vol. 1)
Australia (Vol. 2)
Austria (Vol. 2)
Azerbaijan (Vol. 2)

B

Backward-Looking Justice (Vol. 1)
Bangladesh (Vol. 2)
Belgium (Vol. 2)
Bloody Sunday Inquiry / The Saville Inquiry (Northern Ireland) (Vol. 3)
Bolivia (Vol. 2)
Bosnia-Herzegovina (Vol. 2)
Brazil (Vol. 2)

Brazil: Never Again Project / Projeto Brasil: Nunca Mais (Vol. 3)
Bulgaria (Vol. 2)
Burundi (Vol. 2)

C

Cambodia (Vol. 2)
Causes of Failure of Transitional Justice (Vol. 1)
Center for the Documentation of the Consequences of Totalitarianism / Totalitārisma seku dokumentēšanas centrs (Latvia) (Vol. 3)
Central African Republic (Vol. 2)
Child Soldiers and Transitional Justice (Vol. 1)
Chile (Vol. 2)
Citizens against State Security / Grazhdani sreshtu Darzhavna Sigurnost (Bulgaria) (Vol. 3)
Class B/C War Crimes Trials (Vol. 3)
Colombia (Vol. 2)
Comfort Women (Vol. 1)
Commission for Investigation of the Events in and around Srebrenica between 10 and 19 July 1995 / Komisija za istraživanje događaja u oko Srebrenice između 10. i 19. srpnja 1995 (Bosnia-Herzegovina) (Vol. 3)
Commission for Reception, Truth and Reconciliation / Comissão de Acolhimento, Verdade e Reconciliação de Timor Leste (East Timor) (Vol. 3)
Commission for the Study and Evaluation of the Totalitarian Communist Regime in the Republic of Moldova / Comisia pentru studierea si aprecierea regimului comunist totalitar din Republica Moldova (Vol. 3)
Commission of Inquiry for Human Rights Violations in East Timor / Komisi Penyelidik Pelanggaran Hak Asasi Manusia di Timor Timur (Vol. 3)
Commission of Inquiry for the Assessment of History and Consequences of the SED Dictatorship in Germany / Enquete-Kommission Aufarbeitung von Geschichte und Folgen der SED-Diktatur in Deutschland (Vol. 3)
Commission of Inquiry into Disappearances of People in Uganda since the 25th of January 1971 from 1st July, 1974 to 2nd January, 1975 (Vol. 3)
Commission of Inquiry into Post-Election Violence, the Waki Commission (Kenya)
Commission of Inquiry into Violations of Human Rights (Uganda) (Vol. 3)
Commission of Inquiry to Locate the Persons Disappeared during the Panchayat Period (Nepal) (Vol. 3)
Commission of Latvia's Historians / Latvijas Vēsturnieku Komisija (Vol. 3)
Commission on Wartime Relocation and Internment of Civilians (United States) (Vol. 3)
Commission to Clarify Past Human Rights Violations and Acts of Violence That Have Caused the Guatemalan People to Suffer / Comision para el Esclarecimiento Histórico e las Violaciones a los Derechos Humanos y los Hechos de Violencia que han Causado Sufrimiento a la Población Guatemalteca (Vol. 3)
Commission to Counter Attempts to Falsify History at the Expense of Russian Interests / Komissiia po protivodeistviiu popytkam fal'sifikatsii istorii v ushcherb interesam Rossii (Vol. 3)

Alphabetical List of Entries

Committee for Access to the Former State Security Files, the Bonev Committee / Komissia za dostup do dokumentite na bivshata Darzhavna sigurnost, Komissiata Bonev (Bulgaria) (Vol. 3)

Committee for Disclosing the Documents and Announcing Affiliation of Bulgarian Citizens to the State Security and the Intelligence Services of the Bulgarian National Army, the Kostadinov Committee / Zakon za dustup i razkrivane na dokumentite i za obyavyavane na prinadlezhnost na bulgarski grazhdani kum Darzhavna sigurnost i razuznavatelnite sluzhbi na Bulgarskata narodna armia, Komissiata Kostadinov (Vol. 3)

Committee for Disclosing the Documents and Announcing Affiliation to the Former State Security and General Staff Intelligence Directorate, the Andreev Committee / Komissisa za razkrivane na dokumenti i ustanoviavane na prinadlezhnost kam bivshata Darzhavna sigurnost i bivsheto Razuznavatelno upravlenie na Generalnia shtab, Komissiata Andreev (Bulgaria) (Vol. 3)

Community Justice versus Transitional Justice (Vol. 1)
Compensation Packages (Vol. 1)
Complicity (Vol. 1)
Conflict (Ongoing) and Transitional Justice (Vol. 1)
Congo, Democratic Republic of the (Vol. 2)
Conspiracy of Silence (Vol. 1)
Council for Aboriginal Reconciliation (Australia) (Vol. 3)
Court Trials for Redress (Vol. 1)
Crimes against Humanity (Vol. 1)
Crimes against Peace (Vol. 1)
Criminal Adjudication (Vol. 1)
Criminal Justice (Vol. 1)
Croatia (Vol. 2)
Cuba (Vol. 2)
Cuba Archive (Vol. 3)
Czech Republic (Vol. 2)

D

Decommunization (Vol. 1)
Denmark (Vol. 2)
Determinants of Transitional Justice (Vol. 1)
Development and Transitional Justice (Vol. 1)
Due Process (Vol. 1)

E

East Timor (Vol. 2)
Ecuador (Vol. 2)
Education and Post-Conflict Transitional Justice (Vol. 1)
Efficiency of Transitional Justice (Vol. 1)
El Salvador (Vol. 2)

Equity and Reconciliation Commission / Instance Equité et Reconciliation / Hay'at al-Insaf wa al-Musalaha (Morocco) (Vol. 3)
Estonia (Vol. 2)
Estonian International Commission for the Investigation of Crimes against Humanity / Inimsusevastaste Kuritegude Uurimise Eesti Rahvusvahelise Komisjon (Vol. 3)
Ethiopia (Vol. 2)
Ethnic Cleansing (Vol. 1)
European Court of Human Rights (Vol. 3)
European Union (Vol. 3)
Ex Post Facto Issues (Vol. 1)
Extraordinary Chambers in the Courts of Cambodia (Vol. 3)

F

Fever of Atonement (Vol. 1)
Fiji (Vol. 2)
Forensic Investigations (Vol. 1)
Forgiveness, Legitimacy of (Vol. 1)
France (Vol. 2)

G

Gacaca Courts (Vol. 1)
Genocide (Vol. 1)
Genocide and Resistance Research Center of Lithuania / Lietuvos gyventojų genocido ir rezistencijos tyrimo centras (Vol. 3)
Georgia (Vol. 2)
Germany – the Communist Past (Vol. 2)
Germany – the Nazi Past (Vol. 2)
Geschichtsbewältigung / Vergangenheitsbewältigung (Vol. 1)
Ghana (Vol. 2)
Greensboro Truth and Reconciliation Commission (United States) (Vol. 3)
Guatemala (Vol. 2)

H

Haiti (Vol. 2)
Higher National De-Baathification Commission (Iraq) (Vol. 3)
Historical Injustices (Vol. 1)
History Office, Historical Archive of the Hungarian State Security / Történeti Hivatal, Állambiztonsági Szolgálatok Történeti Levéltára (Hungary) (Vol. 3)
Honduras (Vol. 2)
House of Terror Museum / Terror Haza Muzeum (Hungary) (Vol. 3)
Human Rights Violations Investigation Commission / The Oputa Panel (Nigeria) (Vol. 3)
Hungary (Vol. 2)
Hybrid Tribunals (Vol. 1)

I

Identity and Transitional Justice (Vol. 1)
Impeachment Proceedings (Juicio de Responsabilidades) against Former Dictator Luis García Meza (Bolivia) (Vol. 3)
Independent Commission of Experts / The Bergier Commission (Switzerland) (Vol. 3)
Independent Commission of Historians / Unabhängige Historikerkommission (Liechtenstein) (Vol. 3)
Independent Committee of Eminent Persons / The Volcker Committee (Switzerland) (Vol. 3)
Inquisitorial Justice (Vol. 1)
Institute for National Memory / Ústav pamäti národa (Slovakia) (Vol. 3)
Institute for the History of the 1956 Hungarian Revolution, the 1956 Institute / 1956-os Magyar Forradalom Történetének Dokumentációs és Kutatóintézete, 1956-os Intézet (Vol. 3)
Institute for the Investigation of Communist Crimes and the Memory of the Romanian Exile / Institutul de Investigare a Crimelor Comunismului și Memoria Exilului Românesc (Vol. 3)
Institute for the Study of Totalitarian Regimes and Security Services Archive / Ústav pro studium totalitních režimů/Archív bezpečnostních složek (Czech Republic) (Vol. 3)
Institute of National Remembrance – Commission for the Prosecution of Crimes against the Polish Nation / Instytut Pamięci Narodowej – Komisja Ścigania Zbrodni przeciwko Narodowi Polskiemu (Vol. 3)
Inter-diocesan Project Recovery of Historical Memory / Proyecto Interdiocesano Recuperación de la Memoria Histórica, REMHI (Guatemala) (Vol. 3)
International Center for Transitional Justice (Vol. 3)
International Coalition of Sites of Conscience (Vol. 3)
International Commission for the Evaluation of the Crimes of the Nazi and Soviet Occupation Regimes in Lithuania / Tarptautinė komisija nacių ir sovietinio okupacinio režimo nusikaltimams Lietuvoje įvertinti (Vol. 3)
International Commission of Inquiry on East Timor (Vol. 3)
International Criminal Court (Vol. 3)
International Criminal Tribunal for Rwanda (Vol. 3)
International Criminal Tribunal for the Former Yugoslavia (Vol. 3)
International Historical-Enlightenment and Human Rights Society Memorial (Soviet Union, Russia) (Vol. 3)
International Military Tribunal for the Far East (Japan) (Vol. 3)
International Presidential Commission for Studying the Holocaust in Romania / Comisia Internationala pentru Studierea Holocaustului in Romania (Vol. 3)
International Tribunals (Vol. 1)
International versus Domestic Norms and Actors (Vol. 1)
Investigative Commission on the Kidnapping and Assassination of Former National Representatives Zelmar Michelini and Héctor Gutiérrez-Ruiz / Comisión Investigadora sobre Secuestro y Asesinato Perpetrados contra los ex Legisladores Héctor Gutiérrez-Ruiz y Zelmar Michelini (Uruguay) (Vol. 3)
Investigative Commission Requested by Senator Juan Carlos Blanco Regarding His Conduct in the Ministry of External Relations in the Case of Elena Quinteros / Comisión

Investigadora Solicitada por el Señor Senador Juan Carlos Blanco Relacionada con su Actuación en el Ministerio de Relaciones Exteriores en el Caso de la Señora Elena Quinteros (Uruguay) (Vol. 3)
Iraq (Vol. 2)
Iraqi High Tribunal (Vol. 3)
Israel (Vol. 2)
Italy (Vol. 2)

J

Japan (Vol. 2)
Japan-China Joint History Research Project (Vol. 3)
Judicial versus Nonjudicial Methods (Vol. 1)
Justice Cascade (Vol. 1)

K

Kenya (Vol. 2)
Kosovo (Vol. 2)

L

Latin American Institute for Mental Health and Human Rights / Instituto Latinoamericano de Salud Mental y Derechos Humanos (Chile) (Vol. 3)
Latvia (Vol. 2)
Law of Armed Conflict / International Humanitarian Law / *ius in bello* (Vol. 1)
Liberia (Vol. 2)
Lithuania (Vol. 2)
Lustration (Vol. 1)
Lustration Court (Poland) (Vol. 3)

M

Media and Transitional Justice (Vol. 1)
Military Justice (Vol. 1)
Montenegro (Vol. 2)
Morocco (Vol. 2)
Mothers of the Plaza de Mayo / Asociacion Madres de Plaza de Mayo (Argentina) (Vol. 3)
Mozambique (Vol. 2)

N

Namibia (Vol. 2)
Naming or Not Naming Perpetrators (Vol. 1)
National Commission on Political Imprisonment and Torture, the Valech Commission / Comisión Nacional sobre Prisión Política y Tortura, Comisión Valech (Chile) (Vol. 3)

National Commission on the Disappearance of Persons / Comisión Nacional sobre la Desaparición de Personas (Argentina) (Vol. 3)
National Commission on Truth and Reconciliation, the Rettig Commission / Comisión Nacional de Verdad y Reconciliación, Comisión Rettig (Chile) (Vol. 3)
National Commissioner for the Protection of Human Rights in Honduras / Comisionado Nacional de los Derechos Humanos (Vol. 3)
National Committee for the Investigation of the Truth about the Jeju April 3 Events / Jeju Sasam Sageon Jinsang Gyumyeong mit Myeongye Hoebok Wiwonhoe (South Korea) (Vol. 3)
National Council for the Study of the Securitate Archives / Consiliul Naţional pentru Studierea Arhivelor Securităţii (Romania) (Vol. 3)
National Inquiry into the Separation of Aboriginal and Torres Strait Islander Children from Their Families / The Stolen Generations Inquiry (Australia) (Vol. 3)
National Reconciliation Commission (Ghana) (Vol. 3)
National Reparations Commission / Comisión Nacional de Resarcimiento (Guatemala) (Vol. 3)
National Truth and Justice Commission / Commission Nationale de Vérité et de Justice (Haiti) (Vol. 3)
Nepal (Vol. 2)
Netherlands (Vol. 2)
New Zealand (Vol. 2)
Nigeria (Vol. 2)
Normative Change and Transitional Justice (Vol. 1)
Northern Ireland (Vol. 2)
Nuremberg Trials (Germany) (Vol. 3)

O

Office of the Documentation and Investigation of Crimes of Communism / Úřad dokumentace a vyšetřování zločinů komunismu (Czech Republic) (Vol. 3)
Office of the Federal Commissioner Preserving the Records of the State Security Service of the Former German Democratic Republic / Bundesbeauftragte für die Unterlagen des Staatssicherheitsdienstes der ehemaligen Deutschen Demokratischen Republik (Vol. 3)
Organization of American States (Vol. 3)
Outreach and Transitional Justice (Vol. 1)

P

Pakistan (Vol. 2)
Panama (Vol. 2)
Papua New Guinea (Vol. 2)
Paraguay (Vol. 2)
Paraguay Nunca Mas (Vol. 3)
Parliamentary Investigative Commission on the Situation of Disappeared Persons and Its Causes / Comisión Investigadora Parlamentaria sobre Situación de Personas Desaparecidas y Hechos que la Motivaron (Uruguay) (Vol. 3)
Peace and Justice Service of Uruguay / El Servicio Paz y Justicia (Vol. 3)

Peace Commission / Comisión para la Paz (Uruguay) (Vol. 3)
Peru (Vol. 2)
Philippines (Vol. 2)
Poland (Vol. 2)
Political Police (Vol. 1)
Politics of History (Vol. 1)
Politics of Memory (Vol. 1)
Politics of the Past (Vol. 1)
Politics of the Present (Vol. 1)
Portugal (Vol. 2)
Presidential Commission for the Analysis of the Communist Dictatorship in Romania, the Tismaneanu Commission / Comisia Prezidenţială pentru Analiza Dictaturii Comuniste din România, Comisia Tismăneanu (Vol. 3)
Presidential Commission of Inquiry into Involuntary Removal and Disappearance of Certain Persons (All Island) (Sri Lanka) (Vol. 3)
Presidential Commissions of Inquiry into the Involuntary Removal or Disappearance of Persons (Sri Lanka) (Vol. 3)
Presidential Truth Commission on Suspicious Deaths / Uimunsa Jinsang Gyumyeong Wiwonhoe (South Korea) (Vol. 3)
Property Restitution (Vol. 1)
Prosecute and Punish (Vol. 1)
Purges (Vol. 1)

Q

Quantitative Social Science Methods (Vol. 1)

R

Recognition (Vol. 1)
Reforms of Military, Police, Secret Police (Vol. 1)
Rehabilitation of Political Prisoners (Vol. 1)
Reintegration of Former Combatants (Vol. 1)
Reparations (Vol. 1)
Reparatory Justice (Vol. 1)
Repression (Vol. 1)
Restorative Justice (Vol. 1)
Restorative versus Retributive Justice (Vol. 1)
Retribution (Vol. 1)
Retributive Justice (Vol. 1)
Rewriting History Textbooks (Vol. 1)
Right to Truth (Vol. 1)
Romania (Vol. 2)
Rule of Law and Justice (Vol. 1)
Russia (Vol. 2)
Rwanda (Vol. 2)

S

Serbia (Vol. 2)

Serious Crimes Unit, Office of the General Prosecutor of the Republic of Timor-Leste / Unidade de Crimes Graves, Gabinete da Procuradoria-Geral da República (East Timor) (Vol. 3)

Sierra Leone (Vol. 2)

Simon Wiesenthal Center (Vol. 3)

Slovak Republic (Vol. 2)

Slovenia (Vol. 2)

South Africa (Vol. 2)

South Korea (Vol. 2)

Spain (Vol. 2)

Special Commission on the Dead and Disappeared for Political Reasons / Comissão Especial sobre Mortos e Desaparecidos Políticos (Brazil) (Vol. 3)

Special Court for Sierra Leone (Vol. 3)

Special International Crimes Office / Statsadvokaten for Særlige Internationale Straffesager (Denmark) (Vol. 3)

Special Tribunal for Lebanon / Tribunal Special pour le Liban (Vol. 3)

Sri Lanka (Vol. 2)

State Commission for the Examination of Repressive Policies Carried Out during the Occupations / Okupatsioonide repressiivpoliitika uurimise riiklik komisjon (Estonia) (Vol. 3)

Superior Responsibility for Military and Political Leaders under International Criminal Law (Vol. 1)

T

Taiwan (Vol. 2)

Theater of Violence (Vol. 1)

Torturer Problem (Vol. 1)

Transition Type (Vol. 1)

Tribunal of Opinion (Vol. 1)

Trust and Transitional Justice (Vol. 1)

Truth and Reconciliation Commission / Comisión de la Verdad y Reconciliación (Peru) (Vol. 3)

Truth and Reconciliation Commission / Commission Vérité et Réconciliation (Canada) (Vol. 3)

Truth and Reconciliation Commission (Liberia) (Vol. 3)

Truth and Reconciliation Commission of Yugoslavia / Komisija za istinu i pomirenje (Serbia and Montenegro) (Vol. 3)

Truth and Reconciliation Commission, Republic of Korea / Jinsil Hwahae-reul Wihan Gwageosa Jungri Wiwonhoe (South Korea) (Vol. 3)

Truth and Reconciliation Commission (Sierra Leone) (Vol. 3)

Truth and Reconciliation Commission (Solomon Islands) (Vol. 3)

Truth and Reconciliation Commission (South Africa) (Vol. 3)

Truth Commission / Comisión de la Verdad (Ecuador) (Vol. 3)

Truth Commission / Comisión de la Verdad (El Salvador) (Vol. 3)
Truth Commission of Panama / Comisión de la Verdad de Panamá (Vol. 3)
Truth Commissions (Vol. 1)
Truth Justice and Reconciliation Commission (Kenya) (Vol. 3)
Truth (Truth Seeking and Truth Telling) (Vol. 1)
Turkey (Vol. 2)
Twentieth Century Institute, XX. Század Intézet / Twenty-First Century Institute, XXI. Század Intézet (Hungary) (Vol. 3)

U

Ubuntu (Vol. 1)
Uganda (Vol. 2)
Ukraine (Vol. 2)
UN Sub-Commission on the Prevention of Discrimination and the Protection of Minorities (Vol. 3)
United States Holocaust Memorial Museum (Vol. 3)
Universal Jurisdiction (Vol. 1)
Unofficial Truth Projects (Vol. 1)
Uruguay (Vol. 2)

V

Venezuela (Vol. 2)
Victim Theories (Vol. 1)
Victim's Rights and Redress (Vol. 1)
Vietnam (Vol. 2)

W

Waitangi Tribunal (New Zealand) (Vol. 3)
War Crimes (Vol. 1)
War Crimes Chamber of the Court of Bosnia-Herzegovina (Vol. 3)
Wiedergutmachung (Vol. 1)
World Tribunal for Iraq (Vol. 3)

Z

Zimbabwe (Vol. 2)
Zone of Impunity (Vol. 1)

Thematic List of Entries

List of Methods, Processes, and Practices (Volume 1)

Access to Secret Files
Accountability Mechanisms
Amnesty
Apology
Compensation Packages
Court Trials for Redress
Forensic Investigations
Gacaca Courts
Hybrid Tribunals
International Tribunals
Lustration
Property Restitution
Prosecute and Punish
Purges
Quantitative Social Science Methods
Recognition
Rehabilitation of Political Prisoners
Reintegration of Former Combatants
Reparations
Retribution
Rewriting History Textbooks
Truth Commissions
Unofficial Truth Projects

List of Debates, Controversies, and Key Questions (Volume 1)

Archival Records as Evidence
Art and Transitional Justice
Causes of Failure of Transitional Justice
Child Soldiers and Transitional Justice
Community Justice versus Transitional Justice
Complicity
Conflict (Ongoing) and Transitional Justice

Determinants of Transitional Justice
Development and Transitional Justice
Due Process
Education and Post-Conflict Transitional Justice
Efficiency of Transitional Justice
Ex Post Facto Issues
Forgiveness, Legitimacy of
Identity and Transitional Justice
International versus Domestic Norms and Actors
Judicial versus Nonjudicial Methods
Media and Transitional Justice
Naming or Not Naming Perpetrators
Normative Change and Transitional Justice
Outreach and Transitional Justice
Restorative versus Retributive Justice
Rule of Law and Justice
Superior Responsibility for Military and Political Leaders under International Criminal Law
Trust and Transitional Justice
Truth (Truth Seeking and Truth Telling)
Victim Theories
Victim's Rights and Redress

Glossary of Concepts and Terms (Volume 1)

Accountability
Acknowledgment
Administrative Justice
Armed Conflict
Auratic Sites
Backward-Looking Justice
Comfort Women
Conspiracy of Silence
Crimes against Humanity
Crimes against Peace
Criminal Adjudication
Criminal Justice
Decommunization
Ethnic Cleansing
Fever of Atonement
Genocide
Geschichtsbewältigung / Vergangenheitsbewältigung
Historical Injustices
Inquisitorial Justice
Justice Cascade
Law of Armed Conflict / International Humanitarian Law / *ius in bello*
Military Justice

Political Police
Politics of History
Politics of Memory
Politics of the Past
Politics of the Present
Reforms of Military, Police, Secret Police
Reparatory Justice
Repression
Restorative Justice
Retributive Justice
Right to Truth
Theater of Violence
Torturer Problem
Transition Type
Tribunal of Opinion
Ubuntu
Universal Jurisdiction
War Crimes
Wiedergutmachung
Zone of Impunity

List of Country Studies (Volume 2)

Afghanistan
Albania
Algeria
Argentina
Australia
Austria
Azerbaijan
Bangladesh
Belgium
Bolivia
Bosnia-Herzegovina
Brazil
Bulgaria
Burundi
Cambodia
Central African Republic
Chile
Colombia
Congo, Democratic Republic of the
Croatia
Cuba
Czech Republic
Denmark
East Timor

Ecuador
El Salvador
Estonia
Ethiopia
Fiji
France
Georgia
Germany – the Communist Past
Germany – the Nazi Past
Ghana
Guatemala
Haiti
Honduras
Hungary
Iraq
Israel
Italy
Japan
Kenya
Kosovo
Latvia
Liberia
Lithuania
Montenegro
Morocco
Mozambique
Namibia
Nepal
Netherlands
New Zealand
Nigeria
Northern Ireland
Pakistan
Panama
Papua New Guinea
Paraguay
Peru
Philippines
Poland
Portugal
Romania
Russia
Rwanda
Serbia
Sierra Leone
Slovak Republic
Slovenia

South Africa
South Korea
Spain
Sri Lanka
Taiwan
Turkey
Uganda
Ukraine
Uruguay
Venezuela
Vietnam
Zimbabwe

List of Transitional Justice Institutions and Organizations (Volume 3)

Afghanistan Independent Human Rights Commission
African Union
All-Inclusive Political Dialogue / Dialogue Inclusif Politique (Central African Republic)
Amnesty Commission / Comissão de Anistia (Brazil)
Bloody Sunday Inquiry / The Saville Inquiry (Northern Ireland)
Brazil: Never Again Project / Projeto Brasil: Nunca Mais
Center for the Documentation of the Consequences of Totalitarianism / Totalitārisma seku dokumentēšanas centrs (Latvia)
Citizens against State Security / Grazhdani sreshtu Darzhavna Sigurnost (Bulgaria)
Class B/C War Crimes Trials
Commission for Investigation of the Events in and around Srebrenica between 10 and 19 July 1995 / Komisija za istraživanje događaja u oko Srebrenice između 10. i 19. srpnja 1995 (Bosnia-Herzegovina)
Commission for Reception, Truth and Reconciliation / Comissão de Acolhimento, Verdade e Reconciliação de Timor Leste (East Timor)
Commission for the Study and Evaluation of the Totalitarian Communist Regime in the Republic of Moldova / Comisia pentru studierea si aprecierea regimului comunist totalitar din Republica Moldova
Commission of Inquiry for Human Rights Violations in East Timor / Komisi Penyelidik Pelanggaran Hak Asasi Manusia di Timor Timur
Commission of Inquiry for the Assessment of History and Consequences of the SED Dictatorship in Germany / Enquete-Kommission Aufarbeitung von Geschichte und Folgen der SED-Diktatur in Deutschland
Commission of Inquiry into Disappearances of People in Uganda since the 25th of January 1971 from 1st July, 1974 to 2nd January, 1975
Commission of Inquiry into Post-Election Violence, the Waki Commission (Kenya)
Commission of Inquiry into Violations of Human Rights (Uganda)
Commission of Inquiry to Locate the Persons Disappeared during the Panchayat Period (Nepal)
Commission of Latvia's Historians / Latvijas Vēsturnieku Komisija
Commission on Wartime Relocation and Internment of Civilians (United States)

Commission to Clarify Past Human Rights Violations and Acts of Violence That Have Caused the Guatemalan People to Suffer / Comision para el Esclarecimiento Histórico e las Violaciones a los Derechos Humanos y los Hechos de Violencia que han Causado Sufrimiento a la Población Guatemalteca

Commission to Counter Attempts to Falsify History at the Expense of Russian Interests / Komissiia po protivodeistviiu popytkam fal'sifikatsii istorii v ushcherb interesam Rossii

Committee for Access to the Former State Security Files, the Bonev Committee / Komissia za dostup do dokumentite na bivshata Darzhavna sigurnost, Komissiata Bonev (Bulgaria)

Committee for Disclosing the Documents and Announcing Affiliation of Bulgarian Citizens to the State Security and the Intelligence Services of the Bulgarian National Army, the Kostadinov Committee/ Zakon za dustup i razkrivane na dokumentite i za obyavyavane na prinadlezhnost na bulgarski grazhdani kum Darzhavna sigurnost i razuznavatelnite sluzhbi na Bulgarskata narodna armia, Komissiata Kostadinov

Committee for Disclosing the Documents and Announcing Affiliation to the Former State Security and General Staff Intelligence Directorate, the Andreev Committee / Komissisa za razkrivane na dokumenti i ustanoviavane na prinadlezhnost kam bivshata Darzhavna sigurnost i bivsheto Razuznavatelno upravlenie na Generalnia shtab, Komissiata Andreev (Bulgaria)

Council for Aboriginal Reconciliation (Australia)

Cuba Archive

Equity and Reconciliation Commission / Instance Equité et Reconciliation / Hay'at al-Insaf wa al-Musalaha (Morocco)

Estonian International Commission for the Investigation of Crimes against Humanity / Inimsusevastaste Kuritegude Uurimise Eesti Rahvusvahelise Komisjon

European Court of Human Rights

European Union

Extraordinary Chambers in the Courts of Cambodia

Genocide and Resistance Research Center of Lithuania / Lietuvos gyventojų genocido ir rezistencijos tyrimo centras

Greensboro Truth and Reconciliation Commission (United States)

Higher National De-Baathification Commission (Iraq)

History Office, Historical Archive of the Hungarian State Security / Történeti Hivatal, Állambiztonsági Szolgálatok Történeti Levéltára

House of Terror Museum / Terror Haza Muzeum (Hungary)

Human Rights Violations Investigation Commission / The Oputa Panel (Nigeria)

Impeachment Proceedings (Juicio de Responsabilidades) against Former Dictator Luis García Meza (Bolivia)

Independent Commission of Experts / The Bergier Commission (Switzerland)

Independent Commission of Historians / Unabhängige Historikerkommission (Liechtenstein)

Independent Committee of Eminent Persons / The Volcker Committee (Switzerland)

Institute for National Memory / Ústav pämati národa (Slovakia)

Institute for the History of the 1956 Hungarian Revolution, the 1956 Institute / 1956-os Magyar Forradalom Történetének Dokumentációs és Kutatóintézete, 1956-os Intézet

Institute for the Investigation of Communist Crimes and the Memory of the Romanian Exile / Institutul de Investigare a Crimelor Comunismului şi Memoria Exilului Românesc

Thematic List of Entries

Institute for the Study of Totalitarian Regimes and Security Services Archive / Ústav pro studium totalitních režimů/Archív bezpečnostních složek (Czech Republic)
Institute of National Remembrance – Commission for the Prosecution of Crimes against the Polish Nation / Instytut Pamięci Narodowej – Komisja Ścigania Zbrodni przeciwko Narodowi Polskiemu
Inter-diocesan Project Recovery of Historical Memory / Proyecto Interdiocesano Recuperación de la Memoria Histórica, REMHI (Guatemala)
International Center for Transitional Justice
International Coalition of Sites of Conscience
International Commission for the Evaluation of the Crimes of the Nazi and Soviet Occupation Regimes in Lithuania / Tarptautinė komisija nacių ir sovietinio okupacinio režimo nusikaltimams Lietuvoje į vertinti
International Commission of Inquiry on East Timor
International Criminal Court
International Criminal Tribunal for Rwanda
International Criminal Tribunal for the Former Yugoslavia
International Historical-Enlightenment and Human Rights Society Memorial (Soviet Union, Russia)
International Military Tribunal for the Far East (Japan)
International Presidential Commission for Studying the Holocaust in Romania / Comisia Internationala pentru Studierea Holocaustului in Romania
Investigative Commission on the Kidnapping and Assassination of Former National Representatives Zelmar Michelini and Héctor Gutiérrez-Ruiz / Comisión Investigadora sobre Secuestro y Asesinato Perpetrados contra los ex Legisladores Héctor Gutiérrez-Ruiz y Zelmar Michelini (Uruguay)
Investigative Commission Requested by Senator Juan Carlos Blanco Regarding His Conduct in the Ministry of External Relations in the Case of Elena Quinteros / Comisión Investigadora Solicitada por el Señor Senador Juan Carlos Blanco Relacionada con su Actuación en el Ministerio de Relaciones Exteriores en el Caso de la Señora Elena Quinteros (Uruguay)
Iraqi High Tribunal
Japan-China Joint History Research Project
Latin American Institute for Mental Health and Human Rights / Instituto Latinoamericano de Salud Mental y Derechos Humanos (Chile)
Lustration Court (Poland)
Mothers of the Plaza de Mayo / Asociacion Madres de Plaza de Mayo (Argentina)
National Commission on Political Imprisonment and Torture, the Valech Commission / Comisión Nacional sobre Prisión Política y Tortura, Comisión Valech (Chile)
National Commission on the Disappearance of Persons / Comisión Nacional sobre la Desaparición de Personas (Argentina)
National Commission on Truth and Reconciliation, the Rettig Commission / Comisión Nacional de Verdad y Reconciliación, Comisión Rettig (Chile)
National Commissioner for the Protection of Human Rights in Honduras / Comisionado Nacional de los Derechos Humanos
National Committee for the Investigation of the Truth about the Jeju April 3 Events / Jeju Sasam Sageon Jinsang Gyumyeong mit Myeongye Hoebok Wiwonhoe (South Korea)

National Council for the Study of the Securitate Archives / Consiliul Național pentru Studierea Arhivelor Securității (Romania)

National Inquiry into the Separation of Aboriginal and Torres Strait Islander Children from Their Families, the Stolen Generations Inquiry (Australia)

National Reconciliation Commission (Ghana)

National Reparations Commission / Comisión Nacional de Resarcimiento (Guatemala)

National Truth and Justice Commission / Commission Nationale de Vérité et de Justice (Haiti)

Nuremberg Trials (Germany)

Office of the Documentation and Investigation of Crimes of Communism / Úřad dokumentace a vyšetřování zločinů komunismu (Czech Republic)

Office of the Federal Commissioner Preserving the Records of the State Security Service of the Former German Democratic Republic / Bundesbeauftragte für die Unterlagen des Staatssicherheitsdienstes der ehemaligen Deutschen Demokratischen Republik

Organization of American States

Paraguay Nunca Mas

Parliamentary Investigative Commission on the Situation of Disappeared Persons and Its Causes / Comisión Investigadora Parlamentaria sobre Situación de Personas Desaparecidas y Hechos que la Motivaron (Uruguay)

Peace and Justice Service of Uruguay / El Servicio Paz y Justicia

Peace Commission / Comisión para la Paz (Uruguay)

Presidential Commission for the Analysis of the Communist Dictatorship in Romania, the Tismaneanu Commission / Comisia Prezidențială pentru Analiza Dictaturii Comuniste din România, Comisia Tismăneanu

Presidential Commission of Inquiry into Involuntary Removal and Disappearance of Certain Persons (All Island) (Sri Lanka)

Presidential Commissions of Inquiry into the Involuntary Removal or Disappearance of Persons (Sri Lanka)

Presidential Truth Commission on Suspicious Deaths / Uimunsa Jinsang Gyumyeong Wiwonhoe (South Korea)

Serious Crimes Unit, Office of the General Prosecutor of the Republic of Timor-Leste / Unidade de Crimes Graves, Gabinete da Procuradoria-Geral da República (East Timor)

Simon Wiesenthal Center

Special Commission on the Dead and Disappeared for Political Reasons / Comissão Especial sobre Mortos e Desaparecidos Políticos (Brazil)

Special Court for Sierra Leone

Special International Crimes Office / Statsadvokaten for Særlige Internationale Straffesager (Denmark)

Special Tribunal for Lebanon / Tribunal Special pour le Liban

State Commission for the Examination of Repressive Policies Carried Out during the Occupations / Okupatsioonide repressiivpoliitika uurimise riiklik komisjon (Estonia)

Truth and Reconciliation Commission / Comisión de la Verdad y Reconciliación (Peru)

Truth and Reconciliation Commission / Commission Vérité et Réconciliation (Canada)

Truth and Reconciliation Commission (Liberia)

Truth and Reconciliation Commission of Yugoslavia / Komisija za istinu i pomirenje (Serbia and Montenegro)

Thematic List of Entries

Truth and Reconciliation Commission, Republic of Korea / Jinsil Hwahae-reul Wihan Gwageosa Jungri Wiwonhoe (South Korea)
Truth and Reconciliation Commission (Sierra Leone)
Truth and Reconciliation Commission (Solomon Islands)
Truth and Reconciliation Commission (South Africa)
Truth Commission / Comisión de la Verdad (Ecuador)
Truth Commission / Comisión de la Verdad (El Salvador)
Truth Commission of Panama / Comisión de la Verdad de Panamá
Truth Justice and Reconciliation Commission (Kenya)
Twentieth Century Institute, XX. Század Intézet / Twenty-First Century Institute, XXI. Század Intézet (Hungary)
UN Sub-Commission on the Prevention of Discrimination and the Protection of Minorities
United States Holocaust Memorial Museum
Waitangi Tribunal (New Zealand)
War Crimes Chamber of the Court of Bosnia-Herzegovina
World Tribunal for Iraq

Country Studies

Afghanistan

Transitional justice has been marginalized in Afghanistan's state-building process. The aftermath of the U.S.-led military intervention in Afghanistan was marked by victors' justice: while the Taliban were driven away, commanders and factional leaders with known records of human rights violations and war crimes were included into the government with no attention to accountability. As a result of international pressure, the Afghan government did adopt a five-point Action Plan for Peace, Justice and Reconciliation, popularly called the Transitional Justice Action Plan, in December 2005. However, the Action Plan was not implemented and, a year after its entry into force, the Afghan Parliament adopted a bill granting blanket amnesty for all those involved in the Afghan conflicts. The Amnesty Bill became law in December 2008. The bill remains a clear message that impunity rather than justice prevails in Afghanistan.

The Repressive Past

Afghanistan emerged in the late nineteenth century as part of the British colonial empire and became independent in 1919. Governance ever since has been characterized by attempts to balance power between central governments based in Kabul and regional power holders and between movements to modernize and efforts to maintain customary systems. Poverty and lack of education have further complicated the situation. Throughout its modern history, these internal tensions, which often manifested themselves along regional, ethnic, and tribal lines, have been further compounded and manipulated by external actors. Afghanistan's relationship with its neighbors, and especially the controversy over the Durand Line, the state border that crosses through the Pashtun areas of Afghanistan and Pakistan, is a continuing source of unrest and conflict. Afghanistan has been a battleground on which several international conflicts, including the Cold War and the war on terror, have been fought.

The recent history of conflict in Afghanistan can be divided into five major phases: (1) the communist revolution and People's Democratic Party of Afghanistan (PDPA) government (1978–1979); (2) the Soviet invasion and rule of Afghanistan (1979–1989); (3) the fall of the Mohammad Najibullah government and the civil-war period (1989–1996); (4) the Taliban regime (1996–2001); and (5) the post-Taliban period (2001–present). These phases will be discussed in turn.

(1) The modern conflict in Afghanistan started with the communist revolution of April 27, 1978. Communist politics resonated poorly in Afghanistan, a country of intensely traditional and religious values. In response to the PDPA, anticommunist guerrilla groups emerged from training camps in Pakistan. The PDPA responded by arresting and torturing alleged opposition members. The period of PDPA rule remains poorly documented, but the existing evidence suggests that disappearances, summary executions, and massacres were widespread.

(2) To avoid increasing anarchy and conflict at its southern border and to support the communist movement, the Soviet Union invaded Afghanistan on December 24, 1979. Under a Soviet-led and -supported communist government, summary executions diminished, but arrests, disappearances, massacres, and indiscriminate bombings of rural areas continued. The notorious Afghan intelligence service, established during the Soviet period, was responsible for many arrests, torture, and executions.

Resistance to the Soviet invasion was largely organized along regional, and therefore ethnic, lines. The most successful leaders fighting the "holy war" for the liberation of Afghanistan, the mujahidin (holy warriors), gained power during this period, and many of them remain important figures in Afghan politics today. By channeling funds and support to the mujahidin, Pakistan, Iran, Saudi Arabia, and the United States managed to inject their agendas into the Afghan resistance. The end of the Cold War and the Geneva Accords of 1988 forced Soviet forces to withdraw by the following year, but by 1989 the war had left a million dead and created the world's largest refugee crisis, with approximately 6 million refugees in Iran and Pakistan.

(3) The government established after the Soviet withdrawal survived for three years, at which point President Najibullah was overthrown. He was eventually executed by the Taliban. When the Cold War ended, the United States and the West lost interest in Afghanistan. Civil war and a state of near-anarchy ensued as Afghanistan divided into a number of semiautonomous regions along mainly ethnic lines, and different factions fought for control of Kabul. It is only during the civil war that the conflict was brought to Kabul, with disastrous consequences. For example, in 1994, it is estimated that 10,000 people died from direct shelling by warlords trying to gain control of the capital.

(4) The Taliban, mostly Pashtuns from the Afghan refugee camps in Pakistan, formed in reaction to the lawlessness and abuses of the civil war period. Pakistan played a critical role in building the Taliban into a formidable military force. Their aim was to establish a fundamentalist Islamic government in Afghanistan. Taliban ideology resonated with the religious and cultural mores of the Pashtuns in southern Afghanistan. By 1998, the Taliban controlled 90 percent of Afghanistan. Although the Taliban brought much-craved security to the rural population (albeit through harsh diktat), their policies were vehemently anti-Shia and their behavior in most areas was that of an occupying force. The hard-line Taliban government progressively limited the rights and freedoms of Afghans, partly by enforcing strict dress codes for women and men, forbidding various forms of cultural expression, and barring women from education and employment. The Taliban enforced their decrees through the Department for Promotion of Virtue and Prevention of Vice with punishments that included floggings and public executions. Fighting continued

throughout the country between the Taliban and other ethnic factions, resulting in widespread civilian casualties and numerous massacres.

The Taliban also provided a refuge for Osama bin Laden and al-Qaeda. The attacks on New York and Washington, DC, on September 11, 2001 refocused world attention on Afghanistan. The United States launched the war on terror by attacking Afghanistan with the aim of overthrowing the Taliban regime and its terrorist allies. Coalition attacks from the air were supported on the ground by various Afghan factions, known as the Northern Alliance (many of whom were former mujahidin leaders).

(5) While the United States and its allies were fighting the Taliban, and with much of Afghanistan's territory falling under control of the Northern Alliance, international actors, along with select Afghan delegates, convened in Bonn to establish the Afghan Interim Authority (AIA) and draw a road map for state building. The Bonn Agreement set benchmarks to establish key institutions of a sovereign and democratic state. The Taliban were not included in these talks.

Security has remained a vital concern during state building. Since late 2005, security has deteriorated rapidly, first in the south and southeast of the country and then the west and parts of the north of Afghanistan. Driven out by U.S. forces and their allies in 2001, the Taliban regained strength with support from Pakistan, regrouped, and increased their attacks against the Afghan government and international agencies in Afghanistan. Since 2007, security incidents, including roadside bombs and suicide attacks, increased in the Kabul region and in the north and west of the country. The detention practices of U.S. forces, civilian casualties, and the destruction of property as a result of international military operations also negatively affected the perception of the international military presence.

In 2010, efforts to promote reintegration and reconciliation started with the organization of a government-led Peace Jirga (grand assembly) at which the Afghanistan Peace and Reconciliation Program (APRP) was approved. However, the trust-building efforts between the government and the Taliban came to a halt when the leader of the High Peace Council that oversees the implementation of the APRP was killed in a suicide attack in 2011. While the Afghan government's efforts to promote peace remain in flux, the United States has pushed forward with efforts to enable the Taliban to open an office in Qatar.

Transitional Justice

The fragile peace that prevailed between phases of the conflicts in Afghanistan has never led to accountability for past crimes. The Bonn Agreement of 2001 was not a peace agreement, but rather an agreement between select Afghan leaders, including the Northern Alliance commanders who had supported the U.S.-led military intervention in Afghanistan. As a result, many known human rights abusers were brought into the political fold. Nevertheless, the fall of the Taliban regime and the establishment of a transitional government in late 2001 made it possible to start a discussion about Afghanistan's brutal history of conflict and human rights abuse. The Bonn Agreement left this possibility open by avoiding an amnesty provision and creating a national human rights body, the Afghanistan Independent Human Rights Commission (AIHRC).

A mechanism for transitional justice in Afghanistan was not established as part of the Bonn Agreement. Instead, nascent attempts to develop a transitional justice process in Afghanistan have included: (1) national consultations by the AIHRC and documentation of human rights violations and war crimes committed during all the phases of the Afghan conflict; (2) the development of the National Action Plan for Peace, Reconciliation, and Justice (the Transitional Justice Action Plan); and (3) mobilization of civil society. In addition, (4) some of the vetting processes have included criteria relating to past crimes, and (5) a few war crimes trials have been conducted in Afghanistan and using universal jurisdiction in the Netherlands and the United Kingdom. Preliminary analysis by the International Criminal Court is ongoing.

National Consultations and Documentation

The AIHRC has been a driving force behind transitional justice in Afghanistan. It was given a mandate to address transitional justice both through the Bonn Agreement and the presidential decree establishing the Commission. In 2004, the AIHRC conducted national consultations to identify how Afghans wanted past violations to be addressed. Through its central and regional offices the AIHRC documented the views of more than 6,000 ordinary Afghans from thirty-two of thirty-four provinces and from refugee populations in Iran and Pakistan. Its report, titled A Call for Justice, was published in January 2005.

The consultation showed that ordinary people perceive that impunity is entrenched in Afghanistan, and that perpetrators have attained positions of power despite their continued involvement in human rights violations. The report suggests an urgent need to break with the past and recommends a way forward, including an integrated approach to build trust in Afghanistan's institutions and recognize victims' needs and wishes. The consultation showed strong public support for holding criminals accountable for past crimes through prosecution. Removing war criminals from positions of power (vetting) was highlighted as the next-best option.

In the interim, attempts to document violations went forward. Early suggestions for the establishment of a commission of inquiry were not implemented. In support of the AIHRC's consultation process and future documentation efforts, the United Nations Office of the High Commissioner for Human Rights (OHCHR) undertook mapping of gross human rights violations and war crimes in Afghanistan from 1978 to 2001, on the basis of UN and other existing open-source material. In January 2005, High Commissioner for Human Rights Louise Arbour traveled to Kabul to support the launch of the AIHRC's Call for Justice report. During the visit, Arbour met with President Karzai and gave a copy of the OHCHR's mapping report to the president. The report, which has never been published, was also given to the AIHRC as a resource for its documentation efforts. The AIHRC has undertaken a massive effort to document war crimes in Afghanistan from 1978 to 2001. It has also documented war crimes and human rights violation from 2001 onward. Other existing documentation includes the Afghanistan Justice Project's (AJP) comprehensive report, Casting Shadows.

The National Action Plan for Peace, Reconciliation, and Justice

The Action Plan for Peace, Reconciliation, and Justice was drafted on the basis of the recommendations included in the Call for Justice report. The drafting committee included representatives of the president's office, the AIHRC, and the UN Assistance Mission for Afghanistan (UNAMA) and was supported by the European Union and the Netherlands. The Action Plan was hotly debated and narrowly adopted. The government adopted it in December 2005, just days before the OHCHR national conference on truth seeking and reconciliation. Included as a benchmark in the Afghanistan Compact and the Afghanistan National Development Strategy (ANDS), the current agreements between the Afghan government and its international partners, it has become one of the most important guidelines for the country's transitional justice process.

The Action Plan includes five measures aimed at ensuring that Afghanistan becomes a stable, lawful, and democratic state: (1) according dignity to victims, including through commemoration and the building of memorials; (2) vetting human rights abusers from positions of power and encouraging institutional reform; (3) truth seeking; (4) reconciliation; and (5) expressing opposition to an amnesty and establishing a task force to make recommendations for an accountability mechanism.

Adopting and publicly launching the Action Plan ran into significant delays, and its implementation has been slow. The president and the cabinet favored some elements, but the action on criminal accountability was controversial. Although widely favored by international actors, establishment of an advisory panel on senior appointments received little support from within the government. Awareness of the plan within the ministries responsible for its implementation remains weak. The passage of the amnesty resolution was a severe political blow to the Action Plan. The adoption of the APRP has pushed the Action Plan further off the agenda.

Although the implementation of the Action Plan has faced and will continue to face challenges, the fact that the Afghan government made a formal commitment to transitional justice is important. The Action Plan will continue to provide a framework for the civil society and the international community's support for transitional justice, and it is a tool that civil society can use to pressure the government.

Mobilization of Civil Society

The AIHRC has become the informal leader on transitional justice and has developed its work in the area with considerable success. Its transitional justice unit has about thirty staff members in eleven offices. To support the implementation of the Action Plan, the AIHRC has undertaken a comprehensive mapping exercise covering the 1978–2001 period. The conflict mapping was finalized in 2009.

In early 2009, the AIHRC and partner organizations organized a strategic conference on transitional justice that resulted in the establishment of the Transitional Justice Coordination Group. The group consists of mainly Kabul-based civil society organizations and victims' groups working on transitional justice. Although civil society organizations have cooperated on an ad hoc basis, the establishment of the Transitional Justice Coordination Group is the first real attempt by civil society organizations working in the field of transitional justice to strategically coordinate their activities and support each other. Civil society's engagement in transitional justice remains fragile, but documentation and research, victims' groups, and arts-based mechanisms are emerging. Most civil society initiatives on transitional justice remain centered in Kabul, and outreach to the subnational level has been limited. However, victims' groups have also been emerging at the subnational level, and there is an increasing recognition that national-level advocacy needs to have its roots in local realities.

Vetting

Since 2001, several vetting initiatives have been attempted for candidates for the parliamentary elections, provincial chiefs of police, and senior political appointments. Only the vetting of provincial chiefs of police has included vetting on the grounds of the candidate's human rights record. Vetting of parliamentary candidates has focused on links to illegal armed groups. Vetting on the basis of parliamentary candidates' human rights records was discussed but considered unconstitutional. The advisory panel established to advise President Karzai on his senior political appointments is functioning, but its decisions are often marginalized.

Court Trials

Criminal accountability for past human rights violations and war crimes has been a contested topic in Afghanistan. National courts currently do not have capacity to conduct trials of major human rights violators, and the international community has shown no appetite for an international tribunal. However, a number of criminal proceedings have already taken place for crimes committed during the years of conflict: in 2004, low-level commander Abdullah Shah was found guilty of killing more than twenty people during the civil war period and sentenced to death. The UN Special Rapporteur on extrajudicial killing, Asma Jahangir, and others extensively criticized his execution because of lack of due process. In 2005, Asadullah Sarwary, the head of the Afghan intelligence service from 1978 to 1979, was tried by the Primary Court of National and International Security. He was later sentenced to death, and his appeal is pending at the time of this writing. The principle of universal jurisdiction has also provided limited opportunities for trials against Afghans residing abroad. In the United Kingdom, Commander Zardad was sentenced to twenty years in prison for cases of torture and hostage taking during the 1990s. In the Netherlands, Hesamuddin Hesam, Director of Military Intelligence Service and Habibullah Jalalzoy, Head of the Interrogation Department of the Military Intelligence Service during the Soviet occupation, were sentenced for cases of torture to twelve and nine years in prison, respectively. Another case in the Netherlands resulted in an acquittal, as direct involvement in torture could not be proved. In 2007, the ICC prosecutor formally acknowledged that Afghanistan was under preliminary analysis. Since then there has been little public engagement of the ICC in Afghanistan.

Conclusion

The post-2001 developments in Afghanistan are a clear example that internationally driven state-building cannot substitute for domestic reform, and that there can be no sustainable peace without attention to justice. The Afghan public's demands for justice have been consistently ignored as commanders and factional leaders with known records of human rights abuses have reinforced their positions within both the Afghan government and the illegal economy, and the international community has failed to recognize that promoting stability by any means will only reignite the conflict.

There are several reasons for the slow progress in developing mechanisms to address the legacies of the conflict in Afghanistan. The inclusion of former commanders in the government and the failure to vet parliamentary candidates have resulted in the presence of many individuals with questionable human rights records in the Afghan political elite, and this has had a considerable effect on the political climate in the country. For example, after the launch of the Action Plan, a handful of members of parliament – former commanders – mobilized support for self-amnesty that resulted in the Amnesty Bill. The Amnesty Bill has remained a strong message of the continued power of the warlords and it has obviously complicated the implementation of transitional justice politically. The conflicting agendas of the international actors add challenges to the slow process: the UN, the EU and its member states, and Canada have strongly supported the AIHRC and transitional justice in Afghanistan, while the United States' agenda on human rights and transitional justice has been less clear.

Afghanistan is also a good example of the often repeated truism that there can be no one-size-fits-all approach to transitional justice. The adoption of the Action Plan for Peace, Justice and Reconciliation by the Afghan government was in many ways unique – also compared to other post-conflict societies – but transitional justice has failed to engage with Afghan culture and religion, and insufficient attention has been given by proponents of transitional justice to reaching out to broader cadres of Afghan society for support and for developing a more in-depth understanding of what justice means in an Afghan context.

Sari Kouvo

Cross-references: Accountability; Accountability mechanisms; Amnesty; Court trials for redress; International Center for Transitional Justice; International Criminal Court; Truth (Truth Seeking and Truth Telling).

Further Readings

A Mapping of Human Rights Violations in Afghanistan from 1979 to 2001. United Nations Office of the High Commissioner for Human Rights, 2005 [unpublished].
Blood-Stained Hands: Past Atrocities in Kabul and Afghanistan's Legacy of Impunity. Human Rights Watch, 2005.
Casting Shadows – War Crimes and Crimes against Humanity, 1978–2001: Documentation and Analysis of Major Patterns of Abuse in Afghanistan. Kabul: The Afghan Justice Project, 2005.
Gossman, Patricia. 2006. Truth, Justice and Stability in Afghanistan. In *Transitional Justice in the Twenty-First Century. Beyond Truth versus Justice.* Eds. Naomi Roht-Arriaza and Javier Mariezcurrena. New York: Cambridge University Press.
Kouvo, Sari and Mazoori, Dallas. 2011. Field Notes: Reconciliation, Justice and Mobilization of War Victims in Afghanistan. *International Journal for Transitional Justice,* 5(3): 492–503.
Nader Nadery, Ahmad. 2007. Peace or Justice? Transitional Justice in Afghanistan. *International Journal of Transitional Justice,* 1: 173–179.
Winterbotham, Emily. 2012. *Healing the Legacies of Conflict in Afghanistan: Community Voices on Justice, Peace and Reconciliation.* Kabul: Afghanistan Research and Evaluation Unit.

Albania

The harsh form of communism and the extraordinary degree of suffering suggested that Albania would have pursued transitional justice with vigor after the collapse of the communist regime in 1990. However, the nature of Albania's often haphazard transition from communism to free-market democracy meant that transitional justice was used for essentially political purposes. As a result, the process lost its meaning among the citizenry, and Albania never really engaged in a serious debate about its communist past.

The Repressive Past

Albania's political culture had little experience with democracy until the collapse of the communist regime in late 1990 and the first somewhat free elections in 1991. Albania's communist leaders pursued an extreme form of Stalinism dominated entirely by Enver Hoxha, First Secretary of the hegemonic Albanian Party of Labor, from 1944 until his death in 1985. In its aftermath, the new party leadership of Ramiz Alia only made cosmetic changes to what was an extremely repressive system.

The key instruments for retaining power were a vast secret police network, regular and brutal purges, a profound limitation of foreign contacts, and a system of prison camps and internal exile. All segments of society, including the top party hierarchy, were subject to periodic purges. The courts, also under strict party control, meted out harsh sentences for any deviations from the official political line. The Albanian communist state was not just perceived to be strong – it was strong, and it took very little for a person to end up in jail. Figures on jailed or internally exiled range from lows of 12,000 to 15,000 to highs of between 50,000 and 60,000 out of a population of roughly 2.5 million.

Created on March 20, 1943 as a secret political police, the Directorate of State Security (Drejtorija e Sigurimit te Shtetit), popularly known as the Sigurimi, was one of the most shadowy secret police organizations in Eastern Europe. The communist monopoly on power was assured almost at the moment of liberation from German Fascist occupation in late 1944. The Sigurimi was part of the Interior Ministry, which also exercised authority over the judiciary and law implementation and enforcement. The political police employed some 10,000 full-time agents with military rank, 2,500 of whom were assigned to the People's Army, and, according to Human Rights Watch, reportedly a quarter of the adult population worked as part-time informers. Officers were generally career volunteers, recommended by loyal party members and subjected to careful political and psychological screening before being allowed to join the service. As elsewhere in communist Eastern Europe, they had an elite status and enjoyed many privileges designed to maintain their reliability and dedication to the party.

The Sigurimi included national headquarters and branches in each of Albania's twenty-six districts, and was organized into sections covering political control, censorship, public records, prison camps, internal security troops, physical security, counterespionage, and foreign intelligence. The political control section verified the ideological correctness of party members and ordinary citizens, monitored private phone conversations and correspondence, and purged the party, government, military, and secret forces of individuals closely associated with Yugoslavia, the Soviet Union, and China, after Albania broke off with each of these countries.

Transitional Justice

Albania underwent a bizarre exit from communism, which had huge implications for subsequent attempts at transitional justice. Simply put, Albania had an anticommunist revolution because everyone else had one. In fact, as revolutions swept communist Europe in 1989, it appeared that Albania might have been able to resist the changes taking place. Since 1976, Albania had pursued a destructive policy of self-reliance and seemed capable of continuing to go its own way as one of the most isolated countries in the world. It is worth noting that it was only in December 1990, essentially a year later than elsewhere in the region, that events at University in Tirana "Enver Hoxha" forced some radical changes in communist policies. The nature of Albania's delayed revolution helps better understand the issues of transitional justice and the reasons for its haphazard implementation. Because Albania had no serious dissident movement, the anticommunist leaders and reform-minded communists that emerged in 1990 and 1991 all had relatively solid communist credentials. Very few were willing to dig too deeply into the past and even fewer had any reason to call for a complete opening of the secret police files. However, they all had to work extra hard to prove their anticommunist credentials, and the result was a highly politicized quest for justice.

Reforms of Repressive Institutions

Albania's first multiparty elections in March 1991 were won easily by the communists (known as the Party of Labor since 1948). The nascent Democratic Party, led by Sali Berisha and Gramoz Pashko, lacked adequate time to prepare and had no strong connections to the villages where more than 65 percent of Albanians lived and who feared the implications of property restitution. Transitional justice was delayed by the communist victory, although the party did implement a housecleaning of hard-liners. As the country drifted toward an economic catastrophe in mid-1991 and a national unity government was formed, some very modest steps were taken toward de-communization. In July 1991, the Sigurimi was abolished and replaced by the National Information Service (Sherbimi Informativ Kombetar or SHIK). The agency was allegedly purged of communist sympathizers and within months some 70 percent of its employees were dismissed. The new agency was prohibited from conducting unauthorized investigations or political activity. Despite this superficial purge of the security services, access to secret police files for citizens was never considered nor was there a noticeable outcry from civil society for such access.

The Ruli Report

The first serious attempt at transitional justice was the release of a crucial report by Genc Ruli, the Democratic Party Finance Minister in the unity government formed in the summer of 1991 after the elected communists were confronted with wide opposition to their electoral victory in July 1991. This document became the principal piece of evidence in the first trials against the former regime and the basis of the charges against members of the old regime, and it set the tone for the nature of the debate to come. The report was an audit of the often luxurious spending of the communist elite. It made clear that the communists were to be held to account for their economic crimes, not political actions. Clearly, the country's new leaders felt that in a nation so stricken by poverty and shortages, the public would be more inclined to support actions that focused on financial abuses. Because most of what the communists did was in fact within the laws they themselves had written, the best route for the new leaders was to catch them on preaching one thing – austerity – while practicing another: gluttony. Given that most Albanians lived in total misery, dismantling the system based on privilege seemed to have its advantages.

Ruli's report was incredibly detailed, citing extensive facts and figures on the consumption that occurred while ordinary people went hungry. It noted the overconsumption of products such as alcohol and sausages by the communist elite and various trips abroad for medical care. In the poorest country in Europe, ordinary Albanians lacked access to basic necessities, lived in a system of rationing, and were not allowed to exit the country. The decision to make economic crimes the centerpiece of the process, in hindsight, was a blunder as it trivialized the entire process and thus lost its relevance for most people. However, given the situation at the time, it seemed to make sense. Albania's new leaders argued that the perks enjoyed by communists were unlawful and other charges would have failed when confronted with still communist-controlled courts and that in the midst of a unity government, they still had to cooperate with members of the old regime.

The election of the Democratic Party in March 1992 brought with it the chance for a sustained attempt to deal with the past. By far the biggest single lobby for serious transitional justice was the former political prisoners who played key roles in the Democratic Party's first government. As its raison d'etre was anticommunism, the party's rhetoric at the outset was extremely inflammatory vis-á-vis the past, and one could only conclude that Albania was about to embark on a massive and unprecedented drive for justice. For various reasons, however, the process became more about politics.

Purges and Lustration

In addition to the economic charges that the Democrats leveled against the top elite, they also conducted a massive purge of the state sectors. When analysts suggest that Albania went further than most other countries in what was referred to as lustration, they are referring to the virtual emptying of the public sector. New laws for state employees were couched in terms of strengthening reform but allowed the government to dismiss employees of state-owned firms or agencies without explanation or the right to appeal. People were generally replaced with party loyalists. This process could hardly be called lustration; pseudo-lustration would be more appropriate. It established the terrible precedent in that whenever a government has changed in Albania, thousands of jobs are at stake.

It was only in 1995, three years after its election, that the Democratic Party government introduced legislation that was decidedly different from what started with the Ruli report in 1991. It had the potential to remove communist wrongdoers from the state and government. Coming so long after the 1992 election, the timing suggests that these laws were entirely political in purpose. In 1994, the Democrats had proposed a new constitution, replacing the previous hodgepodge of provisional constitutional laws and amendments and providing for a centralized presidential republic in keeping with the type of administration President Berisha had already established. The government put this crucial matter to a public referendum. The proposed constitution was soundly defeated. The loss generated a real fear that they could lose the elections due in 1996 and most analysts concluded that the hasty introduction of legislation was directly linked to the impending elections. That said, the new law put everyone in one boat – old members of the Politburo, the Communist Party top leadership structure, and reform-minded communists who had been instrumental in bringing change in 1990 and 1991.

In late 1995, the People's Assembly (Parliament) passed Albania's first two lustration laws (known together as the Lustration Laws): Law 8001 of 22 September 1995 on Genocide and Crimes against Humanity Committed in Albania during Communist Rule for Political, Ideological or Religious Motives (the Genocide Law), and Law 8043 of 30 November 1995 on the Verification of the Moral Character of Officials and other Persons Connected with the Defense of the Democratic State, subsequently amended pursuant to a Constitutional Court Decision of 31 January 1996 (the Verification Law). Prima facie, the Lustration Laws seemed to be aimed at ensuring the democratic nature of the Albanian polity by restricting the entry of individuals with antidemocratic tendencies. However, in their context, scope, and implementation, it soon became evident that the Lustration Laws were exploited by the government to selectively purge Albanian politics not of antidemocratic individuals, but rather of anti-Democratic Party individuals, usually belonging to the Socialist or Social Democratic Parties.

The Verification Law provided for a committee (the Verification Committee) responsible for screening potential and actual members of the government, police, judiciary, educational system, and media in order to determine their affiliation with communist-era government organs and state police. To this end, the Verification Committee was granted exclusive rights to use the files of the former secret service Sigurimi and the Albanian Party of Labor. The Verification Law was thus the first Albanian law regulating the use of such files.

Shortly after the Verification Law was introduced, its use as an advantage of the ruling Democratic Party and extreme detriment to the political opposition became clear. After conducting closed-door reviews, the Verification Committee declared that 139 people should be barred from participating in the elections, with the overwhelming number of these coming from opposition parties. International observers, such as Human Rights Watch/Helsinki and the Organization for Security and Cooperation of Europe's Office for Democratic Institutions and Human Rights (ODIHR), expressed concerns, particularly regarding the composition of the Verification Committee and the secretive nature of the reviews. With six of seven members appointed by the Democratic Party, the objectivity of the Verification Committee was in question, and decisions were often subjective. In short, the first round of transitional justice was used by the government to destroy the opposition. Indeed, the Democratic Party won the heavily disputed and much criticized 1996 elections.

In the summer and fall of 1996, Albania saw a dramatic rise in public investment in several large pyramid schemes, which would spell the end of the Democratic Party government and bring Albania close to civil war. In 1997, after international intervention, new elections put the Socialist Party in power, which produced substantial changes to the existing legislation. The laws become much softer: under the new amendments, only former members of the Politburo, former agents of secret police or foreign intelligence agencies, and individuals convicted of crimes against humanity could be lustrated. The scope of the Verification Law was thus drastically reduced; for example, former ministers in the communist government were no longer barred.

Shortly after its victory, the Socialist Party began to reorganize the central administration, judiciary, universities, and state-controlled media, widely replacing Democratic Party supporters with Socialists and recruits from the old guard. The new government also moved quickly to strike down the effects of the Genocide Law. At the request of the newly appointed state prosecutors, Albanian courts reexamined the accusations of crimes against humanity leveled under the Genocide Law against such former communist officials as Alia and former Politburo members Hekuran Isai and Simon Stefani. On October 20, 1997, the Supreme Court acquitted all the accused, ruling that they could not be held liable for actions that were legal at the time they were committed.

No further convictions were made under the Genocide Law for the remainder of its active life, which ended in 2001, and it essentially became a dead letter.

In addition to changes in the Genocide Law, the Verification Law also underwent further changes. On January 15, 1998, Parliament changed the Verification Law again by narrowing the scope of lustration even further. Most notably, the amendments altered the wording of the law that banned "officers" of the National Information Service and Interior Ministry – but including only "senior officers and leading functionaries" among those – no longer called for the lustration of former communist judges and state prosecutors from civil service, and changed collaboration with the Sigurimi in general to include only collaboration with the Sigurimi in political trials and investigations. The Verification Law expired in December 2001.

The Socialists lost the 2005 elections and the reelected Democrats did not add any substantive new legislation until late 2008, when they introduced and passed what they called a "clean hands" lustration law (The Law on the Cleanliness of the Character of High Functionaries of the Public Administration and Elected Persons). It was not radically different from the earlier Verification Law in that it aimed at evaluating public officials' collaboration with the Sigurimi in the period from November 29, 1944 until December 8, 1990 and established a committee to review cases. The law was widely criticized by opposition parties as a political weapon designed to destroy the independent judiciary and ward off potential corruption investigations into government figures. It was condemned as well by international observers, including the Council of Europe and the Organization for Security and Cooperation in Europe, which called the law's sweeping powers unconstitutional. Albania's Constitutional Court suspended the law pending a decision on its constitutionality and sought the opinion of the Council of Europe's Venice Commission. In its October 2009 assessment, the Venice Commission noted several problems with the law, including that it was enacted so long after the end of the communist regime, the categories subject to verification were too broad, many aspects were simply contrary to the rule of law, and it violated Albania's constitution.

File Access

Separate from lustration and yet an integral component of the transitional justice process is the issue of file access. In Albania, the first legislative attempt to regulate the use of Sigurimi files was made with the introduction of the Verification Law in 1995. However, only the Verification Committee was legally permitted to access the files. Prior to the introduction of the law, the files had sometimes been illegally used by individuals with connections in government to coerce or intimidate their political opponents. Smear campaigns and serious allegations were published in newspapers, containing information that could only have been obtained through file access, and it was apparent that the files were selectively opened and manipulated to the detriment or gain of a few individuals.

When the Verification Law expired in 2001, so did the only piece of legislation providing for even limited access to the secret files. Since then, the question of access occasionally surfaces and then quietly gets shelved. File access again appeared with the aforementioned "clean hands" bill of 2008. In addition to its sweeping provisions, it also declared that all Albanian citizens had the right to review their personal files with the former Sigurimi. As noted, the entire law was struck down by the Constitutional Court, so file access was again shelved. File access was granted within the aforementioned law for lustration but it was totally buried within what was a highly controversial piece of legislation, which meant that file access was again shelved. Some might hold up the failure of this law as evidence of the shadowy hand of former communists, pulling the strings of both major parties and preventing the unfortunate Albanian public from discovering the truth about its past; it would seem strange to suggest that in a country with a history of pervasive oppression, unjust imprisonment, exile, and state murder, the public would not demand to know the identities and roles of their persecutors.

Yet although the secret files have always remained closed to ordinary Albanians, there is no public clamor to see them opened, and it does not appear to be on the forefront of public debate. There have been many reasons offered as to why file access never caught the public's attention. Many suggest that Albanians would prefer to close that chapter of their lives. Moreover, the class of politically persecuted, and of former persecutors, is diminishing as a result of death and emigration; some say most of the files were destroyed before 1992, and in any case, top communist officials and the worst perpetrators never had files. Illegal file misuse from 1992 to 1995 also seriously undermined the public's perceptions of the files' integrity. If politically connected individuals could gain access, who is to say they did not destroy their own files or alter those of their opponents? By the time the Verification Committee took control of the files, the public likely already viewed them with skepticism.

Conclusion

Since 1991, Albanians have heard the on-again, off-again tale of transitional justice. They first saw the former communist rulers head to jail for overconsumption, then saw them fall under the rubric of the genocide law, and witnessed the ups and downs of a deeply politicized lustration process, which ensured that the Albania's major political parties became essentially employments agencies. The trials never caught the public's attention as it all seemed so tawdry and made even more ridiculous when governments changed power and the jail terms ended. Albanians also confronted a battle between the two major parties on the past. Each governing party sought to rewrite the history of Albania. In 1992, the Democrats started the process of replacing the communist interpretation of events with their own. A lack of clarity ensured that at first the communist period almost disappeared to be subsequently revised depending on whose was in power. New interpretations did little to generate discussion as they were almost always couched in terms that were totally black and white. While the statues of the communists came down, few memorials to those who suffered appeared. Even Albania's national day is a subject of controversy, with Democrats and Socialists preferring different dates at the end of November. As of late 2009, the governing Democrats were busy reassessing the events of 1997, suggesting that the economic collapse had its roots in diehard communists. In terms of the critical issue of property restitution, even that was somewhat flawed. Emerging from World War II as an almost feudal country, total property restitution was impossible and confusion over just who owned what dogged the entire transition period.

Considering the overarching goals of transitional justice, which do include the quest for revenge but only to lay the basis for national reconciliation and punishing past human rights abuses, one can certainly conclude that Albania has not achieved much. In 1992, when the Democrats came to power, ordinary Albanians had high expectations in all respects, and there was a real need for a serious national debate about the past. While

Albania did pass substantial legislation between 1993 and 1996, these laws have largely been political in origin and application. Despite an abundance of legislation and mass purges in the public sector, then, there was no real attempt to deal constructively with the communist past and there was never a serious national debate. The reintroduction of transitional justice legislation in 2008, nearly twenty years after the end of the communist regime, seemed to only confirm that politics continued to triumph law.

Robert C. Austin

Cross-references: Access to Secret Files; Lustration; Purges.

Further Readings

Abrahams, Fred. 1996. *Human Rights in Post-Communist Albania*. New York: Human Rights Watch.
Austin, Robert and Jonathan Ellison. 2009. *Transitional Justice in Eastern Europe and the Former Soviet Union: Reckoning with the Communist Past*. Ed. Lavinia Stan. New York: Routledge.
Biberaj, Elez. 1998. *Albania in Transition: The Rocky Road to Democracy*. Boulder: Westview.
Imholz, Kathleen. 1995. Can Albania Break the Chain: The 1993–1994 Trials of Former High Officials. *East European Constitutional Review*, 4: 54–60.

Algeria

In January 1992, the interruption by a military coup of the first multiparty parliamentary elections of independent Algeria, won by the Islamic Salvation Front (Front islamique du salut), triggered a bitter civil war that by 1999 left 200,000 dead, 20,000 disappeared, and 1.5 million forcedly displaced persons. The military commanders declared a state of emergency that was lifted only nineteen years later, in February 2011. The Parliament was dissolved, the Constitution suspended, and the President of the Republic forced to resign. In the name of fighting against subversion, the government annihilated or sought to control all Islamic and non-Islamic opposition forces.

Since the April 1999 election of President Abdelaziz Bouteflika, civil peace has been apparently restored, although the military leaders continued to exercise political power behind closed doors under the democratic façade. Despite demands coming from victims, human rights organizations, and UN organs, the Algerian authorities have rejected transitional justice or independent inquiries aimed at establishing the truth about past violations. The Law on Civil Concord of 1999 and the Law on National Reconciliation of 2006 primarily reflect a desire to obscure the state's responsibility in a large number of crimes considered "crimes against humanity" by a UN expert in October 2007, at a Committee on Human Rights session on Algeria. These laws mainly grant amnesty to the military and police perpetrators responsible for gross human rights violations. The vast majority of members of armed groups claiming allegiance to Islam also escape justice.

The Repressive Past

After the coup of January 11, 1992, fomented by the military command, part of the Islamic opposition has engaged in an armed struggle against a regime it considered illegal. Since 1992, the army has ferociously repressed the civilians suspected of supporting the Islamic Salvation Front. The security forces arrested, deported to concentration camps, tortured, executed, or forcibly disappeared tens of thousands of persons. In 1994, to fight the radical Armed Islamic Groups (Groupes islamiques armés, GIA) and the Islamic Salvation Army (Armée islamique du salut, AIS), army-controlled militias were brought into North Algeria.

From 1992 to 1995, the military intelligence services (Département du renseignement et de la sécurité, DRS) sought to infiltrate the armed Islamic groups in an effort to neutralize and control them. Some violence attributed to Islamic terrorists was thus likely committed with government involvement.

This phase of the countersubversive war conducted by the military command peaked in 1997–1998 in localities such as Raïs, Bentalha, Sidi Youcef, Sidi-Hamed, and Rélizane, where each incident left scores of people dead. Claimed by the GIA, the killings stopped only after the September 1998 resignation of President General Liamine Zéroual and his replacement with Abdelaziz Bouteflika, appointed by the military command and elected as a result of rigged elections in April 1999 (Zéroual resigned in September 1998 but stayed as president until April 1999). In September 1999, Bouteflika approved the referendum that passed the Law of Civil Concord that brought peace to the country by granting conditional amnesty to members of armed groups. In 1995, Zéroual had signed a Clemency Law (*rahma*), which provided for no amnesty but promised clemency to repenting perpetrators.

Violence abated after 1999, but in 2007–2008, several spectacular attacks were claimed by the Salafist Group of Preaching and Combat (Groupe salafiste de prédication et de combat, GSPC), which in 1998 became the successor to the GIA (and has also been the target of DRS infiltration and manipulation). Until 2010, soldiers continued to regularly die in ambushes, former anti-GIA militiamen were killed, and the DRS arrested the suspects, arbitrarily detained and tortured them, and kept their whereabouts secret for weeks and sometimes even months.

By 2010, the generals responsible for the 1992 coup were no longer in office. The only exception was the powerful Mohammed Médiène – alias Tewfik – head of the DRS since September 1990, considered the true master of the country. His main partners (and sometimes rivals), army Generals Mohammed Lamari and Khaled Nezzar, had been sidelined, army General Larbi Belkheir died in 2010, and the DRS General Smaïl Lamari died in 2007. But the "young wolves" of the army and the DRS continue to occupy key positions of responsibility and, if previously too openly involved in the "dirty war," were given guarantees of impunity. All are currently active in business and politics.

The responsibility of the security forces and their leaders – often identified by name in hundreds of victims' testimonials collected by Amnesty International, Human Rights Watch, and Algeria Watch – for the massive and systematic human rights violations committed in the name of the state is well established. The involvement of leaders and operatives of armed groups claiming allegiance to Islam in crimes (massacres, rape, bomb attacks, and the like) is also certain. Numerous testimonies of both survivors and former security service members (collected by the previously mentioned nongovernmental organizations and also published in some books and journals) have also confirmed the responsibility of the military commanders and the DRS leaders for some of these crimes and the fact that they made extensive use of infiltration and manipulation techniques. No independent inquiry or serious judicial investigation ever established the identity of those who masterminded the crimes committed "in the name of Islam" since 1992.

This is because the Algerian judiciary is not independent. Magistrates are controlled, or revoked at the slightest infraction, by the DRS, and witnesses are intimidated or bought. The only members of the security forces condemned until now were found guilty of insubordination or criminal offenses with the purpose to push them out of the institutions where they worked. None was convicted for using torture during interrogation or for killing suspects – two common practices for many years. However, many DRS, army, police, and militia members responsible for disappearances are known by name to the victims' families. The involvement of these organs in human rights violations is officially hidden.

The first victims of state violence who publicly asked authorities to account for their actions were the mothers and wives of the disappeared. Since the autumn of 1997, after the great wave of kidnappings of 1994–1996 that resulted in forced disappearances, these families understood that they were not alone, that forced disappearances by security forces were massive and systematic – between 8,000 and 20,000 – and that together they had to face the public. At first, the families asked that the disappeared be released or brought to court. Soon afterward, they demanded to know the truth about the fate of their loved ones. The more confident the families became, facing the ban on public protests and the repression of the law enforcement agencies, the more they insisted that those responsible for these kidnappings be judged.

As a result of its courage and perseverance, this protest movement composed mainly of women – including mothers who had rarely left home before – has proved capable of facing state hostility, in spite of being persecuted by the authorities. They have not hesitated to directly address those who masterminded the kidnappings. In November 1998, for example, the National Association of the Families of the Disappeared (Association nationale des familles de disparus) sent an open letter to the Chief of Staff of the Army, General-Major Mohamed Lamari, who in April 1993 had told his special forces that "the Islamists want to go to heaven. That takes them there and quickly, I don't want prisoners, I want them dead!" (Souaidia 2001, p. 95). These women were the most active in claiming truth and justice. But first they had to win recognition as mothers of abducted and killed sons. Because most of them were veiled, they were considered by the state mothers of terrorists, although, according to testimonies collected by nongovernmental organizations and associations of victims' families, most victims were peaceful supporters of the Islamic Salvation Front.

The Western media and the representatives of the international community first questioned the role of state agents in the violence during the mass killings of 1997. In the heavily militarized regions, checkered by militias and the army, hordes of attackers massacred civilians. The military sealed off the neighborhoods, did not stop the killings, and blocked the rescue efforts. Algerians were shocked and outraged and many of them, despite the risk of prosecution, protested loudly and accused the military power of condoning the massacre and even having directly orchestrated the murders committed by Islamic extremists manipulated by the DRS. The DRS and army generals did not want these cries of alarm to be heard outside Algeria at a time when the international community was noticing the demand to launch an independent international inquiry to establish the facts and responsibilities coming from Algerian and international human rights organizations.

In the face of this outcry, in 1997, the Algerian regime launched an unprecedented diplomatic and media campaign. Thanks to its supporters in the international community, especially France, it avoided a country visit of special UN rapporteurs and scored a coup when the UN Secretary General sent a delegation of international figures, chaired by former Portuguese President Mario Soares, on a "fact-finding visit" to Algeria in July 1998. Upon its arrival, the agenda of the delegation was controlled by Algerian state representatives. The guided tours at the massacre sites led the delegation to question only the role of Islamic terrorists and to ignore the illegal actions of the military. Thus, the delegation's conclusions perfectly matched the expectations of the regime and were limited to a few timid recommendations dealing with the forced disappearances.

Since then, the Algerian regime managed to impose internationally its representation of this bloody decade as the absolute barbarism of the Islamists, counteracted by tough state methods. Through falsifications, intimidation, and promises of compensating victims' families, the forced disappearances have been presented as the regrettable excesses of individual members of security services overwhelmed by events, although they were massive and organized. Whereas the state's responsibility in the forced disappearances has thus officially received lip service, the question of its involvement in some of the mass killings remains to this day an absolute taboo.

The Impossibility of Transitional Justice and the Travesties of Justice

Alongside the struggle of the families of those victimized by the security forces, there has also been the equally legitimate struggle of the families of victims of the terrorist attacks for which self-avowed Islamic armed groups have claimed responsibility. The first organization representing victims of terrorism was created by the government in 1994. Unlike the associations of families of the disappeared, most organizations representing victims of terrorism have been officially recognized. To counter the claims of victims of state repression, the authorities have put forward these other victims to promote the idea, widely accepted by the Algerian mass media, that violence comes only from Islamic terrorists.

Organizations of victims of terrorism have embraced this strategy of state recognition but ultimately, apart from some compensation, their demands were left unanswered. Nevertheless, some of their members wanted the truth about violations committed by suspected Islamists and perpetrators to be prosecuted. The regime could not accept this, likely because stringent legal proceedings would have challenged its claim that "Islamic terrorism" was exclusively responsible for the "red decade" and would have brought to light the DRS's involvement in the violence.

The victims have in common their demand for justice and truth. Trials of "terrorists" were rare until 2007, but they multiplied afterward. Hundreds of people have been charged, judged, and sentenced, but it is unclear whether they committed the terrorist crimes (murders, bomb attacks) of which they were accused. The judicial inquiries that preceded these trials were mere mockeries of justice, and most of the dozens of murders of the 1990s presented by the regime as "political assassinations" remain unexplained. In particular, those of journalists Tahar Djaout (1993) and Saïd Mekbel (1994), of the head of the national labor union Abdelhak Benhamouda (1997), of Abdelkader Hachani, an Islamic Salvation Front leader (1999), of the monks of Tibhirine (1996), or of singer Lounès Matoub (1998) remain unsolved. Similarly, no major massacre has been the subject of serious investigation, and the judiciary never investigated complaints of torture and kidnapping. Some victims have tried to have Generals Khaled Nezzar and Larbi Belkheir indicted for torture in France, but their requests were turned down or dismissed, because the French government did not want to clash with the Algerian regime.

Since 1999, the Algerian authorities have tried to turn the page on the "bloody decade" and present the country as a constitutional state confronted with "residual," if violent, terrorism. They sought pacification through the 1999 and 2006 laws, which stipulate the non-prosecution of members of armed groups, the exemption of their sentences, or the release from prison of those of them who did not participate in massacres, bombings, or rapes. However, the enforcement of these legal stipulations was so imprecise from a judicial viewpoint that many observers felt that authorities enacted those laws mainly to exfiltrate their DRS agents from the rebel camps and to thank the members of armed groups who repented and collaborated with the DRS. The 2006 law is rightly considered a general amnesty for the members of all security forces (belonging to the army, intelligence services, police, and gendarmerie) against whom "all denunciation or complaint should be declared inadmissible by the competent judicial authority" (according to the Decree for the Implementation of the Charter for Peace and National Reconciliation). In addition, any statement inconsistent with the official version of the "national tragedy" became punishable by prison sentence.

To silence the only voices that continue to call for truth and justice publicly in Algeria – the families of the disappeared – since 2006, the state has provided compensation for them, under the condition that they certify the death of their relative and often his/her belonging to a terrorist group. Many of these families, discouraged and impoverished, have accepted this offer, but others have continued their fight for more than a decade. At the time of this writing, 6,400 persons benefited from compensation packages of 6,000 Euros (equal to forty minimum monthly wages) each.

Given this situation, often regarded as hopelessly blocked or desperate, some leaders of associations of victims of violations committed by the state or the armed groups met in March 2007 in Brussels and formed the Coalition of Victims' Associations to develop common demands. This was a positive initiative, given that for years everything was done to divide the victims. Announcing its willingness to create a Commission for Truth, Peace and Reconciliation (Commission pour la vérité, la paix et la conciliation), the Coalition has not yet established a clear strategy to voice the victims' demands for truth and justice. It clarified that the Commission must "respect the duties of justice, truth, memory, dignity, and reparation," but the name of the proposed Commission did not include the word "justice" and nothing was said about the possibility of prosecuting human rights violators.

Unless it defines the conditions under which transitional justice could be envisaged, this project could appear as a mere amendment of the laws proposed since 1999 by the Algerian authorities. Those responsible for the crimes against humanity committed at their instigation by the security forces and for granting amnesty to the Islamic armed groups are still in power. They have effected their own version of transitional justice by enacting the laws on clemency, civil concord, and national reconciliation (in 1995, 1999, and 2006, respectively). The Coalition's main contribution is the search for truth – a goal ignored by the Algerian authorities.

Whereas the regime seeks to install peace and reconciliation through edicts, the Coalition has implicitly advocated the model of the Equity and Reconciliation Commission (Instance Équité et Réconciliation, or IER; see separate entry) created in Morocco in 2004. A very controversial body, it has merely identified the human rights violations of 1956–1999 and prepared a confidential report delivered to King Mohammed VI in 2005.

The public version of the report did not mention the names of those responsible for the crimes and recommended no sanctions against them. In the absence of justice, special attention was given to compensations for victims, a concern reflected both in the project of the Coalition and the Law of National Reconciliation. The Coalition thus favors the exclusion of judicial intervention, precisely like the Algerian government's "reconciliation laws."

Without clarifying its reasons, the Coalition has failed to associate its initiatives with other human rights defenders who continue to think that justice is essential, such as those who claim ties to political Islam (and fight against every human rights violations, perpetrated by state or non-state armed groups) or those close to other human rights defenders claiming ties to political Islam. The Coalition has denied turning down "Islamist" human rights defenders, although most victims of the "years of blood" were Islamic Salvation Front activists or supporters.

In January 1995, representatives of these latter groups were involved in the Sant'Egidio Platform, adopted in Rome by all Algerian political organizations representing the opposition that together "reject violence for gaining and maintaining power," "respect the political alternation of power through universal suffrage" and the "consecration of a multiparty system," and propose to engage in negotiations with the Algerian authorities to end the civil war. The refusal of the Coalition of Victims' Associations to accept those who, claiming ties to political Islam, affirm their will to fight for universal human rights could make a "real and lasting peace" difficult to attain.

Conclusion

If transitional justice is to be adopted in Algeria, it cannot satisfy the majority of victims unless it results from a real political transition toward democracy and sincere negotiations between both state and non-state actors of all persuasions that would find a way out of the crisis that is acceptable for most of them. Both of these conditions seem to be very difficult to achieve at the time of this writing.

François Gèze and Salima Mellah

Cross-references: Equity and Reconciliation Commission.

Further Readings

Algeria-Watch and Salah-Eddine Sidhoum. 2003. *La Machine de mort. Torture et centres de détention secrète*, October. Available at: http://www.algeria-watch.org/fr/mrv/mrvtort/machine_mort/machine_mort.htm (accessed October 15, 2010).

Kervyn, Jeanne and Gèze, François. 2004. *L'Organisation des forces de répression*, Comite Justice pour l'Algérie, September. Available at: http://www.algerie-tpp.org/tpp/pdf/dossier_16_forces_repression.pdf (accessed October 15, 2010).

Mellah, Salima. 2004. *Le Mouvement islamiste algérien entre autonomie et manipulation*, Comité Justice pour l'Algérie, May. Available at: http://www.algerie-tpp.org/tpp/pdf/dossier_19_mvt_islamiste.pdf (accessed October 15, 2010).

———. 2004. *Les Massacres en Algérie, 1992–2004*, Comité Justice pour l'Algérie, May. Available at: http://www.algerie-tpp.org/tpp/pdf/dossier_2_massacres.pdf (accessed October 15, 2010).

Robin, Marie-Monique. 2004. *Escadrons de la mort, l'école française*. Paris: La Découverte.

Souaidia, Habib. 2001. *La Sale Guerre, Le témoignage d'un ancien officier des forces spéciales de l'armée algérienne, 1992–2000*. Paris: La Découverte.

Argentina

Since the reinstatement of democracy on December 10, 1983, Argentina has stood out in Latin America's Southern Cone for implementing a number of transitional justice mechanisms to address human rights violations committed in the 1970s as political violence and military dictatorships swept through the region. Since then, these abuses have been featured prominently in the country's political agendas and public debates.

The Repressive Past

The ousting of Juan Domingo Perón in 1955 and the banning of the Peronist party, in the framework of the Cold War and the Cuban Revolution, inaugurated a cycle of weak civilian governments, military dictatorships, and political radicalization that included the emergence of Marxist and Peronist guerrilla movements. In 1973, with Perón again in the presidency, a death squad known as the Triple A (Argentine Anticommunist Alliance) was organized with official backing to stifle the opposition, operating throughout the country and murdering hundreds of political activists. Upon his death, Perón was succeeded by his widow, María Estela Martínez, who declared a state of siege on November 6, 1974 (Decree 1368). In February 1975, she authorized the armed forces to wipe out subversive action in the province of Tucumán (Decree 265), and in October 1975, she expanded the scope of this authorization to the rest of the country (Decree 2772). From 1973 to 1976, 1,543 political murders were committed, 5,148 people were imprisoned for political motives, and 900 others were forcefully disappeared. After the coup d'etat of March 24, 1976, which brought a military junta headed by General Jorge Rafael Videla, Admiral Emilio Eduardo Massera, and Brigadier Orlando Ramón Agosti to power, forced disappearances became a systematic practice. The disappearances consisted of the detention or abduction of individuals by military or police officers who took them to illegal prisons or camps known as "clandestine detention centers," where they were tortured and usually murdered. Their bodies were secretly buried in unmarked graves, incinerated, or dumped into the ocean, their properties were looted, and often their children were kidnapped or appropriated. Approximately 500 children were disappeared along with their parents or were born in captivity and illegally adopted by members of the security forces, who registered them under false names. As these crimes were committed, the state denied any responsibility for them. While Argentina's human rights organizations place the figure of disappearances at 30,000 victims, 8,960 cases were officially registered in 1984 by the National Commission on the Disappearance of Persons (CONADEP) created by the constitutional president, Raúl Alfonsín (1983–1989, Radical) to investigate the fate and whereabouts of the disappeared (see entry on the National Commission on the Disappearance of Persons, CONADEP), 90 percent of whom were disappeared after the coup. Eighty percent of all disappearances were perpetrated in major cities (Buenos Aires and its metropolitan area, Córdoba, La Plata, Rosario, and Tucumán), 81 percent of the victims were aged sixteen to thirty-five at the time of their disappearance, 70 percent were men, 30 percent were blue-collar workers, 21 percent were students, 18 percent white-collar workers, and 11 percent professionals. Most were Peronist, Marxist, guerrilla, or labor activists. Another 12,000 were imprisoned for the same political reasons, 2,286 were murdered, and an estimated 250,000 – in a population of 25 million – were forced into exile. All Argentines were denied their civil and political rights, and terror pervaded both the public and private spheres.

The dictatorship rejected any claims made against it, including reports from Amnesty International and the Organization of American States' Inter-American Commission on Human Rights (IACHR), both of which visited the country (in 1976 and 1979, respectively) and denounced the repression. Following its defeat in the Malvinas/Falklands War with the United Kingdom in June 1982, the dictatorship became isolated both domestically and internationally. At that point, the numerous allegations made by domestic human rights organizations gained widespread public attention. These organizations included the Permanent Assembly for Human Rights, the Center for Legal and Social Studies (CELS), the Service for Peace and Justice, the Madres de Plaza de Mayo (a group of mothers of disappeared formed in 1977), the Abuelas de Plaza de Mayo (a group of grandmothers of disappeared children), the Argentine Human Rights League, the Relatives of the Detained-Disappeared for Political Reasons, and the Ecumenical Movement for Human Rights. In contrast to other Latin American Southern Cone countries, in Argentina the dictatorship was unable to impose a negotiated transition on the opposition. Nonetheless, on September 23, 1983, a month before the democratic elections, despite meeting with public rejection, the Junta passed the National Pacification Act (Law 22924), known as the "self-amnesty" law, which extinguished all causes of criminal action arising from crimes committed during the "anti-subversive war" (see entry on Amnesty).

Transitional Justice

Since the return to democracy, Argentina has implemented several transitional justice mechanisms, including establishing a commission to investigate the disappearances; prosecuting the material perpetrators of political violence, after initially barring this possibility through laws; granting reparation to victims; and relaying the memory of what happened to the new generations.

Truth Commission, Prosecution, and Punishment

After taking office on December 10, 1983, President Raúl Alfonsín repealed the self-amnesty law as unconstitutional. On December 15, he created CONADEP and ordered the prosecution of seven leaders of the People's Revolutionary Army and Montoneros guerrilla movements for acts of violence committed after 1973 (Decree 157). These leaders were convicted and received sentences ranging from ten years to life in prison. Alfonsín also brought the first three military Juntas to trial (Decree 158), charging them with homicide, illegal arrest, and torture, as the practice of forced disappearances was not a crime established under the Criminal Code. These decrees embodied what came to be known as the "theory of the two evils" because they limited accountability for political violence to the guerrillas and the military juntas and explained state violence as a response to guerrilla violence.

Alfonsín proposed that in the first instance perpetrators be tried in military courts, with the possibility of appeal in federal courts, and supported the principle of presumption of obedience for all acts committed following Junta instructions. He distinguished three categories of perpetrators: "those who planned the repression and issued the orders; those who acted beyond the orders, prompted by cruelty, perversion, or greed and; those who carried out the orders strictly to the letter" (Decree 158). The government understood that the military chain of command and the ideological context in which the repression took place prevented perpetrators from disobeying orders and fully understanding the nature of their actions. In light of this, of these categories only those who arranged the repression and those who acted beyond the orders would be taken to judgment.

The trials were rejected by the armed forces, who demanded recognition for their role in defeating subversion, and by human rights organizations, who called for a bicameral parliamentary commission to investigate state terrorism, for civilian courts to hear cases, and for "trial and punishment for all perpetrators" of the repression.

The official strategy was modified in February 1984 through an amendment introduced by senator Elías Sapag (member of the Neuquén People's Movement and relative of disappeared persons), which excluded from the defense of due obedience anyone who had committed "atrocious and abhorrent" acts. It was also altered on September 21, 1984 by a military court decision that declared Junta orders "indisputable" and demanded both the investigation of subordinates (who the government said it would not prosecute) to determine whether they had acted beyond the orders of their superiors, and the investigation of the disappeared, to determine if they had committed any crimes. In response, in October 1984, prosecutor Strassera requested that the trial of the military Juntas be conducted in the Buenos Aires Federal Appeals Court, as he considered that these acts negated justice.

Proceedings that began on April 22, 1985 were unique in the treatment of state violence in the continent. The prosecution presented 711 cases – mostly resulting from CONADEP's investigation – to prove that the Juntas could be found jointly and indirectly accountable for the construction of a power apparatus used to perpetrate uncountable illegal detentions and systematically torture and eliminate prisoners, pillaging their property. It also aimed to establish that this system exceeded the declared objective of combating the guerrilla movement.

The defense lawyers tried to prove that the commanders were not equally responsible, alleged the validity of the self-amnesty law, denounced the trial's political nature, justified Junta actions as resulting from the "anti-subversive war," claimed the military intervened to combat subversion by request of the Peronist government, and, while stating that the disappearances had begun during that period, tried to discredit any witnesses who denounced disappearances occurring during the dictatorship. On December 9, 1985, the court found the Junta members guilty of illegal repression, as they had fully disregarded the legal instruments available to them and resorted instead to clandestine actions, but rejected the existence of a coordinated campaign. Therefore, it pronounced different sentences for generals Videla and Viola, admirals Massera and Lambruschini, and brigadier Agosti, and absolved the other four defendants. Item 30 of the judgment extended the scope of criminal action against superior officers, all those responsible for orchestrating actions, and anyone who committed abhorrent acts, thus going against the government's intention of limiting judicial action.

This led the Defense Ministry in April 1986 to instruct prosecutors to only examine cases in which "subordinate officers had committed inevitable errors" in response to orders from superiors. The federal court rejected such instruction. In December of that year, the Executive sent Congress the Full Stop Bill, which established that all causes of action not prosecuted within sixty days would be extinguished. Despite rejection from both opposition and human rights organizations, it was passed on December 26, 1986. With the help of the organizations, hundreds of cases were brought in federal courts before the deadline. In April 1987, an officer summoned to testify initiated a revolt in a faction of the army opposed to the proceedings. Some 150,000 people protested the revolt at Buenos Aires' Plaza de Mayo. The government sent Congress a new bill for what would be the Due Obedience Act, which considered all acts, except alteration of identity, abduction of children, and misappropriation of property, to have been committed under coercion and subordinated to superior orders. The law was passed in the lower chamber (May 16, 1987, by a vote of 119 to 59) and within days in the Senate (May 29, 23 to 4). Alfonsín faced two new revolts in January and December 1988 and a guerrilla attack against army barracks in January 1989.

When he came into office, Carlos Menem (1989–1999, Peronist) declared his intention to "reconcile" and "pacify" society by "solving the military question." Despite rejection from the international community and most of civil society, with demonstrations mobilizing 100,000 people, on October 7, 1989, Menem pardoned convicted guerrilla leaders as well as officers convicted for human rights violations, rebelling against Alfonsín's government, and committing repressive actions connected with the Falklands/Malvinas War. Following a new military revolt, on December 29 and 30, 1990, Menem issued Decrees 2741–2746 benefiting Junta members who were serving time, other human rights offenders, and Montonero guerrilla group leader Firmenich. The human rights organizations filed a complaint with the IACHR, which recommended reparation for the victims and declared that the laws and pardons violated the provisions of the American Declaration of the Duties and Rights of Man and the American Convention on Human Rights. Simultaneously, the French, Spanish, Italian, and Swedish courts reopened cases on human rights abuses in Argentina. In 1998, upon request of the Center for Legal and Social Studies, in the cities of La Plata, Mar del Plata, Jujuy and Mendoza initiated "truth" trials, which, although establishing no punitive measures, expanded the scope of responsibilities for the disappearances to include certain companies and trade unionists. On March 24, 1998, the Congress repealed the Full Stop and Due Obedience laws, on motion of center-left legislators and human rights organizations. On August 12, 2003, under the presidency of Néstor Kirchner (2003–2007, Peronist), the Congress declared them null, on proposal of a left-wing legislator. This decision avoided the extradition to Spain of forty-six military officers, requested in July 2003 by the Spanish judge Baltazar Garzón, and enabled the reopening of judicial proceedings. Since then, 49 military and police officers have been convicted – including the most notorious generals Antonio Bussi and Benjamin Menéndez – 555 have been indicted, 211 have died, 17 were absolved and 44 have been on the run. Lastly, Abuelas de Plaza de Mayo has so far located ninety-two abducted or appropriated children and has restored their true identity.

Reparations

Various victims of repression have gradually received reparation. In October 1986, the Alfonsín administration granted pensions (Law 23446) to spouses and children (younger than twenty-five) of disappeared, for an equivalent of the minimum civil servant retirement benefit. In July 1984, under pressure from international and human rights organizations, it commuted the sentences of political prisoners convicted under dictatorship

(Law 23070). Although former political prisoners demanded compensation, in most cases the courts found that the statute of limitations for such action had expired. They appealed to the IACHR, which supported their demands and pressured the Argentine government. President Menem, himself a former political prisoner, promoted several reparation laws. On January 10, 1991, he granted compensation to political prisoners (Decree 70/1991) held without process during the dictatorship, provided they had initiated legal actions before December 10, 1985. Under pressure from human rights organizations, who argued this violated the principle of equality before the law, in November 1991, the compensation was expanded (Law 24043) to cover anyone detained by sole authority of the Executive between November 6, 1974 (declaration of the state of siege) and December 10, 1983. As a result, 12,890 claims were filed. Compensation consisted of an amount equivalent to one-thirtieth of the monthly salary of the highest-ranking civil servant for every day of confinement.

In June 1994, the Organization of American States (OAS) adopted the Inter-American Convention on Forced Disappearance of Persons (Resolution 1256, Twenty-Fourth General Assembly), establishing that such practice constitutes a crime against humanity. Law 24411 of August 1995 deals with cases of persons absent because they were either disappeared or killed by security forces, establishing a monetary compensation of up to US$220,000 for their families. There were 3,151 claims filed by relatives of murdered persons and 8,950 by relatives of disappeared. Madres de Plaza de Mayo opposed this law, arguing it came from the same authorities that were denying justice. They declared that anyone who accepted compensation would be committing an act of prostitution. Other organizations argued that it represented an official acknowledgment of the violations and did not prevent them from furthering their demands for justice. On August 28, 2004, Law 25914 was passed by initiative of President Kirchner to compensate the children of disappeared and/or political prisoners, including abducted or appropriated children. The reparation was equivalent to twenty times the monthly salary of the highest-ranking civil servant (US$23,000). Also by initiative of the Executive, on March 2, 2005, the Senate approved financial compensation of political exiles, a proposal that was eventually abandoned. Relatives of guerrilla victims have also demanded similar compensations from the state. Compensations amounted to official recognition of the psychological and physical damages caused by the state, and expanded and/or confirmed the number of proven reports.

Memorialization

In 1996, on the twentieth anniversary of the coup, public remembrance became a goal of both state and human rights organizations, upon determining the need to transmit the recent past to younger generations. That year, Hijos por la Identidad, la Justicia contra el Olvido y el Silencio (H.I.J.O.S) was formed, representing the descendants of the disappeared who questioned the lack of justice and the "oblivion and silence" of the society, and who valued the political militancy of their parents. In 1998, a Memory Park was created by Municipal Law 46. Located on the banks of the Plata River in Buenos Aires, it included a Monument to the Victims of State Terrorism with the names of persons disappeared or murdered by state terrorism from 1970 to 1983. A commission of city legislators and representatives of human rights organizations debated what date would be set as the start of state terrorism, whether to include among the victims guerrilla members who died in armed confrontations, and whether to engrave only the names of the disappeared who were officially registered or include the 30,000 victims claimed by human rights organizations. Madres de Plaza de Mayo rejected the project, understanding that the participation of authorities would have offended their sons and daughters who "had fought against economic policies that condemned people to hunger and destitution and which are applied by the same people now erecting the Memory Park" (Carta a la Comisión Pro-Monumento a los desaparecidos n.d.), and they threatened to erase the names of their loved ones with a chisel if they were engraved in the monument. Memorials were also built on the sites of former detention centers (Olimpo in Buenos Aires and the Second Army Corps Base in Rosario).

Several memory archives were created, including that of the Provincial Commission of the Memory, in the Province of Buenos Aires (Law 12483/2000), based on the province's Police Intelligence Division records and the National Memory Archive (Decree 1259/2003), and kept by the National Human Rights Secretariat, which also holds CONADEP's files and the records of the military Junta trials. Streets of Buenos Aires were renamed after disappeared or murdered persons (Azucena Villaflor, first president of Madres de Plaza de Mayo, disappeared), as were schools (Father Carlos Mugica, of the Third World Priests' Movement, murdered by the Triple A) and city squares (Rodolfo Walsh, writer and Montonero activist, disappeared). As of 1995, an account of this recent past was incorporated into school curricula, textbooks, and the school calendar.

These initiatives were resisted by the armed forces and the Menem administration. The federal police maintained control over the Olimpo camp until 2005. In 1998, Menem proposed that the most notorious camp – the Naval School of Mechanics (ESMA), where 5,000 disappeared persons were held – be demolished and a "national unity monument" erected in its place. Human rights organizations filed a judicial action to block the initiative, and together with center-left municipal legislators asked that the ESMA be turned into a Memory Museum (Law 392/2000). On March 24, 2004, the "Space for Memory and the Promotion and Defense of Human Rights" opened at the ESMA, under the direction of the national and municipal governments and representatives of the organizations. At the inauguration ceremony, Kirchner challenged the theory of the two evils and asked forgiveness for the "state's silence" during the twenty years of democracy. This led two generals and an admiral to apply for retirement in protest. The opposition also objected his statements because they omitted state initiatives such as CONADEP or the military Junta trial, and while most organizations supported the museum, Madres de Plaza de Mayo rejected it, understanding that it was closing the history. The account of the past to be presented in this memorial is still under discussion. Other former camps, such as La Perla in Córdoba (March 24, 2007) and Automotores Orletti in Buenos Aires (June 2009), were turned into memorials, and another ten are awaiting similar fate. On the thirtieth anniversary of the coup, Kirchner proposed and Congress approved to recognize 24 March as a national holiday. While these initiatives entailed joint efforts by the state and human rights organizations, new conflicts within and between these actors and public debates indicate the persistence of differences in the interpretation of this past.

Conclusion

After twenty-five years of democracy, Argentina's experience with transitional justice has been intense. It was an international pioneer in the creation of truth commissions and stood out for prosecuting the highest perpetrators of state violence, granting reparation to the victims, and relaying to the new generations the memory of what happened. All these mechanisms have been, and are still today, the subject of heated controversies. But without a doubt they have made it possible to overcome the authoritarian intention of leaving the crimes unpunished and forgotten.

Emilio Crenzel

Cross-references: Amnesty; National Commission on the Disappearance of Persons; Prosecute and Punish; Reparations; Truth Commissions.

Further Readings

Barahona de Brito, Alexandra. 2001. Truth, Justice, Memory and Democratization in the Southern Cone. In *The Politics of Memory: Three Decades of Transitional Truth and Justice*. Eds. Paloma Aguilar, Alexandra Barahona de Brito and Carmen Enríquez. Oxford: Oxford University Press.
Carta a la Comisión Pro-Monumento a los desaparecidos. n.d. Available at: http://www.madres.org/asp/contenido.asp?clave=744 (accessed November 10, 2009).
Comisión Nacional sobre la Desaparición de Personas (CONADEP). 1984. *Nunca Más. Informe de la Comisión Nacional sobre la Desaparición de Personas*. Buenos Aires: EUDEBA. Translated as National Commission on the Disappearance of People, *Never Again a Report by Argentina's National Commission on Disappeared people*. New York: Farrar Straus Giroux, 1986.
Guembe, María. 2006. Economic Reparations for Grave Human Rights Violations: The Argentinean Experience. In *The Handbook of Reparations*. Ed. Pablo De Greiff. Oxford: Oxford University Press.
Malamud Goti, Jaime, ed. 2008. *Game without End: State Terror and the Politics of Justice*. Oklahoma: University of Oklahoma Press.
Vecchioli, Virginia. 2001. Políticas de la memoria y formas de clasificación social ¿Quiénes son las "víctimas" del Terrorismo de Estado en Argentina? [Politics of memory and social classification: Who are the "victims" of the State terrorism in Argentina?]. In *La imposibilidad del olvido. Recorridos de la memoria en Argentina, Chile y Uruguay* [The Impossibility of Oblivion. Tours of the Memory in Argentina, Chile and Uruguay]. Eds. Bruno Groppo and Patricia Flier. La Plata: Al Margen.

Australia

At first glance, approaches to transitional justice in Australia seem to be markedly different from transitional justice projects in other countries that have emerged from periods of authoritarianism, genocide, and armed conflict. Australia is a relatively stable liberal democracy that has not undergone significant regime change, internal armed conflict, or political transformation, with the exception of colonization. However, broadly conceived, two interconnected transitional justice strategies have been implemented in Australia to confront the legacy of the colonial past. The first is the Stolen Generations Inquiry into the laws, policies, and practices of the late nineteenth and twentieth centuries that mandated the forcible removal of Aboriginal and Torres Strait Islander children from their families. The second is the broader national policy of reconciliation since 1991 designed to address colonization, dispossession, and the cultural alienation of Indigenous people. The extent to which transitional justice has redressed the colonial practices of the past is a debate that continues to unsettle the Australian nation.

The Repressive Past

The Indigenous people are the original inhabitants of the Australian mainland, Tasmania, and the offshore islands, including Torres Strait. There is dispute surrounding the origins of the first Indigenous migration to Australia, but the most widely accepted time line for the first arrival is around 50,000 years ago. During this period, Australia, New Guinea, and Tasmania formed a single landmass, which enabled people to migrate to Australia from an extensive land bridge across the Arafura Sea, Gulf of Carpentaria, and Torres Strait. It is also possible that people came across the Timor Sea by boat.

European discovery and colonization started from early 1606, culminating in the arrival of the First Fleet of eleven ships into Port Jackson in Sydney Harbor on January 26, 1788 (a date controversially celebrated as Australia Day). The British government deemed Australia *terra nullius* ("land belonging to no one") to justify colonization and claim sovereignty, effectively ignoring the rights of the Indigenous people who occupied the land for many thousands of years. European settlement had disastrous consequences for the Indigenous people, resulting in the physical and psychological decimation of the population through disease, violent conflict, displacement, dispossession, and the disruption of traditional lifestyles and practices. The history of British colonization and the interactions between Indigenous people and European settlers has been a subject of much debate, popularly known as the "history wars." Some argue that there was peaceful annexation and coexistence, whereas others argue that colonization resulted in violent conflict, ill treatment and cultural genocide.

Between 1869 and 1970, approximately 100,000 Indigenous Australian children were forcibly removed from their families by Australian government agencies and church missions. These children are referred to as the Stolen Generations. They were predominantly of "mixed descent" and were placed – by compulsion, duress, or undue influence – into institutions, internment camps, orphanages, or white families. Many of these children were discouraged from having contact with their families or celebrating their Indigenous culture and identity, and in many cases they were forced or taught to reject and abandon their Aboriginality.

Laws and policies for the forcible removal of children existed in every state of Australia. Since federation in 1901, the Australian states retained exclusive power over Indigenous affairs. This gave governments the authority under "protectionist" legislation to remove Indigenous children with relative ease, requiring minimal legal intervention and justification. In 1869, for example, the Aborigines Protection Act (Victoria) established an Aborigines Protection Board to oversee the "protection" of Indigenous people in that state. This law gave the governor of Victoria the power to remove any Indigenous child from their family to a reformatory or industrial school. Likewise in other states, responsibility for the welfare of Indigenous people was assigned to a Chief Protector or Protection Board, allowing the removal and resettlement of Indigenous people, including the removal of children.

In 1905, the Aborigines Act in Western Australia made the Chief Protector the legal guardian of every Aboriginal and "half-caste" child under the age of sixteen years. In 1909, the Aborigines Protection Act in New South Wales gave the Aborigines Protection Board full control and custody of Indigenous children if a court found the child to be neglected under other legislation. Similar legislation was enacted in other states and territories (although in Tasmania, most Indigenous families had been removed to Cape Barren Island where they were segregated from the non-Indigenous mainland population). The Commonwealth Aboriginals Ordinance 1918 extended the power of chief protectors and governors in each state and territory.

In 1937, the first federal government conference on "native welfare" was attended by representatives of all states and the Northern Territory, except Tasmania. The conference marked the formal, national policy of biological and sociocultural assimilation. At the conference it was concluded that "the destiny of the natives of aboriginal origin, but not of the full blood, lies in their ultimate absorption by the people of the Commonwealth." One of the attendees, A. O. Neville, the Chief Protector of Aborigines in Western Australia, believed that biological absorption was the key to "uplifting the Native race." According to the 1997 *Bringing Them Home – Report of the National Inquiry into the Separation of Aboriginal and Torres Strait Islander Children from Their Families,* Neville's idea was "to keep the pure blacks segregated and absorb the half-castes into the white population" where they would be more readily accepted within the non-Indigenous community. The Protector of Natives in the Northern Territory, Cecil Cook, also saw the rise in half-caste children as a significant problem that could be resolved by the disappearance of the Indigenous race. According to Cook, "The problem of our half-castes will quickly be eliminated by the complete disappearance of the black race, and the swift submergence of their progeny in the white."

After 1940, many Indigenous children began to be removed under child welfare legislation if found to be "neglected," "destitute," or "uncontrollable." According to the *Bringing Them Home* report, "these terms were applied by courts much more readily to Indigenous children than non-Indigenous children as the definitions and interpretations of those terms assumed a non-Indigenous model of child-rearing and regarded poverty as synonymous with neglect."

By 1969, all states and territories had repealed legislation allowing for the forcible removal of Indigenous children from their families. Subsequently, Aboriginal and Islander Child Care Agencies (AICCAs) were set up to contest removal applications and provide alternatives to the removal of Indigenous children from their families.

Australia's policies of assimilation inflicted irreparable individual, family, community, and generational damage, resulting in extensive cultural disconnection for members of the Stolen Generations. A three-year longitudinal Melbourne study during the 1980s revealed that those who were removed from their families were less likely than those not removed to have undertaken or completed secondary education, three times more likely to have a criminal record, twice as likely to have been arrested more than once in the last five years, and twice as likely to use illicit drugs. The Stolen Generations Inquiry and the *Bringing Them Home* report also dealt with forms of contemporary child removal under juvenile justice programs and child welfare legislation (see entry on National Inquiry into the Separation of Aboriginal and Torres Strait Islander Children from their Families, the Stolen Generations Inquiry).

Transitional Justice

Criminal prosecution and individual accountability for the laws, policies, and practices of past Australian governments have not played a role in the Australian context because of the incapacity or unwillingness of the legal system to respond to these types of past wrongs. Instead, nonlegal mechanisms such as the Stolen Generations Inquiry, the *Bringing Them Home* report, and the general process of reconciliation characterize Australia's transitional justice approach to dealing with the general effects of colonization and the more specific impact of ideology, policy, law, and practice that resulted in the children being separated from their families. However, some historical landmark legal decisions concerning native title and land rights in Australia may be viewed as part of the overall strategy for confronting the legacy of colonization, dispossession, and cultural alienation (such as the *Mabo* and *Wik* cases). Moreover, a small number of cases have been heard in Australian courts and tribunals regarding compensation, constitutionality, wrongful imprisonment, breach of statutory duty, negligence, and breach of fiduciary duty (e.g., the *Kruger* and *Trevorrow* cases).

The Stolen Generations Inquiry

The National Inquiry into the Separation of Aboriginal and Torres Strait Islander Children from Their Families was established by the Human Rights and Equal Opportunity Commission (now called the Australian Human Rights Commission) in May 1995. The aim was to receive submissions of evidence from Indigenous and non-Indigenous members of the Australian community regarding the laws, policies, and practices of forcible removal of children. In essence, the Inquiry was a form of truth commission, designed to document the experiences of those affected and to investigate and report on the impact of state-sanctioned human rights abuses. In April 1997, the official report was released, titled *Bringing Them Home*. The report found that the policy of forcible removal was racially discriminatory and constituted a form of genocide under international law. Among other things, the report recommended that the Australian government formally apologize to the affected Indigenous communities.

Former Prime Minister John Howard drafted a motion in 1999 of "deep and sincere regret over the removal of Aboriginal children from their parents," but his government refused to issue a formal public apology. According to Howard, "such an apology could imply that present generations are in some way responsible and accountable for the actions of earlier generations, actions that were sanctioned by the laws of the time, and that were believed to be in the best interest of the children concerned." Although not an official public holiday, a National Sorry Day was established by the public since 1998 to commemorate the *Bringing Them Home* report and to acknowledge the wrongs done to the Indigenous people of Australia (celebrated through events across Australia each year on May 26).

The *Bringing Them Home* report clearly demonstrated the importance of the past in the present and in the future, stating that the "devastation cannot be addressed unless the whole community listens with an open heart and mind to the stories of what has happened in the past." According to the former Governor-General Sir William Deane, "[t]rue reconciliation between the Australian nation and its Indigenous peoples is not achievable in the absence of acknowledgment by the nation of the wrongfulness of the past dispossession, oppression and degradation of the Aboriginal peoples." He added that this form of acknowledgment should not perpetuate a form of personal guilt for ordinary Australians, but rather that it constitutes "our identity as a nation and the basic fact that national shame, as well as national pride, can and should exist in relation to past acts and omission, at least when done or made in the name of the community or with the authority of government."

Reconciliation

The Stolen Generations Inquiry and *Bringing Them Home* report form part of a much broader and holistic package of reconciliation and transitional justice in Australia. Reconciliation is not only concerned with fostering cooperation, solidarity, harmony, and respect to build a partnership between Indigenous and non-Indigenous Australians, but it also aims to promote a shared understanding of the legacy of colonization and dispossession, as well as give formal and legal recognition to injustice, self-determination, sovereignty, land rights, economic independence, and identity to Indigenous Australians. It is essentially a framework for creating a mutual, collaborative, and sustainable process for learning about Indigenous history, culture, and society. Reconciliation is thus both practical and symbolic; it not only necessitates a massive overhaul of social and economic policies to bridge the wide gap between Indigenous and non-Indigenous Australians in the standard social indicators of health, education, life expectancy, crime, and living conditions, but also calls for acknowledgment and restitution for past injustices.

The 1967 referendum is often seen as the beginning of the reconciliation movement in Australia, when 90 percent of the Australian population voted to remove racially discriminatory clauses in the Australian Constitution. One section of the Constitution was deleted to enable Indigenous people to be counted in the Census, and another section was amended to give the Commonwealth the power to make laws with respect to all races, and to make laws to the benefit, not the exclusion, of Indigenous people. Additional sources of consciousness raising included: the 1965 Freedom Ride where a group of students organized a bus tour in New South Wales towns to draw public attention to the poor state of Indigenous health, education, and housing; the 1966 Gurindji strikes in the Northern Territory led by Vincent Lingiari, demanding recognition of land and cultural rights; the 1972 establishment of the Tent Embassy on the steps of Parliament House in Canberra for the recognition of Indigenous land rights; and the introduction of the Racial Discrimination Act in 1975 and land rights legislation in 1976.

The formal reconciliation process in Australia began in 1991 with the establishment of the Council for Aboriginal Reconciliation (CAR) as a statutory authority under the Council for Aboriginal Reconciliation Act 1991 (replaced with Reconciliation Australia in 2001). This was voted on unanimously in Parliament. In 2001, CAR presented the federal Liberal government with a Roadmap to Reconciliation and a Final Report to Federal Parliament, which contained four national strategies for reconciliation at the individual, community, organizational, and governmental levels. This included the National Strategy to Sustain the Reconciliation Process, the National Strategy to Promote Recognition of Aboriginal and Torres Strait Islander Rights, the National Strategy to Overcome Disadvantage, and the National Strategy for Economic Independence.

The then-government under Prime Minister John Howard took nearly two years to make a formal response to CAR's recommendations, rejecting most of them. It refused to apologize to the Stolen Generations and it failed to implement institutional and constitutional change, as well as a sustainable approach to reduce the large socioeconomic gap between Indigenous and non-Indigenous Australians.

Recent Events

In 2007, under the Howard Liberal government, an emergency action plan, known as the Northern Territory National Emergency Response (or Northern Territory Intervention) was introduced as a package of changes to welfare, law enforcement, land tenure, and other measures to address claims of rampant child sex abuse and neglect in seventy-three communities in the Northern Territory. The Northern Territory National Emergency Response Act 2007 was rushed through Parliament, receiving bipartisan support. The

Intervention attracted heavy criticism on a number of grounds, including its suspension of the Racial Discrimination Act 1975 (to enable the widespread bans on alcohol sales, the ban on X-rated pornography, and the compulsory quarantining of welfare payments), and the almost complete lack of consultation with the Indigenous community. Since the election of the Labor government, some changes have been made and some proposals have been raised for future amendment. However, the Intervention as it stands has been criticized by the United Nations Human Rights Committee's 2009 report on Australia's compliance with the International Covenant on Civil and Political Rights (ICCPR) and labeled "racist" by the United Nations Human Rights Rapporteur, Professor James Anaya. According to Anaya, the Intervention measures "overtly discriminate against Aboriginal peoples, infringe their right of self-determination and stigmatize already stigmatized communities."

While the Northern Territory Intervention constitutes a major setback for reconciliation in Australia, a number of positive initiatives have been introduced over the past decade. The most significant was the national apology to the Stolen Generations on February 13, 2008. On this day, Prime Minister Kevin Rudd introduced the Motion of Apology to Australia's Indigenous Peoples in Parliament, which was passed unanimously by the House of Representatives. The apology was made on behalf of the Australian Parliament to all Indigenous people for the policies of past governments, including the policies that mandated the forcible removal of children from their families.

In March 2008, the Rudd government signed the historic Close the Gap Statement of Intent in which it committed to develop a long-term comprehensive action plan targeted toward addressing inequalities between Indigenous and non-Indigenous Australians by 2030. The Council of Australian Governments (COAG) National Indigenous Reform Agreement and the Australian government's "Closing the Gap" strategy on Indigenous disadvantage pledged to: close the life expectancy gap within a generation; halve the infant mortality rate of children under the age of five within a decade; halve the gap between Indigenous and non-Indigenous people in education and employment outcomes within a decade; and ensure all four-year-olds, including those in remote areas, have access to early childhood education within five years.

The Challenges Ahead

The National Reconciliation Week is held each year to celebrate the culture and history of Indigenous Australians and to support a dialogue of reconciliation for the nation. Each July, the National Aborigines and Islanders Day Observance Committee (NAIDOC) holds celebrations across Australia to celebrate the history, culture, and achievements of Aboriginal and Torres Strait Islander peoples, organized by communities, government agencies, local councils, schools, and workplaces. Government departments at the federal and state levels have signed up to Reconciliation Plans (RAPs), launched in July 2006 to encourage and support organizations to engage in the national effort to reduce the large life expectancy gap and contribute to reconciliation. Furthermore, on April 3, 2009, the Rudd government made a formal statement of support for the UN Declaration on the Rights of Indigenous Peoples, despite being one of four countries to vote against the Declaration in September 2007.

There are a number of outstanding issues in relation to reconciliation and transitional justice in Australia. First, the gap between Indigenous and other Australians in the areas of life expectancy, infant mortality, education, employment, and imprisonment is of great concern. Commissioned by the COAG, the Overcoming Indigenous Disadvantage (OID) Report released in July 2009 by the Productivity Commission documented an improvement in only about 20 percent of indicators and deterioration in 10 percent of them, concluding that little progress has been made in overcoming Indigenous disadvantage. A second issue is that after the abolition of the Aboriginal and Torres Strait Islander Commission (ATSIC) in 2004, there has been no national Indigenous representative body, although in August 2009, a model for a new body was put forth to provide Indigenous Australians with a national voice.

Third, institutional change such as a national charter of human rights and a treaty are seen as important to the reconciliation process. Many also advocate the removal of discriminatory provisions in the Constitution, such as section 25 (allowing states to disqualify people from voting because of their race) and section 51(xxvi) (allowing Commonwealth Parliament to pass discriminatory laws), and their replacement with a statement about equality and non-discrimination, as well as a preamble that recognizes Aboriginal and Torres Strait Islanders as the first people of Australia. The fourth important issue concerns compensation for the Stolen Generations. The UN Human Rights Committee in 2009 recommended that Australia establish a national compensation scheme for members of the Stolen Generations, but this has received little support from Australian governments and the general community.

While the majority of Australians support reconciliation and various transitional justice strategies, there are mixed views on how to achieve lasting peace and reconciliation in Australia. The Australian Reconciliation Barometer was designed to document the attitudes of Australians toward reconciliation, based on qualitative studies conducted between May and July 2008 in four core areas: awareness, attitudes, perceptions, and action. Significantly, 100 percent of Indigenous and 91 percent of non-Indigenous Australians thus far thought that a shared relationship is important to the nation. However, only 59 percent of non-Indigenous Australians believed that the Indigenous people hold a special place as the first peoples of Australia. In a number of other significant areas, there remains a gulf between the views and attitudes of Indigenous and other Australians.

Conclusion

Transitional justice mechanisms for responding to the past injustices of colonization, dispossession, and the Stolen Generations policies are embraced within a framework of reconciliation in Australia. Much remains to be done to ensure that past wrongs are adequately acknowledged and compensated for, that the socioeconomic gap between Indigenous and non-Indigenous Australians is eradicated, and that positive perceptions within and between Indigenous and non-Indigenous Australians are supported. Like anything, the substantive nature and extent to which these three components – acknowledgment/compensation, social justice, and nurturing healthy relationships – will determine the success or failure of the transitional justice project, of which power and politics inevitably will play a decisive role. Practical, cultural, symbolic, and spiritual dimensions of reconciliation ultimately require investment into fostering Indigenous self-determination and sovereignty in order to promote legitimacy in governmental policy and ensure the preservation and respect for Indigenous culture. Doing so will not only help the nation as a whole come to terms with its repressive past, but also help transcend this past with a buoyant vision of the future.

Nicola Henry

Cross-references: Apology; Council for Aboriginal Reconciliation; Genocide; Historical Injustices; National Inquiry into the Separation of Aboriginal and Torres Strait Islander Children from their Families, the Stolen Generations Inquiry; Reconciliation.

Further Readings

Altman, Jon and Melinda Hinkson, eds. 2007. *Coercive Reconciliation: Stabilise, Normalise, Exit Aboriginal Australia.* North Carlton: Arena Publications.
Australian Human Rights and Equal Opportunity Commission. 1997. *Bringing Them Home: Report of the National Inquiry into the Separation of Aboriginal and Torres Strait Islander Children from their Families.*
Macintyre, Stuart and Anna Clark. 2003. *The History Wars.* Carlton: Melbourne University Press.
Orford, Anne. 2006. Commissioning the Truth. *Columbia Journal of Gender and Law,* 15: 851–883.
Reynolds, Henry. 1999. *Why Weren't We Told? A Personal Search for the Truth about Our History.* Ringwood: Viking Press.

Austria

In postwar Austria, state institutions and private organizations repeatedly attempted to address the atrocities committed on Austrian soil during the Nazi period (1938–1945). Transitional justice initiatives influenced the country's self-perception of its role in the Nazi crimes. Austria considered itself a victim of Nazi Germany until the 1980s, when society accepted that the country had also played an active role in the Nazi war machine (see entry on Germany – the Nazi Past). Transitional justice remains important for Austrian society and politics.

The Repressive Past

In 1938, the Republic of Austria ceased to exist as an independent state when it became part of the Third Reich. During the first weeks of the occupation, between 50,000 and 70,000 Jews, socialists, communists, and others critical of the Nazi regime were arrested and, in most cases, executed. Until the end of World War II, the Schutzstaffel (Protection Squadron, known as the SS) and the police were in charge of public security in Austria. The SS was a paramilitary organization and the most important agency of the Nazi regime. Its members considered themselves superior in racial purity and ability to other Germans and national groups. While initially the SS operated alongside other important state agencies such as the army and the police, by the end of the war it had gained control over all government agencies in an effort to eliminate perceived threats to the Nazi state. The Sicherheitsdienst (Security Service, known as the SD), the most important organ of the SS, sought to detect the regime's enemies. In Austria, it also played an important role in persecuting the Jewish population. Apart from the SS, the police was a further important pillar of the Nazi dictatorship in Austria. The Geheime Staatspolizei (secret state police, known as the Gestapo) was the most feared. Acts of sheer brutality, degradation, and humiliation were part of a daily routine. Apart from terrorizing the general public, the Gestapo was in charge of solving labor disputes and intimidating workers who seemed to lack a proper work attitude. Thousands of laborers were detained, tortured, and often sent to the front lines. During the final stages of World War II, prisoners of war, forced laborers, and foreign laborers became the preferred target of the Gestapo. Its victims faced severe punishment even for minor offenses. Being late for work, for example, led to the deportation of the offender to concentration camps. Male foreign workers, especially from Poland and other Eastern European countries, were publicly executed without legal basis for having "illegal relations" (private relationships) with Austrian or German women. The Kriminalpolizei (criminal investigative police, known as the Kripo) was another division of the Austrian police in charge of investigation and prevention of "non-political criminal activities." Crime prevention included the persecution of the Roma (the Gypsies).

During the Nazi era, concentration camps existed not only in Germany but also in other territories occupied by the Germans. Shortly after the occupation in 1938, the Nazis built the first concentration camp on Austrian soil near the village of Mauthausen, Upper Austria. A number of smaller subcamps were constructed in all parts of the country to accommodate the rising number of inmates and the growing labor demand of the war industry. The Mauthausen concentration camp was a labor and extermination camp equipped with gas chambers and crematories. It was designed to fulfill the political function of exterminating perceived enemies and meeting the demands of the German war industry at the same time. Inmates had to work for German and Austrian companies under inhumane conditions. They suffered from severe malnutrition, constant abuse, and beatings. Those unable to continue to work were murdered. Apart from the gas chambers, a variety of other methods – such as lethal injections, medical experiments, starvation, and drowning – were used to carry out the regime's policy of extermination through work. In the early years of the occupation, inmates mostly comprised German, Austrian, and Czechoslovak socialists, communists, anarchists, homosexuals, and people of Roma origin. Later, prisoners of war and Jews formed the largest categories of inmates. More than 100,000 people lost their lives in Mauthausen.

The Nazi regime's policy of "racial hygiene" was also implemented in Austria. About 10,000 people with a range of conditions thought to be hereditary, such as schizophrenia, epilepsy, and Huntington's chorea, fell victim to the regime's sterilization programs. Compulsory sterilization was also mandated for chronic alcoholism and other forms of social deviance. In addition, the policy of "racial hygiene" led to the killing of several thousand handicapped children in special clinics in the cities of Vienna, Graz, and Klagenfurt. Another 70,000 people considered "useless" were killed under the euthanasia program T4.

Transitional Justice

In April 1945, the Allies gained full control over Austria. The occupied territory was divided into British, French, Soviet, and American zones and governed by the Allied Commission for Austria. As indicated in the Moscow Declaration of 1943, Austria was considered a victim of the Nazi regime and it was in the interest of the Allies to restore peace and order in the occupied country. Austria thus immediately regained independence. An interim coalition government, including socialists, conservatives, and communists, was formed at the end of April 1945.

Immediate postwar transitional justice initiatives were carried out by the occupying powers and the interim coalition government, with the latter gradually gaining more authority to deal with all different types of crimes committed during the Nazi period. There was consensus among the occupying powers and the interim government that such initiatives should lead to the destruction of the Nazi Party (the National Socialist German Workers' Party, Nationalsozialistische Deutsche Arbeiterpartei or the NSDAP) and all its related organizations, the denazification of the entire state apparatus, and the prosecution of the perpetrators. The Americans enforced their denazification policies most vigorously, whereas the British and the French were more pragmatic. Thus, even ranking Nazi members were allowed to remain in administrative government positions in cases where a vacancy would have compromised the reconstruction process. The Russian authorities were instrumental in the establishment of an interim Austrian government and entrusted it with the enforcement of transitional justice policies.

International Court Proceedings

The International Military Tribunal tried twenty-two of the most prominent Nazi leaders in the German city of Nüremberg in November 1945 (see entry on Nuremberg Trials). A series of trials were also held by the U.S. military in order to prosecute other leading Nazis. Of these, the Mauthausen Camp Trials were the most relevant to Austria's postwar transitional justice process. Sixty-one officials of the Mauthausen concentration camp were indicted. In 1946, fifty-eight officials were sentenced to death by hanging and three to life imprisonment. In nine cases, the death sentence was commuted to life imprisonment.

The Prohibition Act and Denazification

The Prohibition Act (Verbotsgesetz) of August 1945 was designed to prevent the reoccurrence of a Nazi state and to provide the legal framework for prosecuting Nazi crimes. The Act stipulated that the Nazi Party and all its related organizations be dissolved and all their property be transferred to the state. Moreover, any attempt to reestablish such organizations was declared a criminal act. Violators faced severe sentences, including the death penalty. According to the Act, all members of the Nazi Party and its related organizations had to register with the authorities. The registration was necessary to start the process of denazification. In July 1947, the government announced that, based on the information gathered through the registration process, a total of 960 people were removed from high-ranking positions in the state and private sector, some 70,000 of 300,000 civil servants were suspended, and 36,000 other employees lost their jobs in the private sector.

The original version of the Act was very controversial. For example, it allowed registered members of the Nazi Party who were not actively involved in party activities to petition for exemption. This regulation caused serious bureaucratic problems, because more than 85 percent of the Nazis claimed that they had not been active members. A further problem was that the Act did not distinguish between those who were key figures in the Nazi Party and those who held lower positions in the Nazi hierarchy. All Nazis were thus equally sanctioned regardless of the scope of their involvement. In 1947, the Prohibition Act was revised and the National Socialist Act (Nationalsozialistengesetz) was implemented.

The new Act defined the criminal offenses contained in the Prohibition Act in more detail and distinguished between those who held key positions in and those who were "mere followers" of the Nazi regime. Within a year after the Act was passed, the first category numbered 43,468 (accounting for 8 percent of all registered Nazis), while the second included 487,067. The new Act extended the compulsory registration to individuals who were not Nazi Party members but who actively supported the Nazi regime. As a result, 22,000 public servants were suspended. Thus, one-third of the public servants in office in 1945 lost their jobs because of the Prohibition Act. Suspension was one of the "atonement measures" (Sühnefolgen) registered supporters of the Nazi party faced. According to two Acts, high-ranking Nazi Party leaders and other highly active regime supporters had to accept a number of atonement measures, including the payment of special taxes and compensation, the deprivation of civil rights, and a ban on holding positions in public institutions. The group of lower-ranking Nazi supporters ("mere followers") faced similar but less harsh punishment.

The Special Courts

The National Socialist Act further established special courts (Volksgerichte) to deal exclusively with crimes mentioned in the Prohibition Act and the War Criminal Act of 1945. In August 1945, the first such court was set up in Vienna. Soon afterward, three others were established in other major Austrian cities. These courts' verdicts were final; no appeal was possible. Sentences were immediately carried out. The Supreme Court (Oberster Gerichtshof, OGH) could void the judgment and request a retrial with different judges if it observed major discrepancies in the way the special court handled the case. Only those who had no past record of any affiliation with the Nazi regime could become special court judges. The special courts were closed in 1955, when the ordinary courts took over the duty of convicting the perpetrators. Between 1945 and 1955, the special courts held about 90,000 pretrial hearings. There were some 28,000 indictments, and main trials took place in about 25,000 cases. Approximately 90 percent of the main trials were held before 1950. Some 70 percent of the 20,000 people standing trial were found guilty. Almost all of the convicted were Austrians. About half of the trials took place in the Vienna special court. On average, every second indictment let to a conviction.

The War Criminal Act and Court Trials

The interim government passed the War Criminal Act (Kriegsverbrechergesetz) in June 1945. The Act was necessary for several reasons. Existing laws did not cover crimes against humanity, such as denunciation and deportation. Moreover, the German Criminal Code, in force at the time when the crimes were committed, addressed offenses such as murder and personal injury, but the sentences were considered too lenient given the nature of the crimes committed by the Nazis. The interim minister of justice referred to the Act as an exceptional law seeking to deal with exceptional crimes. Whereas some legal experts criticized the Act's retroactive provisions for violating legal principles, most jurists did not consider the Act's retroactivity as morally problematic. Some legal theorists argued that at the time the Act was passed, no equal or higher legal norm prohibited or restricted retroactive legislation. Others pointed out that in 1935 the Nazis had amended the German Criminal Code (Article 2) to permit the retroactive prosecution of any action that deserved punishment according to the "sound feelings of the people." In the Declaration of Independence of April 27, 1945, the interim government noted that the Nazis had to be treated under the same exceptional legal framework that they forced upon the Austrian people. The Act covered offenses such as war crimes, transgression of the right to human dignity, expropriation, and denunciation. Sentences depended on the type of crime committed, the role of the accused in the crime, and the crime's systematic or nonsystematic character. The Act provided for lighter sentences in cases where the accused acted on instructions from his superiors. The Act explicitly read that perpetrators could not claim their innocence by stating that they had just executed orders. Amnesty was granted only in cases when the perpetrator could prove that he/she had committed the crime against her/his own will. None of the accused in the postwar trials could provide sufficient evidence to back such a claim. Tougher sentences were given to those who gave orders or committed the same crime repeatedly. Perpetrators were sentenced to death for committing crimes systematically.

The Act defined war crimes as offenses that contradicted the natural requirements of humanity and violated the generally accepted principles of international law. All key government members during the Nazi period and all other high-ranking members of the Nazi party were declared war criminals who had to be sentenced to death. No evidence of their actual involvement in a crime was necessary because it was believed that whoever had held such positions in the Nazi hierarchy was undoubtedly involved in the planning and ordering of Nazi atrocities. More than 10,000 trials were held on the basis of the War Criminal Act. More than half of the cases dealt with denunciation. No high-ranking members of the Nazi regime were tried under the Act. Some were captured by the Allied forces and tried in Nüremberg or in U.S. trials. Others committed suicide or were killed during the closing days of the war. Moreover, a large number of Nazi Party leaders succeeded in fleeing the country under a different name with travel documents issued by the International Committee of the Red Cross.

Amnesty and Prohibition of Nazi Propaganda

Former members of the Nazi regime were prosecuted in Austria, but there were also calls for amnesties. Many former Nazi Party members considered themselves victims of the Nazi terror rather than perpetrators. This view was supported by conservative politicians who were reluctant to lose the 500,000 former Nazi Party members who were looking for a new political affiliation in postwar elections. During the late 1950s, the Austrian political elite agreed to grant amnesty to those involved in Nazi crimes by abolishing the War Criminal Act and amending the National Socialist Act. Since then, war criminals can only be tried for offenses under the more lenient Criminal Code. There is no statute of limitations for Nazi crimes carrying the death penalty before its abolition in 1950. In total, thirty-five trials have been organized since 1957. Of the forty-nine people indicted, twenty-three were found not guilty and twenty found guilty. In five cases, the trials were suspended. The government at the time believed that, after more than ten years of prosecution, the focus of their anti-Nazi efforts should shift from prosecution to prevention and memoralization. The War Criminal Act was thus abolished, but the Prohibition Act remained in force. Trying to reestablish Nazi organizations, contacting or financing such organizations, or producing propaganda material remain criminal offenses in Austria and carry a minimum prison sentence of ten years. If the offender or the action is particularly dangerous, the penalty is life imprisonment. Belonging to organizations that pursue the aims of the Nazi Party carries a minimum sentence of five years imprisonment. Anyone who denies, grossly trivializes, approves of, or seeks to justify the Nazi genocide or other crimes against humanity in a publication, broadcast, other media, or in any other public manner accessible to others faces imprisonment of between one and ten years.

Several hundred offenders have been found guilty recently. The most prominent case involved the British historian David Irving, who denied the existence of the Nazi crimes in 1989 in two speeches. On entering Austria in 2005, he was arrested, charged under the Prohibition Act, and sentenced to a one-year prison term, which he served.

Right-wing activists and members of the right-wing Austrian Freedom Party have publicly criticized the Act for violating the freedom of expression. The general public and mainstream politicians have vigorously denied such claims, and there seems to be consensus among the Austrian political elite not to abolish the Prohibition Act. By passing the Act, the Austrian government made it clear that the Nazi crimes were historical facts that need not be proven again in court. Supporters note that the European Court of Human Rights repeatedly ruled that the Act's provisions were in line with the European Convention of Human Rights. Article 17 of the Convention explicitly grants governments the right to protect their democratic values and institutions. The Act signals that nobody can belittle the numerous crimes against humanity committed by the Nazi regime and gives respect to the victims, especially those who survived the Nazi terror. The Act's supporters consider it inhumane to glorify and/or trivialize the Nazi atrocities in front of those who suffered and still suffer from the psychological and physical pain caused by those atrocities.

Compensation

For more than thirty years, Austrians considered themselves victims of Nazi Germany and systematically denied any direct involvement of Nazi state institutions and ordinary citizens in the Nazi crimes. Austria therefore refused to pay compensation to victims of these crimes. This attitude changed when former UN Secretary-General Kurt Waldheim ran in the 1986 Austrian presidential elections. The campaign was marred by rumors of Waldheim's participation in war crimes (discussed later). Although they could not be substantiated, the allegations triggered public debate about Austria's participation in Nazi crimes. The year 1986 marked a change in Austria's perception of its role in World War II from being solely a victim of the Nazi regime to being a perpetrator. The Austrian Chancellor Franz Vranitzky confirmed this change in a parliamentary speech in mid-1991.

In 1995, the Austrian government established the National Fund of Austria to offer financial compensation to those who fell victim to Nazi injustice or left Austria to escape such persecution. Victims can receive 5,087 Euros as acknowledgment for the Nazi injustice they suffered. There is no deadline for filing an application. As of late 2010, more than 155 million Euros had been paid to 30,000 victims. In 2001, the Fund was also put in charge of paying compensation for withdrawn tenancy rights, household property, and personal valuables and effects. The deadline for application was June 30, 2004. The 23,000 individual applicants received about 8,500 Euros each in the form of lump-sum payments. Most applicants were of Jewish origin.

Austria's new self-perception, together with increasing pressure from associations of victims living in the United States, led during the late 1990s to the establishment by the Austrian government of other special funds, including the Fund for Reconciliation, Peace and Cooperation, and the General Settlement Fund. The Fund for Reconciliation, Peace and Cooperation was set up in 2000 and accepted applications until 2005. The fund offered a total of 436 million Euros as financial compensation to more than 132,000 forced laborers who worked in Austria between 1938 and 1945. The General Settlement Fund, established in 2001, granted victims of the Nazi regime and their heirs compensation for material loss. Those victims who resided on the territory of present-day Austria and, as a consequence of Nazi persecution, suffered loss through either confiscation or a ban on the exercise of their profession could apply for monetary compensation until May 28, 2003. In total, the Fund paid US$210 million in compensation to more than 19,800 applicants representing more than 100,000 individual victims.

Rewriting History Books

The new Austrian self-perception of its role in the Nazi crimes was also reflected in school history textbooks. While those published before the late 1980s portrayed Austria as a victim of the Nazi regime, those published afterward acknowledged its participation in those crimes.

The International Committee of Historians and the Kurt Waldheim Case

Austrian diplomat and politician Kurt Waldheim (1918–2007) served as United Nations Secretary General (1972–1981) and President of Austria (1986–1992). During the 1985 presidential campaign, the World Jewish Congress alleged that Waldheim had served as an officer in the Nazi Stormtroopers (Sturmabteilung, SA) in 1942–1943, and that he had kept these activities hidden. In response, the Austrian government mandated an International Committee of Historians to investigate Walheim's actions between 1938 and 1945. In its February 1988 report, the Committee found that Waldheim served in the SA, but participated in no war crimes. As noted earlier, the 'Waldheim affair' triggered debates on Austria's role in Nazi atrocities.

Conclusion

Transitional justice in postwar Austria has been manifold. Immediately after the war, transitional justice amounted to the prosecution of key Nazi perpetrators and the denazification of state institutions. Another stage began in 1957 with the passing of the Amnesty Act and the growing importance of reconciliation and prevention. In the mid-1980s, the 'Waldheim affair' marked the third stage. Subsequently, Austria no longer considered itself a victim of Nazi Germany and began to acknowledge its active role in the Nazi war machine. As a consequence, more active reconciliation through compensation began in the early 1990s and still positively influences the country's transitional justice efforts.

Christian Schafferer

Cross-references: Compensation Packages; Germany – the Nazi Past; Nuremberg Trials.

Further Readings

Garscha, Winfried. 2000. Entnazifizierung und gerichtliche Ahndung von NS-Verbrechen. in *NS-Herrschaft in Österreich*. Eds. Emmerich Talos, Ernst Hanisch, Wolfgang Neugebauer, and Reinhard Sieder. Vienna: Oebv, pp. 852–883.
International Commission of Historians. 1993. *The Waldheim Report*. Copenhagen: Museum Tusculanum, University of Copenhagen.
Mueller, Felix. 2005. *Das Verbotsgesetz im Spannungsverhältnis zur Meinungsfreiheit: Eine Verfassungsrechtliche Untersuchung*. Vienna: Verlag Österreich.
Stiefel, Dieter. 1981. *Entnazifizierung in Österreich*. Vienna: Europaverlag.

Azerbaijan

After gaining independence from the Soviet Union in 1991, Azerbaijan's approach to transitional justice has tended mainly toward forgiving and forgetting the injustices of the bloody communist past, which resulted in widespread human rights violations from 1920 to 1991, when the country was a Soviet republic. This approach resulted from the nature of the communist regime, post-independence political instability, lack of will on the part of the main political formations, and the Nagorno-Karabakh war between Azerbaijan and Armenia.

The Repressive Past

Created in 1918, Azerbaijan was the first modern parliamentary republic in the Muslim world, and the first predominantly Muslim country to grant women the right to vote shortly thereafter. In April 1920, the country was invaded by Soviet troops and turned into the Azerbaijan Soviet Socialist Republic, which it remained until October 18, 1991, when it proclaimed its independence. As other communist-controlled Soviet republics, Azerbaijan had to endure Stalinist terror campaigns, mass deportations, Russification (the imposition of Russian language, identity, and culture), and mass surveillance effected at the order of the hegemonic Communist Party by the Committee for State Security (Komitet Gosudarstvennoy Bezopasnosti, KGB).

Given that valuable documents were kept confidential, destroyed, or transferred to Moscow immediately before 1991, there are no estimates for either the number of KGB agents who spied on Azerbaijani citizens or the number of Azerbaijanis victimized by the Soviet regime. Some 12,000 Azerbaijani civilians were killed in the Azeri genocide (Soyqırım) from March 30 to April 3, 1918 by the Bolshevik Baku Soviet. Historian Jamil Hasanli (1991) stated that 40,000 people were convicted for imaginary crimes between 1937 and 1938. From 1937 to 1940, 12,000 persons were imprisoned each year. During the 1930s and the 1940s and in the early 1950s, some 70,000 persons were subject to arrest, deportation, and other forms of repression (including 29,000 intellectuals). Historian Eldar Ismayilov (2007) claimed that the events of 1937 should be considered a genocide, because the communist regime planned to execute 1,500 persons every three months during that year. According to military historian Shamistan Nazirli (2006), in 1937, sixteen Azerbaijani generals were executed. Persons who knew foreign languages were killed in order to destroy the intelligentsia. According to historian Ziya Bunyadov (1993), they were called "enemies of the nation" and were killed after court hearings that sometimes lasted only fifteen minutes. Furthermore, Azerbaijanis were deported to Central Asia, Siberia, and remote areas of Russia as "enemies of Bolshevism." According to information of the Embassy of Azerbaijan in Kazakhstan, 28,000 of the 150,000 Azerbaijanis killed during Stalin-era repressions were shot without investigations and judicial rulings. Terror eased after the death of the Soviet dictator Joseph Stalin in 1953. Still, Russification and mass surveillance of the population continued.

On January 20, 1990 (known as Black January), 26,000 Soviet troops invaded Azerbaijan to stop the independence movement. As a result, 130 innocent people died, 744 civilians were wounded, and the country suffered economic damage.

As a result of the independence movement of 1988–1991, Azerbaijan regained its independence in 1991, without experiencing a genuine regime change. The early years of independence were overshadowed by the war with neighboring Armenia over the province of Nagorno-Karabakh, historically a part of Azerbaijan. By the end of the hostilities in 1994, Azerbaijan had lost control of 20 percent of its territory, including Nagorno-Karabakh and seven surrounding regions, some 30,000 Azerbaijani people had been killed by Armenian military forces, and more than a million were displaced. On November 12, 1995, a new constitution was adopted by referendum. Under Article 7, Azerbaijan is a democratic, secular, unitary republic that upholds the principle of separation of powers.

Transitional Justice

Independent Azerbaijan has embraced very limited transitional justice, and as a result has failed to ensure the rights to justice and truth of victims of the communist regime.

Court Trials

Most of the efforts to reckon with the recent past have related to Black January and took the form of attempts to bring perpetrators to justice. After Black January, Parliament established an Inquiry Commission charged with investigating those events. The Commission interviewed more than 2,500 individuals, consulted experts, and gathered relevant evidence. The evidence was sent to the Azerbaijan General Prosecutor's Office in the hope that a criminal case would be lodged, but that hope has to date gone unfulfilled. On March 29, 1994, parliament officially recognized the events of January 20, 1990 as a criminal attempt to block Azerbaijan's independence and mandated the Prosecutor's Office to undertake investigations and ensure that perpetrators were held accountable. As of this writing, this criminal case, known as the 20 January Case, is formally still being heard by the courts and, as such, remains unsolved. According to the Prosecutor's Office, Azerbaijan officially asked Russia to release to it the relevant criminal case files and to find perpetrators who are hiding in Russia. Russia has not answered that request.

To date, no trials have been launched against the communist decision makers and KGB agents involved in human rights violations. However, more than 345,000 victims of unlawful political repression, perpetrated mainly during the Stalinist period in Azerbaijan, including victims deported to Kazakhstan, were rehabilitated, and the investigation of archival materials is now continuing.

Lustration, File Access, Truth Commission, and Rewriting of History Books

Because the country did not make a clear break with the communist past, the new political leaders did not adopt any lustration, vetting, or screening to ban former communist officials and KGB agents from postcommunist politics. Access has not yet been provided to the KGB files, both because most of these files were transferred to Moscow, kept confidential, or destroyed, and are thus unavailable to the Azerbaijani public, and because their opening might incriminate many postcommunist politicians who started their political careers under communism as KBG informers and secret agents. Although after independence lustration has never been seriously debated in the Azerbaijani parliament, in mid-2010, some political parties not represented in parliament presented to the public a bill on limited lustration that would target only the candidates for the positions of president of the republic, member of parliament, and leader of political parties. According to the bill, the ministry of national security should have the right to release information to the press about these officeholders' past affiliation with the KGB and the Soviet Communist Party (Sultan 2010). At the time of this writing, the bill has not been submitted to parliament.

In addition, Azerbaijan has made little progress in establishing the truth about communist crimes. No truth or investigative commissions were set up to identify those responsible for communist-era human rights violations. However, Azerbaijani historians, journalists, and other social scientists have researched the Soviet atrocities and numerous books have been published on the subject independently of the authorities. History textbooks currently used in schools generally neglect Soviet-era violations of human rights and mostly emphasize the Black January events. Television, radio, and the press also play a truth-seeking role. An Association of Victims of Political Repressions is also working in this area. According to its chairman, Rais Rasulzade, the Association seeks to provide the full list of victims of the communist regime and obtain some reparation (in the form of free public transportation, communal services, health care, etc.) for victims of political repression. Meanwhile, information about the victims was published by both governmental and nongovernmental sources. This information is incomplete, because the number of victims it identifies is much lower than the estimated number.

Property Restitution

The Azerbaijani government has allowed for only very limited property restitution. The Law on the Return of Confiscated Houses to the Owners of November 6, 1991 allowed initial owners or their relatives to receive their abusively confiscated houses, if those had not been sold to or used by somebody else already. However, most of the houses confiscated during Soviet times have been occupied by tenants or sold by communist authorities to new owners. Some of the few unoccupied houses have been used by families displaced during the Nagorno-Karabakh war. The vast majority of the original owners were unable to claim their houses back, because the law makes restitution of occupied houses impossible. Although there have been tense public discussions on the need to amend the law or to adopt new legislation and to recognize the property rights of thousands of Soviet-era victims, the government has taken no concrete steps in this regard.

Reparations and Memorialization

In Azerbaijan, reparations have taken the form of administrative compensation and symbolic commemorations. The Presidential Decree of March 31, 1998 created the honor of 'Martyr of 20 January,' awarded posthumously to the victims of the Black January events, while the Presidential Decree of January 1, 2006 granted monthly pensions worth 300 Azeri Manat (around US$380) to the family members of the martyrs. A subway station in the capital Baku was named after January 20, which was also declared a day of mourning. In addition, the National Martyr Lane Cemetery, the National Memorial, and the Martyrs Mosque have been erected in Baku, and numerous books have been published to celebrate the memory of the martyrs of the Black January events.

The victims of communist-era crimes have received no comparable reparations. However, several symbolic measures have been adopted. Since 1991, Azerbaijan has recognized March 31 as the Day of Azerbaijani Genocide to mark the 1918 events. In addition, most of the Soviet names of schools, public institutions, streets, and subway stations have been changed to Azeri names. For example, the Communist Street was renamed İstiqlaliyyət (Independence) Street, and the Bakı Soveti (Baku Soviet) subway station was renamed the Inner City. Moreover, some Russian schools have been closed, Soviet monuments have been removed, and Russian history is no longer a separate subject in schools and universities. Other nationalizing measures have been implemented, including a transition to 'national surnames' that no longer include Russian suffixes like "ov," "yev," "ova," and "yeva."

Conclusion

Azerbaijan has employed only limited transitional justice methods, and thus its approach to dealing with past communist violations was one of forgiving and forgetting. After gaining independence, Azerbaijan did not prosecute perpetrators, established no truth commission, granted no access to KGB files, implemented no lustration, and provided reparations only to relatives of the victims of Black January, but not those of Soviet repressions and mass killings. This limited reckoning with Soviet crimes was the result of the tense political situation following independence; the Nagorno-Karabakh war, which diverted attention from the crimes of the Soviet occupation; the resistance of political elites, mainly drawn from the ranks of the Soviet-era Communist Party, to reveal their past; and fear that transitional justice would have strained Azerbaijan's relations with Russia and its neighbors and would have further divided an already divided society. The current political situation in the country makes vigorous transitional justice unlikely in the near future.

Seljan Mammadli

Cross-references: Court Trials for Redress; Lustration; Property Restitution; Reparations.

Further Readings

Aliyarli, Suleyman. 1996. *Azərbaycan tarixi* [Azerbaijan History]. Baku: Azerbaijan Press.
Bunyadov, Ziya. 1993. *Qırmızı terror* [Red Terror]. Baku: Azerbaijan Press.
Hasanli, Jamil. 1991. *Ağ ləkələrin qara kölgəsi* [Black Shadow of White Stains]. Baku: Genjlik Press.
Javadli, Natig. 2007. *37-ci il hadisələri genosid sayılmalıdır* [The Events of 1937 Should Be Considered as Genocide]. Bizim Yol, November 29. Available at: http://www.bizimyol.az/index.php?mod=news&act=view&nid=6222 (accessed August 20, 2011).
Nazirli, Shamistan. 2006. *Güllələnmiş Azərbaycan generalları* [Executed Azerbaijani Generals]. Baku: Kooperasiya Press.

Qazaxıstanda 150 min azərbaycanlı – Stalin repressiyası qurbanlarının xatirəsinə abidə ucaldılıb [The Memorial for 150,000 victims of Stalin-era Repressions was built in Kazakhstan:], Gunaz TV, June 1, 2008. Available at: http://www.gunaz.tv/aze/37/newsCat/1/newsID/2712 (accessed August 20, 2011).

Sultan, Rufat. 2010. əvəz Temirxan "KQB" casusları haqda qanunun layihəsini də hazırlayıb [Avaz Temirkhan prepared the Law on "KGB" agents], Bakı Xəbər, August 26. Available at: http://baki-xeber.com/new/2010/08/26/get=48396 (accessed August 20, 2011).

Tahirzada, Adalat. 2011. *1937–38-də güllələnən (həbs olunan) şəxslər* [Persons Executed (Convicted) during 1937–38]. Available at: http://www.adam.az/az.php?category=71 (accessed August 20, 2011).

Bangladesh

Bangladesh gained its independence from Pakistan in 1971 in a bloody process that left deep scars and divisions. While most Bengali residents of West Pakistan supported the call for independence, non-Bengali (Bihari) immigrants from India and some Bengalis collaborated with the Pakistani government in its bloody suppression of the movement. During this period, the Pakistani Army and its civilian sympathizers committed systematic human rights abuses, especially against the Hindu minority, while the Bangladeshi guerrillas fighting for Bangladeshi independence (the Mukti Bahini) committed atrocities against Pakistani Army prisoners and the Bihari ethnic group, which supported Pakistan. This legacy of violence prevented Bangladesh from attaining full national integration and has inhibited economic development.

The Bangladeshi government has long planned to initiate transitional justice to bring closure and healing to these deep emotional wounds, but bitter rivalries have consumed Bangladesh's political parties and leadership. Only recently have Prime Minister Sheikh Hasina and her government felt secure enough to take steps to come to terms with the past. The Bangladesh government is trying to devise civil rights protections for the Bihari and Hindu ethnic and religious minorities persecuted during the independence struggle. As part of this process, Bangladesh has negotiated with Pakistan to allow ethnic Biharis to resettle in Pakistan. The Bihari population of Bangladesh is currently 250,000 (0.25 percent of the population), down from 750,000 at independence. Since the establishment of Bangladesh, many Biharis emigrated to Pakistan. Efforts to resettle the remaining Biharis (currently residing in sixty-six camps in Bangladesh) in Pakistan have ground to halt, as Pakistan is reluctant to accept them. Those in the camps remain stateless.

The Repressive Past

In 1947, the overwhelmingly Muslim Bengali population of East Bengal originally welcomed separation from India as part of the new country of Pakistan. The move was largely viewed as a means of escaping the economic and social dominance of the Hindu minority. Pakistan's founder, Muhammad Ali Jinnah, envisioned the country as a homeland for Indian Muslims regardless of their ethnicity. This vision came unraveled almost from the beginning.

Pakistan was established as a multiethnic state with two wings, East Pakistan and West Pakistan. East Pakistan was overwhelmingly Bengali, while West Pakistan was a multiethnic state dominated by the Punjabi ethnic group.

Although Bengalis formed a slim majority of the Pakistani population, the West Pakistanis (particularly the Punjabi ethnic group) dominated the military and West Pakistani feudal elites dominated the economy. They engaged in systematic economic and social discrimination against the Bengali majority, which began to feel marginalized in Pakistan almost from the beginning. The Bengalis' sense of inferiority was confirmed when Jinnah declared Urdu, the language of West Pakistanis, the national language in 1948. In 1952, the Governor General of East Pakistan rejected Bengali demands for an equal status for the Bengali and Urdu languages and banned pro-Bengali demonstrations. On February 21, university students defying the ban were fired on by Pakistan security forces dominated by West Pakistanis, and several students were killed. The movement quickly escalated into a general confrontation with more clashes and the deaths of more demonstrators. The Awami League, East Pakistan's leading political organization, threw its support behind the pro-Bengali demonstrators. Their demonstrations continued intermittently until 1956, when Pakistan adopted the dual language formula.

The Awami League, under the leadership of Sheikh Mujibur Rahman, attempted to address deep Bengali grievances by agitating for more autonomy for East Pakistan throughout the 1960s. The Pakistani military, which dominated the country's political and economic establishment, responded to Awami League demands with increasing repression, culminating in Rahman's arrest in 1966. He was released from prison in 1969 following massive popular demonstrations. The following year, the Awami League won a parliamentary majority, but the military government of Yahya Khan, the Pakistani president, refused to allow Rahman to become prime minister, as required by the constitution, and instead arrested him again on March 26, 1971.

Before his arrest, Rahman publicly declared independence of East Pakistan as the new, predominantly Bengali state of Bangladesh. In response, the Pakistani army launched Operation Searchlight, a sustained military assault on East Pakistan designed to crush the resistance movement. In this operation, the army was assisted by a paramilitary organization called the Razakars. Most members of this group were Urdu-speaking migrants from India to East Pakistan who did not share Bengali cultural roots with the province's majority population. Because most came from the East Indian state of Bihar, they were commonly referred to as biharis by the Bengali majority.

The attempt to crush the independence movement lasted from March until Bangladesh won its independence on December 16, 1971. During this nine-month period of conflict, the army and the Razakars worked from pre-prepared lists, targeting intellectuals, students, and members of the Hindu minority for murder. There are differing estimates regarding the number of Bengalis systematically killed, with official Bangladeshi sources contending that it approached 3 million, while others argue it could be as few as 300,000. It is estimated that between 250,000 and 3 million Bengali women were raped during this period, resulting in at least 25,000 pregnancies. In addition, 10 million Bengalis, mostly Hindus but including large numbers of Muslims, were driven from their homes and forced to seek refuge in India.

Discrimination against non-Muslim minorities is another repressive element of the Bangladeshi past. The tribal population of Bangladesh, amounting to less than 1 percent of the total population, is predominantly Buddhist, with some Christians and Hindus. The remainder of the population shares Bengali ethnicity and speaks the Bengali language. The Pakistan ideology emphasized a common identity for all Indian Muslims who were to share a common Pakistani nationality after the foundation of the state.

It did not take long for the Bengali Muslim population to grow disenchanted with the Pakistan ideal, as they were subjected to discrimination based on their ethnic identity. They began to assert the ethnic identity they shared with the large Hindu minority.

This influential group has played a significant role in the history of the region. Prior to independence, Hindus made up approximately 17 percent of the East Pakistan population. During the Bangladesh War of Independence of 1970–1971, the Pakistan army and the Razakars drove millions of Hindus from Bangladesh. After the establishment of independent Bangladesh in 1971, many Muslim Bangladeshis continued to press for the removal of Hindu citizens to India. Much of this behavior was motivated by economics rather than religious prejudice, as anti-Hindu religious bigotry was not common or well entrenched in Bangladesh. Many prosperous Hindu families were forced to abandon their holdings when they fled to India. This property was often taken over by Muslim families illegally, while opportunistic Muslims conspired to acquire Hindu land confiscated by the Bangladeshi government. Hindus now constitute 9.2 percent of the Bangladeshi population.

During and immediately after the independence struggle, the Awami League propounded the common Bengali identity, downplayed religious differences, and advocated equal rights for all citizens of the country and a secular government kept separate from Islam. After the August 1975 assassination of Sheikh Mujibur in a military coup, leading military officer General Ziaur Rahman (not related to Sheikh Mujibur) took power and restored order. Rahman founded his own political party, the Bangladesh Nationalist Party (BNP). The BNP advocated a strong Islamic identity for Bangladesh and the use of Islamic symbols, the Arabic language, and Islamic legal strictures, while downplaying constitutional protections for Hindus.

Sheikh Hasina, the daughter of Sheikh Mujibur, assumed the leadership of the Awami Party after her father's murder. At the time of this writing, the BNP is headed by Begum Khaleda Zia, the widow of General Ziaur Rahman, who was assassinated in a 1981 military coup. Bangladeshi politics is dominated by the rivalry between these two parties and two families. Both have alternated periods in power. After the Awami Party won a decisive victory in the December 2008 elections, Sheikh Hasina was sworn in as prime minister. Since returning to power, the Hasina government has attempted to become more secure and has revived the reconciliation process in an effort to unite public opinion and score points against the political opposition.

Transitional Justice

Since the end of the Bangladesh War of Independence, subsequent governments have attempted to come to terms with the tragic events of 1970–1971, but domestic political upheaval prevented these programs' implementation. From 1971 to 1975, purges and court trials were used as transitional justice methods. In 1982, the Bangladesh government established a National Martyrs Memorial and a Bangladesh Liberation War Museum, but refrained from adopting other methods. In 2009, parliament amended the International Crimes Tribunal Act of 1973, restoring the previous war crimes tribunals, adopted a property restitution law, and promised trials of purported war criminals.

Banning "Collaborators" from Politics

The Bangladesh Constitution, written in 1972 during Sheikh Mujibur's first year in office, acknowledged the sacrifices of those who fought and died for independence. The Awami League government banned religiously based political parties and proscribed those who "collaborated" with the Pakistani army and government from voting or participating in politics. The government took steps to establish tribunals to convict those guilty of atrocities and war crimes. Sheikh Mujibur called a halt to the process, which became unwieldy and unmanageable, and in 1975, a coup attempt by mid-level officers ended any prospect of reviving the process. After Ziaur Rahman came to power, he nullified the ban against religious parties, moved to integrate "collaborators" into the political mainstream, and did not restore the tribunals. Bengali war veterans estimated that the Ziaur Rahman government released 11,000 persons held by the Awami League government, awaiting trial for war crimes. The current government has no plans to relaunch the vetting program.

Memorialization

Subsequent Bangladeshi governments have taken steps to ensure a measure of symbolic justice. To this end, in 1982, the government established a National Martyrs Memorial and a Bangladesh Liberation War Museum to perpetuate the memory of the 1970–1971 events and pay deference to those who lost their lives and homes.

Court Trials for Redress

In April 2009, parliament restored the previous war crimes tribunals and the prime minister promised to start the trials as quickly as possible. The government appointed a Chief Investigation Officer, formed an investigation agency to probe atrocities committed during the war, and approached the United Nations for assistance. The UN proposed providing four top international experts to help Bangladesh establish a credible process and pledged to examine Bangladeshi legislation to ensure that it complied with international standards, but stopped the process after receiving complaints from Pakistan. The Bangladeshi government also discussed approaching the governments of the United States and Pakistan to request documents related to the events of 1970–1971 to assist in the prosecutions and asking Pakistan to provide the names of Bangladeshi citizens who cooperated with the Pakistani army, but, as of this writing, has not formally done so.

The Bangladesh government has identified 1,779 Bangladeshi individuals guilty of war crimes, including 369 members of the Pakistani Armed Forces. Most are Bengali members of the Jamaat-e-Islami party, which belonged to the pro-government militia Al Badr. The Jamaat-e-Islami is strongly opposed to the Awami League. Critics of the tribunals have accused the government of using the process for partisan political purposes.

The Bangladesh government has established a headquarters for its tribunals in Dhaka, the national capital, and has provided a budget. On March 25, 2010, the tribunals were officially inaugurated, with a staff of three high court judges and six investigators. Although there have been no trials to date, the Bangladesh Law Minister Shafique Ahmed has promised to conclude the process before the current administration ends its term, and the first charges have been filed against senior Jamaat leaders, including Amir Nizami and Secretary General Mojahid.

Property Restitution

The Sheikh Hasina government has also tried to assure civil protections and/or justice for the Hindu minority. In particular, the restoration of 2.5 million acres of agricultural land, factories, and residential property seized from Hindu families during the periods of upheaval would do much to reassure the Hindu community that it has a viable place in Bangladeshi society and could potentially mitigate the ongoing migration of Hindu citizens to India. On November 2, 2009, the Bangladeshi cabinet approved legislation aimed at returning Hindu properties confiscated by the Pakistani government during the 1965 India-Pakistan war to their Hindu owners still resident in Bangladesh. The Vested Property Return (Amendment) Act of 2009 divided this Hindu property into two categories: returnable and nonreturnable. Much of the property has become subject to lawsuits. The returnable property would be free of disputed claims. Property can only be returned to original owners or their heirs, if they are resident citizens of Bangladesh. The Hasina government hopes to compel local governments to publish a list of all such property within six months after the legislation comes into effect. Hindu claimants could then file for the returnable property, while local governments would settle the disputed claims. The Awami League had tried to implement this procedure during its 1996–2001 tenure, but in 2002, the BNP abandoned the process and law was not passed until 2009.

Conclusion

There is a crying need for transitional justice in Bangladesh. The population needs to come to terms with the bloody chapters in the country's history. Millions of Bangladeshis, both Hindu and Muslim, suffered during the attempts by the Pakistani Army and its allies to repress the independence movement. While the establishment of museums and monuments have already been completed, further action will be required before the country can purge the grim memories haunting Bangladeshi society. The current government has taken concrete steps to address these issues by identifying those guilty of human rights abuse and war crimes. It now hopes to make the next step and bring the accused to justice. This has proven to be a complex process, and there is growing frustration with the long delays. The Bangladesh government is also coming to terms with the mistreatment meted out to the country's Hindu minority and is trying to assure equal protection under the law for non-Muslim minorities. Although the Bangladeshi state was founded as a homeland for both Hindu and Muslim Bengalis, the confiscation of Hindu property under various pretexts has helped drive Hindus out of the country and belied the original premise of the country. The correction of this inequity, even forty years after the fact, would work to reconcile Bangladesh's Hindu and Muslim populations.

Jon P. Dorschner

Cross-references: Court Trials for Redress; Pakistan; Property Restitution; Purges.

Further Readings

Azad, Abul Kalam M. 2009. Bangladesh to Seek Evidence from Pakistan, U.S. in War Crimes, *The Daily Star*, Dhaka, Bangladesh, July 4, 4.
Khan, Yasmin, ed. 2008. *The Great Partition – The Making of India and Pakistan*. New Haven: Yale University Press.
Ministers Urge Patience for War Crime Trials, *BDNews24*, November 8, 2009. Available at: http://www.bdnews24.com/details.php?id=146480&cid=2 (accessed May 30, 2010).
Noman, Abu A. B. M. 2009. *Transitional Justice and Witness Protection: Bangladesh Perspective*. Presented at the Second Conference on Genocide, Truth and Justice, Dhaka, Bangladesh, July 30–31.

Rahman, Anisur. 2009. Dhaka Approves Law to Return 1965 Indo-Pak War Hindu Property, *Daily Pioneer*, November 3. Available at: http://www.dailypioneer.com/213032/Dhaka-approves-law-to-return-1965-Indo-Pak-war-Hindu-property.html (accessed May 30, 2010).

Sumita, Benita. 2007. *South Asia and Genocide: A Case for Prevention*. International Association of Genocide Scholars, July. Available at: http://works.bepress.com/benita_sumita/2/ (accessed May 30, 2010).

Belgium

Belgium experienced transitional justice after World War I and World War II, when this parliamentary democracy was occupied by the Germans and some of its citizens collaborated with the invaders. Although the punishment of collaboration after World War II was inspired to a large extent by the trials that followed World War I, its scale was more extensive. After 1944, former collaborators were excluded from Belgian political and social life not just by means of court trials, but also by purges (see entries on Court Trials for Redress and Purges). After both wars, measures were also taken to punish German war criminals.

The Repressive Past

In August 1914, German troops invaded and nearly completely occupied Belgium until November 1918. The invasion was accompanied by atrocities committed by the Germans against Belgian citizens suspected to have acted as *franc-tireurs* (irregular snipers). The Belgian government resided outside the Belgian territory, in Le Havre (France), and operated in exile, while the German military and civil administration governed the Belgian territory. Unemployment was high, and 120,000 Belgian citizens were forced to work in Germany (2,600 of them died there). The Germans aimed to separate administratively, along linguistic lines, the Dutch-speaking north (Flanders) and the French-speaking south (Wallonia). French was the high-status language, used by the Belgian elites. Since the nineteenth century, the Flemish movement strived for the emancipation of the Dutch-speaking Belgians. Some members of this movement collaborated with the Germans and supported the administrative separation of the country. They were called "activists," a term generally used after 1918 for collaborators, even if not all of them were implicated in political collaboration or supported calls to regard Dutch on par with French or to create a separate Flemish state. Many were economic collaborators who had traded with the Germans and were mostly motivated by profiteering.

Nazi Germany occupied Belgium from May 1940 to September 1944, when the country was liberated by Allied troops. The ruling German administration relied on the Belgian administrative, judicial, and economic structures to control the country, maintain law and order, and make Belgium subservient to the German war effort. Members of the collaborationist Belgian fascist parties, the Flemish National Union (Vlaamsch Nationaal Verbond or the VNV) and the francophone Rex, were appointed to leading positions in the central and local public administration. Nazi-inspired economic and political reforms, such as Nazi corporatism in agriculture, industry, and commerce and a single trade union, modified the Belgian political system. Political opponents were persecuted and sent to concentration camps in Belgium and Germany, Jews were deported and murdered, and certain social groups, mostly workers, were forced to work in Germany. Total casualties amounted to 75,000, of whom 29,250 were Jews, 14,545 Resistance members, and 2,952 deported workers. The Belgian Resistance movement was active in the fields of clandestine press, sabotage, intelligence for the Allies, and trade unionism. During the Nazi occupation, the Belgian government was exiled to London, from where it prepared transitional justice programs.

Transitional Justice

During 1918–1922 and 1944–1950 – that is, the periods that immediately followed the end of each world war – the Belgian government adopted several transitional justice measures. The issue of loyalty to the Belgian state was central to the transitional justice legislation. The fact that the ideological and political specificity of Nazism was not considered explains the limited prosecution and punishment of those who persecuted and murdered Jews. During the 1950s and the early 1960s, different legal measures sought to mitigate the long-term consequences of postwar transitional justice. In the early 1950s, most collaborators convicted to imprisonment were liberated: by 1952, only 770 persons out of about 26,000 remained in prison.

Court Trials of Former Collaborators

Collaboration of Belgian citizens with the German occupiers during World War I and World War II was punished by the Belgian Penal Code, which included a section (book two, title one, chapter two) on "crimes and criminal offenses against the external security of the state." Articles 113 and 115 of the Penal Code of 1867 made life imprisonment the sentence for military and economic collaboration, defined as military or economic aid to the enemy. During World War I, the Penal Code was amended to strengthen provisions regarding espionage on behalf of another state and to punish other acts of collaboration such as political collaboration, defined as serving the political aims of the enemy (Article 118bis), and informing, defined as exposing someone to persecution or even death by giving information on him/her to the enemy (Article 121bis). After 1916, these crimes became punishable by death. The Decree-Law of 12 October 1918 on the residence in Belgium of foreigners and persons of foreign origins made possible the internment of foreigners, former citizens of an enemy state, and naturalized Belgian citizens. This measure had an administrative, not penal, character, as people were not subject to a judicial inquiry, but were interned on an administrative basis, because they were seen as a threat to law and order. This internment was designed to prevent espionage and protect the Belgian army during the time. Civil servants at all levels of the administration could be purged if found to have collaborated with the Germans, and thus they could lose their public posts.

Between 1918 and 1922, some 3,900 persons were tried for collaboration by criminal courts, military tribunals, and assize courts. In a military tribunal, the judges were army officers, whereas in an assize court, the accused were tried by a jury of laymen. The number was relatively modest in comparison to the post-1944 figures and scale of the collaboration (activism alone concerned 15.000 people). Former and suspected collaborators were confronted with (symbolic) violence in the form of plunder or destruction of their personal furniture by mobs. All over the country, women collaborators had their heads shaved. In 1929, the government granted amnesty to former collaborationists out of fear that they could gain martyr status. Flemish nationalists used punishment of collaboration to question the legitimacy of the Belgian state. In 1929, the Flemish nationalist August Borms, one of the most emblematic and radical figures of the activist movement, was elected to parliament while serving a prison sentence for collaboration. His election showed that the work of the judiciary was questioned by some electors in Flanders. The jurisprudence and legal doctrine resulting from the post-1918 trials shaped transitional justice after 1944, because the legislation and the Penal Code underwent no fundamental changes between the wars. If anything, legislative amendments introduced between 1934 and 1940 made it easier to punish people (the special intent was abolished for crimes such as political collaboration) and introduced new punishable acts. The Law of 20 July 1939 added Article 135bis to the Penal Code, punishing the receipt by Belgians of gifts, loans, or other advantages in return for propagandizing for a foreign state or for undermining the fidelity of Belgian citizens to the state and the Belgian state institutions.

Before the Nazi invasion, in the name of protecting the existence and neutrality of the Belgian state, its citizens' constitutional civil rights were limited and the involvement of foreign organizations and citizens in Belgian politics was prohibited. The Law of 22 March 1940 on the defense of the national institutions, directed against the Communist Party, punished those who created or directed formations seeking the "destruction of Belgium's independence, the constitutional liberties or the institutions of the Belgian people" or produced propaganda aimed at "the destruction of Belgium's independence, or the constitutional liberties or the institutions of the Belgian people" (Law of 22 March 1940 on the Defense of the National Institutions). This law was designed to protect the army on a temporary basis and was applicable only until the army was demobilized in 1949.

Between 1942 and 1944, the Belgian government in exile in London and the Chief Military Prosecutor W. J. Ganshof van der Meersch, who stayed in Belgium after the invasion but joined the London government in 1943, amended the articles of the Penal Code on military and political collaboration and informing to allow the punishment of acts of collaboration committed in occupied Belgium, which had not been punished until then. The legislation continued to punish those who helped the enemy, obstructed the country's liberation, and undermined the "spirit of resistance." The new amendments stressed continuity with post–World War I legislation.

More innovative was Decree-Law of 6 May 1944 on the Loss of Nationality and the Dissolution of Certain Rights for Crimes Committed against the External Security of the State in Wartime, which added the dissolution of rights (such as to vote, to be elected to public office, to be a solicitor or a teacher, to be involved in the press, cinema, theater, radio, and banking, and to lead a professional or nonprofit organization) to the penalties incurred by those convicted of collaboration with the enemy. The ban was for life. This Decree-Law laid the foundations of the transitional justice program in Belgium, whose basic features remained unchanged, although the legislation was fine-tuned from 1944 to 1950. The transitional justice instrument was the penal law. Sanctions included the death penalty, fines, the denial of political and civil rights, and the ban from political and professional life of collaborators, defined as citizens who had helped the enemy. Transitional justice was carried out by the state, as collaboration was judged only by the military courts and the Resistance had no part in the hearings. Punishment for collaboration protected the state, its institutions, and economic resources, and targeted Belgian citizens or people who had lived in Belgium for a long time, and who had been a threat to the state (including its institutions and the resources it could mobilize against the enemy) by collaborating with the enemy under the occupation regime. If collaborators had profited from their collaboration, the state could confiscate the goods or money thus acquired. In cases of economic collaboration, the state requested and often received damages from the collaborators, on the grounds that economic collaboration had lengthened the war and thus the Belgian state was forced to incur more expenses, which needed to be compensated. In January 1945, the government established an Office for the Sequestration of the Properties of Persons Accused of Collaboration or of Suspected Persons or Organizations to collect the fines and conduct the confiscations ordered by the courts in view of covering damages to the Belgian state. The Office could take over the management of the assets of the convicted and indicted collaborators.

Numerous cases of collaboration were heard by military courts. In all, 52,778 persons were judged by military courts between 1944 and 1950. Penalties varied from short jail terms to the death penalty. Some 242 convicted collaborators were executed. Financial sanctions amounted to 17 billion Belgian Francs (equivalent to US$340 million).

Internments and Purges of Former Collaborators

In August 1944, a month before the end of the occupation, Minister of Justice Circular 340 revived the Decree-Law of 12 October 1918 by ordering the arrest and internment of all citizens of Germany and its allies present on the Belgian territory, and Belgians suspected of having maintained relations with the enemy, including persons who had worn a uniform of the German army or a service connected with the German army, had been connected with German political or paramilitary organizations, had worked for the German public administration units, or had committed misconduct during the occupation and could expect public vengeance. This administrative measure aimed to protect the liberating Allied armies, maintain public order by removing from public space those who had had close relations with the enemy, and protect people against public vengeance expected to arise after Belgium's liberation. Public vengeance also emerged after the return of political prisoners from concentration camps and forced laborers from Germany in the spring of 1945. The internment policy targeted suspected Belgians. The Decree-Law could also be used for the internment of former collaborators who could not be punished immediately after the liberation because the Belgian administrative and judicial authorities had been paralyzed by the German occupier. Internments could be ordered by mayors, military and public prosecutors, and the head of the State Security Office. Many of those placed in internment camps were arrested by the Resistance. Up to 77,000 persons had been interned by February 1945. Alleged collaborators met with (sometimes symbolic) violence, women were shaved, and about 100 persons were killed in revenge.

As already mentioned, Decree-Law of 6 May 1944 denied all people punished for collaboration certain rights in an effort to exclude from public life collaborators who cooperated with the enemy or "put the fatherland in danger." In justifying the measure, the government in exile argued that collaboration should have been punished with loss of citizenship but, because statelessness was a difficult position to be in and the existence of stateless persons had been a source of tension after World War I, the government decided to revoke only the citizenship of collaborators convicted in absentia.

The Decree-Law of 19 September 1945 on the Civic Purge affected 21,889 individuals. Lesser collaboration acts (such as membership in collaborationist parties or organizations) were not heard and punished by the courts, but people who had committed them were denied their civil and political rights for life or twenty years, depending on the nature of the collaboration. Although new, the civic purge fitted the existing mechanisms punishing collaboration. The military courts carried out the civic purge. The military prosecutor identified the persons who met the criteria listed in the Decree-Law (which mentioned organizations, parties, and institutions such as the VNV, Rex, national-socialist youth organizations, and paramilitary organizations). The information was taken from the documentation collected by military prosecutors. These people were deprived of political and civil rights automatically, without any trial or consideration of individual circumstances. The prosecutor's decisions could be appealed with the civil court within fifteen days. The civic purge aimed to bar collaborators from voting in the first postwar elections. In addition, specific regulations were elaborated to purge civil servants, teachers, railway personnel, and those who held public office. Those suspected of collaboration could be sanctioned according to the pre-1940 disciplinary rules of their profession and could lose their job. This purge was often carried out by special commissions. A total of 10,659 civil servants were sanctioned.

The punishment of collaboration and the civic purge mainly affected the prewar fascist VNV and Rex parties, whose leaders had collaborated with the occupier, and people who had volunteered for German (para)military formations. The purge led to elite change when the wartime elite formed of members of collaborationist parties lost their leadership positions. Soon a discourse of victimization developed, because the purged included many close to the Catholic Party in Flanders. Flemish nationalists sanctioned for collaboration presented themselves as victims of the Belgian state that excessively punished Flanders and the Flemish elite. Hoping to regain the Flemish nationalist vote, the Christian Democratic Party (Christelijke Volkspartij, CVP) was responsive to these complaints and favored measures to mitigate the punishment and the civic purge, introduced from 1948 onward. Thus, transitional justice was politicized, influencing the left-right polarization of Belgian politics in the late 1940s, when the Christian Democrats sought to obtain an absolute parliamentary majority. Criticism of the punishment of collaboration led to the creation in 1949 of a new Flemish nationalist party, Vlaamse Concentratie, founded in1949 to participate in the parliamentary elections that year. Amnesty became a central element of the political programs of Flemish nationalists, but was never realized as Flanders and Wallonia had, and still have, radically different opinions on the question. Wallonia identified with the Resistance, was more left-wing, and wanted to make no concessions to former collaborators. Flanders was more right-wing and identified less with the Resistance. Amnesty was demanded by the Flemish Nationalists, who did not repudiate their collaboration. The debate on collaboration and amnesty was reinforced by the language cleavage dividing Belgian politics.

War Crimes

The punishment of the crimes of World War I was complicated by international politics and Belgium's lack of specific legislation to deal with war crimes. After the war, Belgium wanted to take 1,132 persons to court, but this number was reduced to 334 under Allied pressure following German protests. The Allies preferred trials conducted by German courts and German judges. Fifteen war criminals were brought before the Leipzig court. Belgian authorities felt that the court did not take its task seriously, so they withdrew from the trials in Leipzig. The alternative, imposed by the Treaty of Versailles (1919), to bring the war criminals before military court in the country where they committed the crimes was an obstacle for Belgium, whose military tribunals could not judge war criminals from another country. The only possibility left was to judge war criminals before the ordinary courts if the inquiry had started before the ratification of the Treaty of Versailles. These trials were organized in absentia: twenty-eight persons were sentenced to death, two received life imprisonment, and twenty-two were discharged. The legislation on military court jurisdiction remained unchanged, and as a result, this problem reappeared in 1945.

New legal instruments were created. The Decree-Law of 13 December 1944 on the Creation of the Commission of Inquiry on the Violation of Rules of International Law and the Laws and Customs of Warfare established a War Crimes Commission that cooperated with the United Nations War Commission to investigate the war crimes committed by the Germans in Belgium (including the persecution of the Jews). The Belgian Commission had to collect evidence, identify perpetrators, and inform the population and the international community about the war crimes committed by the Germans on Belgian territory. It focused mostly on informing the public. Several brochures on war crimes were published in 1947–1948. War crimes were less a matter of concern for the public than after World War I, because Belgium was no longer the prime victim of German aggression, the war crimes committed in Eastern Europe overshadowed those in the West, and after 1945 war crimes were dealt with at an international level, in Nürnberg, where France represented Belgium.

The Law of 20 June 1947 on the Competence of Military Courts to Judge War Crimes assigned the trial of war criminals to those courts. Previously the Military Courts were only competent for collaboration crimes, which could not be committed by military men of the occupying forces. Giving the Belgian military tribunals the power to judge the crimes committed by German soldiers and officers was justified by their capacity as military men, and the fact that the Belgian military courts had monopoly over crimes related to collaboration, to which war crimes were often linked. Ninety-one war criminals were tried, eighty-three were convicted, of which twenty-one received the death penalty. One person was executed.

Conclusion

After World War I and World War II, Belgium adopted several transitional justice programs aimed at weeding out collaborators and reinforcing loyalty in the state. However, by the early 1950s, the process of coming to terms with the recent past was politicized and used as a bone of contention among the country's linguistic and ethnic groups, each of which had radically different views on the matter. As a result, some of the methods adopted immediately after the end of World War II (especially the civic purge) were drastically limited in scope by the early 1960s.

Dirk Luyten

Cross-references: Court Trials for Redress; Lustration; Purge.

Further Readings

Bourgeois, A. and G. Temmerman. Verslag namens de werkgroep belast met het opmaken van een inventaris van de sociale en menselijke gevolgen voor de slachtoffers van de oorlog, met name ook van de Spaanse burgeroorlog en voor de getroffenen van de repressie- en epuratiewetgeving [Report of the Working Group Making an Inventory of the Social and Human Consequences for the Victims of War, including the Spanish Civil War, and the Victims of Punishment and Purges]. Flemish Parliament, Session 1984–1985, document 290.

Conway, Martin. 1997. Justice in Post-War Belgium. Popular Passions and Political Realities. *Bijdragen tot de Eigentijdse Geschiedenis/ Cahiers d'histoire du temps présent*, 2: 7–34.

Gilissen, J., Paul Cassiers, and François Debroux. 1967. *Crimes et délits contre la sûreté de l'état. Novelles. Droit pénal. Tôme II*. Brussels: Larcier, pp. 113–319.

Gotovitch, José and Chantal Kesteloot, eds. 2002. *Collaboration, répression: un passé qui résiste*. Brussels: Labor.

Huyse, Luc and Steven Dhondt. 1993. *La répression des collaborations. 1942–1952. Un passé toujours présent*. Brussels: CRISP.

Lagrou, Pieter. 2006. Eine Frage der moralischen Überlegenheit? Die Ahndung deutscher Kriegsverbrechen in Belgien. In *Transnationale Vergangenheitspolitik : Der Umgang mit deutschen Kriegsverbrechern in Europa nach dem Zweiten Weltkrieg*. Ed. Norbert Frei. Göttingen: Wallstein Verlag, pp. 326–350.

Rousseaux, Xavier and Laurence van Ypersele, eds. 2008. *La patrie crie vengeance! La répression des «inciviques» belges au sortir de la guerre 1914–1918*. Brussels and Louvain-La-Neuve: Le Cri and CHDJ.

Van Loon, Carolien. 2008. De geschorene en de scheerster. De vrouw in de straatrepressie na de Tweede Wereldoorlog. *Bijdragen tot de eigentijdse geschiedenis/Cahiers d'histoire du temps present*, 19: 45–78.

Bolivia

In 2004, Bolivian authorities declared the period between November 4, 1964 and October 10, 1982 as one of "political violence committed by official agents of unconstitutional governments" (Law No. 2640/11 March 2004). The need to deal with that period's crimes has prompted Bolivia to embrace multiple transitional justice mechanisms, including the first truth commission in Latin America, reparations, and a trial that resulted in the conviction of a dictator for human rights violations. The emphasis was placed on judicial response, as the fight against impunity became the primary method to deal with the convoluted past. Thus, the substantial technical flaws of the aforementioned trial went unnoticed. In any case, the judicial response was limited, because other important periods of dictatorship were not judicially addressed.

The Repressive Past

The 1964 coup d'état, which overthrew the Paz Estenssoro government, was followed by eighteen years during which the military very strongly influenced and, at times, controlled the government. During this period of political instability, frequent government changes were brought about by force, not democratic elections. One of the most notorious episodes of violence was the Massacre of San Juan of June 1967. Twenty-seven miners, suspected of supporting the emerging Latin American guerrilla movement led by the Cuban leader Che Guevara, were killed by the army while holding a meeting. The assault by the death squad was emblematic of the state policy of repression against dissidents considered a danger to government stability.

In 1971, the military leader General Hugo Banzer Suárez became president after another coup d'état. He held office until 1978. In 1974, upon banning opposition parties, Banzer's regime participated in Operation Condor, a state-sponsored campaign supported by the dictatorships of Argentina, Bolivia, Brazil, Chile, and Paraguay, with the goal of suppressing their opponents. The Banzer regime was marked by forced disappearances, torture, and inhuman and degrading treatment (especially of university students).

In 1979, another coup d'état involved an indiscriminate armed attack against innocent civilians, leaving 100 people dead and 500 injured. In early 1980, prominent opposition leaders were killed, including priest and journalist Luis Espinal and four leaders of the opposition party Popular Democratic Union (Unión Democrática Popular, UDP). In an attack launched against a UDP public demonstration, two people were killed and thirteen were injured.

The coup d'état of July 17, 1980, led by army General Luis García Meza, forced the resignation of the first Bolivian woman president (a civilian), Lidia Gueiler Tejada, who had been elected as interim president sixteen days after the 1979 coup d'état. The Bolivian Workers Confederation (Central Obrera Boliviana, COB), the country's main workers union, was attacked by paramilitaries camouflaged in ambulances who killed the political leaders, including prominent opposition leader Marcelo Quiroga Santa Cruz. Other political leaders and state dignitaries were detained. Several miners who tried to resist were killed. García Meza's dictatorship (1980–1981) involved the closing of parliament and the complete replacement of the upper echelons of the judiciary. Power was used to terrify the population by suppressing fundamental freedoms and ignoring civil and political rights (recognized, in an embryonic form, already in the first Bolivian Constitution of 1826). The press was completely censored, the illegal narcotics industry was exploited by the government, and corruption permeated the regime. A notorious crime of this dictatorship was the Harrington Street Massacre of January 15, 1981. Acting on orders of the Interior Minister Luis Arce Gómez, a death squad operation took place on Harrington Street in La Paz, where the Revolutionary Leftist Movement (Movimiento de Izquierda Revolucionario, MIR) held a secret meeting. Eight of nine political leaders present at that meeting were killed.

The serious human rights violations committed by García Meza's dictatorship provoked repudiation within the armed forces. Several riots conducted throughout the country forced his resignation on August 4, 1981. After several temporary regimes, on October 5, 1982, Hernán Siles Suazo was elected president by the reinstalled parliament. This marked the foundation of democracy.

Transitional Justice

Bolivia's transitional justice has included a commission for the investigation of enforced disappearances, court proceedings, reparation measures, and the possible disclosure of military secret files.

The National Commission for the Investigation of Enforced Disappearances

The National Commission for the Investigation of Enforced Disappearances was created pursuant to a presidential Supreme Decree 19241 of October 28, 1982. Adopted only twenty-three days after Suazo assumed the presidency, the commission was Bolivia's first response to the past and the also first truth commission in Latin America. Its mandate was limited to the investigation of enforced disappearances, leaving other human rights violations dating from the same period of time outside its scope.

The Commission was composed of representatives of the government, the Human Rights Commissions of the Bolivian Parliament, the Roman Catholic Church, representatives of the armed forces, the COB, the nongovernmental organization the Permanent Assembly on Human Rights, the Bolivian Red Cross, and the local press. In total, 155 cases of enforced disappearances from 1967 to 1982 were reported by the commission, but no further investigation was undertaken, and the Commission was dissolved in 1984 without submitting a final report.

Impeachment Proceedings

The Commission identified crimes committed under the Banzer and García Meza regimes, but parliament decided to prosecute only the latter, mainly because many members of the legislative and the judiciary held positions during the Banzer regime. Thus, parliament excluded from prosecution the crimes committed before García Meza's coup d'état.

In accordance with the Constitution, in 1986 Parliament authorized impeachment proceedings against former dictator García Meza and his closest collaborators. In Bolivia, impeachment proceedings are also possible after the conclusion of the mandate. The case was heard by the Supreme Court of Justice. García Meza assumed his own defense until parliament ordered his detention in 1989 for his alleged involvement in the robbery of Che Guevara's diaries, which were kept in the Central Bank vault. That same year, García Meza managed to escape and remained at large for five years. The trial, which continued in absentia, combined all charges, including human rights violations and financial and corruption crimes. The most serious crime was genocide, bearing the maximum allowed sentence accorded by the Bolivian Criminal Code at the time of the trial: twenty years imprisonment (Article 138). The genocide charge related to the Harrington Street Massacre. The trial concluded on April 21, 1993 with a conviction and a sentence of the maximum penalty, combining all the charges, of thirty years imprisonment without parole. On March 11, 1994, García Meza was apprehended in Brazil and extradited to Bolivia, where he arrived on March 15, 1995. He is currently serving his sentence in Chonchocoro, Bolivia's maximum-security detention center.

The trial was a historic event given that it was completed, through laudable effort, during a difficult political time given the influence of the armed forces. But the legitimate aim of meting out justice was marred by an artificial, albeit very popular, legal characterization of the facts as a "bloody massacre" amounting to genocide (see entry on Committee against García Meza).

The most prominent collaborator of García Meza to stand trial was his former Minister of the Interior, Luis Arce Gomez, who was convicted for genocide in connection with the Harrington Street Massacre. He received the maximum penalty for this crime, and the maximum sentence (thirty years imprisonment) for the other crimes charged (murder in first degree, armed rebellion, organization of irregular armed groups, and impairment of the freedom of the press). Arce Gomez was tried and convicted in absentia, as during the late 1980s he was extradited to the United States, where he served a lengthy sentence for drug trafficking. Upon completion of his sentence in November 2007, he was released. To avoid deportation to Bolivia, he applied for asylum in the United States, but his request was denied. On July 9, 2009, he was deported to Bolivia. He is also serving his sentence in the Chonchocoro detention center.

Reparations

Law 2640 of 11 March 2004 provides "exceptional reparations to victims of political violence committed during unconstitutional governments." Redress is envisaged for violations such as: arbitrary detention and deprivation of liberty, torture, exile, serious injuries, death that occurred either in the country or abroad as a result of political violence, enforced disappearances, and political persecution (Article 4). With its imprecise provisions, the law is open to interpretation, in particular with respect to reparations. Of the violations mentioned in Article 4, only enforced disappearance is defined by law and the definition of political persecution is entrusted to further regulation.

Supreme Decree 28015 of 22 February 2005 detailed the mechanisms provided by Law 2640. (Supreme Decree 28015 was partially modified by Supreme Decree 29214 of 2 August 2007.) According to Supreme Decree 28015, to be eligible for compensation, the injury from persecution, violence, or political harm must be demonstrated (Article 2(I)(a)). By correlating the law with the decree, one may argue that the criminal conduct required by the law was persecution, violence, or political harm. But this interpretation may not be sound in cases of detention or arbitrary deprivation of liberty, where violence was not an issue. Likewise, the concepts of "political harm" and "persecution" used in the law remain undefined.

Law 2640 provides compensation for harm suffered during the 4 November 1964 – 10 October 1982 period. The maximum amount of compensation is equivalent to 300 minimum monthly wages (which, as of 1 September 2009, were 647 Bolivianos, or the equivalent of US$90). The National Treasury provides one-fifth of the funding, while contributions from private or foreign donors and international organizations cover the rest. Free medical care for victims without medical insurance and coverage of the funeral-related expenses for those without social security are also offered. The Law also provides for "public honors" to be rendered by Parliament to the victims.

The law established the National Commission for Reparations to Victims of Political Violence (Comisión Nacional para el Resarcimiento a Víctimas de la Violencia Política, CONREVIP) to adjudicate and process reparation claims. Its composition (modified by Law 3449 of 21 July 2006) includes one representative each of the Ministry of Justice, the Treasury, the Roman Catholic Church, and the COB, and two representatives of the Parliamentary Human Rights Commissions. If the Commission denies a claim, the petitioner has ten days to ask the Commission to consider new facts or evidence. The decision is binding, although the appeal is judged by the same body that denied the original claim. The appeals procedure is ineffective as the initial decision cannot be reconsidered in the absence of new facts and evidence. This legal framework runs counter to the jurisprudence of the Inter-American Court of Human Rights, which affirmed that due process must be observed in all procedures that entail the determination of rights. One such tenet is the right to petition, including the right to request reconsideration of a denied claim by a different and independent organ. Recently, the Commission has made public guidelines on the specific evidence required to support claims related to the violations covered by the law. Although a useful tool for petitioners, the guidelines do not correct procedural flaws.

File Access

Public interest in truth revelation reemerged when victims and relatives of victims of the dictatorial regimes asked the government to order the armed forces to disclose all of their files related to those regimes. Under public pressure, on May 21, 2009, the Ministry of Defense issued Resolution 0316 that allowed the army to disclose its archives, files, and documents related to military dictatorial regimes to victims or the relatives of victims who request them and can demonstrate a legitimate interest in them. Once the army verifies the petitioner's identity and legitimate interest, access is granted to the archives. The archives can be scrutinized by the victims (or their relatives) in front of representatives of the Ministry of Justice, the nongovernmental organization Permanent Assembly of Human Rights, and a Notary Public. Representatives of all three organizations must be present for victims to access documents (Articles 1–3).

Thus, file access is granted individually. Given that the armed forces determine who bears a legitimate interest and this concept is not defined, disclosure remains entirely within their discretion. As the legitimate interest must be demonstrated through documents, potential petitioners may be prevented from accessing the archives, as it is unlikely that they will have documentation proving the crimes committed years earlier. The required documentation could be found in the same archives whose disclosure is requested. Thus, the method envisaged by the Ministerial Resolution is an inadequate means to reveal the truth.

On April 1, 2010, the Supreme Court of Justice ordered the disclosure of the armed forces' secret files dating from the period between June 1979 and December 1980. Only files from such a limited time period were targeted because the order was granted upon a victim's request (acting as a *partie civile*) in a criminal trial for the alleged crime of armed rebellion (*Fiscal v. Franz Pizzaro Solano and others*). Under public pressure from the Ombudsman and the civil society, the armed forces disclosed to the judiciary some documents whose relevance for establishing fate of the disappeared was questioned by the opposition. Civil society organizations and Arce Gomez, former Minister of Interior (1980–1981) and a convicted criminal, have indicated the alleged existence of other documents in the hands of the armed forces, rejecting the president's claim that such documents do not exist. Investigation commissions were created by the General Attorney's office in Santa Cruz and La Paz to continue the search for the disappeared. So far, no other public mechanism – distinct from the public trial – has been envisaged for truth telling.

Conclusion

Public interest in the impeachment proceedings and its ramifications indicates that the judicial measure can be considered a substantive element of Bolivia's response to the past. However, it concerned only one dictatorial regime, albeit the most nefarious. Such an outcome is in stark contrast to the nonjudicial measures, such as reparation and file access, that have not been confined to a particular regime. In the Harrington Street Massacre, the legal characterization of the facts as genocide ignored that the internationally recognized definition of genocide does not include the (intended) destruction of political groups. This erroneous characterization weakens the value of the criminal trial as a legitimate response to the past, which may contribute to enhancing the domestic judicial system.

As the main purpose of criminal trials is not truth telling, but the determination of individual criminal responsibility, the unfinished work of the Commission for the Investigation of Enforced Disappearances, coupled with the recent adoption of essentially private file access, undermines the chances of achieving broad-based public recognition of the truth. So far the disclosure of the military secret files has not satisfied the reemerged public interest in confronting more elements of Bolivia's repressive past. The overall situation detracts from a transitional justice model built on solid foundations, as it appears to respond only to the particular political context instead of constituting a systematic and conscious response for dealing with the past.

Kai Ambos and Elizabeth Santalla

Cross-references: Access to Secret Files; Court Trials for Redress; Impeachment Proceedings (Juicio de Responsabilidades) against Former Dictator Luis García Meza.

Further Readings

Cuya, Esteban. 1996. *Las Comisiones de la Verdad en América Latina* [Truth Commissions in Latin America]. Available at: http://www.derechos.org/koaga/iii/1/cuya.html (accessed August 31, 2009).
De Mesa Gisbert, Carlos. 2007. Bajo el Signo de las Fuerzas Armadas [Under the Armed Forces Command]. In *Historia de Bolivia* [History of Bolivia]. Eds. José de Mesa Figueroa, Teresa Gisbert, and Carlos de Mesa Gisbert. La Paz: Gisbert.
Hayner, Priscilla. 1994. Fifteen Truth Commissions, 1974 to 1994: A Comparative Study. *Human Rights Quarterly*, 16(4): 597–655.
Hazan, Pierre. 2006. Measuring the Impact of Punishment and Forgiveness: a Framework for Evaluating Transitional Justice. *International Review of the Red Cross*, 88(861): 19–48.
Santalla Vargas, Elizabeth. 2009. Informe sobre Bolivia [Report on Bolivia]. In *Justicia de Transición. Con Informes de América Latina, Alemania, Italia y España* [Transitional Justice. With Country Reports from Latin America, Germany, Italy, and Spain]. Eds. Kai Ambos, Ezequiel Malarino, and Gisela Elsner. Montevideo/Bogotá: Konrad Adenauer Stiftung/Temis. 153–170.

Bosnia-Herzegovina

The pursuit of justice for war crimes in Bosnia-Herzegovina began during the 1991–1995 conflict, with the creation of the International Criminal Tribunal for the Former Yugoslavia (ICTY) by the United Nations Security Council. Despite being headquartered in The Hague and staffed by international personnel, the ICTY remained the principal justice institution for Bosnia in the years after the 1995 Dayton Agreement ended the conflict. However, the introduction of the ICTY's Completion Strategy in 2003 led to the creation of the hybrid War Crimes Chamber (WCC) in Sarajevo and greater capacity-building programs for the local courts. As a result, trials are increasingly taking place before domestic courts. To date, there have been only limited nonjudicial forms of transitional justice and Bosnian civil society remains comparatively weak. Nonetheless, some victims associations and civil society groups have engaged in ad hoc grassroots transitional justice endeavors including memorialization, truth telling and psychosocial healing. These measures have, however, been piecemeal and rarely reached across ethnic boundaries. As time elapses, trials are becoming increasingly difficult and thousands of perpetrators have yet to be tried. This has caused debate to open up on the need for more holistic approaches to transitional justice. In 2008, local actors participated in a consultation process sponsored by the United Nations Development Program (UNDP), which, for the first time since the war, gathered together civil society organizations and representatives of all levels of authority coming from all ethnic communities. This process resulted in a report containing recommendations on creating a comprehensive national Transitional Justice Strategy that was submitted to the Bosnian Council of Ministers in January 2009. If implemented, this strategy has the potential to respond to the needs of many victims beyond those whose cases have been heard by the courts, to expand understandings of transitional justice to encompass more restorative approaches, and to create a forum for greater interethnic cooperation.

The Repressive Past

After World War II, Bosnia-Herzegovina became one of the six constituent republics of the Federal Socialist Republic of Yugoslavia, which was a one-party communist state. Unlike the other Yugoslav republics, Bosnia-Herzegovina had no majority ethnic group; instead, its Muslim, Croat and Serb communities were distributed throughout its territory. As Yugoslavia began to fragment in the late 1980s, tensions heightened between Bosnia's ethnic groups, leading to violence and political crises. Eventually, war broke out in April 1992 when Bosnia-Herzegovina declared independence from the Federal Republic of Yugoslavia, a move which Bosnian Serbs opposed.

During the following three months, Bosnian Serb irregular forces, supported by the Yugoslav People's Army (JNA), waged a bloody campaign against Muslim and Croat communities. Between 1992 and 1995, the Bosnian Serbs pursued a "policy" of "ethnic cleansing" against the Bosnian Croat and Muslim minorities remaining in Bosnian Serb-held areas. Similarly, Bosnian Croat and Muslim forces committed atrocities against Bosnian Serbs. Furthermore, in 1993, Bosnian Croats and Muslims fought a bloody conflict over control of their remaining territories. In this way, each community committed atrocities against the other communities, and often against members of its own community who opposed the war. In addition, the Bosnian Croats and Serbs received military support from their ethnic brethren in Croatia and Yugoslavia (now Serbia). From 1992, the UN sent peacekeepers into the conflict zone, and their inability to stem the violence has been viewed by some as imbuing them with a degree of culpability.

Where the combatant factions sought to "cleanse" their territories of members of "minority" ethnic groups, the "policy" was pursued through massacres, torture, rape, expulsions, arbitrary mass internment, deportation, and extensive property destruction, culminating in the genocide at Srebrenica in 1995 in which Bosnian Serb forces massacred thousands of Bosnian Muslim men and boys. It is estimated that during the conflict up to 200,000 civilians died, more than 20,000 women were raped, there were 715 detention camps, and more than 2 million people were displaced.

Following the Dayton Agreement, the fledgling Bosnian state faced not just a transition from war to peace, but also from communism to liberal, market democracy. However, the war had destroyed most of the political institutions and forced the educated middle classes into exile, which arguably inhibited the development of alternatives to extreme national politics during the transition. Furthermore, much of the country's infrastructure and more than 30 percent of its residential buildings had been destroyed.

Transitional Justice

Since the war, Bosnia, with the support of the international community, has pursued multiple forms of transitional justice to varying degrees, including holding accountable those responsible for war crimes; implementing vetting programs to reform the state's institutions; assisting and compensating injured civilians, former combatants, and families of those who died; undoing the ethnic cleansing by helping those who had been displaced return home; and searching for the missing.

Trials

Trials for crimes committed during the conflict have occurred within four different systems: (1) the ICTY, (2) the WCC, (3) local courts, and (4) courts in other states, including courts elsewhere in the Balkan region, particularly the War Crimes Chamber at the District Court in Belgrade.

Local courts in Bosnia-Herzegovina heard war crimes cases from the outset of the conflict, although these trials lacked due process guarantees and were often ethnically biased. The scale of the atrocities and need for impartial justice was highlighted by a UN Commission of Experts that had been mandated to gather evidence of war crimes in the Former Yugoslavia. The UN Security Council responded to its recommendations by establishing the ICTY, without the consent of the countries of the Former Yugoslavia, in 1993. Its Statute was enacted in a UN Security Council resolution under Chapter VII of the UN Charter, which made cooperation with the tribunal binding on all UN member states. However, it appears that Security Council members were skeptical about what the court could achieve, and it has been suggested by some commentators that they only agreed to establish the tribunal to avoid being forced into greater military intervention.

According to its Statute, the primary goal of the ICTY is to prosecute persons responsible for serious violations of international humanitarian law committed in the territory of the former Yugoslavia. Since its creation, the tribunal has indicted 161 persons and sentenced 60 individuals, and cases related to Bosnia-Herzegovina have dominated its workload. In addition, the February 1966 Rome Agreement between the parties to the Dayton peace accords included the "Rules of the Road" which stipulated that national courts in Bosnia were required to obtain authorization from the ICTY before proceeding with any cases. The rules were intended to remove any suspicion that the cases being pursued were politically motivated rather than based on evidence.

The ICTY was never intended to be a permanent institution, and in 2001, the ICTY Office of the Prosecutor presented the idea of establishing a special war crimes court in Sarajevo. After some reluctance from the Bosnian government, this proposal gained the support of the Office of the High Representative (OHR) (the international body created to oversee the implementation of the civilian aspects of the Dayton Accords) and the UN Security Council, which was eager for the ICTY to complete its work.

The resulting WCC was inaugurated in March 2005. It has jurisdiction over genocide, torture, multiple murders, and rapes, and is empowered to investigate cases referred to it from the ICTY and cases resulting from the prosecution's own investigations. The WCC is part of the Bosnian judicial system, but has substantial international support through the provisions of funds and the involvement of foreign judges and prosecutors. The international personnel were originally due to be phased out in early 2010. However, as a result of international pressure, domestic political difficulties delaying the recruitment of additional national personnel, and stemming from the fact that the first-instance cases in which the international judges were involved were still ongoing, in December 2009, the High Representative extended the mandate of the international personnel until December 31, 2012.

As part of the Bosnian judicial system, the WCC is intended to work with local courts, and whereas the WCC handles the most serious war crimes cases, it is empowered to refer the less 'sensitive' cases to local courts. It is anticipated that the bulk of the remaining cases in Bosnia will be dealt with by the lower courts. However, at present, these courts face numerous difficulties, including a lack of resources, vulnerability to political pressure, and thousands of outstanding war crimes cases. To address some of these problems, Bosnia's Criminal Procedure Code was reformed in 2003 to harmonize legal procedures across Bosnia-Herzegovina and to introduce innovations to speed up trials, such as the use of plea bargains. These innovations have proved contentious, and many victims oppose the greater leniency offered by plea bargains, which so far have only been used domestically in a few cases before the WCC. In addition, in December 2008, the Ministry of Justice adopted the National War Crimes Strategy, which creates a timetable for completing the prosecutions of outstanding war crimes cases, develops criteria to prioritize cases, and establishes a centralized approach to collecting and processing data on ongoing cases across Bosnia. This strategy will complement the Transitional Justice Strategy, which will address the nonjudicial aspects of dealing with the past, including vetting, truth recovery, compensation, and memorials. A draft of this strategy, compiled by a panel of domestic experts and the UNDP, will be submitted to the Bosnian parliament.

Vetting

The need to prevent individuals who are responsible for war crimes from exercising public office was recognized in the Dayton Agreement, which stipulated that persons convicted of war crimes or who are fugitives from war crimes indictments are barred from public office. Furthermore, the Agreement empowered the OHR to remove civil servants from public office for reasons ranging from their wartime record to obstructing the implementation of the peace process. These OHR powers are known as the Bonn Powers and were used by successive High Representatives to remove or ban 185 public officials from office, including senior officials and politicians, although some of these individuals have now been "rehabilitated" by the OHR, which means that the OHR has decided to allow them to reenter public life.

The Dayton Agreement also required the prosecution or dismissal of police officers and public servants responsible for serious violations of minority rights. The vetting of security officials was conducted between 1999 and 2002 by the International Police Task Force (IPTF), established by the UN Security Council in 1995. The IPTF reviewed 24,000 police officers and decertified or barred from their jobs 793 local and state-level police over past and present activities. Unlike the Bonn powers, the UN Security Council, rather than the OHR, was responsible for "rehabilitations" of police officers. This process has been criticized as lacking transparency and clear criteria. These difficulties led to criticisms of the procedures, and some vetted police officers filed complaints with the Bosnian Human Rights Commission. Consequently, in February 2007, the Human

Rights Ministry established a commission to review the dismissals and report to the newly formed government. This marked the first attempt by Bosnia's politicians to assume ownership over a controversial aspect of transitional justice. The police vetting process has also been criticized because since it was completed, some serving police officers have been indicted and convicted of war crimes. Although the IPTF process did attempt to verify all certifications given with the ICTY, it was working under time constraints and political pressure, which often meant that it was unable to conduct verification in great detail. In addition to police officers, high-ranking military officials were vetted by NATO in 2004, a process that triggered similar criticisms of a lack of transparency.

Finally, there was vetting within the judiciary between 2002 and 2004. This was conducted by an internationally appointed Independent Judicial Commission. Its mandate included overseeing the review and reappointment of all judges and prosecutors based on their professional and ethical competence. The procedure adopted required applicants (both serving and eligible judicial or prosecutorial candidates) to prove their competence to perform judicial functions as well as to provide information on their actions during the war. According to the UNDP, the public has been displeased with this reappointment process as prior political or ethnic-based judicial actions were not taken as a basis for disqualification (UNDP 2009, p. 56).

Reparation and Restitution

Bosnia-Herzegovina has yet to adopt a comprehensive national reparations program that could incorporate individual and collective material and nonmaterial forms of reparations for human rights violations. However, there have been a number of discrete initiatives.

First, Bosnia's two entity-level governments, the Bosnian Federation and Republika Srpska, have each adopted legislation to compensate civilian victims of war and their "own" disabled war "veterans" who participated in the various police and military forces that defended the entity. These laws provide monthly payments to those who suffered injury or sexual violence, as well as to the families of those who were killed or are missing, although the amounts vary between the entities. In addition, some municipalities provide additional rights to civilian war victims or disabled war veterans.

Where monthly payments are given, they are provided on the basis of the suffering endured either directly or indirectly by surviving family members. However, the threshold for war veterans to be considered disabled, and hence entitled to financial compensation, is much lower than for civilian victims. Furthermore, the payments given to war veterans considerably exceed those for civilian victims. This unequal treatment has been criticized by the World Bank and the UN Office of the High Commissioner for Human Rights who argued that payments to victims and veterans should be harmonized. This has yet to occur.

Second, individual and collective compensation claims have been brought before the Human Rights Chamber of the Constitutional Court of Bosnia and Herzegovina and its successor institution, the Human Rights Commission within the Constitutional Court, and have led to compensation being awarded. For example, in one case relating to Srebrenica, the Chamber ordered the government of Republika Srpska to investigate the atrocities, make a single payment of 2 million Bosnian Convertible Marks (KM) (1 million Euros) and four additional payments of KM 500,000 over four years to the Foundation of Srebrenica-Potočari.

Third, a significant form of reparation in Bosnia-Herzegovina is restitution, which was provided for in Annex VII of the Dayton Agreement relating to the right of return for refugees and displaced persons. This provision, which was seen as vital to undoing the ethnic cleansing of the war and undermining support for extreme nationalist politicians, provides for the reconstruction of property, including financial compensation for damaged or destroyed property; the removal of legal obstacles to return; the eviction of individuals who are illegally occupying properties; and the creation of socioeconomic conditions to foster sustainable living standards for those wishing to return to their prewar homes. To fulfill its obligations under Annex VII, the Bosnian government developed an implementation strategy in 2002, which was amended in 2008. According to the UN High Commission of Refugees, by March 31, 2009, 1,026,825 refugees and displaced persons had returned, but only 467,427 of these were "minority returns," where individuals returned to their prewar homes in areas where their ethnic community was now in a minority. These figures do not indicate what proportion of minority returns have maintained permanent residency in their prewar homes, and indeed, it appears that such returnees continue to face many obstacles reintegrating.

Finally, memorials have been erected across Bosnia-Herzegovina, although many of these have been built along ethnic lines – for example, Bosniaks building memorials to honor only Bosniak dead. There has been no coordinated policy of memorialization. Furthermore, as yet, there is no official national memorial to those killed during the war.

Truth Recovery

Although the Dayton Agreement mandated that all parties cooperate with the ICTY, side-letters to the Agreement from Bosnian President Alija Izetbegović and Serbian President Slobodan Milošević also committed the parties to establishing a concurrent international commission of inquiry. These letters, which had identical wording on the proposed commission, stipulated that it would be composed of participants from the governments involved as well as distinguished international experts to be named by agreement among the republics of former Yugoslavia, and that it would be mandated to conduct fact finding and other necessary studies into the causes, conduct, and consequences of the conflict, and to issue a report.

Although three separate commissions of inquiry were created by Bosnia's three ethnic communities, there was no movement on creating a national commission of inquiry until the United States Institute for Peace (USIP) organized a round table in July 1997 at which justice and war crimes officials from the Federation of Bosnia and Herzegovina and Republika Srpska requested USIP to develop the concept of creating a truth commission. Subsequently, at a meeting in November 1997 with Bosnian politicians and religious leaders as well as community leaders, intellectuals, and journalists, USIP representatives presented draft legislation to create a truth commission as a complementary body to the ICTY that would document abuses. However, the ICTY was initially resistant as it worried that such a commission could weaken the court by creating a parallel structure with overlapping interests.

The idea stalled until 2000, when more than 100 participants, mainly from local civil society organizations, gathered at round tables on truth and reconciliation in Sarajevo and Banja Luka. These meetings led to the birth of a new organization called the Citizens' Association for Truth and Reconciliation (CATR), which developed a draft Law on the Truth and Reconciliation Commission in 2003. This time the proposals had the ICTY's support and the draft law was submitted to the Parliamentary Assembly of Bosnia-Herzegovina, but it failed to attract political backing and was not considered by the parliamentarians. Subsequently, in 2005, the USIP urged the three chairmen of the Parliamentary Assembly of Bosnia-Herzegovina to initiate talks among eight parliamentary political parties with the aim of developing a draft law similar to CATR proposal. This initiative resulted in the formation of a Working Group that drew up amendments to the CATR proposal to clarify certain matters. This group produced draft legislation to establish a truth commission in May 2006, but a worsening political situation with disagreements on the constitutional makeup of the Bosnia-Herzegovina meant that no attempts were made to translate the May 2006 draft into legislation.

Although an overarching national truth recovery process has yet to be established, three investigative commissions have been established to address crimes committed in particular locations. First, in December 2003, the government of Republika Srpska, under pressure from the then High Representative Paddy Ashdown and in response to a decision by the Human Rights Chamber, created the Commission for Investigation of the Events in and around Srebrenica between July 10 and 19, 1995. The Commission was tasked with locating missing persons and investigating who was responsible for the massacre (see entry on Commission for Investigation of the Events in and around Srebrenica between 10 and 19 July 1995).

Second, in 2006, the Council of Ministers, in response to demands by Serb parties in the Parliamentary Assembly that the suffering of Bosnian Serbs in Sarajevo be investigated, created a Commission for Investigating the Truth Regarding Sufferings of the Serbs, Croats, Bosniaks, Jews and Others in Sarajevo in the period between 1992 and 1995. This commission was mandated to investigate crimes against *all* civilians living within Sarajevo during the war. The commission quickly became controversial because of the lack of consultation in the selection process of members of the commission. This issue was never resolved, and as a result, the commission has yet to begin work.

Third, the Truth and Reconciliation Commission of the Municipal Assembly of Bijeljina was created in mid-2008 in response to a September 2004 report by the International Mediator in Bosnia and Herzegovina, an institution that was created by the international community to mediate disputes between the entity-level governments. The Commission submitted its report to the Municipal Assembly for consideration, but the report was not adopted. As with the Sarajevo Commission, the work of this commission was politicized by the selection process of the commissioners, together with a lack of transparency in its operations.

In addition to the investigative commissions, truth recovery has been conducted by the Missing Persons Institute, which was created by the Bosnian federal government in 2005 (replacing entity-level commissions) to investigate the fate of the thousands of disappeared. Furthermore, there have been some civil society truth recovery initiatives, ranging from documentation efforts on war crimes and missing persons primarily conducted by Research and Documentation Center in Sarajevo, to artistic, cinematic, and literary projects, to intercommunal dialogue and public forums.

In addition, the civil society Coalition for a Regional Commission for Truth-seeking and Truth-telling About War Crimes (REKOM) has proposed a regional truth and reconciliation commission to investigate the causes and crimes related to the conflicts across the Former Yugoslavia. This proposal has received support from 200 organizations and individuals in the region. Similarly, the Igman Initiative, composed of more than 140 organizations and individuals from Bosnia, Croatia, and Serbia, has argued for regional truth recovery and transitional justice processes. However, other than the ICTY, no regional mechanism has been yet established.

Conclusion

In the thirteen years since the Dayton Agreement, it appears that although there have been prosecutions at the ICTY, the WCC, and local courts, other aspects of transitional justice have not been substantially addressed. Today, Bosnia's political system remains fragile; its judicial infrastructure still lacks the capacity to deal with the thousands of outstanding cases; no agreement has been reached on developing national approaches to truth recovery; thousands of people are still missing; there is no comprehensive approach to reparations; and the public remains unsatisfied with the reform of institutions. The persistence of these problems highlights the need for transitional states to develop comprehensive approaches to transitional justice, rather than simply focusing solely on one approach such as trials, which, even if widely and efficiently pursued, have inherent limitations.

Louise Mallinder

Cross-references: Commission for Investigation of the Events in and around Srebenica between 10 and 19 July 1995; Court Trials for Redress; International Criminal Tribunal for the Former Yugoslavia; War Crimes Chamber of the Court of Bosnia-Herzegovina.

Further Readings

Bennett, Christopher. 1997. *Yugoslavia's Bloody Collapse: Causes, Course and Consequences*. London: Hurst & Company.
Hazan, Pierre. 2004. *Justice in a Time of War: The True Story behind the International Criminal Tribunal for the Former Yugoslavia*. College Station: Texas A & M University Press.
Holbrooke, Richard. 1998. *To End a War*. New York: Random House.
Rangelov, Iavor and Marika Theros. 2008. Transitional Justice in Bosnia and Herzegovina: Coherence and Complementarity of EU Institutions and Civil Society. In *Building a Future on Peace and Justice: Studies on Transitional Justice, Peace and Development*. Eds. Kai Ambos, Judith Large, and Marieke Wierda. Berlin: Springer.
UNDP. 2009. Transitional Justices Guidebook for Bosnia and Herzegovina: Executive Summary. UNDP.

Brazil

A decade passed after the last general left power before Brazil began to deal, albeit precariously, with the legacy of massive human rights violations perpetrated during the military dictatorship (1964–1985). Law 9140 dealing with the victims who lost their lives during that period came into force in 1995. Six years later, a commission was formed to analyze requests for reparation made by victims of political persecution. At the time of this writing, not a single perpetrator had been punished for the crimes committed, no profound reform of the security system had been undertaken, and the right to truth was observed only partially.

The Repressive Past

The military dictatorship was constituted in Brazil within the Cold War logic. The dictatorship counted on the support of co-opted sectors of the civil society in its efforts to fight against the so-called internal left-wing subversion (the communist threat) and to reestablish "order" in the country. The regime put in place after the 1964 coup d'état considered all those opposed to its ideas as enemies of the state. There was no rule of law, and fundamental legal principles were constantly disrespected. In addition to the National Security Law, the "legal grounding" for the abuses committed was provided by the Military Criminal Code, the Military Criminal Process Code, and the Law of Military Judicial Organization, all enacted by decree in 1969. They "regularized" the security agencies, transforming them into public authorities allowed to order and carry out the arrest of any person.

The Brazilian dictatorship went through at least three different stages. The first stage lasted from the April 1964 coup d'état to the consolidation of the military-imposed regime. The second began in December 1968, with the adoption of Institutional Act 5 (AI-5), which granted the President of the Republic powers to close the National Congress provisionally, intervene in the states of the federation, and suspend individual rights such as habeas corpus. During this period, repression reached its peak and press censorship was intense. The third stage, which began with the presidential inauguration of General Ernesto Geisel in 1974, was marked by the slow and gradual opening of the political system and extended until the end of the arbitrary regime.

While in power, the military controlled and repressed society and spread fear. There was a network of intelligence services and several "internal defense" operation centers. There was frequent use of exceptional instruments, which reduced or suppressed the right to defense of those accused of crimes against national security. The modes of punishment most often adopted were exile, the suspension of political rights, loss of political or public office, dismissal or loss of trade union office, loss of a public school place or expulsion from a private school, and prison, where torture was a constant practice used indiscriminately, including against pregnant women. The names of the regime's opponents were included in the files of the repression agencies – a move amounting to punishment, as it could hinder or even prevent the entry of those on file into the labor market, for instance. The legislation of the period also contained the death penalty, established by Institutional Act 14 (AI-14) at the end of the 1960s. Officially, it was never used. Many of those considered adversaries of the regime were, however, killed in torture sessions or summary executions. When such deaths were made public, they were said to result from clashes between enemies of the regime and agents of the security forces. Sometimes people were simply said to be missing.

During the first few months of the Geisel government, the military began to avoid the customary claims concerning the causes of death of opponents of the regime: hit-and-run, suicide, or attempted escape. They started covering up arrests followed by death, making the phenomenon of "disappearances" commonplace. At least 150 people were "disappeared" on political grounds by the Brazilian dictatorship. Witness statements made by other prisoners indicate that the disappeared were kidnapped or captured by the repressive forces and tortured. The regime considered them fugitives. Among the most affected was the Araguaia guerrilla group linked to the Communist Party of Brazil

(PCdoB), with sixty-four activists identified. By mid-2009, only four sets of remains out of all the disappeared of the period had been found and identified.

Although exact data concerning the number of victims of political persecution under the military regime is unavailable, it is known that during the dictatorship's first year alone, forty-nine judges and fifty parliamentarians had their positions abrogated. At least 1,400 civilian public servants lost their jobs, and there were 1,200 expulsions from the armed forces. Six state governors were removed from office. Former presidents Jânio Quadros and Juscelino Kubitschek had their political rights suspended. The same fate befell João Goulart, the president toppled by the coup d'état. Intense persecution of the student movement and of trade unions also took place. Nuns and priests were arrested and tortured; convents were surrounded, temples invaded.

The Organization of American States (OAS, see separate entry) condemned the violence in the country. Through the Inter-American Commission on Human Rights, it found the Brazilian state responsible for the arbitrary arrest, torture, and murder of trade unionist Olavo Hansen, who had allegedly committed suicide in 1970. The Commission even asked the then-ruling military for permission to investigate indications of torture in the country, but this request was never granted. Because of representations made to the UN regarding human rights violations starting at least in 1974, Brazil was the object of the organization's confidential procedure. The Brazilian situation remained under examination by the UN Commission on Human Rights until 1976. The results were never published.

Brazil's transition to democracy took years. It was negotiated from the start and defined in a sort of "agreement" among the elites. The commitment was that the military would gradually withdraw from politics, keeping the role of guarantors of public order. Meanwhile, not only would the civilian elites agree that "excesses" had occurred on both sides (the military and its left-wing opponents), but they would also leave the matter to rest by endorsing the idea of a reciprocal pardon, without investigation of – let alone punishment for – the crimes committed over more than two decades. In other words, the Brazilian transition was conducted in a way that prevented the adoption of transitional justice mechanisms at the start of civilian rule.

The dictatorship ended in 1985 without direct elections for president. Tancredo Neves, a civilian, was indirectly chosen to succeed the last general-president by the electoral college imposed by the military, but he died before his inauguration. Senator José Sarney, his deputy, ended up taking office. Sarney was not only a member of the ruling party of the military regime, but an old ally of the military. Shortly after he took office, the book *Brazil: Never Again* (Brasil: Nunca Mais), produced without the government's participation, informed Brazilian society in detail how the system of repression worked and the different forms of torture suffered by political prisoners. Brazilians also learned the identity of 444 torturers, when their names were published in the country's main newspapers (see entry on Brazil: Never Again Project). Including the disappeared, it is estimated that the number of fatal victims of the military stands at 430.

Transitional Justice

A transitional justice policy has never been adopted in Brazil. The main obstacle to progress in settling accounts with the victims and the society is the way in which the

Amnesty Law (Law 6683/1979) has been interpreted by the public ever since its enactment. Specific initiatives and some laws have constituted mechanisms for dealing with part of the legacy of massive human rights violations. Practically all such initiatives have been informed by the logic of the military regime. This has ensured the persistence of the interpretation of the amnesty on the terms conceived by the dictatorship – that is, for the purpose of forgetting the violations and accepting their perpetrators' impunity. So far, the Brazilian state has invested mainly in financial compensation or restitution.

Prosecutions and Criminality

On August 28, 1979, the National Congress passed the Amnesty Law, after discussing and debating it – a process without parallel under the Argentinean and Chilean dictatorial regimes, for example. It had been demanded ever since the first acts of arbitrary punishment took place right after the coup, fifteen years before, by the political opposition and some political prisoners, and increasingly supported by the larger society. By the late 1970s, it not only involved much of the Brazilian people, but also included the support of international groups and personalities from all over the world. Advocates of a general and unrestricted amnesty included Gabriel García Márquez, Jean-Paul Sartre, Jean-Luc Godard, Julio Cortázar, and Simone de Beauvoir; they even signed letters of protest against the crimes of the dictatorship. In Brazil, the amnesty was demanded in a context of recovery of democracy, of return to the rule of law, and of recognition and defense of human rights. Demands were made for an end to torture and the elucidation of "disappearance" cases, in conjunction with the approval of the Amnesty Law. Clearly, the social movements and human rights defense groups did not recognize the possibility that the law might also cover the perpetrators of the crimes of the military regime. But the legislation (which makes no mention of torture) was sanctioned basically on the government's terms, with its interpretation demonstrating more effectiveness in relation to members of the apparatus of repression than to its victims, and it did not interrupt the escalation of atrocities.

The first known case in which the Amnesty Law was applied to prevent human rights violators from being punished occurred in April 1980. The case of three torturers who had left a political prisoner blind four years earlier made its way through the High Military Court. The request for their punishment was turned down, in spite of the violence against the political prisoner having been confirmed in the records attached to the suit and recognized in the sentence of the High Military Court itself.

Although to date not a single perpetrator has been found guilty of crimes committed during the dictatorship, on several occasions the Brazilian state has been held legally responsible for the imprisonment, torture, death, or disappearance of politically persecuted individuals. The first such occasion was in 1978; the case involved the illegal arrest of a journalist, who was tortured to death. The federal government was ordered to pay compensation to his widow and children for not protecting his physical and moral integrity and for the material and moral damage resulting from his death. The judiciary subsequently laid down other penalties along the same lines. All of them recognized the civil responsibility of the state – never the criminal responsibility of its agents.

Initially, the criminal accountability of members of the security forces was championed by the pro-amnesty movement. However, it gradually disappeared from the discourse even of many relatives of fatal victims, a fact that might signal a nonconfrontational strategy on the part of these social actors who have striven mainly for the truth to be known. But this strategy has proved fruitless. Thus, the Brazilian courts were not kept very busy on this point. We know of very few lawsuits forwarded to the judiciary to test the amnesty's limits. This evinces not only the little faith that victims and their families have in the legal system, but also how the notion articulated by the military of forgetting the violations and accepting their perpetrators' impunity has managed to limit those affected by the violence of the period. Doubtless, the fact that torture and homicide are considered crimes of public initiative – with the prerogative for initiating criminal suits resting with the Federal Prosecution Service – contributed to this picture.

Another attempt to punish such crimes began in June 2008. A federal prosecutor from the southern town of Uruguaiana ordered the Federal Police to investigate the kidnapping and disappearance of an Italian-Argentinian left-wing militant and an Argentinian priest in 1980 on the Brazil-Argentina border, and the supposed involvement of civilian and military agents of the dictatorship. The crimes allegedly took place within the framework of Operation Condor, the campaign of political repression involving assassinations and intelligence operations implemented in the 1970s by the governments of the Southern Cone of Latin America, and for years have been investigated by the Italian judiciary because some of the victims were Italian citizens. The Italian judiciary has indicted more than ten members of the Brazilian repressive apparatus and demanded their trial.

Also in late 2008, the Brazilian Bar Association made a formal submission to the Supreme Federal Court questioning the validity of the Amnesty Law for state agents who violated human rights during the dictatorship. In the document, the association asked the Court for a clearer interpretation of Article 1, as it wanted to know whether the amnesty granted to perpetrators of so-called political and connected crimes also applied to public agents accused of common crimes such as rape, forced disappearance, and homicide. In 2010, the Court invalidated the provisions of the Amnesty Law that prevent the sanctioning of severe human rights violations. It is worth remembering that none of the former military presidents is alive. The last to die was João Baptista Figueiredo, in 1999.

In March 2009, the Inter-American Commission on Human Rights of the Organization of American States filed an application against Brazil before the Inter-American Court of Human Rights in the case *Brazil vs. the Araguaia guerrilla movement*. Relatives of the victims have campaigned for access to the records of the repression against the movement since the dictatorship. In 1982, several family members filed a responsibility suit against the Brazilian state to clarify the circumstances in which these opponents of the regime died and to locate their remains. Having exhausted every domestic appeal available, the relatives turned to the IACHR. In the application, the Commission asked the Court to determine the international responsibility of the state for noncompliance with various obligations, the right to personal integrity and the right to life among them. In the introduction to the application, the Commission noted the historic value of the case and saw in it the possibility of the Court affirming the incompatibility of the Amnesty Law with the American Convention on Human Rights, with regard to serious human rights violations.

Restitution

Although compensation had been paid to affected individuals or their relatives since during the dictatorship through isolated court decisions, Brazil's reparative effort only really started in 1995, with the enactment of Law 9140 (the Law of the Disappeared). From then on, the state admitted responsibility for the more serious human rights violations during the dictatorship, including disappearances and deaths of nonnatural causes, in police or similar facilities, of individuals who participated or were accused of participating in political activities between September 1961 and October 1988. Those who lost their lives as a result of police repression, including suicides, or as a result of armed conflicts with public agents were also covered. This recognition – and moral redress, to some extent – was directed with immediate effect at 136 disappeared whose names were listed in Annex 1 of the law. Their families were granted symbolic compensation payments worth US$120,000 at the time. A special commission, whose members were appointed by the president, was established by the legislature to examine reports of deaths not listed in the Annex that occurred for political reasons and of nonnatural causes "in police or similar facilities" (see entry on Special Commission on the Dead and Disappeared for Political Reasons).

In 2002, after more than five years of mobilization, it was the turn of the politically persecuted to have some of their demands met, when Law 10559 came into force. It aimed to redress the losses incurred by those forbidden from conducting their economic activities as a result of persecution suffered during the military regime. To assess and compensate the losses caused to thousands of people by the discretionary use of power, the Amnesty Commission was created within the Ministry of Justice. This body has received some 60,000 requests from victims of the arbitrary period (see entry on Amnesty Commission).

File Access

The files of the military regime started being opened in the early 1990s by the first democratically elected civilian president. He returned to the sub-federal states the records of the Departments of Political and Social Order (DOPS), which had been held by the Federal Police. In the archive of the São Paulo state alone there were 34 tons of paper, including more than 1.5 million records about Brazilians and foreign nationals. It took two years for this material to become available to the general public. Around 1987, the Edgard Leuenroth Archive of the University of Campinas received an important donation: 18 meters of documentation representing the full record of the more than 700 lawsuits of the High Military Court and Supreme Federal Court used in the Brazil: Never Again Project. A microfilm version of this material can be found at the Latin American Microform Project in Chicago.

In 2005, two months after the UN Commission on Human Rights recommended that the Brazilian government "make public all the relevant documents on human rights abuses" that occurred during the military regime, a dozen steel filing cabinets stored by agents of the defunct National Information Service (SNI), National Security Council (CSN), and General Investigation Commission (CGI), which were under the control of the Brazilian Intelligence Agency (ABIN), were sent to the National Archive, an institution subordinated to the Office of the Chief of the Presidential Staff. Access to these documents must observe the inviolability of information about the honor, image, intimacy, and private life of citizens, as spelled out in the legislation. Shortly thereafter, the Ministry of External Relations and the Federal Police forwarded to the National Archive thousands of secret documents produced between 1964 and 1975. Pre-1975 files are no longer secret and may be consulted by directly interested individuals, such as those mentioned by name or their relatives.

In May 2009, the federal government launched the Memories Revealed Web portal of the Reference Center of Political Struggles in Brazil (1964–1985), set up with the aim of making information on the country's recent history available, grouped together in a national network under the administration of the National Archive. The idea is that the center will facilitate the convergence and diffusion of information on the repression and the resistance to the military dictatorship. At the same time, the government asked potential holders of any relevant private collections to hand in their documents to the institution, guaranteeing the donors' anonymity. The existence and location of the collection considered the most important of the period – the armed forces' files – remain unknown.

Conclusion

While the Amnesty Law has so far hindered the development of a transitional justice policy and the Brazilian state has focused on financial compensation, recent initiatives involving the Federal Prosecution Service, the Supreme Federal Court, and the Inter-American Court of Human Rights allow one to imagine new prospects for the process of settling accounts with the larger society and with the victims of the military dictatorship. They all suggest a greater chance for achieving the right to justice.

Glenda Mezarobba

Cross-references: Access to Secret Files; Amnesty; Amnesty Commission; Brazil: Never Again Project; Reparations; Special Commission on the Dead and Disappeared for Political Reasons.

Further Readings

Arns, Dom Paulo Evaristo, ed. 1985. *Brasil: Nunca Mais* [Brazil: Never Again]. Petrópolis: Vozes.
Brazilian National Congress, ed. 1982. *Anistia* [Amnesty]. Brasília: Congresso Nacional, 2 volumes.
Mezarobba, Glenda, ed. 2006. *Um acerto de contas com o futuro: a anistia e suas conseqüências – um estudo do caso brasileiro* [Settling Accounts with the Future: The Amnesty and Its Consequences – A Study of the Brazilian Case]. São Paulo: Humanitas/Fapesp.
———. 2007. *O preço do esquecimento: as reparações pagas às vítimas do regime militar (uma comparação entre Brasil, Argentina e Chile)* [The Price of Omission: The Reparations Paid by the Government to the Victims of the Military Regime (A Comparative Study of Brazil, Argentina and Chile)]. PhD dissertation, School of Philosophy, Letters and Human Sciences, University of São Paulo.
Organization of American States. 2009. *Application to the Inter-American Court of Human Rights – Case 11.552*, March 26. Available at: http://www.cidh.org/demandas/11.552%20Guerrilha%20do%20Araguaia%20Brasil%2026mar09%20PORT.pdf (accessed July 20, 2009).
Presidency of Brazil. 2009. Memories Revealed Web site. Available at: http://www.memoriasreveladas.arquivonacional.gov.br/ (accessed January 27, 2010).
Sabadell, Ana Lucia and Olga Espinoza Mavilla, ed. 2003. *Elaboração jurídico-penal do passado após mudança do sistema político em diversos países: relatório Brasil* [The Legal-Criminal Formulation of the Past after Changes in Political System in Various Countries: Brazil Report]. São Paulo: Brazilian Institute for Criminal Sciences.

Bulgaria

The formerly communist country of Bulgaria did not provide justice in the early stage of transition, a fact that contributed to the spread of nostalgia for the communist past and to cynical social attitudes regarding justice in general. The declassification of the archives of the former State Security (Komitet Durzhavna Sigurnost or the KDS) in 2007 created the main opportunity for coming to terms with the communist past and subsequently for demands for lustration of the former KDS secret collaborators.

The Repressive Past

After the communist takeover of 1944, the Bulgarian Communist Party quickly assumed full control over the police and turned its activities against the party's enemies. Created in 1947, the communist State Security sought to silence the anticommunist opposition in Bulgaria and abroad. It employed 75,000–80,000 part-time informers and 15,000–20,000 full-time officers by the end of the regime in 1989. There were 250,000–300,000 secret informers throughout the communist period.

Political violence was rampant in the early stage of communist rule. Tens of thousands of people were killed without court hearings in late 1944. Between November 1944 and April 1945, the People's Court sentenced 2,600 people to death and 8,000 others to prison terms, in most cases also confiscating the victims' property. The regime's political rivals were sent to prison and labor camps such as the one on the Belene Island. The camp accommodated 4,500 prisoners in 1949, when it opened, and their number declined to 2,323 in 1952. Closed down on January 1, 1953, it reopened in autumn 1956, after the Hungarian revolution. It was again closed on August 27, 1959, when the Politburo ordered the release of all political prisoners. Some 276 political prisoners at the Belene camp returned home, but 166 other "incorrigible recidivists" continued to serve their prison terms at the newly established Lovech camp, which closed down in 1962.

After the camps were closed down, the KDS concentrated its efforts on preventing dissident activities within Bulgaria and silencing the politically active Bulgarian emigrants. There were several cases of murdered Bulgarian emigrants, the most notorious of which involved the writer, journalist, and popular critic of the regime, Georgi Markov, who died on September 11, 1978, after being shot on the Waterloo Bridge in London with poisonous bullets fired from the 'Bulgarian umbrella.' In 2005, journalist Hristo Hristov proved that the plot for Markov's assassination was masterminded by the KDS Intelligence Department with the support of the Soviet KGB, and revealed that Markov's assassin was a Dane of Italian origin, Francesco Gullino, arrested in 1970 in Bulgaria for customs crimes and recruited by the KDS under the codename Piccadilly.

In the mid-1980s, the State Security engaged in the massive persecution of the Turkish minority. In the so-called Revival Process, the Bulgarian authorities obliged ethnic Turks to take on Slavic names. In November 1984, the Politburo asked the Ministry of Interior to take military action and force the minority to change names. The operation met with resistance from the Turkish minority, which gradually became organized in the following months. In the aftermath, the Belene camp was reopened to receive the leaders of the Turkish minority. On March 31, 1989, the Bulgarian communist leader Todor Zhivkov ordered the Minister of Interior to deport 100,000–150,000 Turks from Bulgaria. Relations between the two neighbors greatly deteriorated after some 200,000 Turks left Bulgaria for Turkey. The Revival Process ended officially on December 29, 1989, when the Bulgarian Turks were allowed to return their native names. This was one of the first demands of the emerging Bulgarian civil society, which started to organize itself into political parties and civil movements after Zhivkov was deposed on November 10, 1989.

Country Studies

Transitional Justice

After the collapse of the communist regime, Bulgaria was dominated by the former Communist Party, renamed into Bulgarian Socialist Party in 1990, which resisted the adoption of legislative measures aimed at redressing past human rights violations. The pro-democratic opposition adopted some transitional justice measures, the most successful being restitution of property, but failed to adopt effective lustration legislation and declassification of the secret archives.

Property Restitution

On February 21, 1992, the parliament dominated by the anticommunist Union of Democratic Forces adopted the Law for Restitution of the city properties and the agricultural land. As a result of that law, most of the formerly nationalized city property (real estate and industrial properties) and most of agricultural land, which formerly was included in the communist-type cooperatives, were returned to the previous owners or their heirs. In cases where the property no longer existed, the law provided that previous owners or their heirs be compensated. Property restitution generally enjoyed public support, ultimately contributing to the establishment of a middle class.

Rehabilitation

In 1993–1998, most the verdicts pronounced by the People's Court in 1944–1945 were annulled on a case-by-case basis. The number of the annulled verdicts is yet unknown. On June 25, 1991, parliament adopted The Law for Political and Civil Rehabilitation of Repressed People, which stipulated the judicial rehabilitation of the people who suffered from political repression during the communist period. The law listed several specific court rulings that were annulled; it also rehabilitated all people who were sent to the communist labor camps as well as those who were killed for political reasons without a court ruling. The law was finally amended on August 10, 2010, with a view to rehabilitate more than 100 Orthodox and Catholic priests killed without court hearings in September 1944.

Lustration

In Bulgaria, lustration was short-lived, as it was quickly discredited as a new form of political persecution and witch hunt. Lustration was first legislated as amendments to the 1992 Law on Banks and Banking, which banned from bank managerial positions individuals who had occupied leading positions in the Communist Party (nomenclatura) in the last fifteen years of the communist period. Because the law did not define the term "nomenclatura," the number of persons affected by lustration could not be estimated. Parliament abolished the law in 1997.

In December 1992, parliament adopted the Law on Introducing Additional Requirements for Members of Governing Bodies of Scientific Institutions and the Supreme Accreditation Commission (known as the Panev Bill after the name of legislator Georgi Panev, who introduced it). Dealing with state-owned universities, scientific institutions, and the Academy of Science, the law banned from leadership positions down to the head of faculty department the former Communist Party leaders at the central and local levels, the KDS officers and informers, and individuals who had planned and executed the Revival Process. Because the law mostly affected them, intellectuals, university professors, and public figures organized a bitter campaign against the law in particular and against the concept of lustration in general. As a result, the Panev Bill was abolished in March 1995 by the parliament, at the time dominated by the Socialist Party.

In addition, Article 26 of the November 1998 Law on Public Radio and Television prohibited former State Security officers and informers from being elected as members of the newly created regulatory Council for Electronic Media. In February 2002, the Council removed one of its members after his name was mentioned in an official report as a former KDS informer.

The idea of lustration gained new momentum in late 2010, when the Commission for Declassification of the State Security Archives revealed in an official report that between 1991 and 2010, half of Bulgarian ambassadors and heads of diplomatic missions – including forty-five of the acting Bulgarian ambassadors – had been affiliated with the KDS. The Minister of Foreign Affairs promised to ask the Bulgarian president to withdraw from their posts abroad all those mentioned in the report, and to amend the Law on the Diplomatic Service to prevent such diplomats from obtaining leading positions in the ministry and abroad. In Bulgaria, the president can appoint and withdraw the ambassadors. On January 14, 2011, parliament adopted a special resolution asking the president to withdraw them. The president, himself a KDS informer, announced his reluctance to do that. At the time of this writing, the Law on the Diplomatic Service has not been amended.

Prosecution and Trials

Despite high public expectations in the early 1990s, the trials against former Communist Party officials were unsuccessful; the investigations and trials took too much time to complete; and the few guilty verdicts passed down did not satisfy public expectations for justice and for condemnation of the communist regime in general.

In the early 1990s, prosecutors concentrated their efforts on collecting evidence for cases regarding the misuse of privileges by the communist leadership. In 1990, a lawsuit was filed against the former party-state leader Zhivkov and his right-hand man and chief of cabinet Milko Balev for embezzlement of state funds. In late 1992, Zhivkov was sentenced to seven years in prison; Balev was sentenced to two years. Because of health problems, Zhivkov served his term under house arrest until 1995, when the Court of Appeals overturned the initial sentence on grounds that the trial should not have taken place, because Zhivkov enjoyed immunity as former head of state. In 1993, the last communist Prime Minister Georgi Atanassov and the former Minister of Economy and State Planning Stoyan Ovcharov were found guilty of misusing state funds and were sentenced to ten-year and nine-year prison terms, respectively. In 1994, President Zhelyu Zhelev pardoned Atanassov due to his failing health.

The Chernobyl Case, launched in 1993, prosecuted the communist-era Vice Prime Minister Grigor Stoychkov and Chief Sanitary Inspector Chavdar Shindarov for failing to take the necessary prevention measures and warn the general public of the risk of contamination when the radiation cloud reached Bulgaria after the explosion at the Soviet nuclear plant in 1986. The court sentenced Stoychkov to two years in prison, which he served, and Shindarov to two years probation.

Completely unsuccessful was the Trial on the Concentration Camps, filed in 1992. The top official among the accused was the former Deputy Minister of Interior Mircho Spassov, a key figure in the camp system. Spassov died a month before the trial began in June 1993. The case was then set aside. In 2002, the Supreme Court closed it when the statute of limitation expired.

Under British pressure, Bulgarian authorities launched investigations into Markov's murder (discussed earlier) and discovered that the last two communist Deputy Ministers of Interior, Vladimir Todorov and Stoyan Savov, had destroyed Markov's file in the State Security Archive, which possibly contained all information on the case. Savov took his own life days before the trial hearings began, while Todorov received a ten-month prison sentence for destroying Markov's file. The case of Markov's assassination remains judicially unsolved, although Markov's relatives have struggled hard to learn the truth about his death and despite revelations made by the investigative journalist Hristov.

The Trial on the Revival Process was hotly debated. In 1991, the Military Prosecutor General charged top communist officials – Zhivkov, Atanassov, and Former Minister of Interior Dimitar Stoyanov – with planning the Revival Process. In 1993 and 1997, the prosecution twice prepared a lawsuit against them, but the court returned the case for further investigation on grounds that prosecutors had failed to collect all necessary evidence.

Access to Secret Files

Initially, the Socialist Party fiercely opposed the opening of the archives. When in government, anticommunist parties announced their readiness to open the archives, but fulfilled this promise only partially. In 1990, parliament created the Special Parliamentary Commission on the State Security Archives, chaired by the Socialist Party member Georgi Tambuev. The Commission was unable to survive the public scandal following the publication in a minor newspaper of a list of members of parliament with ties to the KDS, allegedly obtained by the Commission. In April 1991, parliament dissolved the Commission.

The Law on Access to the State Security Documents of 30 June 1997 laid down the procedure by which Bulgarian citizens once monitored by the KDS could access their own secret files. The law allowed for the creation of a commission headed by the Minister of Interior, and authorized to unmask the KDS informers from within the postcommunist political elite. Its authority was seriously limited by the Constitutional Court ruling of September 22, 1997, which forbade the Commission to publicly release the names of the tainted persons for whom no file was found in the secret archive, but only a name card in the State Security card index, because their files were destroyed in 1989–1990. Its first report, filed on October 22, 1997, revealed to parliament the names of twenty-three active politicians who had collaborated with the KDS, including fourteen members of parliament. Minister of Interior Bonev explained that the names of another seventy collaborators could not be revealed because of the Constitutional Court ruling.

To make the procedure more efficient and raise the number of unmasked politicians, on February 28, 2001, parliament revised the law and created the Commission Determining Connections to the Former State Security (see separate entry), chaired by Metody Andreev, a Union of Democratic Forces legislator. The Commission, which included seven members representing parliamentary parties, worked between April 2001 and March 2002, preparing nine reports revealing the identity of some KDS informers and officers turned postcommunist politicians, and verifying the past of members of all postcommunist legislatures and governments. Altogether it verified the pasts of 1,100 postcommunist politicians and disclosed the names of 53 legislators whose affiliation to the KDS was undisputable. The Commission announced that it could not disclose the names of seventy-six tainted individuals because of the limitations set down by the Constitutional Court ruling. Its final report submitted in March 2002 to parliament claimed that the Commission investigated 7,000 individuals, verified 517 of them as former collaborators, but disclosed the names of only 208 because of the Constitutional Court ruling.

On December 19, 2006, parliament adopted Law for Access and Disclosure of the Documents and Announcing Affiliation of Bulgarian Citizens to the State Security and the Intelligence Services of the Bulgarian National Army. Within weeks, parliament elected the Commission for Disclosing the Documents and Announcing Affiliation of Bulgarian Citizens to the State Security and Intelligence Services of Bulgarian People's Army (known as the Kostadinov Commission; see separate entry), chaired by Socialist Party legislator Evtim Kostadinov. The Commission consisted of nine members proposed by parties in parliament and the president. In its Report #7 of July 19, 2007, the Commission revealed the former KDS affiliation of the then-acting Bulgarian President Georgi Purvanov (the former Socialist Party leader). The revelations created a serious political scandal but had no legal consequence. Since June 2007, the Commission has verified the names of postcommunist state dignitaries and public officials. According to the law, the Commission must verify all public officials who worked for the postcommunist legislative, executive, and judiciary at the national level, the members of the local government, state agencies, the leaders of the intelligence services, and the opinion makers (that is, owners, managers, and journalists of all private and public media). The disclosures of the Commission have informative and moral effects, but not lustration effects, because those named do not have to give up their positions.

The 2006 law also stipulated the creation of a "centralized archive" of all communist security agencies (including the Archives of the State Security and the Archives of the Intelligence Service of the Bulgarian People's Army). The centralized archive was placed under the control of the Commission. The Commission is authorized to secure full access to documents for the people affected by the activity of the KDS. From 2007 to 2010, the Commission verified the pasts of 99,389 people and identified 4,600 of them as former KDS collaborators. The Commission reports are publicly available on its Web site and widely reported in the media. As a result, this Commission is the first successful Bulgarian transitional justice institution.

Rewriting History Books

Until 2007, politicians and journalists dominated the debate on the communist past. Declassification in 2007 of the archives of the KDS and other communist state and party institutions facilitated the efforts of several nongovernmental and academic institutions. The Institute for Study of the Recent Past and the Faculties of History at the Sofia University and the New Bulgarian University have published archival papers, articles, and books on the communist period. Their efforts are supported by investigative journalists, who focused on publishing the files of the KDS collaborators.

Conclusion

Bulgaria's postcommunist transitional justice remains ambivalent. Trials against former communist party officials remained unsuccessful and the lustration laws affected very few communist nomenclatura members. In this respect, Bulgaria's experience attests to the fact that far-reaching transitional justice is almost impossible when former elites retain significant political power, and access to secret files is key to postcommunist transitional justice.

Momchil Metodiev

Cross-references: Access to Secret Files; Committee for Access to the Former State Security Files, the Bonev Committee; Committee for Disclosing the Documents and Announcing Affiliation of Bulgarian Citizens to the State Security and the Intelligence Services of the Bulgarian National Army, the Kostadinov Committee; Committee for Disclosing the Documents and Announcing Affiliation to the Former State Security and General Staff Intelligence Directorate, the Andreev Committee; Lustration; Property Restitution.

Further Readings

Andreev, Metodi. 2002. *Decommunization in Bulgaria*. Budapest, March. Available at: http://www.decommunization.org/Decommunization2/Bulgaria.htm (accessed November 3, 2010).
Hristov, Hristo. 1999. *The Secret File on Camps* [Sekretnoto delo za lagerite]. Sofia: Ivan Vazov.
———. 2004. *The Crimes of the Communist Regime and the Attempts after 10 November 1989 to Investigate Them*. Available at: http://www.decommunization.org/Articles/Hristov4.htm (accessed November 3, 2010).
Gruev, M. and A. Kalionski. 2008. *The "Revival Process". Muslim Communities and the Communist Regime: Policies, Reactions and Consequences*. Sofia: Institute for Studies of the Recent Past & Ciela.
Metodiev, Momchil. 2009. Bulgaria. In *Transitional Justice in Eastern Europe and the Former Soviet Union: Reckoning with the Communist Past*. Ed. Lavinia Stan. New York: Routledge, pp. 152–175.

Burundi

Since Burundi's independence in 1962, its people have suffered successive waves of widespread violence, violations of human rights, and genocide. Over a decade after the signing of the Arusha Peace Accords in 2000, which provided for the establishment of transitional justice mechanisms, the process of Burundians' receiving redress for past atrocities has been fraught with obstacles, including tackling the scale and complexity of the conflict and the crimes committed, as well as the lack of both political will and technical and financial resources. Despite the strong desire for truth, justice, and reparation, Burundians still have not received redress for decades of past atrocities.

Repressive Past

Colonized by Germany in 1899 and under Belgian rule after World War I, Burundi claimed independence in July 1962. At independence, a constitutional monarchy was established and both Tutsi and Hutu ethnic groups (amounting to some 15 percent and 84 percent of the population, respectively) were represented in parliament, but not the Twa ethnic group (accounting for only 1 percent). However, issues over access to power and resources – land in particular – persisted, fueling societal divisions and manifesting in ethnic conflict. From 1962 to 1993, Burundi was controlled by a series of Tutsi military dictators. Widespread violence broke out in 1965, 1972, and 1988. In 1972, 300,000 people, mostly Hutus, were killed and 150,000 fled to Rwanda, the Democratic Republic of Congo, and Tanzania (see entries on Rwanda and Congo, the Democratic Republic). Many of the Burundian refugees of 1972 living in Rwanda later fled to Tanzania after the outbreak of genocide in 1993. The violence of 1988 was sparked after the previous year a coup led by Major Pierre Buyoya resulted in 50,000 deaths in the north of Burundi and the flight of tens of thousands of people seeking refuge to neighboring countries.

In 1993, the Hutu-dominated Front for Democracy in Burundi (FRODEBU) won the first democratic elections. The assassination of FRODEBU leader and first Hutu president of Burundi, Melchoir Ndadaye, sparked an intense wave of violence that lasted until the transitional elections in 2005. In retaliation for Ndadaye's assassination by army officers, Hutu extremists massacred thousands of Tutsis. The army (majority Tutsi) responded by massacring Hutus. These cycles of retaliatory violence resulted in 300,000 deaths and the displacement of 1.2 million people from both ethnic groups.

Political violence, including assassinations, coups, and rebellions, spilled over into popular violence, and political elites manipulated ethnic tensions to deadly effect. The scale and scope of violations since 1962 are huge and include acts of genocide, war crimes, and crimes against humanity: targeted killings, massacres, disappearances, rape and sexual violence, torture, arbitrary arrest and detention, recruitment of children into armed groups, and destruction and theft or confiscation of property and land.

Burundians residing inside and outside the country continue to suffer the destructive legacy of violent conflict. Victims, survivors, and conflict-affected communities live with the loss of loved ones and suffer the physical and psychological scars of decades of war. Many thousands of Burundians are landless, as they were driven from or fled their land, their primary or only source of livelihood. Some 38,000 refugees remain in Tanzania and more than 120,000 Burundian women, men, and children are internally displaced, many with no access to land and limited access to services. Women and girls suffered sexual violence and torture, often used as a way of attacking or humiliating the women's ethnic group as a whole. Women and girl survivors of sexual violence often face intense social stigma as a result of what they endured, especially if they are unmarried with a child. Among those marginalized are women and girls who fought as soldiers with armed groups, and those who worked as cooks, porters, and "wives" or sex slaves to commanders.

In addition to specific acts of economic violence and injustice, such as the pillaging or theft of land and property, the protracted armed violence decimated the national economy and destroyed livelihoods. Economic marginalization acutely impacts victims of conflict, many of whom live with physical disability and/or deep psychological trauma for which local authorities and the state are unable to provide adequate support, further limiting access to employment and basic services. The whole population has suffered the economic impacts of conflict, as per capita income fell by almost 40 percent between 1993 and 2007, making Burundi one of the poorest countries in the world.

In August 2000, the Arusha Accords were signed by the major parties of the conflict in Burundi including the government, political parties, and armed groups, with the exception of the rebel armed group Liberation of the Hutu People-National Liberation

Forces (Libération du Peuple Hutu-Forces Nationales de Libération, PALIPEHUTU-FNL). The rebel group National Council for the Defense of Democracy-Forces for the Defense of Democracy (Conseil Nationale pour la Defense de la Démocratie, CNDD-FDD) signed the ceasefire in 2003. The Accords paved the way for democratic elections in 2005, which the CNDD-FDD won to form a transitional government. However, violence continued as the PALIPEHUTU-FNL had not laid down its arms. In December 2008, after the PALIPEHUTU-FNL signed a ceasefire agreement and agreed to drop the ethnic reference in its name (PALIPEHUTU), the renamed Forces for National Liberation (Forces Nationales de Libération, FNL) become integrated into the mainstream political system as a recognized political party and its members were incorporated into the national army and police forces.

Transitional justice remains politically contentious. Political parties, including the ruling CNDD-FDD, have stalled the process and shown lack of political will, because some political leaders have been implicated in serious human rights violations. The CNDD-FDD government has publicly called for amnesty, including for the most serious of crimes, and argued that security was a prerequisite to seeking justice because until recently the country was insufficiently stable to support transitional justice. Others argue that the ten-year-long delay reflects lack of political will and that uncovering truths about and seeking redress for past crimes is fundamental to securing Burundi's peaceful future. Furthermore, the continued politico-ethnic divisions between the ruling CNDD-FDD and the main parliamentary opposition party Union for National Progress (Uprona) will continue to pose challenges to ensuring adherence to the transitional justice process and recognizing its legitimacy.

The international community has played a significant role in transitional justice, brokering negotiations, uncovering violations of human rights, and offering technical advice on international legal and transitional justice issues. Successive UN missions to Burundi have been mandated to support transitional justice. The UN was central in the transitional negotiations after the signature of the Arusha Accords and in setting up the joint UN, government, and civil society steering committee for the National Consultations on Transitional Justice (see discussion later). The international community and nongovernmental organizations, in support of local civil society groups, have been instrumental in advocating for victims' voices to be heard, documenting human rights abuses, and campaigning against amnesty.

Yet, this role has not been without contention. The international community's support for transitional justice may have come at the expense of national government ownership of the process. The UN has faced criticism from some within Burundi for focusing on certain crimes and periods of violence over others, a choice that has an ethnopolitical significance. For example, in the mid-1990s, the international community was accused of emphasizing the cycle of conflict from 1993, which victimized the Tutsi minority, more than the massacres in 1972, when most victims were Hutus.

Legal process and terminology are contentious in this politically sensitive environment, where the country's recent past has been shaped by identity conflicts and characterized by deep ethnic division. Considering these divides, the legal characterization of genocide has acute political implications, as it seems to imply collective guilt on an entire ethnic group. The post-independence conflict was punctuated by massacres and genocide that targeted both Hutu and Tutsi, and all ethnic groups were both victims and perpetrators of crimes. Because certain periods in the conflict in 1965, 1972, 1988, 1991, and 1993 saw more victims from one ethnic group than another, the temporal jurisdiction of the transitional justice mechanisms is pivotal to their perceived impartiality, contextualizing the violence, and contributing to a fuller historical truth. Burundians have been clear that any transitional justice process should be cognizant of this "long view."

Persistent insecurity, combined with concerns over poor governance and reliability of state institutions, including the justice system, jeopardize the legitimacy and viability of the transitional justice process. Civil society has raised fears that the independence of these transitional justice mechanisms risks being compromised by their dependence on the Burundian legal system. These fears relate to the high levels of corruption in the judicial system, which is dependent on the executive whose members have played a role in serious human rights violations, and to the system's limited resources and institutional capacity. This fragile context threatens the transitional justice process, causing victims to fear to come forward. Guaranteeing protection of witnesses is of grave concern.

Transitional Justice

As part of the Arusha Accords (detailed later), transitional justice is deeply entwined with Burundi's journey toward reestablishing peace and reconciliation. The precise goals of its transitional justice project are, however, intensely debated. Peace-building and societal reconciliation, truth revelation, justice, prosecution, reparation, and reform of discriminatory institutions have been cited as main aims. Nevertheless, the official transitional justice process has been beset with challenges and subject to political manipulation. Despite active local civil society support and international pressure, Burundians have yet to see the establishment of a truth commission, the prosecution of perpetrators, the guarantee of nonrepetition of the crimes, and reparations for victims and survivors.

National Consultations on Transitional Justice

Until the National Consultations on Transitional Justice in July 2009, the official transitional justice process remained the remote preserve of the political elite. The Consultations, which cumulated in a final report published in April 2010, aimed to involve Burundians in national reconciliation by collecting their views on the modalities of setting up transitional justice mechanisms. The Consultations, which were headed by a committee made up of government, civil society, and UN representatives, took the form of individual interviews, focus groups, community meetings, and television broadcasts.

Their final report made recommendations based on the respondents' views of key areas, including: the period of time covered by the transitional justice mechanisms; the crimes over which the Truth and Reconciliation Commission (TRC) and Special Tribunal should have jurisdiction; the composition and powers of the TRC and the Special Tribunal; and the nature of reparations and institutional reform. The report concluded that the time period to be investigated should encompass more than four decades, from Burundi's independence on July 1, 1962 to December 4, 2008, which marked the end to the conflict. It stated that the TRC should have the powers to investigate, determine responsibility, and bring victims and perpetrators together to seek reconciliation. It should have mixed national and international composition, and its chair should preferably be selected from civil society or the religious community. The committee set up to select the TRC members should be made up of representatives of civil society, religious leaders, the UN, and the government. The TRC should decide which names to disclose, on a case-by-case basis and in consideration of respect for human rights and presumption of innocence. The TRC should propose measures for reconciliation, while remaining within the strict limits of international norms, particularly in the treatment of alleged perpetrators of crimes under international law and in regards to amnesty. The TRC should submit its recommendations to the government on institutional reforms needed to ensure that these serious past events are not repeated and engage a range of local and national governmental and civil society stakeholders so that reforms are effectively implemented.

The report called for the Special Tribunal to have the mandate and resources that would enable it to: bring to justice those responsible for serious crimes under international law in order to end the tradition of impunity and give voice to victims; ensure the accused a qualified defense; develop an effective program of victim assistance and witness protection taking into account the gender dimension; and contribute to strengthening the rule of law by supporting the reform of judicial institutions and sharing its knowledge and jurisprudence with national courts.

The National Consultations marked an encouraging first step to engage the wider population and respond to communities' views on transitional justice mechanisms, but their ultimate success depends on the translation of the outcomes into concrete action and continued efforts to encourage wide participation. Burundian civil society organizations were key actors in the Consultations as members of the Tripartite Steering Committee and observers, as well as in educating the wider population about transitional justice and the National Consultations. Civil society groups have maintained pressure on and momentum for transitional justice, calling for criminal prosecutions for past abuses and advocating a victim-centered process. Women's associations have campaigned for women's equal leadership of and engagement in the process, and justice for abuses that impacted women, such as sexual violence. International nongovernmental organizations have supported civil society and victim associations. In October 2011, victims' associations signed a Memorandum of Understanding bringing together both Hutu and Tutsi victims' groups to work together in support of victims rights.

Truth and Reconciliation Commission (TRC)

The Accords contained transitional justice provisions for a truth commission and an international judicial commission of inquiry. If this inquiry found evidence of genocide, war crimes, and crimes against humanity, the Accords provided for the establishment of an International Criminal Tribunal by the UN Security Council. In May 2004, the UN established a mission whose final report, the Kalomoh Report, recommended the establishment of a national truth commission of national and international commissioners and of a special chamber within the court system of Burundi. The UN Security Council endorsed the report and requested the initiation of negotiations with the government of Burundi on implementing the report's recommendations (Security Council Resolution 1606/2005). Negotiations with the Burundian government began in March 2006, but the UN and Burundi could not come to an agreement over amnesty for genocide, war crimes, and crimes against humanity, the independence of the Special Tribunal's prosecutor, and the relationship between the TRC and the Tribunal. The transitional justice process stagnated and was not reinvigorated until the UN negotiated for the National Consultations on Transitional Justice.

In July 2011, President Pierre Nkurunziza announced that the TRC would be established in 2012. Days earlier, he nominated the members of a technical committee that later submitted its report on the establishment and functioning of the TRC to the president. At the time of this writing, the president has not yet shared the findings of the report with civil society partners and the international community. It was expected that the report, detailing the legal framework, strategic directions, and the budget of the TRC, would be made public by late 2011. The Arusha Accords stipulated that the Commission should be set up in 2001. Despite the president's announcement, doubts persist over the existence of political will to propel the process forward in a way that is responsive to victims' and the population's views. Fundamental and complex questions remain concerning the relationship between the TRC and the Special Tribunal, their independence (including the independence of the prosecutor), the financial resources made available for these transitional justice institutions, and the time frame for their establishment and working.

Court Trials for Redress

In Burundi, truth seeking is challenging, given the magnitude of violence and number of victims. Attributing accountability is complex; opinions divide on whether victims of earlier atrocities became perpetrators of later violence. The TRC may uncover truths and offer accountability and acknowledgment for victims of violations, but its ability to record an agreed-on account of the past may be limited. The National Consultations uncovered desire for forgiveness and reconciliation, but focus groups also showed desire for judicial investigation and prosecutions for the most serious crimes. Some those who favored reconciliation said that their reticence concerning prosecutions was rooted in fears of reprisals. Much of the movement on transitional justice has centered on truth seeking, both because of the desire to uncover truths and because the issue of criminal responsibility and prosecuting violence is so sensitive. There is little appetite for prosecutions among political leaders who could face trial for their alleged involvement.

The history of impunity is among the obstacles to pursuing prosecutions. Individuals named by victims of abuses and atrocities have not been brought to justice. In 2006 and 2009, a presidential decree released more than 3,000 suspected perpetrators of atrocities. Suspected perpetrators of crimes continue to occupy official posts, even as members of the security forces. Despite security sector reform programs and laws that ban perpetrators from serving in the police or army, there has been no systematic vetting process and the police have not dismissed those accused of war crimes and gross human rights violations. There are continued cases of human rights abuses and intimidation by members of the security forces.

Civil society organizations have raised concerns that the ability of the Special Tribunal to function will be limited by the national judicial system, often cited as remote, inefficient, underresourced, and susceptible to political pressure and corruption. Women's organizations have highlighted the disparity in sentencing for sexual violence, which sees perpetrators of rape receiving lesser sentences than those convicted of theft.

Reparations and Memorialization

Reparations acknowledge the harm inflicted on victims. Victims have called on the government to provide comprehensive material and symbolic reparations. These include support for and medical care for physical and mental health of victims, including HIV testing, treatment, counseling, and other trauma-healing work, and access to education and skills for child victims. Victims have also called for improved access to employment and support for effective socioeconomic integration, and emphasized the importance of symbolic reparations and memorials. Propositions include monuments, community projects and infrastructure named in memory of victims, and national days of remembrance. Victims have also advocated for collective reparations, including improving local communities' access to health care, education, and economic opportunities. There has been no national policy for material or symbolic reparations, as the government asserts that its community development projects, such as the building of hospitals and schools, provide a form of collective reparations. Victims' associations argue that these national development projects benefit the entire population and do not constitute reparations for victims. At some sites of atrocities, monuments have been erected in memory of victims.

The government has refused to register a number of victims' associations, arguing that they do not comply with the provisions in the Arusha Accords, which require state and non-state organizations to have membership from both ethnic groups. Some local associations represent victims of a particular atrocity and therefore are predominately composed of members of one group. It has been argued that this legal argument hides a political motive, as members of the ruling party have been accused of involvement in some of the crimes for which these victims' groups seek justice.

Conclusion

The year 2012 marks a pivotal moment in Burundi's slow and arduous progress toward providing justice for past wrongs and reconciling divided communities, as the TRC is set to begin its work that year. However, concerns remain that the transitional justice process is susceptible to political pressure and that the political will needed to drive the process and ensure national ownership is not present, especially for establishing a Special Tribunal to prosecute the most serious violations. Fears also persist around ensuring the safety of witnesses and victims, particularly considering continued incidences of violence and political instability in the country. Concerns have been raised that adequate psychosocial support must be provided to avoid retraumatizing victims during the truth-seeking and trial processes. Survivors of sexual violence fear stigma if they testify. The Special Tribunal embedded in the national judicial system might lack legitimacy and independence. Victims call for adequate reparations, including medical care, community development projects, monetary compensation, and memorials, yet national resources are limited. Expectations of the transitional justice process are high, and it remains to be seen whether the eventual mechanisms will meet these expectations.

Ruth Simpson, with Aloys Batungwanayo

Cross-references: Congo, the Democratic Republic; Rwanda.

Further Readings

Government of Burundi. 2010. *Report of the National Consultations on the Establishment of Transitional Justice Mechanisms in Burundi*, April 20. Available at: http://www.ohchr.org/Documents/Countries/BI/RapportConsultationsBurundi.pdf (accessed September 15, 2011).

International Centre for Transitional Justice. 2009. The Transitional Justice Process in Burundi. Challenges and Perspectives. *ICTJ Briefing*, April 11. Available at: http://ictj.org/sites/default/files/ICTJ-Burundi-Processus-de-Justice-2011-French.pdf (accessed August 3, 2011).

Nibigira, Concile and Helen Scanlon. 2010. *Gender Peace and Security: The Challenges Facing Transitional Justice Processes in Burundi*, August. Available at: http://www.initiativeforpeacebuilding.eu/pdf/1008burundi.pdf (accessed September 5, 2011).

United Nations Security Council. 2005. *Report of the Assessment Mission on the Establishment of an International Judicial Commission of Inquiry for Burundi*, S/2005/158, March 11. Available at: http://www.securitycouncilreport.org/atf/cf/%7B65BFCF9B-6D27-4E9C-8CD3-CF6E4FF96FF9%7D/Burundi%20S2005158.pdf (accessed August 29, 2011).

———. 2005. *The Situation in Burundi*, S/RES/1606 (2005), June 20. Available at: http://daccess-dds-ny.un.org/doc/UNDOC/GEN/N05/391/59/PDF/N0539159.pdf?OpenElement (accessed September 1, 2011).

Cambodia

During the less than four years of the Khmer Rouge regime, nearly one-quarter of the Cambodian population – between 1.7 million and 2.5 million people – died or disappeared as a result of the policies imposed by the Khmer Rouge. Cambodia underwent three major phases of political transition after the ousting of the Khmer Rouge regime by the Vietnamese. In each phase, various transitional justice mechanisms were undertaken to encourage support for the new government and steps toward national "reconciliation." These three phases were: the People's Republic of Kampuchea (PRK, 1979–1989); the United Nations Transitional Authority in Cambodia (1989–1993); and the Kingdom of Cambodia (1993–present).

The Repressive Past

On April 17, 1975, Khmer Rouge troops, a Cambodian communist insurgency movement led by Saloth Sar, also known as Pol Pot, seized control of the capital, Phnom Penh. This marked the beginning of nearly four years of an experimental transformation of Cambodian society into an agrarian utopia. The Angkar (Organization), the revolutionary movement, was the sole governing power and the owner of all property and means of production. To advance the movement and strip away the past, the Khmer Republic was renamed Democratic Kampuchea.

The Khmer Rouge imposed strict decrees aimed at isolating the country from foreign elements and establishing the "utopia." First, they forced the population out of the cities and towns and into the countryside in order to establish the planned society based on agriculture and total collectivism. Next, they attempted to seal Cambodia from foreign influences by expelling all foreigners, closing embassies, banning the use of foreign languages, and refusing any foreign economic or medical assistance with the exception of China and North Korea. Newspapers and television stations were shut down, radios and bicycles confiscated, currency and the postal system were abolished, and telephone usage curtailed. All businesses were closed, religion banned, education terminated except for a select few, health care for the population curtailed, and parental authority revoked.

The Angkar's polices were largely uniform across the country, with some regional and individual variations. There were no official class distinctions, but most Cambodians were labeled as either Old People (or Base People) and New People. Old People were those who resided in areas controlled by the Khmer Rouge prior to 1975, while New

People were mostly city dwellers, including peasants who resided in the cities at the time of the evacuation. City residents, exposed to foreign influences, were considered politically precarious to the new regime. Most were put to work in forced-labor camps. Over a few short years, millions of Cambodians were exposed to slave labor conditions where they began dying from overwork, disease, and malnutrition.

To enforce their drastic changes, the Khmer Rouge created and maintained a climate of constant terror, violence, and secrecy. They also instituted a vast prison system across the country. The number of prisoners may have easily ranged from 400,000 to 600,000 people. At Tuol Sleng prison in Phnom Penh alone, at least 12,000 people were tortured and executed. Broad segments of the population were marked for extermination: educated urban elite, soldiers from previous regimes, Buddhist monks, repatriated Cambodians, and ethnic populations such as Chams, Khmer of Vietnamese origin, and Chinese. As the leaders' obsession with potential infiltration and treason in their midst increased, they conducted major purges among their own ranks, torturing and killing hundreds of thousands of civilians.

After several years of border wars, Vietnam invaded Cambodia and on January 7, 1979, succeeded in overthrowing the Khmer Rouge regime. The Vietnamese installed a pro-Vietnam government, the People's Republic of Kampuchea (PRK), led by Heng Samrin, a communist Cambodian politician and a defected Khmer Rouge member who had previously served as political commissar and army division commander. Under the Khmer Rouge regime, hundreds of thousands of Cambodians fled to Thailand or Vietnam. Evading capture, Pol Pot, along with 30,000 to 50,000 supporters and cadres, fled to remote areas in the north and west regions of Cambodia. The country did not immediately stabilize – the Khmer Rouge and two other fractions (United National Front for an Independent, Neutral, Peaceful and Cooperative Cambodia [UNFINPCC] under Norodom Sihanouk, and the Kampuchean People's National Liberation Front [KPNLF] under Son Sann) fiercely resisted the new authority, while continued isolation from the international community slowed progress during the subsequent three major transition periods.

Transitional Justice

Cambodia adopted a combination of transitional justice methods to reckon with the crimes of the Khmer Rouge dictatorship, including amnesty, court trials, historical research commission, national day, and memorialization.

The People's Republic of Kampuchea (PRK, 1979–1989)

After the overthrow of the Khmer Rouge regime, the new People's Republic of Kampuchea (PRK) launched limited transition initiatives seeking to entice those still loyal to the Khmer Rouge regime to switch their support to the new government; to assess the damages done by the Khmer Rouge; to deter further fighting; and to bolster national reconciliation. Four initiatives emerged under the PRK: (1) the Kampuchean United Front for National Salvation; (2) the People's Revolutionary Tribunal and National Trials; (3) the Research Committee on Pol Pot's Genocidal Regime; and (4) the Amnesty Decree.

In 1978, the Vietnamese formed the Kampuchean (or Khmer) United Front for National Salvation with Cambodian refugees to overthrow the Khmer Rouge regime.

On December 2, 1978, to gain broader public support, the Front promised pardons and leniency for past wrongdoings to all defecting Khmer Rouge members. When the Vietnamese overthrew the Khmer Rouge regime a month later, the Front leaders formed the core of the new government. Backed by Vietnam, they continued to encourage soldiers and former Khmer loyalists still at large to join the Front. Those who refused were sought after for "reeducation," imprisonment, or even execution for heinous acts committed under the Khmer Rouge.

In August 1979, the PRK established the People's Revolutionary Tribunal (PRT) in Phnom Penh to judge the crimes of the Khmer Rouge regime. The tribunal was to prosecute the two leading members of the Khmer Rouge state of Democratic Kampuchea, Prime Minister Pol Pot and Deputy Prime Minister and Minister of Foreign Affairs Ieng Sary. The new government hoped that by focusing on only the top two leaders it would further encourage Khmer Rouge soldiers and cadres still at large to defect. The trials, held in absentia in a Cambodian tribunal, were assisted by legal experts from Laos, Cuba, India, Algeria, Syria, Japan, the United States, and the Soviet Union. A ten-member jury convicted the two accused of genocide and sentenced them to death, but the sentence was never carried out. Pol Pot died, presumably of a heart attack, while under house arrest by his own people in a jungle base at Anlong Veng on April 15, 1998, while Ieng Sary was pardoned on September 15, 1996, by King Norodom Sihanouk, in agreement with both co-prime ministers, after defecting from the Khmer Rouge. The PRK carried out many other judicial proceedings throughout the country against cadres and lower-ranking Khmer Rouge supporters. How many of these judicial proceedings took place and whether they were implemented as a part of systematic policy is not well documented.

In 1979, the new government established the Research Committee on Pol Pot's Genocidal Regime, which interviewed and gathered petitions, assessed the damage to Cambodia's infrastructure incurred under the Khmer Rouge regime, collected information about crimes, exhumed mass graves, and studied Khmer Rouge documents. On July 25, 1983, the Committee issued its report, detailing its findings province by province. The report is available in the Khmer language at Cambodia's National Library; excerpts translated into English can be found at the Documentation Center of Cambodia. The Committee aimed at gathering petitions from Cambodians to support an appeal by the government to the UN to deny recognition to the Khmer Rouge, but petitions were never presented to the UN. The Committee used those "petitions signed or thumb printed by 1,166,307 people in villages, cooperatives and government offices in 19 provinces" to estimate that nearly 3.5 million people died during the regime (Fawthrop and Jarvis 2004, p. 73). This truth-commission-type process had two flaws: the results were never disseminated to the population, and it was a one-sided process providing no voice to former Khmer Rouge officials and cadres. In addition, the gathering of the petitions was driven more by political goals (the government's desire to gain recognition from the UN) than the goals of truth and reconciliation (Ciorciari and Sok-Khrang 2009, p. 309; Etcheson 2004, p. 42).

On October 5, 1983, a PRK National Assembly of Information and Culture memorandum encouraged local officials to create memorials at sites of former Khmer Rouge prisons and mass graves and recognized May 20 as a Day to Commemorate the Sufferings Inflicted by the Khmer Rouge regime (known as the Day of Hate). As instructed, memorials were constructed in every province and municipality. The infamous Tuol Sleng or S-21 prison became a museum in 1980.

Amnesty was initially granted by the Solidarity Front to encourage broader support for the overthrow of the Khmer Rouge regime. Later, the new government made amnesty conditional on a public request for forgiveness in front of the local authority and full recognition of the wrongdoing coupled with reeducation. This policy was revised to enable more people to join forces with the new government. Despite these attempts at easing defection from the Angkar, fighting continued until the late 1990s.

The United Nations Transitional Authority in Cambodia (1989–1993)

Another set of transitional justice initiatives was adopted after the Vietnamese troops withdrew from Cambodia in September 1989. While fighting continued, negotiations between the government, the Khmer Rouge, and other entities resulted in the 1991 Paris Peace Agreement. The signing of this accord marked the beginning of the operations of the United Nations Transitional Authority in Cambodia (UNTAC), which worked with Cambodian officials to reform the political and legal infrastructure. The UNTAC monitored a ceasefire among all parties, held free and fair elections, and was also instrumental in improving public security, training judges, prosecutors, and police officers on the new Penal Code adopted at the UNTAC's initiative, implementing a program of regular prison visits, and supervising or controlling local police activities. The UNTAC repatriated more than 350,000 Cambodians from Thai refugee camps, but failed to disarm the factions or convince the Khmer Rouge to participate in elections.

The Kingdom of Cambodia (1993–Present)

In May 1993, Cambodia held its first multiparty elections since 1972. The Khmer Rouge boycotted them, claiming that the Vietnamese still controlled the country. With no single party wining majority, a power-sharing arrangement was struck between the royalist party of Prince Norodom Ranariddh (UNFINPCC) and Hun Sen's Cambodian People's Party. This coalition appointed the Royal Government of Cambodia (RGC) led by two prime ministers. In September 1993, the government adopted a new constitution and renamed the country the Kingdom of Cambodia. Pol Pot and the remaining Khmer Rouge went into hiding and continued their resistance and guerilla warfare until 1998, when the revolutionary movement collapsed. The events leading to the collapse marked another key transition period that culminated with the creation of the Extraordinary Chambers in the Courts of Cambodia in 2006 (see separate entry).

The new government initiated several simultaneous actions to end the violence in the northwestern region, close to the Thai border. To encourage defection, the 1994 Law to Outlaw the Democratic Kampuchea Group (that is, the Khmer Rouge) included both screening and amnesty stipulations. Although it did not ban former Khmer Rouge officials from holding public office, the law considered active members "as offenders of the Constitution and offenders of the laws of the Kingdom of Cambodia" (Law to Outlaw the Democratic Kampuchea Group 1994). It offered amnesty to Khmer Rouge members, not leaders, who surrendered to the government within six months (from July 7, 1994 to January 7, 1995). It is uncertain how many defected under this policy, but the "leader" provision was overturned when the King pardoned Ieng Sary in 1996.

In exchange for his defection from the Khmer Rouge to the government, in August 1996, Ieng Sary received both a royal amnesty and a formal pardon by King Norodom

Sihanouk with agreement and acceptance from Prime Ministers Hun Sen and Norodom Ranariddh. The pardon was for Ieng Sary's 1979 in absentia conviction and death sentence for genocide; the amnesty was granted based on the 1994 Law on the Outlawing of the Khmer Rouge. This was a crucial plea bargain deal for the new government. After Sary's royal pardon and amnesty, Ieng Sary led the biggest mass defection of Khmer Rouge military and political forces in western Cambodia to the government. This move reduced the Khmer Rouge by the thousands, weakening them both militarily and economically. It was the key action that led to their collapse.

In June 1997, Pol Pot ordered the murder of Son Sen, the Khmer Rouge Minister of Defense and his confidant of forty years, and of his family, for collaborating with the Cambodian government. Ta Mok, the Khmer Rouge military commander, arrested Pol Pot for Sen's murder and a "people's tribunal" sentenced Pol Pot to life imprisonment. Pol Pot died nine months later.

Within weeks, the Cambodian government seized control of the last Khmer Rouge stronghold. In December 1998, Nuon Chea, former Deputy Chairman of the Communist Party of Democratic Kampuchea, and Khieu Samphan, former Democratic Kampuchea Head of State, surrendered to the government and offered public apologies for the suffering their regime caused. Both apologies were ill-spoken and had little perceived impact. In mid-1997, Hun Sen, with the Cambodian People's Party (CPP) support, led a military coup d'état and seized control of the government, marginalizing Prince Ranariddh. Two years later, the government arrested another key Khmer Rouge leader at large, Ta Mok. Hun Sen and the CPP continue to govern Cambodia at the time of this writing.

Extraordinary Chambers in the Courts of Cambodia (ECCC)

In June 1997, the co-prime ministers asked the UN Secretary-General Kofi Annan to assist in the organizing of a Khmer Rouge Trial, arguing that Cambodia did not have adequate capacity to prosecute former Khmer Rouge leaders. This led to a decade-long negotiation between the UN and the Royal Government of Cambodia and the establishment of the ECCC (the Khmer Rouge Tribunal). The ECCC was established in February 2006, commenced its judicial work in July, and became fully operational in June 2007. Its jurisdiction covers senior leaders and those most responsible for genocide, crimes against humanity, grave breaches of the Geneva Conventions of 1949, and other crimes committed from April 17, 1975 to January 6, 1979.

Developed as a hybrid court within the Cambodian court system, the ECCC has Cambodian and international judges, with a majority of Cambodians. It includes the Pre-Trial Chamber (five judges), the Trial Chamber (five judges), and the Supreme Court Chamber (seven judges). The Pre-Trial Chamber convenes to settle disagreements between the co-prosecutors, between the co-investigating judges, and between the co-prosecutors and the co-investigating judges. It also hears Pre-Trial appeals. The Trial Chamber's decisions can be appealed to the Supreme Court Chamber, whose rulings are final. The ECCC applies both Cambodian and international law, and operates in a civil law system. In addition to being called as witnesses, victims can participate in proceedings as a complainant or a civil party by submitting a Victim Participation form. To join a case as a civil party, the applicant must have suffered direct harm as a result of crimes committed within the ECCC's jurisdiction and the case must be under investigation by the co-investigating judges.

By 2010, the ECCC had arrested and charged five suspects. On July 30, 2007, the co-investigating judges arrested and later charged Kaing Guek Eav (alias Duch), former head of Tuol Sleng, with crimes against humanity and war crimes. Four months later, Ieng Sary Khieu Samphan, Nuon Chea, and Ieng Thirith were arrested and charged with similar crimes. In August 2008, the co-investigating judges indicted Duch for crimes against humanity and war crimes and ordered continued provisional detention until he is brought before the Trial Chamber. Following appeal by the co-prosecutors, Duch was indicted for crimes against humanity, war crimes, murder, and torture under domestic law. The hearings lasted from March 30, 2009 to November 27, 2009. Twenty-four witnesses, twenty-two civil parties, and nine experts testified during the proceedings, which were watched by 28,000 people from the public gallery. On July 26, 2010, Duch was found guilty as charged and sentenced to thirty-five years in prison. The final sentence was reduced to eighteen-to-nineteen years because he had been illegally detained and already spent years in prison. The defense, the prosecution, and the civil parties appealed the judgment.

In September 2010, the ECCC Co-Investigating Judges signed the Closing Order for Case File 002, indicting Ieng Sary, Ieng Thirith, Khieu Samphan, and Nuon Chea for crimes against humanity, grave breaches of the Geneva Conventions of 12 August 1949, genocide, and offenses under the Cambodian Criminal Code of 1956. Hearings commenced in late 2011. More than 2,000 civil party applicants were accepted for participation. This is one of the largest victim participation trials in the history of international criminal justice.

Reparations

The ECCC Internal Rules allow civil parties to seek collective and moral reparations. To be admissible as a civil party, a victim must demonstrate that she/he has suffered direct physical, material, or psychological harm resulting from crimes within the ECCC jurisdiction, and the alleged prejudice must be personal and directly linked to situations under judicial investigation. That means that for Case 002, for example, some former detainees might be eligible to be civil parties because their detention centers are specifically mentioned, whereas others are not.

The ECCC Internal Rules mention as examples of collective and moral reparations: (1) an order to publish the judgment in any appropriate news or other media at the convicted person's expense; (2) an order to fund any nonprofit activity or service that is intended for the benefit of victims; or (3) other appropriate and comparable forms of reparation. Reparations shall be awarded against and borne by convicted persons (ECCC Internal Rules (rev.4) 11 September 2009, article 23).

Rewriting History Books, Commemoration, and Memory

Nongovernmental organizations have supported the ECCC's creation and activity (by recruiting victim participants, creating outreach programs, and providing evidence for the proceedings) and carried out complimentary transitional justice activities. The Documentation Center of Cambodia publishes the monthly *Searching for the Truth* magazine, which summarizes their work in documenting written, photographic, and other materials related to the Khmer Rouge regime and conducting research and interviews with victims and perpetrators. Their Family Tracing File helps families trace their missing loved ones. In 2009, the Center released a revised high school history curriculum and textbook about the Khmer Rouge regime in collaboration with the Ministry of Education. The previous history book, written in 1994, was fraught with political propaganda and was not thoroughly integrated into the school curriculum.

The Center for Social Development (CSD) had organized several public forums in which district and commune chiefs, monks, former Khmer Rouge, and victims of the Khmer Rouge are invited to large public meetings to discuss transitional justice, the ECCC, and reparations.

A plethora of commemorative artistic works has been developed to remember and/or trigger dialogue about the Khmer Rouge past. Recently, the Khmer Rock Opera "Where Elephants Weep" illustrated the difficult return to Cambodia of two former Khmer Rouge child soldiers. "Breaking the Silence," another opera sympathetic to perpetrators, presented the stories of seven perpetrators and victims and allowed for dialogue and discussion when it was performed in Phnom Penh and the provinces.

Many Cambodians artists have painted scenes of murders, tortures, and life under the Khmer Rouge regime. Van Nath's famous paintings portray what happened to him and other prisoners while at Tuol Sleng. In addition, there are numerous films and books about the Khmer Rouge regime. The films often recount personal survivor stories or document specific aspects of the regime. The film "We Want (U) to Know," produced in a participatory approach with villagers, depicted reenactments by the villagers of what happened during the regime. Other well-known movies include the "Killing Fields," "S21: The Khmer Rouge Killing Machine" (2004), and "Out of the Poison Tree."

Conclusion

Three decades after the collapse of the Khmer Rouge regime, Cambodian transitional justice is incomplete, as the ECCC proceedings are still ongoing, with Case 002 commenced in November 2011. It is too early to determine the legacy and impact of the ECCC on deterring future abuses and fostering social reconstruction. How Cambodia will come to final terms with its past remains an open question. While criminal justice remains limited and many younger Cambodians know little about the Khmer Rouge regime, a history curriculum is now in place, which will help develop a national memory of the Khmer Rouge period.

Phuong N. Pham and Patrick Vinck

Cross-references: Amnesty; Extraordinary Chambers in the Courts of Cambodia; Lustration; Property Restitution.

Further Readings

Ciorciari, John and Anne Heindel, eds. 2009. *On Trial: The Khmer Rouge Accountability Process*. Phnom Penh: Documentation Center of Cambodia.
Etcheson, Craig. 2004. *Reconciliation in Cambodia: Theory and Practice*. Phnom Penh: Strategic Implementation International.
Extraordinary Chambers in the Courts of Cambodia. 2009. *Internal Rules [Rev.4]*, September 11. Available at: http://www.eccc.gov.kh/en/documents/legal/internal-rules-rev4 (accessed July 20, 2011).
Fawthrop, Tom and Helen Jarvis. 2004. *Getting Away with Genocide? Elusive Justice and the Khmer Rouge Tribunal*. London: Pluto Press.

Law to Outlaw the Democratic Kampuchea Group, no. 1, NS 94, July 14, 1994.
McGrew, Laura. 2006. *Transitional Justice Mechanisms in Justice Initiatives. Open Society Justice Initiative*, April, 139–150.
Report of the Research Committee on Pol Pot's Genocidal Regime, July 25, 1983. Phnom Penh: Research Committee on Pol Pot's Genocidal Regime.

Central African Republic

The case of the Central African Republic (CAR), which declared its independence from France in 1960, highlights the limited popular impact of internationally led transitional justice and reconciliation efforts in the context of nearly uninterrupted impunity at the domestic level. With government forces pursuing rebellions and armed groups spread across the CAR's territory, the "repressive past" remains present in the lives of many residents.

The Repressive Past

The first few years of the CAR (the former Oubangui-Chari region of the French Equatorial Africa) as an independent country were largely peaceful. The country came under an unwelcome international spotlight in 1979, however, when Jean-Bédel Bokassa, the CAR's military ruler since 1966 and self-proclaimed emperor in 1976, had some 250 schoolchildren who had protested over increases in school fees beaten, arrested, and packed into cells so cramped that many died of suffocation. Amid the international outcry at the abuses, the French removed Bokassa from power. What at the time seemed an aberration in CAR's placid politics foreshadowed growing tensions in the political system.

Early CAR heads of state used the creation of salaried government posts or other forms of patronage as a means of establishing popular support and legitimacy. As a result, the country became increasingly corrupt, poor, and mismanaged. With the waning of the Cold War, the international monetary institutions and international donors such as France assumed increased decision making over national economic policies, emphasized multiparty democracy, and streamlined bureaucracies. As a result, unemployment swelled and the already weak economy plummeted, while the state's perceived need for violence to maintain its power rose.

Feeling his hold on power insecure, President André Kolingba (1981–1993) drew on the politically dormant "primordial tie" of ethnicity, packing the Central African Armed Forces (Forces Armées Centrafricaines, FACA) with his fellow Yakoma tribe members. His successor, Ange-Félix Patassé (1993–2003), did not trust the army and instead devoted the state's security resources to a number of armed militias, loosely constituted along ethnic lines, and other parastatal forces. Although before 1996 the CAR had few small arms in circulation, non-state actors have since begun to receive arms from abroad, and armies and armed groups from all of the neighboring countries have used CAR territory in their operations.

Beginning in 1996, a series of army mutinies and coup attempts erupted over the issue of salary arrears for all but those in the very highest level of government. During this time, Patassé developed a patronage relationship with the Democratic Republic of Congo rebel Jean-Pierre Bemba, leader of the Movement for the Liberation of Congo

(Mouvement pour la libération du Congo, MLC) (see entry on Congo, Democratic Republic). In October 2001, Patassé questioned the loyalty of his longtime supporter and FACA Chief of Staff, General François Bozizé (who had served jail time on Patassé's behalf after a failed coup attempt in 1983). Thus spurned, Bozizé retreated north, where he assembled forces to take the capital. His first attempt, on October 25, 2002, failed. Several hundred MLC soldiers, stationed in the CAR to support the beleaguered Patassé, descended on Bangui and environs in the aftermath. The nongovernmental International Federation for Human Rights (Fédération Internationale des Droits de l'Homme, FIDH) has provided the most extensive documentation of MLC abuses: 200 people were killed, and there were systematic rape campaigns, with 600 cases documented (Fédération Internationale des Droits de l'Homme 2003). Central Africans incorrectly refer to the MLC as the Banyamulenge, or Congolese Tutsi (the assertion is incorrect because the MLC fighters came from western Congo, whereas the Banyamulenge are from the east). The misnomer is rarely uttered without an accompanying shake of the head at the cruelty of these forces.

Upon winning the support of Chadian President Idriss Déby (and other regional governments) and using Chad's territory to regroup and rearm, Bozizé took Bangui in 2003. His forces were approximately four-fifths Chadian (International Crisis Group 2007). Overnight, the rebels became liberators, and the insurgent became president. When presenting their research on the accompanying abuses to the newly formed International Criminal Court (ICC; see separate entry) in 2003, the FIDH leveled charges against Bemba, Patassé, and Abdulaye Miskine (a Chadian/Central African militia leader employed by the president). Bozizé's men also abused the population, but there has been no thorough documentation of their crimes.

Bozizé went on to win democratic elections in 2005 (from which Patassé, then exiled in Togo, was excluded), but his victory did not silence the outcry over the undemocratic origins of his power, as subsequent rebellions launched by his political opponents indicate. An Inclusive National Political Dialogue (funded by the UN Peace-building Commission), held in 2008 between Bozize's government and four internal rebel groups (see later discussion), failed to settle all grievances. Just weeks after the participants in the Dialogue issued their final report in December 2008, another rebel group, the Convention of Patriots for Justice and Peace (CPJP), emerged, just in time to protest its exclusion from the process. The main bone of contention during the dialogue was the near-total amnesty Bozizé had engineered for his forces, which the rebels hoped to secure for themselves as well. Failing that, the issue of the amnesty remained a key lever to use to stall the negotiations and thereby also the presidential elections, which were initially scheduled for April 2010 but repeatedly postponed since then.

Since 2005, several rebel groups have emerged in the country's hinterlands. All claim government persecution and neglect as reasons for taking up arms. The Army for the Restoration of Democracy (Armée pour la Restauration de la Démocratie, APRD) is active in the northwestern prefectures of Ouham (Patassé's hometown) and Ouham-Pende. Its leaders include former Patassé associates like former Defense Minister Jean-Jacques Demafouth, angry at being excluded from power. In 2006, the Union of Democratic Forces for Unity (Union des Forces Démocratiques pour le Rassemblement, UFDR) emerged in the remote and sparsely populated northeastern Vakaga prefecture. Its leadership represents a mixture of "ex-liberators" (people who helped Bozizé take power but broke with him over insufficient compensation for their services) and northeastern residents who complain of discrimination and neglect by the central government.

In response, the government brutally repressed civilians living in the areas home to rebel groups by burning villages, thereby displacing tens if not hundreds of thousands of people. According to Human Rights Watch (2007), government soldiers, particularly Bozizé's presidential guard (Garde Présidentielle, GP) led by Lt. Eugene Ngaikosset, burned 10,000 houses in the northwest and northeast of the country, causing 212,000 people to flee into the bush, where they lived for months. Rebels also abused the Central Africans in their midst through extortion, beatings, kidnappings for ransom, and summary executions.

In mid-2007, the government signed peace agreements with the UFDR and the APRD. Although abuses remained, the broad-scale repression seen in 2006–2007 stopped. Since then, other armed groups have appeared/been established on CAR territory. Some claim rebel status, although they contain fighters from throughout the subregion (Chad in particular). In February 2008, the notorious Lord's Resistance Army (LRA), which originated in Uganda but now consists mainly of Congolese and Sudanese fighters, launched attacks in the CAR in which they abducted, beat, and killed people and looted and pillaged property. The Ugandan army deployed to the CAR to combat the LRA brought some security to main towns, but opportunistic attackers continue to abduct people when they go to tend their fields. Patassé returned to the CAR in October 2009 and stood for election in the 2011 presidential race. Perhaps, with his repatriation, the cycle of rebellion will slow. But the tactic of taking up arms to procure a seat at the government table remains well entrenched in CAR politics, a tendency internationally led dialogues and related peace-building projects may inadvertently sustain by allowing those who make use of the tactic into the political arena.

CAR citizens remain by and large without protection. Their country is larger than Texas (the size of Spain and Portugal combined), with a population of less than 4 million, no infrastructure, and barely any state presence outside the capital. The territory has long been used as a reservoir of resources by armed actors from the region. Well-armed poachers target the country's fast-dwindling elephant herds for their ivory and other animals for both trophies and meat. Other natural resources (diamonds, bamboo, honey) attract raiders. And increasing numbers of (often armed) cattle herders seek out the country's lush grasses as desertification claims old pastures to the north.

Transitional Justice

CAR's transitional justice efforts included a Truth and Reconciliation Commission, court trials, and reforms of the repressive institutions involved in human rights abuses. Impunity in the CAR has also been taken up by the International Criminal Court.

Truth and Reconciliation Commission

In late 2002, as a beleaguered head of state, Patassé, under pressure from France, attempted to open a political dialogue with some political opponents (he excluded his main challenger, Bozizé), but did not remain in power long enough to see it finished. He watched from exile in Togo while, six months after Bozizé's successful March 2003 coup, the CAR named a Truth and Reconciliation Commission (TRC) as part of a broader National Reconciliation Commission, instigated by Bozizé, who was under pressure from France to prove himself. Far from an exhaustive accounting or societal reckoning, the National Reconciliation Commission served particular instrumental functions: it enabled sidelined politicians to return, ask forgiveness, and seek new posts in the government, and helped Bozizé woo donors suspicious of his motives in the aftermath of the coup.

Andre Denamsse, the TRC's chairman, explained its objective as elaborating the causes of insecurity and crisis in the country since independence. With such broad objectives, no resources to compel testimony, and no real power, the TRC could achieve little. The ousted President Patassé was excluded from the hearings. In its final report, issued at the closing of the National Reconciliation Commission on October 6, 2003, the TRC called for greater inclusiveness in Bozizé's transitional government and an end to the impunity enjoyed by state officials who had engaged in wrongdoing and human rights violations, and denounced the myriad predations of former rulers. Beyond such general calls, the work of the Commission resulted in no concrete action. As a result, today few CAR citizens even remember that the Commission was ever convened.

The International Criminal Court Case

The ICC has taken up the issue of impunity in the CAR. On December 21, 2004, Bozizé asked the ICC to open an inquiry into crimes committed on CAR territory since July 1, 2002, the date when the Rome Statute went into effect. The ICC prosecutor Luis Moreno-Ocampo, who opened the investigation on May 22, 2007, emphasized that, although the investigation focused on the events of 2002–2003 that brought Patassé's ouster, it would also monitor ongoing human rights abuses. In October 2007, the ICC opened an office in Bangui and seven months later it had Jean-Pierre Bemba arrested. (After learning that Bemba and his family were planning a U.S. vacation, the Court acted quickly for fear of losing him to exile in a country that is not party to the Rome Treaty.) Bemba was charged with two counts of crimes against humanity (murder and rape) and three counts of war crimes (murder, rape, and pillaging), allegedly committed on the CAR territory between October 26, 2002 and March 15, 2003. Bemba's trial was scheduled to begin in August 2012. He is imprisoned in The Hague.

In the CAR, people were glad that Bemba had been arrested, but, beside a few radio and newspaper announcements, the discussion was relatively muted. The leading domestic victims' advocacy group, the Organization for Compassion and Development for Families in Distress, (L'Organisation pour la Compassion et le Développement des Familles en Détresse, OCODEFAD), which provided substantial research support to the ICC, expressed satisfaction with the arrest but emphasized that new victims of armed conflict are made daily in CAR, and the victims primarily need material reparations and aid because they still suffer mentally and physically from the attacks they endured.

The ICC's greatest impact was on CAR leaders' political strategies. Moreno-Ocampo's public statement that he remained open to investigating ongoing abuses changed Bozizé's attitude toward the Court. On August 1, 2008, Bozizé wrote to UN Secretary General Ban Ki-Moon to explain his fear that the ICC's work in CAR could stall reconciliation in light of the ongoing rebellions, and to ask the ICC to stop its investigations/hearings. To critics, the letter was yet another attempt by the president to orchestrate impunity for himself and his supporters (International Crisis Group 2008). Bozizé later distanced himself from the letter, but analysts and CAR political leaders have since suggested that Bozizé hoped to use the ICC as a political tool.

National Court Proceedings

Total impunity reigns. Complaints can only be made in Bangui, and for a case to be taken up, the bringer of the suit must usually pay initial fees. These hurdles make the courts effectively inaccessible.

The Amnesty Law took effect when Bozizé signed it on October 13, 2008. If it had been designed equitably, the law might have been justifiable as a way of encouraging the rebels to engage constructively with the government, but it immediately became a political tool for the regime. Bozizé wrote the law to cover all abuses (except those falling under the jurisdiction of the ICC) by the state forces and "liberators" who helped him take power since Patassé's ouster in 2003. The law also names certain prominent (notorious) individuals as beneficiaries of total impunity (for embezzlement and human rights abuses), among them Patassé, Demafouth, and Abdulaye Miskine, a longtime militia leader in the region. Meanwhile, amnesty was granted only to those rebel field leaders and rank and file who abided by a narrow time frame of disarmament and dispersion, a stipulation they regarded as unrealistic. Failure to do so would cost them both the amnesty and permission to participate in politics for ten years. In effect, then, the law has done nothing but heighten the suspicion within which the ruling party and its opponents hold each other.

Reforms of the Police, Secret Police, and the Army

Security sector reform, usually in the form of French military assistance and training, has been nearly constant in the CAR, but with few results. If anything, the need for such reforms is today greater than ever. Recent initiative seemed more promising, but has been slow to get off the ground. In 2008, the CAR government, with technical advice and funding from the international community (primarily France, the European Union, and the United Nations Development Program), developed a military framework law (Projet de Loi de Programmation Militaire 2009–2013) that included a five-year plan to fundamentally restructure and expand the armed forces and gendarmerie (from 5,349 soldiers to 7,135 and from 1,729 gendarmes to 3,284). The law passed in December 2009, but hoped-for donors such as the European Union have shown little interest in funding a program to benefit a military that has seen fifteen years of attempted coups, mutinies, and human rights abuses, and whose commitment to reform seems questionable, as evidenced by the government's sluggishness in passing the law (it languished in the National Assembly for more than a year). The challenges do not stop there: many former rebels yearn for integration into the armed forces as part of their disarmament, demobilization, and reintegration process and demand to retain the rank they achieved in the rebel forces. Few have any military training, and incorporating them would be another setback to efforts to professionalize the forces.

Conclusion

Transitional justice in CAR came on the heels of a repressive past that remains ongoing because, instead of experiencing complete regime change, the country has fallen into a cycle of rebellion fueled less by ideological principles and more by a sheer desire to gain a seat at the government table. Other than the ICC's arrest of Congolese former rebel leader and Vice President Jean-Pierre Bemba, impunity for abuses is nearly total. The "wild card" that is the ICC has become an important factor in CAR politics. Public office holders and candidates consider its activities as they maneuver for allies and power; for instance, they debate the most profitable alliances based on varying probability of ICC arrest. A range of internationally supported projects, such as security sector reform (which includes a revision of the judicial system), work, if fitfully, to inculcate a new culture of responsibility to protect civilians, but progress has been slow. Meanwhile, CAR continues to slip on the Human Development Index, sporadic attacks continue (including ongoing raids by the LRA), and daily subsistence becomes increasingly difficult for many.

Louisa Lombard

Cross-references: Congo, Democratic Republic; International Criminal Court; Reintegration of Former Combatants; Uganda.

Further Readings

Debos, Marielle. 2008. Fluid Loyalties in a Regional Crisis: Chadian 'Ex-Liberators' in the Central African Republic. *African Affairs*, 107(427): 225–241.
Fédération Internationale des Droits de l'Homme. 2003. *Central African Republic: When the Elephants Fight, the Grass Suffers*. Paris: FIDH.
Glasius, Marlies. 2009. 'We Ourselves, We Are Part of the Functioning': The ICC, Victims, and Civil Society in the Central African Republic. *African Affairs*, 108(430): 49–67.
Human Rights Watch. 2007. *State of Anarchy: Rebellion and Abuses against Civilians*, 19(14A). New York: Human Rights Watch.
International Crisis Group. 2007. *Central African Republic: Anatomy of a Phantom State*. Africa Report 136. Nairobi/Brussels: International Crisis Group.
———. 2008. *Central African Republic: Untangling the Political Dialogue*. Africa Briefing 55. Nairobi/Brussels: International Crisis Group.
Integrated Regional Information Network. 2003. Central African Republic: Reconciliation Commission Recommends Government Shakeup. IRINNews, Bangui, October 6. Available at: http://www.irinnews.org/report.aspx?reportid=46541 (accessed November 2, 2009).

Chile

In the first years after its return to elected democracy in 1990, Chile applied truth and some reparations measures to the massive human rights violations that had been committed under the military regime of General Augusto Pinochet (1973–1990). Nonetheless, in the context of a heavily controlled ("pacted") and institutionally limited transition, comprehensive justice measures were not attempted and, after the publication of the official truth commission report (Rettig Report) in 1991, a 1978 self-amnesty law was preserved. This cautious, gradualist approach to transition and transitional justice was lauded by many as a model, but others criticized an apparent preference for official downplaying of the issue of past violations. However, in 1998, the concealment of Chile's human rights legacy was definitively reversed by a series of high-profile developments at home and abroad. At home, former dictator Augusto Pinochet retired as commander-in-chief of the army and entered the Senate. Abroad, Spanish magistrate Baltazar Garzón requested

Pinochet's arrest and extradition for crimes against humanity. Pinochet, in London receiving medical treatment, was detained and held for 503 days.

Pinochet's enforced absence placed Chile's transitional justice legacy under the international spotlight and gave a fresh impulse to justice claims by survivors, victims' relatives, and lawyers. By the time Pinochet returned to Chile in 2000, having been declared medically unfit to stand trial in Spain, transitional justice in the country had undergone a revival. New truth, memorialization, and justice initiatives appeared, including a second official truth commission, the Valech Commission, this time to document torture and political imprisonment. By the time of Pinochet's death in 2006, justice in the form of prosecutions had entered a second, active phase in Chile. Pinochet himself was under formal charges for alleged human rights and financial crimes, and hundreds of other former regime agents were also being investigated. By mid 2011, there were 1,446 criminal investigations ongoing against 773 former regime agents. Although Chile's amnesty law remained intact, exceptions and judicial reinterpretations had produced more than 300 final sentences for human rights related crimes. Sixty-six former agents were serving prison sentences at the time of this writing.

The Repressive Past

Chile's September 11, 1973 military coup toppled left-wing president Salvador Allende, putting an end to the "socialist experiment" begun in 1970. Most believed that the military intermission would be brief, but the coup ushered in seventeen years of military rule. General Augusto Pinochet Ugarte quickly centralized power in his own hands, neutralizing or eliminating ideological opponents and possible challengers from within military ranks.

Human rights violations occurred throughout the lifetime of the regime, ranging from an initial complete suspension of civil and political liberties to a total of slightly more than 3,000 officially recognized cases of disappearance or extrajudicial execution, 38,000 of torture and political imprisonment, and more than 100,000 of forced exile. Most acute violations (killings or disappearances) took place in the months immediately following the coup. The regime decreed a state of "internal war," allowing military tribunals to hand out death sentences to civilian functionaries of the deposed Allende government. These actions were justified by propaganda drives including the official publication of "Plan Z" documents purporting to show that the Allende government had stockpiled weapons and was planning to plunge the country into internecine warfare. However, there was no credible armed resistance to the coup itself, and initial regime violence was in effect a one-sided drive to eliminate political enemies. Violence was also employed to compromise military personnel, particularly young conscripts, and to spread terror and compliance among the general population.

After 1974, a second phase saw the institutionalization of repression. Violations such as the suppression of political rights were formalized by declaration or decree. More serious abuses were handed over to a specially created semi-clandestine secret police force, the Dirección de Inteligencia Nacional (DINA). Set up outside existing military hierarchies, the DINA operated through civilian agents and informers as well as security force personnel. Reporting directly to Pinochet himself, the DINA's main task was the extermination of domestic left-wing militants. It established a nationwide network of clandestine detention and torture centers. Overseas operations were coordinated through Operación Cóndor, a region-wide conspiracy between national armed forces in the Southern Cone. Prominent exiles were targeted for assassination. Condor's most emblematic crimes included the car-bomb killings of constitutionalist former Army Commander-in-Chief Carlos Prats in Argentina in 1974, and of ex-Chancellor Orlando Letelier in Washington's Embassy Row in 1976.

The Letelier killing, in which a U.S. citizen Ronnie Moffit also died, was later to be regarded as the DINA's single biggest miscalculation. Reaction from the U.S. State Department reversed much of previous U.S. sympathy for the regime. Denunciations by vocal, well-organized Chilean exiles and their supporters in Western Europe and the United States also began to generate more vigorous international censure. The regime deemed it prudent to make some changes. Decree Law 1876 of August 1977 disbanded the DINA, replacing it with the Centro Nacional de Informaciones (CNI). Clandestine burial sites were dug up and bodies removed and reburied. Files and other physical evidence were destroyed, and an amnesty passed. Decree Law 2191 of April 1978 conceded amnesty for crimes committed between September 11, 1973 and March 10, 1978, except in the case of those already charged or convicted. Given that the latter clause excluded imprisoned regime opponents, the decree is generally regarded as a self-amnesty law. The law, still in force, also excluded certain types of minor offenses and – at U.S. insistence – the perpetrators of the 1976 Letelier assassination.

The most violent manifestations of repression lessened, climbing again slightly after 1982 because of a rise in street protests, armed opposition, and related crackdowns. However, although torture and other abuses continued throughout the period, only thirty disappearances – less than 3 percent of the official grand total – are attributed to the post-1978 phase. Judicial tolerance for atrocities finally seemed to lessen. Perpetrators lacked the explicit legal immunity provided by amnesty – which applied only to crimes committed before March 1978. Although no regime agent was successfully convicted, thorough investigations could sometimes lay the foundations for post-transitional progress. In one example, lower court judge Carlos Cerda was suspended for insisting on a mass indictment of security force personnel in a disappearance case. The case led to journalistic exposes of the intelligence network involved, and a post-transitional reopening of the case used the information amassed by Cerda to lay formal charges (in 2004) against some of those involved.

Mobilization in defense of human rights in Chile played a key role from the earliest days of the dictatorship. The particular shape of this mobilization meant that Chile, almost uniquely, generated a systematic and reliable "paper trail" of documentation and denunciation of repression even while this was ongoing. The Catholic Church became the major umbrella organization for human rights defense. After an initial ecumenical initiative was forcibly dissolved, Cardinal Raul Silva Henríquez founded the specially created Vicariate of Solidarity, Vicaría, in 1976. The Vicaría provided social, medical, and legal assistance to victims and relatives. Legal responses were privileged, in order to emphasize the apolitical nature of the work. Methods included the rote submission of habeas corpus writs (*recursos de amparo*) to still functioning, albeit de facto complicit, national courts. Almost every known case of disappearance or detention was accordingly meticulously documented and then denounced, at home and abroad. As Chile drew close to a negotiated return to electoral democracy at the end of the decade, the justice system thus contained a large universe of opened but unresolved case files. These cases had been sidelined or shelved during the dictatorship, often by referring them to military courts that routinely invoked amnesty. They nonetheless represented a pool of official data and information. The work of the Vicaría and associated organizations had also produced a small group of human rights lawyers with substantial knowledge of repressive patterns and long experience of legal case strategy. Both of these legacies would be significant in the later revival of justice efforts.

Transitional Justice

From 1983, economic crisis triggered social and political protests that paved the way toward a return to elected democracy. Political parties were gradually legalized, and after a long history of fragmentation, most center and left parties – with the exception of the Communist Party – agreed to accept the framework laid down by the outgoing regime for a negotiated mode of transition. This included a nationwide October 1988 plebiscite, destined to confirm or reject a further eight years of Pinochet's rule. Fifty-five percent voted against continuity, but 43 percent voted in favor, showing continuing high levels of support for the political right and the military. However, the Concertación coalition of center-left parties prevailed in the ensuing 1989 presidential election. The incoming government was clearly identified with opposition to the regime and its human rights record. Its freedom to act in a range of matters was limited by the institutional and constitutional constraints it inherited. The 1980 Constitution, which had been drawn up by the regime, set out a model of "restricted democracy." Appointed senators, extremely high voting thresholds for constitutional reform, and a binominal electoral system ensured an effective right-wing veto in the legislature, while Pinochet was to continue as commander-in-chief of the army until 1998.

Early Truth Measures and the Preservation of Amnesty

On the specific matter of human rights, the outgoing regime let it be known that it would not accept attempts to reverse impunity. Pinochet famously threatened that "the day they touch any of my men, the rule of law is over" (*El Mercurio*, June 10, 1989). Early revelations such as the discovery of a mass grave in the northern desert town of Pisagua accordingly did not lead to prosecutions, although they did make headlines. Efforts to investigate financial fraud involving Pinochet's son meanwhile produced a virtual military rebellion, the *"ejercicio de enlace"* (combat readiness exercise). This, together with another, similar episode gave the impression that civilian control over the military was limited or precarious. Incoming president Patricio Aylwin dropped a campaign promise to repeal the 1978 Amnesty Law, declaring instead that justice would be pursued "insofar as is possible" (*en la medida de lo posible*). Truth and reparation measures were, however, carried out. An official truth commission was set up to investigate acts of disappearance and fatal political violence between 1973 and 1990 (see entry on National Truth and Reconciliation Commission of Chile, the Rettig Commission). The commission report was made public in March 1991. In the same month, a decree law created a foundation to erect a public memorial in the capital's General Cemetery to the 2,279 victims who had been officially acknowledged. Financial reparations were instituted, in the form of pensions and health benefits for relatives, plus assistance for returning exiles. A successor foundation to the Rettig Commission was set up (the National Corporation for Reparation and Reconciliation, Corporación Nacional de Reparación y Reconciliación,

CNRR). The CNRR was entrusted with the task of classifying more victims and attempting to locate more than 1,000 people still classified as disappeared (those of the initial 2,279 victim total who had neither been officially executed by the regime nor subsequently located).

Plans to publish the Rettig Commission's findings more widely throughout the country were short-lived. On April 1, 1991, prominent right-wing politician and former regime ideologue Jaime Guzmán – the author of the 1980 Constitution – was assassinated by members of the Frente Patriótico Manuel Rodriguez, a Communist Party offshoot that had led armed opposition to the dictatorship during the 1980s. The specter of a resurgence of political violence derailed further truth and justice measures. Official sponsorship of symbolic reparations also became notably more muted: when the General Cemetery memorial was finally unveiled in 1994, neither the president nor any other senior official attended. Chile's initial period of officially sponsored transitional justice thus drew to an end, with more emphasis on truth and reparations than on justice. Case files that had been sent to the courts as a result of the truth commission's activities continued to meet with stonewalling from judges unwilling to soften the prevailing interpretation of amnesty.

One exceptional justice breakthrough occurred in this period, with the 1993 conviction of former secret police chief Manuel Contreras. Both he and his DINA second-in-command, Pedro Espinoza, were charged and eventually sentenced – to seven and six years, respectively – for their part in the trail of espionage and forgery that had surrounded the 1976 Letelier car bombing. The trial was televised, causing substantial public impact at a time when atrocities were still not widely acknowledged. The outcome led to tensions with the armed forces. When sentences were confirmed on appeal in 1995, military authorities refused to hand Contreras over until a specially built military prison was provided, to be staffed by military guards. It was widely rumored that the armed forces had also obtained guarantees that no further prosecutions would be initiated.

After this first period, the human rights issue declined in political salience, with critics of official policy (human rights organizations, relatives, survivors, and lawyers) soon finding themselves in a minority. The international visibility and profile of these actors also declined, as did their major national support base: the Catholic Church closed the Vicaría in 1992, thereafter adopting a softer, pro-reconciliation discourse. Authorities and public opinion seemed preoccupied with other matters and uneasy with continuing discussion of the human rights legacy of the Pinochet years. This preference for closure was clearly shared by the military and the political right, who denounced political bias in the Rettig report and vigorously opposed sporadic efforts to revive prosecutions during the 1990s.

Those pro-memory or pro-justice actors who continued to operate concentrated their limited resources on keeping existing court cases alive and/or developing private memorialization initiatives. These included the 1996 reclaiming of former torture center Villa Grimaldi, the first such site in the Americas to be opened to the public. The main relatives' organization, the Association of Relatives of the Disappeared (Agrupación de Familiares de los Detenidos Desaparecidos, AFDD) maintained an uneasy relationship with the governing coalition that ran the country in four consecutive terms since 1990 (Presidents Aylwin, 1990–1994; Frei, 1994–2000; Lagos, 2000–2006; and Bachelet, 2006–2010). Although their core justice demands largely remained unmet, the AFDD retained the support of enough Concertación legislators to be able to exercise an effective moral veto over periodic right-wing efforts to legislate further impunity measures. The switch to a right-wing presidency in 2010 (President Sebastian Piñera) predictably increased the distance between relatives' groups and public authorities over justice and related matters.

Post-1998 Change: More Truth, More Justice

The year 1998 was pivotal in Chile's transitional justice trajectory. The existing uneasy accommodation was subjected to internal and external shock waves. In January, Pinochet's pending retirement and entry into the Senate triggered the first full criminal complaints ever lodged against him in person. In September, a slight softening in judicial receptivity produced the breakthrough Poblete-Córdoba verdict, in which higher courts upheld lawyers' long-standing contention that disappearance was an ongoing crime not fully covered by amnesty. On October 16, Pinochet was arrested in the United Kingdom for crimes being investigated in Spain under universal jurisdiction principles. This became the test case for enforceability of international human rights law in the globalized age. The Chilean government took a clear stance against international enforcement, claiming that the principle of sovereignty required Pinochet's immediate return. But they offered veiled assurances that the open domestic cases against him would not be obstructed. Thus, even when Pinochet was finally released by the British Home Secretary in March 2000, his legal troubles were far from over. The day he flew home to a triumphant military reception, human rights lawyers requested that domestic judge Juan Guzmán impeach and bring charges against Pinochet. The truncated justice dimension of Chile's transitional justice settlement had been definitively broken open.

Subsequent legal wrangling over Pinochet's senatorial immunity from prosecution and medical fitness to stand trial continued for many months. Finally, an interview broadcast by a Miami TV channel seemed to contradict the defense's argument that Pinochet was not lucid enough to stand trial. Shortly afterward, the Supreme Court ruled that he could be formally charged in at least one of the human rights cases open against him. The damage done to Pinochet's prestige by convictions of his closest military collaborators and subalterns led new military authorities to gradually distance themselves from the political right. This tendency was confirmed and accentuated by the 2004 discovery of secret bank accounts held in Pinochet's name in the U.S. Riggs Bank. He and his family were being actively investigated for financial crimes and tax evasion at the time of his death, aged ninety-one, on December 10, 2006. The marked sea change in Chile's political scenario was visible in the fact that he was not granted a state funeral or any official honors.

On the judicial front, the accumulation of new and reopened cases against hundreds of former regime officers has not yet produced any change in the text or status of the 1978 Amnesty Law. However, in 2006, an Inter-American Court ruling (the *Almonacid* case) called clearly for Chile to abolish the statute. The government promised legislation to render the norm "compatible" with its responsibilities under international law, but by mid-2011, this legislation had not materialized. In essence, the continued stalemate among political actors over amnesty has perpetuated a preference for delegating the problem into the hands of the judicial branch. Other controversies generated by judicialization include the strain that ongoing court cases place on both witnesses and defendants. Since 2008, there has also been a visible trend toward extremely lenient sentencing by the Supreme Court, still divided on the question of the reinterpretation of amnesty to exclude certain categories of crime.

Significant Moments and Controversies in Chilean Transitional Justice

The status of the domestic amnesty law is a continuing question mark. Post-1998 trials exploited exceptions and loopholes but had not, as of mid-2011, led to its derogation or annulment. Political actors, unable or unwilling to agree on a legislative solution, seemed happy to leave the problem to the courts. Since 1990, lower and upper courts have vacillated between a broad application, closing options for prosecution, and a narrower interpretation recognizing restrictions set out in international law.

Clear and consensual repudiation of past human rights violations has been a slow and contested process. Although in 2004 the commander-in-chief of the army finally publicly recognized abuses and acknowledged limited institutional responsibility, some key political and social sectors still believed that violations had been justified by the prevailing political climate at the time of the coup.

Recent justice breakthroughs have produced their own set of questions. Allowing officers to serve out convictions in military-run facilities has been criticized as unduly lenient. In general, the state's response to renewed private pressure for justice after 1998 was notably lukewarm. Although some legal assistance was provided to relatives bringing cases, political authorities seemed to favor additional truth and reparations measures. In 2000–2001, a civilian-military dialogue round table was convened to aid the search for still disappeared victims. However, the sparse information it uncovered later proved to be unreliable. The 2003–2004 Valech Commission (see separate entry) was a key step forward in acknowledgment and reparation for survivors, but the placing of testimonies under a fifty-year embargo, which ruled out their use in ongoing court cases, was controversial.

Measures during the Bachelet presidency in the area of symbolic politics and acknowledgment also caused debate. Bachelet, herself a former political prisoner and exile, adopted a more welcoming stance to civil society memorialization initiatives. This practice led to right-wing pressure – finally unsuccessful – for her to attend the 2009 inauguration of a monument to assassinated right-wing senator Jaime Guzmán. Bachelet finally announced a national Museum of Memory and Human Rights, standing in effect as her final personal legacy when her term of office ended in early 2010. A bill to create a National Human Rights Institute was significantly delayed when modifications introduced by the political right stripped the proposed institution of any real powers of scrutiny, but the Institute was finally created and came into full operation in 2011, under the subsequent right-wing presidency of Sebastian Piñera.

Finally, the unexpected "reappearance" in November 2008 of a man included in the official register of the disappeared provoked a brief but significant controversy over victim numbers and the reliability of official figures. A further nine cases of misclassification were later discovered, fueling existing pressure for a new and supposedly definitive instance that reconsidered victim lists in 2010 and 2011. On August 26, 2011, the new instance reported final totals of 3,216 recognized cases of disappearance and political execution and 38,254 cases of torture and/or political imprisonment.

Conclusion

Chile's experience of transitional justice seems to fall into two distinct phases. In the first, initial truth and reparations measures were followed by official and public quiescence. In the second, from 1998, domestic changes including judicial reform combined with outside events to trigger a reexamination of the justice dimension of Chile's transitional settlement. This reexamination eventually spread to encompass new official truth and reparations measures and some support for civil society memory initiatives. This second phase, echoing the developments in neighboring Southern Cone countries, suggests that justice dimensions unaddressed close to transition may reemerge where continuing minority pressure is matched by progress in broader institutional democratization. Shifts in judicial receptivity to domestic justice claims and/or international norms seem to be particularly relevant.

Cath Collins and Claudio Fuentes Saavedra

Cross-references: Amnesty; Court Trials for Redress; National Commission on Political Imprisonment and Torture, the Valech Commission; National Truth and Reconciliation Commission of Chile, the Rettig Commission.

Further Readings

Collins, Cath. 2010. *Post-Transitional Justice: Human Rights Trials in Chile and El Salvador*. University Park: Penn State University Press.

Comisión Asesora para la Calificación de Detenidos Desaparecidos, Ejecutados Políticos y Víctimas de Prisión Política y Tortura [Advisory Commission for the Classification of Victims of Forced Disappearance, Political Execution, Political Imprisonment and Torture]. 2011. *Informe de la Comisión Asesora para la Calificación de Detenidos Desaparecidos, Ejecutados Políticos y Víctimas de Prisión Política y Tortura* [Report of the Advisory Commission for the Classification of Victims of Forced Disappearance, Political Execution, Political Imprisonment and Torture]. Santiago. Available at: http://www.comisionvalech.gov.cl/InformeValech.html (accessed September 6, 2011).

Ensalaco, Mark. 2000. *Chile under Pinochet: Recovering the Truth*. Philadelphia: University of Pennsylvania Press.

Fuentes, Claudio and Felipe Agüero. 2009. *Influencias y Resistencias. Militares y poder en América Latina* [Influences and Resistance. The Military and Power in Latin America]. Santiago de Chile: FLACSO-Chile and Catalonia Ediciones.

Lira, Elizabeth and Brian Loveman. 2002. *El Espejismo de la Reconciliación Política: Chile 1990–2002* [The Mirage of Political Reconciliation: Chile 1990–2002]. Santiago de Chile: LOM Ediciones.

National Commission on Political Imprisonment and Torture. 2004. *Informe de la Comisión Nacional sobre prisión política y tortura* [Report of the National Commission on Political Imprisonment and Torture]. Santiago de Chile. Available at: http://www.comisionvalech.gov.cl/InformeValech.html (accessed September 6, 2011).

National Truth and Reconciliation Commission. 1991. *Informe de la Comisión Nacional de Verdad y Reconciliación* [Report of the Chilean National Commission on Truth and Reconciliation]. English translation published by the Center for Civil and Human Rights, Notre Dame: Notre Dame Law School. Available at: http://www.usip.org/publications/truth-commission-chile-90 (accessed September 6, 2011).

Roht-Arriaza, Naomi. 2005. *The Pinochet Effect: Transnational Justice in the Age of Human Rights*. University Park: Penn State University Press.

The Judge and the General. DVD. Directed by Elizabeth Farnsworth and Patricio Lanfranco. US/Chile: Westwind Productions. 2008.

Colombia

Colombia's experience with transitional justice is one of the most belated in Latin America, making the country an outlier in the region. Some have even questioned whether a transition has actually occurred, given that the conflict is ongoing. Yet the paramilitary demobilization started in 2003 was significantly extended by the Justice and Peace Law, which led to the dismantling of the military structure of one of the conflict's main protagonists, the right-wing paramilitary group Autodefensas Unidas de Colombia (AUC), an important decrease in violence levels, and the revelation of key truths framed by a transitional justice discourse centered on local justice.

The Repressive Past

Since the 1960s, Colombia has experienced an ongoing armed conflict between the military forces and left-wing guerrillas, exacerbated by drug-trafficking and right-wing paramilitary activities since the 1980s. While the atrocities committed by the guerrillas were as heinous as those of the paramilitary, this section focuses on the paramilitary because Colombia's transitional justice has targeted the AUC paramilitary more than the guerrillas, which demobilized individually. Colombia's transitional justice, unlike that of its neighbors, has occurred in the midst of conflict. Between 1980 and 2002, the country was one of the most violent in terms of the number of homicides per 100,000 inhabitants and scored a world record in kidnappings. The number of forced displacements remains second only to Sudan. The excesses committed in the internal armed conflict have constituted serious human rights violations against the civilian population. According to the Inter-American Commission of Human Rights (ICHR), these forced displacements and violent crimes have affected more than 2 million individuals. The exact number of victims of the political conflict is unavailable, because the violence associated with the conflict has been accompanied by violence associated with common and organized crime. According to the Attorney General's Office (Fiscalía), 230,516 victims and their families have benefited from the Justice and Peace Law, which regulates paramilitary demobilization. According to Rettberg (2011), who surveyed a representative number of victims of the armed conflict, there is a worrisome proximity between victims and perpetrators; one-fifth of the victims and their families knew their assailants. Her findings also indicate widespread poverty and precarious living conditions for most victims, and an overwhelming number of women and children among them.

Identifying the perpetrators from among left-wing guerrillas and paramilitaries raises a number of challenges. The difficulty is compounded by the fact that the AUC did not fight the state, which in fact benefited from their war against the guerrillas. The latter led to unsavory alliances between sectors of the public force and the paramilitaries. Despite these difficulties, it is generally agreed that the massacres and disappearances were mainly perpetrated by the paramilitaries, whereas kidnappings and land mines were mainly guerrilla tactics.

While paramilitaries have existed in Colombia since the late 1960s, initially as legal self-defense organizations, they rapidly degenerated through their alliances with drug traffickers, leading to the declaration of their illegality in 1989. Their most brutal period occurred between 1997 and 2002, when the AUC reached unprecedented success in terms of territorial control, military organization, and enrolment levels (reaching 13,150, according to *Verdad Abierta*). This period was one of the bloodiest in Colombian history. The paramilitaries' violence went hand in hand with their territorial and political expansion and control of drug trafficking. The overall impact is well illustrated with the generalized growth rate of homicides coinciding with their expansion in 1997–2002, and its immediate drop almost as soon as the paramilitaries demobilized. This was the case in the city of Medellin, one of their bastions from 2003 to 2007. In Colombia, homicide rates peaked in 2002 with 28,837 (that is, 80 homicides per 100,000 inhabitants), a number that contrasts with the 50 percent drop in the total national homicide rates since 2002. Moreover, the nongovernmental Colombian Commission of Jurists documented 14,677 people killed or disappeared outside combat, allegedly by paramilitaries, between July 1996 and June 2007; yet these figures barely reflect a tenth of the currently registered number of victims.

Forced displacements are also numerous. According to the state agency in charge of collecting data on the internally displaced, Acción Social, there are today 3,115,266 displaced persons in Colombia (7.8 percent of the total population). A 2004 survey showed that 46 percent of the internally displaced were running from the guerrillas, 22 percent from the paramilitary, and 1 percent from state forces (Ibáñez 2008). Unfortunately, the annual number of forced displacements has continued to rise even after demobilization.

The recruitment of minors is another problematic issue. Demobilized AUC ex-combatants have confessed to at least 1,020 such recruitments, while data from the Ministry of Defense shows that 2,700 of the demobilized were minors. Ex-paramilitaries have also assumed responsibility for 1,776 disappearances and 1,473 extortions. According to the World Bank and the Colombian Human Rights and Displacement Office (CODHES), between 3.5 million and 4.5 million of hectares of land were expropriated by the paramilitaries, who still control them. Although demobilized paramilitaries have not yet acknowledged the expropriation, scholars have demonstrated that starting in 1997, the paramilitaries acquired vast stretches of land by forcefully displacing small landowners. Other crimes perpetrated by the paramilitaries have not even been documented. For instance, a study by the Ombudsman's Office revealed that 20 percent of displaced women have been victims of sexual crimes. This overwhelming evidence, while still incomplete, is a clear indication of the paramilitaries' repressive past.

Transitional Justice

In Colombia, transitional justice does not stem from a transition to democracy like in most of South America, but from the 2003–2006 demobilization of the AUC paramilitary who claimed to represent more than 90 percent of the active paramilitaries. The state's responsibility was pointedly excluded from the transitional legal framework, despite evidence of involvement, either by inaction to protect civilians from paramilitary attacks, as in the El Salado Massacre (in which forty people were killed in 2000), or by collusion of some army members, as in the recent Falsos Positivos scandal (which involved extrajudicial killings of civilians).

The Legal Framework for Transition

Demobilization and the adoption of transitional justice methods have been gradual and followed three distinct periods. In 2002–2003, after the initial secret negotiations between the Alvaro Uribe government and the AUC leaders, transitional justice was not contemplated. These negotiations culminated in the Ralito Agreement of July 2003. While much of what was discussed then remains obscure, the document that was made public showed an agreement to demobilize and disarm the paramilitaries and to offer monetary reparations to victims. The agreement informed the Bill on Criminal Alternatives, which included generous terms of reincorporation for the paramilitary, but no provisions to guarantee victims' rights to truth, justice, and reparations (such as restitution, compensation, indemnification, rehabilitation, symbolic reparations, and guarantees against repetition). After being criticized by the victims' representatives, the European Union, and national and international nongovernmental organizations, the bill was amended.

The second period started with the passage of the Justice and Peace Law (Law 975 of 25 July 2005) designed to demobilize the paramilitaries and other illegally armed actors, and grant limited rights to the victims. While incorporating transitional justice elements like reparations in an effort to appease its critics, the law offered disproportionate benefits to the paramilitaries and incomplete rights to the victims. As such, nongovernmental organizations like the Comisión Colombiana de Juristas, supported by Human Rights Watch and the Inter-American Commission for Human Rights (IACHR), challenged the law's constitutionality in the Constitutional Court, which upheld the victims' full rights to justice, truth, reparations, and included victims' active participation in the judicial process. The right to justice entailed the state's duty to undertake an efficient investigation leading to the identification, capture, and punishment of those responsible for conflict-related crimes, to guarantee the victims' access to reparation for the harm inflicted, and to adopt measures preventing the recurrence of such violations.

The third period began in May 2006 when Law 975/2005 was turned into a transitional justice instrument by ten Constitutional Court decisions (C-370, C-127, C-319, C-400, C-426, C-455, C-476, C-575, C-719, and C-531, all adopted in 2006), which gave "claws to guarantee the victims' rights" (Uprimny 2006). Even before these decisions, the law had ambitious goals: the search for peace; the prosecution of perpetrators of crimes against humanity; reparations for the victims granted through the National Commission for Reparations and Reconciliation (CNRR); and the reconstruction of historical memory by the Grupo Memoria Histórica, part of the CNRR. But the Court, relying on its past decisions and domestic and international legitimacy, enlarged provisions benefiting the victims and restricted illegal actors' privileges.

The Justice and Peace Law provided for more lenient (up to eight years of jail time) sanctions for those who fully confessed to their war crimes and crimes against humanity after having been demobilized and disarmed. Failure to fully confess and repetition of the offense warranted the imposition of the harsher sanctions provided by the Penal Code. International experts argue that the law is one of the few transitional justice laws in the world that complies with the general requirements of the German Constitutional Court's "proportionality test" and the "Rule of Balancing" between the search for peace and justice. The ensuing transitional justice and the paramilitaries' demobilization constitute a fundamental break with the Colombian tradition of appeasing illegal armed actors through blanket amnesties and outright impunity. Local nongovernmental organizations like Colectivo de Abogados-José Alvear Restrepo still contend that it is a law of impunity because of the leniency of alternative convictions of up to eight year jail time granted to perpetrators of crimes against humanity. While the law is generally accepted, critics point to difficulties with enforcement attributable to the still precarious investigative powers of the judiciary given the law's emphasis on the (punitive) justice component.

Disarmament, Demobilizations, and Reinsertion

The collective demobilization of most AUC leaders and 31,671 AUC paramilitary members in 2003–2006 represented a first step in decreasing terror and violence throughout the country. But the initial demobilization of paramilitaries directed by the Colombian government was improvised. The IACHR members who oversaw the process argued that, by wasting opportunities, the executive hindered the collection of evidence and information from paramilitary members about the crimes of un-demobilized units. Hence, most of the 29,000 demobilized paramilitaries walked free by concealing their involvement in criminal activities, which could not be documented from other sources. Amendments to law 906/2004 adopted in 2009 gave judges discretionary power to cancel prosecution for the demobilized.

There are two notable reasons why so many former paramilitary soldiers were not prosecuted. First, those who walked free were those who did not confess to any human rights violations and for whom there was no evidence of criminal involvement. While they might have been responsible for human rights abuses, they were not the decisions makers or direct perpetrators of atrocities. Trade-offs between justice and peace were accepted, the more so for minor crimes or low-ranking perpetrators. Second, Colombia found it impossible to prosecute all perpetrators given their overwhelming number and its limited prosecutorial resources. As such, it adopted sentence reductions (inspired by German denazification) instead of clemency laws when the retributive goals of justice conflicted with the political objectives of the demobilization of non-defeated powerful illegal armed actors such as the paramilitaries.

According to the government agency in charge of the reinsertion of ex-combatants, Alta Consejería para la Reinserción (ACR), disarmament included 18,051 weapons, 3 million rounds of ammunition, and 13,117 grenades. Although less than one weapon per demobilized was returned, disarmament has not been a priority, whereas the reinsertion of demobilized ex-combatants into society was hotly debated. To the 31,671 demobilized paramilitaries, the Ministry of Defense added another 19,553 former illegal actors (65 percent from the Fuerzas Armadas Revolucionarias de Colombia [FARC] guerrillas), who demobilized individually from 2005 to July 2009. Thus, the total fully demobilized ex-combatants reached 51,224.

The process of demobilization and societal reinsertion is lengthy and its success hard to gauge. According to the ACR, 2,470 (7 percent) of the total 31,671 paramilitary were forced out of the reinsertion program for their continued involvement in criminal activities; 3,500 (9.5 percent) left the program voluntarily; and only 3,000 (9 percent) successfully completed the five-year program in July 2010. To date, 31,999 individuals (of which 22,269 are paramilitaries) are active participants in the ACR reinsertion program. National Police data indicates that 10 percent of the total 51,224 demobilized ex-combatants have been captured for continuing criminal activities. Reinsertion needs time to show fruitful outcomes.

The death of 2,036 (4 percent) demobilized ex-combatants, mostly former paramilitaries, from 2001 to 2009 further undermined reinsertion, because most of these deaths resulted from assassinations. These assassinations constitute a threat for the demobilized, a challenge to any future peace process with the warring guerrillas (which in 1982 were subjected to extermination after a failed peace process), and a reminder of the fragility of the AUC demobilization in the midst of a conflict.

The process of reintegration is well institutionalized and follows accepted international norms and oversight. But victims and the general public have criticized the vast state resources allocated to the reinsertion of perpetrators of atrocious crimes, when almost half of Colombia's population and most victims are poor and receive less attention and resources than the demobilized. While the director of the reinsertion process has publicly acknowledged these problems, its perceived illegitimacy is detrimental to the peace process.

Prosecutions and Trials

According to the government, the Attorney General/Fiscalía should investigate 3,600 of the 31,670 demobilized paramilitaries either facing serious allegations or incriminated for their participation in crimes against humanity by their demobilized colleagues. In 2009, the Fiscalía presented a report analyzing the implementation of the Justice and Peace Law during its first four years. Confirming the findings of the United Nations Refugee Agency (UNHRHC), the report showed that 65 percent (that is, 1,215) of the 1,867 depositions taken from demobilized paramilitaries by June 2009 were completed. These depositions revealed 27,000 crimes affecting 40,000 victims. To date, only one indictment has been prepared. Fourteen demobilized AUC leaders were extradited to the United States for their alleged involvement in drug-related crimes despite opposition from human rights advocates who claim that deportations will lead to a loss of truth for the victims. Still, depositions have allowed for the discovery of 2,000 graves and 2,439 bodies, of which 571 have been identified and returned to their families.

Depositions have also uncovered evidence that enabled the initiation of 209 criminal investigations against politicians, mainly mayors, ex-mayors, and more than one-third of existing members of Congress (102) who financed or supported the paramilitary. The Parapolítica scandal, which revealed the direct involvement of high-ranking politicians and public officials in financing and supporting the paramilitary, represented the largest-ever judicial investigation of ruling elites in the country's history, because most of the accused belonged to parties that supported the Uribe government. As a result, almost a third of Congress members have lost political office until their legal situation is clarified and are currently in jail awaiting trial. Several of them have already been convicted. Depositions helped unveil another major scandal, the Falsos Positivos, which so far has led to the investigation of 140 army members and to the vetting of many high-ranking military officials by President Uribe.

While a significant number of victims has had no access to the Justice and Peace process because of fear or direct intimidation by armed groups or rearmed paramilitaries or lack of resources to attend the hearings, surveys show that 59.4 percent of victims were included into protection programs and another 17 percent of them into government assistance programs. According to the Fiscalía, 27,147 (10 percent) of registered victims have actively participated in the hearings since 2006. But the massive displacement of millions of innocent civilians is still not understood because demobilized ex-combatants have not yet disclosed the systematic practices that led to displacement. Justice results thus remain mitigated.

The Politics of Memory

While the legal framework was designed to institutionalize the search for judicial truth, it also provided for a National Commission for Reparation and Reconciliation (CNRR), responsible for victims' reparations. A CNRR group, the Grupo Memoria Histórica (GMH), documents the historical truth with the goal of reconstructing public memory and may sow the seeds for a future truth commission, an institution not excluded from the Justice and Peace framework. Since 2008, the GMH has produced many reports on some of the most atrocious massacres and human rights violations.

The first report documented the AUC paramilitary's use of extreme cruelty and terror tactics, such as dismembering live individuals in front of their families and friends, and showed its capacity to hide its crimes by turning rivers into graves, reducing bodies to pieces, and making people "disappear." By revealing the links between paramilitary activities and drug trafficking, the report concluded that Trujillo was an ongoing tragedy and questioned the extensiveness and accomplishment of paramilitary demobilization.

The second report documented the El Salado massacres, which involved 42 group massacres that lead to the assassination of 354 individuals. An entire town was stigmatized as guerrilla sympathizers, and 450 paramilitaries committed cruel murders that replicated Trujillo's viciousness. Beyond the massacres and murders, the report revealed the claims of El Salado's residents that the military ignored the strong paramilitary presence days before the massacre, and shared responsibility by confining residents in the town. The report attributed direct responsibility for the massacre to the Colombian state authorities. By doing so, the report was groundbreaking, as it was the first time a national agency condemned the state. In September 2009, the government delivered a public apology for those massacres.

The Colombian media have also played an important role in reconstructing the truth. In particular, the weekly magazine *Semana* and the nongovernmental organization Fundación Ideas para la Paz (FIP) have developed the Web site *Verdad Abierta*, offering accurate information on the details of the Justice and Peace process and giving a voice to victims.

Reparations

This process is just beginning. According to the CNRR Director Eduardo Pizarro, only 2,000 out of the 250,000 registered victims have received economic compensation. The CNRR's latest report (as of this writing) claimed that another 10,000 victims – mainly women who suffered sexual violence and land mine survivors or their families – were to receive compensation by late 2009. These recent reparations include a budget of US$80 million. Some US$150,000 was set aside for compensating 18,000 other conflict victims in 2010. The reparations process, which is expected to end in 2019, is financed from the national budget and the CNRR fund, which also includes private donations from Colombia and abroad and proceedings from the sale of assets confiscated from the illegal armed actors.

Reparations also involve land restitution. According to *Verdad Abierta*, 5,000 million hectares were forcefully taken in recent decades. Experts, public officials, and CNRR members have drafted several land restitution and protection programs, sponsored by the Canadian government and overseen by the International Center for Transitional Justice (ICTJ). Most proposals refer to the period from the 1970s to the early 1990s, when most land confiscation took place, and provide for 400,000 families, according to the state Registry for Land Abandoned as a Result of Violence (Registro Único de Predios y Territorios Abandonados por la Violencia, RUPTA). Proposals diverge when it comes to the size of returned land plots, the entity that should be in charge of land restitution, the provision for alternative dispute resolution mechanisms, and the system of resource generation for a more democratic access to land to prevent land reappropriation. While to date little land has been returned, the process could be supported by the fact that a plurality of social and governmental actors are involved and the Constitutional Court has already provided the standards that land restitution ought to respect. The contribution of the ICTJ and the Colombian think tank DeJusticia in the drafting of these proceedings should also help the land restitution process.

On June 16, 2011, the Congress passed the Law 1448 on the Attention, Assistance and Integral Reparation of Victims of the Internal Armed Conflict, whose effects are yet to be seen at the time of this writing.

Conclusion

Unlike in other countries, in Colombia, criminal justice has been key to demobilization. While in principle criminal justice is not suited for political ends because its outcomes are slow and uncertain compared to those of a truth commission, the incompleteness of the transition to peace and of the demobilization of paramilitary and other illegal armed actors may have justified the predominance of punitive justice over other forms of transitional justice. Although results are still ambiguous, both the dismantling of the AUC military structure and the important truths that have emerged so far within the transitional justice framework make the AUC paramilitary demobilization irreversible. The plans for land restitution also provide for some degree of moderate optimism on a central issue of Colombia's conflict. Yet it remains an uncertain transition in the midst of a prolonged armed conflict.

Elvira Maria Restrepo

Cross-references: Armed Conflict; Conflict (Ongoing) and Transitional Justice; Crimes against Humanity; Criminal Justice; Media and Transitional Justice; Prosecutions; Reintegration of Former Combatants; Reparations; Right to Justice; Right to Truth; Truth and Reconciliation Commission on the Killing of Hostages in the Justice Palace in 1985.

Further Readings

Fundación Ideas para la Paz and Revista Semana Web site. *Verdad Abierta* [Open Truth]. Available at: http://www.verdadabierta.com (accessed October 30, 2009).
http://www.reintegracion.gov.co/Es/prensa/noticias/Documents/febrero11/factINGagosto11.pdf.
http://www.fiscalia.gov.co:8080/justiciapaz/Index.htm.

Ibáñez, Ana Maria. 2008. *El Desplazamiento Forzoso en Colombia: un camino sin retorno hacia la pobreza* [Forced Displacement in Colombia: A One Way Street toward Poverty]. Bogotá: Ediciones Uniandes.

Justice and Peace Law (Law 975/2005). *Diario Oficial* no. 45.980, 25 July 2005.

Orozco, I. 2009. *Justicia Transicional en Tiempos del Deber de Memoria* [Transitional Justice in Times of a Duty of Memory]. Bogotá: Editorial Temis.

Rettberg, Angelika. 2011. Reparación en Colombia. *Un estudio de las necesidades y las expectativas de las víctimas del conflicto armado* [Reparations in Colombia. A Study of the Victims of the Armed Conflict Necessities and Expectations]. In *La desmovilización de los paramilitares en Colombia, Entre el escepticismo y la esperanza* [The Demobilization of the Colombian Paramilitaries. Skepticism and Hope]. Eds. Elvira M. Restrepo and B. Bagley. Bogotá: Ediciones Uniandes.

Reyes, Alejandro. 2009. *Guerreros y Campesinos. El despojo de la tierra en Colombia* [Warriors and Peasants. The Despoil of land in Colombia]. Bogotá: Grupo Editorial Norma.

Uprimny, R. ed. 2006. *¿Justicia transicional sin transición? Verdad, justicia y reparación para Colombia* [Transitional Justice without a Transition? Truth, Justice and Reparation in Colombia]. Bogotá: DeJusticia.

Congo, Democratic Republic of the

For decades, the Democratic Republic of the Congo (DRC) has been wracked by armed power struggles, international interference, and continued atrocities. Parts of the country are still affected by mass violence, preventing a transition from human rights abuses and conflicts toward peace, rule of law, and respect for human rights. Attempts at confronting the past and at using justice mechanisms to stem current violence have been limited. That said, the first case ever tried by the International Criminal Court (ICC; see separate entry) resulted from a 2004 referral for assistance in investigating and prosecuting atrocities committed in the DRC.

The Repressive Past

The years of political turmoil that followed Congolese independence from Belgium in 1960 paved the way for the 1965 coup and three decades of autocratic and corrupt rule under President Mobutu Sese Seko. That period saw the gradual decay of all state institutions and ultimately state collapse, accelerated in 1989 by the loss of support from key Western allies as the Cold War ended. The weakening of Mobutu's regime encouraged the emergence of opposition movements, forcing Mobutu to propose in 1991–1992 a plan to move toward a multiparty democratic system. The move failed and by the mid-1990s, a rebel movement led by Laurent Kabila, a longtime leftist opponent of Mobutu, emerged. Kabila's Alliance of Democratic Forces for the Liberation of Congo (AFDL) launched an insurgency to topple Mobutu. A "war of liberation" followed in 1996–1997 when a regional alliance, spearheaded by Rwanda and Uganda, sent thousands of soldiers to support the AFDL. Rwandan forces accompanying the AFDL fighters pursued remnants of the army and militia that had perpetrated the 1994 Rwandan genocide, killing thousands of civilians, mostly Hutu refugees and local Congolese, in the crossfire (see entry on Rwanda). Hutu extremist commanders who survived the chase later formed the Democratic Forces for the Liberation of Rwanda (FDLR). Confronted by a weak opposition, the AFDL quickly gained control of the DRC. In May 1997, Kabila became the DRC president, while Mobutu fled the country and died in 2007, in Morocco.

Kabila inherited a failed state and an ethnically divided country. He sought to diminish the influence of his foreign allies, removing Rwandan officers from the army. In response, Rwanda threw its support behind the rebel Congolese Rally for Democracy (RCD), led by ethnic Tutsis. Ugandan troops, in turn, instigated the creation of a separate rebel group, the Movement for the Liberation of Congo (MLC), led by the Congolese warlord Jean-Pierre Bemba. Rwandan and Ugandan forces present in the eastern part of the DRC became occupation forces, thus starting a war of occupation in 1998. This second war was fueled by disputes over land, natural resources, and political power.

The conflict devolved into a stalemate that lasted four years. By 1999, the country was divided into four administrative zones, each dependent on foreign backers for survival. The Rwandan-backed RCD-Goma controlled the two Kivus and parts of Katanga, Maniema, and Eastern Kasai provinces. The breakaway Ugandan-backed RCD-Kisangani controlled parts of North Kivu and Oriental provinces, including the Ituri district. The MLC was the dominant force in Equateur province. The Congolese government held onto the western half of the country with the support of Angolan, Namibian, and Zimbabwean troops. Tensions between Rwanda and Uganda over political control and control of the rich mineral resources led the former allies to openly fight on Congolese ground. Rwandan and Ugandan insurgent groups based in eastern Congo, the FDLR and the Ugandan Allied Democratic Forces (ADF), also repeatedly clashed with their respective national armies on Congolese soil. During this period, more than twenty militia groups emerged, exacerbating local disputes in rebel-held areas over land tenure and control of local resources. In Ituri, the war deepened long-standing conflict between Lendu and Hema ethnic groups. More generally, the conflict increasingly evolved along ethnic lines.

A ceasefire was brokered in Lusaka in 1999, leading the UN Security Council to establish a peacekeeping force, the UN Mission in the Democratic Republic of the Congo (MONUC). But fighting continued. Prospects for peace improved after Kabila's assassination in 2001 and the accession of his son, Joseph, to power. Peace talks initiated in Sun City, South Africa, in 2002 led to a Global and All-Inclusive Agreement to end the war. A transition government was established with one president, Joseph Kabila, and four vice-presidents representing the Kinshasa government, the main rebel armed groups, and the political opposition. A new constitution was drafted in 2005, and presidential and legislative elections were held in 2006, when Joseph Kabila was elected president.

Fighting did not end with the peace talks. As violence continued after the signing of the Sun City Agreement, a European Union peacekeeping force intervened to halt the fighting in Ituri in 2003. Peace agreements were brokered with factions that had not participated in the Sun City Agreement. In the Kivu, many RCD soldiers resisted *brassage*, a military integration process requiring soldiers from all regions and armed groups to report to a central training location from where they would be deployed to regions other than those in which they had previously fought. Resistance was fueled by the FDLR's continued presence and the government's failure to investigate the killings of hundreds of soldiers of Rwandan heritage, mainly Tutsis, perpetrated in its garrisons at the beginning of the war. General Laurent Nkunda, a notorious Rwandan-trained Congolese Tutsi, refused to deploy to Kinshasa. He formed the rebel National Congress for the Defense of the People (CNDP), attacking government forces in the town of Bukavu, South Kivu, in 2004. Kabila's election in 2006 resulted in a loss of political and economic power for the Rwandan-backed RCD-Goma. Rwanda subsequently backed the CNDP, claiming that the Tutsi population was not adequately protected from the FDLR in the DRC.

Seeking a way to end the conflict with Nkunda, in 2006, the government entered into a Rwanda-brokered compromise, which called for a limited military integration called *mixage*. *Mixage* allowed Nkunda's troops to be integrated with government forces in North Kivu and, unlike *brassage*, these mixed forces were deployed locally in eastern Congo to conduct military operations against the FDLR. As it failed to bring Nkunda under the government's control, *mixage* was ended in August 2007. In November 2007, the Nairobi Communiqué, signed by the Rwandan and Congolese governments, called for the disarmament of the FDLR and the repatriation of Rwanda refugees, but it had little actual impact on the ground. The January 2008 Goma Conference on Peace, Security, and Development in North and South Kivu led to a ceasefire agreement. Shortly afterward, Nkunda was put under house arrest while in Rwanda, and his second in command, Bosco Ntaganda, took over the CNDP leadership. Ntaganda called for peace and proceeded to integrate CNDP forces with the Congolese army. Concurrently, the Rwandan and Congolese armies began joint operations against the FDLR. Ultimately the operation failed, the FDLR regrouped, and violence again erupted in the Congo.

Throughout both wars, and continuing at this writing, all of the armed groups, including the Congolese army, have committed grave human rights violations, including forced displacement and killing of civilians, abductions, recruitment of child soldiers, rape and other forms of sexual violence, looting and destruction of property. Some 5.4 million deaths may have occurred in the DRC between August 1998 and April 2007. According to the United Nations, in 2006, 27,000 sexual assaults were reported in South Kivu alone. Between 2003 and 2006, Congolese and international aid workers removed 30,000 children from the regular military and other armed groups and returned them to civilian life. In 2010, the Office of the High Commissioner for Human Rights completed a report mapping the violence between 1993 and 2003, confirming the scope of destruction, atrocities, and massive violations of human rights and humanitarian laws. Survey data suggest that half the population has been interrogated or persecuted by armed groups (55 percent), forced to work or enslaved (53 percent), or beaten (46 percent). One in four adults has witnessed sexual violence and one in six had been sexually violated by members of armed groups, often multiple times (see further readings).

Transitional Justice

To confront the heritage of violence and human rights abuses, several transitional justice mechanisms have been initiated. A Truth and Reconciliation Commission (TRC) was created to investigate crimes committed between 1960 and 2006. The amnesties granted to ex-combatants have explicitly excluded war crimes, crimes against humanity, and genocide, allowing for these crimes' prosecution by national courts. The government further requested the ICC's assistance in investigating and prosecuting atrocities, and ICC investigations began in 2004. In practice, these mechanisms have failed to bring justice. The TRC failed to investigate a single case, and there has been no consistent prosecution policy by national courts. The ICC will prosecute only a handful of cases. As such, many alleged perpetrators have been demobilized and/or integrated into the army, and little or no effort has been made to provide reparations for the victims.

Truth Seeking

In 2003, the DRC established a TRC as a result of the 2002 Global and All-Inclusive Agreement. The TRC was to establish a historical record of crimes and human rights violations committed between the country's independence (1960) and the end of the transition period (2006), to identify victims and perpetrators individually or collectively, and to reestablish national unity on the basis of acknowledgment of the facts, forgiveness, reparation, and rehabilitation for victims. The TRC could provide amnesties for acts of war, political crimes, and crimes of opinion, such as propaganda promoting racial or ethnic superiority or hatred.

The TRC's mandate proved impossible to achieve for practical and political reasons. The TRC had to investigate a period of forty-six years, which covered a wide range of violence in different contexts and situations. The TRC was further undermined by the insecurity in large parts of the country and inaccessibility of war-affected communities because of poor infrastructure. More importantly, the selection of commissioners lacked transparency, and the TRC came to be viewed as a political institution. All of the signatories of the Global and All-Inclusive Agreement were represented in the TRC executive committee, but survivors of violence, the general population, and other stakeholders were never consulted about the design and objectives of the TRC. In practice, those responsible for establishing the TRC were the armed groups responsible for violence and violations. This paralyzed the institution. Unable, or unwilling, to conduct credible investigations of past violations, the TRC lost all credibility and international support. It ended its work in 2006 without having investigated a single case. Calls for a second TRC were made in 2008, but political and practical challenges, including insecurity, remain.

Separate from the TRC, the UN Office of the High Commissioner for Human Rights (OHCHR), with support from the government, launched its own investigation in 2008, mapping the violations of human rights and international humanitarian law of 1993–2003. The report published in 2010 listed multiple acts of large-scale and systematic violence, and assessed the ability of the Congolese judiciary to deal adequately with these crimes.

Prosecution

Despite demands from rebel groups for general amnesties, the Congolese government has been reluctant to grant amnesties to armed groups and its own forces. In accordance with international practice and under the guidance of international actors (the UN and the EU), successive agreements seeking an end to the conflicts in the DRC have included broad amnesties that explicitly excluded war crimes, crimes against humanity, and genocide. In 2003, a decree of the Congolese president provided the legal framework for amnesties. Although serious crimes were excluded from amnesty, there has been little effort to investigate and prosecute such crimes.

Domestic Trials

Following Mobutu's dictatorship and the succeeding conflicts, there has been few formal prosecutions for serious crimes. Immediately after Mobutu's fall, dozens of people associated with his government were arrested and held in detention, often without charges.

Standard legal procedures were disregarded and properties confiscated were generally appropriated by soldiers. Most of those arrested were released after paying fines equal in value to the property they had allegedly misappropriated under the previous regime, without ever facing trial.

The denial of justice continues at the time of this writing. The agreements to end the conflicts in the DRC allow the possibility of prosecution for the most serious crimes, excluding them from amnesty, but few cases of serious conflict-related crimes have been tried by the Congolese courts.

In 2002, the enactment of the military justice and criminal codes made it possible to prosecute human rights violations committed after 1996. Civilian courts cannot prosecute serious violations of international human rights and humanitarian laws because no legislation defines such crimes and the implementing legislation for the Rome Statute has yet to be adopted. Whereas civilian courts are perceived as corrupt, inefficient, and ill-equipped, military courts can better comply with the law and the rights of the defendant. By 2008, only a dozen cases concerning low-ranking officials had been prosecuted. While the lack of financial and human resources and poor equipment and infrastructure have hindered the ability to bring forth cases of serious crimes, the low number of prosecutions reflects the unwillingness to prosecute army officers. Aside from alleged perpetrators from within the Congolese forces, leaders of rebel movements have frequently been integrated into the national army with ranks of colonel or general. Members of the armed forces can only be judged by military judges of equal or superior rank. Because military judges are not awarded ex-officio rank, few can hear cases against high-ranking officials. Adding to the poor performances of the military courts, the few officials who have been convicted managed to escape from prison.

The International Criminal Court (ICC)

A signatory of the Rome Statute since September 2000 (ratified in April 2002), the DRC became the focus of the first investigation of the ICC in June 2004. Having monitored the situation in the DRC since mid-2003, the prosecutor announced that he was ready to request authorization from the Pre-Trial Chamber to use his own powers to start an investigation, and indicated that a referral and active support from the DRC would facilitate his work. Congolese President Kabila was reluctant to refer the situation to the ICC because investigations threatened to damage the political transition process and power-sharing agreement. All sides involved in the conflicts committed atrocities, so an investigation could implicate leaders of military and political groups in power. Following intense domestic and international pressure, Kabila referred the situation of the DRC to the ICC in March 2004.

In March 2006, the court unsealed its first arrest warrant regarding the situation in the DRC. The case against Thomas Lubanga focused on charges of enlisting and conscripting children under the age of fifteen years and using them to participate actively in hostilities. In October 2007, the Court unsealed another arrest warrant against two individuals in the case of the *Prosecutor v. Germain Katanga and Mathieu Ngudjolo Chui*. The accused were charged with seven counts of war crimes and three counts of crimes against humanity.

The Congolese government proceeded to arrest and transfer alleged perpetrators to the ICC. Lubanga and Katanga were arrested and detained in 2005 and charged with war crimes under the Congolese judicial system. Prior to their arrests, they had all been militia leaders, and Katanga and Ngudjolo Chui had been integrated in the national army with the ranks of general and colonel. A fourth arrest warrant was unsealed in April 2008 against Bosco Ntaganda for crimes allegedly committed in Ituri. The DRC asked for support from MONUC to apprehend him. By the time the warrant was unsealed, Ntaganda had become Nkunda's CNDP chief of staff, and support for his arrest quickly diminished. In 2008, Ntaganda took over the CNDP after Nkunda's arrest in Rwanda and called for peace, leading to the integration of the CNDP in the Congolese army. In 2009, he assimilated into the Congolese army with the rank of general. Afterward, the government insisted that, in the interest of peace and security, Ntaganda cannot be arrested. Rather, the DRC wishes to choose the timing of its collaboration with the ICC.

One more suspect was arrested in 2010. In accordance with the arrest warrant issued under seals by the ICC judges, the French authorities arrested Callixte Mbarushimana, an FDLR leader, who faces five counts of crimes against humanity and six counts of war crimes, including charges of murder, torture, rape, inhumane acts and persecution, and destruction of property.

Being the first situation for which trials have been held, the investigation and prosecution of alleged perpetrators of serious crimes in the DRC is testing the ICC. The prosecution has been criticized for lack of focus on the highest-ranking perpetrators and government actors, for limited geographic focus on Ituri, for the narrowness of the charges, and for its impact on the peace process, as illustrated by the case of Ntaganda. With the opening of the first trials, the Court has been challenged to operationalize the provisions of the Rome Statute, such as the participation of victims and their representation in the proceedings. The trials of Lubanga and Katanga and Ngudjolo Chu started in January and November 2009.

The International Court of Justice (ICJ)

After the 1998 conflicts, the DRC initiated proceedings before the ICJ against Rwanda, Burundi, and Uganda. In 2001, the cases against Rwanda and Burundi were removed from the Court's list at the request of the DRC. In 2002, the DRC again filed an application instituting proceedings against Rwanda. In 2006, the ICJ found it had no jurisdiction in the case of Rwanda. In 2005, in the case of Uganda, the ICJ ruled in favor of the DRC, finding that Uganda had violated principles of nonuse of force in international relations and of nonintervention, and its obligations under international human rights law and humanitarian law. Following the judgment, Uganda and the DRC were to negotiate reparations, but no payment has been made to date.

Demobilization, Disarmament, Military Integration, and Vetting

The principles of demobilization, disarmament, and reintegration were included in 2002 in the peace negotiations. A *brassage* process, in which former combatants are integrated in mixed units and then relocated to other parts of the country, was adopted. By mid-2007, 150,000 combatants had been processed, 50,000 of whom were integrated into mixed brigades. The integrated combatants were just a fraction of the estimated 330,000 combatants who participated in the conflicts. Several groups, most notably Nkunda's, refused to comply. After negotiations, Nkunda agreed on *mixage* whereby his combatants were integrated in the army and mixed with other brigades, but remained in their areas of operations. The agreement failed and fighting resumed until Ntaganda took over the CNDP and integrated with the army.

Vetting was never discussed. Katanga and Ngudjolo Chui were integrated into the army before the ICC arrest warrant was unsealed, while Ntaganda remained a general in the Congolese army despite the existing warrant of arrest. Given the difficulties of prosecuting high-ranking officials by military courts, many perpetrators now occupy high-level positions in the army.

Reparations

Little has been done in the DRC to provide reparations to victims of conflicts. The TRC included reparations provisions, but given its overall failure, reparations were never realized. The ICC Trust Fund for Victims assists war victims in the DRC. Currently twelve projects are funded in Ituri, South Kivu, and North Kivu. Because no judgments have been concluded, projects have not focused on the specifics of cases under investigation, but rather have taken a broad approach to support victims. Funded projects include counseling, education, community mobilization, shelter, information, microcredit, reintegration of children, and conflict resolution. Given the instrumental roles local disputes, especially ethnically based disputes, had in fomenting and fueling the conflicts, providing reparations is a politically charged challenge.

The UN Security Council pointed to the responsibility of Uganda and Rwanda to pay reparations to the DRC, and the ICJ judgment against Uganda ordered reparations to be paid.

Conclusion

Several transitional justice mechanisms have been implemented in the DRC, but efforts to confront the past have not been systematic. Attempts to expose the truth have been paralyzed by the continued presence and influence of armed groups involved in and responsible for atrocities. The ICC is unlikely to prosecute more than a few cases, and local military courts – the only mechanisms able to address serious crimes – are unlikely to prosecute high-ranking officials. The justice sector remains plagued by corruption and lack the means to conduct free and fair trials.

Patrick Vinck and Phuong Pham

Cross-references: Court Trials for Redress; International Criminal Court; Reparations; Rwanda; Truth Commissions; Uganda.

Further Readings

Davis, L. and P. Hayner. 2009. *Difficult Peace, Limited Justice: Ten Years of Peacemaking in the DRC.* New York: International Center for Transitional Justice.

Democratic Republic of the Congo, 1993–2003: Report of the Mapping Exercise Documenting the Most Serious Violations of Human Rights and International Humanitarian Law Committed within the Territory of the Democratic Republic of the Congo between March 1993 and June 2003. Geneva: United Nations Office of the High Commissioner for Human Rights, 2006.

Legal and Judicial Cooperation Program. 2004. *Democratic Republic of Congo: Justice Is Overlooked by the Transition*. Paris: International Federation for Human Rights.

Prunier, G. 2009. *Africa's World War: Congo, the Rwandan Genocide, and the Making of a Continental Catastrophe*. New York: Oxford University Press.

Vinck P., P. Pham, S. Baldo and R. Shigekane. 2008. *Living with Fear: A Population-Based Survey on Attitudes about Peace, Justice and Social Reconstruction in Eastern Congo*. Human Rights Center, University of California, Berkeley; Payson Center for International Development, Tulane University; International Center for Transitional Justice, New York.

Croatia

In the decade and a half since the end of the Homeland War (Domovinski rat), the Yugoslav conflict that took place on the territory of Croatia in the period between 1991 and 1995, transitional justice in the Republic of Croatia has been marked by slow but steady progress toward addressing the legacy of human rights abuses inherited from the armed conflict. Especially since 2000, the rise of democratic politics in the country has been accompanied by major advances in the institutional processes and public debate about transitional justice. Despite this positive trend, transitional justice in Croatia continues to face major challenges associated with limited political will, public support, and institutional capacity and impartiality, which often retard and complicate the process of dealing with the repressive past.

The Repressive Past

A year after holding multiparty elections, Croatia declared its independence from the Socialist Federal Republic of Yugoslavia in June 1991. Shortly thereafter, the Homeland War began with the attack of the Yugoslav People's Army (Jugoslovenska Nardona Armija or the JNA) on Croatian territory. On December 19, 1991, the Assembly of the Serbian Autonomous Region of Krajina, together with Serbs from other parts of Croatia, declared independence from Croatia and formed the Republic of Serbian Krajina (Republika Srpska Krajina or RSK). The complex conflict that continued over the next four years was fought between the JNA and RSK forces on the one side and Croatian army and police forces on the other, as well as various special units affiliated with the regimes in Belgrade and Zagreb at the time. Although serious human rights violations were committed on all sides of the conflict, this section emphasizes the abuse attributed to Croatia's armed and police forces, which should have been addressed by the Croatian state through the process of transitional justice.

About one-third of the territory of Croatia was controlled by JNA and Serb forces by the end of 1991. The war involved heavy bombardment of towns and cities and extensive property destruction, including the JNA siege and leveling of Vukovar and the shelling of Dubrovnik and other Dalmatian cities. Violence subsided and a number of ceasefires were declared between 1992 and 1994, but human rights abuse continued throughout that period. In particular, Croatian forces conducted a number of special operations to regain Serb-held areas, such as Operation Medak Pocket, near Zadar, and Operation Maslenica, near Gospić. In operation Medak Pocket, for example, at least 100 Serbs were killed, including 29 civilians, and more than 150 homes were destroyed. Another upsurge in violence marked the final months of the war, such as Operation Flash, conducted by Croatian forces in Western Slavonia, and the Serb shelling of

Zagreb in the summer of 1995. The Croatian army regained control of most of the RSK territories in Operation Storm, which peaked in August 1995, but its follow-up activities continued for several more months. Operation Storm was accompanied by the fleeing and forcible removal of between 150,000 and 200,000 Serb civilians from Krajina, and included widespread intimidation, killing, plunder, and destruction of property of the local Serb population. Pursuant to the terms of the Erdut Agreement of November 1995, the Croatian government agreed to peacefully reintegrate Eastern Slavonia, Baranja, and Western Sirmium and reestablished political and legal authority over those territories in January 1998. In December 1995, Croatia signed the Dayton Peace Agreement, committing itself to a permanent ceasefire and the return of all refugees.

The Homeland War in Croatia, like the conflict in neighboring Bosnia-Herzegovina, was marked by widespread campaigns for "ethnic cleansing," a strategy for establishing control over territory through the expulsion and displacement of civilian populations. This strategy was pursued on all sides in the conflict and, alongside expulsions, involved various techniques of harassment and intimidation, wanton destruction of cities and villages, plunder and destruction of property, torture and inhumane treatment, and killings. In this context, attacks on civilians were effectively deployed as a method of warfare rather than constituting a side effect of the hostilities. Although they remain disputed, the figures for refugees and internally displaced persons during the war illustrate the dynamic of ethnic cleansing quite well. For example, the estimated number of Croatian Serbs who became refugees during the armed conflict is approximately 300,000 – more than half of the total Serb population in Croatia at the start of the war.

The legacy of mass atrocity and human rights abuse inherited from the Homeland War was complex and contested in Croatia. On the one side, there were serious crimes committed by the JNA, RSK forces, and Serbian special units, such as the shelling of Vukovar and the massacre at Ovčara at the start of the war. On the other, operations such as Medak Pocket and Storm had implicated Croatia's armed and police forces in expulsions and killings on a large scale. The Croatian public and the Serb minority in the country have remained divided in their memories of the war, demands for addressing the wartime abuse, and perceptions of the process of transitional justice.

Transitional Justice

In the first five years after the end of the Homeland War, transitional justice in Croatia was plagued by pervasive ethnic bias and was mostly limited to large-scale prosecution of Serbs for war crimes. Since 2000, the process of transitional justice has gained greater momentum and credibility and has expanded to incorporate a broader range of mechanisms and public debates on criminal prosecution, institutional reform, addressing the issue of missing persons, reparations, and truth telling. These mechanisms, as well as their limitations, are discussed in turn.

Criminal Prosecution

The political landscape of the Republic of Croatia remained largely unchanged in the first five years after the end of hostilities and continued to be dominated by the figure of President Franjo Tudjman and his political party, the Croatian Democratic Union (Hrvatska Demokratska Zajednica or the HDZ). Tudjman's rule in the transitional period retained many of the features that had marked his wartime regime: nationalist mobilization and rhetoric, control of the public sphere through the media, suppression of the Serb minority, and intolerance and attacks against critics of the regime. In this environment, transitional justice became largely sidelined or distorted. In particular, concern for the abuse of the Serb minority during the recent conflict was mostly limited to a small segment of civil society that included independent media and human rights groups, such as the weekly *Feral Tribune* and the Helsinki Committee for Human Rights. Under Tudjman's regime, hardly any ethnic Croats were indicted for criminal acts associated with the armed conflict. By contrast, that period was marked by the initiation of proceedings against large numbers of Croatian Serbs for war crimes and genocide.

Croatia adopted Law 110 on General Amnesty in October 1996, providing an amnesty from criminal prosecution and procedure for acts committed during the armed conflict, with the exemption of serious violations of humanitarian law that have the character of war crimes. According to statistics published by the Chief State Attorney of the Republic of Croatia, between 1991 and 2005 in Croatia, 4,814 individuals were reported for criminal acts against international law, investigations were launched against 3,280, and 1,428 were indicted. By the end of 2006, 611 individuals were sentenced and 245 acquitted. With very few exceptions, these cases were initiated in the 1990s against ethnic Serbs and members of the JNA and were marked by serious failures of due process: widespread prosecution in absentia, joint indictments against large groups of defendants, convictions based on insufficiently established facts, and failure to apply the facts to the law. Overcharging of low-level perpetrators for minor crimes was common and after 1995 this practice included the charge of genocide. The prosecution of Serbs for war crimes in the 1990s entrenched ethnic bias in the administration of justice and collective conceptions of responsibility and, in practical terms, obstructed the process of refugee return and reintegration after the end of the armed conflict. Among the Serb minority in the country, war crimes trials have been interpreted as an instrument of revenge, rather than justice, and a continuation of wartime policies of ethnic cleansing.

The state's approach to the prosecution of war crimes began to change after the death of Tudjman in late 1999 and reflected the overall trajectory of democratization in the country, associated with the emergence of a new political constellation and consensus on the desirability of Croatia's integration into the European Union. These developments have been stabilized since 2003, when the HDZ returned to power under the leadership of Ivo Sanader. Three main trends have marked the shift in Croatia's policy toward criminal prosecutions in the new century: reviewing the problematic war crimes caseload from the 1990s; initiating criminal proceedings against members of Croatia's police and armed forces; and improving state cooperation with the International Criminal Tribunal for the Former Yugoslavia (ICTY) in The Hague.

The setting up of a review process for the war crimes caseload inherited from the 1990s has revealed both the scale of judicial misconduct and the continuing challenges faced by the Croatian judiciary. During the course of 2004, a review of all investigation files was carried out and proceedings were dropped for 448 individuals, overwhelmingly Serbs, either for lack of evidence or because their offenses were exempt under the Law on General Amnesty. Despite this effort, in 2008, Croatia was still seeking more than 1,000 war crimes suspects, including 400 based on convictions in absentia, and had issued more than 600 international arrest warrants. The judiciary has been overwhelmed by large numbers of retrials in recent years, as the Supreme Court has began to reverse decisions of lower courts and Serbs previously convicted in absentia have begun to return to Croatia and exercise their right to a new trial. The efforts of the top tiers of the Croatian judiciary to address the legacy from the 1990s and to discourage the initiation of new proceedings in absentia have often encountered resistance from lower courts, especially in areas heavily affected by the war, where ethnic bias in the administration of justice remains a concern.

War crimes trials of members of Croatia's police and armed forces were virtually nonexistent until the end of Tudjman's regime in 2000. During the Račan and Sanader governments, the courts have begun to prosecute abuses committed on the Croatian side of the conflict, including high-ranking officers from the army and police such as Mirko Norac, Rahim Ademi, and Branimir Glavaš. When a court in Rijeka indicted General Norac in 2001 for crimes committed in Gospic ten years earlier, the indictment provoked an explosion of nationalist press and antigovernment demonstrations – 150,000 people gathered at the biggest rally in Split. Since then, four county courts have been designated and equipped to prosecute the most serious war crimes cases (in Zagreb, Osijeak, Rijeka, and Split), including cases transferred back to Croatia from the ICTY, and nationalist backlash against such trials has become muted. In the first decade of the twenty-first century, however, the majority of war crimes trials in Croatia continued to take place where the crimes had been committed and involved mostly Serb defendants. Despite improvements in the quality of proceedings, ongoing concerns included ethnic bias in the selection of suspects and offenses for prosecution, discrepancies in sentencing practices, intimidation of witnesses, and insufficient support for victims and witnesses. While political pressure on the judiciary diminished, the prosecution of members of Croatia's army and police often reflected certain institutional reluctance (*Ademi and Norac* case) and retained its capacity to spark controversy and politicization (*Glavaš* case).

Finally, state cooperation with the ICTY emerged as one of the most controversial and divisive issues in Croatia's politics and public debate throughout the early years of the post-Tudjman period. On the one hand, ICTY indictments and requests for transfer of suspects to its jurisdiction portrayed high-ranking generals as criminals, calling into question their status as heroes in Croatian national mythology. On the other, cooperation with the ICTY became a main condition and obstacle for Croatia's progress toward integration in the EU, at a time when Europe had emerged as a consensus project for the state. When the ICTY indicted General Janko Bobetko in September 2002 for crimes committed in Operation Medak Pocket, the Račan government struggled to avoid international isolation while, at the same time, asserting the argument of the nationalist opposition and the associations of war veterans, which presented the indictment as an attack on the legitimacy of the Homeland War. Even more controversy was created when the ICTY indicted General Ante Gotovina – framing Operation Storm as a campaign for ethnic cleansing – and the EU suspended accession talks with Croatia over its failure to arrest and extradite him to The Hague. The crisis, however, revealed important changes in Croatia's approach to the issue of transitional justice. The discourse of Sanader and the HDZ, now in power, reaffirmed the country's commitment to the rule of law and Europe. Furthermore, the government provided key intelligence that led to the arrest of Gotovina on the Canary Islands later that year. In protest, war veterans groups managed to mobilize 50,000 people at a rally in Split, but these voices had become marginalized and largely limited to the fringes of Croatia's political scene. Since then, accession negotiations with the EU have resumed and have provided a framework that has shaped both the policy and public discussion of transitional justice in Croatia.

Institutional Reforms

Croatia did not adopt a legislative framework for implementing lustration or vetting as mechanisms of transitional justice, either in relation to the communist regime from the pre-1991 Yugoslav era or the 1991–1995 Homeland War. In the period between 1990 and 1996, however, approximately 2,200 judges and prosecutors were dismissed or not reappointed without any clear criteria, suggesting that the purge of the judiciary was politically or ethnically motivated. The opposition Croatian Party of Rights initiated the adoption of lustration legislation in 1998–1999, but the proposal was rejected by the majority of Members of Parliament. Despite pressure by civil society organizations in recent years, in particular the Helsinki Committee for Human Rights, the issue of vetting and lustration for perpetrators of human rights violations dating back to the Homeland War has been largely ignored by the political class. The lack of currency of this transitional justice mechanism in Croatia is usually attributed to a widespread tendency to frame human rights abuse from the conflict as a side effect of the legitimate struggle against the JNA and Serb rebels, on the one hand, and important continuities between Croatia's wartime and postwar transitional elites, on the other.

Missing Persons

In 2007, the total number of Croatian citizens still considered missing was slightly more than 2,000, including 1,093 missing persons from 1991 (mostly ethnic Croats) and 916 missing from 1995 – mostly ethnic Serbs who went missing during operations Flash and Storm. From the beginning of the conflict until the end of 2007, the total number of exhumed mortal remains was 4,402 (from 143 mass graves) and the number of identified persons was 3,484. While the 1991 and the 1995 lists were kept separate for a number of years, since 2006 the Office for Captured and Missing Persons of the Republic of Croatia has integrated the numbers for missing Serbs and Croats. The Croatian government has been criticized by families of missing Serbs and human rights groups for being too slow at carrying out the exhumation of bodies of missing Serbs (only five out of some twenty known burial sites were dealt with by 2007). Families of the missing persons, both Serb and Croat, have also been critical of the slow process of identifying the bodies after their exhumation.

Reparations

The legislative framework for reparations in Croatia has been criticized for de facto favoring members of the military and their families and discriminating against civilian victims of the war and, in particular, ethnic Serbs. In 2007, the number of civilian victims who received compensation in the form of state pension was around 3,000. Very few Serb returnees benefited from such compensation because of their inability to provide medical documentation and other evidence necessary to obtain the status of civilian victims of war.

The liability of the Croatian state for damages caused by terrorist acts or by state organs is regulated by the Law on Responsibility for Damages Caused by Terrorist Acts and Public Demonstrations (117/2003) and the Law on the Responsibility of the Republic of Croatia for Damages Caused by Members of the Croatian Armed and Police Forces during the Homeland War (117/2003). A number of civilian victims, mostly ethnic minorities, have sought compensation for nonmaterial damages from the courts. Analysis of this jurisprudence until 2008 suggests that their compensation claims were mostly unsuccessful, as courts invoked the statute of limitations for war damages or rejected state liability altogether. More successful were claims for damages based on completed criminal proceedings, where individual criminal responsibility had already been established. The most controversial aspect of reparations in Croatia has been the issue of return and reconstruction of property. In particular, it concerns problems arising in the so-called tenancy rights cases (involving Croatian Serbs who lost their special tenancy rights over state-owned flats during the war) and the reconstruction of destroyed and damaged property owned by Serbs in Croatia.

Truth Telling

Transitional justice in Croatia in the first fifteen years of postwar transition did not involve the creation of an official truth commission or fact-finding body, or any significant initiative in that direction at the national level. At the time of this writing, however, Croatian civil society is actively involved in a regional initiative for the establishment of a regional truth commission. The initiative for RECOM, as the proposed commission is popularly known in the region, reflected a widespread sentiment that truth seeking and truth telling in the former Yugoslavia could be adequately pursed only within a regional framework, and a belief that the legitimacy of a regional body depends on the support and engagement of local civil society. The general tasks of the envisioned body would involve establishing the facts of mass atrocities and human rights abuse that took place during the conflicts on the territory of the former Yugoslavia throughout the 1990s, as well as addressing the issue of missing persons in the region.

The Coalition for RECOM was launched in 2006, spearheaded by three organizations: the Humanitarian Law Center in Belgrade, the Research and Documentation Centre in Sarajevo and Documenta in Zagreb. Since then, the Coalition has conducted broad consultations with civil society actors in Bosnia-Herzegovina, Croatia, Kosovo, Montenegro, and Serbia, including major events (Regional Forums in the five capitals) and numerous workshops, meetings, and discussions at the grassroots level. The consultation phase of the initiative for RECOM in the Western Balkans has engaged with human rights groups and other nongovernmental organizations; associations of victims, war veterans, and refugees; journalists, academics, and public intellectuals; judges and prosecutors; members of political parties and parliaments; as well as youth and other social groups. By the end of 2009, the Coalition for RECOM had expanded to incorporate representatives of broad segments of civil society in the region and was preparing to move the consultative process into its second stage: deliberations on the mandate and structure of the proposed regional fact-finding body. The last phase, as envisioned by the Coalition for RECOM, would involve addressing the post-Yugoslav publics, parliaments, and governments, as well as international actors such as the UN and the EU, in order to secure public and official support for the establishment of RECOM.

Conclusion

During the first decade and a half after the end of the Homeland War, the process of transitional justice in Croatia was slow, painful, and often accompanied by divisive and contested politics. The policy of criminal prosecution expanded and stabilized after 2000 to address more adequately and impartially the wartime legacies of abuse, and some progress has been made in relation to the issues of missing persons and reparations. The major challenges to full-blown transitional justice in the Republic of Croatia stem from the ambivalent attitudes toward the repressive past prevalent among the political class and the Croat majority in the country. Although the record of transitional justice has improved in the context of Croatia's bid for EU membership, very often this process has addressed European institutions but continued to ignore Croatian Serbs.

Iavor Rangelov

Cross-references: Amnesty; Bosnia-Herzegovina; Court Trials for Redress; International Criminal Tribunal for the Former Yugoslavia; Lustration; Montenegro; Reparations; Serbia; Unofficial Truth Projects.

Further Readings

Humanitarian Law Center (Belgrade) and Documenta (Zagreb). 2008. *Transitional Justice in Post-Yugoslav Countries: Report for 2007*. Belgrade: Humanitarian Law Center. Available at http://www.hlc-rdc.org/Publikacije/1470.sr.html (accessed November 19, 2009).
Jovic, Dejan. 2009. Croatia after Tudjman: The ICTY and Issue of Transitional Justice. In *Chaillot Paper No.116: War Crimes, Conditionality and EU Integration in the Western Balkans*. Eds. Judy Batt and Jelena Obradović. Paris: Institute for Security Studies.
Peskin, Victor and Mieczyslaw P. Boduszynski. 2003. International Justice and Domestic Politics: Post-Tudjman Croatia and the International Criminal Tribunal for the Former Yugoslavia. *Europe-Asia Studies*, 55(7): 1117–1142.
Rangelov, Iavor. 2006. EU Conditionality and Transitional Justice in the Former Yugoslavia. *Croatian Yearbook of European Law & Policy*, 2: 365–375.
Søberg, Marius. 2007. Croatia since 1989: The HDZ and the Politics of Transition. In *Democratic Transition in Croatia: Value Transformation, Education and Media*. Eds. Sabrina P. Ramet and Davorka Matić. College Station: Texas A&M University Press.

Cuba

The revolutionary regime in Cuba (declared communist in 1961 by supreme leader Fidel Castro) began on January 1, 1959. At the time of this writing, the sole cosmetic change in leadership has been a succession of power from Fidel Castro to his younger brother Raúl in 2006. Regime continuity impedes efforts at transitional justice, although groups outside the island have documented repression and sought compensation for victims through non-Cuban court systems.

The Repressive Past and Present

The Castro regime sought to eliminate all accused collaborators of the toppled Fulgencio Batista dictatorship (1952–1959), including Batista-affiliated government contractors, businesspeople, provincial governors, mayors, aldermen, bank presidents, judges, members of the armed and police forces, university professors, Catholic priests and other religious leaders, and anyone unable to prove their loyalty to the revolution, immediately after the founding of the revolutionary regime. Documented total cases to date indicate about 4,000 deaths by firing squad alone. The famous Argentine rebel Ché Guevara ordered more than 100 of these executions and some were by his own hand. The regime held closed kangaroo trials, or sham legal proceedings held by biased parties, resulting in predetermined guilty verdicts for alleged counterrevolutionary activities. The Ministry for the Recovery of Misappropriated Assets confiscated vast and valuable properties from the so-called Batista collaborators. These events, together with religious persecution, imprisonments, hard labor, indoctrination, and the fear of Soviet influence, led to the first wave of Cuban refugees, mostly to the United States. An unknown number of refugees were convicted in absentia for abandonment of the island and counterrevolutionary acts.

Early supporters of the Cuban Revolution soon turned on Fidel Castro when his promises of restoring democracy and competitive elections never materialized. The regime jailed those who openly criticized the Revolution and its increasingly communist tendencies. Property confiscations went beyond those of accused Batista collaborators. All bourgeois, capitalist elements, such as lawyers, bankers, farmers, cattle ranchers, and commercial and industrial enterprise owners, became targets. Owners of income-generating residential properties lost them, and property titles and ownership promised by the Cuban regime to tenants were never delivered. Within the first decade, even owners of small firms and plots were affected by confiscatory measures. Anti-Yankee (a derogatory term for U.S. citizens) rhetoric was employed to garner support domestically and abroad from enemies of U.S. interventions. The agrarian reforms of 1959 and 1963 transferred to the state vast lands and agro-industries owned by Cuban nationals and foreigners, including several hundred thousand acres owned by U.S. citizens. Nationalization legislation authorized the seizure of private properties of all sizes and monetary value at the beginning of the Revolution and, in 1968, of several thousand remaining small businesses. With few exceptions, no compensation was paid.

The failed Bay of Pigs invasion of April 1961, when Cuban exiles together with U.S. citizens mounted a U.S. government-backed attack against the island in the hope of inciting opposition among Cubans and ousting the Cuban regime, resulted in the imprisonment or execution of those who were captured by Cuban combatants. The attack prompted increased repression on the island in order to quash any possibility of counterrevolutionary cooperation with outside forces. Nevertheless, dissident activity increased on the island and was punished by imprisonment, torture, and forced exile. As in other communist countries, the regime encouraged citizens to report on family, friends, and neighbors, and a vast network of secret informers was recruited throughout the island. According to former Cuban intelligence officer Juan Antonio Rodríguez Mernier (1994), Cuba's Ministry of the Interior (MININT) employed 100,000 persons in the 1980s, at the time when the population numbered 10 million. Additionally, 500,000 agents produced most MININT intelligence data and 3 million intelligence sources were available for service when needed. Cuban regime defector Manuel Beunza, a former high-ranking intelligence officer, has corroborated these figures. This facilitated the revelation of dissident or counterrevolutionary activity, creating an environment of paranoia and distrust.

The Cuban regime shut down Catholic and other private schools in order to consolidate state control over education and to commence communist indoctrination. Parents feared the indoctrination of their children and the loss of their parental rights to the state. In 1960, James Baker, headmaster of the American Ruston Academy in Havana, and Father (later Monsignor) Bryan O. Walsh, Director of Catholic Welfare Bureau, organized the evacuation of 200 students whose parents were considered opponents of the regime. From November 26, 1960 to October 22, 1962, 14,048 unaccompanied Cuban children were sent to the United States by their parents in the so-called Operation Pedro Pan program. The Catholic Church placed children in camps until foster parents were identified. Jewish Family and Children's Services arranged for the 396 Jewish children in the group to be placed immediately with Jewish foster parents. The Operation sought to ultimately reunite children with their parents who had stayed behind in Cuba. Sometimes it took years for parents to escape Cuba and in a few cases parents never made it out of the island. State control over children was officially validated in Articles 37, 38, and 39 of the 1976 Cuban Constitution, which read that the communist state controls education and parents are obligated to educate their children to be useful citizens in a socialist society.

The Cuban regime rid the country of many opponents by permitting mass migrations to the United States. On September 29, 1965, Castro announced that those who wanted to leave could do so through the Cuban port of Camarioca. Thus, hundreds of Cuban exiles in boats retrieved 2,979 relatives until November 15, 1965. Refugees had to apply to the Ministry of the Interior to receive permission to exit the island. That same year, recognizing the danger of these trips for those who took them, U.S. President Lyndon Johnson announced that he would welcome all Cuban refugees. From 1965 to 1973, the Cuban and the U.S. governments organized about 3,000 "freedom flights" from Varadero to Miami in which 265,000 Cubans left the island on American planes. The US$12 million program was financed by the U.S. government and assisted by religious and volunteer agencies that attempted to disperse the refugees around the country. In 1980, Castro again declared that all those who wished to leave Cuba could do so, including the homosexuals, a group the Revolution had attempted to "reeducate." As a result, some 125,000 Cubans left in the Mariel Boatlift mass exodus, in which the Cuban regime surreptitiously placed on boats violent criminals and mentally ill emptied out from its prisons and psychiatric facilities as a condition of allowing refugees to depart. Although Cubans had fled to the United States on boats and rafts since 1959, the end of Soviet subsidies in the early 1990s, following the dismantling of the Soviet Union in 1991, and the ensuing dire economic straits, resulted in thousands of Cubans escaping to the United States on stolen or hijacked boats and makeshift rafts. The refugees, known as *balseros* or rafters, numbered in the tens of thousands between 1991 and 1994. As of 2004, some 80,000 rafters lost their lives while attempting to escape. The regime aggressively tried to stop the exodus by shooting refugees or sinking their vessels to drown them. *The Miami Herald* houses searchable online databases for Operation Pedro Pan, the Freedom Flights, and the Mariel Boatlift.

In the mid 1990s, a nascent independent press created an international stir. The Cuban regime briefly imprisoned and state agents frequently harassed some journalists. In 1998, the Varela Project, inspired by Czechoslovakia's Charter 77, collected signatures for a petition asking the Cuban authorities to observe the democratic rights protected by the international conventions the country had signed, such as the International Covenant on Civil and Political Rights. Seventy-five human rights activists, including twenty-five Varela Project members and twenty-nine independent journalists, were arrested in

Cuba's Black Spring (March 2003). Some of the families of the imprisoned who were harassed, monitored, and lost their jobs chose exile as life in Cuba became unbearable.

Transitional Justice

Without regime change in Cuba the possibilities to enact transitional justice are limited. One of the greatest risks in Cuba's lack of change is that the regime learned from fallen communist countries. That is, there has been time to take measures to ensure that the redress of wrongs committed by them will be made more difficult. The expressed desire of exiles and dissidents to deal with the past and present repression in Cuba varies from "forgive and forget" to trials and prosecution for all involved with the regime.

Truth and Memory

Although a Truth Commission cannot yet be established because the current communist regime denies any wrongdoing, foundations for this option have been established. The Cuba Archive of the Free Society Project, founded in 2001 in the United States and made up of academics, human rights activists, and professionals, documents the loss of life (political disappearances and fatalities) resulting from the Cuban Revolution, from the 1952 Batista coup d'état to the present time. The project compiles cases based on bibliographic and primary sources and provides pictures of victims when available. The goal is to provide a springboard for "constructive remembering" so that the atrocities and injustices will not be repeated after the expected collapse of the Cuban communist regime.

More than half a century has passed since the revolutionary takeover. Therefore, many of the earliest surviving victims are quite elderly. To help capture their experiences, Cuban-American filmmaker Rafael Lima created two documentaries about political prisoners, "Presidio: The Trip Back" (2003) and "Plantados" (2006), which are available from the University of Miami and have entered Cuba via channels not approved by the Cuban government. The visual medium of these testimonies is crucial to educating current and future generations about the systematic destruction of family and life by the Cuban communist regime.

Compensation

In 1996, the U.S. Congress amended the Foreign Sovereign Immunities Act to allow U.S. citizens victimized by terrorist acts and state sponsors of terrorism to sue for damages. In 2002, Congress passed the Terrorism Risk Insurance Act to pursue assets of state sponsors of terrorism such as Cuba, which provides safe haven for members of terrorist organizations from around the world, including the United States. Victims and their families who are U.S. citizens have used this legislation to sue the Cuban government in an effort to tap into frozen Cuban assets in U.S. bank Chase Manhattan. In 1996, Cuban MiGs shot down four members of Brothers to the Rescue, an organization whose volunteer pilots flew missions over the Florida Straits looking for rafters. Three of the four pilots shot down were U.S. citizens. Their families used the legislation to sue for wrongful death and were awarded US$187 million. The Clinton administration (1992–2000) initially rejected the release of frozen Cuban funds to pay the award, because

President Bill Clinton claimed that these judgments interfered with U.S. foreign policy. He relented in 2001, the day before he left office, allowing the families of Armando Alejandre, Carlos Alberto Costa, and Mario M. de la Peña to collect US$96.7 million. Cuba's frozen assets are largely depleted since several families have collected millions of dollars in damages in other lawsuits against the Cuban government.

Restitution of Property

The U.S. government is the only one of the countries whose citizens were affected by confiscations, such as Canada, France, Spain, Switzerland, and the United Kingdom, that has not signed a bilateral compensation treaty with the communist Cuban government and accepted compensation payments for properties owned by its citizens, largely because payments would be inadequate (payments to the signatory countries were pennies on the dollar). These properties are currently estimated to be worth billions of dollars. Cash compensation payments for properties confiscated from U.S. and Cuban citizens will be virtually impossible with the depleted frozen funds and a Cuban Treasury bankrupted by decades of economic mismanagement and the funding of missions intended to garner international support for the Cuban regime.

Cuban exiles attempted to create a registry of confiscated properties that would purportedly have been used to organize and facilitate the resolution of claims, but a lack of trust on the part of potential claimants thwarted this endeavor. Academic groups such as the Association for the Study of the Cuban Economy (ASCE), founded in 1990, have also provided conference presentations and publications, including privatization plans and recommendations on how to best resolve property claims.

Documenting and Reporting Crimes

The Cuban Democratic Directorate (Directorio) was founded in 1990 by students outside of Cuba to aid in the regime change of the island. This organization, informed through its in-country contacts, reports on its Web site, electronic newsletters, and publications on daily repressive acts of the Cuban regime. This provides information that could be used by a postcommunist government to determine how and if to punish the perpetrators of crimes and to rehabilitate the victims. Together with Directorio, Mothers and Women against Repression (M.A.R. por Cuba), founded in 1994 in Miami, brings awareness of human rights abuses in Cuba around the world and lobbies foreign governments and organizations to support opponents of the regime. M.A.R. differs from other Latin American women's groups in that members have not necessarily lost children or spouses to Cuban prisons and executions. These organizations have the support of governments, dissidents, exiles, and others from former communist Czech Republic, Estonia, and Poland that could pressure a postcommunist government in Cuba to right its predecessor's wrongs.

Conclusion

The length and continuing existence of Cuba's communist regime makes it virtually impossible to achieve justice for its victims. In light of events in formerly communist countries, members and collaborators of the Cuban regime have taken steps to protect themselves from future prosecution and the potential reversal of their policies. Many elites' children and relatives live abroad and hold dual citizenship. Officials own real estate around the world, particularly in states friendly to the regime. The option of exile to countries such as Venezuela or Spain (while their communist-tolerant administrations are in place) may allow perpetrators of human rights abuses to find protection from extradition and prosecution. The end of Soviet subsidies led the Cuban regime to open up to foreign investment, including in confiscated properties. This complicates future claims. Additionally, the passage of time has allowed for the option of destroying property registries and state security files. The political will on the island to redress the past is virtually impossible to measure unless a transition from communism begins in earnest.

Tania C. Mastrapa

Cross References: Cuba Archive; Property Restitution; Rehabilitation of Political Prisoners.

Further Readings

DeCosse, Sarah A. 1999. *Cuba's Repressive Machinery: Human Rights Forty Years after the Revolution*. New York: Human Rights Watch.
Directorio. Official Web site. Available at: http://www.directorio.org (accessed September 27, 2010).
Freedom Flights Database. Available at: http://www.miamiherald.com/2008/12/10/807685/search-the-freedom-flights-database.html (accessed September 27, 2010).
Mariel Boatlift Database. Available at: http://www.miamiherald.com/cgi-bin/mariel/index (accessed September 27, 2010).
Mastrapa, Tania. 2011. *Confiscated Fate*. Miami: Blaker Books.
Operation Pedro Pan Database. Available at: http://www.miamiherald.com/cgi-bin/pedropan/search (accessed September 27, 2010).
Rodriguez, Ana. 1995. *Diary of a Survivor: Nineteen Years in a Cuban Women's Prison*. New York: St. Martin's Press.
Rodríguez Mernier, Juan A. 1994. *Cuba por dentro: el MININT*. Miami: Ediciones Universal.
Valladares, Armando. 1986. *Against All Hope*. New York: Alfred A. Knopf.
Werlau, Maria. 2009. *Che Guevara's Forgotten Victims. Cuba Archive*. November 12. Available at: http://cubaarchive.org/home/images/stories/che_guevara_report_11.12.2009.pdf (accessed November 14, 2009).

The Czech Republic

The Czech Republic implemented one of the most comprehensive transitional justice programs among postcommunist countries. These policies had strong retributive undertones, aspiring to punish, exclude, and condemn persons deemed responsible for the systematic human rights violations committed during the 1948–1989 period, and to rehabilitate and compensate the victims of repression. Many policies were controversial in their design, implementation, or both; in particular, the public was disappointed that the authorities were able to bring only a dismal number of perpetrators to justice.

The Repressive Past

The Czech Republic and Slovakia share a common Czechoslovak past. Founded in 1918, Czechoslovakia was divided during World War II, was renewed after the war, became a Federation in 1968, and peacefully separated at midnight on January 1, 1993. While both successor states share the same legacy of the communist regime of 1948–1989 (see entry on Slovakia), they differ in two respects. First, the Czech lands had a larger total population and more political prisoners. Of 250,000 persons condemned for political reasons in communist Czechoslovakia, more than 200,000 were condemned in the Czech lands, where more than 10 million of Czechoslovakia's 15 million people lived. Second, the overwhelming majority of the signatories of Charter 77, a major opposition movement with human rights agenda, came from the Czech Republic. These differences might help explain the different transitional justice approaches adopted by the Czech Republic and Slovakia.

Transitional Justice

The groundwork for transitional justice in the Czech Republic was laid in 1990–1993. Most of this time, the Czech Republic was part of the Czech and Slovak Federation, which was dissolved on December 31, 1992. The independent Czech Republic continued to implement transitional justice, although most of the laws it passed merely extended the Czechoslovak legal framework. Among the most important transitional justice methods it has adopted, in rough chronological order, are: rehabilitation; restitution and nationalization of property; lustration; symbolic condemnation; court trials; and access to the secret archives.

Rehabilitation

The first major law to deal with the past was Act 119 on Judicial Rehabilitation passed by the Federal Assembly in April 1990, just weeks prior to the first democratic elections. The Act sought to: (1) invalidate all of the communist regime's judicial decisions concerning political crimes; (2) eliminate disproportional hardship caused by repression; (3) provide social rehabilitation and adequate material compensation to affected persons; and (4) determine that persons who had violated the communist laws would face legal consequences. The Act further cancelled unjust criminal judgments concerning subversion, treason, and other political "crimes." Cases that did not clearly fall within the list of political crimes could be reopened. Former political prisoners were entitled to receive CSK 2,500 (US$95 in 1995) for each month of imprisonment and other additional remedies whose total could not exceed CSK 30,000 (US$1,145) per year. The period of detention/imprisonment was also considered for the purposes of recalculating pensions.

The Act was relatively well implemented, but it had several shortcomings. The first problem concerned the so-called outstanding punishments. Former political prisoners had usually been charged with political and "nonpolitical" crimes. While the former cases were annulled, the latter cases had to be reopened; this was particularly insensitive considering the elderly victims who, as a result of lengthy procedures, may not have cleared their names and/or received no compensation during their lifetime. Another problem was that victims received financial compensation up to a maximum of CSK 30,000, while the remaining amount was to be given to them in government bonds. Naturally, the depleted economy could hardly afford lump-sum payments. By contrast, members of the repressive apparatus received generous retirement packages. Many political prisoners were disappointed with the government compensating their secret policemen, prison wardens, and torturers.

The Law 87/1991 on Extra-Judicial Rehabilitation widened the scope of rehabilitation for people who had not been convicted of political crimes, but were victims of state persecution because they had been involved in democratic activities or were members of socioeconomic, religious, or other groups. The redress covered those who had been for such reasons imprisoned in labor camps, expelled from schools, or dismissed from employment.

The meager financial compensation and the limited number of persons entitled to such compensation have since led to the approval of other laws. These include Act 198/1993 on the Illegality of the Communist Regime and on the Resistance against It expanded compensation of former political prisoners by authorizing the government to issue directives to compensate former political prisoners. The first such compensation directive, Government Directive 165, was issued in 1997. Act 261/2001 compensated persons interned in military labor camps. Government Directive 102/2002 compensated persons in military camps of forced labor, including the infamous Auxiliary Technical Battalions, which detained persons who were deemed to be too politically unreliable to be drafted to the Czechoslovak People's Army. Act 172/2002 compensated persons abducted to the Soviet Union or detained in camps run by the Soviet Union in other states. Government Directive 122/2009 compensated university students who could not complete their education for political reasons, while Government Directive 135/2009 provided additional compensation to persons rehabilitated by the Rehabilitation Law of 1990 by granting them CZK 1,800 (US$89) for each month of their imprisonment or detention.

Restitution of Property

The Czech Republic implemented one of the most ambitious restitution programs in history. It aspired to return real (immovable) and personal (movable) properties, which were nationalized during the Communist Party rule and which were in possession of the state, to the original owners or their heirs. The most important was the Law on Extra-Judicial Rehabilitation, noted earlier. The government argued that the Act would only be concerned with alleviating some material injustices caused during the communist regime, thereby stating that full material compensation for communist injustices would be impossible. Prime Minister Marián Čalfa, who introduced the bill, argued that any delay in restitution would affect the stability of ownership rights and consequently impair the inflow of foreign direct investments. According to the Act, the state had to return property to citizens who were also permanent residents in the country.

The restitution of property had mixed effects. On the positive side, restitution was viewed – in contrast to other privatization methods – as a clean and transparent method of privatizing the state economy. On the other hand, restitution created problems. Those who had been forced to emigrate from the country and could not return were excluded from the restitution process. This effectively alienated many Czechoslovak émigrés. Furthermore, the litigation resulting from unsuccessful restitution claims significantly burdened the judiciary, including the Constitutional Court. Another problem associated with the restitution was a return of property with legal obligations from the past. Many properties were returned to the owner with tenants whose lease and rent were legally protected. This created a financial burden for the owner, who had to subsidize the tenants or otherwise provide them with alternative accommodation; there were uncertainties for tenants who feared for their future, as the government was gradually lifting regulated rent.

Another major property restitution issue was the restitution of churches and religious congregations. Although several relevant laws were passed and implemented, the issue has not been satisfactorily settled within the two decades following the fall of communism.

Nationalization of Property

Before November 1989, the Communist Party of Czechoslovakia (KSČ) and the Socialist Association of the Youth (SSM) used, or were in possession of, vast properties, such as administrative buildings, hospitals, and leisure facilities across the country. Governmental Directive 212/1990 prevented the Communist Party from using state-owned properties. Later, the newly elected Federal Assembly approved two constitutional laws that nationalized the property of the Communist Party of Czechoslovakia (Act 496/1990) and the Socialist Association of the Youth (Act 497/1990), thereby returning it to "the people." Parliament argued that both organizations unjustly possessed the property of the people and, for this reason, the property should be returned to the people. The reference to "the people" was not a coincidence: it was a symbolic rebuke of the organizations which were self-proclaimed champions of "the people" and frequently abused the word in its policies and rhetoric. Despite this, the Communist Party of Bohemia and Moravia – a successor of the Communist Party of Czechoslovakia in the Czech Republic – has a significant material base.

Lustration

Czechoslovakia was the first country to approve a Lustration Law (Act 451/1991 that Prescribes Certain Additional Prerequisites for the Exercise of Certain Positions Filled by Election, Appointment, or Assignment in State Organs and Organizations). In addition, the Czech National Council passed a minor lustration law (Act 279/1992 on Certain Additional Prerequisites for the Exercise of Certain Positions Filled by the Assignment or Appointment of the Members of the Police of the Czech Republic and Members of the Prison Service of the Czech Republic). The most frequently cited objectives of the Lustration Law mentioned by legislators during parliamentary debates were: personnel discontinuity and minimal justice; national security and public safety; the need to protect the rights of lustrated personnel and to regulate the process in order to prevent wrongful accusations; truth revelation; and the protection of the territorial integrity of the increasingly fragile Federation (David 2011).

The law had forward-looking and backward-looking dimensions. The backward-looking provisions defined those to whom the law would apply, and concerned a variety of fundamental communist-era bodies: the members of the State Security (StB, secret police); its collaborators at specified levels; Communist Party officials from a district level and above; the political management of the Corps of National Security; members of the paramilitary People's Militias; members of the purge committee, which facilitated the dismissal of hundreds of thousands of people from their employment in the aftermath of the communist takeover in 1948 and after the Soviet-led invasion to Czechoslovakia in 1968; and other groups. (Persons who held high-ranking positions in the Communist

Party during the Prague Spring of 1968 were exempt from the law.) The forward-looking elements of the law defined the positions from which persons who fell into the aforementioned categories would be barred: leading positions in the state administration, such as the Army, the Ministry of Defense, the Security and Information Service, the Police, the offices of the constitutional organs, the public media, and the management of state-owned enterprises. The requirements also concerned academic officials in management positions and applied to all judges, assessors, prosecutors, investigators, state notaries, and some security-sensitive concession-based trades.

Individuals who held or applied for a position specified by the act were required to submit both a certificate issued by the Ministry of Interior concerning their work for, or collaboration with, the secret police and an affidavit that they did not belong to other groups specified in the Act. If an individual belonged to any group specified in the Act, the person's superior was required to terminate his/her employment or otherwise to demote him/her to a position that went unspecified by the Act. There was no formal room for discretion for authorities to accept mitigating circumstances. The Lustration Law also stipulated higher legal protection. Any person could object to the termination of his/her employment at a second-level regional court and could appeal the decision at the High Court. Further guarantees were provided by existing laws. According to the Supreme Court, the truthfulness of the certificate issued by the Ministry could be challenged on the basis of civil procedures. Thereafter, a person could submit a constitutional complaint if his/her rights were encroached. The publication of the lustration certificate was impermissible without a written consent of the citizen.

The law was originally intended to be a transitional law valid for five years, until the new democracy became more stable. It was extended (Act 254/1995) for another five years in September 1995, and indefinitely extended in October 2000 (Act 422/2000).

Although all major political actors (except the communists) in the Federal Assembly agreed on the need to cleanse the state apparatus from the remnants of the former regime, they disagreed about its scope and method. President Václav Havel signed the original law, although he considered it too strict. Havel vetoed both extensions of the lustration laws because it delayed the approval of civil service law. In 1992, a group of opposition legislators challenged the law at the Constitutional Court, which nullified several provisions but upheld the law. In December 2001, it again upheld the law and its extension. Internationally, the law was initially criticized by human rights organizations, the International Labor Organization, the Council of Europe, the U.S. Department of State, journalists, and academics, who alleged that it discriminated on the basis of political opinion, constituted collective punishment, and was retrospective. Later, however, scholars and the European Court of Human Rights acknowledged the need for transitional states to conduct lustration.

Symbolic Condemnation

Parliament also approved several declaratory laws that aimed at the symbolic condemnation of the previous regime. Act 480/1991 on the Period of Non-Freedom declared that the communist regime of 1948–1989 violated human rights and its own laws. Act 198/1993 on the Illegitimacy of the Communist Regime and on the Resistance against It explicitly condemned the regime and hailed anticommunist resistance. The law was predominantly declaratory and enumerated injustices of the regime and condemned it, the regime, the Communist Party, and its supporters.

Prosecution and Criminality

Statutes of limitations were major obstacles to the prosecution of communist crimes. The new political elite sought to extend them, arguing that the communist state had not been interested in prosecuting executioners of its own crimes. For this reason, the Rehabilitation Act 119/1990 stipulated that the statute of limitation for communist-era crimes redressed by that law would not expire before January 1, 1995. In 1993, the Act on the Illegitimacy of the Communist Regime stated that the communist regime (1948–1989) could not be considered as a period of limitations for the purposes of the statute of limitations. A group of deputies considered this retroactive, and hence a violation of the rule of law, and requested the Constitutional Court to review the law. The Court upheld it.

In spite of the legal possibility to prosecute crimes, dismally low number of cases were prosecuted and punished. By 2008, the Office of the Documentation and Investigation of Crimes of Communism had completed the investigation of 97 cases concerning 123 persons and forwarded them to the District Attorney, who returned 32 cases for further investigation and initiated prosecution of 74 cases concerning 100 persons. Twenty of the seventy-four cases were returned to the attorney by the judge. The courts sentenced thirty persons, mostly members of the security apparatus; among them, eight received prison sentences (the longest being five years' imprisonment) and twenty-two received suspended sentences with a probation period.

File Access

Initially, the government did not allow people to learn of the identities of those who informed on them to the communist authorities. Capitalizing on that silence, former dissident Petr Cibulka published a leaked list of secret collaborators in 1992. Act 140/1996 on the Access to Files Created by Activity of the Former State Security allowed everyone to gain access to his/her file, although the names of the secret informers were blacked out. According to Act 107/2002, everyone also had access to the files of secret collaborators, and to other files, unless they posed a threat to persons or to interests of the Czech Republic and its security.

The law was very controversial: many liberal intellectuals feared the files were not reliable and that people would not be able to assess them critically. President Havel criticized the law, but signed it. In March 2003, the Ministry of the Interior officially published the names of all secret informers on its Web site. Several actors and singers (like Jirina Bohdalova), however, claimed that they did not collaborate with the secret police. After winning their court battle with the Ministry of the Interior, which was unable to provide acceptable evidence, information about them had to be removed from the lists.

The access to secret files further was expanded by Act 499/2004 (the Archives Law) and Act 181/2007, which also created an Institute for the Study of Totalitarian Regimes (see separate entry). Access to secret police files in the Czech Republic is now without major restrictions.

History Textbooks

Soon after the end of the communist regime, students received new textbooks that did not explicitly adhere to the Marxist-Leninist ideology, but the persistence of inherited historical stereotypes seems difficult to eradicate. Although not referring to the leading role of the Communist Party, a postcommunist revised edition of a history textbook originally from 1988 contained problematic ideological undertones. For instance, a chapter on ancient Mesopotamia mentioned that "the ruling class and the priests enriched themselves at the expense of other citizens" (Blažek 2005). The mother of an eleven-year-old pupil criticized the use of this textbook, objecting to "the support for the class hatred without highlighting the cultural contributions of ancient civilizations" (Blažek 2005).

Conclusion

A relatively large number of transitional justice measures have dealt with the communist past in the Czech Republic. The laws were of inconsistent quality. The implementation of transitional justice was poor in cases of prosecution of communist crimes; more than 200,000 people were condemned for political reasons (many of them in absentia) on the territory of the Czech Republic during the communist regime, but fewer than 10 individuals responsible for that regime's crimes were condemned to jail after 1989.

A nationwide opinion poll conducted in 2010 assessed the utility of transitional justice in the Czech Republic. Victim-centered reparatory measures were seen as the most efficient transitional justice policies, while property restitution, social acknowledgment and rehabilitation of victims, and their financial compensation were seen as the most successful policies (although, aside from the issue of property restitution – which 51 percent found successful – fewer than 50 percent of respondents considered each of the other measures successful). Punishment was viewed as the least successful policy, followed by lustration. In the overall assessment, 38.6 percent saw transitional justice as a success, while 24 percent disagreed (David 2010).

Roman David

Cross-references: Access to Secret Files; Ex Post Facto Issues; Lustration; Office for the Documenting and Prosecution of Crimes of Communism; Property Restitution; Rehabilitation of Political Prisoners; Reparations; Slovak Republic.

Further Readings

Blažek, J. 2005. Šesťáci mají dějepis plný třídního boje [The sixth class has history full of class struggle], *Mlada fronta Dnes*, December 16. Available at: http://zpravy.idnes.cz/sestaci-maji-dejepis-plny-tridniho-boje-fcq-/domaci.asp?c=A051215_210229_domaci_pat (accessed April 30, 2010).
Cepl, V. and M. Gillis. 1996. Making Amends after Communism. *Journal of Democracy*, 7(4): 118–124.
David, Roman. 2003. Lustration Laws in Action: The Evaluation of Lustration Policy in the Czech Republic and Poland. *Law & Social Inquiry*, 28(2): 387–439.
———. 2010. *Twenty Years of Dealing with the Past in the Czech Republic*. Dataset on file with the author.
———. 2011. *Lustration and Transitional Justice: Personnel Systems in the Czech Republic, Hungary, and Poland*. Philadelphia: University of Pennsylvania Press.
David, Roman and Susanne Y. P. Choi. 2005. Victims on Transitional Justice: Lessons from the Reparation of Human Rights Abuses in the Czech Republic. *Human Rights Quarterly*, 27(2): 392–435.

Nedelsky, Nadya. 2009. Czechoslovakia, and the Czech and Slovak Republics. In *Transitional Justice in Eastern Europe and the Former Soviet Union: Reckoning with the Communist Past*. Ed. Lavinia Stan. London: Routledge, pp. 37–75.

Priban, Jiri. 2007. Oppressors and Their Victims: The Czech Lustration Law and the Rule of Law. In *Justice as Prevention: Vetting Public Employees in Transitional Societies*. Eds. Alexander Mayer-Rieckh and Pablo de Greiff. New York: Social Science Research Council, pp. 309–346.

Denmark

Transitional justice in Denmark primarily revolves around the aftermath of World War II. The transitional justice measures adopted immediately after the occupation of Denmark by Nazi Germany from 1940 to 1945 focused on purging persons who in various ways had collaborated with the occupiers. Today, the history of the occupation is preserved by numerous museums and substantive research in the field is still conducted by a number of institutions.

The Repressive Past

Denmark was occupied by Nazi Germany in a swift operation on April 9, 1940. During the first years of the occupation, Germany gave Denmark favorable terms compared to the situation in the other occupied countries. The Danish government and parliament continued to function and retained most of the control over domestic policy. King Christian X remained the head of state, and the police and judicial system carried on their work under Danish authority. Germany was formally represented by a Reich Plenipotentiary (Reichsbevollmächtigter).

The Danish government remained in place until August 29, 1943. By then, the population had become increasingly hostile to the Germans and the resistance movement had become more active. Following a series of strikes, mass demonstrations, and sabotage in August 1943 (the so-called August Rebellion), the Germans presented the Danish government with an ultimatum demanding that the death penalty be instituted in cases of sabotage. The government refused, and as a result it was dissolved by the Germans, who then instituted martial law. The Danish politicians did not form a new government, because at this point a continuance of the previous government's collaborative policy (*samarbejdspolitik*) was against the prevailing public opinion. Instead, the daily affairs of the various departments of the government were left in the hands of the highest-ranking public servants, the permanent secretaries (*departementschefstyret*). They had no authority to make political decisions and were meant to merely keep the administration going in a nonpolitical manner. A committee of thirteen key politicians (*13-mandsudvalget*) supervised their work and was consulted in all matters of importance. The Danish Parliament did not reconvene until the country was liberated on May 5, 1945 by British forces.

The Crimes

On June 22, 1941 – the date of the launch of the German invasion of the Soviet Union – the German forces demanded that all Danish communists be arrested. The Danish government, still functioning at that point, complied with the request. Using secret registers, 339 communists were arrested by the Danish police and detained in a work camp in Horserød. Subsequently, about half of them were transferred to the Stutthof concentration camp in Poland, where twenty-two of them died. On August 22, 1941, a unanimous Danish Parliament issued the Communist Act, which lifted the immunity of three communist members of Parliament, allowed detention of suspected communists, and banned communist parties and organizations in Denmark. On September 8, 1941, the Danish Supreme Court stated that the Act was constitutional. However, there has been general agreement that at least parts of the Act violated the Danish Constitution.

After the fall of the government in 1943, Denmark was fully subjected to the Nazi regime. Following a decree from Hitler, the Germans carried out a countrywide raid against all Danish Jews on the night between October 1 and 2, 1943. Assisted by Danish civilians, however, the vast majority of the Jews escaped to neutral Sweden.

As a result of controversies between the police force and the occupying authorities regarding the participation of Danish policemen in anti-regime sabotage, the Germans arrested 1,960 of the 10,000 Danish police officers in September 1944. They were subsequently deported, first to the Neuengamme concentration camp and later on to Stutthof/Buchenwald. The Danish police force was dissolved, and the police work in Denmark was taken over by the Germans.

In total, approximately 850 members of the resistance movement were killed in action, in concentration camps, or by execution during the occupation. About 1,000 Danish citizens were killed in air raids, during civil disturbances, or in reprisal killings (known also as clearing-murders). The groups that suffered the most fatalities were sailors and fishermen, who continued their work during the war. About 1,000 were killed, most of them by submarines. In addition, 850 sailors lost their lives in the service of the Allies.

Transitional Justice

On the morning of May 5, 1945, a "liberation government" comprising politicians and members of the resistance movement presented itself to the public. First and foremost, it instigated the purge of the Danish collaborationists. Otherwise, Denmark generally returned to the form of government that was in place before the war. As soon as May 9, 1945, Parliament reopened with – for the most part – the same members as before the government stepped down in 1943. The continuity in the political system was remarkable and illustrated that Denmark was privileged in comparison with other occupied countries. The "liberation government" remained in power until a general election was held in October 1945.

The Purge of Collaborationists

The legal framework of the purge was issued by the Danish parliament according to ordinary procedure. However, the drafting process and the content of the relevant acts were unusual. The first initiatives to the purge had already been taken during the last period of the occupation. In the autumn of 1943, a leading group of the resistance movement, the Freedom Council (Frihedsrådet) had published a pamphlet titled *When Denmark Is Free Again*, which laid down some principles to be followed in a purge after the war. According to the Freedom Council, the existing legislation was insufficient and needed to be supplemented in order to encompass all the kinds of collaborationism that had taken place.

Afterward, efforts to draft new legislation were made by both the legal committee of the Freedom Council and a group of civil servants. The latter was established by politicians, who until August 1943 had been responsible for the policy toward the German occupants. The two groups disagreed on the extent to which the legislation should be applied retroactively. In the end, the resistance fighters prevailed, and the new provisions of the Civil Criminal Code were given retroactive force throughout occupation of Denmark. However, acts committed in compliance with statutes and orders enacted by Danish authorities from April 9, 1940 to August 29, 1943 were exempted from punishment. Another point of disagreement was whether the collaborationists should be judged by special tribunals or ordinary judges. On this matter the original draft was amended after the war. The resistance movement's proposal for special tribunals was abandoned, and ordinary judges were appointed to handle the cases.

Immediately after the liberation in May 1945, the official preparations of the purge began. The Civil Criminal Code and the Administration of Justice Act were amended by Act 259 of 1 June 1945 on Amending the Civil Criminal Code Regarding Treason and Other Threats to the State, which listed the crimes with which the collaborationists could be charged, and Act 260 of 1 June 1945 on Amending the Administration of Justice Act Regarding the Processing of Cases on Treason and Other Threats to the State, which established the rules on the election of judges for the cases under Act 259.

The first sentences that were delivered were generally severe and took as their starting point the minimum sentence of four years prescribed by section 3 of Act 259. This practice gave rise to substantial public criticism and protests that the jail sentences tended to be too long. Nevertheless, as a result of political objections and lack of political will, the minimum sentence was not lowered until June 1946, when The Civil Criminal Code was amended by Act 356.

Denmark signed the London Treaty on the Prosecution and Punishment of Major War Criminals in September 1945. In July 1946, Act 395 of 12 July 1946 on Punishment for War Crimes was passed. Of the seventy-seven criminals tried under this act, seventy-one were sentenced to punishments from one year imprisonment to death. None of these death sentences were executed. The leading German war criminals – Reich Plenipotentiary Dr. Werner Best, the Higher SS-Führer Günther Pancke, and the Chief of Police Otto Bovensiepen – were charged with war crimes, and more specifically killings, interrogation methods entailing serious abuse, and deportation. They were all convicted by the Danish Supreme Court on March 17, 1950, and received prison sentences of twelve years, twenty years, and life, respectively.

In total, approximately 40,000 people were arrested on suspicion of collaboration (including economic collaboration), propaganda, service to the German military or police, service as informants to the Germans, and other charges. Of these, 13,521 received some kind of punishment, and many were convicted of more than one crime. The largest group by far was composed of those convicted for armed collaboration. Thus, 7,500 received prison sentences for having served in various armed bodies with relation to the occupiers, including active service at the front (about 3,000) and service as airport guards or in other German military installations (4,500). Approximately 2,000 were punished for their service with the German police or police-like units. Approximately 1,100 were sentenced to prison for their work as informers, and about 600 for serious crimes such as murder or violence committed in the interest of the occupiers. Some 1,100 were found guilty of economic collaboration, whereas 600 (including the 50 leaders of the Danish

National-Socialist Party) were imprisoned for having helped the enemy in different ways. Seventy-eight were sentenced to death, but of these death sentences only forty-six were carried out. The majority of the convicted collaborationists received prison sentences of less than four years.

In 1947, the Danish state started a practice of pardoning. It primarily benefited individuals who had received longer sentences as most minor collaborationists had already served their time and been released. About 26 percent of all prisoners (approximately 3,600) served their full sentence. The authorities responsible for pardons were the Ministry of Justice and the Appeals Board of 1 June 1945. The Appeals Board was charged with the task of reviewing judgments with a view to determining whether there was reason to reduce the sentences. In relevant cases, the board would submit its recommendation to the Ministry of Justice. In addition, the Ministry of Justice instigated the so-called half-time pardons, which meant that collaborationists who had served half of their sentence were eligible for a pardon on the king's birthday or the Danish national day. By 1953, the last war criminals had been released from Danish prisons, whereas the last person convicted under the amendments to the Civil Criminal Code was released in 1960.

There has been considerable criticism of the Danish purge. One serious charge is that too many people served too severe sentences, and that the "big fish" who were tried at a late stage were given a more lenient treatment that the "smaller fish" who were the first to stand trial. In addition, it has been argued that not enough consideration was given to the fact that the official Danish policy had been based on cooperation until the autumn of 1943.

Financial Compensation to Victims

The Act on Compensation for the Victims of the Occupation Period (Lov om erstatning til besættelsestidens ofre, cf. Consolidated Act 136 of 23 February 1995 amended by Act 1018 of 4 December 1996) was originally passed in October 1945 and remains in force. Section 1(1) prescribes that Danish citizens are to be financially compensated if they incurred disease or injury during the time from April 9, 1940 to the end of the war, and therefore have suffered loss in their ability to work. The disease or injury must be a result of acts of war in Denmark, including searches, arrests, internments, and deportations carried out by the occupying power.

The Act primarily defined the victims of the occupation period as Danish citizens who: (1) were deported to a prison or a concentration camp abroad; (2) served for at least six months on Danish or foreign ships under allied control in war-zone waters; (3) were actively involved in the work of the resistance movement in Denmark for at least one year, if this work produced significant physical or psychological damage; and/or (4) sailed on Faeroese fishing boats or fish transportation ships in war-zone waters for at least six months in order to transport war supplies to allied ports outside of the Faroe Islands. Persons, including surviving family, who showed "nationally unworthy behavior" were not eligible for compensation. The Act is now fully administered by the National Board of Industrial Injuries (Arbejdsskadestyrelsen).

Truth-Seeking Mechanisms and Archives

Truth seeking regarding the German occupation of Denmark has been – and still is – primarily undertaken by academics. The Danish State Archives collect and store historical sources and make them available to the public. The State Archives include, for example, private accounts from resistance fighters and papers and other materials from the occupation period. In 1998, the creation of a database (Guide to the Museums and Archives of the Occupation Period) containing all significant material from 1940 to 1945 was initiated. Most of the collections from the Resistance Museum and the Danish State Archives have already been registered, but the conclusion of the project is still some years ahead. It aims to publish all the information online. Also, the archives of the Museum of Danish Resistance can be used for study purposes by professional researchers as well as private individuals. A number of privately owned archives and collections such as the Historical Collection from the Occupation Period (Historisk Samling fra Besættelsestiden 1940–45) exist as well.

Preservation of Memory

One of the official Danish "flag days" is April 9. The flag is at half-mast on all public buildings until noon to mark the first day of the German occupation in 1940. Another flag day is May 5. On the eve of the liberation, May 4, it is tradition to put lit candles in the windows to symbolize the end of the blackouts during the war. Many Danes still follow this tradition.

The German occupation of Denmark from 1940 to 1945 is probably the best-described period in Danish history, and it continues to be the subject of substantive research. The memory of the occupation is preserved, for example, by numerous museums across Denmark. Some, like the Resistance Museum in Copenhagen, also undertake research. In addition, research in the field is conducted by several institutions, including the Danish Institute for International Studies, Holocaust and Genocide.

Conclusion

The German occupation of Denmark and the transitional justice measures that were subsequently adopted continue to be the subject of considerable research and public debate. During the past decades, substantial research has been conducted regarding the popular memory of the occupation period. In 2004, a member of parliament officially requested that the prime minister establish a truth commission based on the South African model, which was to shed light on various aspects of the occupation and particularly the collaborative policy. The prime minister at the time responded that while the occupation is one of the most thoroughly studied periods of Danish history, there may still be aspects of the collaborative policy that need further scrutiny. However, he did not find it appropriate to establish a truth commission.

With a view to contributing to transitional justice in other countries and ensuring that Denmark will not serve as safe haven for perpetrators of serious crimes committed abroad, a Special International Crimes Office (Statsadvokaten for Særlige Internationale Straffesager) was set up in 2002 as a part of the Danish Prosecution Service. The office is nationally responsible for investigating and possibly prosecuting serious crimes, including genocide, crimes against humanity, war crimes, terrorism, and torture, committed abroad by persons residing in Denmark.

Pertaining to future prospects of transitional justice, there is an ongoing public debate on whether measures should be adopted with regard to the Danish colonial administration in Greenland. For example, a Greenlandic member of the Danish parliament requested in August 2009 that the prime minister officially apologize to twenty-two Greenlandic children who, in an experiment conducted in the early 1950s, were forcibly removed from their parents and placed with Danish foster parents or in orphanages. The prime minister refused further action on the matter and stated that "the Danish government regards the colonial era as a concluded part of the common history of Denmark and Greenland" (Unofficial Translation of Prime Minister Lars Løkke Rasmussen's Answer 2009). When it comes to responding to the forced removal of children from Aboriginal communities, Denmark has yet to match Canada and Australia (see entries on Indian Residential Schools Truth and Reconciliation Commission/Pensionnats indiens Commission de Verite et de Reconciliation [Canada]; Truth Commission into Genocide in Canada; and National Inquiry into the Separation of Aboriginal and Torres Strait Islander Children from their Families, the Stolen Generations Inquiry [Australia]).

Astrid Kjeldgaard-Pedersen

Cross-references: Access to Secret Files; Compensation Packages; Complicity; Court Trials for Redress; Germany – the Nazi Past; National Inquiry into the Separation of Aboriginal and Torres Strait Islander Children from their Families, the Stolen Generations Inquiry (Australia); Purges; Special International Crimes Office; Truth (Truth Seeking and Truth Telling); Truth and Reconciliation Commission, Canada: Truth Commissions.

Further Readings

Kirchhoff, Hans. 2004. *Samarbejde og modstand under besættelsen – En politisk historie* [Collaboration and Resistance during the Occupation Period – A Political Story]. Odense: Syddansk Universitetsforlag.
Kirchhoff, Hans and Jens Andersen. eds. 2002. *Gads Leksikon om dansk besættelsestid 1940–45* [Gad's Encyclopedia on the Period of Occupation in Denmark]. Copenhagen: Gads Forlag.
Tamm, Ditlev. 1985. *Retsopgøret efter besættelsen* [The Purge after the Occupation Period]. 2 volumes, 2nd edition. Copenhagen: Jurist- og Økonomforbundets Forlag.
Unofficial Translation of Prime Minister Lars Løkke Rasmussen's Answer of 18 August 2009 to Question no. S2770 Posed by MP Juliane Henningsen on August 10, 2009. Available at http://www.ft.dk/samling/20081/spoergsmaal/s2770/svar/641544/714409.pdf (accessed November 17, 2009).

East Timor

Transitional justice mechanisms were implemented in East Timor in the wake of violent reactions to the UN-supervised popular referendum held in August 1999, when a considerable majority of the population expressed its desire for political independence from Indonesia. Given that many of those suspected of human rights violations had relocated to Indonesia, the main obstacles faced by transitional justice in East Timor concerned limited national jurisdiction and the Indonesian government's reluctance to cooperate.

The Repressive Past

In the beginning of the sixteenth century, East Timor became a colony of Portugal. Despite skirmishes with the Dutch and the British, Portugal kept its grasp on the Timorese territory until 1974, when the Carnation Revolution upset the Portuguese political landscape (see entry on Portugal). The toppling of Portuguese dictator Antônio de Oliveira Salazar's authoritarian government triggered the extinction of Portuguese colonies overseas.

In 1975, in the aftermath of the Vietnam War, the Western world was shocked by the victory of the communist North over the United States-backed South. The power struggle in East Timor was shaped by these turbulent times of extreme political polarization between communism and capitalism. On August 11, 1975, the recently established pro-capitalism party, the Timorese Democratic Union (União Democrática Timorense, UDT), launched an armed campaign in the Timorese capital, Dili, prompting reaction from the opposing communist party, the Revolutionary Front of an Independent East Timor (Frente Revolucionária de Timor-Leste Independente, Fretilin), igniting a civil war that, in turn, left deep scars in the country's political history. This episode ended in November 1975 with Fretilin the victor and a unilateral declaration of independence, reflecting the tone of communist discourse.

As a reaction to this movement, other political organizations in East Timor were quick to claim Portuguese Timor's integration into Indonesia through the Declaration of Balibó of November 1975. Already before this date, Indonesia had commenced military operations along its frontiers with East Timor, aimed at undermining the country's weak government. Mohammed Suharto's dictatorship in Indonesia, avowedly anticommunist, was considered the best antidote against the expansion of communism in Asia and accordingly received strong support from the United States and Australia.

Indonesia finally overthrew the Fretilin government on December 7, 1975, initiating an occupation that lasted twenty-four years and was never considered legitimate by the United Nations. Indonesian forces brutally cracked down on surviving oppositional forces. In the late 1970s, the Indonesian government deployed its military forces to eliminate Fretilin's armed resistance movement ensconced in the countryside. These incursions resulted in gross human rights violations against the armed opposition and the civil population. In the 1980s, resistance to Indonesian occupation was reorganized as a guerilla movement and obtained increasing clandestine support in villages scattered throughout the countryside. As Timorese society became more militarized and increasing numbers of young people were armed, levels of violence surged dramatically. Human rights violations were committed by militants fighting both for and against independence, despite the latter's clear military and logistical superiority. Among the massacres that victimized segments of the pro-resistance population was the Santa Cruz Massacre, in Dili, in November 1991. Nearly 200 people were killed by Indonesian troops during a peaceful memorial procession to the Santa Cruz Cemetery. The massacre, reported by two foreign journalists, drew considerable international attention.

During the years of Indonesian occupation, the resistance movement overcame the polarization between communists and pro-capitalists and greatly expanded. Fretilin was replaced by the National Council for the Reconciliation of Timor. This entity reflected the shift away from the movement's original identification with communism toward a language of nationalism and pacifism.

Suharto remained as head of the Indonesian government until 1998 and, despite growing attention from the international community, the political deadlock with East Timor remained unresolved. With the end of the Suharto regime, the United Nations mediated agreements between Portugal and Indonesia, a process that culminated with the referendum of August 30, 1999, in which 78 percent of the East Timorese population chose independence over autonomy, despite the militia's threats and intimidation in favor of Indonesian occupation. The massive mobilization of the pro-independence movement was met by harsh violent action of militias backed materially and logistically by the Indonesian police and military. According to the UN, 250,000 Timorese were forced to flee to the island's western areas, hundreds of civilians were assassinated, and 80 percent of the country's infrastructure was burned down by militiamen.

On October 25, 1999, the UN Security Council established the United Nations Transitional Administration in East Timor (UNTAET) with the goal of rebuilding destroyed facilities and creating basic conditions for political independence. For the first time in its history, the UN assumed total administration of a national government, taking on all executive, legislative, and judicial functions. Brazilian diplomat Sérgio Vieira de Melo came to personify the UN government of East Timor. East Timor finally became independent on May 20, 2002, a date that also marks the conversion of UNTAET into the United Nations Mission of Support in East Timor (UNMISET), an organization conceived to provide assistance to the country's government and assure local political stability.

Transitional Justice

Transitional justice in East Timor ensued shortly after the violent episodes of 1999 and was intended to identify and/or punish its perpetrators. Although organizations such as the Commission on Reception, Truth and Reconciliation have defined the 1974–1999 period as subject to investigation, in practice, efforts have been concentrated on more recent cases of rights violations. Transitional justice has been carried out in a composite manner, combining two distinct methods to deal with the problems arising from social trauma. The first method focuses on restoration and is based on the premise that the conditions for keeping peace are paramount, even if this requires placing lesser emphasis on the punishment of those responsible. The second method, guided by the premise of retribution, mobilized traditional judicial procedures and was grounded on the expectation of punishment.

The Restorative Model

The formal justice system put in place by the UN in East Timor after the violent outbursts in 1999 was extremely fragile and unprepared to deal with the quantity and complexity of cases of alleged violence. The provisional government deemed it convenient to combine court procedures with the restorative method practiced by truth commissions in other transitional regimes. Not only is restorative justice sensitive to local cultural variations, it is also considered a quicker and more cost-effective way of dealing with past human rights violations.

The Commission on Reception, Truth and Reconciliation (CRTP; see separate entry), the United Nations' main effort in this area, was established in 2001 (through UNTAET Regulation 2001/10) after the Congress of the National Council of the Timorese Resistance, which took place in 2000. Importantly, this commission's mandate excluded the investigation and judgment of more serious crimes, which were left for the Panels for Serious Crimes and for the Serious Crimes Unit (see separate entry), both of which were units of the hybrid tribunal described later.

In East Timor, the restorative method was set up in a social situation where victims and perpetrators were likely to know each other. This is because many of the young Timorese who fought against independence as members of the lower ranks of the Indonesian militias were recruited from the villages that eventually became the targets of their aggression. Most of them never returned to their villages for fear of retribution and afterward were forced to live in precarious exile conditions elsewhere in the country. Others returned and resumed a tense daily life, as face-to-face interaction with their erstwhile victims was frequently unavoidable. Both situations were far from ideal for the restoration of peace.

Given this context, the restorative method concentrated on producing the conditions for former aggressors to return to their original social environments. It was expected that confrontation between victims and confessed aggressors would provide a cathartic ritual and stabilize social relations. The revelation of truth was therefore associated with the goal of reconciliation. The victims were called on by commissioners to forgive their former aggressors and to produce deals to compensate the community for its sufferings. This was meant to minimize future conflict and quell feelings of vengeance.

The criticism of this restorative model can be summed up in two main arguments. The first one states that CRTP rituals better served the interests of confessing aggressors, who by doing so escaped judicial prosecution, than of victims, who received minimal compensation for their suffering and none of the explanations they felt deserved. Perhaps feeling pressured by an atmosphere in which the commissioners were overwhelmingly focused on reconciliation, many victims might have publicly shown support yet been opposed to it in private. Another criticism relates to the commission's mandate, which was incapable of satisfying the demand for truth because the jurisdiction of the commission was limited only to minor criminal offenses. As a result of this limited mandate, the CRTP concentrated its investigative efforts on the actions of lower-echelon soldiers, sparing their leaders.

The restorative principle was also embodied in the Commission of Truth and Friendship (CTF; see separate entry), established in 2005. Unlike the CRTP, which was linked to the UNTAET, the CTF was binational, jointly created by the Indonesian and Timorese governments, as the latter had achieved independence at this point. This commission, which ended its work in 2008, had the double mission of establishing a conclusive truth concerning the serious rights violations that took place in 1999 and recommending actions that could contribute to peace.

Although it had the power to grant amnesty, much like the Truth and Reconciliation Commission in South Africa (see separate entry), it did not do so. Rather, it prioritized the attribution of institutional – not individual – responsibility for the violent episodes of 1999. The underlying assumption was that individual criminals were acting according to a clearly defined institutional context, and therefore the violence had not been the result of random, isolated, or spontaneous action. In line with CRTP's conclusions, the CTF's report held that the 1999 violence in East Timor was orchestrated by the civil and military arms of the Indonesian government and involved an asymmetry of power between pro-autonomy militias, acting in tandem with Indonesian interests, and pro-independence groups, linked to the Timorese. According to the report, Indonesian institutions coordinated with militias in East Timor, providing them with logistical and material support, with full awareness of the gravity and extent of the violence. In sum, it became clear that there had been well-organized cooperation based on the common political objective of eliminating the pro-independence movement.

The CTF's activities were very controversial. The prerogative of granting amnesty combined with the holding of private hearings with witnesses and individuals suspected of rights violations aroused strong suspicion concerning the commission's true objective. Collecting testimony in private, shielded from public scrutiny, seemed to contradict the formal objective of producing the truth. Criticism subsided with the publication of the commission's report, which renounced the possibility of amnesty and kept to the purpose of clarifying past events and making recommendations for the reconciliation process.

Although the restorative method in East Timor used different institutional forms and occurred in distinct political periods, there is a common strand in critiques of the CRTP and CTF. Both are said to have produced frustration because they did not reach the leaders who ordered the abuses that occurred during the 1999 violence.

The Retributive Method / Retributive Justice

After the 1999 public referendum, the UN sent an Investigation Committee to East Timor with the mission of investigating recent episodes of violence and recommending ways to deal with past crimes and judge those responsible. The International Criminal Court's recommendation of investigating the crimes committed at the time of the referendum – following the framework of the International Criminal Tribunal for the former Yugoslavia and of the International Criminal Tribunal for Rwanda – was not followed. Instead of a court, the UN suggested two institutional solutions: one consisted of asking the Indonesian government to create an ad hoc court to try suspects of serious crimes committed in East Timor, and the other involved the creation of a hybrid tribunal model to be based in Dili, the capital of East Timor. This experiment would later inspire transitional justice methods/institutions in Cambodia and Sierra Leone (see entries on Cambodia; Hybrid Tribunals; International Criminal Court; International Criminal Tribunal for the Former Yugoslavia; International Criminal Tribunal for Rwanda; Sierra Leone).

With regard to the first option, the Indonesian government, yielding to international pressure, created a national ad hoc court, based in Jakarta, to judge suspects. This was supposed to be the flagship court for the condemnation of the criminals associated with the serious crimes in 1999, who had moved to Indonesian territory. Although the court ultimately condemned six of those accused of crimes against humanity, it received strong criticism for not delivering the expected results.

According to David Cohen (2003), the successful yet few condemnations ultimately processed by the court must be attributed to the personal commitment of judges who withstood an openly hostile political environment and carried on with the prosecutions, and not to the efficacy of the judicial system, which failed as a whole. Among its failures, Cohen pointed to its neglect of relevant witnesses and available evidence. Moreover, by failing to identify those responsible, it did little to undermine the Indonesian version of events, which downplays the possibility of orchestrated violence in 1999. According to the Indonesian government, the violence in East Timor was the result of the clash between pro- and anti-integration armed groups, in which no Indonesian security units participated.

This version, however, sharply contrasts with the findings of the International Commission of Inquiry for East Timor and the Truth and Friendship Commission (see separate entries). Most importantly, its findings also contradicted those reached by the Commission of Human Rights Abuses in East Timor (KPP HAM; see separate entry), which had been appointed by the Indonesian National Commission on Human Rights (Komnas HAM), and whose conclusions served as the legal base for the creation of the ad hoc court.

The Indonesian ad hoc court was not the only judicial response to the crimes in East Timor. The experiment with a hybrid tribunal in East Timor ensued a few months after the UNTAET was installed and became part of the endeavor to rebuild the national justice system. This involved shared responsibility between the judicial institutions of East Timor and the UN. Despite this formal resolution, the international facet of the court became more salient because the Timorese were not fully prepared to deal with institutional procedures foreign to their traditional practices.

The tribunal was composed of three complementary units: the Special Panels for Serious Crimes, the Serious Crimes Unit, linked to the Office of the General Prosecutor of the Republic Timor-Leste, and the Public Defenders' Office.

The Special Panels for Serious Crimes were created in May 2000 (through UNTAET Regulation 2000/15) and were based at the Dili District Court, which was created shortly before by the UN (UNTAET Regulation 2000/11) as part of the effort at institutional reconstruction. The Special Panels, constituted by two working units, were given exclusive jurisdiction to deal with accusations of genocide, war crimes, crimes against humanity, torture, and sex crimes committed from January 1 to October 25, 1999. Each panel was composed of three judges, two foreign and one Timorese, according to the court's mixed composition rule.

The establishment of panels was connected with the creation of the Serious Crimes Unit (SCU, see separate entry), based at the East-Timor Office of the Prosecutor-General (UNTAET Regulation 2000/16). This is the court's UN-sponsored prosecutorial arm, whose personnel are mostly international employees. Despite its subordination to the Prosecutor-General, in practice the SCU maintained its operational autonomy.

The Public Defender's Office did not require special legislation and thus remained subordinated to Indonesian law that continued to be in effect during the transition period in East Timor (as long as it was compatible with human rights international standards). In contrast with the panels and the SCU, the Public Defender's Office did not rely on an international staff and was instead composed solely of Timorese lawyers. Note that when the UNTAET was established, the Timorese legal experts were mostly associated with the Indonesian government and had fled in fear of retaliation. Those who remained and were incorporated into the newly created structure did not have the professional experience required, as opposed to the international attorneys used to conducting prosecutions. The asymmetry between the defense and the prosecution – a departure from the international standards required for fair judicial procedures – drew much of the criticism aimed at the court.

Yet the core of dissatisfaction with the hybrid court – and the retributive paradigm as a whole – pertains to its failure to bring to justice the main responsible figures for the crimes of 1999 who took refuge in Indonesia. The objective of investigating the violent episodes of 1999 and punishing those responsible was defeated by the lack of cooperation from the Indonesian government, which refused to extradite witnesses and the accused to the court's seat in Dili. The court's limitations were further aggravated by the lack of resources for its functioning. Its funding was considerably lower than the amount received by ad hoc courts.

Conclusion

Transitional justice experiences in East Timor combined the retributive and restorative paradigms of justice in judicial and nonjudicial bodies, and involved the governments of East Timor and Indonesia. Despite the diversity of the institutional models and the specificity of the criticism aimed at each one of them, there is one source of discontent that is common to all: only criminals linked to the lower ranks of the concerted violence of 1999 were prosecuted. Except for the sentencing in Jakarta, those connected to the higher ranks of the Indonesian military who ordered the violence escaped judicial and nonjudicial efforts. Transitional justice in East Timor still carries the burden of this failure.

Cristina Buarque de Hollanda

Cross references: Cambodia; Commission for Reception, Truth and Reconciliation; Commission of Human Rights Abuses in East Timor; Commission of Truth and Friendship; Hybrid Tribunals; International Center for Transitional Justice; International Commission of Inquiry for East Timor; International Criminal Court; International Criminal Tribunal for the Former Yugoslavia; International Criminal Tribunal for Rwanda; Serious Crimes Unit, Office of the General Prosecutor of the Republic Timor-Leste; Sierra Leone; Truth and Friendship Commission; Truth and Reconciliation Commission, South Africa.

Further Readings

Cohen, David. 2003. *Intended to Fail: The Trials before the Ad Hoc Human Rights Court in Jakarta.* New York: International Center for Transitional Justice. Available at: http://www.ictj.org/images/content/0/9/098.pdf (accessed January 13, 2010).

Katzenstein, Suzanne. 2003. Hybrid Tribunals: Searching for Justice in East Timor. *Harvard Human Rights Journal*, 16 (Spring). Available at: http://www.law.harvard.edu/students/orgs/hrj/iss16/katzenstein.shtml (accessed January 13, 2010).

Silva, Kelly Cristiane da and Daniel Schroeter Simião, eds. 2007. *Timor-Leste por trás do palco: cooperação internacional e a dialética da formação do estado* [East Timor Backstage: International Cooperation and State Building in East Timor]. Belo Horizonte: Editora UFMG.

Ecuador

After experiencing a series of civilian and military dictatorships during the 1970s, from 1984 to 1988, Ecuador experienced systematic human rights violations at the hands of the right-wing Social Christian Party (Partido Social Cristiano), whose control over the judiciary hampered the prosecution of human rights violators and ensured their impunity. As many political and military leaders associated with the dictatorships retained significant political clout even after 1988, when the four-year administration of President Leon Febres Cordero Ribadeneira ended, investigations into human rights violations have been carried out mostly by the press and human rights organizations. Such work was often blocked by administrative and judicial state bodies, a frequent tactic in Ecuador where authoritarian practices and a culture of impunity have affected all efforts to bring to justice those responsible for past human rights violations.

Political Background

Human rights violations have characterized Ecuadorian politics since the country's birth in 1830. In the conflicts that were played out during the twentieth century, different groups fought for supremacy using any means at their disposal, often causing serious human rights abuses. From 1970 to 1972, President José María Velasco Ibarra held power as a "civil dictator" after dissolving the National Congress. In 1972–1976, General Guillermo Rodríguez Lara ruled as a single dictator, while in 1976–1979, a military triumvirate (comprising the Air Force commander Luis Leoro Franco, Army commander Guillermo Durán Arcentales, and Navy commander Alfredo Poveda Burbano) controlled the country.

During the military dictatorship of 1972–1979, human rights violations took the form of excessive use of force in repressing student protests and illegal detention of individuals demonstrating against the government. Repression of labor protests and strikes was the norm during this period. The most infamous violation of human rights was the Aztra Massacre of October 18, 1977, in which the police killed more than 100 workers of the Ingenio Aztra, a sugar cane plantation, who had occupied the company's offices to protest against poor working conditions. The exact number of victims is unknown, because many bodies were thrown into the boilers of the sugar plant or tossed into a river nearby. The perpetrators of the massacre were never prosecuted. The government completely controlled the judiciary, and the three rulers appointed the Supreme Court Justices. However, there is little evidence to suggest that human rights abuses were a focus of government policy or that an organized machinery of repression and extermination existed.

The return to democracy in 1979 heralded a new era dogged by instability and the power struggle between the traditional right (represented by the Social Christian Party) and a populist and progressive movement, named first the Concentration of People's Forces (Concentración de Fuerzas Populares) and then the Ecuadorian Roldosista Party (Partido Roldosista Ecuatoriano). The first democratically elected president, Jaime Roldós Aguilera (representing the Concentration), died tragically in a plane crash two years after taking office. The 1984 elections were won by the Social Christian leader Febres Cordero with the support of the right-wing electoral coalition National Restoration Front (Frente de Restauración Nacional). Febres Cordero's rule was characterized by systematic human rights violations.

Thus, the worst human rights violations took place not under the dictatorial regimes of the 1970s, but under the democratically elected regime of President Febres Cordero (1984–1988), backed by the United States. Initially accepted by the population, the government's authoritarian style and arbitrary application of punitive measures met the popular demand to address the security problem evidenced by high crime rates and the proliferation of subversive Marxist-leaning groups. The regime also played on the public's fear of the alleged subversive threat, magnified by the media and the state bureaucracy.

During the late 1970s and the early 1980s, subversive left-wing groups emerged in Ecuador. The most prominent was Alfaro Vive Carajo (AVC), whose members were targeted by the government in its fight against subversion. Despite staging bank robberies and abducting wealthy individuals, the AVC lacked strong military power and organizational structure. Formed in the early 1980s by upper-middle-class individuals and university student leaders, the AVC became most active after 1984, as a consequence of the radical policies of the Febres Cordero's right-wing government.

To combat the AVC, special police and army groups were formed to repress subversion and tackle political dissidence and left-wing groups. Fully backed by the government, these groups were offered rewards for the capture, dead or alive, of AVC leaders. This is why they went beyond their initial remit of combating subversion and targeted government opponents. In one incident that took place in 1987, the Socialist legislator Diego Delgado Jara was severely beaten and left for dead. Organized police and army groups multiplied under the banner of combating subversion and organized crime. These groups operated throughout the country, mostly in the cities of Quito and Guayaquil. Human rights violations such as torture, rape of prisoners, forced disappearances, and summary executions became commonplace. International security experts were also hired. Some of them (such as Ran Gazit) provided training in torture and repression methods. One year later, in 1988, Febres Cordero was accused, and absolved, of embezzlement, when it was found that these experts were paid from the public purse (see further discussion later in this entry).

The government intentionally exaggerated the insurgency phenomenon to incorporate intelligence and repression agencies like the Criminal Investigation Service, the Flying Police Squadrons, and the Special Army Operations Group into the state structures and to foster a climate of terror and fear in order to weaken and dismantle trade unions, workers' movements, opposition parties, newspapers refusing to toe the government line, Catholic priests identified as being close to working-class movements, and student organizations.

Reported cases of human rights violations soared between 1984 and 1988. There were 126 cases of homicide by the security forces, 240 people tortured, 200 people held incommunicado, 500 people arbitrarily deprived of their freedom, 7 citizens disappeared, and 100 homes illegally entered. The most notorious cases were those of teacher Consuelo Benavides Cevallos and the Restrepo Arismendi brothers (see later discussion).

Some of these cases went to the Inter-American Court of Human Rights, and President Fabián Alarcón Rivera (1997–1998) realized that the resulting case law, involving the search for the disappeared and the handing over of bodies, was unfavorable to his country. The Ecuadorian Attorney General Office preferred a monetary solution, whereby the victims' families received a total of around US$1 million. Because of this payoff, political groups involved in human rights violations felt less urge to investigate further. It was generally believed that the financial compensation would definitely close the human rights violations case, although from a legal standpoint their reopening could not be excluded. Ultimately, the government, through the Offices of the Public Prosecutor and the Attorney General, achieved impunity for the human rights violations of 1984–1988. The demands for justice and truth of the victims' relatives were reduced to mere financial claims.

Thus, the culture of impunity continued even after 1988, as those who violated human rights during the Febres Cordero regime retained significant political clout. Paradoxically, Febres Cordero himself acquired greater power once he left the presidency. (The Ecuadorian president is indirectly elected by the Congress.) As Mayor of Guayaquil (1992–2000) and Congressman (2000–2007), he exerted total control over the Supreme Court of Justice and the Office of the State General Prosecutor. Investigations into human rights violations were thus further hampered by the absolute power his party and close circle of friends wielded over the Ecuadorian justice system. Real power was exercised by those controlling the judicial functions and not those who had been democratically elected.

Since 2000, the Ecuadorian democracy was repeatedly destabilized by several failures and breakdowns, in which the Social Christians and Febres Cordero played pivotal roles. Many breakdowns resulted from the lawsuits the Social Christians filed against their political enemies. Indeed, all five presidents who succeeded Alarcón after 1998 have been subject to prosecution. Weeks after parliament removed him from the presidential office, Lucio Gutierrez spent the August 2005–January 2006 period in prison, charged with subversion.

Transitional Justice

Ecuador has adopted court proceedings, a truth commission, and financial compensation as transitional justice methods.

Court Proceedings

On December 4, 1985, Benavides Cevallos and farm worker Serapio Ordóñez were detained in the parish of Cube, the Esmeraldas province, by members of the Navy on suspicion of being linked to the AVC. Days later, Ordóñez was released. As the Ecuadorian authorities refused to disclose any information, Cevallos's family concluded that she was disappeared by the Navy. In 1988, the family confirmed that the body of an unidentified woman found with gunshot wounds three years earlier was Cevallos.

In August 1988, a multiparty Congress commission investigated this forced disappearance. Its report, published in January 1989, established that the Navy detained Cevallos on December 4, 1985, and registered her detainment six days later. She was immediately transferred to Quito and placed under police custody, a fact denied by the police. Then the Navy returned her to Esmeraldas, after subjecting her to torture and sexual assault. The report included the testimony of Ordóñez, who declared that he and Cevallos were detained and tortured by the Navy, and that the Navy compiled a false document supposedly signed by Cevallos, stating that she had been released in good health. The commission implicated seven Navy members, three police members, and three former ministers of the Febres Cordero government in Cevallos's detention and the deliberate attempt to cover up the truth about her death. The report was formally submitted to the Congress and the Supreme Court of Justice in January 1989. In May 1992, the Court agreed to hear the case. In 1995, ten years after Cevallos's death, the Court convicted two Navy officers and one lower-ranked Navy member of her death. Higher-ranking officers and former ministers implicated by the commission went unpunished. In response to this impunity, in 1996, a complaint was lodged by human rights organizations at the Inter-American Court of Human Rights (see entry on Organization of American States). The complaint was settled two years later with an agreement between the Ecuadorian state and the Cevallos family. The Court declared that the state had violated the rights enshrined in Articles 3, 4, 5, 7, 8, and 25 of the American Convention on Human Rights, while the agreement settled the nature and amount of reparations. The state was asked to continue its investigations and to punish all those found guilty of the human rights violations referred to in the ruling of the Inter-American Court.

The case of the Restrepo Arismendi brothers epitomizes the impunity of the Febres Cordero government. In January 1988, the police arbitrarily detained Carlos Santiago and Pedro Andrés Restrepo Arismendi, aged seventeen and fourteen, respectively. The boys were taken to the detention center of SIC-10, a repressive police group. After days of torture, one boy died. His brother was then killed to eliminate the surviving witness. From the outset, the state wove a complicated web of misleading information with the intention of hindering investigations into the killing. It used investigators to spy on the Restrepo family and report back to their superiors in the police. The location of the two bodies remains unknown, despite searches by the Offices of the Public Prosecutor, the Ombudsman, and the Attorney General. The case was filed with the Inter-American Human Rights Commission in August 1997. Facing the possibility of international condemnation, in May 1998, the Ecuadorian state accepted responsibility for the brothers' disappearance and deaths and agreed to prepare a detailed report on the events surrounding the disappearance, to prosecute the guilty parties who had yet to be convicted, to carry out an exhaustive search of Lake Yambo (where the bodies were allegedly dumped after being dismembered), and to pay an indemnity. The Inter-American Commission ratified this out-of-court agreement in October 2000.

One year after leaving office in 1988, Febres Cordero faced a lawsuit for embezzlement (noted earlier) related to hiring Israeli security expert Ran Gazit with money from the "Reserve Funds," a special non-audited account at the disposal of the president. Evidence showed that the services provided by Gazit consisted mainly of instructing the Ecuadorian police on torture and how to combat insurgent groups. The lawsuit ended with a stay of proceedings. This initiated the government's absolute control of the judicial system by means of legislative agreements establishing periodic changes among Supreme Court Judges.

Truth Commission

Executive Decree no. 305 of 3 May 2007 created the Truth Commission (see separate entry) made up of four reputable reputed human rights defenders with the mandate to investigate violations committed from 1984 to 1988 as well as isolated human rights violations perpetrated under subsequent governments. Despite its shortcomings and errors, the Commission's Report, submitted to the president on July 7, 2010, was the first serious attempt at uncovering and investigating the recurring and systematically suppressed human rights violations of 1984–1988. (Human rights violations committed during the military dictatorship of the 1970s have not been subject to investigation). At the time of this writing, none of the cases included in the Commission's Report has come to court.

Financial Compensation

The transitional justice process also consisted of the financial compensations, already mentioned previously, paid to victims' families in the cases of Consuelo Benavides and Restrepo Brothers, and amounting to US$1 million and US$2 million, respectively. At the time of this writing, no compensation packages have been offered to other individual victims or victims' groups.

Conclusion

Since the early 1990s, Ecuador has engaged in very limited transitional justice, as the attempts it made always served certain political purposes of the ruling elite. Furthermore, no effective results have been achieved with respect to prosecuting those in positions of command at the time when the human rights violations took place. The Truth Commission was perceived by the civil society as another means of achieving the government's political goals, especially with regard to the removal of the impunity enjoyed by those responsible for the serious human rights violations of the 1984–1988 period and subsequent isolated cases. As Correa's government is slowly losing credibility, in particular as a result of its inability to address the country's unemployment and to control crime, the work and results of the Truth Commission will likely be discredited, making any future transitional justice process very difficult.

Kai Ambos and Ramiro García Falconí

Cross-references: Truth Commission, Ecuador.

Further Readings

Ambos, Kai. 2008. *El marco jurídicio de la justicia de transición* [The Legal Framework of Transitional Justice]. Bogotá: Temis.
España Torres, Hugo. 2000. *The Witness*. Quito: Editorial El Conejo.
Inter-American Court of Human Rights. Benavides Cevallos v. Ecuador. Fund, Damages and Costs. Judgment of 19 June 1998. *Series C No. 38*.
Tamayo, Eduardo. 2008. *Cases of Resistance to Authoritarianism*. Quito: Alianet.

El Salvador

El Salvador's transitional justice began in the early 1990s, with a negotiated peace process sponsored by the United Nations to end a twelve year anti-insurgency civil war. Peace agreements were signed in 1991 and 1992 between government forces and left-wing guerrilla movement the Farabundo Martí National Liberation Front (Frente Farabundo Martí para la Liberación Nacional, FMLN). The agreements established that a truth commission would be set up, under UN auspices, to investigate the extreme military, paramilitary, and death squad violence that had claimed tens of thousands of lives over the preceding decade (see entry on Truth Commission, El Salvador). Its final report was the only one in Latin America that named specific perpetrators. The Commission was also empowered to make binding recommendations for lustration, victim reparations, and institutional reforms. The report and subsequent UN observer mission heralded important structural changes, including the downsizing of the Salvadoran armed forces, reorganization of its police force, and introduction of a Human Rights Ombudsperson's office. But justice measures were cut short by a sweeping amnesty law, passed just days after the truth commission report was published.

Overall, El Salvador illustrates the "peace for justice" trade-off. A relatively successful peace process was widely believed to require both early amnesty and subsequent continued impunity for past human rights violations. Successive Salvadoran governments since transition have defended amnesty as the cornerstone of continued peace and political stability. El Salvador was also an example of transitional justice without political replacement, as the peace accords did not bring about immediate elections. Although the FMLN was transformed into a recognized political party, the presidency and congress remained under the control of the right-wing National Republican Alliance (Alianza Republicana Nacionalista or ARENA) party. The first major political change came in 2009, when FMLN candidate Mauricio Funes was elected president. This prompted expectations in some quarters that official truth and justice policies might change. However, there has been relatively little visible social demand for addressing the past, in a country that also suffers from extremely high levels of social violence and continued poverty.

The Repressive Past

El Salvador's twelve-year-long political violence (1980–1992) was a confrontation between a revolutionary armed left and an exceptionally brutal counterinsurgency response, carried out by civil-military governments in informal alliance with right-wing death squads. Atrocities were committed on both sides. The army employed scorched-earth tactics in the countryside, and the FMLN used kidnapping, political assassination, and other violations of international humanitarian law in pursuit of their revolutionary objectives. The UN-sponsored Truth Commission found that state forces had been responsible for most fatal violence, attributing 80 percent of documented incidents to them and only 5 percent to the FMLN and its allies. A full death toll for the Salvadoran conflict is elusive. It is also difficult to draw an exact distinction between numbers of war dead and victims of human rights violations. Experts put the figure at 50,000 to 70,000 people. The UN estimated that by 1982, almost 1 million people – 20 percent of the total population – had fled the country or were internally displaced.

The violence employed during the war was both intense and extreme. Mutilated corpses were deliberately discarded in public spaces in order to sow terror among the civilian population. Repression was targeted only to a limited degree at political insurgents: a lack of formal structure and a largely rural population employed in plantation-style agriculture meant that violence against the organized left quickly spilled over into the settling of old scores over deep-rooted historical injustices. Right-wing death squads acted to defend the interests of a handful of powerful traditional elites, who saw their privileges threatened by the rise of social organizing in the countryside.

The Catholic Church, which took an early and outspoken role in defense of human rights, soon became a direct target of repression. Three of the most notorious war atrocities involved Church personnel. Two – the 1980 assassination of iconic San Salvador Archbishop Oscar Romero and the rape and murder of four U.S. churchwomen later that year – took place during the peak of violence. The final one, the 1989 murder of six Jesuit priests and two coworkers, was a watershed. The killings were carried out by an army patrol, under cover of an unexpected FMLN assault on the capital, San Salvador. Although unsuccessful, the FMLN operation proved that the anti-insurgency war had reached a stalemate. This fact, plus widespread international revulsion over the Jesuit killings, helped shift U.S. policy preferences toward a negotiated, rather than military, solution to the conflict. Within months, the Salvadoran authorities had been persuaded by U.S. advisers to accept the mediation of other Central American countries and the UN.

In the preceding decade, atrocities had been routinely denied by the national government and the U.S. authorities. El Salvador's conflict became a proxy war. The United States, concerned about the threat of communism in its "back yard," advised, directed, and bankrolled the Salvadoran counterinsurgency offensive from Washington and through an extensive diplomatic presence on the ground. But concerns over the Salvadoran military's human rights record eventually led the U.S. Congress to introduce certification requirements including demonstrable improvements in the human rights situation as a condition for further military aid. The question of human rights reporting and statistics became highly politicized, with Congress growing impatient with continued State Department denials of widely rumored atrocities. In one famous incident, U.S. journalist Mark Danner traveled to the northern village of El Mozote just days after its entire population – some 500 people, including 100 children – had been slaughtered by an army patrol. Only one villager survived to tell the tale. Danner's reporting, however, was brushed aside by U.S. embassy personnel, who claimed that it was simply too dangerous for them to travel to the area to verify Danner's account.

Transitional Justice

Truth measures were more prominent than formal justice efforts in El Salvador's negotiated political transition, although some military officers were forced into retirement in Latin America's closest equivalent of Eastern European lustration (see separate entry). Reparations have targeted former combatants more than civilians, with pensions and resettlement plans for the war wounded used as an incentive for demobilization.

Truth Telling

El Salvador's major truth initiative was the Truth Commission that worked from July to December 1992. The three Commissioners were internationals, as were many of their staff. This was intended to improve the Commissioners' own safety and ensure objectivity in a still polarized political situation. The commission heard testimony around the country and preserved anonymity without offering witness protection. In March 1993, it published its report, From Madness to Hope, which contained a selection of illustrative cases, named around forty military officers and several FMLN leaders, asked that all of them be banned from future public office, strongly criticized the Supreme Court's "glaring inability" to enforce the law, and recommended the replacement of all its judges. These measures were strenuously rejected, although both the FMLN and the government had endorsed the terms of the Commission's mandate in advance and had promised to respect its recommendations. The government was also extremely unhappy about the Commission's decision to name individual perpetrators, a policy it had tried to reverse in the weeks leading up to the report's release via intense lobbying of the UN.

It was not until the United States threw its weight behind the pressure for resignations that the army command was restructured in June 1993. A second commission, known as the Ad Hoc Commission, had been working alongside the better-known Truth Commission. The Ad Hoc Commission, which was made up of three Salvadoran civilians, reviewed service records and made recommendations for dismissals on the basis of human rights considerations. This mechanism, also included in the peace accords, was a last-minute compromise. The promise that the armed forces would be purged had persuaded the FMLN to abandon its previous insistence on its militants being allowed to enlist in the regular army after transition. The Ad Hoc Commission's final report, containing 103 names (including those of the serving Defense Minister and most of the high command), was completed in September 1992, months before the Truth Commission report. The list caused controversy and tension in government circles. Then the Truth Commission report came out, reinforcing the Ad Hoc Commission's findings. After the United States threatened to cut off military aid until restructuring was carried out, the named officers were finally retired, on full pensions.

Institutional Reform and Democratization

Institutional change was the least direct but perhaps the most successful area of Salvadoran transitional justice. The country continues to suffer from high levels of poverty and common criminality, but the installation of the basic infrastructure of a democratic state was a substantial achievement. Fragile transitional compromises held across a range of areas. The FMLN became a recognized political party, and the strength of the regular army was substantially reduced. The various militarized police forces were replaced by a single National Civilian Police, to which former FMLN combatants could apply to be admitted. Judicial reform continued, and over time the introduction of congressional approval of appointments led to the admittance into the judiciary of some progressive figures associated with the local human rights community. To underline its new commitment, El Salvador signed up to a significant number of international human rights treaties and set up a Human Rights Ombudsman's office to monitor state performance.

Justice in the Form of Prosecutions

Justice measures in El Salvador have largely been restricted to the nonjudicial purging mechanism mentioned earlier. Even this was later partially reversed, as some named individuals appealed against their bans from public office. They successfully claimed it was unconstitutional to suspend their political rights on the basis of a nonjudicial process.

Formal justice in the form of trials was extremely scarce in El Salvador both before and after transition. Although the United States and others generously funded reform of the country's rickety judicial system during the war, its investigative capacity, professionalism, and impartiality remained highly questionable. In the 1980s, FMLN perpetrators were occasionally imprisoned on the basis of forced confessions, but when the violence came from the government's side, the tendency was to produce sporadic verdicts seemingly designed for international consumption. Three low-level national guardsmen were tried and imprisoned in 1984 for the murder of the U.S. churchwomen, but the question of higher orders was not explored. The complete failure of efforts to investigate the killing of Archbishop Romero is perhaps explained by the fact that Roberto d'Aubuisson, named by the Truth Commission as having ordered the assassination, was the founder of the ruling ARENA party and an influential military figure.

The third emblematic killing of the 1980s, the Jesuit murders, again produced an erratic trial outcome. The original state prosecutors resigned, alleging official obstruction of their investigation. They later had to leave the country after receiving death threats, as did the judge. The verdicts had little legal or logical coherence, with one soldier found innocent of crimes to which he had confessed, and others exonerated for only some of the eight simultaneous killings. The perpetrators were initially sentenced to more than twenty years, but it was widely known that an amnesty law was in the pipeline and that the sentences were unlikely to be fully served. Indeed, shortly after the convictions and just days after the publication of the Truth Commission report, the Salvadoran congress rushed through Legislative Decree 486, the General Law for the Consolidation of Peace. This broad amnesty law sought to extinguish civil and criminal liability (Article 4c), as well as rule out sanctions for some kinds of judicial malpractice.

An early domestic challenge to the law's constitutionality failed, with the courts ruling that amnesty was a "purely political question" that abolished not only the penalty for a crime but also the crime itself. The amnesty law had broad political support, presented as a necessary and legitimate measure to end the scourge of civil war. It genuinely benefitted perpetrators on both sides of the conflict. There was also a relative lack of social appetite for accountability because of the sheer scale and breadth of civilian suffering during the war and a demobilizing effect caused by political party and UN domination of the peace process and its immediate aftermath. Nongovernmental organizations working to identify and locate victims' remains, or to trace displaced children forcibly adopted by military personnel during the war, found that administrative rather than formal judicial channels offered the best chance of success. Despite some external efforts to restart judicial accountability during the late 1990s, the 1993 Amnesty Law has largely continued to block domestic prosecutions.

The Jesuit case fueled efforts at domestic change in Salvadoran transitional justice. The Institute for Human Rights of the Jesuit-run Universidad Centroamericana José Simeon Cañas in San Salvador became active on behalf of the Jesuit congregation and the victims' relatives as part of a broader commitment to justice for victims. But efforts to reopen the domestic case were repeatedly rebuffed by the powerful attorney general, who upheld the "preemptive" invocation of amnesty to preclude any new investigation. Domestic cases therefore tended to fall at the first hurdle, even after the Supreme Court ruling of September 26, 2000 handed the initiative back to judges by opening a loophole whereby individual judges had to decide whether amnesty should apply to crimes committed during the presidential period that straddled the transition (1989–1994). Judges proved unwilling or unable to take up the gauntlet. In 2004, a final domestic rebuff over the Jesuit case led the congregation to accept long-standing outside offers to submit a transnational case in Spanish courts (see later discussion).

Regional and Transnational Legal Activity over El Salvador

The human rights situation in El Salvador became a focus of attention for the international human rights community during the 1980s, following widespread condemnation of U.S. policy toward Central America during the Reagan administration. The involvement of international organizations in the country continued after the end of the war in 1992, but their focus shifted from urgent right-to-life concerns related to past massacres and death squad activity to postwar reconstruction and development. The UN mission in El Salvador was first scaled down and then withdrawn in the mid-1990s. The late 1990s saw a revival of interest and activity from overseas-based nongovernmental organizations over the justice situation in El Salvador. The revival was prompted in part by the 1998 arrest in England of former Chilean dictator Augusto Pinochet, an unexpected development that forced widespread reexamination of the prospects for "late justice" for past human rights violations in Latin America. A small U.S.-based nongovernmental organization, the Center for Justice and Accountability (CJA), was formed in 1998 to explore the possibilities of legal action in the United States on behalf of victims of atrocities committed elsewhere. The actions would take the form of civil claims based on two U.S. domestic statutes: the Alien Tort Claims Act (ATCA), an eighteenth-century law originally designed to protect foreign nationals who had been victims of piracy on the high seas; and the Torture Victim Protection Act (TVPA), a more recent counterpart law that extended similar protection to U.S. citizens.

The first TVPA claim over events in El Salvador was lodged in May 1999, in the Florida courts, by relatives of the four U.S. churchwomen murdered in 1980. Prompted by the chance discovery that two former Salvadoran generals involved in the case were living a comfortable retirement in Florida, the case was spearheaded by lawyer Bill Ford, brother of one of the victims, and by the U.S. nongovernmental organization the Lawyers' Committee for Human Rights (LCHR). The case, *Ford et al. v. García and Vides-Casanova*, concluded with a jury trial in October 2000. The result was disappointing for accountability advocates: after hearing expert testimony about the war in El Salvador and requesting guidance about principles of command responsibility, the jury found that the two defendants could not be held liable for the actions of their subordinates.

In the interim, the CJA prepared an ATCA case against the same defendants. *Romagoza, González and Mauricio v. García and Vides-Casanova* drew on eyewitness testimony from torture survivors living in the United States and resulted in a multimillion-dollar award in July 2002 against Eugenio Vides-Casanova and José García. Both men were former Ministers of Defense, and García had also been head of the National Guard from 1979 to 1983. The award, which went through various stages of appeal and reversal, was finally reinstated in 2006, leading directly to proceedings against García in 2009 for immigration fraud. Two more CJA cases against Salvadoran defendants were also successful, with awards made in 2003 and 2004, respectively, against Alvaro Saravia and Nicolas Carranza for their roles in the Romero assassination and other extrajudicial killings.

In November 2008, the CJA took part in its first criminal action over El Salvador. It joined with the Spanish nongovernmental organization Human Rights Association of Spain (Asociación Pro-Derechos Humanos de España) and relatives to bring a case for the Jesuit murders in the Spanish courts. The case, admitted in January 2009, is not an example of universal jurisdiction because it relies in part on the Spanish citizenship of five of the six murdered priests, but represents the first fully transnational criminal case over past human rights violations in El Salvador. The groups responsible for the case and its civil claim predecessors have also attempted to form links with domestic nongovernmental organizations, as overseas cases aim to increase domestic accountability.

At the regional level, the Inter-American Commission and Court for Human Rights (see entry on Organization of American States) received dozens of complaints about the human rights situation in El Salvador, in particular after 1995 when the country first recognized the Court's contentious jurisdiction. The *Serrano* case, brought by the mother of two young girls who disappeared in 1982, was elevated from the Commission to the Court in 2003. A 2005 verdict found in favor of the plaintiff, ordering the Salvadoran state to undertake symbolic and material reparations and to renew efforts to resolve the case in domestic courts. The verdict noted and for the most part respected the Salvadoran government's position that the Court should only rule on events taking place subsequent to the 1995 acceptance of its contentious jurisdiction.

After the *Serrano* verdict, the Salvadoran government requested a special audience with the Inter-American Commission on Human Rights. At the session, which took place in 2007, the government put forward various experts, including former FMLN peace negotiator Salvador Samayoa, to attest to the central role of the 1993 amnesty in securing continuing stability in El Salvador.

Conclusion

El Salvador's application of transitional justice mechanisms remains limited. The UN-sponsored Truth Commission of 1992 significantly contributed to truth telling by naming perpetrators and thus assisting in the security force purging and institutional rebuilding that marked the early transitional period. El Salvador's continued emphasis on the preservation of impunity through amnesty has, however, begun to look outdated, as other Latin American countries move toward a gradual application of "late justice" through prosecution. Other limitations include the lack of follow-through on practical and symbolic reparations measures to victims, as distinct from former combatants.

Since 2000, Salvadoran authorities have seemed hostile to human rights concerns, sidelining the Ombudsman's office whenever it expressed strong views about past impunity or present abuses related to a crackdown on gang warfare. This indifference was expressed in the failure to carry out specific Truth Commission recommendations including a monument to victims, which civil society groups had to erect privately. Moreover, after a counterproposal to grant a posthumous public honor to the notorious d'Aubuisson was narrowly defeated in Congress in 2007, a local ARENA mayor erected a monument to him in a San Salvador public square. Despite positive signals from the new government, including the first-ever public apology for state atrocities in January 2010, it remains to be seen whether the 2009 political shift to a left-wing administration will bring any progress in transitional justice. Substantial change in the justice arena seems challenging given the continuing stake of both main political parties in the legal protection afforded by amnesty.

Cath Collins

Cross-references: Organization of American States; Truth Commission, El Salvador.

Further Readings

Call, Charles. 2002. Assessing El Salvador's Transition from Civil War to Peace. In *Ending Civil Wars: The Implementation of Peace Agreements*. Eds. Rothchild E. Cousens and S. Stedman. Boulder: Lynne Rienner Publishers, pp. 383–420.

Cañas, Antonio and Héctor Dada. 1999. Political Transition and Institutionalization in El Salvador. In *Comparative Peace Processes in Latin America*. Ed. C. Arnson. Stanford: Stanford University Press/Woodford Wilson Center Press, pp. 69–95.

Collins, Cath. 2010. *Post-Transitional Justice: Human Rights Trials in Chile and El Salvador*. University Park: Penn State University Press.

Holiday, David and Rubén Zamora. 2007. The Struggle for Lasting Reform: Vetting Processes in El Salvador. In *Justice as Prevention – Vetting Public Employees in Transitional Societies*. Eds. Alexander Mayer-Reickh and Pablo de Grieff. New York: SSRC, pp. 80–119. Available at http://www.ssrc

.org/workspace/images/crm/new_publication_3/%7B57efec93-284a-de11-afac-001cc477ec70%7D.pdf (accessed November 20, 2011).
Popkin, Margaret. 2000. *Peace without Justice: Obstacles to Building the Rule of Law in El Salvador*. University Park: Penn State University Press.
Stanley, William. 1996. *The Protection Racket State – Elite Politics, Military Extortion, and Civil War in El Salvador*. Philadelphia: Temple University Press.
Truth Commission of El Salvador [Comisión de la Verdad para El Salvador]. 1993. *From Madness to Hope: The 12-year War in El Salvador*. UN Publication S/25500. Available at: http://www.un.org/en/documents/ (accessed August 3, 2010).

Estonia

Post-communist Estonia's approach to transitional justice has been heavily predicated on its view of the Soviet period as an illegal foreign occupation and annexation, thus casting transition justice as the process of dealing with the repression committed by a foreign power, and not by Estonia itself. To be sure, some Estonians were implicated in the repressive acts committed in the country between 1940 and 1991, when Estonia was occupied by the Soviets, and between 1941 and 1944, when it was occupied by the Nazis. The aim has been to establish the historical truth in relation to past repression, to bring to justice (where still possible) those involved in mass repressions, and to commemorate through symbolic acts the memory of those repressed. Lustration has been limited to a "written oath of conscience" that was initially demanded of civil servants and elected officials, and to identifying those who were actively employed by the Soviet and Nazi security agencies. No blanket employment bans or retributive policies have been enacted to date.

The Repressive Past

In the summer of 1940, the Soviet Union occupied and annexed Estonia along with the other two Baltic states of Latvia and Lithuania. Almost immediately, the Stalinist regime began its repression with the arrest, deportation, and sometimes killing of scores of former Estonian political, military, economic, and intellectual elites. It also sought to quickly impose the Soviet economic system with the nationalization of private property. Another level of terror was unleashed on the night of June 13–14, 1941, when the NKVD (the Soviet political police, a precursor to the KGB) carried out the mass deportation of 10,000 men, women, and children seen as politically dangerous or otherwise suspect. This repression remained etched in the minds of Estonians, becoming a touchstone for much of the opposition to Soviet rule.

During the three years of German occupation, the Nazis carried out repression against Estonian Jews (some 1,000 killed out of 5,000) and any remaining communists (6,000 killed, including family members). Thereafter, the Nazis transported more than 7,500 Jews from other parts of Central and Eastern Europe to be killed in concentration camps in Estonia. In addition, a number of Estonians were recruited into special police battalions to help with rounding up Jews in Belarus and Poland. While the killing of Jews in Estonia was limited in comparison to other areas of Nazi occupation, it remained a sensitive historical topic, given that thousands of Estonian men joined the Wehrmacht in 1943–1944; one key motivation was to forestall the return of the Soviet Union and its terror.

After Soviet rule was reestablished, renewed repression was carried out not only against Nazi collaborators and former members of the German army, but also against 10,000 "Forest Brothers" – anti-Soviet armed resistance fighters active in the countryside. Roughly 2,000 of these fighters were killed and another 8,000 arrested, of whom 4,000 later died in prison. (In all, 30,000 persons are believed to have been part of the movement through the mid-1950s.) Lastly, the Stalinist authorities carried out a second wave of deportations in March 1949, this time encompassing some 20,000 kulaks or individuals resisting the forced collectivization of agriculture. Following Stalin's death in 1953, repression was eased, although arrests based on "political paragraphs" of the Soviet Criminal Code continued up to 1988 (reaching 500).

Transitional Justice

To cope with this past of foreign occupation, mass killings, and postwar KGB repression, Estonia has adopted a six-part approach to transitional justice, involving: (1) decrees and laws rehabilitating all individuals convicted for political crimes during the Soviet era and providing them with special social rights, including pension supplements and other benefits; (2) an extensive program of property restitution and/or compensation to rectify the Soviets' nationalization of property in 1940; (3) a requirement (in force until December 31, 2000) that all individuals seeking either elected or appointed office in state institutions or the civil service sign "a written oath of conscience" in which they disavowed any participation in past repression; (4) a procedure for identifying and, if necessary, making public the names of those individuals directly involved with the KGB or Nazi security services operating in Estonia from 1940 to 1991; (5) a policy of investigating and prosecuting individuals suspected of having participated in crimes against humanity and genocide during the Stalinist era; and (6) commemorative events, campaigns, and investigative commissions dedicated to clarifying the past and preserving this memory for the future.

Victim Rehabilitation

The rehabilitation of individuals convicted of political crimes during the Stalinist era was one of the first demands voiced across the Soviet Union as a result of Mikhail Gorbachev's policy of *glasnost* (openness). This imperative arose also in Estonia and already in December 1988 the Estonian Soviet Socialist Republic's Supreme Soviet passed a law acknowledging the irremediable suffering caused by Stalinist terror and condemning in unequivocal terms the deportations of innocent people. As a follow-up measure, the Supreme Soviet Presidium elaborated in February 1990 a detailed list of more than thirty different sections of the Russian Criminal Code (in force in Estonia during Stalinist rule), in relation to which previously repressed people were to be rehabilitated. These sections included infamous provisions such as anti-Soviet agitation and counterrevolutionary activity.

When in March 1990 Estonia elected its first free parliament, the Supreme Council, this body passed yet another law allowing individuals to request rehabilitation for any Soviet conviction, if they could prove that they had acted in the struggle for the independence of the republic or against injustice wrought upon the Estonian people. Yet despite these juridical steps, it was not until December 2003 that Estonia passed a law defining a particular legal status for repressed persons along with special social and other rights to which these individuals were entitled. The law was the result of an important lobbying effort by nongovernmental organizations representing repressed persons, and support from prominent members of the conservative Res Publica party, which formed the government after winning the 2003 parliamentary elections.

Property Restitution

After the Soviet takeover of Estonia in 1940, communist authorities nationalized all private property, including land, factories, assets, commercial establishments, and large private homes. A half-century later, in June 1991, the Estonian Supreme Council adopted the Bases for Property Reform Act, which mandated an extensive policy of property restitution, meaning either the return of nationalized property (if it was still extant) or the payment of compensation in the form of special privatization vouchers. The law was meant to spur an overall return to private property and market capitalism, but it was also seen as a justice policy in order to right the wrong of unilateral property seizure by the Soviet regime.

The law established a deadline of December 31, 1991 by which all previous owners could file restitution claims. The measure defined the pool of eligible claimants broadly by including the spouse of a child of a previous owner and the grandchildren of a previous owner and "other descending relatives." Within months, thousands of claims began to flood into local government offices, totaling 220,000 by the time the whole process was over. Throughout the 1990s, officials spent innumerable hours reviewing these claims and gathering additional archival documents in order to decide each case. Ultimately, 5,000 buildings (both commercial structures and residential dwellings) and 202,000 land plots (equaling 1.4 million hectares) were returned by October 2004. In addition, a total of 8.27 billion Estonian Kroons (US$600 million) worth of compensation vouchers were issued by the Estonian state. Still, the restitution policy was controversial, because in many dwellings the Soviets had installed new tenants, who suddenly had to live at the mercy of the old owners. In this respect, many saw the policy as having created a new injustice for those turned into "forced renters" of these buildings. According to estimates, the tenants amounted to 22,500 families or upward of 100,000 people.

The Written Oath of Conscience

Alongside the victims of past repression, the perpetrators of these crimes also slowly came under scrutiny beginning in late 1991. The venue for this debate became a special Constitutional Assembly, convened in September 1991 as part of a broader agreement to work out a new constitution for the restored state. After long deliberations, the Assembly agreed in early 1992 to instate a special written oath of conscience (*süümevanne*) required of all persons seeking either elected or appointed (i.e., civil service) office in Estonia (whether national or local) through December 31, 2000. Under the oath, the person would avow that he/she had never been a member of any foreign security service or participated in the active persecution of fellow citizens. Although the statement was somewhat formal, later legislation allowed state authorities to contest in court the authenticity of someone's oath. If untrue, that person could be dismissed from his or her position. In the end, such investigations surfaced only a handful of times, resulting in only one conviction (in which the member of a municipal council was stripped of his mandate), before the measure expired in 2000.

The oath was legally codified in a special Implementation Act of the Constitution that specified a range of other transitional provisions for the new legal order. During deliberations, the Assembly also considered a harsher lustration clause that would have explicitly prevented top Communist Party leaders from running for local or national office and serving in local or national government posts until December 31, 2000. This proposal was dropped when the Supreme Council reviewed the Act for final approval.

Revealing the Names of Former Security Agents

The second measure aimed at perpetrators of repression stemmed from a law passed in 1995 establishing a procedure for securing information about, registering, and, whenever necessary, making public the names of individuals found to have actively worked for the Soviet and Nazi security services. Specifically, people who had been employed by or had collaborated with the Gestapo, the KGB, the Soviet military intelligence agency (GRU), or any of their predecessors were given until April 1, 1996 to register with the Estonian Security Police Board and to disclose their full past involvement with such organs in a written affidavit. If they did not register and sufficient evidence was gathered against them by the Board, their name could be published thereafter in the *Riigi Teataja* (State Gazette) as a past agent or accomplice of a foreign occupier. In the law, the net was cast fairly wide to include people who had served not only as full-time employees of such security services, but also as occasional informants or collaborators. Yet, in practice, attention focused only on full-time employees. In return for such disclosures, the law promised that, if such information did not indicate participation in a criminal act, it would be kept as a state secret in perpetuity by the Board and no harm would come to the confessor. Moreover, even if evidence was gathered on someone who did not register, that person could contest the charges in front of a confidential court of law.

Following the adoption of the law, observers estimated that as many as 20,000 people might come under the measure's rather broad definition of collaboration. In fact, only 1,153 people contacted the Board by the April 1, 1996 deadline. This set the stage for the Board to begin its own investigations into the past of those persons who had not come forward. From 1998 to 2008, the Board released the names of just 616 people (138 women and 478 men), all of whom had worked for the KGB. The Security Police Board never disclosed the sources for its investigations but, given the degree of detailed career information released about each individual, the revelations appear to have been based on personnel records taken over from the Soviet Estonian branch of the KGB. Each disclosure included full details of the KGB department(s) in which the person worked, the position(s) the person held, and the approximate dates of employment. For some individuals, this service went back to 1944. Moreover, as mandated by law, the lists have included the individual's current employer and position. While this appears to be a sweeping disclosure, the provision has been defended as necessary to make the public (including employers) aware of where these people once worked.

Prosecuting Crimes against Humanity

Given the nature of Stalinist repression in Estonia and the occurrence of two large-scale deportations in 1941 and 1949, the notion of crimes against humanity has also become an important dimension to transitional justice. Yet attempts to incorporate these crimes into the legal system by identifying the legal categories under which they could be placed have not been easy from a legal or political viewpoint. For example, it was not until November 1994 that the Estonian parliament passed a special amendment to the old Soviet Estonian Criminal Code defining these offenses. In June 2001, the Code was completely redrafted and fuller definitions of both crimes against humanity and genocide were enacted, drawing on the 1998 Rome Statute of the International Criminal Court. Authority for investigating and prosecuting these crimes was given to the Estonian Security Police Board and the State Prosecutor's Office.

Since 1994, investigations by these two organizations have focused on four types of crimes. The first concerns crimes against humanity and war crimes committed by the occupying Soviet authorities in 1940–1941, including the June 1941 deportations. It was under this category that the first trial of a suspected Stalinist-era war criminal began in June 1996. An ex-NKVD operative, Vassili Riis, stood accused of having given the order for the arrest or deportation of 1,061 people from the island of Saaremaa in June–July 1941. Yet, given Riis's advanced age at the time (eighty-six), the proceedings became subject to repeated delay, until in February 1998 Riis died. A similar scenario ensued with Idel Jakobson, a communist accused of involvement in up to 1,800 cases of repression from 1940 to 1945. Barely a year into his court proceedings, Jakobson passed away.

A second set of suspected crimes against humanity relates to those committed during the Nazi occupation. These crimes have already received considerable attention from other international authorities. The only major outstanding case in Estonia has involved an Estonian living in Venezuela, Harry Männil, who worked for four months in the Nazi security police. Holocaust memorial groups have accused Männil of involvement in the arrest of numerous people (including Jews), many of whom were later killed. Männil has insisted that he was responsible for the legitimate arrest of communists and other collaborators with the previous Soviet regime. In December 2005, the State Prosecutor's Office discontinued an investigation against the eighty-five-year-old Männil for lack of evidence.

In 2000, a third category of crimes against humanity emerged in Estonian judicial practice, when the Supreme Court overturned a lower court ruling convicting an ex-NKVD agent of killing three partisans opposed to the reestablished Soviet regime in 1946. The court found that the accused, Karl-Leonhard Paulov, could not be convicted of murder. Because the killings had been perpetrated against innocent civilians and without trial, they fell under the category of crimes against humanity as defined by the Nuremberg War Crimes Tribunal, to which the Soviet Union was a party at the time they took place. The Court thus demanded a retrial, and in July 2000 a lower court sentenced Paulov to eight years imprisonment. Paulov died shortly thereafter, but his case opened the way for a broader investigation of KGB and other Soviet activities against Estonian armed resistance, which began in 1944 and lasted until 1978, when the last partisan was captured. As a result, in 2003, Vladimir Penart was convicted of having indiscriminately killed anti-Soviet partisans in 1953–1954.

Lastly, in 1995, the Security Police Board opened separate investigations examining the culpability of persons involved in the mass deportations of March 1949. Whereas initially the Board began its inquiries under the heading of crimes against humanity, this definition was changed in 2001 after the revamped Estonian Penal Code provided a more specific definition of the crime of genocide. Given the mass nature of the deportations and their ethnic character (their aim was to break the back of the ethnic

Estonian rural population), this historical period acquired its own significance or place in relation to retrospective justice. Since the early 2000s, the authorities have charged seventeen people with crimes against humanity in connection in the 1949 deportations. Arnold Meri was charged with acts of genocide. Eight of the eighteen were convicted, all receiving suspended sentences owing to their advanced age. The remaining ten died either before or during their trial.

In regard to both the third and fourth types of crimes against humanity, Estonia took the major step of classifying the actions of the occupying Soviet authorities to pacify the civilian population as a possible crime against humanity or genocide. This was important because the Soviet Criminal Code at the time did not contain reference to such crimes, thus implying that Soviet agents could not be convicted for these offenses ex post facto. Yet Estonia has maintained that because these acts took place during an illegal occupation, they do constitute a crime against humanity under international law as defined, for example, by the Nuremberg Tribunal and in force also during that time in the Soviet Union. This legal interpretation, in turn, received affirmation in 2006, when the European Court of Human Rights rejected the appeals of three Estonians seeking to overturn Estonian court rulings convicting them of crimes against humanity during the postwar Soviet period.

Symbolic Justice

Symbolic justice began in Estonia with the removal of countless Soviet-related memorials and the renaming of streets. Although these actions caused little controversy, a flashpoint did erupt in the spring of 2007, when the Estonian government decided to relocate a Soviet war memorial known as the Bronze Soldier in downtown Tallinn. The move sparked two days of rioting by Russian-speaking youths, who protested what they saw as a desecration of their historical identity. The controversy showed that stark differences continue to exist between ethnic Estonians and the Russian minority (amounting to 25 percent of the country's population) over the interpretation of the past.

In terms of public commemorations, there are three official days of remembrance: June 14 (the 1941 deportations), August 23 (the Molotov–Ribbentrop Pact), and September 22 (the day when the Soviets reentered Tallinn in 1944 and began their second occupation of Estonia). Additionally, in June 2001, President Lennart Meri undertook a unique tour of Estonia to commemorate the sixtieth anniversary of the first Soviet deportations and to present thousands of Estonians who had been repressed under the Soviets with a special pin depicting a cornflower – the national flower of Estonia – broken in two. The Broken Cornflower campaign became an eminent example of symbolic recognition, with the seventy-two-year-old president (himself a postwar deportee to Siberia) often talking at length with the recipients of the honor. Based on this initiative, the broken cornflower became the official pin accorded to individuals duly certified as having been repressed.

Lastly, a number of civic organizations, investigatory commissions, and research organizations have been set up to perpetuate the memory of both Soviet and Nazi repression. A victims' organization, Memento, founded in 1989, continues to operate. In 1992, Memento was instrumental in the creation of the State Commission for the Examination of Repressive Policies Carried Out during the Occupations (see separate entry). Some years later, President Lennart Meri convened an additional International Commission for the Investigation of Crimes against Humanity (see separate entry). Both commissions received extensive state funding and published numerous research reports on the extent of Soviet and Nazi crimes in Estonia. Several local nongovernmental groups document the past, including the Occupation Museum in Tallinn and the Estonian Repressed Persons Records Bureau.

Conclusion

While Estonia's approach to transitional justice has been multifaceted, its focus has been mostly on dealing with Soviet-era repression, given the latter's long duration and degree of terror (including deportations). There has been considerably less interest in broaching internal Estonian issues like the Estonian citizens who served in the Communist Party or collaborated with the KGB. On this score, Estonians have preferred to look to the future, to solidify their restored statehood, to obtain admission to the European Union and NATO, and eventually to leave their history of occupation behind them.

Vello Pettai

Cross-references: Crimes against Humanity; International Commission for the Investigation of Crimes Against Humanity; International versus Domestic Norms and Actors; Lustration; Politics of History; Property Restitution; Rehabilitation of Political Prisoners; State Commission for the Examination of Repressive Policies Carried Out during the Occupations.

Further Readings

Birn, Ruth Bettina. 2001. Collaboration with Nazi Germany in Eastern Europe: The Case of the Estonian Security Police. *Contemporary European History*, 10: 181–198.
Kahk, Juhan, ed. 1991. *World War II and Soviet Occupation in Estonia: A Damages Report*. Tallinn: Perioodika.
Mälksoo, Lauri. 2001. Soviet Genocide? Communist Mass Deportations in the Baltic States and International Law. *Leiden Journal of International Law*, 14: 757–787.
Salo, Vello, Ulo Ennueste, Erast Parmasto, Enn Tarvel, and Peep Varju, eds. 2005. *The White Book: Losses Inflicted on the Estonian Nation by Occupation Regimes 1940–1991*. Tallinn: Estonian Encyclopedia Publishers. Available at: http://www.riigikogu.ee/public/Riigikogu/TheWhiteBook.pdf (accessed July 13, 2010).
Weiss-Wendt, Anton. 2008. Why the Holocaust Does Not Matter in Estonia. *Journal of Baltic Studies*, 39: 475–498.

Ethiopia

From 1974 to 1991, the Derg Marxist-Leninist military junta, led by Colonel Mengistu Haile-Mariam, ruled Ethiopia as one of Africa's most brutal and authoritarian regimes. During the political purges of 1977–1978 (known as the Red Terror), tens of thousands of Ethiopian intellectuals, dissenters, and opposition party members and sympathizers were imprisoned, tortured, and killed. The Ethiopian People's Revolutionary Democratic Front (EPRDF) toppled the junta in May 1991. Since then, hundreds of officials of the former regime have been detained in an effort to make them accountable for the atrocities of the 1974–1991 period. Lustration and property restitution programs have also been launched.

The Repressive Past

Ethiopia's history includes wars and political violence. The most recent violent regime changes were the military 1974 coup d'état against the imperial reign of Emperor Haile Selassie I, and the 1991 defeat of the Marxist-Leninist military junta of Colonel Haile-Mariam by the EPRDF insurgents. In the first case, political violence occurred after the regime change, when the military leadership used terror and purges to consolidate its power after ousting Emperor Selassie. In the second case, the use of military force and political violence helped the EPRDF wrestle power away from the Derg and achieve regime change.

The Red Terror campaign occurred after the 1974 revolution that toppled the monarchy. That year, a popular movement of students, peasants, and workers overthrew Emperor Selassie I, who had ruled Ethiopia since 1930. In the revolutionary disarray, a military junta seized power, overthrew and jailed the Emperor, suspended the constitution, dissolved parliament, and established a provisional military government. The military takeover abolished the quasi-feudal government structure of Emperor Selassie. No attempts were made to hold the imperial regime accountable for its political and human rights abuses. Rather, the military regime made sweeping arrests of those associated with Selassie's reign and executed sixty generals, ministers, and high-ranking officials. By late 1974, Emperor Selassie was secretly killed and buried in the basement of the royal palace, without any public trial or even secret hearing.

Following these summary executions, systematic and atrocious human rights violations occurred in 1975–1988. To begin, in the days before May Day 1977, the youth committees of the leftist Ethiopian People's Revolutionary Party (EPRP), which opposed the military junta, planned a nationwide demonstration demanding the establishment of a civil government. The Derg thwarted this plan in the so-called May Day Massacre, when it preemptively killed hundreds of young people planning to participate in the demonstration. The carnage continued for days, during which the bodies of more than 1,000 slaughtered students and intellectuals were left in the streets. Families who identified the bodies of the murdered youth were asked to pay for the bullets that were used to kill their sons and daughters before they could take the corpses for a proper funeral.

In July 1977, a "ferreting-out" campaign directed against so-called antirevolutionary and reactionary elements resulted in the death of more than 1,000 people and the arbitrary detention of even more persons accused of belonging to different political parties, notably the Ethiopian Peoples' Revolutionary Party (EPRP) and the All-Ethiopian Socialist Movement (Ma'ison). This event anticipated the notorious Red Terror urban campaign. Borrowed from the Russian revolutionary lexicon, the Red Terror meant the liquidation of counterrevolutionaries. In Ethiopia, the Red Terror was the most systematic and infamous campaign of official human rights violations perpetrated by the Derg. Officially launched in November 1977, the Red Terror massacre lasted until 1979. In it, the Derg killed a generation of mostly young intellectuals without any resort to the rule of law.

The number of casualties of Red Terror remains disputed. Estimates range from 150,000 to 500,000 persons killed all over the country during the Red Terror period, depending on which internal conflict going on at the time is included in the count. The entire Derg era was characterized by serious human rights violations that constituted state-sponsored terror in the form of sexual abuse, summary execution, torture, arbitrary arrest, detention, disappearance, unlawful dispossession of property, the use of food aid as a political tool, and forced resettlement.

The Derg military junta was toppled in 1991 by the EPRDF, a coalition of ethnic insurgent movements led by the Tigray People's Liberation Front (TPLF). Colonel Haile-Mariam fled the country to Zimbabwe on May 21, 1991. Ethiopia's capital, Addis Ababa, fell to the EPRDF forces on May 28, and a provisional government was established on June 1, with Meles Zenawi, the TPLF and EPRDF chairman, as the executive head of state. Days later, Zenawi promised the Ethiopian people a new and broad-based democratic government composed of representatives from all opposition movements and distinguished Ethiopians unconnected to the Derg. Parliament was dissolved and leading civil servants and military officials started to surrender to the new government, together with tens of thousands of Derg soldiers who flocked into Addis Ababa.

During the unstable period that followed the EPRDF takeover, only a few people took the law into their own hands to punish the collaborators of the Derg regime. The new government carried out mass arrests of key officials from the former regime and the Workers' Party of Ethiopia, the communist party established by the junta in 1987. Simultaneously, Peace and Stability Committees were established by the government in Addis Ababa with a broad mandate to investigate, arrest, and detain suspected human rights violators of the Derg regime. Many of those arrested were brought to the Committees and the police by former victims or their families who recognized the perpetrators in public. During the first months of the EPRDF government, more than 2,000 military and civilian officials were detained, as were several thousands more shortly thereafter. After preliminary investigations, several hundred were released after short detention periods.

Transitional Justice

When assuming power in 1991, the EPRDF government potentially had the full range of transitional justice mechanisms available for how to deal with Deng-era perpetrators of the gross human rights violations. However, Prime Minister Zenawi acknowledged that the TPLF had made the decision to use criminal prosecutions before forming the government. According to Zenawi, it was important for the EPRDF to restore justice and to show the people that no official can carry out human rights violations with impunity (interview with the author, January 16, 2002). Thus, a general amnesty was not considered, as it would send the wrong signal to people and future politicians. However, other transitional justice instruments were applied, including lustration of Derg regime members and collaborators and property restitution. Furthermore, a method most often associated with restorative justice was incorporated into the mandate of the Special Prosecutor's Office as a corollary objective of the trials, focusing on recording the brutal offenses perpetrated against the Ethiopian people.

Criminal Prosecution

The EPRDF government decided to use Ethiopia's court system and Penal Code to prosecute members of both the Derg junta and the Workers Party of Ethiopia and collaborators of the military regime for the massive human rights violations of the 1974–1991 period, without introducing international jurisdiction in the process. To this end, Proclamation 22/1992 established the Special Prosecutor's Office (hereafter the Office) with a mandate to investigate and prosecute those responsible for committing offenses by abusing their public position under the Derg regime. The objectives of the Office were ambitious: (1) to prosecute officials of the Derg regime responsible for thousands of killings; and (2) to record the atrocities by compiling all the written evidence available and by soliciting oral testimonies from victims and victims' families.

The Office submitted the first charges in October 1994, marking the beginning of the Red Terror trials, which were heard in courts throughout the country. Initially, the trials were welcomed by large segments of the Ethiopian population who looked forward to finding out the truth about their missing relatives and seeking accountability for the injustices committed by the Derg. The international community also supported the initiative, providing funding and assistance with legal capacity building to the Office and for public defense attorneys for the accused. Later, international support waned as the trials were delayed and increasingly politicized.

The Office divided the accused into three groups: the first group included top level policy makers and senior government and military officials of the junta; the second included military and political field commanders who carried out orders and passed them on; and the third was composed of individuals "on the ground" who carried out the brutal human rights violations. The first group totaled 106 people (many charged in absentia), including Colonel Haile-Mariam, former Prime Minister Captain Fikreselassie Wegederesse, and former Vice-President Colonel Fiseha Desta. Their trial, called the main trial, was heard at the Federal High Court in Addis Ababa. Second and third group cases were heard in regional supreme courts throughout Ethiopia, primarily in the areas were atrocities had occurred. Initially, the Office charged 5,198 political and military officials of the Derg regime, of which 2,258 were tried in regional supreme courts by delegation from the federal High Court.

A number of charges, all based on Ethiopian state laws, were brought against the accused. The first charge was of public provocation and preparation to commit genocide, causing the deaths of thousands of supporters of different political groupings. Another charge was that of genocide in violation of the 1957 Ethiopian Penal Code. According to the Code, genocide charges can be based on the intent to destroy, in whole or in part, a political, ethnic, racial, or religious group. Derg officials were accused of intending to annihilate political groups like the EPRP, which opposed their policies. Additional charges included unlawful detention and abuse of power. The defendants in the main trial were collectively and independently charged with 209 accounts of genocide, aggravated homicide, grave and willful injury, abuse of power, and unlawful detentions.

After a prolonged trial, the verdict against the Derg leaders was passed in December 2006, while the sentencing was decided in early 2007. Fifty-five top political and military officials of the Derg military junta were convicted and sentenced, twenty-two of them in absentia. The Court accepted most charges, but released one defendant who defended his case against all charges. All but one of the defendants were found guilty of genocide. There was one dissenting judge on the genocide verdict. Judge Nuru Saiid argued against the Ethiopian Penal Code's protection for political groups against genocide, which had been repealed during the Derg. As the Convention on the Prevention and Punishment of the Crime of Genocide (1948) does not protect political groups, and the Ethiopian state had legitimately sought to protect itself from attack from political groupings, Saiid argued that the Court should not convict the defendants of genocide and incitement to commit genocide.

The Court, with one dissenting judge, rejected the Office's request for death penalty of key defendants because of extenuating circumstances and because the aim of punishment is to reform, not to exact revenge. Instead, the Court sentenced forty-eight defendants to life imprisonment and the others to long-term imprisonment.

The Office appealed the verdict to the Federal Supreme Court, which concluded in May 2008 that the imposition of the death penalty on the defendants as requested by the Office was justified and reasoned and would serve as a warning to other officials in similar positions. Accordingly, the Supreme Court imposed the death penalty on eighteen respondents. The sentence needed approval from the head of state to be carried out. Some of the defendants also appealed the High Court's verdict and sentencing, but all these appeals were rejected by the Supreme Court.

Notwithstanding their ambitious overall objective of making the Derg regime and its officials accountable for their gross human rights violations and by restoring justice in Ethiopia, the Red Terror trials have been criticized by both domestic and international actors for seriously breaching the rights of the accused. Criticisms were voiced against the inefficient procedures and working methods of the Office and the courts (both the High Court and the regional courts); the legal restrictions imposed on the defendants, which undermined the rights of habeas corpus and timely access to evidence; and detentions without proper investigation. The Office's wide powers to detain suspects indefinitely and without review by the courts led to arbitrary detention. Many detainees were released by the courts after years in detention without any charges being brought against them. The severe delays in the court proceedings (some detainees spent more than ten years in prison without their cases being heard) violated the right of the accused to be brought promptly before a court of law. The administration of the trials was criticized for taking too long and for bringing defendants before different judges who had not heard earlier witnesses or examined previously presented evidence, thus breaching principles of fair and speedy trial. All trials in the regional court have been held, but appeals are still ongoing in certain regions.

Lustration

After assuming power in 1991, the transitional government collectively disqualified all former officials of the Derg military junta and members of the Workers' Party of Ethiopia at different ranks from their public positions. Thousands of people employed in ministries, courts, mass organizations (for urban dwellers, peasants, women, and youth), and security forces were thus dismissed. All security institutions, including the army and the police, were completely dismantled and their personnel were discharged. The civil and political rights of the former officials, members and collaborators of the Workers' Party – such as the right to political assembly and to vote – were also restricted. Additionally, as part of the verdict in the Red Terror trials, the Court ruled that the individuals sentenced to lifetime imprisonment could not participate in elections and were permanently barred from all public offices, while those sentenced to twenty-five to thirty-five years in prison could not participate in elections and hold public office for five years from their date of release.

Restitution of Property

In 1991, the new government also launched property restitution. Many people were arbitrarily evicted from their private properties by the Derg regime. Laws and procedures that allowed victims to reclaim their properties were promulgated in 1995, including Proclamation 110/95 for the review of illegally confiscated properties. As a result of individual initiatives and investigations by the government, some victims recovered their properties, which included dwellings and other buildings, manufacturing firms, coffee-processing plants, service enterprises, dairy farms, and vehicles. At the time of this writing, many restitution claims by victims are still under investigation, and their outcomes are pending.

Reconciliation

By establishing a trial process, the EPRDF effectively broke with the violent practice of the past where new power-holders summarily executed, imprisoned, or exiled members of the old regime. The new practice of making them accountable in courts was by comparison a reconciliatory move. The decision to undertake the trials in the society where the atrocities took place, instead of international tribunals, and to allow the hearings to be presided over by Ethiopian nationals instead of foreign experts, in hearings open to the general public, sought to "cleanse old wounds" and heal the societal trauma inflicted by the Red Terror.

In addition, the secondary mandate of the Office is explicitly geared toward restorative justice, as the Office must record the atrocities carried out by the Derg by compiling all the written evidence available and by soliciting oral testimonies from victims and their families. These records, which should be made accessible and available for the public and for further studies and research, unveil the horrendous acts committed, in order for the truth about the Red Terror to become public knowledge in Ethiopia. The recording was intended to have a reconciliatory effect in the society at large, as knowing the truth about the atrocities would heal both individual and collective grievances, in addition to educating the people in order to prevent the recurrence of repression in the future.

Allowing victims of human rights abuses to have their say in court and venting their personal grievances as part of a truth-telling process may also promote societal healing. The impact of the trials on the public discourse was noticeable in the first years of the process, as public and private news media covered the hearings and people discussed testimonies. However, as the trials were delayed and accusations of human rights violations by the EPRDF government started to emerge in the late 1990s, public interest dropped and many started to question the legitimacy of the government to undertake the trials as human rights violations could continue to be carried out with impunity.

Conclusion

The ambitious objectives of the ruling EPRDF of restoring respect for human rights and accountability for crimes committed by the Derg military junta have not been adequately met. The effort of making Derg officials accountable for their crimes is commendable, but the many deficiencies of the trials violated the human rights of the accused and undermined the principles of a fair trial. Furthermore, human rights violations continue to be carried out with impunity at the time of this writing, albeit on a smaller scale than during the Derg. This situation undermines the core values and principles of human rights and justice intended to be strengthened and protected by the post-Derg transitional justice process.

Kjetil Tronvoll

Cross-references: Court Trials for Redress; Lustration; Property Restitution; Reconciliation.

Further Readings

Author's interview with Meles Zenawi, January 16, 2002.
Babile Tola. 1997. *To Kill a Generation: The Red Terror in Ethiopia*. Washington, DC: Free Ethiopia Press.
Dadimos Haile. 2000. *Accountability for Crimes of the Past and the Challenges of Criminal Prosecution: The Case of Ethiopia*. Leuven: Leuven University Press.
Girmachew Alemu Aneme. 2006. Apology and Trials: The Case of the Red Terror Trials in Ethiopia. *African Human Rights Law Journal*, 6(1): 64–84.
Kissi, Edward. 2006. *Revolution and Genocide in Ethiopia and Cambodia*. Lexington: Lexington Books.
Tronvoll, Kjetil, Charles Schaefer, and Girmachew Alemu Aneme, eds. 2009. *The Ethiopian Red Terror Trials*. Woodbridge: James Currey Publishers.

Fiji

As a consequence of British colonial-era policies and their legacies, Fiji's history has been marked by sharp racial divisions in politics between its two largest populations: ethnic indigenous Fijians (*i taukei*) and Indo-Fijians (whose ancestors came to the country from South Asia). The legacies of colonial policies are a form of structural repression that each group experienced. Historical differences underlie perceptions of unjust arrangements of political and economic power between ethnic Fijians and Indo-Fijians; these perceptions have created a set of grievances used by political leaders to justify policy preferences and political actions. Most prominent in its post-independence history, Fiji has experienced the overthrow of elected governments in 1987, 2000, and 2006. Accompanying each of these successful or purported coups was a period of acute repression, followed by attempts to achieve some form of reconciliation. These attempts at reconciliation generally have not attempted full-scale transitional justice, but have focused largely on developing new political institutional arrangements.

The Repressive Past

Political leaders in Fiji contest what components of history represent past repression. The memories of colonial-era repression exemplify this division. For ethnic Fijians, the colonial era resulted in a decreased control over collectively owned land, stemming from the granting of leases to sugar-farming operations. (Collective Fijian entities still own nearly 90 percent of the land in the country; the remainder of the land was alienated by colonists and the colonial administration in the early colonial era.) In addition, colonial-era regulations tied Fijians closely to their villages, limiting their participation in the formal economy and formal educational system. The system of indirect rule required Fijians to remain in their villages or face penal sanctions.

The vast majority of Indians in the country during the early colonial era were brought as indentured laborers to work on sugar plantations. These *girmityas* – a term based on *girmit*, an abbreviation of agreement, or the indenture contract – were sometimes induced to signing the contract by misrepresentation. They then faced a dangerous journey from the subcontinent to Fiji, difficult work and living conditions, and were, essentially, exploited for the benefit of Colonial Sugar Refining, the Australia-based company that held a virtual monopoly on sugar production. Harsh discipline – whipping by supervisors for minor infractions – and cramped, poor-quality living conditions made plantation life for many unbearable, as evidenced by high suicide rates. After the five-year indenture, a majority of *girmitiyas* chose to remain in Fiji, often settling on land as tenant farmers.

Along with "free" immigrants from the subcontinent, these former indentured laborers started to form a more permanent Indian population in Fiji. Their descendants, in particular, began to argue for political representation in the colony. When this representation was finally granted, the Indo-Fijian members of the Legislative Council held a disproportionately small number of seats. During the late colonial era, this uneven representation continued: people of European descent held a number of seats far disproportionate to their population. Further, ethnic Fijians achieved the franchise for their Legislative Council representatives only during the last decade of colonial rule.

During the postcolonial era, which started in 1970 when Fiji gained its independence from the United Kingdom, Fiji maintained separate communal representation, as seats in Parliament were allocated on the basis of ethnicity. This communal representation also continued to favor the European and other smaller ethnic groups (referred to as General Electors), as they were allocated more than 15 percent of the seats in the Lower House, despite comprising less than 5 percent of the population. In addition to the Lower House, an Upper House (Senate) was appointed and, by design, contained a majority of ethnic Fijian members. Additionally, the Fijian members appointed to the Senate by the Great Council of Chiefs (an apex body of high ethnic Fijian chiefs) held veto power over any changes to specific legislation related to Fijian interests and land.

From 1970 until 1985, politics in Fiji largely represented a split between the Indo-Fijian-backed National Federation Party and the Alliance backed largely by ethnic Fijian and General Elector voters. The founding of the Fiji Labor Party – a multiracial leftist party – in 1985 and its decision to contest the 1987 election with the National Federation Party as the Coalition resulted in significant change. The Coalition, under the leadership of Dr. Timoci Bavadra (an ethnic Fijian from the west of Fiji), won a small majority of seats in Parliament.

Shortly after the coalition took power, disaffected ethnic Fijians launched the *taukei* movement, claiming the coalition government was hostile to ethnic Fijian interests. Members of the movement held marches, established roadblocks, and engaged in sporadic violence, such as firebombing offices of prominent Indo-Fijian leaders. One month after Bavadra and the Coalition took power, Lieutenant Colonel Sitiveni Rabuka led a coup, taking over Parliament on May 14, 1987, and establishing an interim government. During this period, the interim government initiated a constitutional review; the *taukei* movement and the Great Council of Chiefs, among other Fijian leaders, called for establishing a constitution that guaranteed ethnic Fijian political supremacy. In addition, the government introduced a ban on sporting, recreational, and commercial activities on Sundays, reflecting fundamentalist Methodist beliefs of a segment of the ethnic Fijian population. In addition, there were instances of continued small-scale rioting, bombing, and harassment against Indo-Fijian leaders. After Coalition and Alliance leaders reached an accord brokered by the Governor General on an alternative way forward for the country, Rabuka staged a second coup on September 25, 1987 against the Governor General, declared Fiji a republic, and appointed a military government. After three months, during a significant portion of which there was heavy press censorship, Rabuka handed power to an interim civilian regime with a mandate to establish a new constitution. Even under this civilian regime, instances of extrajudicial violence against critics of the regime continued.

In 1990, the interim government promulgated a new constitution that mandated that the president and prime minister shall be ethnic Fijians. The constitution also provided that ethnic Fijians would constitute a majority in Parliament. All voting for Parliament would strictly follow racial lines. The constitution also mandated "protection and enhancement" of ethnic Fijian interests, serving as the foundation for a number of policies designed to increase the number of ethnic Fijians in government jobs, receiving scholarships, and running businesses. As a result of a combination of intra-ethnic Fijian divisions and external pressures, Fiji undertook a second constitutional review in the mid-1990s. The resulting 1997 constitution, while still preserving race-based representation for two-thirds of the seats in Parliament, established seats open to citizens from any background for the first time in Fiji. In addition, the 1997 constitution provided no limitation on the race of the prime minister.

In 1999, the Fiji Labor Party formed the Peoples' Coalition with a number of ethnic Fijian parties on the anti-Rabuka side of intra-Fijian dispute in the earlier part of the decade. The Peoples' Coalition – and particularly the Mahendra Chaudhry-led Labour Party – enjoyed a large victory over a less formal coalition between Rabuka's Soqosoqo ni Vakavulewa ni Taukei (Fijian Political Party) and the National Federation party. In May 1999, Chaudhry was sworn in as the first Indo-Fijian Prime Minister of Fiji. During the following year, some ethnic Fijian political leaders and a relaunched *taukei* movement criticized Chaudhry's leadership and some Coalition policy proposals. On May 19, 2000, a group of armed militants (including both members of the Army's elite Counter-Revolutionary Warfare Unit – CRW – and civilians) stormed Parliament, took members of the Peoples' Coalition government hostage, and declared a coup. George Speight (a civilian), the public leader of the coup, claimed to be acting to protect ethnic Fijians' interests. The takeover of Parliament led to large-scale looting in Suva. During the ensuing period, members of the Peoples' Coalition were held hostage for fifty-six days and suffered physical abuse. During this same period, Indo-Fijians in rural areas suffered thefts, arson, rape, harassment, and other forms of intimidation, which were particularly severe at Muaniweni in the interior of Viti Levu near Suva.

The military, under Commodore Voreqe (Frank) Bainimarama, rejected the purported coup, but had President Ratu Sir Kamisese Mara stand aside to allow Bainimarama to take over effective control of government. Bainimarama then abrogated the 1997 constitution. Bainimarama appointed an interim government headed by Laisenia Qarase. In early July, the Great Council of Chiefs appointed Ratu Josefa Iloilo president and the military negotiated a release for the parliamentary hostages. Within two weeks, the military captured and arrested the main set of rebels, including Speight, who had violated the agreement by not surrendering their weapons. In November, members of the CRW attempted a mutiny against Bainimarama. In the aftermath of this failed attempt, a number of the attempted mutineers experienced extrajudicial violence after being captured. The High Court held on November 15, 2000 that the 1997 constitution required the reinstatement of the Peoples' Coalition government. When this decision was affirmed by the Court of Appeal in March, the president dissolved Parliament, reappointed Qarase as an interim prime minister, and called for elections under the 1997 constitution. These elections witnessed Qarase's new Soqosoqo ni Duavatani Lewenivanua (SDL, United Fiji Party) winning a narrow victory over Chaudhry's Labor Party.

After 2004, Bainimarama increasingly criticized Qarase and the SDL's pro-ethnic Fijian policies as racially divisive. When SDL won another narrow victory in the 2006 election, Bainimarama continued his criticisms, issuing a series of demands. After attempts by New Zealand to broker negotiations between Bainimarama and Qarase failed, Bainimarama took over the government on December 5, 2006. In January 2007, Bainimarama handed executive authority back to President Iloilo who then appointed Bainimarama as interim prime minister. In April 2009, when the Court of Appeal overturned a High Court decision and held the dismissal of Qarase was illegal, Iloilo abrogated the 1997 constitution and again appointed Bainimarama as prime minister. Since December 2006, there have been instances of harassment and limitation on movement of SDL political leaders and critics of Bainimarama. In addition, news media have faced censorship as well as deportation of expatriate editors.

Transitional Justice

While there has been some degree of common agreement that there is a need for reconciliation or other forms of transitional justice to respond to the history of coups in Fiji, political leaders have sharply disagreed about what forms this justice should take. In particular, leaders have disagreed about the extent to punish perpetrators, the need to root out "shadowy figures" behind the coups (political leaders and business owners who have been thought to offer support to the coups), and the causes of the coups (and, therefore, the appropriate response to prevent ongoing problems). Underlying each of these differences is ambivalence on the part of some leaders toward the coups. In the aftermath of Speight's attempted 2000 coup, for instance, a number of ethnic Fijian leaders (including Qarase in an interview on the public affairs television show "Close Up") stated that they "supported the cause, but not the method" that Speight used.

Constitutional Review/Reform

During the periods of rule by interim and military governments after the 1987 coups, there were few attempts at reconciliation or transitional justice. Instead, many of the reforms represented forms of victors' justice. The ethnic Fijian leaders in power during this era held the cause of the coup to be Fijian economic disadvantage and concern about losing political power. As a result, these governments undertook a constitutional review, culminating in the 1990 constitution that mandated ethnic Fijian political dominance and economic support for ethnic Fijians. Further, Rabuka, military officials, and police officials were all granted immunity from prosecution for their involvement in and actions supporting the 1987 coups.

When intra-Fijian disputes about leadership and the budget and issues concerning the governance of concessionary policies toward ethnic Fijian commercial ventures threatened Rabuka's leadership, he turned to Indo-Fijian members of Parliament to secure his position as prime minister. In return for this support – and in response to international pressures as well as a provision in the 1990 constitution – Rabuka agreed to establish a Constitutional Review Commission. In 1995, Sir Paul Reeves – the Maori former Governor General of New Zealand – was selected to chair this commission. The other two commissioners (Tomasi Vakatora and Brij V. Lal) were selected, respectively, by Rabuka and Jai Ram Reddy (the leader of the opposition and head of the National Federation Party). The Constitutional Review Commission held consultation meetings throughout the country and prepared a lengthy report concerning the place of the Constitution in Fiji, elections, and governance. The process culminated in the drafting of the 1997 constitution.

The 1997 constitution – both in the process leading to its drafting and its final form – represented an attempt to achieve transitional justice by reforming institutions of government by decreasing (but not eliminating) the influence of race in Fiji's political life and by fostering national unity. Generally, the 1997 constitution included many progressive provisions, adapted, from among other documents, South Africa's post-apartheid constitution. Chapter 2 of the 1997 constitution was a compact representing the essential framework of agreement of how to govern the diverse country. The constitution also included a chapter calling for social justice to address socioeconomic inequalities among all groups in Fiji. Finally, the 1997 constitution introduced seats in Parliament not pre-designated on a racial basis. The initial draft, prepared by the Constitutional Review Committee, called for two-thirds of all seats to be open, leaving a minority of seats designated on a communal basis. During the process of approving the draft constitution, however, Parliament reversed the ratio, meaning that two-thirds of the seats remained communally designated. In gaining approval for the constitution, both Rabuka and Reddy undertook extensive efforts, culminating in Reddy addressing the Great Council of Chiefs. Despite the process of extensive consultation, some ethnic Fijian political leaders rejected the changes to the constitution. Furthermore, the numerous progressive elements of the 1997 constitution were not self-executing, but required Parliamentary action to implement.

After Speight's attempted coup in 2000, the interim government's assessment of the cause of the coup and appropriate response differed little from Speight's assessment (and from the response after the 1987 coup). The Qarase-led interim government initiated a constitutional review premised on the belief that ethnic Fijians needed greater political and economic power. This work, however, was cut short by private action pursued through the judiciary. Most famously, in Chandrika Prasad's case, High Court judge Anthony Gates held that the 1997 constitution remained the supreme law in Fiji and that Qarase's interim government was not legal. Prasad, a displaced farmer from Muaniweni, received legal support from the Fiji Human Rights Commission, under the leadership of Dr Shaista Shameem. Despite the acclaim *Chandrika Prasad v. Republic of Fiji* has received, its legacy was severely weakened by subsequent developments in Fiji. First, the Court of Appeal decision affirming much of Gates' opinion in *Prasad* (as well as subsequent decisions on related cases, including the opinion of a three-judge panel headed by Gates in 2008 in a case brought by Qarase) strengthened the basis for extra-constitutional action on the basis of necessity. More importantly, the decision was not self-executing. After the Court of Appeal decision, Qarase arranged for new elections rather than hand power back to Chaudhry's Peoples' Coalition – a course of action to which Chaudhry acceded. (A subsequent attempt to challenge these actions by the nongovernmental organization Citizens Constitutional Forum was rejected by the courts.)

Trials

After the 2001 election, Fiji conducted a series of trials of some of the people involved in the 2000 coup attempt. In 2002, Speight was convicted of treason and sentenced to death, although the president subsequently commuted the sentence to life in prison. In 2004, the sitting Vice President Ratu Jope Seniloli and five others (including a sitting member of Cabinet) faced trial for treason for their part in Speight's actions in 2000. Seniloli was convicted and sentenced to four years imprisonment. He was, however, released by order of SDL Attorney General Qorinasi Bale after serving slightly more than three months. This early release – as well as the limited number of individuals tried and convicted – brought criticism from military leaders, including Bainimarama, that the SDL government was protecting people involved in the 2000 coup in an attempt to cultivate political support.

Reconciliation Measures

The SDL government also developed and partially implemented a program of reconciliation for the events of 2000. The SDL established a Ministry of National Reconciliation. In October 2004, the Ministry along with other government leaders sponsored a Reconciliation Week that culminated on Fiji Day (the anniversary of the country's independence). The events included traditional reconciliation ceremonies to seek forgiveness for transgressions. These events, however, were attended mainly by supporters of the SDL. Chaudhry, other Labor party leaders, and members of civil society organizations criticized the events as non-genuine and insufficient to establish restorative justice. The SDL also proposed the establishment of a Reconciliation and Unity Commission through its Promotion of Reconciliation, Tolerance, and Unity bill. By holding hearings concerning "the causes, nature and extent of the violations of human rights" associated with the events in 2000, the Commission would have prepared a report on the events and their implications for preventing politically motivated violations of human rights in the future. While the Commission could have offered some potential for restorative reparation and compensation for some victims of events in 2000, the bill came under heavy criticism from Bainimarama, Chaudhry, and civil society organizations for enabling the Commission to grant amnesty for individuals involved in the 2000 coup attempt. The SDL government did not pass this bill prior to the 2006 election, but planned to revise the legislation afterward. The Reconciliation Bill was one of the items that Bainimarama criticized in advance of his takeover of government in December 2006. President Iloilo granted Bainimarama and the military amnesty for their actions in 2006.

In some respects, Bainimarama's coup in 2006 was an attempt to undo the previous response to the 2000 coup. Bainimarama had initially selected Qarase to serve as interim prime minister in 2000. In his statements in 2006, Bainimarama claimed that had he known the path Qarase would follow, he would not have appointed him. In his takeover address, Bainimarama has argued that his work in leading government is to undo the legacy of racial politics in Fiji and avoid what he labeled as the "divisive policies" of the SDL.

The Bainimarama-led government instituted the Peoples Charter for Change, Peace, and Progress; the final version of the Peoples Charter identifies its goal of rebuilding Fiji "into a non-racial, culturally vibrant and united, well-governed, truly democratic nation." The Peoples Charter initiative is based on the belief that racial division has hampered the country's development by distorting its political leadership. As such, the Peoples Charter envisions a process of forward-looking transitional justice by enhancing governance, building a cohesive national identity, and achieving sustainable development. In its final version, the Peoples Charter calls not only for reform of institutions and political leadership, but also for increased involvement of the population in governance. While the process of revising the draft Peoples Charter involved a large number of participants, there was limited participation of political parties opposed to the Bainimarama-led government. Further, the Peoples Charter largely lists a set of policy goals, while not identifying the means to achieve these goals. As such, the Peoples Charter is largely a framework document rather than a legally binding program.

Conclusion

Transitional justice in Fiji has largely reflected the political concerns of those seeking to implement processes of reconciliation or forward-looking reforms. In this respect, transitional justice efforts in the country have largely been instances of victors' justice, often leading to outcomes that others experience as repressive. In large measure, this dynamic is attributable to how important control over government has been for attempts as transitional justice. Further, while many attempts at transitional justice acknowledge the importance of colonial-era legacies, the attempts at transitional justice in Fiji have been unable to address these pre-independence events despite the importance of this history in shaping contemporary political dynamics. Reconciliation efforts narrowly focused on the rule of law and formal democratic requirements continue to ignore these colonial legacies and make it less likely to achieve a transition to equal justice. The injustices a government may address are in many cases legacies from previous generations that have left poor people – particularly the rural poor, foremost of whom are those who have been displaced from land when leases were not renewed – economically and socially disadvantaged. These effects have been compounded by the economic losses associated with coups (out-migration, decreased investment, and declines in tourism, a main source of foreign exchange earnings). Well-governed social justice provisions targeted on the basis of economic need, rather than racial background, may help overcome these legacies and, perhaps, provide a foundation for victim-led reconciliation efforts.

Erik W. Larson

Cross-references: Amnesty; Conflict (Ongoing) and Transitional Justice; Court Trials for Redress; Reconciliation.

Further Readings

Ali, Ahmed. 2004 [1979]. *Girmit: Indian Indenture Experience in Fiji.* Suva: Fiji Museum / Ministry of National Reconciliation and Multi-Ethnic Affairs.

Lal, Brij V. 1992. *Broken Waves: A History of the Fiji Islands in the Twentieth Century.* Honolulu: University of Hawaii Press.

Larson, Erik and Ron Aminzade. 2009. Nation-Building in Post-Colonial Nation-States: The Cases of Tanzania and Fiji. *International Social Science Journal,* 192: 169–182.

Reeves, Sir P., T. R. Vakatora, and B. V. Lal. 1996. *The Fiji Islands – Towards a United Future: Report of the Fiji Constitution Review Commission.* Suva: Government Printer.

Robertson, Robbie and William Sutherland. 2001. *Government by the Gun: The Unfinished Business of Fiji's 2000 Coup.* Annandale NSW: Pluto Press / Zed Books.

France

Following the shock of its military defeat by Germany in June 1940, the authoritarian Vichy regime replaced the Third Republic, a parliamentary regime, from July 10, 1940 to August 10, 1944. Democracy was then reinstituted with the annulment of most Vichy legislation, general elections, and the creation of a Fourth Republic. Courts of justice tried those who had collaborated with the Germans. Amnesties and amnesia hid, until the 1970s, the responsibility of Vichy political, judicial, and administrative powers as instruments of political and racial policies. True memory of these "dark years" came slowly back to light among the French people, and reparations were finally granted to some of the victims or their survivors. No reconciliation between Vichy and Gaullist France was ever attempted.

The Repressive Past

The Vichy regime started on July 10, 1940 with a Constitutional Law passed by a majority of the Parliament of the Third Republic, in effect giving all powers to Marshall Philippe Pétain, a respected figure of World War I. He issued a series of acts de facto replacing the parliamentary regime of the Third Republic: the Parliament was suspended, the Republic became a "French State" headed by Pétain as Chief of State, with "Labor, Family, Homeland" replacing the traditional motto "Liberté, égalité, fraternité." No formal or informal opposition was allowed: only the regime's voice was expressed in controlled and censored press and state radio broadcasts. Political parties and trade unions were abolished. All state employees had to swear allegiance to Pétain, whose picture was everywhere.

The Vichy authoritarian and anti-Semitic regime was not imposed by the German victors: it was a French initiative inspired by French rightist, fascist, and conservative groups, a reaction against the democratic parliamentary regime of the Third Republic and the communist/socialist Popular Front government of the 1930s. Vichy initiated anti-Semitic laws as early as October 1940, which excluded Jews for racial reasons from state employment and allowed the confiscation of their business and personal property. Foreign Jews were interned in camps without judicial oversight. Other victims were communist and socialist leaders and supporters, resistance fighters against the German occupation (treated as terrorists), and civil servants – all of whom were targeted for political reasons – and freemasons and trade unionists, who were targeted for social and economic reasons. Punitive measures varied according to group and included harassment, registration, dismissal from public or private functions, confiscation of property, internment, and deportation of Jews to German extermination camps; arrest, imprisonment, torture, killings, or deportation of resistance fighters and political opponents to

German concentration camps; investigation and harassment of freemasons and trade unionists; deportation of workers to Germany for forced labor; and dismissal of civil servants on racial or political grounds.

Those responsible for these crimes were the Vichy political leaders, whose edicts were the bases for the regime's constitutional acts, legislation, and regulations applied by all administrative and judicial authorities, and by the citizens. Enforcement was carried out by the Vichy administration, prefects, police, and judges. The official administration was supplemented from 1943 onward by a national parapolice force known as the Milice, composed of 45,000 armed volunteers fighting against the Resistance and the communists.

The number of French and foreign Jews deported from France with the complicity of the Vichy authorities was 76,000; fewer than 3 percent survived. Around 100,000 people lost their lives in Resistance activities, and 130,000 resistance fighters were deported to German camps. Some 35,000 civil servants were dismissed, 60,000 freemasons were investigated, 6,000 harassed, 549 (of 989 deported) died in German camps, and 750,000 French workers were sent to Germany as conscript labor.

The Vichy regime collapsed when most of France was liberated from German occupation by the Allies (mainly American and British), and a de facto provisional government of France, led by General de Gaulle, took over in August 1944. The transition was difficult. War was not finished in Western Europe until the German surrender on May 9, 1945. There were revolutionary armed (communist) movements in a few regions, the French were still torn between their early respect and faith in Marshall Pétain, who had stopped the war in 1940, and the new Gaullist authorities – yet unelected – who had the prestige of the long-awaited Liberation that included the Resistance-assisted military successes of the Allies. There was an urge for revenge and punishment of the Vichy leaders and other collaborators, including those who had arrested, tortured, or executed members of the Resistance. There was also an element of social revenge against the elite and private vendettas, which led to illegal trials, purges, and summary executions.

Transitional justice measures were adopted unevenly: the restoration of order and political and judicial measures came first. However, there was no effort at reconciliation, and the truth about the role of Vichy and its participation in the persecution of the Jews were obfuscated for more than thirty years. Reparations for victims and survivors were obtained only scarcely and slowly.

Transitional Justice

In a period of turmoil, France's return to democracy required that order be restored and maintained and that the executive, legislative, judicial, and administrative powers be reestablished and effective.

Restoring Order

An (unelected) Provisional Government was set up in June 1944 in Paris, followed by a new government of "national unity" in September. General Charles de Gaulle was elected president on November 13, 1944. The government replaced the French Committee of National Liberation, an advisory body created in Algiers in June 1943. A consultative Assembly of 248 members was created in November 1944 to give advice to the provisional government and make proposals. In liberated France, a decree (*ordinance*) of 1944 created seventeen Commissioners of the Republic, who replaced the Vichy prefects (government-appointed senior administrators with authority over regions of France). They had wide powers, including a role in the purges. They could suspend all legislative and regulatory texts, and were to take all measures and decisions to maintain order and the functioning of public administration and private enterprises. They were authorized to suspend from their functions all elected officials and civil servants, and to halt the implementation of tribunals' judgments. During the post-liberation period when the German troops had left and the Vichy authorities had not yet been replaced by an effective administrative and police structure, there was little or no control over Resistance groups' initiatives in different regions. It took time, negotiations, and persuasion of local populations for de Gaulle-appointed Commissioners to assume effective power in their regions.

Restoring Democracy

The Ordinance of August 10, 1944 reestablished republican legality by declaring null and void all Pétain's constitutional Acts. The newly reconstituted democratic parties, Socialists and Christian Democrats, wanted a return to the parliamentary system of the Third Republic. De Gaulle wanted a new constitution with a strong executive and a weak parliament to replace the past ineffectiveness of the Third Republic. The Communists, first hoping for a Soviet-type revolution, realized its impossibility in a country with a large Allied military presence and without popular support. After a failed coup, they participated in elections and coalition governments, with the support of de Gaulle, who encouraged their integration into democratic institutions and needed their support for the reconstruction of France's railways, mines, and industry.

General elections and a referendum were held in October 1945 (the last elections were held in 1936): the French voted against a return to the institutions of the Third Republic and elected a Constituent Assembly. In October 1946, a further referendum approved the Constitution of the Fourth Republic, another parliamentary regime. It reaffirmed the rights and freedoms of the Declaration of the Rights of Man and of the Citizen of 1789 and proclaimed that "every human being, without distinction of race, religion or belief, possesses inalienable and sacred rights" (Preamble of the Constitution of the Fourth Republic 1946, paragraph 1). The Republic's motto – "liberty, equality, fraternity" – was reinstated as well as its founding principle: government of the people, for the people, and by the people. Finally, De Gaulle's wish for a strong executive was satisfied when a new Constitution was adopted in October 1958, giving birth to the Fifth Republic.

Justice

In March 1944, in Algiers, the National Council of the Resistance adopted its program. Among the measures to be adopted after the Liberation was the "punishment of traitors and the eviction from the administration and professional life of all those who have dealt with the enemy or have actively associated themselves with the policy of the governments of collaboration" (Charte du Conseil national de la Résistance 1944, Article 2).

An estimated 11,000 summary executions of alleged collaborationists were carried out before and after the Liberation.

In the post-Liberation period, two concerns had to be reconciled: respect for legal norms and the need to judge quickly. Three types of official courts were instituted: the courts of justice, in each French department (county); the civic courts charged with less important cases, also in each department; and, at the national level, the High Court of Justice that judged the members of the Vichy governments and senior officials, admirals, colonial governors-general, and diplomats. These jurisdictions started functioning in October 1944, with the aim of replacing progressively the various extralegal bodies that carried out "people's justice" in the aftermath of the Liberation.

A governmental ordinance of June 1944 authorized the trial and punishment of all civil servants for acts of collaboration with the enemy and for having undermined the [democratic] institutions and public liberties. The ordinance referred to Articles 75 of the Penal Code adopted in July 1939, which stated: "Shall be guilty of treason and punished by death: 4. Every French citizen who, in wartime, will entice military personnel or sailors, to enter the service of a foreign power.... 5. Every French citizen who, in wartime, will entertain intelligence with a foreign power or with its agents, with a view to facilitate the enterprises of this power against France" (Ordonnance relative à l'épuration administrative sur le territoire métropolitain 1944).

An ordinance of August 1944 instituting the punishment of "national indignity" targeted "every French citizen recognized as guilty of having, after 16 June 1940, either given direct help voluntarily in France or abroad to Germany or to its Allies, or having voluntarily undermined the unity of the nation or the freedom and equality of the French" (Ordonnance instituant l'indignité nationale 1944). Members of governments having exercised their authority in France between June 16, 1940 and the establishment of the Provisional Government of the French Republic were liable to be charged with this crime. The ordinance also applied to those having had a directing function in national, regional, or departmental services of the propaganda of these governments and of the Commissariat on Jewish Affairs, which coordinated the anti-Jewish policies of Vichy France. It listed a number of bodies of collaboration, participation in which would be treated as a crime. Publishing articles or books, giving lectures favoring the enemy, and promoting collaboration with the enemy, racism, or totalitarian doctrines would also be considered criminal.

The ordinance established "special sections" – an unfortunate term in view of the infamous *sections spéciales* created by Vichy – attached to the departmental courts of justice. There was no right of appeal on substance, but only recourse to the Court of Cassation on procedural grounds. Judgments of national indignity could order the withdrawal of all civic and political rights, ineligibility to representative functions, vetting and exclusion from public functions, legal and teaching positions, associations and trade unions, leading positions in the media, and positions as managing directors and members of governing boards of industrial and business firms. The duration of these punishments would be no less than five years.

Some of these punishments recalled the anti-Jewish exclusion laws of Vichy. The difference was that the Vichy laws applied to Jews because they were Jews, who were not charged with any offense, nor judged by an established tribunal, with no right of appeal, and without limitation of time. The post-Liberation ordinance prescribed punishments on an individual basis, based on a tribunal's judgment, for a set period of time. Indicted persons had legal assistance.

Responding to the potential charge of discrimination against Vichy supporters and collaborators, the introduction to the ordinance on national indignity noted that the principle of equality before the law is not opposed to a separation between good and bad citizens in order to distance from positions of command and influence those among the French who disregarded France's ideals and interests during the most painful period of its history. On the charge that the ordinance had retroactive effect – a violation of the Penal Code – the introduction replied that the system of national indignity was not part of the criminal order, but was based on the terrain of political justice, and its judgments could not be pronounced beyond six months after the liberation of the entirety of France.

The High Court of Justice judged Philippe Pétain, Pierre Laval, 106 ministers, secretaries of state and high-level civil servants between March 1945 and January 1949. Sentences included eight death sentences of which three were executed, forced labor of various durations, and national indignity; there were three acquittals and forty-two cases were dismissed.

The number of cases judged by the Courts of Justice, which ceased functioning in 1951, was 57,954, and those judged by the Civic Chambers 69,797. They included 6,763 death sentences, of which 767 were executed. Other sentences were for forced labor or imprisonment. Almost 50,000 persons were sentenced to national indignity. Between 22,000 and 28,000 civil servants were subjected to disciplinary measures. By 1947, 2,300 military officers had been dismissed.

Courts of justice were abolished in 1950 and replaced by military tribunals. The High Court of Justice ceased functioning also in 1950, but was reconvened in 1954 and in 1960 to try escaped suspects who had returned to France.

A 1951 law granted amnesty to all those who had committed acts for which the punishment involved loss of civil rights and a prison sentence of less than fifteen years. The law did not apply to grave crimes or judgments of the High Court. With the second amnesty law of 1953, all remaining prisoners of the judiciary purge, except those guilty of the most serious crimes, were released, marking the end of France's post-Liberation purges. Of the 40,000 individuals sent to prison in 1945 for acts of collaboration, only 4,000 remained by jail in 1951 and none by 1964.

Presidential pardons and commutations were widely used to soften unduly harsh verdicts and bring some order in the chaos of postwar jurisprudence. Beside these judiciary measures, the Vichy administration was subject to an administrative purge (*épuration*). More than 11,000 civil servants were subject to disciplinary measures or forced retirement, out of 50,000 cases reviewed by purge committees. Purges were also applied in economic, intellectual, artistic, and media circles through internal purge committees in each trade sector. The French remained divided over those who felt betrayed by the alleged excessive indulgence of the judges or of purge committees and those who felt victimized by their excessive severity. These quarrels have now passed into history.

Reconciliation Measures

No measures were taken to reach reconciliation between the "two Frances" of 1940–1944. Governments following the Vichy period first tried to erase all traces of that period, by legislation, justice, and by pretending that the crimes committed then by the French, or with the assistance or complicity of the French state, its leaders, its administration and police, and by citizens were solely the responsibility of the German occupiers, and not that of the French. It took thirty years to correct this misconception. French presidents (de Gaulle, Pompidou, Giscard d'Estaing, and Mitterand) held that those crimes should not be revealed or punished in the interest of the civil and social peace in France. This position was maintained until the 1970s, which witnessed the publications of history books, the showing of films, the revelation of the truth at the trials of Klaus Barbie, Paul Touvier, and Maurice Papon, and the courageous admission of France's responsibility for Vichy's crimes by Jacques Chirac on July 16, 1995 – as well as through the passage of time and the emergence of new generations neither involved nor concerned with the Vichy period. Known as the Butcher of Lyon, Barbie was the Gestapo member who personally tortured prisoners and was responsible for the deaths of some 4,000 people. Touvier was the first Frenchman to be convicted for crimes against humanity for his collaboration with the Vichy government, whereas Papon, the secretary general for police in the Bordeaux Prefecture responsible for the deportation of 1,600 Jews, was later convicted and sentenced for complicity for crimes against humanity. There were no specific mechanisms for bringing together victims and perpetrators, except during the Tribunals' sessions when the plaintiffs faced the perpetrators.

Reparation

As a direct consequence of Chirac's 1995 speech, a decree created a Mission of Study on the Spoliation of Jews of France in 1997. The Mission was to establish an inventory of the spoliations, which had affected 300,000 to 330,000 persons.

Altogether, the Mission found that access to 80,000 bank accounts and about 6,000 bank safes had been blocked, 50,000 aryanisation procedures had been initiated, more than 100,000 objects and works of art as well as several million books pillaged, and 30,000 apartments emptied. The total value of these spoliations (that is, property confiscations) was estimated at the 2006 equivalent of 1,554 billion Euros. The Commission of Indemnification of Victims of Spoliations Effected as a Result of Antisemitic Legislative Measures in Force during the Occupation was created in 1999 as a consultative body. By April 2007, 23,591 requests had been recorded: 22,208 recommendations were adopted for indemnification for a total amount of 316.4 million Euros. Sums related to banking spoliations represented 31.4 million Euros. The average amount of indemnification was 27,934 Euros. Most of the recommendations concerned elderly persons, often of modest means.

In 2000, the government instituted a measure of reparation for children of Jewish deported parents in the form of monthly life pension of 3,000 Francs (450 Euros) or a one-time payment of 180,000 Francs (27,450 Euros).

Preserving Memory

Memory preservation of the Holocaust was actively assumed by Jewish organizations through documentation gathering, publications, memorials, celebrations, and political lobbying. Other groups maintained the memory of resistance and deportations. Programs referring to Vichy France and the Holocaust were only included in state school curricula in the 1980s. By 1982, most school manuals were already mentioning the role of the

Vichy regime in the deportation of the Jews. A Ministry of National Education order issued on April 25, 1988 included the history of World War II and the Holocaust in the public high school curriculum. Access to archives on that period was slowly liberalized.

Conclusion

The transition of France from the Vichy regime to democracy was done promptly and effectively with regard to the country's constitutional institutions and a reaffirmation of democratic and human rights. Still, justice, closely linked to political and social constraints, had its own excesses before a return to traditional judicial principles and procedures was accomplished. The recognition that the state owed a debt to victims, particularly the Jewish ones, took years, and reparations were only authorized slowly. The role of Jewish organizations, historians, and human rights associations was decisive in convincing post-Vichy governments to take action against political opposition and simple bureaucratic obstruction. Only time and new generations allowed the Vichy years to be recognized as what they were – a "dark period" of repression.

Yves Beigbeder

Cross-references: Amnesty; Apology; Germany – the Nazi Past; Prosecute and Punish; Purges; Reparations.

Further Readings

Beigbeder, Yves. 2006. *Judging War Crimes and Torture, French Justice and International Criminal Tribunals and Commissions (1940–2005)*. Leiden: Martinus Nijhoff Publishers.
Charte du Conseil national de la Résistance, Algiers, March 15, 1944. Available at: http://www.ldh-france.org/1944-CHARTE-DU-CONSEIL-NATIONAL-DE (accessed November 7, 2009).
Mission d'étude sur la spoliation des Juifs de France. 2000. *La persécution des Juifs de France 1940–1944 et le rétablissement de la légalité républicaine. Recueil des textes officiels 1940–1999* [The Persecution of French Jews 1944–1944 and the Restoration of Republican Legality. Collection of Official Documents 1940–1999].
Novick, P. 1968. *The Resistance versus Vichy. The Purge of Collaborators in Liberated France*. London: Chatto & Windus.
Ordonnance instituant l'indignité nationale, August 26, 1944. Paris: Gouvernement provisoire de la République française.
Ordonnance relative à l'épuration administrative sur le territoire métropolitain, June 27, 1944. Paris: La Documentation française.
Paxton, R. O. 2001. *Vichy France, Old Guard and New Order, 1940–1944*. New York: Columbia University Press.
Preamble of the Constitution of the Fourth Republic. 1946. Available at: http://www.elysee.fr/elysee/anglais/the_institutions/founding_texts/preambule_to_the_27th_of_october_1946_constitution/preambule_to_the_27th_of_october_1946_constitution.20243.html (accessed November 7, 2009).
Rousso, H. 1991. *The Vichy Syndrome, History and Memory of France since 1944*. Cambridge, MA: Harvard University Press.

Georgia

Georgia has yet to reckon with the crimes and the abuse of power committed during the Soviet era (1921–1991) and the post-Soviet conflicts with the breakaway regions of South Ossetia and Abkhazia. Its August 2008 war with Russia produced a new set of human rights violations on all sides, weakening still further the prospects for justice in the republic.

The Repressive Past

Russia annexed Georgia in 1801, but the republic declared its independence in 1917, following the collapse of the Russian empire. Georgia was forcibly incorporated into the Soviet Union in 1921, after the Red Army invaded the country and toppled its moderate Social Democratic, pro-Menshevik government. During the next decade, the Soviet state seized Georgia's private factories and collectivized its peasant lands in a violent process designed to impose communist economic policies and political rule. Pro-Bolshevik Georgians were installed in positions of authority in political, economic, and cultural institutions in the newly created Transcaucasian Soviet Federated Socialist Republic. In 1936, Georgia assumed the status of a separate Soviet republic.

Josef Stalin, a seminarian turned revolutionary from the Georgian town of Gori, eventually became a member of the inner circle of the Bolshevik Party. By 1928, he achieved undisputed leadership of the Party and elevated many of his Georgian comrades to key positions in Moscow. The most brutal of Stalin's colleagues was Lavrentii Beria, formerly the First Secretary of the Georgian and then Transcaucasian Communist Party in the 1920s and early 1930s. Stalin appointed Beria to head the Soviet secret police (the People's Commissariat for Internal Affairs or NKVD, the predecessor of the KGB or Committee for State Security) in 1938, during the Great Purge. Although Beria reduced the tempo and number of executions of "enemies of the people," he remained responsible for the terror through which Stalin governed, including the Gulag, the archipelago of forced labor camps.

Some 50,000 Georgians perished during the Great Purge (1936–1938), while tens of thousands of other Georgians suffered from subsequent repression waves. In 1944, at the height of World War II, more than 100,000 Meskhetian Turks were deported from Meskheti (renamed the Samtskhe-Javakheti region) to Central Asia on suspicion of collaborationist attitudes. Mortality rates from such operations often exceeded 25 percent. Until 1991, thousands of ethnic Georgians were placed under surveillance by the KGB.

In the late 1980s, the political opening (*perestroika*) of Soviet leader Mikhail Gorbachev aimed to rejuvenate, but managed to destabilize, Soviet socialism. One of the architects of this reform was Foreign Minister Eduard Shevardnadze, former head of the Georgian Ministry of Internal Affairs and First Secretary of the Communist Party of Georgia. As *perestroika* unfolded, Georgian nationalism intensified, and new anti-Soviet elites mobilized the population against Moscow. In March 1991, a referendum on independence received the support of 99 percent of Georgians. Georgia declared its independence the following month.

Even before the referendum on independence, nationalists assumed control of the Georgian legislature, the Supreme Soviet. In November 1990, the body elected as its chairman Zviad Gamsakhurdia, a Tbilisi State University literature professor, who became the first president of independent Georgia in May 1991. Gamsakhurdia's erratic and increasingly dictatorial leadership helped plunge Georgia into political and ethnic turmoil. The Georgian National Guard and paramilitary groups forced him out of office in 1992. Under Shevardnadze, elected president in 1995, the law enforcement and security agencies developed a reputation for brutality and impunity, and paramilitary groups operated freely. This abuse of power, coupled with dramatic economic decline, motivated liberal reformers to challenge the president at the polls. After the opposition condemned the parliamentary elections of November 2003 as rigged, widespread peaceful demonstrations (known as the Rose Revolution) forced Shevardnadze to resign. Mikheil Saakashvili, the pro-Western opposition leader, won the 2004 presidential election.

The Russian-Georgian War of August 2008 created new human rights abuses, further complicating the identification of perpetrator and victim. The conflict resulted from mounting strains between Russia and Georgia, and between Georgia and its two breakaway regions of South Ossetia and Abkhazia. Georgia's use of military force to reestablish control over the regions, protected by Russia since 1991, domestic Georgian politics, and the clashing regional interests of Russia and the United States led to the outbreak of the war. Saakashvili risked military action to reunite the fractured country in the hope that the groundswell of support for reunification in Georgia would silence growing domestic opposition to his increasingly authoritarian rule. He also believed that Russia would not retaliate because he enjoyed the support of the United States. Saakashvili miscalculated. Russian forces quickly defeated their Georgian adversary, and Moscow soon thereafter supported the formal declarations of independence by Abkhazia and South Ossetia.

All sides in the war engaged in gross human rights violations. Russian forces bombed Georgian villages and Gori, allegedly using cluster bombs. Ossetian militia groups attacked Georgian civilians living within Ossetia and along the border with Georgia proper, while Georgia allegedly used cluster munitions and other forms of indiscriminate violence against civilians in the war zone. Hundreds of South Ossetian and ethnic Georgian civilians and combatants were killed in the conflict.

Transitional Justice

Although Georgia endured Soviet repression for seventy years, its postcommunist political elite did not forcefully address the crimes of the Soviet past. Part of the problem is the complex and often contradictory character of that past, particularly the Stalinist era. The cult of Stalin had remained strong in Georgia after his death in 1953. Reacting to the attacks on Stalin and Stalinism by Nikita Khrushchev, Stalin's successor, widespread demonstrations fueled by wounded nationalism engulfed Tbilisi in March 1956. Perhaps hundreds of protesters were killed when Moscow called in the Red Army to quell the disturbances. Many Georgians still harbor deeply ambivalent feelings about the dictator, and Georgia's Ministry of Culture continues to maintain a large museum in Gori, Stalin's birthplace, dedicated to the dictator. Its permanent displays celebrate Stalin's life and rule, providing only a hint of his mass crimes, which included tens of thousands of Georgian victims.

After 1991, Georgia's reluctance to engage in transitional justice also reflected the preferences of powerful groups that were enriched through nepotism and widespread corruption and saw little need or utility in reopening the past. Transitional justice was further hampered by the survival of numerous Soviet elites, the continuation of ethnic tensions, and the weakness of the liberal political opposition.

Access to Secret Archives

Some 230,000 secret files dating from 1921 to 1991 had been stored in the basement of KGB headquarters in Tbilisi. Part of this archive and other sensitive files were transferred to Moscow in 1991, while many archival documents that remained in Tbilisi were destroyed by fire during the conflict that erupted in December 1991 between Gamsakhurdia's supporters and the Georgian National Guard. After the violence subsided, the 20,000 files that survived in poor condition were transferred to the Archive Administration of the Ministry of Internal Affairs for repair and storage, but the Georgian political authorities denied access to them. After 1995, President Shevardnadze opposed the opening of the files, maintaining that during communist rule "tens of thousands" of ordinary Georgians were forced to collaborate with the KGB and other security organs. File access would thus "reopen old wounds" and lead to "a new wave of resistance, mistrust and hatred" (Georgian President Opposes Lustration, 1997).

Shevardnadze's decision may have also reflected fear for his own political position – during the Soviet period he had close ties with the Georgian KGB and also served as head of the Georgian police. Whatever his motivation, Shevardnadze's depiction of Georgians as primarily victims of Soviet coercion broadly simplified and distorted history. Not only Russians but also Georgians perpetrated crimes against fellow Georgians during Soviet times. When Beria took over the NKVD in 1938, he thoroughly purged the organization and seeded it with his Georgian supporters, who then terrorized the Soviet Union, including their native republic.

Under Saakashvili, the government provided limited access to the former KGB archives. The Archive Administration of the Ministry of Internal Affairs also continued to restore the fragile, fire- and water-damaged files. On its Web site, the Ministry notes that, upon petition, it would endeavor to provide "documentary information" about relatives who died "during the Great Purge" (From the History of the Archives). At the time of this writing, there are no public data on how many people have accessed the secret files compiled on them or their relatives during Soviet times.

Lustration

After his election in 2004, President Saakashvili promised to put forward a lustration law, but took no action. In 2005, lustration was taken up by opposition parties. Two years later, a draft lustration law proposed by the opposition Democratic Front was voted down by the ruling National Movement Party on the grounds that it would be ineffective or detrimental to its own purpose, because the lists of former KGB agents in Georgia had been removed to Moscow and were inaccessible. Lustration, the critics maintained, would expose only some of the former agents, thus leading to further injustice. The ruling party was divided on the issue, and a minority faction argued in favor of the proposed law and an even harsher variant. For its part, the opposition maintained that lustration, despite its inherent shortcomings, was important as a symbolic rejection of the Soviet past. However, senior members of the ruling party again expressed the government's disinterest in lustration during discussions in 2008–2009.

Parliament addressed lustration again in 2010, when the Democratic Front proposed the Liberty Charter package of measures, which included possible political and occupational restrictions on former communist officials and agents, and a ban on the public display of Nazi and Soviet symbols. The bill's lustration provisions resembled those debated in 2007. In an unusual display of compromise between the government and the opposition, the bill was passed on its first reading by a vote of seventy-five to one. According to the bill, representatives of parties in parliament would serve as members of a state commission created by the president. The commission would determine appropriate measures against former Soviet agents and officials, but their deliberations – and the lists of individuals subject to lustration – were to remain confidential. However, when the Georgian parliament adopted lustration in May 2011, the law failed to authorize a commission comprised of members of parliament. Instead, it invested the Ministry of Internal Affairs with important powers over lustration, raising fears among liberals that the process would stall or be politicized.

Reforms of the Secret Police

Under Gamsakhurdia's leadership, the Supreme Soviet of Georgia purged the top ranks of the republican KGB, ignoring protests from Moscow. In May 1991, after he became president of Georgia and shortly before the collapse of the Soviet Union, Gamsakhurdia made final the break with Moscow of the Georgian KGB, by then renamed the National Security Committee. After Gamsakhurdia was ousted, the Georgian State Council abolished the Ministry of State Security and formed an Information and Intelligence Bureau, appointing Irakli Batisashvili as its head. Although these reorganizations shattered the identification of the Georgian security services with the Soviet Union and Russia, they never established strong legislative controls or oversight functions. In early 1993, Shevardnadze restored a measure of political stability to an unstable Georgia after becoming head of state. However, the internal security forces remained under his personal control.

Court Proceedings

No Soviet-era perpetrators have been brought to justice in post-Soviet Georgia. By contrast, after the 2008 war, both Russia and Georgia have availed themselves of international justice mechanisms, but with limited results, by filing cases with the International Court of Justice, the International Criminal Court, and the European Court of Human Rights (see separate entries). The case lodged by Georgia against Russia in the International Court of Justice in 2008 for alleged acts of forced displacement of ethnic Georgians in Abkhazia and South Ossetia was dismissed in April 2011 on procedural grounds. The 1965 international convention on ethnic discrimination, which Georgia invoked, requires that the parties to a dispute first attempt to negotiate a settlement, a condition that was never satisfied. The charges brought by Georgia and Russia against each other in the International Criminal Court are still under preliminary investigation at the time of this writing, and it is unclear when or if the competing claims will be adjudicated.

After the 2008 war, Georgians also lodged complaints against Russia with the European Court of Human Rights, claiming that Moscow violated their right to life, humane treatment, and the protection of their property. Residents of South Ossetia and members of the Russian military who had served as peacekeepers in the region took the same course of action against Georgia. In January 2011, the European Court dismissed 1,549 of the

3,300 cases against Georgia because of the failure of legal representatives of residents of South Ossetia and members of the Russian Army to respond to requests for information. The remaining claims, on both sides, were still under investigation at the time of this writing.

Sorting out the mutual allegations arising from the war is likely to be complicated by the findings of the Independent International Fact-Finding Mission on the Conflict in Georgia issued in late 2009. The mission, funded by the European Union, maintained that the 2008 war began with a Georgian military assault on South Ossetia, but that Russia had earlier contributed to tensions in the region and that ethnic Georgians were victims of ethnic cleansing during the war.

Reconciliation

No reconciliation programs have been implemented to bridge the divide between the communist-era victims and victimizers. In addition, the Georgian government's impulse for reconciliation with South Ossetia and Abkhazia is weak. The State Ministry for Reintegration, which works toward the reunification of South Ossetia and Abkhazia with Georgia proper, has emphasized the importance of confidence-building measures, particularly the use of social, economic, and cultural cooperation for political bridge building with the two regions. Observers contend, however, that trust will remain in short supply as long as the Saakashsvili government uses threatening language or force to resolve disputes. Better prospects may lie in the Georgian opposition, which recognizes the historical mistreatment of the Abkhaz and Ossetian minorities by ethnic Georgians.

Saakashvili's weakening of Georgian democracy in the years before the war undermined the very institutions (the press, parliament) that might have restrained him from taking military action. Yet domestic opposition to Saakashvili remained strong before and after the war. Georgian opposition leaders, such as Irakli Alasani, former ambassador to the United Nations, argue that the most effective way to win back South Ossetia and Abkhazia is to make reintegration into Georgia more attractive by strengthening Georgian democracy.

Rewriting History Books

In post-Soviet Georgia, officially sanctioned textbooks have evaluated communist rule as a negative experience for the Georgian nation in political, economic, demographic, and moral terms. They often use the concept of "totalitarianism" to explain the pervasive, destructive impact of the Soviet system, which attempted to create a *Homo Sovieticus* indifferent to public morals, rule of law, or private property. Some textbooks include instructional materials suggesting that the fundamental source of the Soviet repression of Georgia was communist ideology, not Russian imperialism, although Russia formed the core of Soviet Union. The most thoughtful of the textbooks examine the complexity of Soviet "patriotism" during World War II, when some Georgians fought with devotion for the Soviet cause, while others joined the ranks of the Axis in a desperate bid to overturn Soviet rule in Georgia.

In 2010, in another reaction to the Russian-Georgian War, the Georgian government began to promote an "occupation" textbook condemning without qualification two centuries of rule by the Russian and Soviet empires. The textbook provoked controversy in Russia and Georgia, where some teachers, scholars, and politicians voiced concern over an adversarial narrative hindering efforts at reconciliation and justice.

Memorialization

Until 2008, the most notable example of using public space to evaluate the Soviet past was the opening in 2006 of the Museum of Soviet Occupation as part of Georgia's Independence Day celebration. Influenced by similar permanent exhibitions in Latvia and Estonia, the Georgian museum uses text and other media to narrate seventy years of Soviet occupation. Yet the continued existence in Gori of the Stalin museum and a six-meter bronze statue of the dictator on a nine-meter pedestal were reminders of Georgia's difficulty with reckoning with the Soviet era.

This ambiguity started to dissolve shortly after the Russian-Georgian War of 2008 when the Ministry of Culture announced plans to turn the Stalin Museum into a Museum of Russian Aggression. Although this transformation had yet to occur, in mid-2010, the huge statue of Stalin in Gori was moved to the grounds of the Stalin Museum. The government then announced that a monument to the victims of the totalitarian regime and of the Russian-Georgian War would be erected where the Stalin statue had stood. At the time of this writing, work on the monument had not yet started.

New efforts were also undertaken to rename streets with a clear identification with the communist era, using as replacements the names of soldiers who died in the 2008 war. In July 2010, the parliament unanimously approved the government's proposal that February 25 be named Occupation Day to mark the date in 1921 when the Red Army entered Georgia's capital and toppled its government. It also instructed public institutions to develop methods of remembrance in order to educate the public about the Soviet and Nazi totalitarian regimes.

If defeat in the 2008 war led the Georgian government to intensify its negative assessment of the Soviet past, other factors encouraged and legitimated this course of action. In 2009, Latvia dedicated June 17 as Soviet Occupation Day, and in June 2010, Moldova established June 28 as its Soviet Occupation Day (see entries on Latvia and Moldova). In its resolution naming February 25 as Occupation Day, the Georgian parliament linked its decision to this broad movement to condemn the Soviet era, expressing its support for the European Parliament and the OSCE Parliamentary Assembly in their decision to declare August 23, the date of the Molotov-Ribbentrop Pact, as a remembrance day for the victims of the Nazi and Soviet regimes.

Identifying oppressive expansionism as the hallmark of Russia's relationship with Georgia, the Saakashvili government challenged representations of historical events in which Russia or the Soviet Union is viewed in a positive light. In 2009, to make way for a new parliament building in the town of Kutaisi, the government demolished a large memorial to Georgia's role in defending the Soviet Union against the German invasion in World War II. Of the 700,000 Georgians who fought in the Soviet Army during World War II, 300,000 died in the conflict (Georgia's population was 3,540,000 in 1939). The Kremlin and several Georgian politicians protested the memorial's destruction, and in 2010, two Georgian opposition leaders attended a ceremony in Moscow that unveiled a monument commemorating the one destroyed in Kutaisi. In May 2011, the Georgian parliament officially recognized the mass repression and deportation of ethnic

Circassians by the Russian empire in the 1860s as genocide. The resolution passed on a vote of ninety-five to zero, but with many abstentions by members of the opposition.

Conclusion

The pursuit of transitional justice in Georgia is a multidimensional problem embedded in layers of history. The Soviet Union committed mass crimes and abuses of human rights against ethnic Georgians over seven decades. Yet Georgians also controlled the Soviet state during the most repressive years of the communist era. Georgians were also responsible for widespread abuse against regional minorities, including the Ossetians and the Abkhaz, who themselves resorted to violence and coercion against ethnic Georgians when given the opportunity. This tangled web of crime and repression makes the pursuit of transitional justice extremely complex. The political divisions among ethnic Georgians create further difficulties. Georgian elites often use the Soviet past to weaken their opponents, not to pursue transitional justice. Opposition parties have rallied in front of the Museum of Soviet Occupation under banners that condemned President Saakashvili as the "Bolshevik of the 21st Century" (Georgia Marks 1921 Red Army Invasion, 2009). The case of Georgia demonstrates that the pursuit of transitional justice will falter without consensus among elites and legitimate political institutions.

Thomas Sherlock

Cross-references: Access to Secret Files; Court Trials for Redress; European Court of Human Rights; International Criminal Court; Latvia; Lustration; Moldova; Russia.

Further References

Frichova, Magdalena. 2009. *Transitional Justice and Georgia's Conflicts: Breaking the Silence*. New York: International Center for Transitional Justice.
From the History of the Archives. Available at: http://archive.security.gov.ge/en/history.html (accessed February 4, 2011).
Georgia Marks (1921) Red Army Invasion, *Civil Georgia*, February 25, 2009. Available at: http://www.civil.ge/eng/article.php?id=20474&search=kgb (accessed February 4, 2011).
Georgian President Opposes Lustration. *RFE/RL Newsline*. December 9, 1997. Available at: http://www.friends-partners.org/friends/news/omri/1997/12/971209I.html (accessed February 4, 2011).
Independent International Fact-Finding Mission on the Conflict in Georgia. 2009. *Report*, September, 3 volumes. Available at: http://www.ceiig.ch/Report.html (accessed September 12, 2011).
Lustration amid Stalin Debates, *Civil Georgia*, February 17, 2007. Available at: http://www.civil.ge/eng/article.php?id=14650 (accessed February 4, 2011).
MPs Pass "Liberty Charter" with First Reading, *Civil Georgia*, October 28, 2010. Available at: http://www.civil.ge/eng/article.php?id=22794&search=tortladze (accessed February 4, 2011).

Germany – the Communist Past

Reckoning with the communist past in the German Democratic Republic (GDR) began shortly after the collapse of the old regime in the fall of 1989. Efforts and public interest have waned since their zenith in the first half of the 1990s, when policy makers were driven by motives and challenged by problems similar to those of other postcommunist countries, yet uniquely conditioned by the country's division from, and proximity to, democratic West Germany. Although the major political players in East and West

Germany united in agreement on the basic principles of retroactive justice as early as the spring/summer of 1990, the details sparked disputes before and after unification of the two states on October 3, 1990. West German anticommunist attitudes strengthened the voice of the East German opposition and marginalized the successor to the Socialist Unity Party (SED, which had been the GDR's ruling communist party), the Party of Democratic Socialism (PDS), in setting policy but not discourse. The legacy of West Germany's handling of the National Socialist past influenced approaches to confronting communist rule. As a whole, Germany's national identity continues to be shaped predominantly by its National Socialist past.

The Repressive Past

Toward the end of World War II, the United States, the United Kingdom, the Soviet Union, and, later, France agreed to a temporary division of Germany into four zones of occupation, with the Soviet Union in charge of the eastern part. Soviet denazification efforts soon also served the purpose of repression against real and alleged foes of the new communist order. Intimidation and repression of political opponents played a crucial role from the onset and remained a cornerstone after the GDR was founded on October 7, 1949.

Following a pattern seen in other Central and Eastern European countries, repression was most pronounced in the early stages of communist rule. Purges, intimidation, blackmail, show trials, kidnapping, assassination attempts, and imprisonment aimed to eliminate any political opposition. In June 1953, demonstrations against the regime that started in Berlin and spread to other cities were brutally crushed by Soviet tanks. Several people died, thousands were arrested, and more than twenty executed. As part of a general amnesty, many political prisoners were released in 1956. The relaxation of repression proved short-lived; the period of "thaw" ended a few months later.

Between 1945 and the building of the Berlin Wall in August 1961, approximately 3 million citizens crossed the border from East to West, voting with their feet against the imposition of communist rule. Deadly fortifications along the intra-German border and the Wall stopped the exodus. The few loopholes for escape that remained were gradually sealed. Estimates of how many people paid with their lives trying to cross the border to West Germany vary widely but approximately total at least 100. The Berlin Wall infused new life into the SED regime, allowing it finally to consolidate its rule. From now on, repression emphasized psychological intimidation and harassment; they remained the ultimate recourse and exposed the regime's vulnerability.

Since the 1950s, special criminal units of the People's Police and the Ministry of State Security (commonly referred to as the Stasi) were responsible for upholding internal order. Most repression was executed by organs of the state security, which directed both foreign intelligence and domestic surveillance. Founded in 1950, the insignia of the Ministry highlights its role as shield and sword of the communist party; full-time personnel were trained as "party soldiers" and increased from 2,700 in 1950 to more than 91,000 by the fall of 1989, when its ratio to the population was about 1:180, making it the largest security service in Eastern Europe. Its officers depended on a wide network of political informers – in 1989, more than 170,000 out of a population of 16.6 million. Among the informers were approximately 1,500 West German citizens. The Stasi had its own interrogation and detention facilities, among them prisons in Bautzen and

Berlin-Hohenschönhausen. During the tenure of the GDR, approximately 180,000 people were in custody for political reasons.

Political prisoners were not the only ones affected by the tentacles of communist authorities. To safeguard socialism, private lives were compromised and violated by such regime infractions as forced adoptions, resettling of citizens who lived along the border with West Germany, aborted careers, wire tapping, illegal opening of mail, and forced entry into homes.

Changes in the international environment and the regime's desire for international respectability made suppressing and isolating East German citizens from Western influence more difficult. To release pent-up reform pressure in the 1970s and 1980s, the SED government increasingly allowed or forced critics to move to West Germany. In particular, the forced exile of singer and songwriter Wolf Biermann in November 1976 aroused attention in the West and protest in the East. More people began to petition to leave the GDR legally, willingly exposing themselves to harassment by the authorities and even imprisonment. From 1963 on, the West German government literally bought out political prisoners from the cash-strapped GDR government; ransom was paid for about 33,500 people overall. By the middle of the 1980s, more than 10,000 people left the GDR annually with official blessing. Some 650,000 people emigrated between 1961 and 1989.

This controlled exit strategy weakened organized opposition within the GDR but could not suppress it entirely. By summer 1989, the Stasi estimated that about 2,500 people were involved in opposition groups, many of them church-based. Public reform pressure mounted in the summer and fall of 1989. The regime's fortieth anniversary celebrations in October 1989 were interrupted by demonstrations that quickly escalated to mass protest. In rapid succession, the old leadership under Erich Honecker resigned, the Berlin Wall opened, a new transitional government was instituted, and round-table talks commenced. Democratic elections took place in March 1990, and their outcome accelerated the move toward unification of East and West Germany on October 3, 1990.

Transitional Justice

Immediately after the fall of the Berlin Wall in November 1989, public pressure forced East German political leaders to address egregious government abuses. Efforts continued under the democratically elected GDR government, which set the agenda and path for transitional justice in a unified Germany. The Unification Treaty of August 31, 1990, which became effective on October 29, 1990, framed incorporation of the East into West Germany; it included the basic guidelines for transitional justice agreed on by the two governments. Unification returned a federal structure to former GDR territory. It fell on the Land Berlin and the five (re)established *Länder* (states) to execute most transitional justice measures, prompting regional variation in policy setting and implementation.

Germany's approach to transitional justice was comprehensive in scope and execution, but legal-administrative outcomes were defined by restraint and pragmatism. They focused on file access and vetting, reparations, criminal justice, and rehabilitation. Concrete policy measures were largely completed by 2005; interest in transitional justice has long been relegated to the back burner in both East and West. Government attention focuses on interpreting and commemorating the history of the GDR, activities that have turned out to be more conflict-prone than anticipated.

File Access and Vetting

The list of grievances against the former communist government was long, but none aroused more public anger than the role of the state security. Outraged citizens stormed its headquarters when the reformed GDR government under Hans Modrow failed to disband it; in Berlin and many other cities, grassroots activists disrupted the Stasi's attempted destruction of files. How to deal with those who had worked either formally or informally for the Stasi and what to do with the files were matters of heated debate in the spring and summer of 1990. The Stasi law passed by the GDR parliament became an amendment to the Unification Treaty; its major principles were incorporated into the Stasi Records Act of December 1991, passed by the all-German parliament, the Bundestag.

The task of organizing, reconstructing, archiving, and researching Stasi files was imparted to the Federal Commission for the Records of the State Security Service of the former German Democratic Republic (henceforth, BStU, the German acronym). Allowing individuals access to their secret police files was the core of the new law and its most controversial and novel aspect. Concerns that it would result in acts of vengeance have not materialized, and Germany's model has been emulated in several countries in Central and Eastern Europe.

The German practice raised important questions about who should be allowed access and under what conditions; ongoing clarifications were included in several amendments to the Stasi Records Act. The conflict culminated in the lengthy debate and court proceedings over the files of former Chancellor Helmut Kohl. The final outcome affirms the difficulty of aligning individual and public rights. Information about public figures can be released in exceptional cases but remains limited to aspects of their public lives. File access is strictly regulated: individuals can examine their own files, and under certain conditions researchers and journalists can gain access to records. Text passages may be blackened out to protect the privacy rights of those who had been affected by Stasi activities; the names of those who worked for the Stasi, on the other hand, are seen as a record of history and are not subject to the same restrictions.

Reasons for exceptional dismissal in the public sector – civil servants and elected politicians – focused on active involvement with the German security service and crimes against humanity; SED functionaries per se were not reviewed. Thus, a major role for the BStU is review of institutional inquiries into whether an individual had worked for the Stasi; it is also consulted with regard to pension, compensation, and rehabilitation claims of those who were persecuted under the SED regime. The agency is restricted to providing information on whether and in what capacity an individual worked for the Stasi, but has no role in decision making. Some high-profile cases in the political and literary world drew attention to ambiguities in Stasi involvement; prominent among them, Manfred Stolpe, then-prime minister of Brandenburg; Gregor Gysi, popular leader of successor party of the PDS (now, after the merger with a West German group, the Left Party); and author Christa Wolf. With time, both the stigma of Stasi involvement and public interest waned.

Whether a person was hired or dismissed differed widely from region to region and between sectors of public service employment. The Land parliaments used different criteria to hire and fire; inquiries were lengthy and often obsolete by the time a decision was made. In the first half of the 1990s, vetting procedures coincided with dismissals and early retirement schemes stemming from the downsizing of bloated administrative structures and economic restructuring. Calculating their true extent is difficult, but the number of dismissals was modest compared to the overall pool of reviews, numbering 1.7 million to date. Vetting procedures were scheduled to expire in 2006 but the Seventh Amendment to the Stasi File Law, which passed the Bundestag in December 2006, extended the period of investigations to 2011. From the opening of the BStU in 1991 to June 2009, 6.4 million inquiries have been recorded, 2.6 million related to information requests, access to, and release of, files; more than 1.5 million people inspected their files. Despite a decline in applications, interest remains high; for example, in 2008, the agency handled almost 84,000 requests.

For some time, public interest in the Stasi has only been spurred by new stunning revelations about particular individuals or media events, such as the release of the Oscar-winning movie, *The Lives of Others*, which dramatizes the Stasi's insidious work and effects on citizens and exposes the difficulty of clearly delineating victims and perpetrators. Demands for renewed scrutiny of those who worked for the Stasi surface with some regularity, but the political will to reopen this chapter of transitional justice has dissolved.

Restitution and Compensation

In June 1990, the East and West German governments agreed on a Joint Statement on the Resolution of Outstanding Property, which became part of the Unification Treaty (Appendix III) along with the East German Property Act of September 1990. People who sought reparations included those who had lost their property as a result of nationalization and collectivization under Soviet occupation and later under the GDR government. The majority had fled the GDR.

Jewish victims of the Hitler regime also presented claims. In contrast to the West German government, GDR leaders had denied them any recompense, claiming to have rooted out any remnant of fascism on their soil. Jewish reparation claims were honored after 1990 but are covered by different laws and not subject to expiration. Possessions expropriated during Soviet occupation from May 8, 1945 to October 1949 were excluded but later covered in the Indemnification and Compensation Act of 1994. For all others, after heated debates, the two German states agreed on "restitution before compensation" as the legal framework. Arguments in favor of restitution included the anticipated high financial costs of compensation. West Germans emphasized the right to property and the precedent of restitution to victims of Nazism, whereas some East German negotiators favored compensation. Yet from the beginning, major exceptions to restitution were made and later extended in several amendments to the Property Act. Examples included property used for communal purposes and "special investment purposes" or acquired in good faith by GDR citizens. In response to concerns that restitution in-kind would slow down the process of privatization, the Investment Acceleration Act of 22 March 1991 allowed greater use of compensation.

Myriad agencies administered the difficult task of sorting out about 800,000 claims covering 2.3 million different assets. By 2000, more than 90 percent of all cases had been closed; deadlines had long expired. Overall, about 22 percent of claims resulted in restitution and another 5 percent in compensation. The principle of restitution of individual property was used in only a few cases; when restitution occurred, it was mostly public property. This outcome obscures the heated emotional battles over the process: many assets were claimed by several parties, and while property was in the hands of East Germans, many claimants came from West Germany and abroad. Overall, restitution was contested, and uncertainty about the outcome unsettling to the parties involved.

Criminal Justice and Prosecutions

Initially, criminal trials focused on electoral fraud, abuse of authority, and corruption. The list of criminal charges rapidly grew to include border shootings, denunciation, doping of athletes without consent, perversion of justice, cruelty against prisoners, extortion of property, and economic crimes. All groups in the newly elected GDR parliament favored the prosecution of "regime crimes," and the Unification Treaty reiterated the mandate to prosecute crimes committed between 1949 and 1990 for up to ten years. Only the prosecution of homicides could be pursued as long as 2030. Demands for amnesty arose during the 1990s but never garnered sufficient political support.

Criminal proceedings could only take place when actions had been punishable under East German and West German law. In case of conflict, the milder punishment had to be applied. Specialized criminal investigative agencies and departments were set up in Berlin and the five *Länder*. Because Berlin was the center of the old regime, its offices managed most of the caseload; during their existence from 1991 to 2000, these offices employed up to 700 individuals.

The legal framework restricted prosecution to egregious government and human rights abuses. The lack of codified national laws to define what constitutes egregious violations complicated the process and contributed to the daunting number of cases. According to the work of Klaus Marxen, Gerhard Werle, and Petra Schäfter, an estimated 75,000 criminal cases were investigated, involving about 100,000 people. In the end, about 1,000 proceedings involving 1,737 individuals ended up in court; 753 were found guilty. Most were released on parole or had to pay fines. Only about forty people served limited jail time. The last court cases ended in 2005; homicide cases can still be pursued, but few, if any, new trials are expected to take place.

High-profile cases – for example, involving Erich Honecker, Egon Krenz, and Erich Mielke – caught the attention of the media, as did some trials involving border guards. Honecker, leader of the GDR from 1971 to 1989, was brought to trial but released on grounds of age and terminal illness in January 1993. He emigrated to Chile where he died in May 1994. Ironically, Mielke was sentenced for the murder of two policemen in 1931 but not any actions during his tenure as head of the Stasi from 1957 to 1989. He was released on account of his advanced age. They are only the tip of the iceberg. More than a third of the defendants were sixty-four years and older and often unfit for trial. Krenz, who briefly led the GDR in 1989, and two other high-ranking functionaries of the SED regime were sentenced to prison terms for their role in orders to kill individuals attempting to escape from the GDR. They appealed the ruling of the Berlin trial court; German courts as well as the European Court of Justice upheld the convictions. Krenz served three of his six-and-a-half-year term. Former dissidents have criticized the lack of interest and resolve in pursuing criminal justice as well as the leniency in judgments. Defenders argue that the rule of law prevailed over retribution.

Rehabilitation and Compensation

Compared to vetting and restitution, issues of rehabilitation and compensation received less public attention but struck a nerve with victims. Shortly before unification, the GDR parliament passed a rehabilitation act, and the Unification Treaty reaffirmed the commitment to rehabilitation and compensation, but not until November 1992 did the Bundestag directly address the concerns of those who had suffered most under the GDR regime. Additional acts followed in 1994, 1997, 1999, and 2007. Rehabilitation of victims was mostly concluded by the end of 2002, although application deadlines have been extended several times; they are now scheduled to end in 2019. By 2002 (the last date for which data have been made available), about 8,500 of more than 35,000 claims to administrative rehabilitation were granted; almost half of more than 96,000 petitions of professional rehabilitation were approved; and criminal rehabilitation affected about 188,000 citizens. Rehabilitation was accompanied by financial restitution, and by the end of 2002, about 617 million Euros had been paid out.

It took much longer to settle a pension plan for victims of the SED regime who had been incarcerated in GDR prisons. A need-based plan finally passed in 2007; it potentially affects about 170,000 citizens who were in custody for at least six months. Critics have pointed to the slow response and the relatively meager compensation of victims (up to 250 Euros per month, depending on the financial situation of the applicant).

Remembering the Past

From the onset, research and civic education about the communist past and retroactive justice were deemed complementary, informing and reinforcing each other. Transitional justice is short-lived; history lessons and memory politics, on the other hand, are pillars on which national identities are built. Germany has a long history and an extensive network of institutions for political education. New ones were added, prominent among them a government-funded foundation devoted to a better understanding of communist rule (Stiftung zur Aufarbeitung der SED-Diktatur). It resulted from the proceedings of the Commission of Inquiry for the Assessment of History and Consequences of the SED Dictatorship in Germany (1992–1998).

Other institutions are also accorded a place in "telling the truth" about the communist regime. For example, the BStU acts as an important player in the academic study of the state security through both its own scientific staff and granting media and researchers access to material. Its role extends to the public dissemination of knowledge about the Stasi, for example, in the form of exhibitions, publications, guided tours of the Stasi archives and former headquarters, public lectures, and film screenings. In all cases, central offices in Berlin and those in the *Länder* coexist, cooperate, and share in educational endeavors.

However, efforts to interpret the communist past and integrate it into a national narrative in unified Germany have proven difficult. In discourse and identity, the National Socialist past prevails, and many victims of communist persecution feel overlooked. Attempts have been made in recent years to include the communist regime explicitly in commemoration concepts. The more official interpretations tend to couch the experience of the GDR predominantly in terms of its dictatorial features, the more many citizens in the former GDR recoil; they feel that this tactic unfairly neglects their daily lives and distorts their biographies. Battles of memory ensue. Other challenges include ignorance about, and disinterest in, GDR history.

Conclusion

Transitional justice measures served multiple goals: to bring justice to the victims of the SED regime, to punish those who misused power, and to unearth the "truth" about the vanished GDR regime. They have been addressed in material and symbolic ways, but demands for justice have staying power, even if public and political interest moves on. By definition, retroactive justice is controversial in trying to balance demands for corrective actions with the reconciliation deemed important for building a political community. East/West exchanges added further complexity. Western resources, such as personnel, finances, and administrative and legal infrastructure, facilitated swift and comprehensive retroactive justice policies, but they were accompanied by alienation and suspicion between East and West Germans and different levels of interest and involvement. While many East Germans were directly affected, most West Germans remained spectators.

Helga A. Welsh

Cross-references: Access to Secret Files; Commission of Inquiry for the Assessment of History and Consequences of the SED Dictatorship in Germany; Compensation Packages; Court Trials for Redress; Geschichtsbewältigung; Office of the Federal Commissioner for the Records of the National Security Services of East Germany, Gauck Agency; Rehabilitation of Political Prisoners; Reparations; Property Restitution.

Further Readings

Bruce, Gary. 2008. Access to Secret Police Files, Justice, and Vetting in East Germany since 1989. *German Politics and Society*, 26: 82–111.
Gieseke, Jens, with Doris Hubert. 2006. *The GDR State Security. Shield and Sword of the Party*. 2nd edition. Berlin: The Federal Commissioner for the Records of the State Security Service of the former German Democratic Republic.
The Lives of Others. 2006. VHS. Directed by Florian Henckel von Donnersmarck. Munich: Wiedemann & Berg Film Productions.
Marxen, Klaus, Gerhard Werle, and Petra Schäfter. 2007. *Die Strafverfolgung von DDR-Unrecht. Fakten und Zahlen* [The Prosecution of Injustice in the GDR. Facts and Figures]. Berlin: Stiftung zur Aufarbeitung der SED-Diktatur.
McAdams, A. James. 2001. *Judging the Past in Unified Germany*. Cambridge: Cambridge University Press.
Sa'adah, Anne. 1998. *Germany's Second Chance. Trust, Justice, and Democratization*. Cambridge, MA: Harvard University Press.
Welsh, Helga A. 2006. When Discourse Trumps Policy: Transitional Justice in Unified Germany. *German Politics*, 15: 137–152.

Germany – the Nazi Past

Nazi Germany committed atrocities on a monumental scale. After Germany's defeat in World War II, the occupying powers engaged in transitional justice policies that varied across the four occupation zones, especially between the Soviet Occupation Zone and the three western zones under American, British, and French authority. Yet in all zones, these measures included systematic efforts at criminal prosecution for Nazi wrongdoing, large-scale denazification programs, the restitution of stolen property, and compensation for surviving victims. The sovereign Federal Republic of Germany (FRD, or, until 1990, West Germany) and German Democratic Republic (GDR, or East Germany) continued to pursue transitional justice during the Cold War, as has done the Federal Republic of Germany after the 1990 reunification. This makes the German experience of transitional justice among the most widespread, systematic, varied, and long-lasting to date.

The Repressive Past

The Nazi regime (1933–1945) was among the most brutal and repressive in human history. It committed widespread violence against persons and property, within Germany and across Europe. Upon Adolf Hitler's ascension to power in January 1933, the Nazi regime began to imprison real, potential, and imagined political opponents in "wild" concentration camps subsequently regularized as institutions for "protective custody," a euphemism for the extrajudicial incarceration of political opponents and social groups deemed undesirable by the regime. These included Jews, Romani, "asocials" and the "work-shy" (the chronically unemployed), recidivist criminals, homosexuals, and Jehovah's Witnesses.

All aspects of the German state and much of civil society were brought under control of the Nazi party. The regime employed state and party organizations for repressive purposes, as well as the army, paramilitary formations (the Sturmabteilung, or SA, and the Schutzstaffel, or SS), the police, and the feared secret police (Gestapo). Private industry cooperated extensively in Nazi repression through the appropriation of Jewish property and the use of slave labor during the war. Professionals like physicians and jurists were also deeply implicated. In effect, almost all of organized German society was involved in Nazi repression and atrocities to some extent.

Nazi repression was political, racial, eugenic, and economic. Political repression included the outlawing of all parties save the National Socialist German Workers (or Nazi) Party and the harassment and imprisonment of political opponents, especially socialists, communists, clergy, and the regime's conservative opponents. Many of these died in concentration camps. A violent purge of the Nazi party in June 1934 resulted in 150 murders and the incarceration of 1,000 individuals. Another 200 were executed in the aftermath of the failed attempt to assassinate Hitler and stage a military coup on July 20, 1944. The violent wartime suppression of resistance in occupied territories was another form of political, and often racial, repression.

The Nazi regime is notorious for its racially motivated atrocities. Nazi ideology professed a socially Darwinist vision of "scientific" racism, which held that racial conflict was the driving force of history and that lesser races were dangerous and corrupting, among whom Jews posed a particular threat. Once in power, the Nazis reorganized society in line with these beliefs, beginning with policies of racial exclusion and discrimination within Germany and extending to racial genocide throughout Europe. New legislation disenfranchised and discriminated against Jews, who were progressively barred from most professions, prohibited from marrying non-Jews, and had their property "Aryanized" (expropriated by the state and transferred to non-Jewish owners at submarket prices). The intent was to force Jews to emigrate by making living conditions in Germany intolerable. Once the war began, emigration became impossible, and with the conquest of territory the number of Jews living under German control expanded exponentially. The Nazis aimed to reconfigure the populations of their newly acquired "living space" in Eastern Europe along racial lines by removing much of the local Slavic population through deportation and enslavement. Jews were confined to newly created Eastern European ghettos, to which Jews from elsewhere were deported. With the invasion of the Soviet Union in June 1941, the Nazis moved from repression and discrimination to outright murder, as mobile killing units (Einsatzgruppen) began to massacre Jews in the rear areas of the front. In 1942, extermination centers were set up in Poland, where European Jews were deported and killed, mainly in gas chambers.

The genocide of the Jews (the Holocaust or the Shoah) claimed 5.4 million to 6.2 million lives, while 200,000 to 500,000 Romani were also killed for racial reasons. Other civilian populations, especially in Eastern Europe, were targeted for large-scale ethnic cleansing, racial discrimination, and mass murder. Germans killed around 2 million Poles (including forced laborers – see later discussion). Nineteen million Soviet civilians – including Soviet Jews killed in the Holocaust, deaths from war-related famine, and civilians killed during military operations or in the course of the anti-partisan warfare, often as a result of deliberate massacres – died in the war. An additional 3.3 million Soviet prisoners of war (POWs) were either killed in German custody or died as a result of negligent camp conditions. More than 1 million civilians were killed in Yugoslavia, many in the course of the civil war unleashed by the German occupation. Hundreds of thousands of civilians died elsewhere in occupied Europe, as a result of German aerial bombardments, famines, and massacres.

Nazi racial ideology called for the exclusion, expulsion, and extermination of racial undesirables, and eugenic measures to improve the "racial health" of the German population. The July 1933 Law for the Prevention of Genetically Diseased Offspring authorized the forced sterilization of 400,000 Germans suffering from nine "hereditary" conditions, including epilepsy, manic depression, "feeblemindedness," and alcoholism. Between January 1940 and August 1941, 70,000 mentally and physically handicapped individuals were killed in the official "euthanasia" program, and 60,000 more afterward, with government encouragement but without formal orders. Homosexuals and Jehovah's Witnesses were subject to "protective custody" in concentration camps, where hundreds were killed or died.

The Germans also committed economic crimes. They operated a massive system of forced and slave labor in support of their war effort, both inside and outside concentration camps. In the summer of 1944, 7.5 million foreign workers were registered in the Reich. At least 500,000 forced laborers working outside the concentration camps died. Some 1.2 million prisoners died in concentration camps, not including Jews murdered immediately upon arrival as part of the extermination process. The Nazi regime's massive and systematic plunder of private property began with the prewar Aryanization of Jewish property in Germany and was extended to both Jewish and non-Jewish property in occupied territories. Occupied countries were also expected to cover Germany's occupation costs. Between the direct and indirect expropriation of Jewish property in Germany and abroad and the imposition of occupation costs on foreign territories, two-thirds of Germany's war expenditures were covered through expropriation.

Transitional Justice

Germany surrendered unconditionally on May 8, 1945, thus ending World War II in Europe. The country was divided into four occupation zones, one each for the Americans, British, French, and Soviets. During the occupation period and after, Germany was subject to extensive transitional justice. In all four occupation zones and the subsequent independent German states (founded in 1949), measures were taken to pursue justice for Nazi crimes, to remove Nazis from public life, and to compensate surviving victims. Given the political and economic differences between the Soviets and the Western Allies, and later between the communist GDR and the liberal democratic FRG, transitional justice was pursued differently in East Germany and West Germany. During the early phases of the occupation, the presence of four-power institutions (especially the Control Council for Germany) and the lingering remnants of inter-allied cooperation meant that there were some common parameters for transitional justice throughout Germany. By the time the two separate sovereign states were founded, almost nothing remained of this common foundation. The landscape of transitional justice in postwar Germany was thus unusually complex, varying across space and over time. Still, there were three main elements to transitional justice in Germany after World War II: criminal justice, denazification, and restitution/reparations.

Criminal Justice

After the war, more than 95,000 Germans and Austrians were convicted of Nazi crimes, mostly in the courts of the formerly occupied European countries, in keeping with the territoriality principle first articulated in the Moscow Declaration of October 1943. Nearly 3,000 persons were convicted in West European courts, mostly in France. Far more trials took place in Eastern European courts: 26,000 Germans and Austrians were convicted in Soviet, 21,000 in Czechoslovak, and 5,000 in Polish courts. Tens of thousands of non-Germans were convicted as collaborators throughout Europe (50,000 in Hungarian and Czech lands).

In Germany, the occupation authorities held numerous trials, of which the Nuremberg Trials (see separate entry) are the best known. The Americans convicted 1,416 individuals in U.S. military courts (mainly at Dachau), the British 1,000, the French 780 defendants in military courts, and the Soviets nearly 5,500 defendants in their occupation zones.

Meanwhile, the Germans and Austrians convicted more than 32,000 Nazi perpetrators. There were 4,667 convictions in the German courts of the three western occupation zones and 8,059 in the German courts of the Soviet zone through 1949. Subsequently, there were 1,989 convictions in the FRG courts through 2005, and more than 4,700 in the GDR courts through 1989. Austrian courts convicted 13,000 defendants before special People's Courts (Volksgerichte) through 1955 and a further 18 before regular courts after 1956. More than 320,000 Germans and Austrians were investigated or indicted for Nazi crimes. Thus, almost 30 percent of those investigated for Nazi crimes were convicted in a court of law. The extent of due process in these trials varied considerably, from exceedingly fair trials in the FRG in the 1960s to blatant show trials in the Soviet Union in the late 1940s.

The prosecution of Nazi criminality can be divided into three phases. The initial phase of intensive and strenuous prosecution lasted through 1949. The vast majority of

Nazi trials took place in this period, characterized by the most severe sentences. Starting in the 1950s, there was a sharp decline or complete cessation of trials. In Germany, responsibility for Nazi trials devolved entirely to German courts. In West Germany, during the 1950s, a small number of trials were organized. These trials were conducted under ordinary German statutory law, not international law. After manslaughter fell under the statute of limitations in 1960, all trials had to be for murder. In East Germany, the drop-off in prosecutions was dramatic. While in 1951 there were 259 convictions in West German courts and 332 in East German courts, by 1956 there were 23 convictions in West Germany and only a single conviction in East Germany. Outside of Germany, the prosecution of Nazi criminality was halted in the 1950s, a period of formal and informal amnesties and clemency proceedings. Thus, by the end of the 1950s, virtually all convicted Nazi criminals had been released from prison. After the late 1950s, West Germany saw a renewed wave of prosecutions, albeit on a much smaller scale. This was spurred both by a series of high-profile Holocaust trials, which made it clear that many egregious perpetrators remained at large, as well as pressure emanating from effective East German propaganda campaigns highlighting the reintegration of former Nazis into West German public life. In both 1965 and 1968 (the peak years after 1953), there were sixty-seven convictions each. More importantly, several very high-profile cases attracted media attention, the most important being the Ulm Einsatzkommando Trial (1958), the Frankfurt Auschwitz Trial (1963–1965), and the Düsseldorf Majdanek Trial (1975–1981). These helped put Nazi crimes, the Holocaust in particular, at the center of German public debates.

The other major fault line in the history of criminal trials for Nazi crimes is geographic. There were far more trials in Eastern Europe and East Germany than in the west, mostly because of the geography of Nazi atrocities, which disproportionately took place in Eastern Europe, and the fact that, in the context of the Cold War, Nazi trials came to serve different political functions in the two regions. Clearly, all Nazi trials, even the most summary proceedings, as in the Soviet Union, to some degree sought genuine justice for Nazi wrongdoings. Yet these trials were always also political. In Germany, these differences were particularly acute. In the western occupation zones/Federal Republic, these trials had largely pedagogical purposes. By demonstrating the evils of Nazism, aggressive war, dictatorship, and racism, they delivered a democratizing education and sought to transform German political culture. In the East, the trials also had a pedagogical dimension, but the focus was less on dictatorship and more on imperialism and capitalism. By the time of the Waldheim trials in East Germany in 1950, the trials also helped foster Stalinization. The Waldheim trials were summary proceedings against 3,000 defendants transferred to German jurisdiction from Soviet internment camps. In four months, they were almost all convicted and sentenced to at least ten years in prison, without due process or concrete evidence. As Walter Ulbricht, then-General Secretary of the Socialist Unity Party, put it, the defendants were "undoubted enemies of the building of socialism" and needed to be put in jail (Werkentin 1994, p. 99).

The success of Nazi trials in Germany is open to debate. A sizable number of cases were investigated, prosecuted, and resulted in convictions, but, given the scale of Nazi crimes, they represented only a small fraction of those implicated in Nazi atrocities. Moreover, only a tiny minority of those convicted served full sentences. It is also doubtful that the trials had much pedagogical impact in Germany. Germans, west and east, constructed narratives of German wartime suffering, in which they figured largely as the first victims of Nazism.

Lustration (Denazification)

At the Yalta Conference in 1945, the Allies declared that, among their postwar goals, one was to "wipe out the Nazi Party [and] remove all Nazi and militarist influences from public office and from the cultural and economic life of the German people" (United States Department of State 1955, p. 970). Denazification, the major tool for achieving this goal, was implemented differently in each of the four occupation zones. American practices set the standards for the West, being adopted by the French and British as well. The Soviets went their own way.

In the American zone, denazification was first carried out by the Americans, who later turned over responsibility for its implementation to the Germans. The Joint Chiefs of Staff Directive 1067 of April 1945 required that all "more than nominal" Nazis be "removed and excluded from public office and from positions of importance in quasi-public and private enterprises." Persons who might "endanger" the occupation were subject to automatic arrest. By August 1945, 80,000 persons had been arrested and 70,000 others had been removed from their jobs. Then, the U.S. Forces European Theater Directive of 7 July 1945 mandated that persons in important positions in public life or, after September 1945, private industry fill out a questionnaire detailing their affiliations and activities during the Third Reich. Persons meeting any of 125 specific conditions (for instance, Nazi party office holders or SS officers) were automatically removed from their positions. The American Occupation Government "Special Branch" could recommend but not mandate dismissal for less implicated individuals. The criteria for evaluation were very schematic, given the large numbers of cases to be evaluated. Only formal affiliations and offices were taken into account, not an individual's actual activities in office. By March 1946, more than 1.2 million questionnaires had been evaluated. Twenty-four percent of all public sector employees (139,996 persons) were dismissed, with a further 8 percent being recommended for dismissal but not actually dismissed. In the private sector, 68,568 persons were dismissed. In total, during the American-controlled phase of denazification, 338,892 persons were either dismissed or refused permission for reemployment. (By the end of the war, there were roughly 6 million Nazi party members in Germany).

From the very start, Germans were highly critical of what seemed to them an overly rigid and draconian lustration process. As virtually all former Nazi party members had to fear for their economic future, denazification helped create solidarity between active Nazis and more nominal party members. Critics within the American military government worried that denazification paralyzed public administration. In response, the military government transferred authority for denazification to German authorities with the Law for the Liberation from National Socialism and Militarism of 5 March 1946, later adopted in the French and British zones. Under the law, all "active supporters" of the Nazi regime were to be "excluded from influence in public, economic, and cultural life." Unlike the previous American practice, the new law required a careful evaluation of each individual case that went beyond "external markers" like party membership. The law required all Germans aged eighteen or older to fill out elaborate questionnaires regarding their activities in the Third Reich. Prosecutors sorted defendants into one of five categories: (1) major offenders, (2) incriminated, (3) less incriminated, (4) fellow travelers, and (5) exonerated. Special lay courts (Spruchkammern), whose members were chosen by political parties, then evaluated the individual cases. The burden of proof before these courts was reversed. Defendants had to prove their innocence, which created great controversy in the German public sphere. Major offenders could be sentenced to up to ten years in a labor camp, while, along with incriminated persons, they lost their pensions and faced a mandatory prohibition from any but "common employment" for five to ten years. Less incriminated persons could be prohibited from high-level employment for up to three years.

In practice, the Spruchkammern reintegrated, rather than excluded, former Nazis into German society. Because the Spruchkammern were required to re-vet all cases, including those of persons previously dismissed by the Americans, they could overturn earlier findings. The Spruchkammern were far milder than the American Special Branch. By the end of 1949, the Spruchkammern had categorized 1,654 persons as major offenders, 22,122 as incriminated, and 106,422 as less incriminated (the three categories subject to employment bans).

Unlike the Americans, the Soviets involved Germans (especially communists) in the process from an early date. The Soviet Military Government set up state and provincial governments in July 1945 and these pursued independent and distinct denazification procedures, leading to considerable regional variation in the Soviet zone. Thuringia pursued a very "mild" policy aimed at high-ranking, "active" Nazis, whereas Saxony sought to remove all incriminated party members based on rank and function. This led to different results. As of October 1, 1945, 90 percent of public-sector employees in Thuringia had been Nazi party members, compared to 17.9 percent in Saxony. By late 1946, 390,478 persons in the Soviet zone had been dismissed from their positions or refused re-employment. These are slightly higher than comparable figures for the American zone. The major difference is that in the west, dismissed public-sector employees were typically replaced by elderly personnel who had worked in Weimar Republic, while in the east, they were replaced by communist or socialist cadres. Thus, denazification came to consolidate Socialist Unity Party power in East Germany.

In 1947, the Soviets made 64,578 dismissals, but then Soviet Military Government Order 201 rehabilitated all nominal Nazi party members and created German commissions to examine remaining serious cases. These commissions dismissed 11,167 persons. Thus, the Soviet zone was the first to pursue an official policy of rehabilitation. In all of Germany, 520,000 persons were dismissed, transferred to lesser positions, or refused re-employment in the course of denazification.

Restitution and Reparations

Efforts to provide compensation to surviving victims were extensive, diverse, and complicated. They included: (1) efforts to restore expropriated or Aryanized property to its rightful owners, (2) global reparations paid to either to successor states (like Israel) or to nongovernmental organizations (like the Conference on Jewish Material Claims against Germany), and (3) programs for direct reparations to individual survivors.

The Soviets, with their skepticism toward private property, were more concerned with securing reparations for the harm done to their own country. In the Soviet zone/GDR, only Jewish communal property was returned on a limited basis. The Americans, by contrast, wanted to see Aryanized property returned to its rightful owners. After failed efforts to convince the Germans to pass restitution laws, the Americans promulgated a Restitution Law for their zone in November 1947 (followed by the British and the French in 1948 and 1949). All property within the three Western Zones/Federal Republic taken from victims of Nazi persecution or discrimination (overwhelmingly but not exclusively Jews) had to be returned. If it could not be returned because it had been destroyed, compensation was to be paid. Over strenuous German objections, no exemptions were made for property purchased in "good faith" by third parties. Because the state had resold most Aryanized property to private persons, the Restitution Laws directly affected individual Germans and were unpopular. Concerted efforts to effect repeal or drastic reductions in the course of negotiations for the Transfer Treaty (1955) granting West Germany full sovereignty largely failed. Roughly 3–3.5 billion DM worth of property was returned by the time the statutes expired in 1966. An additional 4 billion DM were paid for direct claims on the government under a 1957 restitution law regulating government obligations.

Efforts to win compensation for harm and suffering for Nazi victims were no less controversial. Reparations aimed to cover all harm – to health, life, and career opportunity – not included in the restitution laws. Only victims of racial, religious, or political persecution were included. This left out most victims of Nazi eugenic crimes (of the forced sterilization or euthanasia programs). For most of the postwar period, only residents and former residents of Western Germany were eligible, which left out millions of victims, especially in Eastern Europe. Reparations were paid to groups (states or nongovernmental organizations) or to individuals.

The most important group reparations were paid to Israel by the FRG through an agreement reached in March 1953. For the Germans, reparations to Israel assisted the domestic rehabilitation of former Nazis by shifting the focus away from individual criminal guilt to the more abstract harm done by the regime. They also won for Germany substantial international goodwill. Accepting "blood money" from Germany was deeply controversial in Israel, but the young state desperately needed material assistance and saw reparations as an act of limited justice. Although negotiations were complicated by German resistance and objections from Arab states, the FRG agreed to pay 3 billion DM to Israel and additional sums to the Jewish Claims Conference, including 450 million DM for Jewish victims living in the (western) diaspora.

The process of winning direct reparations for individual victims was the most drawn out. In late 1949, the South German Länderrat (council of state governments) promulgated a reparations law that authorized reparations for victims of racial, religious, or political persecution, Germans or displaced persons, resident in the U.S. occupation zone, as of January 1, 1947. Parallel, but not identical, laws were subsequently passed in the British and French occupation zones. These laws were recognized as valid at the federal level after the founding of the FRG in 1949. Although broadly similar in recognizing claims for compensation by victims of racial, religious, or political persecution, these laws differed substantially in financing, procedures, and payment levels. In the British zone, for instance, reparations were paid for wrongful imprisonment, whereas physical harm or loss of livelihood was treated under pension law. In the American zone, all forms of harm were dealt with under reparations law. There was initially no unified federal law on reparations for victims of Nazi crimes. The Germans resisted any increase in payments or expansion of eligibility. In this context, negotiations with Israel provided a decisive impetus to unify and reform domestic reparations procedures. In 1953, a unified Federal Indemnification Law was passed (amended and expanded in 1956 and 1965). It offered compensation to victims of racial, religious, or political persecution for harm to life, body, or health, to freedom, property, or professional advancement. Eligibility was initially restricted to persons who lived in (or had lived in) West Germany prior to December 31, 1952, but later it was extended to the German Reich's 1937 borders.

The FRG government initially estimated that its total reparations payments would run to 5–10 billion DM. By the late 1990s, however, the German government had made total payments of more than 100 billion DM. Under the Federal Indemnification Law, four-fifths of this went to individual claimants, half of them Jews living in Israel. This did not include payments by individual corporations to their former slave laborers. In the postwar period, many companies negotiated such payments individually. As they were exempted from civil liability by German courts, companies only made payments voluntarily. East Europeans were largely excluded from such payments during the Cold War, although they had constituted the vast majority of slave laborers. After unification, payments were finally made to East European slave laborers, who had previously been excluded from German reparations programs because they had not lived within the boundaries of the former German Reich. The average payment came to a mere 550 DM per person.

Conclusion

Efforts at transitional justice in Germany, by Germans and their postwar occupiers, were both extensive and mixed in their results. If 95,000 Germans were convicted of Nazi crimes, this represents perhaps one in six perpetrators. Denazification had little lasting impact on the composition of West German elites. In the east, where its results were more durable, denazification helped consolidate a Stalinist dictatorship. Restitution and reparations paid out massive sums of money to victims of Nazi repression, yet the per capita payments were often so pitifully small as to make little difference in people's lives. Germany thus serves as a case study in the limits of transitional justice. Even with the most sustained efforts, some crimes are too enormous to be repaired. The political fate of post-conflict societies can often depend more on the geopolitical circumstances in which they find themselves than on any specific set of transitional justice measure undertaken.

Devin Pendas

Cross-references: Nuremberg Trials.

Further Readings

Frei, Norbert. 2002. *Adenauer's Germany and the Nazi Past: The Politics of Amnesty and Integration.* New York: Columbia University Press.

Goschler, Constantin. 2005. *Schuld und Schulden: Die Politik der Wiedergutmachung für NS-Verfolgten seit 1945.* Göttingen: Wallstein.

Pendas, Devin. 2009. Seeking Justice, Finding Law: Nazi Trials in the Postwar Era, 1945–1989. *Journal of Modern History*, 81(3): 347–368.

Reichel, Peter. 2001. *Vergangenheitsbewältigung in Deutschland. Die Auseinandersetzung mit der NS-Diktatur von 1945 bis heute.* Munich: Beck.

United States Department of State. 1955. *Foreign Relations of the United States. Conferences at Malta and Yalta, 1945.* Washington, DC: U.S. Government Printing Office.

Vollnhals, Clemens. 1991. *Entnazifizierung: Politische Säuberung und Rehabilitierung in den vier Besatzungszonen, 1945–1949*. Munich: DTV.

Werkentin, Falco. 1994. Strafjustiz im politischen System der DDR: Fundstücke zur Steuerungs- und Eingriffpraxis des zentral Parteiaparates der SED. In *Steuerung der Justiz in der DDR*. Ed. Hubert Rottleuthner. Cologne: Bundesanzeiger, pp. 93–133.

Ghana

It was only recently that Ghana formally engaged in transitional justice, in spite of its checkered political history. In 2001, following the electoral victory of the opposition New Patriotic Party (NPP), transitional justice became a priority of the government, and it chose a non-retributive process. The following year, a Truth and Reconciliation Commission (TRC) was established with a focus on restorative justice.

The Repressive Past

Ghana's political history is characterized by a mix of civilian dictatorships and military rule. Since attaining independence from Great Britain on March 6, 1957 and until its fourth attempt at democratic rule on January 7, 1993, Ghana was governed by four military regimes, which spanned a total of twenty-two years. The legacy of the civilian and military dictatorships included political and ethnic conflicts, various types of massacres, and human rights violations inflicted upon Ghanaian citizens. These infringements damaged the society and left an indelible mark on the minds of the victims. They also divided society along ideological lines and provoked a rift between the civilian population and the military.

The first of the military takeovers occurred on February 24, 1966, nine years after the country attained independence. The coup overthrew Ghana's first President, Kwame Nkrumah, and his Convention Peoples Party (CPP), and established the National Liberation Council (NLC). The NLC ruled between 1966 and 1969. The overthrow was provoked in part by flagrant abuses of individual rights under the CPP post-independence government. In his attempt to consolidate powers and to respond to perceived subversive activities by the opposition – mainly the National Liberation Movement (NLM), which, together with other opposition political parties, became the United Party – Nkrumah introduced harsh laws to tame opposition to his rule. Among these measures was the Preventive Detention Act of 1958, which gave the government discretionary powers to arrest and to keep in custody for unlimited time any person deemed a threat to national security. The evolution of Nkrumah's political heavy-handedness continued in 1964 when Ghana became a one-party state. Several members of the opposition became victims of these measures. At the time of the military coup, more than 300 people were in detention without trial. Prominent among the causalities was J. B. Danquah, one of the six big personalities in Ghana's political history, also known as the "Doyen of Ghana Politics." Danquah was twice arrested and eventually died in custody in 1965.

The NLC intervention aimed at arresting the increasingly autocratic rule by Nkrumah's CPP and therefore presented itself as an interim government with goals to return the country to civilian rule. Nonetheless, the NLC regime showed no greater respect for human rights. In its three-year reign, it overstepped its bounds, and atrocities were committed against its opponents. Governing by decrees, the NLC introduced the infamous "protective custody," a measure that violated the principle of habeas corpus. Leading CPP members were detained. In addition, several investigative bodies were established and prosecutions took place with the objective of demonizing the previous CPP government. Properties belonging to the CPP officials were seized and attempts were made to suppress the CPP and the socialist-leaning ideology of Nkrumah, ban the opposition groups, and allow the state to control social, economic, and infrastructural development.

Not surprisingly, before the NLC disengaged from politics in 1969, it inserted an indemnity provision into the new 1969 constitution to prevent any inquiries into its rule. The vendetta against the CPP continued during the civilian constitutional government that took over from the NLC. The Progress Party headed by Kofi Busia took over political power in October 1969 following an NLC-supervised transitional election. The Progress Party was the offshoot of the NLM/United Party. Not only did the Progress Party fail to contest the indemnity provisions inserted by the NLC into the 1969 constitution, but sympathizers of the CPP regime continued to suffer victimization and administrative injustices. The era of the Progress Party rule witnessed Ghana's first experience with lustration, exemplified in what has famously become known in Ghana's political history as Apollo 568, as a result of which hundreds of civil servants were dismissed from their positions because of their suspected political affiliations with the CPP. The Supreme Court ruled for the reinstatement of the affected workers, but Busia's Progress Party refused. The silence and failure of the Progress Party government to confront the injustices of the NLC regime marked the genesis of a culture of impunity regarding military interventions and their associated brutalities. And the continuous distaste for the CPP, which began under the NLC, signaled the beginning of the cycle of vengeance and vendetta in the nation's political history.

Barely three years of constitutional rule under the Progress Party had passed when the military again intervened on January 13, 1972. This second intervention lasted for close to eight years and was marked by internal changes. The military junta was first named the National Redemption Council (NRC) and later changed to the Supreme Military Council (SMC I). The NRC/SMC I was first headed by General Ignatius Kutu Acheampong. The regime cited corruption and mismanagement as the principal reasons for its coup, although it was clear that the military leadership sympathized with the CPP, and its ideological orientation mimicked that of the CPP as well. Following a palace coup that toppled General Acheampong in 1978, the SMC I became SMC II, with General Akuffo as the new head of state. Under the regimes of SMC I and SMC II, Ghana saw little change in the incidence of human rights abuses. Opponents of the regime were regularly detained after inadequate or nonexistent trials. The abuses became more frequent and extensive during the latter days of General Acheampong's leadership. University students' protests against the government over mismanagement of the economy and rising cost of living were met with repression, including detention, torture, and killings. Several opponents, especially those belonging to professional bodies like the Ghana Bar Association and former members of parliament, ministers, and other state dignitaries representing the Progress Party, were arrested, detained, and jailed for no reason. Eventually, most of them were compelled to go into exile.

While Ghanaians were grieving over military viciousness under SMC II and advocating a return to civilian rule, yet another military coup took place on June 4, 1979. The coup that toppled the SMC II was staged by junior officers of the Ghana armed forces.

This mutiny against senior officers and the army leadership was led by a young Air Force officer, Flight Lieutenant Jerry John Rawlings. Rawlings, who was in custody facing a court martial after the failed coup attempt of May 1979, was released from custody by his colleagues and made the leader of the mutinies. The June 4 uprising instituted the Armed Forces Revolutionary Council (AFRC) and lasted for three months. The short rule by the AFRC was arguably the bloodiest military intervention in Ghana's history. The period witnessed the purging of the military establishment through execution of three former military heads of state, including General Akwasi Amankwa Afrifa, who had been the head of state during the NLC regime and had long retired from the army at the time of the coup.

Furthermore, several senior military officers who had held offices under the NRC/SMC I/SMC II regimes were either executed by firing squad or subjected to the jurisdiction of special/secret courts, which sat in-camera, denied defendants access to legal representation, and sentenced these officers to long jail terms. Private individuals, businessmen, and market women were persecuted and had their assets confiscated or commandeered for corruption and in some cases were sentenced to long prison terms by these same secret courts. Again, some people were compelled to go into exile. Still, the AFRC continued the process already set in motion by SMC II to return the country to civilian democratic rule. The AFRC supervised the scheduled democratic elections, and on September 24, 1979 handed over power to the civilian, democratically elected government of Hilla Limann and his Peoples National Party (PNP). The 1979 transition was the third attempt at democratic governance in Ghana. Before exiting, however, the AFRC took a cue from the military government in 1969 and inserted indemnity clauses into the Third Republican Constitution. Once again, victims of human rights abuse under military rule had no opportunity to seek redress for the violations.

Twenty-seven months into the new civilian democratic administration, Ghanaians witnessed a "Second Coming" of Rawlings, who again seized power by force on December 31, 1981. The coup overthrew the PNP government, replacing it with the Provisional National Defense Council (PNDC), which ruled for more than eleven years. The PNDC was a revolutionary government made up of both military and civilian elements. For the next eleven years, Rawlings and his PNDC ruled Ghana with an iron fist. Responding to several violent attempts to destabilize its rule, the PNDC dealt ruthlessly with suspected opponents. On June 30, 1982, the country witnessed the abduction and murder of three high court judges and a retired army major, allegedly by a pro-government death squad. At the time of their abduction, the judges were hearing cases lodged by victims of the AFRC rule. This incident was one of the most gruesome acts committed under the PNDC. Although some of those responsible were subsequently apprehended, publicly tried, and executed, the public later learned that some of the top PNDC functionaries had been connected to the execution but not brought to trial.

The two Rawlings regimes – the short-lived AFRC regime of 1979 and the PNDC regime of 1981–1992 – are viewed as the most appalling periods of human rights violations in the nation's history. These periods, in particular the eleven-years-long PNDC "socialist-inspired revolution," also described by Kwame Boafo-Arthur as a "decentralized structure of tyranny and violence," saw flagrant arrests of men and women, who were stripped naked and publicly flogged either for hoarding essential commodities or for selling them above government-set prices. Abductions, torture, secret killings, and disappearances were frequent occurrences throughout the PNDC regime. More than 300 people were reportedly extrajudicially killed or declared missing during that time. Unlike the previous military interventions, which targeted political elites – members and sympathizers of the overthrown governments – the Rawlings regimes introduced new sets of victims as they targeted the rich and property-owning class.

It was with this military-dominated political history that Ghana made yet another attempt at democratization in 1993. This turbulent political history led to deep-seated cleavages, rancor, and bitterness in the Ghanaian social fabric.

Transitional Justice

An active policy to address past human rights abuses was a priority for the newly elected President John Agyekum Kufuor, representing the NPP government, in his inaugural address on January 7, 2001. The following month, the president repeated his promise in his maiden address to parliament. In July 2001, Attorney General and Minister of Justice Nana Akufo-Addo sent parliament a bill intended to establish a truth and reconciliation commission for Ghana. Six months later, a law was enacted setting up the National Reconciliation Commission (NRC). The transitional justice approach adopted in Ghana was non-retributive, victim-centered, and aimed at promoting reconciliation among Ghanaians.

The National Reconciliation Commission

The NRC represented the first formal approach to transitional justice in Ghana. As a manifesto promise of the NPP during the December 2000 elections, the NRC was established almost ten years after the political transition to democracy in 1993. By then Rawlings had transformed himself into a civilian and his PNDC had converted into a political party – the National Democratic Congress (NDC) – that successfully contested the 1992 transitional election. Rawlings was reelected for a second and final term in 1996. Ghana's 1992 Constitution provides for only two terms of four years each for the presidency. Rawlings was thus barred from contesting in the 2000 elections. His continuous rule as the head of a civilian government during the first eight years of democratic administration ensured that no formal transitional justice mechanism could be implemented. It was not until his NDC lost to the main opposition party, the NPP, in December 2000 that discussion of transitional justice ensued. The timing of the NRC is thus significant in the transitional justice discourse because it contradicted the conventional assumption that the transitional justice process is initiated at the outset of political transition.

The political process leading to the establishment of the NRC also marked a contrast with past experiences where state-investigative bodies were set up through executive decrees. The NRC was established by Ghana's parliament, through a legislative process that was reasonably long, open, consultative, and participatory. There was widespread public discussion of the NRC Bill following its introduction to parliament, an international conference to learn best practices was organized, and civil society made substantial inputs into parliamentary deliberations. There was also a robust debate in parliament following nationwide public forums seeking views of ordinary Ghanaians, who were generally supportive of the government-initiated national reconciliation. It must be said, however, that the main opposition in parliament, the NDC, after vigorously participating in debates, refused to vote and walked out of the Chamber during voting. Notwithstanding, the process achieved popular legitimacy.

The discussions leading to the creation of a transitional justice institution represented sharply divided opinions. Opposition to any form of transitional justice, mainly from the NDC, argued that human rights violations in Ghana had been isolated and not systematic as in other countries in Africa and elsewhere and, therefore, not warranting a transitional justice mechanism. They also submitted that it was better for the nation to forget the past as democratization gained momentum. By conducting retrospective investigations into the past, old wounds will be raked and the nation might not be able to deal with their ramifications. On the contrary, supporters of the proposals, mostly coming from human rights groups and activists as well as civil society organizations, put forward that the political legacies of Ghana required some form of remembrance, acknowledgment, and justice if the country was to transcend the politics of vindictiveness. The NPP government, for its part, argued forcefully that the NRC was the beginning of a process of wiping the slate clean and bringing the cycle of vengeance and vendetta to an end.

In short, advocates of the NRC found it prudent to revisit the past, not necessarily for revenge or vengeance, but to draw critical public attention to societal wrongs committed in the name of the state, and to face the future with a renewed national purpose and reconciliation. As an internally driven policy agenda, with no manifestation of international pressure, the debate for and against the NRC favored its creation. Significantly, entrenched self-imposed amnesty provisions inserted into the 1992 Fourth Republican Constitution by the PNDC as part of the transitional arrangements foreclosed any formal judicial inquiry into the military regimes associated with Rawlings and other previous rulers. Thus, a judicial response to addressing the injuries suffered by victims of human rights abuses in the periods of unconstitutional rule, which characterized most of Ghana's post-independence life, was impracticable.

Although some Ghanaians preferred to see perpetrators of heinous crimes tried and punished, the indemnity clauses made Ghana's transitional justice victim-focused and perpetrator-friendly. In other words, Ghana's adoption of a restorative justice mode of transitional justice occurred, in a sense, by default. The mandate of the NRC was limited to only seek the truth of Ghana's dark past and recommend appropriate ways to restore the dignity of and respect for victims of state violence. The law establishing the NRC tasked it to promote national reconciliation among the people of Ghana by seeking to document the true, complete, and historical record of violations and abuses of human rights inflicted by the state. The NRC also had to make recommendations to the government for redress of wrongs committed within the periods specified in the law, including reparations for victims and institutional reforms. Persons who appeared before the NRC to give evidence were not to be subjected to any civil or criminal proceedings if they offered incriminatory evidence in the course of their testimonies. Finally, the NRC did not have the mandate to recommend punishment or prosecution for persons found to have perpetrated human rights abuses.

The NRC, as the main transitional justice institution, was inaugurated in May 2002 and commenced public hearings in January 2003 after taking statements from victims and witnesses. One of the controversial hearings that came before the NRC referred to the 1982 murder of the three high court judges and a retired army officer. Fresh evidence presented to the NRC suggested that the former President Rawlings and the former national security chief during the PNDC era, Captain Kojo Tsikata, were implicated in the incident. Rawlings allegedly possessed recorded information from one of the confessed suspects, Amartey Kwei. Before dying by firing squad, the suspect had given the information to Rawlings that purportedly implicated Tsikata. The Special Investigative Body (SIB) set by the PNDC to investigate these murders made adverse findings of complicity against Tsikata. To unravel this piece of news, the NRC invited Rawlings to produce this tape before it. The public expected that Rawlings would refuse to honor the invitation from the NRC because of his party's opposition to the NRC. In addition, the party saw the NPP's investigation as a witch hunt, an attempt to demonize Rawlings and his associates. Contrary to public expectations, Rawlings did appear, but only to claim that he could not find the tape. Beside these public hearings, the NRC investigated key state institutions to ascertain their role into human rights abuses.

After eighteen months of statement taking and nationwide televised public hearings, the NRC submitted its report to the president in October 2004. The NRC received more than 4,000 statements and conducted public hearings on about 1,800 of them. Its report made several recommendations, including for monetary reparations, restitutions, memorialization, and institutional reforms. The NPP government accepted in whole the findings and recommendations of the NRC report. It started implementing aspects of the recommendations, in particular monetary compensation to victims, in October 2006 during its second term in office (see entry on the National Reconciliation Commission).

Conclusion

The NRC project symbolized the most official and comprehensive effort to redress past wrongs in Ghana. Although it does not employ criminal justice, it has contributed to the development of an empirical database of postcolonial human rights abuses that can inform any major reform of state institutions. Through the truth discovered in its report, notwithstanding its limitations, the NRC has provided valuable lessons to help prevent a repetition of past mistakes. The next phase of the NRC institution is crucial for the future prospects of transitional justice in Ghana. The failure to comprehensively implement the recommendations in the report, including critical institutional reforms, memorialization, and apologies, may spell doom for any meaningful transitional justice. If Ghana's past experience with reports such as this is anything to depend on, then it may be accurate to suggest that the future of the NRC rich report will, at best, be confined to the shelves to gather dust. The NDC party, which opposed this process from the onset to the end, assumed political office on January 7, 2009, following a December 2008 election victory. The NDC has yet to demonstrate any commitment to follow through with the implementation of the outstanding recommendations.

Franklin Oduro

Cross-references: Amnesty; Lustration; National Reconciliation Commission; Restorative versus Retributive Justice; Truth Commissions.

Further Readings

Boafo-Arthur, Kwame. 2005. National Reconciliation or Polarisation? The Politics of Ghana's National Reconciliation Commission. In *The Crisis of the State and Regionalism in West Africa: Identity, Citizenship and Conflict*. Eds. W. Alade Fawole and Charles Ukeje. Dakar: Codesria.

Gyimah-Boadi, Emmanuel. 2006. Ghana's Transitional Justice. In *Transitional Justice and Human Security*. Eds. Alex Boraine and Sue Valentine. Cape Town: International Center for Transitional Justice.

Haynes, Jeff. 1991. Human Rights and Democracy in Ghana: The Record of the Rawlings' Regime. *African Affairs*, 90: 407–425.

Oduro, Franklin. 2005. Reconciling a Divided Nation through a Non-Retributive Justice Approach: Ghana's National Reconciliation Initiative. *International Journal of Human Rights*, 9: 327–347.

Oquaye, Mike. 2004. *Politics in Ghana, 1982–1992: Rawlings, Revolution and Populist Democracy*. Accra: Tornado Publications.

Guatemala

Guatemala has been marked by intense dynamics of conquest, violence, racism, and inequality. As a result of a brutal war (1960–1996), 45,000 persons disappeared, more than 600 villages were completely destroyed, 200,000 persons were forced into refugee camps in Mexico, and 1 million Guatemalans were internally displaced. Widespread torture and extrajudicial assassinations occurred. Accounting for the violent past has been seen essential in a transition to a more peaceful future. In Guatemala, the persistence of impunity accompanied efforts to achieve justice and accountability. The central transitional justice mechanism, the Commission to Clarify Past Human Rights Violations and Acts of Violence That Have Caused the Guatemalan People to Suffer (Comision para el Esclarecimiento Histórico, CEH; see separate entry), was the first official body to address war violence. Guatemalan civil society, with international support, continues to push for criminal trials and reparations, and has used the CEH report, *Memory of Silence*, as a call for justice, not amnesty.

The Repressive Past

Guatemala is a nation of 11 million people. About 60 percent of the population identifies itself as Mayan. The extremes of wealth and poverty are an issue of access to and ownership of land. Historians have traced the skewed land tenure, and consequent development of a racist and exclusionary state, to the Spanish conquest, when the best lands along the coast were grabbed by the conquistadores and organized into *latifundios*, and the indigenous population was driven into the northern highlands. During the 1900s, the inequities between the rich, primarily Ladino land-owning class, and the Mayan peasantry increased.

In 1952, President Jacobo Arbenz Guzmán's agrarian reform threatened the holdings of the U.S. United Fruit Company, which wielded tremendous influence with the U.S. administration. A coup, sponsored by the U.S. Central Intelligence Agency (CIA), overthrew Arbenz in 1954 and buried the agrarian reform. Peasants were forced off the land and executed/persecuted; land became even more concentrated in the hands of the traditional elites and the foreign fruit companies, in cooperation with the military. A series of military governments followed.

After the 1960s, Guatemala experienced a protracted guerrilla struggle. The insurgency reached its highest level of popular participation in 1981, when armed insurgents numbered 6,000. In 1982, several guerrilla organizations formed the Guatemala National Revolutionary Unity (Unidad Revolucionaria Nacional Guatemalteca, URNG).

After a crackdown against urban activists in 1978, and fueled by concerns related to the victory of the Sandinistas in Nicaragua in 1979 and the growth of the rebel army in El Salvador, in 1981, the Guatemalan army took the war to the highlands. The counterinsurgency campaign, which sought to destroy the rebels' support base, left the highlands and its majority Mayan population in ruins. The 1981–1983 period saw intense violence and the massive displacement of the highland population, as 1.3 million people fled their communities. Tens of thousands were killed. Hundreds of highland villages were wiped out.

The army's counterinsurgency program militarily dominated the highlands by employing the strategy of "draining the pond in order to kill the fish" (the pond being the population and the fish the insurgents), but the hundreds of thousands of Guatemalan refugees in UN camps in neighboring Mexico brought international attention to the military government's atrocities. In 1985, the Guatemalan army, responding to international pressures, allowed elections to build a democratic facade for its continuing control. The advent of electoral democracy was seen as an extension of the military's 1982 National Security Doctrine, which sought to eradicate the internal enemy through military and political means, not a genuine democratic transition. The army called elections an example of how politics is an extension of war by another means.

The first elected president, the Christian Democrat Vinicio Cerezo, assumed office in 1986. He claimed that the very existence of a civilian president represented democratic transition and carefully referred to violence as a feature of the past. During the period between the election and Cerezo's assumption of the presidency, several decrees assured both amnesty for the military and its continued hegemony as an institution.

Despite the advent of civilian presidents, human rights violations continued. So did the protests. A growing movement organized around the principle of the "right to the truth" demanded an end to repression and military rule. In 1984, despite considerable risk, the newly formed Mutual Support Group for Family Members of the Disappeared (Grupo de Apoyo Mutuo, GAM) began protests in front of the National Palace, with pictures of missing relatives. The GAM, uniting urban activists and rural Mayans, organized extensive marches and demonstrations that were met with fierce repression: two of the founding members were killed in 1985.

As internal pressures by civil society resulted in increased repression rather than reforms, pressures built from outside of Guatemala, with demands to put an end to the armed confrontation between the government and the URNG. The military believed that it had little need to negotiate with the URNG, which it defeated during the counterinsurgency of the 1980s. The URNG called for negotiations, but the government refused to negotiate with "terrorists." International and regional pressures, however, forced the Guatemalan government to accept negotiations with the rebels. Costa Rican President Oscar Arias launched an initiative for negotiated settlements to the region's conflicts. The accord (Esquipulas II) signed in 1987 committed the region's states to open internal dialogues between belligerent parties. Resolving Guatemala's armed conflict was necessary for the region to move forward.

Transitional Justice

In Guatemala, transitional justice took the form of a truth commission, a truth-gathering project developed by the Catholic Church, exhumations of graves of former victims, and court cases lodged in Guatemalan, Spanish, and international courts.

The Commission to Clarify Past Human Rights Violations and Acts of Violence That Have Caused the Guatemalan People to Suffer (CEH)

During peace negotiations with the URNG, the Guatemalan government felt little need to allow for transitional justice, while the military felt that it did not have to account for its actions against the insurgents. The URNG had limited power to apply in terms of demands for judicial accountability for military officers for human rights violations. The army threatened to accuse URNG commanders of human rights violations as well, and in the end the military and the insurgents found it easier to agree on amnesty for each side. The demands for truth would be addressed by creating the CEH – a form of "transitional amnesty" more than "transitional justice."

The idea of creating a truth commission was discussed in 1991 by civil society groups in meetings designed to formulate a position on the negotiations between the government and the URNG, which began in earnest in 1994. Human rights were seen as the necessary starting point, because the persistence of repression in Guatemala was a threat to negotiations. The topic of a truth commission proved so contentious that the parties failed to agree on the details. Anxious to sign the Global Human Rights Accord (and launch the peace process), the parties separated the issue of the truth commission as a distinct negotiation point. Members of the negotiating team reported that this was among the most difficult accords to negotiate.

While negotiating the Global Accord in 1994, the military came to accept that a commission addressing the armed conflict would be established. This acceptance grew out of a perceived separation between court justice and historical clarification. According to the government, many human rights abuses were excluded from judicial redress by the amnesty laws of 1985–1986. A commission, not the courts, was the appropriate place to address them.

The military insisted that the truth commission cover the entire war period, from the rise of the insurgency in 1960 to the signing of the final peace in 1994, and both "internal and external factors" in order to present a picture of Guatemala as swept up in the winds of the Cold War, as well as the responsibility of the Catholic Church, the University of San Carlos, and the labor movement in the conflict. The intention was to burden the commission with an impossible amount of work, and thus to ensure superficiality, while including those elements of Guatemalan history vindicating the military's violence.

The Accord for the Establishment of the Commission to Clarify Past Human Rights Violations and Acts of Violence That Have Caused the Guatemalan People to Suffer was signed on June 23, 1994. The word "truth" was conspicuously absent from the title. The Accord called for a three-member body consisting of an international chairperson and two Guatemalans, which would operate for six months, with the possibility of extending its mandate by another six months. The Commission was to "clarify" human rights violations and acts of violence; to prepare a report on the internal and external factors; and to formulate recommendations. The Accord read that "the work, recommendation, and report of the Commission shall not delineate responsibilities or have judicial purposes or effects" (Kritz, 1998, vol. 3).

The Accord, made public in 1994, was received with disappointment. The Commission, as mandated, lacked the authority to name or punish offenders. The Accord guaranteed no financial reparations for the victims, but empowered the Commission to make recommendations to encourage "harmony and peace" in Guatemala. Language such as "the Commission shall recommend... measures to preserve the memory of victims, to foster a culture of mutual respect and observance of human rights, and to strengthen the democratic process" (Commission to Clarify Past Human Rights Violations and Acts of Violence That Have Caused the Guatemalan People to Suffer 1999) was equally vague in regard to concrete reparations. Critics worried that the Commission would encourage impunity. The military was seen as the victor in this round of negotiations.

While most analysts attribute the faults of the Accord to the relative weakness of the rebels at the negotiating table, neither of the negotiating parties was interested in seeing a serious airing of the truth of the violence in Guatemala. URNG commander Jorge Ismael Soto Garcia (a.k.a. Pablo Monsantos), a member of the negotiating team, said that when the idea of the truth commission was first raised, the military claimed that they had evidence documenting human rights abuses by the URNG and supporting claims that the four URNG *comandantes* were war criminals. The military insisted that if past human rights abuses were resolved in the courts, for every prosecuted member of the military, a URNG member would also be charged. According to Soto Garcia, the guerrilla delegation was "unaffected" by this threat, feeling sure that the body of evidence implicating the armed forces in atrocities was much greater. However, a truth commission might have damaged high-level guerrilla commanders, given the military's superior ability to control information and make the most out of information in the report that would be damaging for the guerrilla commanders as they sought to enter politics in Guatemala.

The URNG *comandantes* saw the utility in the military's demand for a truth commission that would blame both sides for the war and the violence. Such an "objective" version of the war excused the URNG *comandantes'* lesser violations and credited the rebels with a far greater agency than they ever actually had in combat. By promoting a version of history that discussed, and excused, the army and the guerrilla equally, the URNG would achieve the parity it lacked on the field. The URNG sought a return to Guatemalan politics and needed to appear as significant protagonists in the nation's history. While neither the government/military nor the URNG were enthusiastic about seeing the Commission, the victims had no voice at the negotiating table.

The public viewed the Commission with skepticism, but continued to provide data in the form of victims' statements. On February 25, 1999, the Commission presented its report, *Memory of Silence*. In addition to 3,500 pages of information on atrocities, including more than 600 massacres, the Commission found the state responsible for 93 percent of the violations and called it genocide. The report was surprisingly strong, given that the victims and civil society had no voice in the Commission's creation, and the political transition following the 1996 Firm and Lasting Peace agreement effected a partial transformation of the structures of power. As the one concrete outcome of the peace process, and in the absence of other arenas for political contestation, the CEH became an arena for unresolved conflicts.

Inter-Diocesan Project: Recovery of Historical Memory (REMHI)

Prior to the formal conclusion of the peace negotiations, the Catholic Archbishop's Office of Human Rights (hereafter the ODHA) established in 1994 the REMHI project (see separate entry), which trained more than 800 Guatemalans to travel throughout the countryside and encourage survivors to document their testimony. The REMHI, which was the first organized effort to elicit widespread discussion concerning the nature and impact of the violence, collected more than 2,000 testimonies.

REMHI's testimony takers (*animadores de la paz*) were trained to encourage Guatemalans to talk. The Church stated that it "does not want more hate, or vengeance" but "wants the truth to be known because from the truth comes forgiveness.... To speak is to begin healing, and relieve the pain" (REMHI, "Hablemos la Verdad Recuperemos Nuestra Historia"). REMHI's testimony-taking sessions in rural communities began with prayer, and several REMHI *animadores* stressed that judgment lay with God; to forgive was to be a good Christian.

The ODHA and the REMHI project had conflicting motives. Many of the intellectual architects of REMHI were social scientists interested in collecting and analyzing data that would contribute to a deeper understanding of Guatemalan reality. The ODHA and the Catholic Church were interested in Christian forgiveness and Christian burials. The Church, which lost many followers during the violence to death, migration, exile, and conversion to Evangelical faiths, saw the truth-gathering efforts and exhumation projects as a means to regain status in rural communities affected by the violence.

In 1994–1996, REMHI established a precedent for visiting rural communities and engaging in testimony taking. The project was carried out before the formal cessation of armed hostilities, in an extremely fluid context. Its creators saw their work as contributing to the future work of an official truth commission, if one ever came to fruition.

Exhumations

Concurrently with REMHI, rural communities exhumed the graves of massacre victims. Survivors often knew where the bodies were buried in "clandestine cemeteries." Sometimes, those who escaped the massacre had returned and hastily buried their dead loved ones; other times, the military ordered survivors to bury the dead. The persistence of terror precluded the acknowledgment of these sites of mass graves, although these were often located in or near the village center.

In 1992, the Guatemalan Forensic Anthropology Team (Equipo de Antropologia Forense de Guatemala, EAFG) began working with support from Clyde Snow, a University of Oklahoma professor, who had gained a reputation for his ability to determine the fate of the "disappeared," sometimes on mere scraps of bone (Joyce and Stover, 1991). The physical evidence produced in exhumations, combined with survivors' testimonies, was organized by the Center for Legal Action on Human Rights (CALDH) to prepare cases against the Guatemalan military for crimes against humanity and "local genocide," the massacres in the highlands. In Plan de Sanchez, Baja Verapaz region, and San Martín, Chimaltenango region, CALDH helped communities prepare their cases in view of launching trials if amnesty could be overcome. Both communities presented strong cases against the highest-level officials considered responsible for the violence: Efrain Rios Montt, Oscar Humberto Mejia Victores, and Romero Lucas Garcia.

The EAFG published several studies detailing the exhumations (EAFG, 1997). With the evolving sophistication of the scientific methods of forensic anthropologists, the evidence produced became more credible and powerful. The EAFG also published simplified, cartoon versions of its work. The accessibility of the information fueled movements around rural Guatemala, and demands for exhumations increased; by 2004, the EAFG had completed more than 300 exhumations.

The Myrna Mack Court Case

Efforts to address the violence also included pressures for justice in the legal case regarding the murder of anthropologist Myrna Mack, who had conducted research concerning the internally displaced in the highlands. She was stabbed to death in Guatemala City on September 11, 1990. The press pointed out that Mack was murdered because she conducted research on the reality of life for highland Guatemalans affected by the violence. Internationally, Mack's colleagues protested the loss. The attention generated by this effort, combined with massive local protest, made it impossible for the government to ignore the issue.

The government argued that Mack's murder was the work of common criminals and refused to conduct a serious investigation. Myrna's sister, Helen Mack, pursued the case herself by collecting evidence that eventually convicted in 2002 in Guatemala one of the assassins, a member of the president's security police. She has also sought to hold three high-ranking army officers accountable for having planned and issued the orders to the assassin. This court case, and the work of the foundation established in Myrna Mack's name, has generated considerable movement in the area of judicial reform, but to date has led to no further prosecutions.

Justice in Regional and International Courts

The National Reconciliation Law of November 1996 amnestied all those who participated in the armed conflict, although Article 8 prohibited the granting of amnesty for "genocide, torture or forced disappearance." The law allows Guatemalan judges reluctant to prosecute state officials to judge individual cases, and places the burden on the victim to prove charges: the perpetrator can seek to have a case dismissed based on the fact that it occurred during the armed conflict. While attempts have been made to bring more than a dozen genocide cases in the Guatemalan courts, these cases have met with significant obstacles, from legal maneuvers in the form of appeals to dangerous threats against those involved in such cases. Cases against the state or individuals have rarely been taken up in Guatemalan courts.

More than 100 Guatemalan human rights cases have been taken up in the Inter-American system. Until 2000, the Guatemalan government stonewalled the Inter-American Commission on Human Rights and refused to accept responsibility for human rights cases presented to the Inter-American Court. After 2000, in a bid to improve Guatemala's international image, the government admitted limited responsibility and agreed to implement the Court's decisions involving reparations to victims.

The Guatemalan state's more collaborative stance toward the Inter-American Court falls far short of achieving accountability, because the Court lacks the ability to determine individual criminal accountability; it is often unclear what kind of responsibility the Guatemalan government is accepting (for obstruction of justice or actual responsibility for the crimes committed); and collective reparation measures have been at best modest and at worst divisive for the communities affected by the violence (Merskey and Roht-Arriaza, 2007).

Guatemalans, human rights advocates, and lawyers trained in transnational jurisprudence have pursued cases abroad under the principle of universal jurisdiction (see separate entry). Stymied by impunity and inadequate judicial remedies at home, Guatemalans have found European courts receptive to the idea that some crimes are so heinous as to make them "crimes of international concern" and, hence, appropriate for investigations and trials although the alleged crimes occurred far from the seat of the court.

In 1999, Mayan activist and Nobel laureate Rigoberta Menchú Tum and others filed in the Spanish National Court in Madrid a complaint that charged eight prominent Guatemalans, including Montt, Victores, and Garcia, with genocide, torture, terrorism, summary execution, and unlawful detention. The case addressed atrocities in the communities of Plan de Sanchez and Rio Negro, the murder of Menchú's relatives, and violations against Spanish nationals living in Guatemala. The court heard testimony from victims and expert witnesses in 2008.

Conclusion

Many expected that confining discussions of the violence to the CEH would prevent prosecutions. Yet, the CEH interpreted its mandate for the benefit of the victims, not of the signatories to the peace negotiations, and exceeded expectations with the strength of its final report. The CEH's final report provides opportunities for judicial measures. In building a legal case around genocide, the CEH attempted to bypass its built-in weakness: the restriction regarding judicial implications. However, the lack of justice in national courts indicates the persistence of impunity. In sum, Guatemala's transitional justice experience demonstrates both the power of the truth and the truth about power. The CEH, the REHMI, the exhumations, and the Myrna Mack trial show the desire to achieve accountability for human rights abuses, despite the very real risks to activists. However, the lack of investigations, prosecutions, and reparations indicates that the efforts to achieve truth and justice have yielded few material consequences.

Amy Ross

Cross-references: Amnesty; Commission to Clarify Past Human Rights Violations and Acts of Violence That Have Caused the Guatemalan People to Suffer; Reparations; Truth Commissions.

Further Readings

Commission to Clarify Past Human Rights Violations and Acts of Violence That Have Caused the Guatemalan People to Suffer. 1999. *Guatemala: Memoria del Silencio* [Memory of Silence]. Available at: http://shr.aaas.org/guatemala/ceh/mds/spanish/toc.html (accessed November 3, 2009).

Equipo de Antropología Forense de Guatemala. 1997. *Las Masacres en Rabinal: estudio histórico de las masacres de Plan de Sanchez, Chichupac y Rio Negro*. EARG; Guatemala City.

Joyce, Christopher and Eric Stover. 1991. *Witnesses from the Grave: The Stories Bones Tell*. Boston: Little, Brown and Company.

Kritz, Neil. 1998. *Transitional Justice: How Emerging Democracies Reckon with Former Regimes*. Washington, DC: U.S. Institute for Peace.

Mersky, M. and N. Roht-Arriaza. 2007. Guatemala. In *Victims Unsilenced: The Inter-American Human Rights System and Transitional Justice in Latin America*. Washington, DC: Due Process of Law Foundation, pp. 7–32. Available at: http://www.dplf.org/uploads/1190403828.pdf (accessed November 3, 2009).

Oficina de Derechos Humanos del Arzobispado de Guatemala. 1999. *Guatemala: Never Again!* New York: Orbis Books.

———. 1998. *Guatemala: Nunca Más, Informe Proyecto Interdiocesano de Recuperatión de la Memoria Histórica*. 4 vols. Guatemala City: Oficina de Derechos Humanos del Arzobispado de Guatemala.

Oglesby, E. 2007. Educating Citizens in Postwar Guatemala: Historical Memory, Genocide, and the "Culture of Peace". *Radical History Review*, 97: 76–98.
Oglesby, E. and A. Ross. 2009. Guatemala's Genocide Determination and the Spatial Politics of Justice. *Space and Polity*, 13: 21–39.
Ross, A. 2006. The Creation and Conduct of the Guatemalan Commission for Historical Clarification. *Geoforum*, 37: 69–81.
———. 2004. Truth and Consequences in Guatemala. *Geojournal*, 60: 73–79.
Schirmer, Jennifer. 1998. *The Guatemalan Military Project. A Violence Called Democracy*. Philadelphia: University of Pennsylvania Press.

Haiti

Haiti's experience with transitional justice has been short. In an attempt to deal with a three-year period of intense violations (1991–1994), a truth commission was hastily appointed in 1995. But other mechanisms of transitional justice have never been implemented, even though the country has a long history of violent abuse. And the long-standing complicated political and security situation in the country to date has precluded any further thought of transformation.

The Repressive Past

Haiti and the island of Hispaniola were discovered by Christopher Columbus in 1492. The import of slaves from Africa began in 1520. By 1697, when the western half of the island was ceded to France, French trade from the island included goods produced almost entirely by slave labor in the settlement. The population of Haiti grew quickly. By the mid-1700s, the colony was populated by 36,000 whites who ruled over 700,000 black slaves, freed slaves, and mulattoes through a series of authoritarian laws. In 1791, an organized slave revolt began. When the French abolished slavery in 1794, the Haitian revolution began in earnest, but was quashed three months later. Haitians, however, continued their fight. Twelve years later, the Haitians defeated the French army. On January 1, 1804, Haiti declared independence.

From 1843 to 1915, most of the twenty-two presidents served less than two years in office, a result of political and economic instability. Throughout this time, the plummeting Haitian economy forced thousands of Haitians across the Dominican border for work. It is estimated that between 20,000 and 30,000 Haitians obliged to work in Dominican banana plantations were massacred in the Dominican Republic during that time for dissenting against the Haitian government. In 1915, the U.S. fleet invaded Haiti, and the Americans installed a proxy government in Port-au-Prince, the country's capital, held in place by thousands of American security forces.

Black Haitians were frustrated with the ruling class of whites and mulattoes, and began to agitate for change. A black Haitian, Dumarais Estimé, was elected in May 1946 on a tide of rising popular discontent, but he was deposed four years later. In December 1950, his successor, Colonel Paul Magloire, pushed for mulatto elite rule, and was willing to support them with military backing. Support was also provided by the Roman Catholic Church and the U.S. government. Magloire was ousted in May 1956. Five provisional governments and a civil uprising that lasted for one day followed.

François "Papa Doc" Duvalier was elected president in September 1956 on a platform of *noirisme*, meaning the advancement of blacks and the rejection of Western domination.

His pro-Haitian transformations quickly turned to repression and tyranny, and an estimated 30,000 to 60,000 people were killed during his time in office. His personal army, a group of supporters nicknamed the *tonton macoutes*, helped carry out Duvalier's reign of terror. Yet the United States continued to support the once democratically elected Duvalier. When Papa Doc died in 1971, his nineteen-year-old son, Jean-Claude, was installed as president. Although "Baby Doc" eased many of the oppressive policies for a short while, eventually he, too, cracked down on dissidents within the country. As the economic situation worsened, further aggravated by the growing worldwide oil crisis, dissent among Baby Doc's critics grew. He was forced to leave Haiti in 1986.

A progressive group of liberation theology Roman Catholic priests was influential among Haitian peasant groups, cooperatives, and the peasant vigilante groups that had sprung up in defense against the *tonton macoutes*. The group was headed by Father Jean-Bertrand Aristide, and stood for justice, openness, and participation, the values on which Aristide later campaigned. Aristide was elected president with 67 percent of the popular vote in 1990. Slightly more than six months from the day he took office, the military engineered a coup against him, and Aristide was forced into exile, first in Venezuela and later in Washington, DC.

In 1991 and for the next three years, a campaign of torture was waged against Aristide's supporters by the regime of General Raoul Cédras, which was responsible for forcing Aristide into exile. A series of provisional governments, all backed by the armed forces under Cédras, ruled the country. Throughout this time, the country was shaken by extreme violence against Aristide's supporters. At least 5,000 were killed, and thousands more were abused by Haitian military and police officials. More than 50,000 attempted to escape by boat to the United States. An estimated 300,000 went into hiding within the country itself. In some areas of the country, whole populations were targeted and killed, while in others, top supporters of Aristide were murdered. On July 3, 1993, the United States brokered the Governor's Island Accord, signed by Aristide and Cédras. Aristide was further undermined when Cédras and his supporters were awarded large sums of money for their cooperation. On October 15, 1994, Aristide returned to power in Port-au-Prince. He stepped aside after he finished serving his one term in office, as per the terms of the constitution. His successor, Réné Préval, who had served as Aristide's prime minister and had been forced into exile with Aristide, assumed power with Aristide's backing. Aristide was reelected in 2000 with 92 percent of the electoral vote, and returned to office in February 2001. He left office in 2004. Préval was reelected in 2005. For the next several years, and at the time of this writing, periods of extreme violence continued.

Transitional Justice

The idea of transitional justice in Haiti was contemplated and attempted once, and then only briefly. President Aristide convoked the National Truth and Justice Commission (Commission nationale de vérité et de justice) when he returned to power in 1995. The Commission was jointly supported by the International Organization of American States and the United Nations Permanent Mission to Haiti (International Civilian Mission in Haiti or MICIVIH).

Aristide himself called for and established the truth commission, which ran from March to December 1995. The idea of such a commission had been conceived by the Haitian diaspora living in Montreal, Canada, many of whom were wealthy elites who were themselves strong supporters of Aristide. The Commission was largely supported by those who aligned with Aristide and those who had been abused at the hand of Cédras. Yet the internal situation in Haiti, created by the uneven power brokering that had established the uneasy peace between Aristide and Cédras, was such that there was considerable backlash and threats of violence against the Commission and against Aristide's supporters.

The Commission was established to look into the events that had taken place between 1991 and 1994, and to establish some record of what had taken place. These findings were expected to lead to subsequent prosecutions. In large part, these failed to materialize because the Commission's patron, Aristide, left office as the report was presented. Furthermore, because much of the girding of the truth commission had come from international participants – both commissioners and staffers – when they withdrew at the completion of the Commission's work, that level of support was also effectively withdrawn.

The Commission was, therefore, unable to have any major and lasting impact. For those who were involved in its work, the revelation of the considerable violence and numbers of abuses that had taken place was staggering. But for those outside of its sphere, it went largely unnoticed. The report led to no discernible reforms or changes in the community.

Other discrete peace-building and political transformation initiatives, supported by international governments and their agencies, continued. These included army demobilization, police training, judicial reform, and a reduction in drug trafficking. Yet, because of both lack of donor support and persistent corruption, violence has resurged.

The Haitian courts have subsequently tried some of those who were involved in the violations committed between 1991 and 1994. Yet judicial practices are neither free nor fair. In 2005, the Supreme Court overturned the convictions of thirty-eight paramilitary and army leaders who had been found guilty in 2000 for murder and torture in the 1994 Raboteau massacre. Most of those convicted were in exile at the time and so were tried in absentia. The Supreme Court called for the release of all those convicted after finding that the lower court that originally had tried the men had lacked the authority to hear the case. The decision was seen as a severe blow to efforts to fight impunity. People who testified in the trial suffered reprisals when some of those who were in exile returned. This is a hazard of carrying out transitional justice in unstable situations.

Conclusion

The Commission nationale de vérité et de justice was unable to have any major impact. It did not secure any kind of foothold for transitional justice-related activities. Future prospects for confronting these and other atrocities look doubtful, as extremely high levels of violence and poverty have prevented the organizational structure of the state from functioning properly for several decades. The earthquake that struck Haiti in January 2010 will significantly hamper efforts at justice and state-building for the foreseeable future.

Joanna R. Quinn

Cross-references: Armed Conflict; Causes of Failure of Transitional Justice; Conflict (Ongoing) and Transitional Justice; National Truth and Justice Commission; Truth Commissions.

Further Readings

Amnesty International. 1998. *Haiti: Still Crying Out for Justice*. AMR 36/02/98.
Brody, Reed. 1998. International Aspects of Current Efforts at Judicial Reform: Undermining Justice in Haiti. In *The (Un)Rule of Law and the Under-Privileged in Latin America*. Eds. Juan Mendez, Guillermo O'Donnell, and Paulo Sérgio Pinheiro. Notre Dame: University of Notre Dame Press.
Dupuy, Alex. 1997. *Haiti in the New World Order: The Limits of the Democratic Revolution*. Boulder: Westview.
Rotberg, Robert I., ed. 1997. *Haiti Renewed: Political and Economic Prospects*. Cambridge, MA: The World Peace Foundation.

Honduras

In Honduras, the transition from military to civilian rule in 1981 was followed by gruesome human rights abuses that stifled domestic transitional justice efforts during the 1980s. With the changing international environment and election of new leadership in the early 1990s, the country began taking on the challenges of reconciling with the past. Most notably, the Honduran truth commission report, *The Facts Speak for Themselves*, which investigated the 1980–1993 period, was released in 1993. The number of prosecutions has increased since the 2000 repeal of the amnesty laws, but these have been only marginally effective because of a struggling judicial system and the still-powerful military.

The Repressive Past

While Honduras did not experience a serious rebel threat or widespread civil war as its neighbors did in the 1980s, the spillover effects of those conflicts had a significant impact on the country's politics and led to extensive human rights abuses on the part of security forces similar to those seen in Guatemala and El Salvador (see separate entries). Having ruled the country intermittently during the 1960s and the 1970s, the Honduran military turned government over to civilian authorities in 1981.

Despite some high-profile incidents (see later discussion), these military governments were not associated with widespread human rights abuses and instead made attempts to redistribute land to landless peasants. These efforts met with resistance from landed elites, but also prompted pressure from peasant organizations and trade unions to move more quickly, resulting in illegal land occupations. Thus, the armed forces intervened in land disputes and were involved in human rights abuses in the late 1970s. In 1975, they attacked the headquarters of a peasant organization and tortured and disappeared several people. The armed forces were aware of the pushes toward communist activity in Honduras and surrounding states, and among the first targets of military activity were individuals suspected of belonging to Salvadoran guerrilla organizations.

Concerted campaigns of torture, disappearances, arbitrary arrests, and political murders began after the transition to civilian rule and coincided with the intensification of the civil war in El Salvador and the U.S.-sponsored counterrevolutionary war against the Sandinistas in Nicaragua. These neighboring conflicts drove increased U.S. interest in Honduran politics, which meant heavy U.S. assistance in equipment and training for the Honduran military and the establishment of territory held by anti-Sandinista counterrevolutionary (often called "contra") forces along the border with Nicaragua.

In the early 1980s, the United States trained hundreds of Honduran military and police officers at the School of the Americas at Fort Benning, Georgia, in the Panama Canal Zone, and the at International Police Academy in Washington, DC, and by bringing military advisors to Honduras from other Latin American countries such as Argentina, who had been practicing brutal interrogation methods in their own countries for years. The result for Honduras was the inauguration of military-sanctioned death squads, including the Military Intelligence Battalion 3–16, a special security services unit under the direct command of the Armed Forces General Staff, which carried out kidnappings, interrogations, and executions. Its members operated in civilian clothes and used unmarked vehicles in order to deny military involvement in the abductions and disappearances. The heaviest human rights abuses in the country occurred from 1981 to 1984. Hundreds were kidnapped and tortured, and at least 179 were disappeared. The 1984 internal power struggle, which removed General Gustavo Alvarez Martinez from his post as Commander-in-Chief of the Armed Forces, was the turning point in the conduct of the Honduran military. The new military leadership put an end to the systematic campaign of official death squad activity against leftist activists, but the country's human rights record remained exceptionally poor, with arbitrary arrests and use of torture in investigations still commonplace well into the 1990s.

Transitional Justice

Because of the sharp increase in systematic human rights abuses after the transition from military to civilian government and the persistence of those violations, efforts to pursue truth, justice, and reconciliation in Honduras took on a unique character. Domestic avenues for transitional justice did not open up until the early 1990s. Thus, at the height of the campaign against suspected leftists, the Inter-American Court of Human Rights served as the chief outlet for truth telling and legal action against the Honduran government, hearing three high-profile cases related to presumed disappearances. Beginning in the 1990s, Honduras turned to domestic transitional justice mechanisms including a truth commission, institutional reforms, and attempts at criminal prosecutions.

The Inter-American Court of Human Rights

Among the first cases decided by the Inter-American Court were those dealing with disappearances by state security forces in Honduras. As a supranational judicial body established by the Organization of American States (see separate entry), the Court serves as a forum for legal action only when all domestic legal remedies have been exhausted. The Court proved to be the legal avenue that Hondurans needed during the 1980s.

Relatives of the disappeared filed suit with the Honduran government from 1981 to 1984, but the state dismissed the cases, forcing those families to turn to the Inter-American Court. The families of Saúl Godínez Crúz and Angel Manfredo Velásquez Rodríguez accused the Honduran government of forced disappearances, petitioning the Inter-American Commission of Human Rights, which brought the case to the Court on behalf of the injured party. On July 21, 1989, the Court handed down decisions in both cases, ruling in favor of the families and ordering the Honduran state to pay damages. The proceedings were significant not only for the reparations ordered for the families, but also for the investigation into disappearances in Honduras and the activities of the military more broadly. The Court found the state responsible for forced disappearances, established that the government had carried out or condoned a campaign of disappearances from 1981 to 1984, and secured important testimony from military officials and uncovered new information about Battalion 3–16, thus serving a vital truth-telling function. The Court also called attention to the ineffectiveness or unwillingness of the Honduran executive and judiciary to investigate and punish human rights violations in the country.

The Court's truth-telling functions are important because the testimony gathered and the information established was a form of justice even when the verdict was not in favor of the plaintiffs. An earlier case against Honduras, brought on behalf of Francisco Fairén Garbi and Yolanda Solís Corrales, found that the state had not been proven responsible for their disappearances, but established knowledge of the patterns of abuses in the country at the time, illuminating other rights violations such as clandestine detention. The case effectively argued the insufficiency of domestic legal remedies stemming from intimidation of and threats against attorneys and judges.

Truth Commissions

In the early 1990s, the government's attitude toward the human rights situation in Honduras began to change. In 1992, Dr. Leo Valladares Lanza, a member of the Inter-American Commission on Human Rights, was appointed to the newly created position of Honduran National Commissioner for the Protection of Human Rights and tasked with investigating human rights violations in the country. The following year, Roberto Reina, a former president of the Inter-American Court of Human Rights, was elected President of Honduras. His human rights background made him a natural ally in the work of the National Commissioner for the Protection of Human Rights (see separate entry), and he supported the idea of prosecuting and punishing those found to be responsible for rights violations in the truth commission report. In this same period, the Cold War ended and the Central American peace process brought an end to the civil wars among Honduras's neighbors, thereby removing the main reasons for political repression in the country. U.S. interest in and support of the Honduran military decreased dramatically, causing military power to decline and allowing for the political opportunity to open the truth commission investigation in 1992. Fourteen individuals and organizations such as the Centro de Estudios Legales y Sociales (CELS) and SOA Watch, an organization committed to lobbying to close the School of the Americas, contributed research assistance.

Commissioner Valladares published his initial report in 1993. He was keenly aware of the need to issue his findings quickly in order to serve the families of the disappeared. Unlike the Truth Commission in El Salvador (see separate entry), the Valladares report was entirely a domestic undertaking, leading him to see it as an opportunity to demonstrate the effectiveness of the country's institutions under its changing democracy. Valladares wanted the transitional justice effort to extend beyond the truth commission and include other methods. He stated that the truth commission report was not meant to take the place of the judicial action.

The Honduran Truth Commission was limited in its scope, focusing chiefly on disappearances. Through new investigatory work and reliance on the work of the Inter-American Court in the *Godínez Crúz* and *Manfredo Velásquez* cases, Valladares reported that at least 184 people were disappeared by Honduran security forces from 1980 to 1993.

The number was later revised down to 179. The report sought to illuminate the relationship between the United States and the Honduran armed forces, particularly in regard to the formation, training, and operation of Battalion 3–16. The United States was consistently uncooperative, blocking the release of documents and refusing to provide information. Domestically, Valladares also faced opposition from a still-powerful military that also hampered future prosecutorial efforts.

In June 2009, the Honduran armed forces ousted President Manuel Zelaya in a coup d'état, in response to his efforts to hold a referendum to convene a Constitutional Assembly to change the constitution – in large part to eliminate presidential term limits, his critics argued. The proposed referendum drew condemnation from Congress and was declared unconstitutional by the Supreme Court. The coup drew international condemnation, and Honduras was suspended from the Organization of American States (OAS). International actors did not recognize Zelaya's successor, former president of the Honduran Congress Roberto Micheletti, as the new head of state. In an effort to reintegrate with the international community, Honduras established a Truth Commission to investigate events and alleged human rights abuses surrounding the coup. The Commission began its work in May 2010.

This Commission is unrelated to the truth commission of the 1990s or the work of the National Commissioner for the Protection of Human Rights. The new Commission has been controversial since its inception. Supporters of the coup government argued that such investigations would only increase divisions in the country. With the election of Porfirio Lobo to the presidency through constitutional means in late 2009, many argue that it is time to move on. Meanwhile, critics have charged that because the Truth Commission was established by the coup government, it cannot be trusted to deliver a reliable, impartial report on Zelaya's ouster. In June 2010, Honduran human rights defenders established an independent organization known as the True Commission to register testimony, investigate, and document human rights abuses connected to the 2009 coup d'état.

Domestic Prosecutions

Achieving domestic legal accountability for state-sponsored human rights abuses in Honduras has met with mixed success. Honduras reformed many of its government institutions to deal more effectively with the problem of impunity for human rights abuses. President Reina set up the Special Prosecutor for Human Rights, which opened its first case in 1995 by charging ten army officers for attempted murder and illegal detention of university students in 1982. Afterward, more charges were filed, with at least thirty-eight members of the armed forces investigated for human rights abuses. Colonel Juan Blas Salazar Mesa was found guilty by the First Criminal Court, but he was not punished because of the amnesty laws of 1986 (Decree 31–86) and 1991 (Decree 87–91). Many officers cited the amnesty laws as reason enough not to cooperate with prosecutions, going into hiding, and refusing to appear in court. In 2000, the Supreme Court declared that the amnesty laws were inapplicable in the case of the 1982 kidnapping of university students in which Mesa was accused (No. 20–99 of 26 June 2000). While this decision did not universally declare the amnesties unconstitutional, it did allow prosecutors to appeal for exclusion of amnesty protections, making trials possible and requiring decisions on a case-by-case basis.

Since this change, there has been some progress in bringing perpetrators to justice. Cases are still most often dismissed by the courts for insufficient evidence or significantly delayed because of lack of cooperation from the military in granting access to information, but there have been a few successful prosecutions. In May 2003, Colonel Salazar Mesa was sentenced to four years in jail for the kidnapping of university students that he was tried for in 1995. Three other members of the army were convicted of human rights violations in 2004 and 2005 and received sentences ranging from two to twelve years in prison. While the formal barriers to prosecution have been removed, Honduras has continued to face difficulties in curtailing the power of the military and compelling its cooperation in coming to terms with the past. Military jurisdiction over human rights trials ended with the 1982 constitution (Article 91) and the 1984 Constitutive Law of the Armed Forces (Decree 98–84), but the military remains uncooperative with civilian courts. Many members of the infamous Battalion 3–16 still serve in important positions in the Honduran military today, and the military remains a powerful political actor, as demonstrated by the 2009 coup d'état that ousted President Manuel Zelaya.

Conclusion

While Honduras still faces serious challenges in making a clean break with the past and providing justice for its citizens, the country's experience with transitional justice is positive. In the 1980s, those affected by political repression had to look to international actors for justice. In the 1990s, Honduras began to open the book on the past and sought to face the truth about the campaign of disappearances and patterns of violence in the country, even as prosecutorial efforts continued to be stymied by amnesty laws and the ability of the military to manipulate the judicial system in cases of human rights trials. More recently, there has been progress in holding members of the armed forces legally accountable for their actions. Thus, Honduras has consistently, if very slowly, managed to move forward in pursuing justice.

Brett J. Kyle

Cross-references: El Salvador; Guatemala; National Commissioner for the Protection of Human Rights; Organization of American States; Truth Commission, El Salvador.

Further Readings

Center for Justice and Accountability. 2009. *Honduras: Battalion 316: Torture & Forced Disappearance*. San Francisco: The Center for Justice and Accountability. Available at: http://www.cja.org/article.php?list=type&type=254 (accessed January 1, 2011).

Godínez-Cruz v. Honduras. 1989. San José: Inter-American Court of Human Rights.

Kaye, Mike. 1997. The Role of Truth Commissions in the Search for Justice, Reconciliation, and Democratisation: The Salvadoran and Honduran Cases. *Journal of Latin American Studies*, 29(3): 693–716.

Manfredo Velásquez v. Honduras. 1989. San José: Inter-American Court of Human Rights.

Popkin, Margaret and Naomi Roht-Arriaza. 1995. Truth as Justice: Investigatory Commissions in Latin America. *Law & Social Inquiry*, 20(1): 79–116.

Sriram, Chandra. 2004. *Confronting Past Human Rights Violations: Justice vs. Peace in Times of Transition*. New York: Frank Cass.

Valladares, Leo. 1994. *Honduras: The Facts Speak for Themselves: The Preliminary Report of the National Commissioner for the Protection of Human Rights in Honduras*. New York: Human Rights Watch.

Hungary

Although there were various attempts at some type of reckoning with the past, transitional justice efforts in Hungary often ran into constitutional or political obstacles. Despite heated debates, Hungary's transitional justice belongs to the milder types among former communist countries. At the same time, debates about the past continue to flare up regularly in political discourse.

The Repressive Past

The Hungarian People's Democracy's (1949–1989) history includes different periods. The most repressive years were between 1949, when the multiparty system was eliminated, and 1953, when Soviet dictator Josef Stalin died. During this period, the state security service – Államvédelmi Hatóság (ÁVO then ÁVH) – terrorized the population, exercising control over both public and private life. Real or suspected opponents of the communist system, members of the propertied and bourgeois class, and those of the churches were interned, imprisoned, or sentenced to forced labor. Show trials targeted members and leaders of the communist party (Hungarian Workers' Party – MDP). According to estimates, 3,000 people were purposefully killed by the regime and approximately three times as many were "indirect" victims, whose death could have been avoided by humane treatment. Cautious de-Stalinization ("thaw") began after Stalin's death, when in June 1953 Imre Nagy became the prime minister.

Pressure for reforms built, and on October 23, 1956, an anticommunist uprising broke out. After two weeks of armed combat and the reorganization of public life (the multiparty system was reestablished and workers' committees formed), on November 4, 1956, the Soviet Red Army attacked the capital and crushed the uprising. Led by János Kádár, the reorganized communist party (Hungarian Socialist Workers' Party, HSWP) strengthened the communist regime with bloody repression (200 to 300 people were executed and 15,000 were imprisoned, while 200,000 fled the country), culminating in the 1958 execution of former Premier Imre Nagy and his comrades.

Two amnesties (1960 and 1963) marked the start of normalization, and the Kádár regime, operating under the slogan of "who is not against us is with us," became known as the "happiest barrack" in the Soviet camp. If the 1950s were characterized by open repression and terror, after the 1960s, "liberalization" offered people relatively undisturbed private life, traveling privileges, and economic freedoms by accepting the private "second economy" in exchange for their tacit acceptance of the system. Despite the regime's "liberal" façade, secret services (Division III/3 – domestic surveillance, or counter interior reaction group) monitored the population, especially the cultural institutions (media, theaters, universities, and churches), and continuously harassed the opposition. By 1989, approximately 170,000 people were under surveillance by the security services, which employed 50,000 agents (in a total population of 10.4 million). Informers were recruited using methods ranging from ideological conviction and promises of social advancement and privileges to threats. Sanctions for nonconformist behavior or opposition activities included the denial of privileges (passports), education, or job opportunities, in more severe cases arrests and police investigation, and in some high-profile cases forced emigration. Prison sentences, however, were rare during these years.

During the 1980s, mounting economic troubles and the changing international environment led to reform movements within the party and the appearance of various opposition groups. Inspired by the Polish example of the Round Table Negotiations, in 1989, the newly organized opposition and the HSWP negotiated around the National Round Table. Their pact paved the way to the free elections of March 1990, ousting the communists from power. The Hungarian Republic was proclaimed on the symbolic date of October 23, 1989 (the anniversary of the 1956 uprising). Division III/3 was dissolved in February 1990, less than a month before the first free elections, by the outgoing communist government.

Transitional Justice

While embracing a forgive-and-forget approach, Hungary did implement a number of transitional justice programs, including restitution and rehabilitation, court trials, screening and vetting, access to secret files, and memorialization.

Restitution and Rehabilitation

Rehabilitation in high-profile cases already started during the last days of the People's Republic: on June 16, 1989, Imre Nagy and other martyrs of the 1956 uprising were given a government-sanctioned ceremonial reburial attended by 250,000 people, including cabinet members and Prime Minister Miklós Németh, and their conviction was nullified in court later that summer. The first postcommunist parliament enacted a law about the memory of the 1956 uprising, while the second, socialist-led coalition did the same for Imre Nagy. On June 23, 2000, parliament designated February 25 the memorial day of the victims of communism (the day when, in 1947, Independent Smallholder MP Béla Kovács was arrested by the Soviet authorities and deported to the Soviet Union). Act 12/1991 terminated special pensions paid for contributing to the defeat of the 1956 uprising, while those who suffered injustice caused by the state (loss of freedom or life for political reasons) between May 1939 and 1990 were entitled to compensation (22/1992).

Compensation for lost property was also high on the agenda. The debate focused on redress or re-privatization. Initially two of the three members of the right-wing coalition government that took power in May 1990 (the Christian Democrats and the Independent Smallholders' Party, ISP) favored returning nationalized or confiscated property to original owners, but the strongest coalition party, the Hungarian Democratic Forum (HDF), rejected it, and in the end this view prevailed. The only exception was the churches: they were handed back many of their former buildings deemed necessary for their religious or cultural activities (23/1991). The compensation laws instead offered vouchers for property lost after 1948 (25/1991) and between 1939 and 1948 (24/1992). Vouchers could be used to purchase property or to receive social security or pension-type payments. Approximately 1.8 million people applied for such redress. Most recipients – mainly elderly people – used the vouchers to buy the apartments they rented from the state, while many people not interested in getting property sold their vouchers to entrepreneurs.

Although the ISP campaigned almost exclusively with the program of land re-privatization in order to undo the injustice of the forced collectivization during the 1950s, the Constitutional Court rejected the distinction between various forms of property. However, lands in agricultural collectives were designated for compensation, which could be bid for at auctions. While doubtless rectifying a grave injustice committed during communism, land privatization contributed to the dismantling of successful agricultural collectives and created small, unviable, and uneconomical parcels, delivering a severe blow to a hitherto thriving Hungarian agriculture.

Retroactive Criminal Justice

On September 2, 1991, deputies Zsolt Zétényi and Péter Takács of the ruling HDF submitted to parliament Bill 2961 on the Prosecutability of Offenses between December 21, 1944 and May 2, 1990. This "bill of justice" proposed to amend the Hungarian Criminal Code by suspending the statute of limitation (which lapses after thirty years) for certain crimes (treason, premeditated murder, and aggravated assault leading to death) not prosecuted for political reasons. Despite the length of the time period involved, the bill's primary target were crimes committed during and immediately after the 1956 uprising. Taking the elapsed time into account, the bill recommended that the courts alleviate or commute sentences for communist crimes without restriction, taking into consideration factors such as the age or the possibly altered character of the defendants. The bill's sponsors argued that during the indicated period the Hungarian government did not enjoy full sovereignty because of Soviet and communist influence, and criminal prosecution was greatly influenced by extralegal political considerations (on December 21, 1944, the first provisional National Assembly convened after World War II, and on May 2, 1990, the first freely elected parliament met). Given that prosecution was often prevented or hampered by the authoritarian regime, and could only be carried out in the new *Rechtsstaat* (rule of law), the statute of limitation should be regarded as "tolled" (or suspended/not applicable) during the indicated period. The bill was enacted on November 4, 1991, a symbolic date, which marked the anniversary of the Soviet attack on Hungary to crush the 1956 uprising.

The bill was fiercely debated both by parliament and society. The arguments focused on three main issues. The first pertained to a fundamental dilemma of transitional justice: whether the country should focus on forward-looking reconciliation and productively engage society's energy, or satisfy society's moral value system and sense of justice as the basis for healthy social development, as supporters argued. In this debate the opposition accused the government of trying to divert attention from pressing social and economic problems and its own inept governing. Second, concerns were raised about the length of the elapsed time, which would, on the one hand, render providing evidence beyond doubt very difficult, and on the other, as former dissident János Kis pointed out, lead to the conviction of very old people more than thirty years after their crimes. But this delayed conviction defeated the purposes of criminal prosecution to prevent future crimes and prompt the convicted to atone.

The third and decisive argument addressed the principles of the rule of law, which prohibited retroactive legislation. This debate highlighted differences with respect to legal theory (natural vs. positive law), the nature of transition (whether the laws of the dictatorship should be respected – here the supporters of the law referred to the Nuremberg trials), and the constitutional order of the new regime, the choice between models of "legislative supremacy" and "higher law constitutionalism." Although the bill's liberal and socialist opponents invoked the rule of law, its supporters also made references to it, claiming that restoring the rule of law means punishing capital crimes, and the general principles of the *Rechtsstaat* must not be used to leave grave violations of the law without consequences.

This was exactly the rule-of-law argument that prevented the bill from coming into effect. President Árpád Göncz refused to promulgate it and sent it instead to the Constitutional Court for legal review. The Court's Resolution 11 on Retroactive Criminal Legislation of 5 March 1992 struck the law down, because it violated legal certainty, used vague language (underdefined terms like "political reason" and "treason"), and emphasized that the transition was based on legal continuity with the communist regime.

Following this failure, Law 90/1993 on Procedures in the Matter of Certain Criminal Offenses during the 1956 October Revolution and Freedom Struggle had a narrower focus. It was based on international law and restricted the scope of potential defendants to those who committed violence (by firing into crowds of unarmed people) during the 1956 uprising. The law invoked international law (the Geneva Convention) by stating that in 1956, Hungary was at war and thus acts committed during the suppression of the uprising and the subsequent reprisals were war crimes and crimes against humanity, thus not subject to the statute of limitation. Although a modified version of this law passed constitutional scrutiny, only a handfull of trials were held on its basis and no more than three or four resulted in conviction and prison sentence. The European Court of Human Rights exonerated one defendant, János Korbely. Thus, although Hungary made early attempts at prosecuting criminal acts committed during communism, they proved unsuccessful and disappeared from the agenda.

Screening and Vetting

The secret police files and the past of citizens who acted as communist-era police informers were at the center of attention from the very beginning of Hungarian democracy. In September 1990, deputies Péter Hack and Gábor Demszky of the largest opposition party, the liberal Alliance of Free Democrats (AFD), proposed that all secret police files be opened and made public for those interested. They argued that this would fulfill two important transitional justice goals: advance knowledge about the past and inform the people about the past of politicians who competed for their votes. It would have only covered those who filled public positions, and everyone was to be given the opportunity to contest the allegations, or resign his or her position before facing potential public disgrace. As an added bonus, such a public handling of the files could also prevent their use for blackmail, settling of accounts, or other illegitimate purposes. However, the governing coalition did not support this motion, and rumor had it that they were afraid of losing their parliamentary majority, had their representatives been screened and forced to resign.

Toward the end of its term, this conservative coalition itself raised the issue of the secret service files. According to Law 23/1994 on the Background Checks of Individuals Holding Certain Important Positions (or the Lustration Act), public officials were to be screened by a three-judge committee to see whether they had carried out any activity related to domestic intelligence, were members of the World War II–era fascist Arrow Cross Party or the law-and-order militia squads (*pufajkás*) in 1956/1957, or were Communist Party or government officials who had received information from state security services. Those found to have belonged to the aforementioned categories were called on to resign, and if they refused, their names were to be published. In the political atmosphere of that time it was assumed that the screening of those who did not inform, but only received information, was directed against the postcommunist Hungarian Socialist Party (HSP), which by then scored high in the polls, and the inclusion of militia members was meant to disqualify Gyula Horn, HSP's leader and prime ministerial hopeful, who was a *pufajkás* following the 1956 uprising (the failed "bill of justice" would also have affected him). But the HSP, which won the 1994 elections with a landslide, was not significantly affected: its political heritage was well known by the citizens, so the revelations did not prove embarrassing enough for them to prompt resignation.

The Constitutional Court found some parts of the law unconstitutional, based on the right to privacy. The Court thus restricted screenings to public persons, excluding, for example, lower-ranked judges and university professors. An amended version (67/1996) passed by the socialist-liberal coalition further restricted screening to those public officials who have to take an oath before parliament or the president of the Republic, or are elected by parliament. Although the statute would have lapsed by 2000, the conservative cabinet led by Viktor Orbán and his party (Fidesz) extended it for another four years (93/2000) and, despite the Court's constitutional reservations, increased the number of people to be screened from 900 to 17,000, including judges, prosecutors, and national and local party leaders. By this time the idea of lustration became closely tied with the ongoing political battles, and support for screening divided along political affiliation: the right insisted on lustration, while the left wanted to take the issue off the agenda. Many argued that the nature of the Hungarian transition did not allow the exclusion of former elites from politics. The liberals continued insisting on the complete openness of the files, without sanctions going beyond public knowledge.

In 2002, following a narrow socialist-liberal electoral victory, Péter Medgyessy became the prime minister of the new HSP-AFD coalition. Soon afterward, the right-wing daily *Magyar Nemzet* published a document attesting that during the late 1970s he was a secret officer of Division III/2 (counterintelligence). Based on that information, the right-wing opposition demanded his resignation, and the incident caused temporary fractures within the coalition. While legally Medgyessy could assume his position and was not compelled to disclose his past, the case directed attention at the shortcomings of the screening law. While public persons had to be screened for III/3 involvement, details about other secret services, such as counterintelligence, remained classified because they continued operation, once again raising the problems of continuity between the "national interest" of the communist and postcommunist regimes. Until then there had been a general consensus that only those working for domestic intelligence could be condemned as contributing to the maintenance of the communist system, whereas other branches of secret services carried out activities vital for the defense of national interest.

The case put lustration back on the political agenda. A parliamentary commission led by AFD deputy Imre Mécs (a former death row inmate after the 1956 uprising) investigated the secret service connections of all postcommunist ministers and deputy ministers. The right-wing opposition refused to participate in the commission, which nevertheless presented its finding to the Speaker of Parliament, suggesting that since 1990, every cabinet had members who had collaborated with the communist security services, but there were no further consequences. The Constitutional Court declared the commission unconstitutional, as it violated fundamental rule of law principles such as legal certainty and predictability.

At the same time, the screening law was taken up anew. The AFD again insisted on complete openness and the accessibility of all files, while Fidesz proposed a Czech-type lustration excluding from public life everyone connected to any branch of the secret services, as well as former members of the Politburo, Central Committee, and independent party secretaries. In 2003, the government amended the 1996 law to include all secret service divisions in the screening law, and wanted to extend vetting to the churches, but this proposition was voted down in parliament. Two years later, after the court ruled that clergy members were public persons, demands for a thorough investigation of churches mounted.

Access to Secret Files

Citizens' access to the secret service files concerning them was regulated by the Constitutional Court verdict 60/1994 on the screening law, which granted such access. Act 67/1996 created the History Office for this purpose, but it provided only limited access to the files by victims: the name of the police agent who reported on them was not disclosed to victims. This practice came under widespread criticism, because most found that the informers' right to privacy enjoyed disproportional advantages over the victims' (and society's) right to information. Following the scandal of his past involvement with Direction III/2, Prime Minister Medgyessy invited experts to formulate suggestions. Led by Lâszló Sólyom, former Constitutional Court Chief Justice (and President of the Republic since 2005), the committee concluded that because before the transition Hungary was not a rule-of-law state, the secret service past must not be classified, although exceptions prompted by authentic national interest can be made. Act 3/2003 founded, as the legal successor of the History Office, the Historical Archive of the Hungarian State Security where all secret documents are brought together. There, the names of informers are made available to their victims, and researchers and private persons have access to information on public figures.

Memorialization and Rewriting of History

Since 1989, a number of monuments, memorials, and museums have been dedicated to the memory of the victims of communism. The best known is the House of Terror, opened in 2002 in Budapest (see separate entry). But memorialization has occasionally been tainted by controversy. The local press has debated at length the fact that in the cemetery dedicated to the victims of the 1956 Revolution, the so-called National Place of Memory, a number of World War II criminals are buried. The new history textbooks present new approaches to the communist period, the 1956 revolution, and the Kádár era. They unequivocally condemn communism as a dictatorship and detail the post-1956 reprisals, naming some of the best-known victims. They also mention the role of opposition movements and emphasize the damage even the more benign Kádár regime inflicted on the society.

Conclusion

Hungary experimented with all types of transitional justice: compensation, access to files, retroactive criminal justice, and vetting. However, constitutional (rule of law) principles were interpreted to significantly constrain the possibilities at the disposal of lawmakers. Furthermore, because debates about transitional justice soon became an integral issue in partisan struggle, lustration lost its initial significance as a method of coming to terms with the past, and was used as a weapon against political opponents. This is clearly demonstrated when compromising information is revealed, as public reaction is usually determined by political sympathies. That a significant segment of the population remembered the Kádár regime not as the period of repressive dictatorship but of relative calm, security, and moderate prosperity quelled public interest in bringing former communist officials or secret service agents to justice. At the same time, political analysts and intellectuals still insist on a thorough investigation of the files and blame many ills in political and social life on the lack of a complete and thorough reckoning with the past.

Csilla Kiss

Cross-reference: Access to Secret Files; Court Trials for Redress; Ex Post Facto Issues; History Office; Lustration; Prosecute and Punish; Purges.

Further Readings

Halmai, Gábor, ed. 2003. *Ügynökök és akták [Agents and files]*. Budapest: Soros Foundation.
Kiss, Csilla. 2006. The Misuses of Manipulation: The Failure of Transitional Justice in Post-Communist Hungary. *Europe-Asia Studies*, 58(6): 925–940.
Oltay, Edith. 1993. Hungary Attempts to Deal with Its Past. *RFE/RL Research Report*, 2(18): 6–10.
———. 1994. Hungary's Screening Law. *RFE/RL Research Report*, 3 (15): 13–15.
Stan, Lavinia. 2007. Goulash Justice for Goulash Communism? Explaining Transitional Justice in Hungary. *Studia politica*, 7 (2): 269–292.

Iraq

The 2003 overthrow of Saddam Hussein's government by the U.S. invasion provided Iraq the opportunity to pursue transitional justice to gain accountability and justice for the egregious human rights abuses perpetuated by the ruling Baath party. Neither the United States, as the occupying power, nor the post-Saddam Iraqi government developed an integrated strategy for transitional justice. Iraq's main transitional justice institutions, the Iraqi High Tribunal and the Higher National De-Baathification Commission (see separate entries), contributed to the sharpening of sectarian differences between Arab Sunnis and Shias, which fueled the civil war of 2004–2007. Sectarianism remains a major obstacle to social reconciliation.

Repressive Past

Iraq's human rights record has been dismal for the past thirty-five years. The Baath party regime that seized power in July 1968 arrested hundreds of its opponents, staged show trials, and executed more than fifty people, many of them publicly hanged, in its first eighteen months in power. Through arrests and executions, it all but destroyed the rival Communist Party. It expelled 40,000 Fayli (Shia) Kurds to Iran in 1971–1972. After the bloody suppression of the Kurdish revolt in 1974–1975, the Baath regime forcibly displaced hundreds of thousands of Kurds who lived along the Iranian and Turkish borders. Some were relocated to larger towns, others to the south; their villages were razed. The regime also pursued an Arabization policy in Kurdish areas in an effort to change the demographic balance; Arab settlers were brought in by the regime to replace forcibly dislocated Kurds. As opposition to the secular and socialist Baath party surfaced in the Shia-dominated south, the regime cracked down on the Shia religious establishment, expelled tens of thousands to Iran, and executed members of al-Dawa, an underground Shia Islamist party.

Abuses escalated under Saddam's brutal regime (1979–2003), which used terror to keep itself in power. An elaborate set of overlapping security services moved ruthlessly against any perceived or potential opposition. Special courts empowered with the death penalty were set up outside the civilian judicial system to try political crimes. Arbitrary arrest, arbitrary/indefinite detention, torture, disappearance, extrajudicial killings, forced deportations, and mass reprisals were common. Saddam's ill-fated invasions of Iran (1980) and Kuwait (1990) dragged Iraq into devastating wars. Following the invasion of Kuwait, the United Nations imposed comprehensive economic sanctions against Iraq that lasted until 2003. The sanctions created desperate conditions for Iraqi civilians, and hit children, the aged, and the sick particularly hard. Most of the population relied on inadequate food rations and medical and educational systems.

While nearly all Iraqis suffered under Saddam's rule, the scale, scope, and duration of the repression varied widely across Iraq's three main communities, Sunni Arabs, Shia Arabs, and Kurds. Although his was a secular regime, Saddam relied on his fellow Sunnis for support. Sunnis dominated the officer corps, the security and intelligence services, the Baath party, and the government. Dissent was still crushed, but overall the Sunnis fared the best under Saddam. In a 2004 poll, only 23 percent of Sunnis believed Iraq was better off without Saddam.

In the Shia south, Saddam's regime used a carrot-and-stick strategy throughout the 1980s. It moved harshly against intensifying opposition by Islamist parties; following several assassination attempts by al-Dawa against leading government officials, the regime executed Ayatollah Muhammad Baqir al-Sadr and made membership in al-Dawa punishable by death. Thousands were executed. Iraq expelled Shias of "Iranian origin" to Iran, although those targeted had lived in Iraq for generations; 200,000 were deported in the 1980s. As he needed the loyalty of the Shias, who comprised the bulk of the army's foot soldiers during the Iran-Iraq war (1980–1988), Saddam poured development money into Shia areas. But after Iraq's crushing 1991 defeat in Kuwait, returning soldiers ignited an uprising that quickly consumed the south. The regime suppressed the revolt, killing tens of thousands. The Iraqi High Tribunal has found nearly a dozen individuals guilty of crimes against humanity for this incident. Saddam later drained the southern marshes, where deserters and political opponents often sheltered, also destroying the unique culture of the resident Marsh Arabs. Today only 20,000–40,000 March Arabs remain, most of the rest having been displaced. Some believe this incident constitutes genocide.

The Kurdish population suffered grievously under Saddam's regime. The genocidal 1988 Anfal campaign killed 50,000 to 180,000 people, destroyed 2,000 villages and 12 larger population centers, deported hundreds of thousands, and devastated rural Kurdistan's economy and infrastructure. Chemical weapons were used against civilians in the town of Halabja in March 1988, killing 5,000. The 1987–1989 larger campaign against the Kurds destroyed 4,000 villages and depopulated large swathes of Kurdish territory near Iraq's borders. Another notorious act was the 1983 killing of 8,000 men and boys of the Barzani tribe, which led a major Kurdish party. Like the Shias, the Kurds rose up in 1991; when Saddam's army moved north, 1.5 million Kurds fled to Iran and Turkey. Confronted with a massive refugee crisis, the United States, Great Britain, and France established a "safe haven" inside northern Iraq so the Kurds could return safely; the Iraqi Kurds were outside Baghdad's control until 2003.

The collapse of the Saddam regime in 2003 profoundly altered Iraq's sociopolitical order. The ruling Sunnis found themselves out of power, while the main targets of Saddam's wrath, Shias and Kurds, took control. The American Coalition Provisional Authority turned power over to the interim Iraqi Governing Council in June 2004, and American troops continued to provide security until 2009. The United States formally handed over security duties to the Iraqis in June 2009, and all American troops were withdrawn in December 2011.

Transitional Justice

Efforts to bring Saddam to justice via a formal legal process go back to the 1990s. During the 1991 uprising, the Kurds captured eighteen tons of documents. Upon reviewing the files, Human Rights Watch determined that the Anfal campaign constituted genocide. It tried unsuccessfully to have a case brought against Iraq at the International Court of Justice. The group Indict was established in 1996 to begin developing cases against Saddam's regime for eventual international criminal persecution.

Iraq's main tools to deal with its past are lustration and court trials, with fitful efforts at other types of reconciliation. The United States has played an enormous role in Iraq's pursuit of transitional justice. Following its removal of Saddam's regime, it banned the Baath party, issued a sweeping de-Baathification decree, endorsed and supported a domestic Iraqi tribunal, and pushed the Iraqi government toward reconciliation measures with the Sunnis.

Prosecutions

Most Iraqis wanted to see former regime officials stand trial for their crimes, although summary execution or other punishment (usually torture) was also frequently mentioned as a suitable outcome. A domestic court that would apply the death penalty had wide support. The United States endorsed such a court even before the invasion had begun. This idea came in for heavy criticism from the United Nations, European Union, and human rights organizations, which all opposed the use of the death penalty and believed that Iraq's judiciary had been too compromised by Saddam's rule to undertake fair and impartial trials.

The statute for the Iraqi High Tribunal was announced in 2003, and American forces captured Saddam only a few days later. The statute established a court that was exclusively Iraqi, with international personnel only in advisory capacities. In a tacit recognition that the Iraqis lacked the capacity to put on trials to international standards, in March 2004, the United States established the Regime Crimes Liaison Office (RCLO) to administer the court's day-to-day operations; train judges, prosecutors, and other tribunal personnel; assist with the writing of statements and decisions; pay for most of the court's budget; organize documents and other evidence; conduct investigations, especially those requiring forensic support; build facilities; and provide security. The inclusion of the death penalty, the establishment of the Iraqi High Tribunal while Iraq was under occupation, and the large American role combined to keep the UN and most EU states from involvement with the court.

The High Tribunal brought its first cases in a difficult climate. As sectarian violence engulfed the country in 2005–2006, proceedings against Saddam unfolded in the Dujail case. A minor incident by Iraqi standards, Dujail involved the execution of 148 men and boys from Dujail as punishment for a failed 1982 assassination attempt against Saddam. Faced with a deteriorating security environment in 2005, the Shia-led government pushed hard for proceedings against Saddam – from charging, to the trial, to the inevitable execution – to move as quickly as possible. Several judges lenient toward Saddam were removed during the Dujail and Anfal trials. Prime Minister Nuri al-Maliki, in his determination to see Saddam executed in 2006, had the hanging go forward although it fell on a Sunni religious holiday.

The government's actions seemed calculated to help it shore up its support among Shias, and to send a message to the Sunni insurgents that the regime could never be brought back into power. But its interference in the tribunal's work backfired. The Tribunal's capacity to present its proceedings as an impartial exercise in justice was tainted, and Sunnis viewed its trials as yet another manifestation of the Shia-led government's hostility toward them. Once Saddam, the Tribunal's most important defendant, was executed, the tribunal's proceedings no longer commanded the interest of many Iraqis.

The Tribunal continued to operate into 2010 with judgments handed down in seven cases involving offenses committed by Saddam's regime. While the Tribunal has held some of the worst offenders in Saddam's regime accountable for their crimes, it falls short on other important benchmarks. Serious breaches of fair trial standards occurred, especially with regards to ensuring the rights of the defendants; politicization compromised its domestic legitimacy, while the death penalty and the perception of victors' justice harmed its international reputation; and it helped harden Iraq's sectarian divide.

Lustration

In May 2003, the Coalition Provisional Authority head Paul Bremer issued Order #1 and Order #2. Order #1 banned individuals who were in the top four levels of the Baath party from public employment. Baathists in the top three layers of management in government ministries, affiliated corporations, and other government institutions (i.e., hospitals and universities) were also dismissed. Order #2 disbanded the Iraqi army, dismissed employees at the Ministry of Defense, and automatically disqualified anyone at or above the rank of colonel or in the intelligence services from a public-sector job. Senior party members, including anyone at or above the rank of colonel, could not receive termination payments or pensions.

In 2003, the Iraqi Governing Council established the Higher National De-Baathification Commission (HNDBC). Its head, Ahmad Chalabi, was a controversial Iraqi Shia exile well known for his hard-line position that all Baathists should be removed from public life. The HNDBC wielded tremendous power and pursued de-Baathification more zealously than had the Coalition Provisional Authority. But its procedures lacked transparency and consistency, and criteria for reinstatement or exemption were unclear. To appeal, individuals had to prove they had not committed any crimes and would lose their pensions if the appeal was denied.

For many observers, these two orders were the biggest mistakes of the U.S. occupation. They unfairly assumed guilt based solely on party rank. Many Baath party members had joined for pragmatic and not ideological reasons and had not committed any crimes, yet were dismissed, while individuals who had committed offenses but were at a lower level or were not Baathists were not punished. Within months, Order #1 decapitated the state bureaucracy, throwing civil administration into disarray. Some 38,000 public-sector employees, including 12,000 teachers, were dismissed, and disbanding the army produced 400,000 unemployed men. Tens of thousands lost their pensions. The dismissals created widespread economic dislocation. Many employed people were their families' sole breadwinner, and those banned from government jobs had few options as there were almost no jobs available outside of the public sector.

De-Baathification hit the Sunnis hard because of their large representation in the bureaucracy and the military. They saw the process as a campaign to marginalize and punish their community, and complained that de-Baathification in practice meant de-Sunnification. Sunni disaffection fueled the growing insurgency.

By April 2004, the United States changed its stance, considering the implementation of de-Baathification poor, uneven, and unjust. The United States began to bring vetted senior officers, even if ex-Baathists, into the new security forces, which had a glaring shortage of officers. Interim Prime Minister Iyad Allawi, a Shia and former Baathist, supported the reincorporation of Baathists, whose human capacity the new government desperately needed. Bremer and Allawi both tried unsuccessfully to disband the HNDBC.

Convinced that reincorporating the Sunnis into governance and security structures could defuse the insurgency, the United States kept pressing Iraq to adopt a more conciliatory de-Baathification policy. But the powerful Shia Islamist parties that dominated Iraq's governments after mid-2005 took a hard line against reintegrating ex-Baathists. Some Shia-controlled ministries went beyond HNDBC dismissals, purging nearly all Sunni employees, while the HNDBC turned a blind eye to Shia Baathists. Viewing the HNDBC as a partisan instrument wielded by a vengeful Shia government, Sunni political representatives made reforming or ending de-Baathification their top priority. In 2007, the United States made the adoption of a revised de-Baathification law a benchmark of progress for the Iraqi government.

The Accountability and Justice Law of 2008 was not an improvement over the old system. Despite structural and procedural changes, the new Accountability and Justice Commission (AJC) was the HNDBC under a different name. Under the law, many of those dismissed were eligible for pensions. Some 38,000 people at the group level of the Baath, the lowest of the four levels covered by de-Baathification, could keep or return to their jobs, with some restrictions. But group members could no longer work in the interior, defense, and foreign affairs ministries. Any person previously employed by a Baathist security or intelligence agency, irrespective of party membership or personal conduct, was to be retired. Sunnis are unhappy with the law, and have pressed demands for its revision, but the Shia Islamist and Kurdish parties insist there will be no changes. In 2010, the AJC threw Iraqi politics into turmoil when it attempted to disqualify candidates both before and after the March parliamentary election.

De-Baathification was fundamentally unfair. Rather than vet individuals, it assumed complicity in wrongdoing by virtue of membership in the Baath. Criteria for exemption and reinstatement were never made explicit, making its implementation arbitrary and highly politicized. Its deeply divisive nature helped plunge Iraq into civil war. Genuine reform of the process is needed if Iraq is to successfully manage its sectarian tensions.

Reconciliation

Desperate to end the civil war, the United States pushed hard to move al-Maliki's government toward reconciliation with the Sunnis. This included reforming de-Baathification, greater incorporation of the Sunnis into governance and the security forces, and amnesty for some insurgents. As a member of al-Dawa, which had suffered enormously under the Baath, al-Maliki was reluctant to politically reincorporate ex-Baathists and resistant to efforts to negotiate with the insurgents. The other main Shia parties staked out even more hard-line positions.

In early 2007, a rift opened between al-Qaeda in Iraq and the other Sunni insurgents, leading some Sunni tribal shaykhs to begin to cooperate with U.S. forces against al-Qaeda in a movement known as the Awakening. These shaykhs formed voluntary, locally based security forces in Sunni areas. Dubbing them the Sons of Iraq, the United States paid members US$300 a month each. Within a year, the Sons of Iraq had 91,000 members, 80 percent of them Sunni. The United States also brought its troop total in Iraq from 130,000 to 160,000 by mid-2007. These developments brought violence down sharply after mid-2007, but the Awakening further complicated reconciliation efforts. Through 2008 and 2009, the United States gradually transferred responsibility for the Sons of Iraq to the Iraqi government, which eyed them warily, concerned that the (armed) Sunnis would turn against it again once U.S. forces withdrew. The Sunnis in turn distrusted and feared the government. Responsibility for vetting the Sons of Iraq and dealing with Awakening leaders rested in the Implementation and Follow-Up Committee for Reconciliation (IFCNR) formed by al-Maliki in June 2007.

According to the Amnesty Law of February 2008, individuals accused or convicted of conflict-related crimes could apply for amnesty. Those accused of serious crimes, which included murder and terrorism, were ineligible. The law was concerned with pretrial detainees who had spent long periods of time in custody without a hearing or trial. The United States and the Iraqi government each held 23,000 detainees, mainly suspected Sunni insurgents and militiamen loyal to the Shia cleric Muqtada al-Sadr.

Progress toward reconciliation remained limited into 2009. Al-Maliki promised jobs in the security forces and the public sector to Sons of Iraq members, but by mid-2009, only 5 percent had been placed and salary payments were delayed. The arrest of fifteen Awakening leaders in April 2009 heightened Sunni misgivings about the government's intentions. Despite American willingness to allow even high-ranking ex-Baathists into the political process if they renounced violence, al-Maliki firmly resisted. Fundamental differences exist between al-Maliki and the United States on reconciliation issues. Implementation of the amnesty was slow, and the small number of detainees released by late 2008 was offset by new arrests. One year after the law's passage, 6,300 detainees were released. Following a spate of bombings in March–April 2009, al-Maliki called for revisions to the amnesty law, which he blamed for releasing "major terrorists" responsible for the bombings. He also lashed out at the outlawed Baath party, calling it "full of hate." He later supported the AJC's efforts to disqualify candidates in 2010. Progress in reconciliation will depend greatly on which party dominates in the future. Al-Maliki and his allies remain committed to de-Baathification, whereas Allawi's coalition views it as harmful and destabilizing.

Reparations

Several institutions provide reparations to victims of the Baath party regimes: the Commission for the Resolution of Real Property Disputes (CRRPD), the Iraqi Prisoners and Politically Dismissed Foundation, and the Martyrs Foundation. Of these, only the CRRPD is functional. New legislation created the CRRPD in November 2005, which succeeded the earlier Iraqi Property Claims Commission (IPPC) created by the Iraqi Governing Council in 2004. Both the IPPC and the CRRPD are headed by Ahmad al-Barrak, a moderate Shia lawyer and human rights activist who served on the Iraqi Governing Council.

The CRRPD is an independent government commission that decides claims for compensation for property illegally or unfairly seized by the regime from July 17, 1968 to April 9, 2003. It decides claims for properties seized or confiscated for ethnic or sectarian reasons, or taken unfairly or unlawfully. Properties taken for the purposes of land reform and legitimate public use are excluded. The deadline for filing claims was extended indefinitely. By early 2009, the commission had received 153,000 claims, of which more than 41,000 were from the Kirkuk area, and issued 67,000 decisions. Only about 30,000 of those decisions are final and a mere 1,000 claims have been paid.

Decisions on claims are made by one of the thirty-two judicial committees spread across all of Iraq's provinces. Appeals are heard by the Cassation Commission in Baghdad, comprising seven judges who assess whether the case was decided in accordance with the law. When it overturns a decision, the case goes back to the judicial committee, which must review the case in light of the Cassation Commission's ruling. A successful claimant can accept compensation in lieu of the property. In March 2006, amendments to the law governing the CRRPD made the Ministry of Finance responsible for settling successful claims. The party returning the property may receive compensation as long as the property was not a gift of the regime. Compensation is based on the property's current value.

The CRRPD faces several challenges. Its process is slow and mired in bureaucracy. At its current pace, the Cassation Commission will need nearly three decades to finish its caseload. The commission does not accept claims for destroyed property, or for real property disputes occurring since Saddam's overthrow, despite the significant displacement that has taken place. Enforcement of its decisions is weak; if the current occupants refuse to leave, eviction is rare. A number of its staff have been killed, including the head of the Cassation Commission in 2007, and al-Barrak was the target of an assassination attempt in late 2008.

Conclusion

Transitional justice by definition requires a transition, but in the Iraqi case, the transition collapsed into a sectarian civil war. In the highly polarized and violent atmosphere of post-Saddam Iraq, the Iraqi High Tribunal and HNDBC functioned as politicized instruments whose activities seemed directed against the Sunnis by a vengeful Shia government. The Shia parties that have dominated Iraqi politics have been unwilling to countenance substantive reconciliation measures, and the reparations process covers only one category of those who suffered under the Baathist regimes. There has been no overarching strategy guiding or unifying the various transitional justice methods being employed. While these measures have allowed some of those responsible for Iraq's dreadful human rights record to be held accountable, they sadly fall far short of being impartial and fair efforts at justice.

Beth K. Dougherty

Cross-references: Amnesty; Court Trials for Redress; Higher National Debaathification Commission; Iraqi High Tribunal; Lustration; Reparations.

Further Readings

Newton, Michael and Michael Scharf. 2008. *Enemy of the State: The Trial and Execution of Saddam Hussein*. New York: St. Martin's Press.

Scharf, Michael and Gregory McNeal, eds. 2006. *Saddam on Trial: Understanding and Debating the Iraqi High Tribunal*. Durham: Carolina Academic Press.

Sissons, Miranda. 2008. *Briefing Paper: Iraq's New Justice and Accountability Law*. New York: International Center for Transitional Justice.

Stover, Eric, Hanny Megally, and Hania Mufti. 2005. Bremer's "Gordian Knot": Transitional Justice and the US Occupation of Iraq. *Human Rights Quarterly*, 27: 830–887.

Stover, Eric, Miranda Sissons, Phuong Pham, and Patrick Vinck. 2008. Justice on Hold: Accountability and Social Reconstruction in Iraq. *International Review of the Red Cross*, 90: 5–28.

Israel

Questions of transitional justice have preoccupied Israeli society and have defined its identity and ethos since the country was established in the aftermath of World War II and the Shoah (Holocaust). How to "address the legacies of past human rights abuses, mass atrocity, or other forms of severe social trauma, including genocide or civil war, in order to build a more democratic, just, or peaceful future" (*Encyclopedia of Genocide and Crimes against Humanity* 2004, vol. 3, p. 1045) has been one of the central themes of the Israeli experience. The fact that this case deals with crimes committed by other states before Israel's founding makes it an unusual but still valid example of transitional justice.

Israeli identity has been formed partly in response to the Shoah, which resulted in the extermination of some two-thirds of the European Jews. The memory of the Shoah and the plight of the survivors continue to shape the Israeli public discourse. Commemoration days, school trips to Poland, memorials, and museums keep public and private memory alive. Many Jewish Israelis are descendants of Eastern, or Sephardic, Jews who fled Arab countries before and after the establishment of Israel, but the ethnic cleansing of the Arab world of most of its Jewish minority between 1941 and the 1970s has not yet influenced the Israeli narrative as deeply as the Shoah, maybe because most of the state's founding fathers were European, or Ashkenazi, Jews and the Israeli political and social system was dominated by the Ashkenazim until the 1980s.

The Repressive Past

The terms "Shoa" (calamity) and "Holocaust" (burned sacrifice) describe the persecution and destruction of European Jews by Nazi Germany and its allies from 1933 to 1945. While they started immediately after Adolf Hitler's rise to power in Germany, the Jews' exclusion and persecution became continent-wide only after the Germans conquered and annexed most European countries. Following the German attack on Poland and the start of World War II in 1939, hundreds of thousands of Jews in Eastern Europe were placed into ghettos, where many of them starved, died from disease, or were killed. Mass killings started after Germany's invasion of the Soviet Union in June 1941. Moving behind the frontlines, paramilitary death squads (Einsatzgruppen) shot around 1.5 million Jewish men, women, and children and buried them in mass graves.

On January 20, 1942, the Nazi leaders discussed the organization of the "Final Solution to the Jewish question" at the Wannsee Conference in the Berlin suburb. At the meeting,

Reinhard Heydrich presented a plan, presumably approved by Hitler, for the deportation of the Jewish population of Europe and French North Africa (Morocco, Algeria, and Tunisia) to German-occupied areas in Eastern Europe and the use of the Jews fit to work for road-building projects. During that meeting, the Nazi leaders planned the murder of as many as 11 million Jews from Europe and North Africa.

Afterward, deportations began from Western and Central Europe to the newly established death and labor camps in Poland, where people where either gassed on arrival or worked to death. In slightly more than a year, from 1942 to 1943, roughly one-third of the European Jewry was thus murdered. The last to be killed were the Jews of Hungary. Most of them were deported to and killed at Auschwitz in the spring and summer of 1944, shortly before the liberation. With the Nazi death machine working until the last days of German collapse in May 1945, only about a third of European Jewry survived. The number of Holocaust victims is estimated between 5.85 and 6.1 million.

Transitional Justice

After World War II, the surviving Jewish communities in Europe and the Yishuv, the pre-state Jewish commonwealth in the British Mandate of Palestine, were not in a position to help create a new system of universal human rights and justice. With very few financial and human resources at their disposal, they had other urgent priorities such as rehabilitating and resettling the hundreds of thousands of Jewish survivors and refugees and reconstructing Jewish life in Europe or elsewhere. Soon they also became involved in the struggle leading up to the establishment of the state of Israel in 1948 following the UN Resolution 181 for the partition of Palestine.

During the first fifteen years after it was established, Israel was preoccupied with military and economic survival. Borders had to be stabilized, infrastructure had to be built, the economy had to be developed, and immigrants had to be absorbed. Dealing with the recent past was not a priority, as people were busy building new lives. Between 1948 and 1951, Israel's population more than doubled. Nobody in Israel wanted to listen to what the Shoah survivors had to say. Transitional justice came only much later.

From Revenge to Justice

After World War II, as the enormity of the Shoah became clear, there were individual acts of revenge perpetrated by organized groups, mostly consisting of former Eastern European Jewish partisans and of Jewish soldiers from Palestine serving with the Jewish Brigade in the British Army in Germany and Italy. Beginning in 1945, they hunted down an unknown number of Nazi war criminals, who were then either killed on the spot or tried in improvised martial courts. A better-known revenge operation was organized by the former partisan and later Israeli writer Aba Kovner, who founded the organization Nakam (revenge). On April 14, 1946, at the Langwasser internment camp near Nuremberg, Nakam poisoned bread distributed to 12,000–15,000 German prisoners of war, mostly SS members. Some 200 prisoners fell ill, but none died. Kovner was arrested and sent back to Palestine. Revenge attempts were then abandoned and denounced by mainstream Jewish leaders as impractical and immoral. In the end, Simon Wiesenthal's approach – seeking justice, not revenge – was followed. A survivor himself, after his liberation from Nazi camps he started to hunt down Nazi war criminals and to collect data and information on war crimes to be used in court and to educate the public.

The Plight of the Displaced Persons

The pursuit of revenge was seen as deflecting resources from the immediate challenges of refugee relief and the struggle to establish a Jewish state. Reconstructing Jewish life in Europe and building a Jewish state, not hunting down Nazis – that is, the triumph of life over death – was seen as the proper kind of revenge. With tens of thousands of Jewish survivors and refugees housed in Displaced Person Camps in Germany, Austria, and Italy and the future of Palestine still unsettled, the Jewish refugees and displaced persons had to be cared for. As hygienic conditions were initially very bad, many died in the weeks following their liberation in 1945. The Allies often kept former Jewish prisoners in the very camps where they had been liberated and where they lived with refugees from Eastern Europe, including former Nazi collaborators. This caused great friction.

By the summer of 1945, the U.S. President Harry Truman commissioned Earl G. Harrison, the Dean of the University of Pennsylvania Law School, to survey the Displaced Persons Camps. Harrison recommended that Jews should be recognized as a distinct nationality, housed in exclusively Jewish camps, and aided in their emigration from Germany. By the end of that year, Jewish camps were set up with the help of the United Nations Relief and Rehabilitation Administration (UNRRA), the American Jewish Joint Distribution Committee (JOINT), and other organizations. Within a year, Jewish displaced persons began to organize and take over the camps. With the help of American Jewish servicemen and the American Jewish community, an infrastructure, complete with social, religious, health, and educational services, was set up.

As repatriation proved impossible because of the violent anti-Semitism still rampant in Eastern Europe and the communist takeovers, the camps became permanent and grew in population as more and more Jewish survivors fled the East. After the 1946 pogrom in the Polish town of Kielce, in which 42 Jewish survivors were murdered, more than 150,000 Polish Jews fled to the West. By 1947, the number of Jewish displaced persons reached 250,000. While camps grew and began to resemble full-fledged Jewish towns or villages, the future of the displaced persons remained uncertain. Repatriation was not ruled out, but most countries remained closed and immigration to Palestine was severely restricted after the 1930s. Drawing attention to their plight, the displaced persons influenced international opinion in the run-up to the November 1947 UN resolution on the partition of Palestine. After the state of Israel was created and American legislation increased immigration quotas, most Jewish displaced persons left for Israel and the United States. The last camp closed in 1957.

Restitution

Restitution (Wiedergutmachung; see separate entry) brought transitional justice back onto the public agenda in the early 1950s. Without resources to cope with the challenges of state-building and risking economic breakdown, the Israeli government of David Ben Gurion decided to demand and accept German restitution. In 1951, the authorities made a claim for compensation worth US$1.5 billion from Germany, both because Israel had absorbed 500,000 Holocaust survivors and because the Nazis had robbed Jewish property worth at least US$6 billion. The German government of Konrad Andenauer agreed to consider restitution on moral grounds and because the acceptance of guilt was thought to help West Germany's readmittance into Western Europe.

In 1951, the Conference of Material Jewish Claims against Germany was established in New York, where World Jewish Congress President Nahum Goldmann convened a meeting of twenty-three major American Jewish and international Jewish organizations. The Conference was to lead the fight for restitution and compensation. The reparations issue provoked a heated public debate in Israel, where many opposed the idea of accepting money from Germany on grounds that justice could not be done and atonement was not possible. Widespread and violent demonstrations followed the negotiations, which started in 1952. In 1953, a deal was struck and approved by the German and Israeli parliaments in the face of heavy opposition. The US$845 million that Germany paid in the form of goods helped stabilize the Israeli economy and integrate the new immigrants. There were also individual payments to more than 278,000 Holocaust survivors, who received lifetime pensions under the West German Federal Indemnification Law of 1952. Hundreds of thousands of other survivors received one-time payments.

Justice: The Eichmann and Demjanuk Trials

The Adolf Eichmann trial of 1961 changed the way Israelis looked at the Shoah and brought the past back into public discourse. The abduction in Argentina by the Israeli foreign intelligence service (the Mossad) of one of the central planners of the genocide of European Jews and the subsequent trial in Jerusalem served as a national catharsis. During the fourteen-week-long public trial, more than 1,500 documents were presented, 100 prosecution witnesses (90 of whom were Nazi concentration camp survivors), and dozens of defense depositions delivered by diplomatic couriers from sixteen countries were heard or read. For the first time, a full picture of events emerged, the survivors could freely speak about their experiences, and the Israeli public listened to them. Seeing themselves as fighting Jews defending against the threat of being driven into the Mediterranean sea, young Israelis had looked down on survivors who, they believed, had not fought back against the Nazis. This perception changed as a result of the trial. Eichmann was convicted, sentenced to death, and executed in 1962.

His abduction and trial gave the impression that Israeli justice had global reach. The state of Israel was able to defend itself and the Jewish communities worldwide against present threat, as well as to seek out the perpetrators in hiding and bring them to justice. However, Eichmann's trial was for a long time the only Nazi war crime trial in Israel, and by comparison, 6,489 Nazi war criminals were sentenced in Germany from 1945 to 1993. In Israel there was only one other Nazi war crime trial, that of John Demjanuk, a Ukrainian living in the United States who was believed to be a notorious guard at the Treblinka death camp. After being extradited to Israel in 1986, Demjanuk was found guilty of crimes against humanity and condemned to death in 1988. Because of serious doubts about his identity, the Israeli Supreme Court overturned the sentence and released him in 1993. Afterward he relocated to the United States. Suspected of having committed war crimes as a guard at the Sobibor death camp, in 2009 Demjanuk was again extradited to Germany, where he was tried in Munich. He died in March 2012 before his appeal was heard.

Remembrance: Yad Vashem

Thus, in Israel, Nazi war crime trials were largely a symbolic affair, serving remembrance, which became central to Israeli identity during the 1970s. Central to this process was Yad Vashem, one of many organizations that have worked to document the Shoah since the 1940s. Receiving official status by a special law adopted by the Israeli parliament in 1953, Yad Vashem was located next to Mount Herzl on the Mount of Remembrance in Jerusalem. It includes a documentation center and a memorial site serving as an educational facility, research center, and memorial site, where religious and state ceremonies remembering and honoring the dead are held annually. It contains the Holocaust History Museum, the Children's Memorial, the Hall of Remembrance, the Museum of Holocaust Art, the Valley of the Communities, a synagogue, an archive with 130 million pages of documentation and 100,000 photos, a research institute, a library with 123,000 books, a publishing house, and an educational center serving students and teachers from Israel and abroad. Non-Jews who saved Jews at personal risk are honored by Yad Vashem as "Righteous among the Nations." More than 2,000 trees have been planted in their honor.

Yad Vashem seeks to collect all the names of the 6 millions Shoah victims and to preserve them in the Hall of Names. With 800,000 visitors in 2009, Yad Vashem is one of the most visited sites in Israel. Students and soldiers are taken there on a regular basis. Together with regular school trips to Poland for events such as the March of the Living in Auschwitz, Yad Vashem has become central to shaping Israeli identity. Since the 1990s, the centrality of Holocaust remembrance in the Israeli-Jewish discourse and Israeli politics has come under sharp criticism from post-Zionist intellectuals, journalists, and historians on grounds that an identity based only on past persecution foments a paranoid mindset that might prompt Israel to overreact in the conflict with the Palestinians and make it miss the chance for establishing peaceful relations. Nevertheless, the identification of Israelis with the victims of the Shoah has grown and shows no sign of abating. Israeli schoolchildren are regularly taken to Poland to visit the camps or to take part in the annual March of the Living in Auschwitz, an international program that brings Jewish teens from all over the world to march from Auschwitz to Birkenau in an effort to educate them about the horrors of the Holocaust. This may be attributable to perceived and real existential threats, Israel being one of the very few states in the world today being regularly threatened with annihilation and genocide.

Conclusion

While Israel was created as a Jewish state in the aftermath of one of the greatest tragedies that ever befell the Jewish people, efforts at transitional justice have been few. After its establishment, the new state was too busy consolidating its borders and building a society from scratch to deal with transitional justice related to the Shoah. The question did come up with Wiedergutmachung from Germany, but transitional justice efforts remained feeble. Only two Nazi war criminals were brought to justice in Israel, and their trials served mainly educational purposes. After the Eichmann trial, Israeli identity was partly formed as an answer to the "Shoah experience," and school trips to Holocaust memorials became an important feature in the upbringing of new generations. The concept of transitional justice will likely be brought up in any future settlement of the

Arab-Israeli conflict dealing with the displacement both of Palestinian Arabs and the expulsion of Jews from Arab countries during the 1940s–1960s.

Simon Erlanger

Cross-references: Wiedergutmachung.

Further Readings

Brenner, Michael. 1997. *After the Holocaust. Rebuilding Jewish Life in Postwar Germany.* Princeton: Princeton University Press.
Encyclopaedia of Genocide and Crimes against Humanity, vol. 3. New York: Macmillan Library Reference.
Friedländer, Saul. 1997. *Nazi Germany and the Jews: The Years of Persecution, 1933–1939.* New York: Harper Collins.
———. 2007. *The Years of Extermination. Nazi Germany and the Jews, 1939–1945.* New York: Harper Collins.
Gilbert, Martin. 2008. *Israel. A History.* London: Black Swan.
Lentin, Ronit. 2000. *Israel and the Daughters of the Shoa: Reoccupying the Territories of Silence.* Oxford: Berghahn Books.
Sachar, Howard. 2007. *A History of Israel: From the Rise of Zionism to Our Time.* 3rd edition. New York: Alfred A. Knopf.
Segev, Tom. 1998. *1949: The First Israelis.* New York: Henry Holt and Co.
———. 2000. *The Seventh Million: The Israelis and the Holocaust.* New York: Picador.
———. 2010. *Simon Wiesenthal: The Life and Legends.* New York: Doubleday.
Tobias, Jim and Peter Zinke. 2000. *Nakam. Jüdische Rache an NS-Tätern.* Berlin: Konkret.

Italy

Punitive measures were initiated against the Fascist regime and its representatives first in the southern regions of Italy occupied by the Allies in 1943 and then throughout the country after the end of World War II. These measures consisted of court trials, purges, the reaffirmation of civil and political rights, and compensation for the victims of the regime. Transitional justice was implemented mainly in 1943–1946 and from the 1990s onward. An amnesty law passed in 1946 signaled Italy's desire to settle accounts with Fascist crimes and perpetrators.

The Repressive Past

The Fascist regime lasted from October 28, 1922 (the "March on Rome" and King Victor Emmanuel III's decision to ask General Benito Mussolini to form a new government) to July 25, 1943 (Mussolini's arrest and the appointment of Marshal Pietro Badoglio as head of government). At its height in January 1941, Mussolini's Italian empire included Ethiopia, Eritrea, central Somalia, Libya, Albania, Slovenia, western Greece, southern France, and the Dalmatian coastline of Croatia. After September 8, 1943 (the day of the armistice between Italy and the Allies), the country was divided into two. In the northern part occupied by the German troops, the Italian Social Republic was established, whereas the southern regions of Italy were under Allied control. The southern and northern parts were reunited at the end of World War II, when northern Italy was liberated from Nazi control.

In the occupied regions, an active armed resistance (Resistenza) grew, which from 1944 was led by the Northern Italian National Liberation Committee (Comitato di

Liberazione Nazionale dell'Alta Italia, CLNAI). This Committee was part of the Central Committee of National Liberation (Comitato Centrale di Liberazione Nazionale, CCLN), a resistance organization. Given the alliance between Nazi Germany and the Italian Social Republic, the Resistance fought both a liberation war (against the Germans) and a civil war (against Fascist Italians).

To become the country's Fascist leader, Mussolini had to accept the monarchy, which was formed during the Risorgimento of 1861, when most of the states of the Italian Peninsula and the Kingdom of the Two Sicilies united under King Victor Emmanuel II, and to concede some freedom to Catholic associations. In 1929, he signed the Lateran Pacts with the Catholic Church, as a result of which the Catholic-controlled city of Rome joined the Italian Kingdom. Despite these concessions, historians do not dispute the totalitarian aspirations of the Fascist regime, which sought the elimination of political and trade union freedoms and the creation of a single-party and single-trade union regime; control of the press and of the right to form associations; obligatory party membership for civil servants; enrolling the youth in regime-sponsored associations; and promoting and controlling free time (after work), propaganda, the cult of the leader, aggressive nationalism, a revisionist foreign policy, and warmongering.

In 1926, the death penalty was reintroduced for political crimes against the state and the heads of state. In 1937, the Mussolini regime introduced racist legislation banning marriages and sexual relations between Italians and people of African descent. After September 1938, complex and rigid laws discriminated against Jews, progressively removing them from government employment, the professions, schools and universities, and limiting their ownership of personal property and real estate. There were 47,252 Jews living in Italy in 1938.

The police was used as a repressive institution. A police-controlled Special Tribunal for the Defense of the State tried anti-Fascist "subversives." The much-feared tribunal, known for the harsh sentences it gave for the most trivial political offenses (including telling political jokes while drunk), imposed a total of 27,735 years of imprisonment, 42 death sentences (of which 31 were carried out), and 3 life sentences. The police files of the Central Political Records Office, which included information on individuals considered dangerous by the regime, were reorganized in 1925–1926, and then their number increased with the addition of about 130,000 new files. Some 15,000 opponents of the regime were interned under Mussolini's rule.

After its creation in 1943, the Italian Social Republic accentuated the repressive aspects of the Fascist regime in order to counter armed and unarmed resistance groups that were increasingly taking an active stand against the Republic and the German occupation. The Charter of Verona (the Republic's constitutional program approved by the Republican Fascist Party congress on November 17, 1943) decreed that "those belonging to the Jewish race are foreigners. During this war they belong to a hostile nationality" (Paragraph 7). Republican institutions aided the deportation of Italian Jews to the death camps organized by the German occupiers.

Given the Italian Fascist regime's collaboration with Nazi Germany, it is impossible to establish how many individuals were victims of the Fascist regime and how many were victims of German occupation. We know that 23,826 political prisoners were deported to German concentration camps (10,000 died there), 44,000 partisans were killed, and 15,000 civilians were killed in massacres (mainly committed by the German armed forces, at times with the collaboration of the Republican Fascists). Some 650,000 Italian soldiers of the former Royal Army were interned in Germany after the armistice for refusing to fight for the Nazi Germany and the Italian Social Republic. Of them, 20,000–30,000 were executed or died of improper living conditions, with the effective acquiescence of the Italian authorities. Of 6,806 Italian Jews deported by the German Schutzsraffel (SS) with the collaboration of the Italian authorities, 5,969 were killed in death camps, and 322 died in Italy (of these, 42 committed suicide or died in escape attempts).

Transitional Justice

The mechanisms of transitional justice put in place after Mussolini was ousted from power in July 1943 included criminal proceedings, purges, the reaffirmation of civil and political rights (such as property rights), and compensation for the victims. Their adoption and application in the southern territories of Italy occupied by the Allies in September 1943 were influenced first by the Allied Military Government (AMG) and then by the Allied Control Commission (ACC), which operated until late 1945. Many measures were adopted before Italy was completely liberated, when its northern and central regions were still occupied by German troops.

Ivanoe Bonomi was the CCLN leader and the prime minister between June 1944 and June 1945. His government included representatives of all six parties that belonged to the CCLN (Christian Democracy, the Socialist Party of Proletarian Unity, and the Communist, Action, Liberal, and Labor Democracy parties). Although Bonomi headed the CCLN government, there were tensions between the government and the CLNAI regarding the severity of the punishment of Fascist crimes and purges, as the more extreme policy advocated by the CLNAI was blocked by the moderate forces within the government and the society. After the national uprising of April 25, 1945, and accompanying the court trials launched against those involved in war crimes, there was a ferocious and uncontrolled settling of accounts with the Fascists and Nazi collaborators, in the course of which 10,000–45,000 Fascists were killed, without trial, mostly by communist partisans and activists, or after summary trials held by extrajudiciary tribunals controlled by the Resistance.

The High Court of Justice

The High Court of Justice was instituted by Decree-Law 159 of 27 July 1944 on Sanctions Against Fascism, which stipulated the removal of top state employees who (1) had actively participated in the political life of the Fascist regime, (2) had clear Fascist sympathies, and (3) had received career nominations or promotions through the Fascist hierarchies. The Court was composed of a presiding judge and eight members "nominated by the Council of Ministers from among high magistrates, serving or retired, and prominent figures of unimpeachable rectitude" (Article 2). The Court was to try the Fascist party leaders and members of the Fascist government guilty of "having annulled constitutional guarantees, destroyed popular freedoms, created the Fascist regime, compromised and betrayed the fate of the country, and led it to the present catastrophe" (Article 3). It operated in conjunction with the High Commissariat for the Punishment of the Crimes of Fascism (Alto commissariato per la punizione dei delitti e degli illeciti del fascismo), established by the Royal Decree-Law 134 of 26 May 1944 on Punishment for the Crimes of Fascism. The High Commissioner could refer to the Court other individuals, not belonging to the three categories mentioned previously, to be tried for their crimes.

As Decree-Law 159 had limited application, and moderate parties opposed radical measures, the most important Fascist party leaders who had not been executed by the partisans in April 1945 were not tried by the High Court. (Top leaders like Mussolini, Roberto Farinacci, Achille Starace, Alessandro Pavolini, and Fernando Mezzasoma were all executed without trial by the partisans.) Thus, the High Court failed to condemn those who had the greatest responsibility for Fascist crimes and, with some exceptions, only tried minor figures responsible for serious crimes but lacking political stature. Second-echelon Fascist leaders paid for their crimes, sometimes with their lives, but top leaders emerged unscathed from the trials.

The only trial of Fascist Party leaders held before the High Court was that of former Finance Minister Giacomo Acerbo, Education Minister Giuseppe Bottai, State Minister and Senate Speaker Luigi Federzoni, and State Minister Edmondo Rossoni, accused of the crimes specified in Article 3 of Decree-Law 159. On May 28, 1945, Acerbo was sentenced to thirty years imprisonment; the other three received life sentences. Except for Acerbo, the accused were all tried in absentia and amnestied soon after. Between September 1944 and October 1945, the High Court held sixteen trials against ninety-nine defendants: there were four death sentences, six terms of life imprisonment, and other minor sentences. After Italy was liberated in April 1945, the Court extended its jurisdiction to the entire country. But in October 1945, it ceased hearing cases, limiting its activity to assess the behavior during the Fascist period of the Crown-appointed senators.

The Extraordinary Courts of Assizes (the People's Courts)

The Extraordinary Courts of Assizes were established by Decree-Law 142 of 22 April 1945 on the Institution of the Extraordinary Courts of Assizes for the Crimes of Collaboration with the Germans to judge "those who, after 8 September 1943, had committed crimes against allegiance to, and the military defense of, the State, envisaged by article 5 of the Decree 159 of 27 July 1944 by means of any form of intelligence, correspondence or collaboration with the German invader or by assistance afforded to the latter." These extraordinary provincial tribunals were set up in every Italian province to try Fascist Republicans who actively participated in the civil war that was fought alongside the war of liberation in the German-occupied territories. They were presided over by a magistrate, appointed by the presiding judge of the Court of Appeal, and composed of four jurors, drawn from a list of citizens indicated by the Committee of National Liberation of the provincial capital. The Decree-Law 625 of 5 October 1945 transformed the Extraordinary Courts into special sections of the ordinary Courts of Assizes.

These courts organized 20,000–30,000 trials and handed down 500–1,000 death sentences, many terms of life imprisonment, and long detention periods. The justice they administered reflected, especially during their first months of activity, the climate of hatred toward the Fascist Republicans and the desire for avenging the crimes of repressing anti-Fascist and partisan activity. Many trials of the perpetrators of torture, executions, brutality, and collaboration were conducted under public pressure, in courtrooms full of anti-Fascists and victims' relatives. As such, not all trials were fair. As time passed, a more prudent attitude emerged, sentences became more lenient or were replaced with acquittals, and many initial sentences were annulled or reduced by the Courts of Appeal and the Court of Cassation. Thus, only ninety-one death sentences were carried out. In late 1947, these courts ceased to operate, and pending trials were referred to ordinary Courts of Assizes.

Amnesty

After the People's Courts ceased their activity, the government decided to limit the possibility of punishing crimes committed during the Fascist period. The need to pacify the country, the subsiding of anti-Fascist sentiments, and the increased influence of the moderate segments of the society all led to issuing the amnesty by means of the Presidential Decree 4 of 22 June 1946, known as the Togliatti Amnesty for the name of the communist justice minister who promoted it. Other amnesties and pardons followed in the 1950s, supplementing the benefits provided by Decree 4.

Even though seen by most political parties as necessary, the amnesty was issued too soon and on an excessively large scale, undoubtedly before the task of punishing the Fascists responsible for the worst crimes had been completed. Those who, according to Article 3 of the Decree-Law 4/1946, were guilty of serious crimes because they held "high-ranking positions in the civilian, political or military power structures" or were responsible for "massacres, particularly brutal tortures, murder or pillage" or crimes committed for profit should have been excluded from amnesty. Its broad application made amnesty unpopular, as individuals responsible for grave crimes, former Fascist Party leaders, murderers, and torturers were also pardoned. As a result of the amnesty of the 1950s, all those who supported the Fascist regime, collaborated with the German occupiers, and had been sentenced for their crimes were freed.

War Crime Trials

In postwar Italy, preoccupation with the Fascist past allowed Italians to forget the crimes committed in colonial wars in Libya and Ethiopia and during the first three years of World War II, when Fascist Italy was allied with Nazi Germany. Fascist symbols (including monuments and murals of Mussolini's quotes) were removed and April 25 became a national holiday celebrating the Resistance and the war of liberation. But democratic Italy charged no former perpetrators of war crimes and made no extraditions to countries like Yugoslavia and Greece, which called for the prosecution of Italian war crimes.

Under German occupation, 15,000 Italian civilians were killed in reprisals or terrorist attacks against the population, meant to discourage or repress Resistance activity. After the war, the Allies tried Field Marshal Albert Kesselring and other German generals in Italy in British military courts, whereas successive Italian governments refused to hand over or try the Italian military personnel accused of war crimes by countries that had been under Italian occupation during World War II. Most German generals were sentenced to death, but their death sentences were immediately commuted to life imprisonment and then shortened by British authorities. As such, during the 1950s, all convicted German generals, apart from Maltzer, who died in prison, were released.

After 1947, the Italian military tribunals tried lower-ranking German officers for massacres committed in Italy, but there were few trials relative to the number of massacres. Two well-known trials were held in July 1948 in Rome and in October 1951 in Bologna. In 1948, SS Lieutenant Colonel Herbert Kappler was sentenced to life imprisonment for the massacre perpetrated in the Ardeatine Caves, in which 335 Italians (including Jews) lost their lives. In 1951, SS Major Walter Reder was sentenced to life imprisonment for a series of massacres, including the one in Monte Sole (Marzabotto), where 770 civilians fell victim. Kappler made a daring escape from the Rome military hospital on August 15, 1977, while Reder was pardoned in 1985. After NATO was created in 1949, the trials were discontinued so as not to embarrass Germany, a NATO ally of Italy.

New trials of German officers resumed in Italian military tribunals in the late 1990s, after hundreds of judicial files detailing war crimes committed by Germans against Italians were discovered. The files were illegally shelved by the General Military Prosecutor Enrico Santacroce in 1960 and hidden in Rome in Palazzo Cesi, the General Military Prosecutor's Office, because Italian politicians did not want to embarrass the Germany, a NATO ally, by asking for the extradition of German war criminals. About twenty trials have been held to date, with the defendants in absentia. The only exception was the trial of former SS officer Erich Priebke, sentenced to life imprisonment in 1998 for the Ardeatine Caves massacre. Priebke is serving his sentence in Italy under house arrest. Defendants in most other trials were also sentenced to life imprisonment, but because German law did not allow their extradition, they continued to live at liberty in Germany.

Purges

The purges of public administration and the private sector divided the Allies and the Italian government, and also the Italian political parties, which held different views regarding the rapidity, scope, and means to rid the country of Fascists. Purges were such a divisive subject that they led to the fall of both the Bonomi cabinet in December 1944 and the Ferruccio Parri cabinet a year later.

Immediately after liberating southern Italy in 1943, the Allies purged the civil administration of Fascist collaborators, but purges were stopped after the Italian government regained control of the country. In effect, the Italian government was allowed to decide who and when to purge, and it preferred reconciliation. In 1943–1945, between 10,000 and 20,000 individuals were removed from public posts because of their Fascist past, but not all these dismissals were definitive because many of them were reversed on appeal. After 1946, purges ceased and most of the people who had been removed from public administration were allowed to return to their posts. In February 1948, pending cases lodged in courts of appeal were discontinued and purged officials and civil servants were brought back to service. The purges conducted in private firms were even less incisive.

Restitution, Rehabilitation and Reparation

Three categories of victims benefited from the restitution of confiscated property, the abrogation of laws discriminating on racial or political basis and the victims' reintegration into their workplaces (rehabilitation), and material or moral compensations for political or racial persecution (reparation). They were: (1) victims of racial persecution subjected to the anti-Jewish racial legislation; (2) victims of political persecution; and (3) deportees to German concentration camps.

Article 31 of the Supplementary Conditions of the Armistice with Italy signed on September 29, 1943 by the Italian government, and the Allies stated: "All Italian laws which imply discrimination on the grounds of race, color, faith or political opinion will, if this has not already been done, be abrogated, and the persons detained for such reasons will, in accordance with the orders of the United Nations, be freed and released from any legal impediment to which they have been subjected." But Italian regulations meant to abrogate discriminatory legislation were ineffectual. Issued between 1944 and 1947, they were very specific and covered only a limited number of cases. The property restitution program was inefficient, as those who sought the return of expropriated property faced many bureaucratic obstacles – regulations were ambiguous, procedures very complex, and often victims were obliged to undertake long and humiliating appeals against the decisions of the administrative organs in order to have their right to restitution guaranteed.

Reintegration into the workplace of former racial and political victims, including deportees to the Nazi camps, was more complete in public institutions than in private firms. However, even in public institutions, the damage the readmitted employees had suffered in terms of their lost careers, because of racial discrimination, was not recognized.

Victims of political and racial persecution were granted retirement packages and the possibility for promotion and recovery of lost salary, but procedures have been complex and cumbersome. Relevant regulations adopted after 1943 were still being implemented in 2003.

Conclusion

In 1943–1945, the Allied-controlled southern Italy used court trials and purges as methods to reckon with the crimes of the Italian Fascist regime and the German occupation, while the Resistance movement engaged in extrajudicial trials in which many Fascist collaborators were sentenced to prison terms and even death. In 1946, after the Italian government retook control over the entire country, these punitive measures were replaced by the government's desire for national unity and reconciliation, even at the risk of forgetting Fascist crimes and not punishing perpetrators. The 1946 amnesty program stopped punitive justice measures in their tracks, but amnesty might have come too early. Purges failed to remove Fascists from the judiciary and the police, and reparation, rehabilitation, and restitution programs have had only a symbolic value.

Paolo Pezzino

Cross-references: Amnesty; Court Trials for Redress; Germany – the Nazi Past; Property Restitution; Purges; Reparations; Victim's Rights and Redress.

Further Readings

Baldissara, Luca and Paolo Pezzino, eds. 2004. *Crimini e memorie di guerra* [Crimes and Memories of War]. Naples: L'ancora del Mediterraneo.

D'Amico, Giovanna. 2006. *Quando l'eccezione diventa norma. La reintegrazione degli ebrei nell'Italia postfascista* [When the Exception Becomes the Rule. The Reintegration of the Jews in Post-Fascist Italy]. Turin: Bollati Boringhieri.

Franzinelli, Mimmo. 2006. *L'amnistia Togliatti. 22 giugno 1946: colpo di spugna sui crimini fascisti* [The Togliatti Amnesty. 22 June 1946: Throwing in the Sponge over Fascist Crimes]. Milan: Mondadori.

Pavan, Ilaria. 2004. *Tra indifferenza e oblio. Le conseguenze economiche delle leggi razziali in Italia* [Between Indifference and Oblivion. The Economic Consequences of the Racial Laws in Italy]. Florence: Le Monnier.

Woller, Hans. 1997. *I conti con il fascismo. L'epurazione in Italia 1943–1948* [Settling Accounts with Fascism. The Purges in Italy 1943–1948]. Bologna: Il Mulino.

Japan

For Japan, coming to terms with the war crimes and atrocities committed by its military in the Asia-Pacific region during World War II remains a highly sensitive historical and political issue. Several attempts to address and redress these crimes were made right after the war, but they were mostly done at the state level. Reconciliation and justice for individual victims, especially in other Asian countries, were highlighted in the 1980s, and since the 1990s there have been belated attempts to officially apologize, compensate, and memorialize. "History problems" with its neighboring countries are still an issue for Japan and have hindered the country diplomatically.

The Repressive Past

In World War II, Japan fought in the Asia-Pacific region as an Axis Power against the Allies. Some of the Japanese military's actions constituted war crimes. For example, Japan's treatment of prisoners of war (POWs) was regarded as abusive, inhumane, and against the Geneva Convention, which Japan signed in 1929 without ratifying. As the war developed and Japanese supply routes were shattered by Allied attacks, Japanese units and their POWs faced shortages of food, water, and medicine, leading to serious hunger, disease, and sometimes death. Japanese soldiers, themselves treated inhumanely, mistreated their POWs also because they had been told that for a solider to become a POW, rather than to commit suicide, was disgraceful. An often cited example is the Bataan Death March. In April 1942, American and Filipino POWs captured by the Japanese army in the Philippines were forced to march and bear an uncomfortable train ride to a detention center 100 kilometers away, during which 30,000 POWs died of malnutrition, disease, and maltreatment. Many Australian and British POWs were killed in a similar march in North Borneo. Some 62,000 POWs (and 200,000 civilians from other Asian countries) endured severe work conditions, abuses, and food deprivation during the construction of the Burma-Thailand Railway. About 12,400 POWs died as a result. Another notorious case involved the lethal chemical and biological weapons experiments conducted by Unit 731 in China on more than 3,000 POWs.

Serious war crimes were also committed against civilians in other Asian countries, including China. When Japanese soldiers entered Nanjing in 1937, they attacked the population brutally, killing local inhabitants and looting, raping, and committing arson. The Chinese government estimated the death toll at 300,000, while the International Military Tribunal for the Far East prosecutor believed it reached 200,000. Japanese right-wing critics have, however, downplayed and even denied the massacre. Recent research conducted by Japanese researchers suggests that the death toll ranged from 20,000 to 200,000. Such widely different estimates reflect ideological bias and different uses of the term "atrocity," targeted time periods, and methodologies used to estimate population demographics. Civilians in other Asian countries under Japanese occupation also faced severe abuses, looting, and raping. In Singapore and Malaysia, many of those opposed to Japan's occupation were killed or subjected to forced labor and maltreatment. Koreans and Taiwanese, who were under Japanese colonial rule at the time of the war, also suffered torture, forced labor, and sexual slavery. The Japanese living in Japan too suffered as the wartime regime suppressed antiwar activists, controlled dissemination of information, recklessly continued the war beyond the country's resource capabilities, and forced the nation to endure serious poverty and hunger.

Overall, at least 3.1 million Japanese (including 800,000 civilians) died during World War II. The war in the Asia-Pacific region also resulted in the deaths of 92,000–100,000 Americans, 22,694 Russians, 29,968 British, 27,600 Dutch, 10–35 million Chinese, 200,000 Koreans, 1.1 million Filipinos, 30,000 Taiwanese, 100,000 citizens from Malaysia and Singapore, and a large number of Australians and Pacific islands inhabitants. In total, more than 19 million people in Asia were killed as a result of the war and of the Japanese occupation.

Transitional Justice

The crimes of World War II were addressed with the help of court trials, purges, reparations, official apologies, compensation packages, and memorialization. Immediately after the war, court trials were pursued vigorously by the United States and its Allies. Reparations through postwar peace and bilateral treaties at the state level were settled and the Cold War set in. Afterward, Japan geared up for postwar recovery and economic development, while placing suffering from the atomic bombs dropped on Hiroshima and Nagasaki at the center of its national war experience. The memory of war and war guilt gradually faded, and until the 1980s, there was no attempt to further address war crimes.

Court Trials

After Japan's defeat in 1945, the Allies' immediate response to Japanese atrocities was the criminal punishment of Japanese wartime leaders. Based on the Proclamation Defining Terms for Japanese Surrender (the Potsdam Declaration) of July 1945, the International Military Tribunal for the Far East (the IMTFE or the Tokyo Trial; see separate entry) was established in January 1946. The tribunal prosecuted twenty-eight political and military wartime leaders for crimes against peace, war crimes, and crimes against humanity; two defendants died during the hearings, and one case was dismissed because of mental illness. All other defendants were convicted in November 1948. Seven of them were sentenced to death. The trial disclosed to the Japanese people and the world many untold facts about Japanese wartime policy and the war crimes and atrocities perpetrated by the Japanese military, and highlighted the individual responsibility of wartime leaders. The IMTFE was more focused on substantiating crimes against peace (aggressive war) than crimes against humanity. It was conducted in the context of Allied postwar occupation and the Cold War, and efforts focused more on demilitarizing and democratizing Japan than pursuing justice for individual victims. Accordingly, the tribunal kept silent about the responsibility of Emperor Hirohito, the human experiments conducted by Unit 731, and the alleged Japanese use of chemical and biological warfare in China, and downplayed the atrocities perpetrated against Asian civilians under Japanese occupation. These issues, which have remained serious diplomatic and transitional justice problems, were only raised later.

While the Tokyo Trial focused on wartime leaders' responsibility for crimes against peace, those responsible for ordering or committing war crimes like the killing of innocent civilians and the maltreatment of POWs were judged under minor war crimes trials (so-called Class B/C War Crimes Trials) established by Australia, China, France, the Netherlands, the Philippines, Soviet Union, United Kingdom, and the United States in their territories previously occupied by Japan. Each country operated trials in its jurisdiction and under its own special national military courts. Of the 55,000 individuals taken into custody, 5,700 were tried, 984 were sentenced to death, 475 to life imprisonment, and 2,944 to limited prison terms. Among those indicted were 173 Taiwanese and 148 Koreans who, as Japanese colonial subjects, were forced to work for the Japanese Imperial Army; of these, more than 40 were executed. These figures exclude trials conducted by the Soviet Union, details of which are still unknown. Among those judged in these trials were individuals, including commanders, responsible for the Bataan Death March and the Burma-Thailand Railway construction. The procedures and verdicts of the minor trials were affected by serious problems like the absence of interpreters, wrongful arrests, and legal procedural deficits. In 1951, Japan signed the San Francisco Peace Treaty with the former Allied Powers and accepted the judgments of the IMTFE and Class B/C war crimes trials (Article 11).

Purges

Also based on the Potsdam Declaration, an extensive purge was conducted against individuals associated with militarism or ultranationalism, including war criminals. In the first two and a half years, more than 200,000 individuals were purged from socially and politically influential public positions. But purging and vetting were incomplete, and after the occupation of Japan by the Allied forces ended, the Japanese society welcomed back former Class A war criminals and suspects. In 1951, Mamoru Shigemitsu, sentenced to seven years in prison, was paroled only to become the minister of foreign affairs three years later. Nobusuke Kishi, arrested as a Class-A war crimes suspect, was released from jail in 1948 and then purged, but he became the prime minister in 1957. Purges and court trials were an important element of the Allied (especially U.S.) occupation policy to demilitarize and democratize Japan. With the development of the Cold War, the United States renounced punishing wartime leaders and elites and instead collaborated with them as important allies against communism. This policy shift was reflected in the lenient settlements set out in the 1951 San Francisco Peace Treaty.

Reparations

Article 14 of the San Francisco Peace Treaty stated that "except as otherwise provided in the present Treaty, the Allied Powers waive all reparations claims of the Allied Powers, other claims of the Allied Powers and their nationals arising out of any actions taken by Japan and its nationals in the course of the prosecution of the war, and claims of the Allied Powers for direct military costs of occupation." Japan relinquished all of its assets oversees. Based on Article 16, the country has paid, through the International Committee of the Red Cross, 4.5 million pounds sterling (that is, some US$7 million) to compensate POWs. As the treaty did not prohibit individual states that formerly were under Japanese occupation from claiming reparations for damage and suffering, Japan negotiated individually with Burma, the Philippines, Indonesia, and Vietnam. China did not sign the peace treaty in 1951, but communist authorities waived claims when they reestablished diplomatic relations with Japan in 1972. Korea was not invited to the

San Francisco conference in 1951, but in 1965, South Korea reestablished diplomatic relations with Japan and settled claims and reparation issues under a bilateral treaty. Based on these treaties, the Japanese government has argued that all reparation matters have been legally settled.

Official Apologies and Compensation

In the late 1980s, acknowledging and addressing Japan's past war crimes and war responsibility became issues of public interest. After Emperor Hirohito died in 1989, the mass media and the public debated his responsibility for the war and critically looked back on the Showa period (1926–1989), while Asian victims of Japan's war crimes and abuses asked for reparations. The democratization and economic development of other Asian countries increased interest in human rights, and the end of the Cold War allowed individual victims to present their sufferings publicly and seek redress.

In 1991, former Korean "comfort women," who were forced to work at Japanese military brothels during World War II, brought their claims before Japanese courts, asking the Japanese government for an official apology and compensation. Facing these legal actions, the Japanese government launched an official inquiry. In August 1993, Chief Cabinet Secretary Yōhei Kōno admitted that "the then Japanese military was, directly or indirectly, involved in the establishment and management of the comfort stations and the transfer of comfort women," who often "were recruited against their own will" and "at times, administrative/military personnel directly took part in the recruitments." Kōno expressed apology and remorse to all wartime comfort women for their pain and suffering.

At the same time, the Japanese government argued that all compensation issues had been legally and collectively settled with the countries concerned and was reluctant to respond to individual claims. Still, admitting moral responsibility for their sufferings, in 1995, the government supported the creation of the Asian Women's Fund, which disbursed donations from Japanese citizens worth 565.5 million yen (some US$6 million). The Fund provided former comfort women "atonement money" (about 2 million yen, or US$22,000, per person), medical and welfare support, and an apology letter from the Japanese prime minister. The project compensated 285 victims from the Philippines, Korea, and Taiwan. Seventy-nine Dutch individuals who were interned in Indonesia and worked as comfort women received medical welfare support worth 3 million yen (some US$32,000) each. In total, the Japanese government provided medical welfare support worth 750 million yen (US$8 million).

Dissolved in March 2007, the Fund was criticized from various quarters. Some victims, especially from South Korea, refused compensation not officially granted by the Japanese government. The Kōno statement was criticized by right-wing groups and politicians, including Prime Minister Shinzō Abe, for accepting without firm evidence the Japanese government's involvement in "forcing" comfort women to work "against their will." To compel the Japanese government to assume its legal responsibility to compensate and to end the culture of impunity for wartime sexual violence, in December 2000, the Women's International War Crimes Tribunal on Japan's Military Sexual Slavery was held in Tokyo. The tribunal was initiated by a Japanese nongovernmental organization and supported by international organizations. This people's tribunal handed down its final judgment in The Hague, the Netherlands, in December 2001. The judgment acknowledged the appalling sexual violence conducted against women under the "sexual slavery system" as a crime against humanity and found Emperor Hirohito and military and political leaders guilty of crimes against humanity.

Legal actions taken by former comfort women stimulated other victims to follow suit. Recently, Chinese and Korean victims of forced labor and Chinese victims of biological experiments asked for compensation, but most of the fifty cases presented to Japanese courts were rejected on grounds that claims were settled collectively, at the state level, by bilateral peace treaties.

Memory, Reconciliation, and History Textbook Controversies

In June 1982, the Japanese media reported that the Ministry of Education, during the textbook authorization process, which checks and examines the appropriateness of nominated books as to be used at school, required that some textbooks downplay the aggressive aspect of the Asia-Pacific War. The report, later proven inaccurate, caused anger and protest from the Chinese and South Korean governments, which interpreted it as a sign that the Japanese government denied past wrongdoings. In 1985, Prime Minister Yasuhiro Nakasone visited the Yasukuni shrine, which is said to hold the souls of the 2.5 million Japanese, most of them soldiers, who died in war since the 1868 Meiji Restoration. The shrine is controversial because it is also said to hold the souls of twelve of the defendants convicted at the Tokyo Trial and two defendants who died during the Trial. Nakasone's visit was strongly criticized by neighboring Asian countries. Around that time several cabinet ministers publicly denied the aggressive nature of Japan's war and the Nanjing massacre. They were later forced to resign. These events raised doubts about the Japanese government's commitment to coming to terms with the past. At the same time, since the 1980s, academic research and media reports on Japan's war crimes and atrocities have multiplied and the Japanese have taken an interest in addressing atrocities conducted in their name.

In the face of growing public interest and emerging support for victims' plight, in the 1990s, the Japanese government started to face the past, examine its responsibility, and seek ways to redress wrongdoings. Political changes facilitated this process. In 1993, for the first time since 1955, a coalition government that excluded the conservative Liberal Democratic Party (LDP) was formed. In August 1993, Prime Minister Morihiro Hosokawa publicly stated that Japan's aggression and colonial rule caused unbearable suffering and sorrow to people in many countries. Two years later, in August 1995, Prime Minister Tomiichi Murayama of the Social Democratic Party, which has actively pursued transitional justice, admitted that during World War II, Japan, "through its colonial rule and aggression, caused tremendous damage and suffering to the people of many, particularly Asian, countries," and he apologized to victims. This statement has been reaffirmed as the government's view by all of Murayama's successors, including those representing the LDP.

This statement, and the fact that since the mid-1990s Japanese history textbooks have mentioned comfort women, angered right-wing politicians and nationalists. The view that Japan's war was self-defensive in nature and it aimed to free Asian countries from Western imperialism, and the downplaying or denial of the Nanjing massacre, fueled the neonationalist or revisionist movement in the late 1990s. The movement was led by the Japanese Society for History Textbook Reform (Atarashii Rekishi Kyōkasho wo

Tsukuru Kai), established in 1997. Including public figures, academics, and an influential cartoonist, the society argued that Japanese history textbooks and history curricula, which stress the aggressive nature of Japan's war and war crimes committed by Japanese forces, were not "balanced" but masochistic, and that this unbalanced view fueled the "apologetic" position adopted by the Japanese government and people. Other countries saw the movement as a sign that Japan was ignoring its past, but opinion polls showed that was not the case. A poll conducted in 1993 by the *Yomiuri Shimbun* newspaper showed that Prime Minister Hosokawa's statement was supported by 53.1 percent of respondents, while 24.8 percent disagreed. One year later, another poll conducted by the *Asahi Shimbun* newspaper showed that 72 percent of respondents believed that compensation to victims of Japanese occupation and colonialism was insufficient.

As a result of the debate on history textbooks, Japan's relationship with China and South Korea worsened, especially in 2001–2006, when the LDP Prime Minister Junichirō Koizumi paid annual visits to the controversial Yasukuni shrine. In 2001, the Japanese Society for History Textbook Reform drafted a textbook for junior high school pupils, which was approved by the Ministry of Education, Culture, Sports, Science and Technology. Although only 0.4 percent of schools adopted it initially (this percentage rose to 1.7 percent in 2009, when the Society published the third edition), the textbook was presented in neighboring countries as the majority/official view in Japan, creating a huge row in China and South Korea.

The controversy over history textbooks harmed Japan's diplomatic relations with its neighbors and stirred up nationalistic sentiments on both sides. Whereas China and South Korea argued that Japan did not recognize its past wrongdoings and responsibility and the Japanese society was leaning toward the right, Japan believed that its neighbors played the "history card" for political and economic reasons. As such, Japanese started to express frustration relating to how long and how much the country was asked to apologize and compensate for its World War II behavior. This national sentiment fueled sympathy for the revisionist movement.

Joint History Research Projects

Against a backdrop of the increasingly heated debates over history, in 2001 the Japan-Republic of Korea Joint History Research project was launched to recognize the importance of promoting mutual understanding of accurate facts and recognition of history. The project, covering ancient to contemporary history, issued its first report in 2005. Its second report, released in March 2010, examined history textbooks in both countries. The reports noted that the two countries disagreed on some aspects of their understanding of modern and contemporary history and expressed dissatisfaction with the way in which the other side teaches modern history topics like comfort women, the Japan-Korea Annexation Treaty of 1910, and Japan's official apology.

As Sino-Japanese relations worsened in 2006, the Japanese government proposed the creation of the Japan-China Joint History Research Committee, consisting of intellectuals and academics from both countries, aimed at fostering objective historical analyses and promoting mutual understanding. The Committee completed its final report in January 2010, but the section on modern history was not made public at China's request. Both committees emphasized the important steps they took toward promoting mutual understanding, but noted that a sizeable gap exists in the three countries' understanding of and attitudes vis-à-vis recent history.

Conclusion

After World War II, when Japan was under American occupation, court trials, reparations, and purges were pursued. Serious attempts to redress the suffering of individual victims in other Asian countries occurred much later, in the 1990s, when Asian victims started to demand official apologies and compensation. Recently highlighted issues regarding the understanding of historical events and their country's war responsibility proved salient to the Japanese, who realized that reconciliation with neighboring countries might become increasingly difficult in the future. The Japanese still struggle with the memory and memorialization of the war, but after 2005, journalists and scholars have started to reexamine the past in much more nuanced manner, overcoming past taboos and ideological debates.

Madoka Futamura

Cross-references: Apology; China; Compensation packages; Court Trials for Redress; Democratization and Transitional Justice; International Military Tribunal for the Far East; Prosecute and Punish; Public Identification of Perpetrators; Purges; Reconciliation (Complexities of); Reparations; South Korea.

Further Readings

Asian Women's Fund. Digital Museum: *The Comfort Women Issue and the Asian Women's Fund.* Available at: http://www.awf.or.jp/index.html (accessed April 17, 2010).
Funabashi, Yoichi, ed. 2003. *Reconciliation in the Asia-Pacific.* Washington, DC: United States Institute of Peace Press.
Futamura, Madoka. 2008. *War Crimes Tribunals and Transitional Justice: The Tokyo Trial and the Nuremberg Legacy.* London: Routledge.
Ministry of Foreign Affairs of Japan. Historical Issues Q&A. Available at: http://www.mofa.go.jp/policy/q_a/faq16.html (accessed April 17, 2010).
Onuma, Yasuaki. 2002. Japanese War Guilt and Postwar Responsibilities of Japan. *Berkeley Journal of International Law,* 20(3): 600–620.
Statement by the Chief Cabinet Secretary Yohei Kono on the result of the study on the issue of 'comfort women. August 4, 1993. Available at: http://www.mofa.go.jp/policy/women/fund/state9308.html (accessed April 17, 2010).
Statement by Prime Minister Tomiichi Murayama, on the occasion of the 50th anniversary of the war's end. August 15, 1995. Available at: http://www.mofa.go.jp/announce/press/pm/murayama/9508.html (accessed April 17, 2010).
Tanaka, Yuki. 1996. *Hidden Horrors: Japanese War Crimes in World War II.* Boulder: Westview.

Kenya

After several false starts, the Kenyan government began in 2008 to put in place transitional justice mechanisms. Most observers, however, are cautious about the extent to which these measures will prove effective. As the government includes many senior politicians who are widely believed to be complicit in past abuses, it might still lack the political will to act against its own members. If this is the case, democratic rule will have failed to end the impunity that characterized decades of authoritarian rule. The International Criminal Court (ICC; see separate entry), however, could well prosecute a number of senior officials in its stead.

The Repressive Past

Four distinct periods of Kenyan history could be subjected to transitional justice mechanisms. The first is the British colonial period, in particular for the wide-scale abuses committed during the Mau Mau rebellion, a low-intensity insurgency between 1952 and 1957 that sought to end British rule. In response, the British declared a state of emergency and instituted a number of harsh measures, including the detention of leaders of the nonviolent Kenyan independence movement, the internment of at least 80,000 Kenyans in concentration camps, and a forced resettlement program that affected up to one million Kenyans, mainly those belonging to the Kikuyu ethnic group. Both sides committed atrocities. The number of Kenyan deaths exceeded 10,000 and might have been several times that number, while fewer than 100 Europeans were killed, including both security forces and civilians. Credible allegations have been made that British officials made widespread use of torture and committed other grave violations of human rights, including summary executions.

The second period covers the rule of Prime Minister and then-President Jomo Kenyatta, from independence in 1963 until his death in 1978. Even though Kenya was nominally a multiparty democracy during this period, the Kenya African National Union (KANU) monopolized political power. Under Kenyatta, the ruling party used repressive means to retain its dominance, including unlawful detention, the use of torture, and a few instances of alleged political assassination.

Third, under the presidency of Daniel arap Moi, in power from Kenyatta's death until his own retirement in 2002, the government became significantly more repressive, especially after a failed coup attempt in 1982. The government outlawed opposition parties, instituted a one-party state, and arrested dissenters, many of whom it detained without trial and tortured. In the early 1990s, pro-democracy activists faced violent repression. Nonetheless, the movement snowballed and, with additional pressure from Western aid donors, caused the government to liberalize the political system and grant greater civil and political rights. The 1992 and 1997 multiparty elections returned Moi to power, a result made possible by fraud, intimidation, gerrymandering, and other nondemocratic practices, facilitated by a divided opposition.

During the struggle for political pluralism and alongside the 1992 and 1997 elections, senior KANU and government officials organized and financed attacks on people belonging to ethnic groups that generally supported the opposition but lived in KANU-dominated zones. Exploiting and stoking preexisting popular resentment against "nonindigenous" groups, especially around land issues, these state and party leaders trained and paid private militias and armed groups to attack members of minority ethnicities, as well as destroy their housing, livestock, and other possessions. Over the course of the decade, some 1,500 people were killed and hundreds of thousands displaced in so-called ethnic clashes, at the time the gravest and most systematic abuses of human rights in Kenya since independence.

The fourth period to which transitional justice could be applied is the presidency of Mwai Kibaki, first elected in 2002, marking the end of KANU rule. In particular, accountability could be pursued for the political violence linked to the highly contested 2007 presidential election results. As in the 1990s, but in a span of only two months, more than 1,100 people died and at least 350,000 were forced to leave their homes, businesses, and land because of their ethnicity and presumed political affiliation. Unlike in previous years, the violence was not only organized and perpetrated by state agents and ruling party officials, but also by opposition supporters in response to what they considered to be a stolen election. Senior politicians and businessmen from both sides are widely believed to have planned and coordinated the deadly attacks.

Transitional Justice

A systematic and neutral investigation of, and follow-up to, past abuses was unimaginable while Moi and KANU remained in power. A few commissions of inquiry found specific senior officials responsible for large-scale political violence, ethnic cleansing, and other grave crimes, but the government never prosecuted, let alone convicted, a single person of involvement. Mwai Kibaki and his National Rainbow Coalition (NARC), elected in 2002, had promised to investigate prominent cases of corruption and presumed political assassination, including the murder of Foreign Minister Robert Ouko in 1990, after he threatened to reveal information on high-level corruption, and the murder of American priest John Kaiser, who had provided important testimony against government figures. As under Moi, however, neither of these inquiries resulted in any prosecutions. Similarly, during his first term, Kibaki's government failed to prosecute senior officials, including Cabinet ministers, responsible for massive corruption schemes under both Moi's and Kibaki's presidencies. Kibaki appointed a Task Force on the Establishment of a Truth, Justice, and Reconciliation Commission. The government ignored the task force's recommendations on the establishment of such a commission, published in 2003, but the report arguably did sow the seeds of future action.

The main reason that Kibaki did not seriously complete any transitional justice measures was that, during his first term (2003–2007), he presided over a broad-based coalition that had formed just before the 2002 elections. Because opposition unity was a key strategy to defeat KANU, NARC took into its fold a number of prominent defectors from KANU, including many of those responsible for the worst abuses of the past. Once in power, the NARC alliance partially unraveled, and Kibaki depended on the support of KANU members of parliament, which further impeded accountability for crimes committed under KANU rule, which many civil society organizations and some politicians had been advocating.

Transitional justice gained a new impetus from the crisis that followed the December 2007 elections. Two separate processes emerged, one broad and the other narrow. Both resulted from the internationally brokered National Accord between Kibaki and his main challenger, Raila Odinga, which led to a grand coalition government and ended postelectoral violence. First, in an agreement signed in March 2008, both sides committed themselves to the creation of a Truth, Justice and Reconciliation Commission (TJRC; see separate entry), mandated to inquire into human rights violations from independence in December 1963 up until the signature of the National Accord at the end of February 2008. (Because of ethno-regional groups' general identification with the presidencies of either Kenyatta or Moi, it would be extremely divisive politically for investigations not to cover both periods.) Parliament passed the legislation establishing the commission in December 2008, with the goals of establishing a record of violations, identifying and recommending the prosecution of the perpetrators and reparations for victims, and fostering reconciliation.

The process of appointing commissioners and defining the commission's mandate advanced only slowly. The government did not consult widely before drafting the legislation. A number of Kenyan civil society groups and international human rights organizations, such as Amnesty International, have criticized the legislation for not granting the commission sufficient independence. The government retains the decision-making power over whether to prosecute or grant amnesty, even for crimes for which amnesties are prohibited under international law. Many also objected to insufficient provisions for witness protection and reparations for victims. Moreover, there is no indication how any reparations will be financed, as the commission is underfunded, suggesting a lack of government commitment to the process.

The July 2009 appointment of Bethuel Kiplagat as TJRC chair proved highly controversial. Even though he was broadly respected for his conflict mediation role in several countries in the Horn of Africa, numerous civil society organizations considered Kiplagat too closely associated with some of the abuses of the Moi regime to be credible as the head of the commission. Debates over the TJRC leadership overshadowed the commission's actual activities, as some groups walked out of or boycotted its inaugural public meetings, which began in early 2010.

Concurrently, a separate March 2008 agreement mandated the creation of a Commission of Inquiry into Post-Election Violence (see separate entry). The Waki Commission (named after its chair, Justice Philip Waki) issued its report in October 2008, which addressed the question of accountability for serious abuses. The government subsequently endorsed its recommendations, including the establishment of a Special Tribunal to try those responsible for the worst human rights violations during the post-electoral crisis. The prosecutor and two of the tribunal's three judges would be foreigners, in order to provide the credibility and independence that Kenyan courts currently lack. Any official charged with an offense would be suspended from duty and anyone convicted would be ineligible for public office. Other recommendations addressed a major reform of the police force, which was responsible for roughly one-third of the deaths in the post-election violence, often through shooting unarmed demonstrators in the back.

To try to force the coalition government to act, despite the fact that several cabinet ministers and members of parliament would probably be among the accused, Justice Waki presented former UN Secretary-General Kofi Annan, who had led the mediation team, with a list of a dozen senior officials allegedly responsible, widely believed to include Cabinet ministers, members of parliament, and prominent businessmen, as well as the police commissioner. If the Kenyan government did not set up the Special Tribunal by March 2009, later extended to May and then August 2009, Annan would turn the list over to the International Criminal Court (see separate entry), which could then begin proceedings. Faced with this threat and under strong pressure from Western aid donors, the Kenyan government announced it would comply. In July 2009, frustrated by government foot-dragging, Annan handed over the Waki envelope – and boxes of accompanying evidence – to the ICC prosecutor.

The government's first attempt to introduce enabling legislation failed to achieve the required two-thirds majority in parliament. Many members of parliament expressed a preference for a hybrid court in which the United Nations would play a more active role, citing the Special Court for Sierra Leone as a model (see entries on Hybrid Courts; Special Court for Sierra Leone). Others expressed a preference for trying cases using existing national institutions, while some considered any Kenyan process to be overly prone to political interference, preferring that the cases be tried only by the ICC. Kenyan civil society organizations were also divided in their preferred scenario. Some politicians who may have played a role in the post-electoral violence supported the Kenyan courts option because they believed it would be more easily subverted, or favored inaction, which risked ICC involvement, because they did not expect the latter to be effective.

The government's second attempt to introduce legislation to create a hybrid tribunal was never even tabled at parliament. The cabinet was unable to agree on the modalities and instead committed the government to reforming the national judiciary and the police – a Herculean task – after which it would begin prosecutions. This declaration of intent was insufficiently plausible to convince Kenyans – and presumably the ICC – that the government was serious about accountability. This was confirmed when backbench Member of Parliament Gitobu Imanyara introduced a private member's bill to establish the tribunal: although the government officially supported it, the bill's third version was effectively stillborn because, whenever it was due to be debated, a boycott by legislators prevented the assembly from achieving quorum.

Together, these nascent transitional justice mechanisms would investigate the three post-independence periods outlined earlier. The Special Tribunal and the TJRC would both have jurisdiction over the 2007–2008 post-electoral violence. The tribunal would pursue an estimated 100–200 of those who bear the greatest responsibility, whereas the commission would cover a broader range of abuses since independence. With the Special Tribunal highly unlikely to be established, it is left to the ICC to fill the accountability gap. This can only be partial, as it would prosecute only a handful of "big fish" (the most prominent cases), and remains conditional on the ICC prosecutor convincing the Pre-Trial Chamber to authorize an official investigation. This step would be bypassed if the Kenyan government officially referred the matter to the ICC, which it has steadfastly refused to do, despite pledging its utmost cooperation with any eventual ICC investigations and prosecutions.

Only the colonial era will not be addressed by any official mechanism. However, in May 2009, three Kenyan men and two women, backed by the Kenya Human Rights Commission (a nongovernmental organization) and the Mau Mau War Veterans Association, announced their intention to sue the British government through the British judicial system in order to obtain compensation for unlawful imprisonment, assault, and torture during the Mau Mau uprising. If successful, thousands of other cases could follow. The British government maintains that upon reaching independence, the Kenyan state inherited responsibility for any abuses committed under colonial rule.

Conclusion

Despite the end of authoritarian single-party rule in 1991 and the opposition's eventual victory in 2002, amid promises to investigate past abuses and end impunity, transitional justice in Kenya has advanced only in fits and starts. For more than fifteen years, none of the efforts undertaken ever achieved any accountability. It took an acute crisis, in which more than 1,100 people died and hundreds of thousands were displaced, and prolonged negotiations under international mediation to put the issue of accountability for grave violations of human rights back on the national agenda in early 2008. The Truth, Justice and Reconciliation Commission was launched in 2009, but it lacks prosecutorial powers, while the Special Tribunal is unlikely ever to be created. Without any serious national attempts to prosecute perpetrators, only the ICC could partially fill the judicial void and achieve accountability for past abuses, albeit in only a very small number of cases.

Stephen Brown

Cross-references: Commission of Inquiry into Post-Election Violence; Hybrid Courts; International Criminal Court; Special Court for Sierra Leone; Truth, Justice and Reconciliation Commission.

Further Readings

Brown, Stephen. 2003. Quiet Diplomacy and Recurring "Ethnic Clashes" in Kenya. In *From Promise to Practice: Strengthening UN Capacities for the Prevention of Violent Conflict*. Eds. Chandra Lekha Sriram and Karin Wermester. Boulder: Lynne Rienner.
Hansen, Thomas Obel. 2009. Political Violence in Kenya: A Study of Causes, Responses, and a Framework for Discussing Preventive Action. ISS Paper 205. Pretoria, South Africa: Institute of Security Studies.
Human Rights Watch. 2008. *Ballots to Bullets: Organized Political Violence and Kenya's Crisis of Governance*. New York: Human Rights Watch.
Musila, Godfrey M. 2009. Options for Transitional Justice in Kenya: Autonomy and the Challenge of External Prescriptions. *International Journal of Transitional Justice*, 3: 445–464.
Waki Commission. 2008. *Report of the Commission of Inquiry into Post-Election Violence*. Nairobi.

Kosovo

Historical, ethnic, and nationalistic problems, together with the gross human rights violations committed during the Kosovo armed conflict, made transitional justice processes and mechanisms a necessary ingredient in building the post-conflict Kosovar society. For Kosovo to come to terms with its legacy of large-scale past abuses, it needed to ensure accountability, serve justice, and achieve reconciliation.

The fact that Kosovo's transitional justice was conducted on a territory with an evolving but uncertain future status and by an international administration presented a number of challenges and opportunities. The result has been that transitional justice mechanisms controlled by the central government (such as individual prosecution, administrative reparation, and institutional reforms) were privileged over those involving stronger community and citizen participation (such as truth telling and reconciliation).

The Repressive Past

Different theories have been presented to explain Kosovo's ethnic development. For many Albanian historians, modern Albanians are the original inhabitants of Kosovo because they descend from the Illyrians that inhabited the geographical area of modern Albania and Kosovo since the Bronze Age. The Albanians, which make 90 percent of Kosovo's current population, also base their claim to the land on this demographic dominance. However, many Serb historians argue that, when Serbs arrived in the Balkans in the seventh century, the region was dominated by South Slavs. For Serbs, the Albanian demographic domination of Kosovo is the result of the fifteen-century Ottoman invasion and its introduction of Islam, and the seventeenth-century great exodus of Serbs. For them what matters most is their national and spiritual heritage in Kosovo. The connections of the Serbian Orthodox Church to Kosovo and the Serbian history of protecting Kosovo from outside invaders, as was the case with the 1389 Battle of Kosovo, make many Serbs feel that Kosovo is the heart of the Serbian nation.

Despite their claim to be the original and demographically dominant inhabitants of Kosovo, the Kosovar Albanians became a political and demographic minority when Serbia reacquired control over the territory from the Ottoman Empire in 1912. Since then, a vicious circle of violence and hatred started between the Kosovar Albanians and Serbs. The central government in Belgrade used the Kosovar Serbs to oppress the Kosovar Albanians. In their struggle for political, social, and cultural rights, the Albanians fought not only against the oppressive regime in Belgrade, but also against its Serb representation in Kosovo.

A very important victory for Kosovar Albanians was achieved in 1974 when the constitution of the Socialist Federal Republic of Yugoslavia recognized Kosovo as an autonomous province of Serbia with status almost equivalent to that of a republic. This recognition, however, intensified the Albanian national movement, which organized riots and called for Kosovo's independence in the 1980s. As the communist regime weakened in the late 1980s, Kosovar Serbs who already were feeling threatened by the new Albanian self-assertiveness (which included some intimidation, pressure, and violence on the part of extremist Albanians to push Serbs out of Kosovo), felt even more the urge for ethnic solidarity with other Serbs in Yugoslavia. Serbian nationalism grew significantly. Serbian nationalist leaders such as Slobodan Milosevic exploited the fears and claims of the Kosovar Serbs of maltreatment to achieve his political goals. In 1989, Milosevic instituted a new constitution that revoked the Kosovo's autonomous status. The Kosovar Albanian leaders responded in 1991 by organizing a referendum, declaring Kosovo's independence, and forming an unofficial government led by Ibrahim Rugova. Milosevic reacted with more repressive measures.

Albanian nationalists did not support Rugova's passive resistance methods in confronting Milosevic abuses. In 1996, they created the Kosovo Liberation Army (KLA) and started an insurgency and guerrilla warfare. In its counterinsurgency warfare, Milosevic's army, police, and paramilitary forces targeted not only the KLA but also the Kosovar Albanian civilian population. Serbian forces engaged in indiscriminate killings, rapes, torture, forced displacements, and ethnic cleansing. Attempts for a negotiated solution were fruitless. After Yugoslavia refused to endorse the 1999 Rambouillet negotiations, the international community became frustrated with Milosevic's lack of compromise. NATO undertook a three-month bombing campaign against Serbia, which in turn accused NATO of killing a significant number of civilians. At the same time, Serbian security and military forces took advantage of the withdrawal of the Organization for Security and Cooperation in Europe (OSCE) observer mission to systematically cleanse villages of ethnic Albanians. This ethnic cleansing led to killings of many civilians and to a massive displacement of more than 850,000 Albanians out of Kosovo.

The Independent International Commission on Kosovo estimated that 7,494 to 13,627 Kosovar Albanians were killed during this conflict. Some victims were shot, others were burned alive, and still others were killed by beating, shelling, bombardment, and indiscriminate gunfire by Serb forces. Amnesty International estimated that, during the conflict, more than 3,000 ethnic Albanians were victims of enforced disappearances by Serbian police, paramilitary, and military forces. In addition, 800 Serbs, Roma, and members of other minority groups were abducted, reportedly by KLA members, during and after the war. Other documented forms of gross human rights violations committed by Serb forces during the Kosovo conflict included rape and sexual assault, torture, cruel and inhuman treatment, the use of human shields, and placing civilians at risk of harm. Serious crimes such as violations of medical neutrality, arbitrary detention and violation of right to a fair trial, destruction, looting, pillaging of civilian property, and confiscation of documents were also documented.

A military technical agreement stipulating the withdrawal of all Serbian government forces from Kosovo was signed by NATO and the military leaders of the Former Republic of Yugoslavia on June 9, 1999. The UN Security Council Resolution 1244/1999 placed Kosovo under the UN Interim Administration Mission in Kosovo (UNMIK) for a transitional administration while working out Kosovo's final status. On February 17, 2008, the Kosovo Assembly declared the province's independence. As of October 30, 2010, 71 of 192 UN member countries had formally recognized Kosovo. With the backing of the General Assembly, Serbia – which rejected Kosovo's independence – sought an advisory opinion on the legality of Kosovo's independence declaration under international law. On July 22, 2010, the International Court of Justice gave its advisory opinion saying that Kosovo's unilateral declaration of independence did not violate international law. This advisory opinion, although criticized by Serbia, was a positive step toward Kosovo's independence.

Transitional Justice

In Kosovo, transitional justice has focused on the pervasive human rights abuses that followed Kosovo's first declaration of independence in 1990. The key method has been individual prosecution for gross human rights violations. Reparation for victims of Kosovo conflict has been explored, while truth seeking and reconciliation have remained slow or absent.

Individual Prosecution

Prosecution was carried out concurrently both by the International Criminal Tribunal for the Former Yugoslavia (ICTY; see separate entry) and by UNMIK and Serbian courts. The ICTY's power to prosecute persons responsible for serious violations of international humanitarian law committed in former Yugoslavia since 1991 included violations committed during the Kosovo conflict. Under this power, Milosevic was indicted on May 24, 1999 for his crimes in Kosovo. Although he died in 2006 before his trial was completed, the ICTY rendered its very first case on Kosovo on February 26, 2009 (*Prosecutor v. Milan Milutinovic*, IT-05-87-T), convicting five senior Serb officials for crimes committed during a campaign of terror and violence directed against the Kosovar Albanians in 1999. By February 2009, the ICTY indicted nine of the most senior Serb and Yugoslav officials for crimes allegedly carried out in Kosovo by Serb forces. The ICTY's contribution to Kosovar transitional justice was very significant. By prosecuting individuals involved in crimes committed in Kosovo, the court promoted justice. By documenting the historical background and the context of those crimes, it contributed to the search for truth and laid grounds for reparation claims by the victims.

The UNMIK, established by the Security Council Resolution 1244 as Kosovo's transitional civil administration, had responsibility to maintain civil law and order. This mandate was interpreted to include reestablishing the justice sector and seeking accountability for gross human rights committed during the Kosovo conflict. This involved the reconstruction of judicial infrastructure and personnel and decisions concerning which laws should be applicable in transitional Kosovo.

Under the transitional civil administration, security forces from different countries present in Kosovo needed to conduct their policing, arrests, and business according to a uniform standard. This required a regulation on the applicable law. In his first regulation introduced as the Special Representative of the Secretary General (SRSG), Bernard Kouchner ordered that the laws applicable in Kosovo prior to March 24, 1999 should continue to apply insofar as they do not conflict with internationally recognized human rights standards. For members of the Kosovar Albanian legal community, this decision was outrageous because it was tantamount to reestablishing the oppressive Milosevic regime. Kosovar Albanian judges and prosecutors refused to apply this law, opting instead to apply laws that were in force before the revocation of Kosovo's autonomous status in March 1989. International security forces were thus confused as to whether to follow Kouchner's regulation or go along with the Kosovar Albanian practice. In response, Kouchner amended the provision on the applicable law to meet the practices followed by Kosovar Albanian judges and prosecutors. His regulations 24/1999 and 25/1999 stated that applicable law in Kosovo will be the regulations promulgated by the SRSG, including subsidiary rules; the law came into force in Kosovo on March 22, 1989. In criminal trials, however, defendants had the benefit of the most favorable provision in the laws in force in Kosovo between March 22, 1989 and the date of issuance of the two regulations. In 2003, Kosovo acquired its own Criminal Code and Code of Criminal Procedure. The Provisional Criminal Code, promulgated by UNMIK regulation 25/2003, contained provisions related to both national and international offenses. The first Kosovar Ministry of Justice was created in 2005.

The reconstruction of the judiciary's physical infrastructure was also a challenge. Court facilities, equipment, and legal documents were destroyed during the conflict. More serious was the lack of human capacity in the justice sector. Prior to the conflict, the justice sector was dominated by Serbs. After the conflict, the majority of the Serbs left and those who remained were unwilling to serve. Since the revocation of Kosovo's autonomy in 1989, Albanians had little or no access to legal education and legal professions, and so judicial expertise in post-conflict Kosovo was seriously lacking. The emergency judicial system counted only forty-seven judges and prosecutors of which forty-one were Albanians and none was Serb. The situation was so bad that of 526 individuals interviewed as part of the very first effort to recruit judges and prosecutors in Kosovo in 1999, only 48 met the minimum criteria. To solve the problem of shortage and inadequately trained local lawyers, the SRSG approached lay judges and in 2000 instituted a twinning system allowing international judges and prosecutors to work side by side with their Kosovar counterparts.

In June 2008, Kosovo counted 302 local judges, 83 local prosecutors, 15 international judges, and 11 international prosecutors. Representation of ethnic diversity in the judiciary remained poor: in 2007 it was 88.7 percent Albanian, 4.9 percent Serb, and 6.5 percent other ethnic groups.

The presence of international judges and prosecutors helped increase the capacity of local lawyers and portray the judiciary as more independent and impartial, although it remained Albanian-dominated. Still, despite their experience in international and comparative law, international lawyers lacked the knowledge of local law and local practices. Their limited number made it difficult to assess their effectiveness and impact in the Kosovar justice system.

The lack of capacity of local judges and prosecutors, the Serbs' suspicion of the partiality of a justice system dominated by Albanians, and the continued ethnic tensions made it difficult for Kosovar courts to prosecute gross human rights violations committed during the conflict. To overcome these challenges, UNMIK started the process of establishing the Kosovo War and Ethnic Crimes Court (KWECC) to address serious ethnic and war crimes. This court was to be staffed with multiethnic Kosovar and international judges, prosecutors, and staff. Because of the political impasse that followed its adoption, criticisms by the Kosovar Albanian legal community, and lack of funding, the court was never operational. In 2000, the United Nations abandoned this idea.

To deal with the challenges this court was supposed to respond to, UNMIK strengthened its hybrid courts by involving at least one international judge in cases concerning war and ethnically related crimes ranging from genocide to kidnapping. The limited number of international judges and prosecutors, however, made it impossible for them to sit in all cases involving serious ethnic related crimes. For example, the trials of cases related to the March 2004 massacre were delayed because of the low number of international judges. By July 2009, only 400 prosecutions had been initiated in 1,400 cases reported to the police after the massacre. The lack of international judges also justified the need to let some cases be tried by a bench of Kosovo Albanian judges, who imposed sentences inconsistent with the gravity of the offenses.

Overall, the Kosovar domestic courts' record in prosecuting war crimes or serious ethnic crimes, such as those committed during the March 2004 violence, has remained poor compared to the progress made by war crimes chambers in Sarajevo or Belgrade. The European Union Rule of Law Mission in Kosovo (EULEX), which since December 2008 has taken over the UNMIK's justice responsibilities, has promised to make the prosecution of war crimes a priority.

In addition to the ICTY and UNMIK courts, there are also Serbian courts, such as the Serbian War Crimes Chamber of Belgrade and the so-called parallel court system operating in the northern part of Kosovo bordering Serbia. The War Crimes Chamber was established in 2003. Among the seven prosecution cases before this Chamber in 2008, there was the *Prosecutor v. Suva Reka* trial, relating to the killing of Kosovar Albanians in 1999. In June 2009, this court sentenced three former members of a notorious Serb paramilitary unit called the Scorpions to twenty years in prison. It also charged seventeen former KLA members for murdering at least fifty-two Serbs, Roma, and ethnic Albanians and raping many women in the town of Gnjilane. This Chamber has been praised by international human rights organizations for its efforts to hold alleged perpetrators accountable for war crimes despite limited funds, inadequate political support, and little public awareness of its work.

Transitional justice in Kosovo has also been affected by parallel courts operating both in Kosovo and in Serbia proper. These are remnants of the courts that existed before Serbia was forced out of Kosovo in 1999, and have continued to operate along UNMIK courts. Although most of these courts are now located in Serbia proper, they have branches in Kosovo. They apply Serbian law and serve mainly the Kosovar Serb community. Most Kosovar Serbs approach these parallel courts either because they did not trust the UNMIK Albanian-dominated courts or they needed their judgments to be recognized in Serbia. OSCE research indicated that between June 1999 and January 2003, the parallel municipal and district courts heard or facilitated 5,300 matters arising out of Mitrovice/Mitrovica region alone. These courts have been problematic in their handling of criminal cases. They have been accused of handing down lenient sentences to Serb defendants, and there has been a problem of double jeopardy because defendants tried before parallel courts could still face a second trial on the same charges before UNMIK courts. Parallel courts also impact relations between Kosovar Albanians and Kosovar Serbs, because as long as each ethnic group relies on the law it perceives to be more favorable to it, national unity and reconciliation will remain difficult.

Reparation

In 2000, UNMIK adopted Regulation 66 on Benefits for War Invalids of Kosovo and for the Next of Kin of Those Who Died as a Result of the Armed Conflict in Kosovo. This reparation program offers benefits to victims of all ethnic groups and their families. Benefits include financial payments for war invalids, free access to the medical care provided in governmental health centers and rehabilitation centers, exemption from sales tax, excise tax, and customs duties on vehicles adapted for the specific disability, and financial payments for the next of kin of those who died as a result of the armed conflict in Kosovo. A special fund to provide special benefits for eligible beneficiaries was established and administered by the Department of Health and Social Welfare. In February 2006, Kosovo adopted the Law on the Status and Rights of the Families of Martyrs, KLA War Invalids and Veterans, and the Families of the Civilian Victims of War, providing financial and other benefits for the families of deceased and injured members of the KLA and other armed groups. An amendment to this law was proposed in May 2008 to recognize the right of families of the disappeared to receive compensation and to know the truth about the disappearance of their family members. The status of martyr includes everyone who sacrificed his/her life for Kosovo's freedom, including activists who contributed to the national cause, individually or as an organized group, and were murdered by the enemy between May 9, 1945 and December 30, 1991. In addition to this administrative reparation, judicial reparation was recognized in Kosovo: legislation in both Serbia and Kosovo provides that civil suits can be brought against both public officials and non-state actors for their criminal acts.

The reparation program has shortcomings. According to Amnesty International, most civilian victims of serious human rights violations committed in Kosovo have not received adequate, effective, and prompt reparation proportional to the gravity of the violation and harm they suffered. Because Regulation 66/2000 covers only the period of the armed conflict between February 27, 1998 and June 20, 1999, it excludes victims of abductions committed after June 1999. The Law on the Status and Rights of the Families of Martyrs, KLA War Invalids and Veterans has also been criticized for creating serious discrepancy between the rights afforded and benefits awarded to the dependants of military and civilian victims. Finally, most civil suits brought to court for reparation have been unsuccessful mainly because the Kosovo Supreme Court decided in 2004 that claims against the state must be brought within five years of the violation, thus excluding most claims from reaching the courts.

Challenges in addressing the issue of property rights and property restitution have also weakened the reparation system in Kosovo. Hundreds of thousands of minorities, mainly Serbs forced to leave their property because of the armed conflict, insecurity, or expulsion, found their property destroyed or occupied. To find legal remedy outside the existing poor judicial system, the Kosovo Property Agency (KPA) and the Kosovo Property Claim Commission (KPCC) were created to adjudicate and resolve property conflicts. This process did not produce the expected results. By February 2009, there were still 50,000 to 60,000 outstanding claims on damaged, destroyed, or illegally occupied property as a result of the conflict. Through intimidation and corruption, title documents were validated by municipal officials to unlawful owners, making it difficult for the rightful owners to prove their ownership. Also, some KPA/KPCC decisions are not enforceable and those enforced led, sometimes, to post-eviction incidents between the property owner and those they evicted.

Truth Seeking and Reconciliation

The history of Kosovo shows that local Albanians and Serbs were never integrated. The Kosovo conflict was the result of this division and contributed to its deepening. Following the 2004 massacre, the UN Secretary General reported to the Security Council that most Kosovar Albanians do not wish to create a truly multiethnic society or are even determined to prevent it. Despite this evidence, the UNMIK administration and the post-independence Kosovar government have avoided the costly and painful journey of interethnic reconciliation. Not much has been invested in creating an interethnic dialogue and searching for the truth about Kosovo's history, ethnic conflict, massacres, abductions, and disappearances. The lack of interest in learning and facing the truth about Kosovo's past and in building interethnic reconciliation is likely to continue to undermine efforts toward building a democratic, multiethnic, and stable Kosovo.

Despite the positive impact of initiatives such as the "internal dialogue with communities" by the prime minister and the "Contact Group Plus" by international partners, after the 2004 massacre, these initiatives failed to develop into a nationwide dialogue on ethnic reconciliation in Kosovo. Truth-seeking and reconciliation mechanisms remain a missing, but important and necessary, ingredient in rebuilding Kosovo.

Conclusion

Transitional Justice in Kosovo is an ongoing process that will continue to evolve as Kosovo's status is defined. In this development, it will be necessary to build on the success achieved in justice and institution-building. Overcoming future challenges requires ensuring justice to both Kosovar Albanians and Kosovar Serbs and pursuing policies based on truth seeking and reconciliation between all citizens.

Jean-Marie Kamatali

Cross-references: Court Trials for Redress; International Criminal Tribunal for the Former Yugoslavia; Reparations.

Further Readings

Amnesty International. 2009. *Kosovo: Burying the Past: 10 years of Impunity for Enforced Disappearances and Abductions in Kosovo*. Available at: http://www.amnesty.org/en/library/asset/EUR70/007/2009/en/ccf25c64-d299-46ee-83d4-a8835f8bf970/eur700072009eng.pdf (accessed October 19, 2010).

Baylis, Elena A. 2007. Parallel Courts in Post-Conflict Kosovo. *The Yale Journal of International Law*, 32(4): 1–59.
Independent International Commission on Kosovo. 2003. *The Kosovo Report, Conflict, International Response, and Lessons Learned*. Available at: http://www.reliefweb.int/library/documents/thekosovoreport.htm (accessed October 20, 2010).
Property Rights in Kosovo: A Haunting Legacy of a Society in Transition. 2009. New York: International Center for Transitional Justice.
Vickers, Miranda. 1998. *Between Serb and Albanian, A History of Kosovo*. New York: Columbia University Press.

Latvia

Transitional justice was launched in Latvia in the late 1980s at a time when the country was part of the Soviet Union, and continued after the republic became independent in 1991. As in other Soviet republics, Mikhail Gorbachev's *glasnost* and *perestroika* policies allowed Stalinist crimes to be investigated, made public, and denounced. Postcommunist Latvia's transitional justice has tried to overcome Soviet imperialism and the legacy of Latvia's Nazi past.

The Repressive Past

During World War II, Latvia was subject to Soviet and Nazi occupation. While the three years of Nazi rule led to the elimination of the majority of the Latvian Jews, the forty-six years of Soviet dictatorship dramatically changed Latvia's demographic composition by increasing the number of non-Latvians in its total population.

On June 17, 1940, the Soviet Union occupied Latvia by virtue of the 1939 Molotov-Ribbentrop pact signed with Nazi Germany, which assigned the country to the Soviet sphere of influence. Latvia had been part of the Russian Empire until 1918, when the republic first declared its independence. Following rigged elections, in which only one preapproved list of candidates was allowed, in 1940, Latvia was "voluntarily" integrated into the Soviet Union at the request of the fraudulently installed parliament. Most political leaders of the Latvian interwar republic (1918–1940) and senior army officers were imprisoned; some were shot on the spot without trial, others deported to the Gulag, the vast Soviet prison and labor camp system. The Communist Party of Latvia became the only party permitted to function and the republic's ruling force. Because the party was very weak at the time of the Soviet invasion, its ranks were filled up with Russian communists or "Latvian Russians," Latvian communists who fled to Soviet Russia after Latvia became independent in 1918. This contributed to the perception of foreign rule resulting from Latvia's subordination to the central Moscow government.

The Soviet repressive regime was installed and maintained by means of terror, implemented by the Latvian branch of the feared secret political police, the People's Commissariat for Internal Affairs (Narodnyy Komissariat Vnutrennikh Del, NKVD), precursor to the KGB. The NKVD arrested and tortured those who resisted Soviet rule or engaged in "anti-Soviet activities," and carried out the first mass deportations. On the night of June 13–14, 1941, more than 15,000 civilians, including children, were deported and sentenced to work in the Gulag or forced to live in special settlements in Siberia.

In July 1941, Latvia became part of the Reichkomissariat Ostland of Nazi Germany, after which the elimination of the Jewish and Roma population began. Mass killings – committed by Nazi troops and Latvian collaborators, including the infamous Arajs Commando – took place at Rumbula, Bikernieki, and other sites. Formed of ethnic Latvians, the Arajs Commando allegedly killed 26,000 Jews. Other Latvian members of the Nazi Security Service (Sicherheitsdienst) and the Latvian Auxiliary Police force also engaged in crimes. By the end of the year, almost the entire Jewish population of Latvia (who numbered nearly 70,000) was eliminated. In addition, some 20,000 Jews brought from Austria, Germany, and Czechoslovakia lost their lives in Latvia at the time.

After the Soviet Union reoccupied Latvia in 1944, more mass deportations followed. At least 119,000 people were persecuted between 1944 and 1953. Deportations targeted supporters of Latvia's independence (the "nationalists") and those who resisted the introduction of collective farming (the "kulaks"). In the mass deportations of March 25–30, 1949 alone, 42,125 civilians – including 10,987 children under the age of sixteen – were moved to Siberia. In need of workers and farmers, the Latvian collective farms and industrial enterprises hired migrants from other Soviet republics, mainly Russia. This changed the republic's demography, as the percentage of Latvians fell from 75 percent in 1935 to 60 percent in 1959. After Stalin's death, the surviving deportees were allowed to return to Latvia – the majority of them in 1956, the last one in 1966 – but they continued to face discrimination.

The leaders of the Communist Party of the Soviet Union (CPSU) did not allow the Latvian Communist Party to retain a degree of self-rule, as they did in Eastern Europe. In 1958–1959, some Latvian communist leaders, including the deputy chairman of the Latvian Council of Ministers Eduards Berklavs, unsuccessfully tried to install national communist rule and stop further mass migration of Russian workers to Latvia. Berklavs was exiled and 200 other Latvian Communists fell victim of inner-party purges and lost their jobs.

The KGB replaced the NKVD in 1954. When the Latvian KGB was dissolved in 1991, it employed about 4,300 full-time agents and an unknown number of part-time informers. The KGB also secretly used academics and scientists traveling abroad as "passive" informers required to submit mandatory reports to their home institution after every trip. Before Gorbachev came to power, the KGB engaged in mass surveillance to root out dissent and opposition against the communist and Soviet system. Under Gorbachev, the KGB reduced the number of its activities and agents in Latvia, destroyed some of its files, and could no longer open private letters without good reason. A 1990 law permitted the destruction of documents pertaining to secret informers and agents who no longer worked for the KGB. By virtue of this law, the "preventive measures" archive was destroyed and most other files were moved to Russia.

As a result, independent Latvia was left with 6,923 alphabetical cards containing the names of agents and informers, but not explaining their role in and the nature of their collaboration with the secret police, and 4,819 agent cards giving no precise information on the agents' secret activities. Those listed might have been regular collaborators, or informers who were never used, scientists reporting on a conference abroad, or informers who offered only trivial information on their targets. The most active agents may not be named at all, because the files of party members were regularly destroyed. File cards not referring to victims are kept with the Center for Documentation of the Consequences of Totalitarianism (see separate entry).

Transitional Justice

Soviet authorities made little effort to come to terms with the Nazi past, except through the overall condemnation of Nazis and their collaborators and the prosecution of some major Nazi criminals in 1946–1947. Gorbachev allowed only limited reckoning with Stalinist crimes without condemning the activity of the KGB, which he restricted without dismantling. Only after 1991 did Latvia reckon with its Nazi and Soviet pasts with the help of vetting, court trials, rehabilitation and restitution programs, access to the communist secret files, and symbolic justice. The focus was mostly on Soviet crimes.

Vetting/Lustration

Latvia limited the involvement of former communist officials and KGB agents in post-communist politics through restrictive election and citizenship laws without adopting a separate lustration law.

In 1993, a parliamentary group for the study of KGB documents identified five deputies, including the Minister of Foreign Affairs Georgs Andrejevs, as former secret agents. Andrejevs stepped down, while insisting that his collaboration was limited to reporting on his visits abroad to international conferences. Andrejevs and three other deputies were later cleared of charges when their collaboration could not be proven.

Article 5 of the Saeima (Parliament) Election Law of 25 May 1995 declared ineligible individuals who "belong or have belonged to the salaried staff of the USSR, Latvian SSR or foreign state security, intelligence or counterintelligence services" and "after January 13, 1991 have been active in the CPSU (Communist Party of Latvia), Working People as International Front of the Latvian SSR, the United Board of Working Bodies, Organization of War and Labor Veterans, All-Latvia Salvation Committee or its regional committees" (The Saeima Election Law 1995). These organizations were either communist or had opposed Latvia's independence after January 13, 1991, the day when the Soviet special troops (OMON) unsuccessfully tried to reimpose Soviet control over the Baltic republics.

The 1995 law partly responded to the candidacy of Alfreds Rubiks, the last First Secretary of the Latvian Communist Party, who at the time was serving an eight-year prison term for his involvement in the failed 1991 coup. In the 1993 Saeima elections, Rubiks became a deputy, but parliament invalidated his mandate, considering him ineligible to occupy a deputy seat because of his role in the coup. In 1997, Rubiks was released from prison but was banned from running for parliament by the 1995 Election Law. The ban did not refer to the European elections, so in 2009, Rubiks won a seat in the European Parliament. Similarly, Tatjana Zdanok, leader of a pro-Russian-minority coalition, was unable to run for the Saeima because of the 1995 Election Law, but in 2004 and 2009 she was elected as member of the European Parliament.

Article 9 of the Election Law on Cities and Town Councils, District Councils and Pagasts Councils of 25 January 1994 banned the same categories of people as the 1995 law from being nominated to and from holding council positions. Both election laws amounted to lustration laws, but no separate lustration law was passed. In 2006, President Vaira Vīķe-Freiberga vetoed a lustration proposal on grounds that few of those named in file cards were agents (this veto was not sufficient to prevent the law, but parliament followed the president's lead and ultimately did not pass a lustration law). At that point, debates on the citizenship law, which initially excluded two-thirds of Latvia's Russian-speakers from citizenship and declared them ineligible to seek public office, and the incompleteness of the KGB archive, which precluded the identification of secret agents, had dampened support for vetting.

Independent Latvia restored its statehood on the basis of continuity with the interwar republic of June 17, 1940, before the two foreign occupations. The Resolution on the Renewal of the Republic of Latvia Citizens' Rights and the Fundamental Principles of Naturalization of 15 October 1991 led to the temporary exclusion of 700,000 residents, mostly Russian-speaking migrants who had arrived in Latvia during Soviet times. Instead of automatically receiving Latvian citizenship, they had to undergo naturalization, which included an exam in the history and language of Latvia and an oath on the Latvian constitution proving their loyalty to the new independent republic. Although most of those excluded from automatic citizenship were ethnic Russians, ethnicity did not lead to exclusion. One-third of ethnic Russians residing in Latvia in 1991 had been citizens of interwar Latvia, being therefore entitled to automatic citizenship.

Naturalization began after the adoption of the 1994 Citizenship Law, which foresaw a "window system" enabling only certain age groups to be naturalized every year. Clearly, Latvian authorities wanted to temporarily exclude Soviet migrants – the "occupiers," as the nationalist Latvian press called them – from the body politics and test their loyalty to the republic through naturalization. The naturalization process was rigid until the Citizenship Law was amended in 1998, but afterward it has been open to noncitizens who have been permanent residents of Latvia for five years, pass the examination in the Latvian language and history, and give the oath to the Latvian constitution.

Naturalization amounted to vetting because Article 11 of the Citizenship Law disqualified individuals involved with the Soviet regime or supportive of "totalitarian ideas." According to the law, citizenship was denied to persons who

(1) through the use of anti-constitutional methods have turned against Latvia's independence, its democratic parliamentary state system or the existing state authority in Latvia; 2) after May 4, 1990, have propagated fascist, chauvinist, national-socialist, communist or other totalitarian ideas or have stirred up ethnic or racial hatred or discord; 3) are officials of institutions of a foreign state authority, administrative or law enforcement body; 4) serve in the armed forces, internal forces, security service or the police (militia) of a foreign state; 5) after June 17, 1940, have chosen Latvia as their residence directly after demobilization from the USSR (Russian) Armed Forces or USSR (Russian) Interior Armed Forces and who, on the day of their conscription/enlistment, were not permanently residing in Latvia; 6) have been employees, informants, agents or have been in charge of conspiratory premises of the former USSR (LSSR) KGB or other foreign security service, intelligence service or other special service; ... 8) after January 13, 1991, have acted against the Republic of Latvia through participation in the CPSU (LCP), Working Peoples' International Front of the Latvian SSR, United Council of Labor Collectives, Organization of War and Labor Veterans, or the All-Latvia Salvation Committee and its regional committees or Latvian Union of Communists those involved in the Soviet repressive regime, the former KGB and Soviet army officers.

In addition, "if a person who has submitted a naturalization application is called to criminal liability or with regard to him/her a discovery case on establishing cooperation with the KGB is initiated, the application review shall be interrupted until a court decision takes effect or the case is terminated" (The Citizenship Law 1994). Some 132,175 noncitizens obtained Latvian citizenship from 1995 to 2009, but in mid-2009, there were still 350,000 noncitizens in Latvia.

Court Trials

Postcommunist Latvian authorities did not prosecute Nazi crimes, but indicted those responsible for Soviet crimes. Some Nazi criminals were punished after World War II, but Soviet crimes could be investigated only after 1991. In 1946, seven Nazi officials, including SS leader Friedrich Jeckeln, were convicted by the Soviet Criminal Court in Riga and publicly hanged. Soviet trials did not match international standards, but the death sentence of convicted Nazi war criminals symbolized the condemnation of the Nazi regime. After 1991, Latvians believed that the top priority was to rehabilitate Latvian victims of Soviet terror and to condemn and convict Soviet criminals.

Criminal adjudication of Soviet crimes started in 1995. The Justice Ministry Department of Investigations of Crimes of the Totalitarian Regime (Totalitāro režīmu noziegumu izmeklēšanas nodaļa, TRNIN) has worked together with the Center for Documentation of the Consequences of Totalitarianism to prosecute human rights violators. The criminal reappraising of the past was complicated by the fact that the most brutal crimes were committed in the 1940s–1950s, and thus most perpetrators were dead or very old or were Russian citizens who could not be prosecuted in Latvia.

Only nine investigations ended in criminal charges. Only Alfons Noviks, head of the Latvian NKVD and then the Latvian State Security, who was responsible for the mass deportation of 1940–1941 and the arrests, executions, and mass deportation of 1944–1953, served jail time. Charged with crimes against humanity/genocide, in December 1995, Noviks was convicted to life in prison but died three months later at the age of eighty-eight. Several trials were called off because of the poor physical or mental condition of the accused or because the defendants died before their appeal was decided. In the case of Mihails Farbtuhs and Vasilijs Kononovs, the European Court of Human Rights overturned the verdict of the Latvian courts on procedural or health grounds. The classification of Soviet deportations as genocide is widely accepted in Latvia, but not by foreign legal scholars.

Rehabilitation and Restitution

The rehabilitation of victims of the communist regime started under Gorbachev and included the rehabilitation of those purged from the Latvian Communist Party in 1959, most notably Berklavs' return from exile.

Property was returned to its pre-Soviet owners by virtue of the Law on the Denationalization of Building Properties of 30 October 1991, which repealed Soviet nationalization of large homes and farms. Because the law aimed to restore the property status prior to the Soviet and the Nazi occupations, Jewish private property was also restored to owners or their descendants. When privatization was introduced in 1992, allowing for the transfer of state-owned property to private hands, it was considered that the property had to be returned to its rightful owners, and only when they did not claim it could the property be sold to other parties.

Access to Secret Files

Because the KGB documents left behind in Latvia are fragmentary, the Latvian postcommunist authorities have been reluctant to grant access to the extant secret documents to citizens. As such, file access is limited and granted only for governmental and research purposes. In 1996, the Saeima rejected a draft law that would have allowed publication of, and public access to, KGB agent files. Parliament saw the legislative proposal as running counter to the privacy protection stipulations of the European Convention of Human Rights, which Latvia had just signed. In 2004, President Vīķe-Freiberga asked for the KGB files not to be published until 2014. Parliament agreed.

The Rewriting of History and the Truth Commission

Rewriting history and filling in the blanks created by Soviet propaganda started under Gorbachev. The Latvian independence movement brought to light the secret Molotov-Ribbentrop Pact to explain that Latvia was forcibly occupied by the Red Army and annexed by the Soviet Union. Since 1990, Latvian authorities have stressed the notion of occupation in Latvia's history, although Russia still maintains that the Baltic states voluntarily joined the Soviet Union and profited from this union.

In 1998, President Guntis Ulmanis founded the Commission of the Historians of Latvia (see separate entry) to investigate human rights abuses perpetrated between 1940 and 1956 under the Nazi and Soviet occupations. The Commission organizes annual conferences and publishes research reports. This presidential, permanent Commission of Latvian and international scholars was set up after commemorations of the Latvian Legion, a World War II military organization serving under the SS Nazi symbol, proved the need for research and education on Latvia's history. The Commission of Historians answered these needs.

The rewriting of history seeks to educate Latvians and the international community about Latvia's recent history. In an effort to educate schoolchildren, the post-Soviet textbooks portray the Latvian perspective on World War II and emphasize the republic's occupation and forceful annexation to the Soviet Union. Noncitizens wishing to receive Latvian citizenship must pass a history exam, which tests their knowledge of the consequences of the Hitler-Stalin Pact for Latvia, the Soviet mass deportations, and the Holocaust.

Symbolic Justice

Independent Latvia adopted a number of symbolic measures to reckon with its past. The Law on the Cessation of Activities of Some Social and Socio-political Organizations of 24 August 1991 banned the Communist Party, its youth organizations, the pro-Soviet International Front of the Working People of Soviet Latvia (the Interfront), and other organizations that opposed Latvia's independence. After Latvia's 1991 independence, all Soviet symbols and statues of communist leaders were dismantled and streets were renamed.

Since 1990, Latvia has commemorated the victims of the Soviet and Nazi dictatorships. Three national commemoration days are dedicated to the Victims of the Genocide of the Totalitarian Communist Regime (March 25, June 14, and the first Sunday in December). The Genocide of Jews is commemorated every year on July 4, but victims of the Nazi occupation are remembered to a much lesser degree than victims of communism.

After 1990, Latvian governments have issued several declarations stating the Latvian perspective on World War II and the country's occupation. Among these are the 1990 Declaration on the Condemnation and Prohibition of Genocide and Anti-Semitism in Latvia, the 1996 Declaration on Latvia's Occupation, and the 2005 Declaration on the Condemnation of the Totalitarian Communist Occupation Regime Implemented in Latvia by the Soviet Union. In 2000, Latvia became a member of the Task Force for International Cooperation on Holocaust Education, Remembrance, and Research.

Conclusion

Independent Latvia has sought to come to terms with its Soviet more than with its Nazi past. This is partly because the Soviet past was more recent and affected the Latvian ethnic majority. While Latvians readily admit that they were victims of the Soviet regime, they have been reluctant to recognize themselves as victimizers under the brief Nazi occupation of 1941–1944. Latvia's transitional justice choices were limited by the unavailability of the KGB secret files. The inability to prosecute Soviet human rights perpetrators has led to an emphasis on vetting through election and citizenship laws and on the commemoration of the victims of Soviet repression. This exacerbated the victimization of the Latvian nation and hindered the integration of Soviet-era migrants into the Latvian society.

Katja Wezel

Cross-references: Access to Secret Files; Centre for Documentation of the Consequences of Totalitarianism; Commission of Historians of Latvia; Court Trials for Redress; Politics of Memory; Rewriting History; Truth Commission; Vetting.

Further Readings

Crimes against Humanity: Latvian Site. Available at: http://vip.latnet.lv/LPRA/angliski.htm (accessed September 30, 2009).

Jansons, Ritvars and Indulis Zālīte. 2001. LSPR valtsts drošības dienesta izveidošana un tā galvenie represīvie uzdevumi 1944–1956. gadā [The Establishment of the Institutions of State Security in the Latvian SSR and their Main Repressive Tasks 1944–1956]. In *Totalitarian Regimes and their Repressions Carried out in Latvia 1940–1956, Commission of the Historians of Latvia, vol. 3.* Ed. Irēne Šneidere. Riga: Institute of the History of Latvia, pp. 373–476.

Jaskovska, Eva and John P. Moran. 2006. Justice or Politics? Criminal, Civil and Political Adjudication in the Newly Independent Baltic States. *Journal of Communist Studies and Transition Politics*, 22(4): 485–506.

KGB Documents online. Available at: http://www.kgbdocuments.eu (accessed January 19, 2010).

Nollendorfs, Valters and Erwin Oberländer, eds. 2005. *The Hidden and Forbidden History of Latvia under Soviet and Nazi Occupations 1940–1991, Symposium of the Commission of the Historians of Latvia*, vol. 14. Riga: Institute of the History of Latvia.

The Citizenship Law of 1994, 1994. Available at: http://www.humanrights.lv/doc/latlik/citiz1.htm (accessed June 25, 2010).

The Saeima Election Law of 25 May 1995, 1995. Available at: http://www.legislationline.org/documents/action/popup/id/4909 (accessed November 2, 2009).

Wezel, Katja. 2009. Latvia's Soviet Story. Transitional Justice and the Politics of Commemoration. *Atslēgvārdi/Keywords* 2. Available at: http://www.satori.lv/staticPage/show/id/Keywords2 (accessed December 17, 2009).

Liberia

Liberia suffered through one of the worst civil wars of the late twentieth century. During the height of the conflict, approximately a half-dozen different groups were fighting for control of the country and its valuable natural resources. Over the course of the more than two-decade-long civil war, some 250,000 Liberians were killed out of a population of approximately 3 million. At its worst point, more than 1.5 million people were estimated to have been internally displaced by the conflict. A further 750,000 fled to neighboring countries. Human rights violations in the later stages of the conflict, particularly after Charles Taylor's election in 1997, were particularly brutal. Summary execution, torture, rape, looting, and burning of villages were widespread practices by government and rebel forces. After securing rebel-held areas, government forces employed these tactics to punish perceived rebel sympathizers. Hundreds of civilians were forced into military service or labor by all sides. It is estimated that more than 20,000 children were pressed into fighting in the civil war, but observers believe the number was much higher.

Since the Accra Comprehensive Peace Agreement was reached in 2003, Liberia has begun the process of addressing past human rights violations. To date, the centerpiece of Liberia's transitional justice strategy has been the Liberian Truth and Reconciliation Commission (TRC), which was agreed to in the peace accords. The TRC concluded its investigation in mid-2009. After previewing its findings in early 2009, the commission's final report was released on July 1, 2009. The report includes a range of additional transitional justice measures intended to further victims' healing and provide accountability for perpetrators, the most controversial being the recommendation that fifty individuals, including current President Ellen Johnson Sirleaf, be banned from public office for their role in the conflict. The fate of Charles Taylor and other leaders of the warring factions has been a controversial subject in Liberia because many remain influential in post–civil war politics.

The Repressive Past

The origins of Liberia's civil war were rooted in long-standing animosity. Historically, Liberia's population was divided between Americo-Liberians and indigenous Liberians. Americo-Liberians are the descendants of freed American and Caribbean slaves who settled in Liberia beginning in 1820. Indigenous Liberians are the descendants of African ethnic groups who inhabited what is now Liberia when the first Americo-Liberians arrived. From the very start, relations between the two groups were rancorous as Americo-Liberians viewed indigenous Liberians as barbarous while indigenous Liberians thought that the Americo-Liberians' slave past made them inferior.

Americo-Liberians have never made up a large portion of Liberia's population (approximately 3 percent by recent estimates). Yet, until Samuel Doe's coup in 1980, they dominated Liberian politics and economy. Indigenous Liberians were able to advance in society, but they needed to adopt the ways of Americo-Liberians in order to do so. Indigenous Liberians were not granted the right to vote until 1946, but property qualifications meant that most continued to be disenfranchised. Following the death of President William Tubman in 1971, his vice-president, William Tolbert, assumed the presidency. Tolbert broke with his predecessors and pursued modest political liberalization. However, these changes created rising expectations that the government did not live up to.

Economic inequality remained stark in late-1970s Liberia. At the time, despite their small numbers, Americo-Liberians controlled more than 60 percent of the country's wealth. Tensions came to a head in 1979 when Tolbert's proposal to increase rice prices led to the Rice Riot, which government forces brutally suppressed. Sensing the government's weakness, the opposition pushed for concessions, which, in turn, weakened Tolbert's support within his own party. In the midst of this instability, Samuel K. Doe led seventeen indigenous soldiers in a coup on April 12, 1980. Tolbert was assassinated, and less than two weeks later, thirteen top government officials were tried and publicly executed.

Doe's takeover marked the first time that indigenous Liberians had controlled the country. However, interethnic conflict would soon create more instability. Doe was from the Krahn ethnic group. Other groups soon chafed under the preferential treatment given his ethnic kin. Moreover, Doe's army, which was dominated by fellow ethnic Krahns, terrorized the rival Mano and Gio ethnic groups of Nimba County. Through intimidation and fraud, Doe won the presidential election in October 1985. Doe's regime proved to be brutal and repressive.

As a result, on December 24, 1989, Charles Taylor's National Patriotic Front of Liberia (NPFL) launched an insurgency campaign from Ivory Coast. By the following June, Taylor's rebels were battling Doe's army in the Liberian capital of Monrovia. In July, the Independent National Patriotic Front of Liberia (INPFL), a rebel splinter group led by Prince Johnson, also entered Monrovia. On August 24, 1990, the first Economic Community of West African States Monitoring Group peacekeepers arrived in Monrovia to attempt to curb the fighting. The peacekeepers were attacked by Taylor's forces, who denounced the intervention. On September 9, 1990, the INPFL captured Doe and tortured him to death.

By November 1990, the Economic Community of West African States succeeded in organizing the first of many peace talks. However, cease-fires and peace agreements were repeatedly broken over the next several years. Finally, on August 17, 1996, the Economic Community mediated a new peace deal and a transitional government was organized to hold elections. On July 19, 1997, Taylor won the presidential election through voter intimidation; most of his major rivals were other warlords.

The Taylor regime brought a new level of brutality to Liberia and its neighbors. Taylor's NPFL and, after 1997, his Liberian government provided significant military and logistical support to Sierra Leone's Revolutionary United Front (RUF). The RUF is one of the most brutal rebel groups in recent memory, employing murder, mutilation, and amputation against thousands of Sierra Leonean civilians. Civil war in Liberia reignited between April and July 1999, when dissidents began launching attacks on Liberia from neighboring countries – first the Joint Forces of Liberation for Liberia, and then the Liberians United for Reconciliation and Democracy (LURD) and the Movement for Democracy in Liberia. Taylor's government stepped up attacks against members of the Mandingo, Krahn, and Gbandi ethnic groups who were accused of siding with the rebels.

For its part, LURD appeared to target Kissi civilians for its worst abuses, perhaps because Taylor's RUF allies once had a stronghold in a Kissi area of Liberia.

Horrified by the tactics of the RUF, the international community intervened in neighboring Sierra Leone's civil war first. They recognized, however, that the conflicts were not wholly separate. On March 7, 2001, the UN Security Council concluded that Taylor's support of the RUF was a threat to international peace and security and authorized the imposition of sanctions against Liberia. Bans on trade in arms and diamonds and foreign travel restrictions on senior government officials were imposed. After May 2002, when elections marked the culmination of Sierra Leone's peace process, fighters began to trickle into Liberia and many joined the various warring factions. With Taylor's government weakened and increasingly isolated, the rebels gradually pushed from rural areas to the suburbs of Monrovia by 2003.

International pressure and the government's failing battlefield fortunes led Taylor to agree to peace talks, which began in Accra, Ghana, on June 4, 2003. Taylor quickly returned to Liberia, however, to escape the international arrest warrant following the unsealing of an indictment by the Special Court for Sierra Leone. Some of the fiercest fighting of the entire civil war occurred over the next two months following Taylor's return to Liberia as factions vied for advantage. On July 6, 2003, under continued international pressure, Taylor agreed to go into exile in Nigeria.

Although Taylor was rumored to continue to pull strings from Nigeria, a peace agreement was finalized quickly following his departure. On August 11, Taylor transferred power to his vice-president, Moses Blah, and left Liberia. Liberia's warring parties signed the comprehensive peace agreement on August 18. Three days later, Charles Gyude Bryant was selected by the parties to head a power-sharing transitional government. On September 19, the UN Security Council authorized a 15,000-strong peacekeeping force, the United Nations Mission in Liberia (UNMIL), which began its mandate on October 1. Two years later, on October 11, 2005, internationally supervised elections were held for president and the legislature. Johnson-Sirleaf won the presidency in a runoff election on November 8.

Transitional Justice

Given the nature and scope of the violence, there has been significant interest in transitional justice in Liberia. Little progress was made on implementing the terms of the peace accords during the transitional government, as it was corrupt and inefficient. Only once Johnson-Sirleaf took office did significant reform begin. In many respects, Liberian society remains fragile. After the signing of the peace accord, more than 100,000 combatants were disarmed and demobilized, but many are alienated from their communities and lack economic opportunity. Thousands of individuals are believed to have committed human rights violations during the course of the civil war. Tens of thousands of refugees and internally displaced persons have returned to shattered communities and what is left of their homes. The TRC has been relatively uncontroversial, but has not yet completed its work. There is significant disagreement in Liberia about what, if anything, to do in addition.

The Truth and Reconciliation Commission

Although the 2003 Accra Peace Agreement included provisions for the TRC, it was signed into law by the National Transitional Government on June 10, 2005. The shape of the commission that emerged in the legislation was the result of significant consultation with victims and civil society groups. Meetings were held around the country to gain input. Subsequently, the UNMIL, the UN Development Program (UNDP), and the Transitional Justice Working Group (a coalition of nongovernmental organizations) brought together seventy civil society groups in July 2004 to craft a bill. Shortly thereafter, a meeting of civil society representatives, government officials, and international experts finalized the text of a draft bill, which was presented to the government in September 2004. Following the bill's passage, in October 2005, Bryant appointed the TRC's nine commissioners. The TRC was formally inaugurated in February 2006 by newly elected President Johnson-Sirleaf. After a few months of preparation, the TRC was officially launched on June 22.

The TRC was given a two-year mandate to investigate and publish a report documenting the gross human rights violations, violations of international humanitarian law, and economic crimes that occurred in Liberia between January 1979 and October 14, 2003. It was empowered to recommend the prosecution of the worst offenders and amnesty for those who made "full disclosures of their wrongs" and displayed "remorse for their acts." Amnesty, however, could not be recommended for serious violations of international humanitarian law and crimes against humanity or by the TRC's Diaspora Project, which operated in parallel in the United States. In addition, the TRC was asked to provide recommendations on reparations as well as legal and institutional reforms.

Although the international community was attracted to the truth commission idea because it was perceived to be less of a threat to stability, the UN and EU donor governments were slow in fulfilling the pledges they had made to the TRC. It had an initial estimated budget of US$13 million, but it was subsequently cut back to US$8 million. As a result of funding problems, the commission was forced to shut down virtually all of its work for approximately one year. As a result of the delay, public hearings scheduled to be held around the country beginning in early 2007 were postponed until early 2008.

The Liberian TRC is noteworthy for being the first truth commission to systematically reach out to the diaspora community, primarily in the United States. It did so by working with a national advisory committee of Liberian community members and the nongovernmental organization the Advocates for Human Rights. By the end of the conflict, it was estimated that more than 40,000 Liberians had come to the United States. In the fall of 2006, statement taking was pilot-tested in Minnesota, the state with the largest Liberian population in the United States. Subsequent volunteer training, outreach, and statement taking were launched in a number of major metropolitan areas in the United States as well as in the Buduburam Refugee settlement outside Accra, Ghana, and in London, Great Britain. The effort is entirely volunteer-based, with more than 600 individuals contributing their time.

As the TRC concluded its public hearings, it convened a National Conference, which issued the Virginia Declaration in mid-June 2009. It recommended the implementation of the following additional transitional justice measures: the creation of a special court to prosecute perpetrators who were in leadership positions; the use of Palava hut ceremonies, a forum for communal arbitration and cleansing, for perpetrators who have acknowledged wrongdoing and expressed remorse; the prohibition from public service of perpetrators who committed crimes against humanity; the construction of memorials for victims; the provision of individual reparations in the form of psychosocial services, educational scholarships, microloans, livestock and agricultural support, and food aid;

and the provision of collective reparations in the form of psychosocial support centers, support for communal farming, and priority funding for infrastructure projects. The declaration urged that these programs be funded in part by cash or in-kind contributions by perpetrators; the provision of any amnesties should be individualized and granted only to individuals who were either younger than age eighteen at the time of the crime or who did not violate international law and cooperated fully with the TRC; and the creation of follow-up bodies, namely the Independent National Human Rights Commission to ensure the implementation of TRC recommendations and the Peace and Reconciliation Commission to promote reconciliation around the country. The commission's final report repeated these suggestions and named fifty individuals, including Sirleaf, who should be banned from public office.

Trials

As of mid-2009, perpetrators of human rights violations in Liberia have avoided punishment for their crimes. In May 2012, Charles Taylor was convicted for crimes committed in Sierra Leone. On June 4, 2003, Taylor was indicted by the Special Court for Sierra Leone (SCSL) on seventeen counts of war crimes committed in support of the RUF (the SCSL later decided to concentrate on only eleven counts). On March 17, 2006, President Johnson-Sirleaf formally asked Nigeria to turn Taylor over to the SCSL, which it did on March 29. Taylor entered a formal not guilty plea on April 4, 2006. On June 16, 2006, the UN Security Council issued Resolution 1688, which authorized Taylor's transfer to The Hague, where he would be tried in the International Criminal Court's facilities. The trial formally began on June 4, 2007. Almost immediately, the trial was postponed until January 7, 2008 because several procedural issues. The prosecution rested its case on February 27, 2009 and the defense case was scheduled to begin in mid-July 2009.

Taylor's son also has been put on trial outside of Liberia for human rights violations. On December 6, 2006, Chucky Taylor was indicted by a U.S. federal grand jury in Miami for torture and conspiracy to torture, the first time anyone had been charged under the U.S. Federal Extraterritorial Torture Statute. Under his father's regime, Taylor had headed Liberia's Anti Terrorist Unit, which terrorized the population between 1999 and 2003. In October 2008, Chucky Taylor was found guilty. He received a ninety-seven-year sentence in January 2009.

The relationship between the TRC and prosecution remains a subject of ongoing discussion and controversy within Liberia. As the TRC began its work in 2006, a group calling itself the Forum for the Establishment of a War Crimes Court issued a series of statements condemning the TRC as a travesty of justice because it did not provide for the punishment of those responsible for the violence. The public, at least initially, also supported prosecution. A late 2004 survey by the Transitional Justice Working Group found that nearly 60 percent of respondents supported prosecuting the leaders of the warring factions. By contrast, President Johnson-Sirleaf and the TRC repeatedly asserted that the country has selected the option of truth and reconciliation and that there was no interest in prosecuting Charles Taylor in Liberia. The Liberian government and foreign governments believed that trials would threaten the peace process. The TRC also said that it opposed arresting Taylor's associates. TRC Chairman Jerome Verdier expressed concern that ex-combatants are avoiding the TRC out of fear that their testimony would be used in subsequent trials. For his part, Charles Taylor's lawyers have used Liberian courts to attempt to prohibit the TRC from hearing testimony regarding his alleged crimes on the grounds that Taylor was not present to defend himself and that the TRC's proceedings could prejudice his trial at The Hague.

As it conducted hearings and heard testimony around the country, however, the TRC changed its position on prosecutions. Its December 2008 preliminary report urged prosecutions, as did the June 2009 Virginia Declaration. The recommendation to establish a special court and to use Palava hut forums was intended to expedite prosecutions and recognize that the national justice system was severely damaged by the war. In Liberia, there is a shortage of personnel, many of whom fled the country or were killed. Resources and infrastructure are lacking. As a result, the TRC's view on trials is now more aligned with many civil society groups and religious organizations. Liberian politicians, by contrast, have not warmed to the proposal. They argue, for example, that a special court would lack jurisdiction over foreign fighters, who played a significant role in atrocities committed during the civil war. The argument is also self-serving as several politicians are alleged perpetrators.

Vetting Procedures

The Accra Peace Agreement also contained provisions for restructuring Liberia's police and military. Of the two, police reform has been more challenging. The agreement established a vetting procedure to screen individuals in the police force for alleged human rights violations during the civil war. Applicants' names were checked against lists of names of individuals accused of human rights abuses, which were maintained by UNMIL and the SCSL. If they passed this hurdle, applicants' names were posted for public notice to allow anyone to come forward with accusations. Overall, the system has worked imperfectly. Human Rights Watch criticized the vetting process for its limited resources, a lack of clear criteria for making judgments, and a failure to adequately engage the public. The U.S. government, through a private contractor, managed the restructuring of the military. Unlike the police, the national army was fully demobilized after the peace accord so there has been less continuity in personnel. As a result, vetting of the army has been somewhat more successful.

Conclusion

Liberia's transitional justice experience remains a work in progress. It remains to be seen what sort of long-term impact the TRC will have in Liberian society. It has been very transparent about what its final recommendations will be. The fate of its recommendations and their impact on society will be dependent on the political climate. The government's willingness to undertake a reparations program, even if it does not involve cash payments, is unclear. To date, foreign donors have displayed a willingness to contribute funds for memorial projects. Prosecutions, however, have prompted the most concern from politicians and civil society groups. Given the perceived stakes involved, the government will approach it with great delicacy, if at all.

Eric Wiebelhaus-Brahm

Cross-References: Court Trials for Redress; Sierra Leone; Special Court for Sierra Leone; Truth and Reconciliation Commission of Liberia.

Further Readings

Amnesty International. 2007. *Liberia: Time for Truth, Justice and Reparation for Liberia's Victims*. AI Index: AFR 34/001/2007. Available at: http://www.amnesty.org/en/library/info/AFR34/001/2007/en (accessed June 25, 2009).

Ellis, S. D. K. 1999. *The Mask of Anarchy: The Destruction of Liberia and the Religious Dimensions of an African Civil War*. New York: New York University Press.

Human Rights Watch. 2005. *Liberia at a Crossroads: Human Rights Challenges for the New Government*. September 30. Available at: http://www.hrw.org/en/reports/2005/09/30/liberia-crossroads (accessed June 25, 2009).

———. 2002. *Back to the Brink: War Crimes by Liberian Government and Rebels*. May. Available at: http://www.hrw.org/legacy/reports/2002/liberia/ (accessed November 7, 2009).

Liberian Truth and Reconciliation Commission. *Final Report*. Available at: https://www.trcofliberia.org/reports/final (accessed November 7, 2009).

Liberian Truth and Reconciliation Commission. Official Web site. Available at: https://www.trcofliberia.org/ (accessed November 7, 2009).

Liberian Truth and Reconciliation Commission Diaspora Project. 2009. *A House with Two Rooms: Final Report of the Truth and Reconciliation Commission of Liberia Diaspora Project*. Available at: http://www.theadvocatesforhumanrights.org/Final_Report.html (accessed October 27, 2009).

Lithuania

Since proclaiming its independence from the Soviet Union in 1990, Lithuania has followed the policy of "a thick dividing line" (*riebaus brūkšnio politika*) regarding the crimes committed during the Nazi and Soviet periods. This phrase, coined by the Lithuanian historian and politician Arvydas Anušauskas, accurately describes the fact that both society and government have tried to distance themselves from the past. Nevertheless, unlike most other postcommunist states, the term "genocide" has been used to describe the political repression and deportations carried out under Soviet leader Joseph Stalin in 1940–1941 and 1944–1953.

Despite powerful rhetoric and extensive memory work (creating monuments, marking the places of resistance, and publicly honoring the victims), juridical transitional justice (lustration and trials) has been very slow and largely ineffective because of the lack of reliable evidence and the strength of the former communist leaders in postcommunist politics. Lithuania's democratization allowed many reformers from the previous oppressive regime to maintain their political influence by changing their political orientation, but they have been unwilling to allow trials and other more stringent forms of transitional justice.

The Repressive Past

Lithuania's first Soviet occupation (1940–1941) was marked by the nationalization of private property, mass deportations, and political repression. The country's occupation by Nazi Germany (1941–1944) was equally cruel, and 90 percent of Lithuania's Jewish community perished during World War II. The second Soviet occupation (started in 1944) was marked by nationalization, the forced creation of collective farms, mass deportations, and political repression, which continued until Stalin's death in 1953. After the war, a strong armed resistance movement against the Soviet authorities emerged, but was eventually quashed. Many of its members and their families were primary targets for deportation and political repression.

During 1940–1941 and 1944–1952, Lithuania lost 780,922 people. At least 132,000 of its residents were deported to remote areas of the Soviet Union, including Siberia and Kazakhstan, and another 150,000 were sent to Soviet prison camps (the Gulag). The losses experienced during 1940–1953 amounted to 33 percent of the country's population in 1940. Post-Soviet Lithuania has described the massive losses and political repression experienced under Stalin as genocide, although, according to extant documents, deportations and political repression were not carried out according to ethnic criteria. This repression aimed to eliminate the "anti-Soviet elements" and speed up the collectivization of agriculture.

The Soviet secret police – the People's Commissariat for Internal Affairs (Narodnyy Komissariat Vnutrennikh Del, or the NKVD), later known as the Committee for State Security (Komitet gosudarstvennoy bezopasnosti, or the KGB) – played an important role in Sovietization, a process that aimed to subdue anti-Soviet resistance and create a Soviet nation. In 1940–1941, the NKVD targeted army officers, policemen, secret agents, government employees, and factory owners of independent Lithuania, and their relatives (labeled enemies of the state), who were threatened, intimidated, tortured, and/or deported. In 1944–1953, the Soviet security services resumed their activities, expanding the list of the enemies of the state to include those resisting Sovietization and collectivization, and used cruel methods like public humiliation and leaving the dead bodies of tortured victims in public squares for relatives and the general public to see them.

The Soviet regime extensively employed intimidation and terror even after 1953 in order to maintain its control over the republic's social and political life and to suppress dissident, anti-Soviet, and nationalist activities. In 1961, there were 1,181 KGB agents in Lithuania, a number that remained roughly unchanged until the early 1970s, when the political police started to target specific groups of people, including those with relatives (and contacts) abroad or engaged in dissident activities. During the 1970s and the 1980s, the KGB moved away from using terror and physical brutality, but expanded its surveillance activities. For example, in 1971 it kept secret files on 525,000 Lithuanian residents who corresponded with people abroad.

The Lithuanian Soviet regime was challenged by resistance, including the rise of the "folklore movement" (students and intelligentsia singing folk songs and studying history and pagan religions) and influential *samizdat* illegal publications like *The Chronicle of the Lithuanian Catholic Church* (Lietuvos Bažnyčios Kronika). In addition, the Final Act of the Conference for Security and Cooperation in Europe, signed in 1975 in Helsinki, inspired dissident activities closely scrutinized by the KGB. In the early 1980s, many dissidents were tried in Soviet courts and jailed. Nevertheless, after Soviet leader Mikhail Gorbachev introduced *glasnost* (openness) in 1987, dissident groups like Lietuvos Laisvės Lyga (the Lithuanian Freedom League) commemorated the victims of Stalinist deportations and political repression and challenged the official Soviet history.

Transitional Justice

Given the number and severity of Nazi and Soviet crimes and the fact that many victims were still alive and politically active, the independent Lithuania was unable to "forgive and forget." Even Sąjūdis, the movement that helped the republic declare its independence from the Soviet Union, took its name from a partisan resistance movement that was active after World War II. Commemoration of the Nazi and Soviet atrocities was at the heart of numerous public demonstrations in the late 1980s and early 1990s, when Sajūdis was active. The slogans during demonstrations explicitly demanded transitional justice by claiming that "KGB=SS" (that is, the Soviet political police was equivalent to the Schutzstaffel, the Nazi praetorian guard centrally responsible for perpetrating the Holocaust) or asking for "Freedom for Political Prisoners" and the condemnation of the Molotov-Ribbentrop Pact between Nazi Germany and the Soviet Union, which assigned the Baltic states to the latter in 1939. These demonstrations aimed to encourage Lithuania to confront its repressive past. This process has included the use of restitution, rehabilitation, lustration, and criminal adjudication.

Restitution and Rehabilitation

After independence, the Lithuanian government produced legislation to return property nationalized during Soviet times to the rightful owners or their descendants. If restitution was impossible, compensation was awarded in the form of assets, land, or money. Legal and practical difficulties plagued the restitution process, including lack of documentation and competing claims to the same property. Because of historical reasons related to the change in the country's borders (Poland occupied eastern Lithuania in 1920–1939) and the destruction or loss of reliable documentation, property restitution has been especially slow in eastern Lithuania, home to the country's Polish minority. Tensions have also related to communally owned property. The Restitution Act I-283/1990 on the Status of the Catholic Church in Lithuania mentioned the return of religious property, not of nonreligious communally owned property. The Jewish community (re-registered in 1991) has faced challenges related to the return of its property, including religious artifacts, because of the difficulty of proving its relationship to the many prewar Jewish communities. In addition, there have been competing claims made by several Jewish religious communities, both in Lithuania and abroad.

Many cultural artifacts and other valuables were taken out of Lithuania during the Soviet period. In 1992, a referendum demanded that Russia, as the successor to the Soviet Union, provide compensation for the damage caused by the Soviet occupation. However, compensation was not made, as Russian legislation prohibits the return of any items seized by the Red Army during World War II to their previous owners (see entry on Russia).

Following Law VIII-342/1997 on the Legal Status of Persons Who Suffered from the Occupations in 1939–1990 (revised in 2007), the full scale of the damage wrought by the occupying regimes is still unknown. The law described victims of the Nazi and Soviet regimes as political prisoners, deportees, and forced migrants (expellees), and mandated the Genocide and Resistance Research Center of Lithuania (see separate entry) to conduct research aimed at helping former victims claim such legal status and the accompanying social services.

Founded in 1993, the Center is a successor to the Commission for Research into Stalinist Crimes, a volunteer organization that sought to record the names of the former deportees and political prisoners. This name recording launched the restoration of the historical truth, which was important for former anti-Soviet resistance fighters, who were the primary targets of deportations, but demonized during Soviet times as "enemies of the state." Rehabilitation started in the early 1990s, when the identification of victims of the Soviet regime coincided with international organizations' investigation of Lithuanian Holocaust perpetrators. Responding to the international pressure, Lithuanian authorities then blocked the rehabilitation of several hundred individuals accused of perpetrating war crimes and crimes against humanity. The Special Investigations Division of the Prosecutor General's Office was established in 1991 to reexamine and overturn "all other unfounded and unjustified decisions" on rehabilitation made during the early 1990s. This process proved difficult, given the lack of reliable information. In 2004, the Prosecutor's General's Office initiated only three requests to revoke rehabilitation.

Lustration

Attempts to pursue lustration started immediately after independence. A resolution adopted by the Supreme Council (the Soviet Lithuanian legislature) in March 1990 deemed cooperation with the KGB and its agents an activity that hurt the interests of independent Lithuania and promised that collaborators who ended their relationship with the KGB and committed no serious crimes would face no moral, legal, or other consequences. In August 1991, the Supreme Council formed the Temporary Commission to Investigate KGB Activities to find out whether former KGB operatives were still employed in key government institutions. Law I-2166/1991 on the Security and Spy Agencies banned former collaborators with foreign secret services like the KGB from being employed in Lithuanian private and public institutions.

The law proved difficult to implement, and thus there was no full-scale lustration. Since 1990, when right-wing parties like the Homeland Union (Tėvynės Sąjunga) won elections, lustration and reckoning with the Soviet past have been revived, while leftist political parties have been less critical of the Soviet past. There was interest in lustration in 1991–1992 (when right-wing leader Vytautas Landsbergis chaired the Supreme Council) and a slowdown in 1993–1996 (when leftist parties formed the government). When center-right parties won parliamentary elections in 1996, transitional justice intensified, and partial lustration took place in 1998–1999, when some former KGB collaborators acknowledged their past.

Lustration is hampered by lack of reliable documentation on 90 percent of the former KGB agents (many files were destroyed or removed from Lithuania before 1991). This lacuna raises the question of whether lustration can be morally justified and fair. Law VIII-1436/1999 on the Registration and Acknowledgment ("confession") of Those Who Secretly Collaborated with the Soviet Special Services asked former KGB collaborators to acknowledge their past within six months of the law's publication (by June 8, 2000) to a five-member Lustration Commission, whose members were appointed by the Prosecutor General's Office, the Genocide and Resistance Research Center, and the State Security Department. This led to 1,500 "confessions," coming from former KGB operatives or persons who merely came in contact with the KGB. The Lustration Commission, which also identifies and publicly announces the names of former KGB operatives who refuse to voluntarily confess their past, has struggled to carry out its mandate because of a lack of resources (its staff is unpaid) and political support (from the leftist parties that won the 2000 elections). In 2010, the Commission had 200 files left to examine. The Commission is scheduled to be disbanded in 2012.

Law VIII-1436/1999 banned former KGB operatives from working for the Lithuanian national and local government, educational institutions, banks, "strategic businesses" (in communications), and private intelligence and security companies for ten years, unless they "confessed" their activities. As "confession" meant forgiveness, 1,589 former agents acknowledged their association with the KGB. In the so-called reservists scandal of 2005, three leading politicians were accused of having served as former KGB agents. An investigative parliamentary commission created to explore their past concluded that belonging to the KGB reserve did not constitute full and conscious collaboration with the KGB because membership in the KGB reserve was equivalent to being drafted in the Soviet military. (Those drafted into the KGB reserve were trained to conduct intelligence activities. They had certificates showing that they were members of the military, but the special code indicated that they were part of the KGB reserve. Unlike active-duty KGB operatives, they were not engaged in gathering intelligence; they were merely prepared for similar activities.) The commission recommended that the investigation of former KGB collaborators be pursued further and that lists of collaborators be made public. Parliament ignored these recommendations.

In June 2010, parliament amended Law VIII-1436/1999, which prevented former KGB agents from working in private businesses and industries related to national security. Following a European Human Rights Court ruling, it eliminated restrictions on former KGB agents working in the private sphere. Former KGB agents who did not reveal their identities and did not "confess" were banned from important leadership positions in the government, including those appointed by parliament, the president, the prime minister, and the cabinet of ministers. Restrictions applied only to agents identified as such by the Lustration Commission. Given the lack of reliable data and the difficulty of establishing cooperation with the KGB in the courts, the Lustration Commission has been unable to prove to the courts that people accused of collaboration with the KGB were in fact agents. Although in some cases the Commission obtained the case number demonstrating collaboration with the KGB, the courts deemed this evidence inconclusive.

There is little public interest in lustration, but the Lithuanian Union of Political Prisoners and Former Deportees, which includes about 40,000 members, and well-known dissidents like Nijolė Sadūnaitė recently received public attention as defendants in a defamation trial. The plaintiff, Algis Klimaitis, accused the Union of insulting him by openly referring to him as the KGB agent code-named Kliugeris. In 2006, the Lustration Commission, drawing on archival documents, determined that Klimaitis had cooperated with the KGB, but Klimaitis appealed the verdict, arguing that he was not a "real" KGB agent because he was not aware that he was listed in the KGB documents. This trial shows the weakness of the Lustration Commission, which has been unable to work with the courts in presenting the collected evidence and convincing the courts that it is valid.

Court Trials

As many documents were destroyed and many victims, perpetrators, and witnesses are dead, it has been almost impossible to conduct fair trials concerning atrocities committed during the twentieth century. Lack of political will also explains the limited impact of trials related to the Soviet "genocide" and the Holocaust.

Law I-2477/1992 on Responsibility for the Genocide of the Residents of Lithuania mandated the prosecution of those responsible for committing crimes against humanity on the territory of Lithuania. The Prosecutor's Office alone has the right to conduct investigations into the grave crimes committed during the Soviet and Nazi occupations. The law made the Genocide and Resistance Research Center responsible for gathering evidence relevant to such trials.

It is estimated that more than 50,000 people were responsible for the Soviet genocide in Lithuania (Anušauskas 1996), but in 1990–1998, only one criminal case related to that genocide reached the Lithuanian courts. In 1990–2009, 237 pretrial cases related to Soviet-era crimes against humanity and war crimes were initiated. However, about one-third of these cases were thrown out because the perpetrators were dead and/or it was difficult to gather reliable evidence. Only twenty-five pretrial cases reached the courts, and thirty-seven people were charged. Many of them were seriously ill and could not face trial, and others died during the process.

The international community, including the Simon Wiesenthal Center (see separate entry), has repeatedly reprimanded the Lithuanian government's slow progress on Holocaust-related cases. In 2008, there were twenty-two pretrial cases related to the Holocaust. Between 1990 and 2008, the Lithuanian courts heard nineteen Holocaust-related criminal cases in which ten people were found guilty (five of them died during the trial). The Prosecutor's Office has argued that many Lithuanian citizens who participated in the Holocaust were tried by the Soviet Union shortly after World War II for war crimes and crimes against humanity, and that repeated trials of such individuals are prohibited by international and Lithuanian law. The trials of individuals accused of crimes against humanity tended to be widely publicized and were often accompanied by many acrimonious debates over how and whether to punish the perpetrators. The trial and conviction of Stalin-era torturers Kiril Kurakin, Petras Bartasevičius, and Juozas Šakalys are a case in point. The three men, who were in their late seventies, received sentences from three to six years for crimes committed while serving in the NKVD. The sentences were reduced because of their poor health. The old age and poor health of the accused also complicate trials of people accused of committing crimes against humanity during the Holocaust.

Given the many difficulties associated with such trials, symbolic measures such as commemorations of victims of political repression and deportation and educational programs developed by institutions such as the Genocide and Resistance Centre and the International Commission for the Evaluation of the Crimes of the Nazi and the Soviet Occupation Regimes in Lithuania (see separate entry) have gained importance. In June 2000, frustrated by the state's inability to effect transitional justice, former political prisoners and deportees organized "The Anti-Communist Congress and Tribunal" to evaluate the crimes of communism, condemn the Soviet ideology, and prove that the "communist doctrine is criminal." It included a staged trial, complete with charges presented by the victims, statements by the prosecution, evidence supplied by the victims, witness testimony, and staged speeches by the defense. This attempt to denounce communism (as an ideology and a political system) as criminal received recognition from the Lithuanian Right. Leftist politicians ignored the event.

Gaining more international visibility for communist-era crimes has become one of Lithuania's main foreign policy goals after accession to the European Union. Together with Polish, Latvian, and Estonian policy makers, Lithuanian politicians tried to draw attention of the European institutions to the World War II experience of the "other"

Europe. Landsbergis, a Lithuanian representative in the European Parliament, was unable to gain support for the ban of communist symbols. However, some recognition has been obtained. On May 9, 2005, the European Commission's Europe Day Commission Declaration 49/05 made reference to the suffering of those "for whom World War II was not the end of dictatorship." That year, the European Parliament Resolution, "The Future of Europe Sixty Years after the Second World War," acknowledged the suffering in communist Europe.

The International Commission for the Evaluation of the Crimes of the Nazi and Soviet Occupation Regimes in Lithuania

The International Commission (see separate entry), founded in September 1998 by President Valdas Adamkus to establish the truth about the Nazi (1941–1944) and the Soviet (1940–1941 and 1944–1990) occupations, promotes international cooperation among historians and nongovernmental organizations interested in memory, advises government officials on historical issues, and develops projects related to education and civil society building.

Presidential Decree 159/1998 outlined the Commission's mission. According to the Commission Web site, its search for the historical truth will help address moral and psychological barriers that hinder the creation of a democratic society. Its mandate reflects the belief that international actors can significantly impact democratization and transitional justice. So far, the Commission has been unable to find a common voice with which to interpret the past, partly because its members embrace competing perspectives on the past.

The Commission helped establish sixty-six tolerance education centers targeting pre-university students and teachers, prepared educational materials for the centers, provided training for secondary school teachers, and helped commemorate Nazi and Soviet victims. Its Tolerance Education Program opens avenues for international cooperation because it embraces new approaches to Holocaust education. This agenda is supported by international actors like the United States Holocaust Memorial Museum and Yad Vashem Holocaust History Museum (see separate entries).

Conclusion

Postcommunist Lithuanian attempts to address the wrongs of the past have yielded few tangible results. Lustration has been incomplete and inconsistent, while criminal trials of those who committed crimes during the Soviet and Nazi regimes have been few. Thorny historical legacies have impeded other legal processes. The slow and inefficient restitution of property owned by Lithuanian Jews before World War II, the lack of progress in addressing cases related to crimes against humanity, and competing victimhoods related to the Nazi and the Soviet regimes (for example, some view the use of the term "genocide" to describe the crimes of the Soviet regime as relativization of the Holocaust) have fueled tensions between actors interested in the restoration of historical truth. The internationalization of several transitional justice processes (such as addressing the legacies of both the Soviet and Nazi totalitarian regimes) has led to the creation of an international commission focused on education about the past, and intense public debates which have helped consolidate democracy and create an open society.

Dovilė Budrytė

Cross-references: Genocide and Resistance Research Centre of Lithuania; International Commission for the Evaluation of the Crimes of the Nazi and the Soviet Occupation Regimes in Lithuania; Lustration; Reparations; Restitution of Property; Simon Wiesenthal Center; United States Holocaust Memorial Museum; Yad Vashem Holocaust History Museum.

Further Readings

Anušauskas, Arvydas. 1996. *Lietuviu tautos sovietinis naikinimas 1940–1958 metais* [The Destruction of the Lithuanian Nation by the Soviets, 1940–1958]. Vilnius: Mintis.
———. 2008. *KGB Lietuvoje: Slaptosios veiklos bruožai* [The KGB in Lithuania: Various Aspects of Its Secret Activities]. Vilnius: Spaudos praktika.
Budryte, Dovile. 2005. *Taming Nationalism? Political Community Building in the Post-Soviet Baltic States.* Aldershot: Ashgate.
Jaskovska, Eva, and John P. Moran. 2004. Justice or Politics? Criminal, Civil and Political Adjudication in the Newly Independent Baltic States. *Journal of Communist Studies and Transitional Politics,* 22(4): 485–506.
Kuti, Csongor. 2009. *Post-Communist Restitution and the Rule of Law.* Budapest: Central European University Press.

Montenegro

Since its declaration of independence on June 3, 2006, Montenegrin transitional justice has been hesitant and ambivalent. The country at first seemed unwilling to truly address its complicity in the crimes committed during the communist period and the subsequent Yugoslav wars of the 1990s (see entry on Serbia). However, substantive efforts taken in 2009 suggest that the authorities in Podgorica, the country's capital, are finally prepared to address past crimes.

The Repressive Past

The Socialist Federative Republic of Yugoslavia (1945–1992) resulted from World War II and the vicious multisided civil war of 1941–1945, reaching a high level of ferocity in Montenegro. In 1941–1945, the countryside was subjected to Red Terror, orchestrated by the antifascist, communist Partizan commanders Arso Jovanovic and Mose Pijade. Partizan mass graves were established throughout Montenegro. Possibly 55,000 Montenegrins out of a prewar population of 400,000 died during the Red Terror and the concomitant Serbian ultranationalist Chetnik and German reprisals.

Perhaps the utter devastation of Montenegro during the civil war, especially of its urban intelligentsia, explains why the country was spared the worst of the post-1945 "settling of accounts," the efforts of the ruling Communist Party to punish Nazi perpetrators and collaborators. In the spring of 1945, surviving Montenegrin Chetnik units attempting to flee to Slovenia were largely destroyed by the Partisans. One thousand Montenegrin "community organizers," notably high-school teachers and university professors, were "liquidated" in high-profile show trials conducted by People's Courts of the wartime communist secret political police, the Organization for the People's Defense. Immediately after 1945, the communists confiscated and nationalized church lands, industrial plants, and urban dwellings.

A second period of repression occurred after 1948, following Yugoslav communist leader Josip Broz Tito's break with Joseph Stalin. Precipitated by the arrest and execution of prominent Montenegrin Partisan General Arso Jovanovic, Tito instituted sweeping purges that targeted the "Pan-Slavist" tendencies within the Communist Party of Yugoslavia, including Montenegro. Some 12,000 out of 60,000 party members killed at this time were Montenegrin. Eighty percent of them were subjected to party "administrative procedures" and sent to one of twelve penal colonies, where many prisoners died because of harsh living and working conditions. Military tribunals and People's Courts summarily executed the remaining 20 percent of purged party members.

Tito instituted another purge after 1954, when chief ideologue Milovan Djilas broke with the Yugoslav regime over economic policy. These purges were relatively mild compared to the events of 1945 and 1948, being primarily directed at Montenegrin cultural figures. Although the Yugoslav State Security Administration, the communist secret political police (UDBa) under Yugoslav Interior Minister Aleksandar Rankovic, maintained a tight grip over the country, the 1950s witnessed relative liberalization. Pressure for reform gained momentum after the fall of Rankovic in 1966, with reform movements taking place within the Croatian and Serbian Leagues of Communists. There was no comparable reformist tendency within the Montenegrin League by the time Tito ushered in a new period of repression following his crackdown on the reform movements after 1971.

In the regime's last two decades, the federal Service for State Security (SDB, successor to the UDBa) and military intelligence (KOS) closely monitored subversive threats putatively orchestrated by émigré groups in the West, while the republic-level SDB monitored society for "internal threats" posed by cultural dissidents, ultranationalists, and nonconformists. The regime's surveillance activities were greatly facilitated by Article 173 of the 1974 Constitution, which mandated citizens to report any "hostile activities" to the authorities.

After Tito's death in 1981, the Serbian League of Communists implicitly encouraged and co-opted nationalist movements in Serbia, Montenegro, and Kosovo as a response to centrifugal forces, notably Albanian and Croatian nationalism. Growing nationalism and the federal leadership's failure to fashion an effective response ultimately led to the violent disintegration of the country in the Yugoslav wars of 1991–1999. Although no fighting took place and very few war crimes or crimes against humanity were committed on Montenegrin soil, the Montenegrin elites were apparently complicit in the irredentist and annexationist designs of Serbian President Slobodan Milosevic, and supported Milosevic's "Anti-Bureaucratic Revolution" of the late 1980s, which stripped the Serbian provinces of Kosovo and Vojvodina of their autonomy. Montenegrin hard-liners may also have envisioned a Greater Montenegro incorporating the towns of Dubrovnik and Konavle in Croatia, which in 1180–1389 belonged to the medieval Serbian province of Zeta, predecessor to modern Montenegro.

On April 27, 1992, Serbia and Montenegro reconstituted the Yugoslav Federation. Although reformists in the League of Montenegrin Communists (renamed the Democratic Party of Socialists in 1991) broke with Milosevic after 1997, initiating a slow process culminating in the country's independence in 2006, there are many unresolved issues dating from the Yugoslav wars. Since 2006, the country has adopted an extremely hesitant attitude to transitional justice, partly because of the need to consolidate a new constitutional settlement after independence. Elites seem reluctant to address many issues arising from the country's past.

Transitional Justice

Despite recently adopted legislation, Montenegrin transitional justice remains incipient. It is far too early to assess the effectiveness of many of the inchoate mechanisms instituted to date and the level of political commitment to address the past. The country has been a laggard in lustration and restitution/compensation but a Balkan pioneer in promoting truth revelation through comprehensive freedom-of-information legislation, including access to secret police files. War crimes trials, begun in 2009, will further test Montenegro's determination in pursuing transitional justice.

Restitution and Reparations

Under the Yugoslav Law 52/1996 on the Rights of Civilian War Invalids, victims of human rights abuses are denied the right to compensation unless they can satisfy extremely narrow criteria. A victim is defined as a person who has "suffered from the enemy during the war, who has sustained injuries in conducting war operations, who has been hurt by ammunition leftovers or by enemy subversive or terrorist actions." The extremely rigorous burden of proof required to establish victim status, which excludes crimes committed by non-state actors, such as paramilitaries, or state agents in the absence of a formal declaration of war, as well as Montenegrin jurists' very selective choices regarding evidence allowed to be introduced, effectively precludes judicial redress for abuses suffered at the hands of UDBa or SDB between 1945 and 1992 and seriously limits cases dating from the Yugoslav wars.

In one high-profile case, the government awarded compensation to the families of Bosniaks who were forcibly "repatriated" in 1992 to the Republika Srpska, where they were executed. In civil proceedings brought by the victims' families between 2000 and 2008, in twenty-five of thirty-eight first instances decisions, the independent Montenegrin state was found responsible and ordered to provide compensation. Upon appeal, these lower court decisions were overturned by the Constitutional Court (subject to an appeal ruling from the Supreme Court). In December 2008, the government agreed to grant compensation to nine families. This political decision was prompted by a desire to buttress the regime's human rights credentials in its accession negotiations with the European Union. In the absence of rigorous war crimes legislation, most victims have very little recourse to judicial redress and instead must try to deal with the Ministry of Justice on an ad hoc basis.

Podgorica has been much more proactive in addressing the issue of compensation for communist-era forced expropriation of private property. Restitution Law 01–458 of 23 March 2004 provided for restitution in kind, where possible, with cash compensation or substitution of other state land when physical return is not possible. Its primary purpose was to facilitate the privatization of state-owned assets pursuant to the Ownership Transformation Act 51 of 1994. Separate legislation on property confiscated from religious communities was also envisaged, but its implementation stalled because of a lack of political will and administrative inertia.

The Restitution Law was severely criticized. Claims had to be filed with the municipal restitution commission where the property is located within eighteen months of the commissions' establishment. These commissions have been accused of political bias and lack of independence. The lack of a systemic registry of pre-1945 landownership raises the possibility of capricious decisions. And there has been very little progress on the issue of compensation for the seizure of church lands, especially those of the Serbian Orthodox Patriarchate.

Lustration and Vetting of Public Officials

At this writing, a draft bill remains before the Parliamentary Committee for the Political System, Judiciary, and Administration. Diplomats do not believe that Speaker Ranko Krivokapic (representing the government) will permit the draft legislation to make it out of committee stage. Montenegro's current lustration efforts are likely to be even less successful than measures taken during the late Yugoslav era.

If enacted, Law 58/2003 on Accountability for Human Rights Violations would have made Serbia and Montenegro pioneers in vetting in the former Yugoslavia. It allowed a nine-member parliamentary commission to examine individual responsibility for human rights abuses, as opposed to party or organizational culpability, retroactive to 1976, the year when Yugoslavia ratified the International Covenant on Civil and Political Rights. Officials to be vetted included the president, prime minister, members of parliament, municipal politicians, judges, prosecutors, university rectors, the governor and vice-governor of the National Bank, private bank directors, military officers, and tax administrators. Although parliament elected its members, the commission never started functioning because of a lack of funding and personnel support.

The law was seemingly adopted to placate the international community. While Montenegro's governing Coalition for European Montenegro (headed by the Democratic Party of Socialists, the DPS) did not block the passage of the law, it was at best tepid toward it. Upon adoption, the law was never implemented by the Montenegrin government. The current draft law before parliament, introduced by two small opposition parties, incorporates many features of the earlier, unenforced Serbian law. At this writing, this bill remains stalled in parliament.

The failure of successive Montenegrin governments to address lustration clearly shows the political dynamics that have blocked the country's transitional justice efforts after the Yugoslav wars. Montenegro, like Slovenia and Slovakia, has been characterized by a remarkable lack of political and administrative elite turnover. The governing DPS ruled the country prior to 1989 as the League of Montenegrin Communists. Consequently, they have a vested interest in obstructing legislative proposals that conceivably could screen them out of office. The main opposition party, the Socialist People's Party of Montenegro, which split from DPS in 1997 over the question of links with Serbia, shares many of the government's reservations about lustration. Both parties represent similar constituencies that would have the most to lose from any meaningful lustration provisions. Since independence, the two parties have formed a de facto partnership to block any attempts at screening public officials.

Smaller parties have been divided on the issue. The Liberal Party and the Movement for Democratic Change introduced the legislation to the Committee for the Political System, Judiciary, and Administration, but have received very little support. The New Serbian Democracy party, representing Montenegro's Serb minority, is hostile to the proposed bill, while DPS's coalition partners, the Croatian Civil Initiative and the Party of Bosniaks, oppose it in exchange for other concessions. The Democratic Union of Albanians, the Albanian List, and the Albanian Coalition have been at best lukewarm toward the draft bill.

Various factors at the elite and societal level explain the systematic opposition toward lustration. Elites with strong ties to the former regime are unlikely to condemn it. They also maintain that Montenegro was only tangentially involved in the crimes of the Milosevic and Tito regimes and that their post-conflict priority must be reconstruction, not transitional justice.

There is also very little public engagement with the legacy of Montenegro's Yugoslav history. A few nongovernmental organizations have unsuccessfully tried to place the country's past excesses on the public agenda. Investigative journalism, especially the reports of the human rights activist Aleksandar Zekovic, has also brought alleged war crimes to light.

Access to Secret Police Files

In contrast to its ambivalent approach to lustration and compensation, the government has been a regional pioneer in allowing its citizens access to communist-era secret police files. In 2005, Montenegro became the first former Yugoslav republic to pass a Freedom of Information Act (Act 69/2005) and an Access to Secret Files Act (Act 77/2005). Under Article 3 of Act 69/2005, all public information, including secret police files, is subject to disclosures, with narrow exceptions on the grounds of "harm to individuals" or "public interest." These exceptions do not apply if disclosure reveals the misuse of power, criminal offenses, or egregious misadministration. Act 77/2005 permits citizens to personally review any files maintained on them after 1945 under the classification "internal enemy." The National Security Agency must answer requests within two weeks. Denials of access can be appealed to the Administrative Court. Final authorization for the release of files resides, in theory, with an independent and impartial judiciary, and not the public service.

This legislation built on Presidential Decree 15/2001, permitting citizens to review secret political police files under the classification "internal enemy." Although an important milestone toward greater openness and transparency, the decree lacked the force of parliamentary legislation, and bureaucratic decisions were not subject to judicial review. Subsequent legislation, drafted and guided through parliament by Deputy Prime Minister and Interior Minister Dragan Djurovic, addressed its deficiencies and omissions by providing for judicial review and parliamentary oversight of the new agency responsible for the communist-era secret police files.

Despite the provision for judicial review, in addition to subsequent reforms of the judiciary, serious lacunae continue to undermine the effectiveness of the legislation. As no law on official secrets defines the nature or the categorization of these secrets, everything may be marked as a state secret. Under Article 18 of the Law 01–457-2/2005 on the National Security Agency, state secrets are not disclosed if such disclosure could "endanger implementation of Agency activities or risk the security of another person." Also, citizens have no way to ascertain whether the secret police maintained additional files on them under a different category, whether their names were contained in files on other people, or whether files including them existed under collective titles (political parties, nongovernmental organizations, etc.) or certain events. The National Security Agency's internal decree addressing these issues has not been published in the *Official Gazette* as of the time of this writing. Established in March 2005 as a state authority autonomous from the Interior Ministry, the Agency is responsible for the Yugoslav-era secret political police files. The Parliamentary Committee for Security and Defense monitors its budget and activities.

In 2002–2007, 90 of the 327 requests to review secret police files were approved. In half of the other cases, authorities stated that no files existed. This process clearly reflected another problem dating from the Yugoslav era: the civil service's excessive secrecy and opacity. Both the Law 45/2001 on Civil Service and the Law 60/2003 on General Administrative Procedure impose mandatory obligations on civil servants to secrecy and confidentiality, allow public servants to vet file disclosure requests on grounds of unspecified "national security" and "harm to individuals," and necessitate internal reviews of applications. The courts have yet to reconcile the contradiction between internal civil service codes and Act 77/2005.

Truth Commission

The government has shown very little enthusiasm for establishing a Montenegrin truth commission to assess the country's past, especially the Yugoslav wars. Montenegrin authorities have always maintained that such a truth revelation endeavor can only succeed if implemented at a regional, not national, level. They plausibly argue that there is a lack of will in other formerly Yugoslav states, notably Serbia, to enact comprehensive legislation pertaining to secret police files, a necessary prerequisite for a truth commission to function properly.

The fate of the short-lived Truth and Reconciliation Commission of Serbia and Montenegro (see separate entry) suggests that Podgorica's concerns are valid. This body was decreed by President Kostunica in March 2001, without any prior parliamentary or public debate. Its mandate was narrowly restricted to tracing the causes of the war and not its effects (completely disregarding the communist past). Investigating authority to identify war crimes and human rights abuses, including subpoena power over secret police files, was explicitly denied. The Montenegrin government viewed the Commission as a Serbian public relations exercise. Considering that none of its nineteen members were Montenegrin, these concerns seemed valid. The Commission was disbanded in early 2003, after achieving nothing of importance.

Court Trials

Prior to 2009, only a single war-crimes trial (dealing with the Yugoslav wars of the 1990s) took place in Montenegrin courts, involving the high-profile trial, conviction, and sentencing of Nebojsa Ranisavljevic for the 1992 abduction and murder of nineteen Muslim civilians in Bosnia-Herzegovina. Montenegro's delayed record of court trials is explained by the need to redesign its judicial system after declaring independence. The country's legal transitional justice framework is codified in recent laws passed by the Montenegro Parliament and, more problematically, the Yugoslav-era Federal Assembly. This latter corpus of laws, which still provides the foundation for Montenegrin jurisprudence, is subject to review by the Constitutional Court to ensure its compatibility with the 2007 constitution. Many Yugoslav-era laws have been modified to harmonize them with the constitution or, in some cases, struck down.

Since independence, Montenegrin authorities have proactively implemented comprehensive reforms of the judiciary and the Office of the Supreme State Prosecutor. Law 22/2008 on the Amendments of the Law of Courts established two special chambers for the processing of cases related to organized crime, terrorism, and war crimes within the High Courts of Podgorica and Bijelo Polje. In conjunction with Law 69/2003 on the State Prosecutor of Montenegro, which strengthened this office's independence, the Montenegrin judiciary was given more robust tools with which to pursue four cases of alleged war crimes.

Recently these war crimes investigations came closer to resolution. On November 27, 2009, the trial of six policeman, including Deputy Interior Minister Miroslav Markovic, commenced in the High Court of Podgorica over the alleged deportations of eighty-three Bosniak refugees in May 1992 near Herzeg Novi. The trial is an explicit acknowledgment by the government that serious crimes were possibly perpetrated in the name of the state. In August 2009, four former Montenegrin reservists of the Yugoslav National Army (JNA) were indicted and arrested for the torture and inhumane treatment of 169 Croatian civilians and prisoners of war at the Morinj prison camp in 1991–1992. Seven Montenegrin JNA reservists were indicted and arrested for the murder of twenty-three Kosovars near Rozaje in April 1999. Investigations continue into alleged crimes against humanity committed by seven Montenegrin soldiers and policeman in 1999 in the Bukovica region, where twenty-four of thirty-nine villages were ethnically cleansed and thousands were forced to flee. Allegedly, seven civilians were killed and seventy-four tortured by the security personnel under investigation. On May 15, 2010, the High Court of Bijelo Polje sentenced the defendants in the Morinj to prison sentences ranging from fourteen months to four years.

These trials will show if Montenegrin courts can prosecute alleged war criminals. The prosecutors' ability to access top secret files from the National Security Agency remains a concern. During the Herzeg Novi investigations, Supreme State Prosecutor Vesna Medenica frequently filed grievances with the Administrative Court over access to documents. The presiding judges may come under political pressure to avoid embarrassing the government. These concerns are especially salient in the Herzeg Novi trial. The defendants are expected to try to introduce a signed order from then republican police minister, General Pavle Bulatovic, that instructed his subordinates to "arrest Muslims between the age of seven and seventy and to hand them over to the Republika Srpska authorities" (Amnesty International, 2008). If authenticated and allowed into evidence, this documentation would raise the sensitive issue of command responsibility, including the role, if any, played by Montenegro's senior military and political leaders, including Prime Minister Milo Djukanovic.

Despite serious obstacles facing successful war crimes prosecutions, these trials represent Montenegro's best attempt to address its past and should complement the ongoing trials at the International Criminal Tribunal for the Former Yugoslavia (ICTY; see separate entry). The domestic prosecutions are intended to punish those responsible for war crimes and crimes against humanity and establish a historical record. It is hoped that successful prosecutions of the high-profile defendants in the Herzeg Novi trials can mitigate Montenegro's "culture of impunity" (Amnesty International 2008).

Conclusion

Montenegro remains relatively untested in its approach and political commitment to transitional justice. Since the end of the Kosovo War in 1999, the country has been preoccupied with achieving its independence and, subsequently, post-Yugoslav consolidation and reconstruction, not post-transitional justice. There has also been very little societal or elite engagement to address the darker aspects of Montenegro's communist and postcommunist wartime past. The current war crimes trials and the courts' willingness to enforce access to secret police files will indicate if Podgorica is prepared to substantively address this past.

J. Robert Nicholson

Cross-references: Access to Secret Files; Court Trials for Redress; International Criminal Tribunal for the Former Yugoslavia; Lustration; Serbia; Truth and Reconciliation Commission of Serbia and Montenegro.

Further Readings

Amnesty International. 2008. *Report, 2009*. New York: Amnesty International.
Aucoin, Louis and Babbitt, Eileen. 2006. *Transitional Justice: Assessment Survey of Conditions in the Former Yugoslavia*. Belgrade: United Nations Development Program.
Cohen, Lenard. 2001. *Serpent in the Bosom: The Rise and Fall of Slobodan Milosevic*. Boulder: Westview Press.
Humanitarian Law Center. 2007. *Transitional Justice in Post-Yugoslav Countries – 2008 Report*. Belgrade: Humanitarian Law Centre.
Organization for Security and Cooperation in Europe. 2010. *Factsheet of the OSCE Mission to Montenegro*. Podgorica: OSCE.

Morocco

King Hassan II (1961–1999) was a brutal dictator who subjected thousands of Moroccans considered a threat to his regime to arbitrary arrest, torture, and enforced disappearance. Since the early 1990s, a gradual process of dealing with the past has taken place, culminating in 2004 with the creation of the Moroccan Equity and Reconciliation Commission (Instance Équité et Réconciliation, IER; see separate entry), which is the first truth commission in the Arab world. The IER, established by King Mohammed VI to examine the crimes committed under the rule of his own father, has investigated some of the worst abuses in Morocco and provided reparations for victims and their families.

The Repressive Past

Until the twentieth century, Morocco was ruled by the Alawi monarchy, whose claim to be the direct descendants of Prophet Muhammad made them both the temporal and spiritual rulers of the country. From 1912 to 1956, the country was a protectorate of France (in the south) and Spain (in the north), but in 1956 it regained its independence and the monarchy was restored. The country is a constitutional monarchy, with political power concentrated in the royal palace and limited powers retained by an elected parliament. Although stable and tolerant of minorities, Morocco remains very poor, with high rates of unemployment and low levels of literacy.

The period of widespread repression, known as the "years of lead" (*les années de plomb*), began shortly after the country gained its independence from France in 1956. Violence was rooted in the struggle for independence that spawned regional revolts and two major political parties. To eliminate opposition, regions that had joined in the anticolonial struggle were subsequently subjected to severe crackdowns under the first post-independence ruler, King Mohammed V. Among these regions was the Northern Rif, whose 1958 revolt was brutally crushed by the Royal Armed Forces, resulting in thousands of deaths.

Hassan II inherited the throne in 1961 and consolidated his power through a combination of rewards (land grants, business deals, and well-paid government positions offered to his political rivals) and punishments (against dissenters, including Marxists, trade unionists, intellectuals, farmers, and Islamists). During the 1960s and 1970s, which saw the worst abuses, the left-leaning National Union of Popular Forces Party (UNFP) suffered the brunt of persecution. Its leader, Mehdi Ben Barka, was forced into exile in France and later forcibly disappeared in Paris in 1965. The two unsuccessful attempted coups d'état of 1970–1971 provoked wide-scale arrests, military trials, and executions of those suspected of involvement. In 1973, fifty-eight members of the armed forces who received prison sentences in connection with the coup d'état were transferred to the Tazmamert secret detention center, known for its brutal conditions. The trials did not observe due process standards. Punishment was meted out broadly, sometimes drawing in family members who were imprisoned together for decades at a time.

The Sahrawis of the Western Sahara, a former Spanish colony, were also targeted for repression. An armed conflict between the government and the local armed group, Popular Front for the Liberation of Saguia el-Hamra and Rio de Oro (the Polisario Front), erupted when in 1979 Morocco annexed the region, which had been jointly administered by Morocco and Mauritania since 1975. During the 1980s, many Sahrawis who opposed Moroccan control of the region were disappeared, detained or tortured. An UN-sponsored cease-fire was instituted in 1991, but the region has continued to experience violence and human rights abuses. The Moroccan establishment still refuses to acknowledge the crimes perpetrated against the Sahrawis, and this silence has made dealing with crimes problematic. Considered a high security threat, access to the region is strictly controlled, hampering investigations into abuses.

Morocco's "years of lead" were characterized by a wide variety of abuses. Approximately 50,000 people were victims of violations that ranged from arbitrary detention and torture to extrajudicial execution and forced disappearances. Survivors of torture in Moroccan prisons have written autobiographical accounts of captivity in dark and cramped cells deep within secret detention facilities. The total number of disappearances is estimated between 1,000 and 2,000 victims. The fate of hundreds of disappeared persons remains unknown.

The use of secret detention centers was widespread during the "years of lead." Derb Moulay Cherif was a secret detention center in Casablanca used mostly for political prisoners, secret trials, and torture. In Tazmamert, a secret prison built for those implicated in the coup attempts of 1971–1972 with the apparent goal to exterminate the inmates, fifty-eight officers were sentenced to anywhere from three years to life. Dar al-Mokri was the most notorious of eleven private villas in Rabat, where political prisoners were sent after spending time in detention centers. Qal'at M'gouna held Sahrawi and Moroccan prisoners who, in many cases, were later forcibly disappeared. Agdz was used primarily to hold Sahrawis from 1977 to 1983.

In the late 1980s, human rights violations abated in Morocco because of the end of the Cold War and the publication of victims' testimonials and Amnesty International reports detailing the secret human rights violations and life in the secret prisons whose existence King Hassan II had consistently denied. In 1991, in response to these developments, the king released more than 330 "disappeared" persons, some of whom had been imprisoned for up to eighteen years. The release helped break the silence around claims of abuse, provided a rare glimpse into Morocco's secret detention centers, and encouraged the families of other disappeared to harbor hopes for their return.

Transitional Justice

Since 1990, Morocco has established several institutions with transitional justice responsibilities, but has yet to prosecute perpetrators, remove them from public positions, and provide a formal apology to victims on behalf of the state for its role in violations.

The Human Rights Advisory Council

In 1990, King Hassan II established a Human Rights Advisory Council (Conseil Consultatif des Droits de l'Homme) to advise him on matters concerning human rights. In the Council's inaugural speech, the king talked about the need for truth and reconciliation, but made it clear that he would not tolerate open criticism of the state or himself. The Council amended the Code of Criminal Procedure provisions dealing with incommunicado detention periods, limited the terms of all police custody procedures, created a functional bail system, and helped legislate the right to counsel. After the king asked it in 1998 to examine pending cases of disappearances and to clear them, the Council identified only 112 cases of missing persons who it labeled "repentants" or "disappeared" – a much lower number than that documented by local and international human rights organizations. Of the 112 persons identified, 56 were declared dead, 12 were declared alive, and 44 had "unknown fates." The list included neither Sahrawis nor details on those declared dead. The Council asked the king to create a committee to further investigate the cases, to publish the findings of the investigation, and to provide families with death certificates.

Two independent human rights organizations, the Moroccan Association for Human Rights (AMDH), established in 1979, and the Moroccan Organization for Human Rights (OMDH), established in 1989, became prominent public voices. In 1993, a Ministry for Human Rights was established, and steps were taken to integrate former "enemies" of the state into the public administration. Long-exiled human rights defender, Abderrahmane al-Youssoufi, was appointed as prime minister.

The Independent Arbitration Panel

In April 1999, the Council recommended to the king that he establish a body to compensate victims of past human rights violations. The king approved this request just two weeks before his death in July 1999. Upon assuming the throne, King Mohammed VI acknowledged state responsibility for disappearances, took steps to break with the repressive elements of the past, fired the feared Interior Minister Driss Basri, and appointed an Independent Arbitration Panel to determine the levels of compensation for cases of arbitrary detention and enforced disappearance between 1956 and 1999. The Panel comprised three Supreme Court justices (one of whom served as Panel chair), four Council members, one Interior Ministry representative, and one Justice Ministry representative. The Panel operated under the auspices of the Council.

The Panel, which worked between 1999 and 2003, accepted 5,127 applications between September 1 and December 31, 1999. The 6,000 applications received after the December 31, 1999 deadline were not considered. In total, 8,000 people testified at 196 general hearings and nearly 400 individual hearings. The Panel rendered 5,488 judgments: 3,681 applications were successful; 889 were rejected (because they were not related to forced disappearance or arbitrary detention); 750 were remitted for future deliberation; and 133 were deemed to lack sufficient evidence. For the successful cases, the Panel awarded US$100 million. The awards ranged from US$600 to US$300,000.

The Panel acknowledged the state's responsibility for human rights abuses and provided substantial compensation to victims and families, but was also criticized for the disparity in the amounts of individual awards and the lack of transparency in explaining the criteria used for determining awards. Another criticism related to the fact that awards were proportionate to a person's income at the time of the violation. Victims who were high-income earners received larger compensation awards than those who were not, even when the crimes they suffered were equivalent. The Panel failed to satisfy the families' requests for death certificates, the return of bodily remains, mental and physical health care, and an official acknowledgment of abuse by the state. The Panel did not investigate extrajudicial executions, accepted applications during a very short time period, undertook no investigation of individual or institutional responsibilities for past violations, and did not include the public in its work. Despite these criticisms, it set an important regional precedent in the area of reparations for state-sponsored human rights violations, and paved the way for the activity of the IER.

The Equity and Reconciliation Commission (IER)

The king inaugurated the Commission on January 7, 2004 in Agadir. The IER comprised a president and sixteen members appointed by the King upon the Council's recommendation. Nine were Council members, including the president. The IER included several former political prisoners and torture survivors, again including the president. Although the IER staff included many women in key positions, the IER had only one female commissioner. At the height of its activities, the IER employed 200 staff working in various capacities.

On April 10, 2004, a royal decree approved the IER's mandate. The IER investigated violations committed during the period starting with independence in 1956 and ending with the date of the inception of the Arbitration Panel in 1999. It was to establish the truth about past violations, provide reparations to victims and families, and recommend measures aimed at preventing future abuses. These objectives sought to redress criticisms raised against the Arbitration Panel. Instead of adopting a narrow view of reparations, the decree recognized reparations as comprising "medical and psychological re-adaptation, social integration, settlement of administrative, legal, and professional problems, and restitution of property" (Article 9). The IER could investigate cases unresolved or unaddressed by the Panel. The Commission was to situate past violations in historical context, contrast them to the values of human rights and democracy, determine the responsibility of state organs, clarify specific incidents by gathering forensic and factual evidence about unsolved cases, and recommend measures to preserve memory and guarantee the non-repetition of the violations. The mandate prohibited the publication of findings of individual responsibility as part of the truth-seeking process, but allowed the Commission to establish "the nature and amplitude of the violations" within its remit.

Violations under investigation included only enforced disappearances and cases of arbitrary detention committed by state agents or individuals acting on behalf of the state, but the IER recognized that those crimes may entail the violation of the rights to life, liberty, and judicial protection. The mandate defined the crimes of enforced disappearance and arbitrary detention as systematic manifestations of the government's brutality against its people, not simply incidents of individual excess. The IER investigated violations committed throughout Morocco, including the Western Sahara, and encouraged Moroccans forced into exile during the "years of lead" to submit information about their cases. The IER lacked subpoena or search-and-seizure powers. Still, public officials had the legal obligation to cooperate with all its requests for information and evidence, as the IER's mandate had been approved by royal decree.

On January 12, 2004, commissioners announced they would accept applications for compensation from victims for one month. By February 12, the IER had received 13,000 submissions, which were added to the thousands of unexamined applications submitted to the Arbitration Panel. The one-month deadline was not enforced for unresolved cases of disappearance. In early 2005, the reparations working group presented a comprehensive analysis and proposal to the IER plenary that comprised individual, collective, material, and symbolic forms of reparation, including the conversion of former detention centers into homes for the poor and cultural centers. In September 2005, the outline of its proposed national reparations program was presented in a National Forum attended by hundreds of state and non-state representatives, including many victim groups and human rights organizations.

The IER took statements from thousands of victims and families, conducted in-depth investigations into many complex or unresolved cases, and traveled to more than thirty districts throughout the country. It clarified many cases of missing persons, categorizing them as enforced disappearances, deaths in prison, or deaths in the context of a riot or conflict. The Commission also organized televised national forums on prison literature, state violence, and the importance of truth and reconciliation, and prepared twenty studies on constitutional human rights protections, security sector reform, and the promotion of democratic values and practices.

The Commission's most visible work was the seven public hearings it organized for victims in regions known for relatively high levels of past repression. Commissioners envisioned the hearings as an educational tool that could help restore victims' dignity. All public hearings were widely attended, in some cases by senior advisers to the king, government ministers, opposition party leaders, diplomats, international press, and representatives of human rights organizations. Some hearings were broadcast live on Moroccan television and radio.

The IER was criticized for unwillingness to co-opt human rights organizations, inability to compel testimony from perpetrators, and its limited mandate that fell short of full truth and accountability. The fact that the IER president and half of the other commissioners retained their positions with the Advisory Council diminished the IER's independence. The IER, however, represents the most comprehensive investigation of violations ever undertaken in Morocco. It compiled a massive and detailed database on victims, violations, and perpetrators (including an archive of more than 22,000 personal testimonies from victims and their families), and created a broad definition of possible reparations for victims, ranging from monetary awards to economic, social, and institutional remedies. The IER submitted its final report to the king in late 2005.

Since then, substantial progress has been registered in implementing the IRE's recommendations. By 2010, some 9,000 victims received a combined US$85 million in individual compensations. The Advisory Council signed agreements with ministries and official agencies to provide victims and their families with state-sponsored medical care and vocational training, and in 2008 launched a program to manage and fund communal reparations in eleven regions. The IER's legal and institutional reform recommendations were not implemented.

Conclusion

Morocco has adopted a number of transitional justice methods in order to confront the human rights violations of the "years of lead," including the first truth commission ever created in an Arab country and a generous, if contested, program of reparations for a significant number of victims. However, additional steps should be taken to confront the legacy of mass abuse. Court proceedings, truth-telling initiatives, official apologies, and institutional and legal reforms could be used to address the legacy of the past, achieve national reconciliation, and build a culture of human rights.

Lavinia Stan

Cross-references: Equity and Reconciliation Commission.

Further Readings

Hazan, Pierre. 2008. The Nature of Sanctions: The Case of Morocco's Equity and Reconciliation Commission. *International Review of the Red Cross*, 90: 399–407.

Opgenhaffen, Veerle and Mark Freeman. 2005. *Transitional Justice in Morocco: A Progress Report*. New York: International Center for Transitional Justice. Available at: http://www.ictj.org/images/content/1/9/197.pdf (accessed February 5, 2011).

Mozambique

The civil war of 1976–1992 pitted the ruling communist party, Liberation Front of Mozambique (Frente de Libertação de Moçambique, FRELIMO), against the rebel movement, Mozambican National Resistance (Resistência Nacional Moçambicana, RENAMO). As, after the conflict, the two belligerent parties opted to reject accountability through transitional justice, the FRELIMO government unconditionally amnestied crimes committed during the civil war. However, survivors living in central Mozambique, the epicenter of the strife, claimed that civil war–related spirits compelled them to revisit the past in community courts in order to settle accounts with their former torturers. These popular experiences produced meaningful transitional justice processes that undermined attempts by the central Mozambican government to sustain a culture of impunity for civil war crimes.

The Violent Past

Both before and after gaining its independence from Portugal on June 25, 1975, Mozambique experienced a series of prolonged wars. From 1964 to 1974, the country faced an anticolonial war between the nationalist and revolutionary liberation movement, FRELIMO, and the Portuguese colonial regime. During this war, the colonial forces perpetrated numerous war crimes throughout the country, while FRELIMO persecuted and killed a number of Mozambican dissidents. After ten years of anticolonial war, Mozambique attained independence shortly after the Carnation Revolution unfolded in Portugal in April 1974. FRELIMO formed the first postcolonial government and imposed one-party rule. By offering shelter and support to other African independence movements, the new Mozambican state became the target of the white-dominated governments of neighboring Rhodesia and South Africa. As such, in 1976 Mozambique was invaded by the Rhodesian Army, which committed serious crimes, including the notorious Inhazonia massacre of August 1976 in the central province of Manica. Rhodesia also provided military support to the armed rebel movement RENAMO.

The Rhodesian invasion marked the beginning of the protracted civil war between the FRELIMO government and the RENAMO rebels. Seen as one of the most viciously destructive wars during the mid-1980s in Africa, it created an overwhelming humanitarian disaster. The war engulfed the entire country and also involved foreign troops from Apartheid South Africa, Rhodesia, and Zimbabwe, as well as military instructors from the Soviet Union, Cuba, and the United Kingdom. Both FRELIMO and RENAMO perpetrated serious human rights violations and crimes. As each belligerent party considered the civilians living under territories controlled by their military rivals as supporters of the enemy, these civilians were made direct targets of the violence, which included village destruction, aerial bombardments, forced conscription, torture, mutilation, indiscriminate killings of those suspected of collaborating with "enemy forces," kidnapping and rape of young girls and adult women, compulsory marriages, forced starvation, and death by landmines. Severe drought brought extreme famine, resulting in a massive exodus and many deaths. It is estimated that during the civil war, 1 million people died and 4 million took refuge in neighboring countries.

In the midst of this grave man-made and natural humanitarian disaster, soldiers, militias, and *mujibas* (the RENAMO para-police forces) instigated deep divisions in communities within the war zones. Neighbors and relatives became suspicious of each other, spied on each other, and engaged in acts of betrayal, torture, and murder.

By the late 1980s, the impossibility of a military resolution to the war was evident. To boost peace prospects, in 1990, the FRELIMO government passed a new constitution introducing a multiparty system, cultural and religious pluralism, and economic liberalization. From 1990 to 1992, the government and RENAMO undertook peace negotiations brokered by national and international mediators (mainly Christian religious groups) in Rome, Italy. Negotiations aimed "to get a focus on what unites and rule out what divides" the belligerent parties (Igreja 2008, p. 544). Accountability through transitional justice was perceived as divisive and was thus precluded from negotiations. On October 4, 1992, the FRELIMO and RENAMO leaders signed the General Peace Agreement. Ten days later, the FRELIMO government passed Amnesty Law 15/1992 on crimes committed between 1979 and 1992.

While it prevented the indictment of human rights perpetrators and made it impossible for them to be brought before the courts, the amnesty law did not end the struggle to determine responsibility for the violent past. In their participation as members of the Mozambican Parliament, FRELIMO and RENAMO have demonstrated their irreconcilable views about the origins of the civil war and used the memories of the war to accuse each other of serious crimes. As a result of these memory wars, the parliamentary members of RENAMO have made appeals for the creation of a truth and reconciliation commission similar to that of South Africa. However, the FRELIMO party has dismissed these calls. Outside the national parliament, among urban civil society groups there is not much debate about the deployment of transitional justice mechanisms to address the legacies of the civil war. But civil war survivors of violence have continued their quest for justice.

Transitional Justice

The Amnesty Law and FRELIMO's political dominance severely restricted Mozambique's transitional justice. The country launched no court trials against perpetrators of war crimes and created no truth commission. In the years immediately following the civil war, the political and civil society elites did not engage in serious debates about how to settle accounts with the perpetrators of serious human rights violations and war crimes. Because both FRELIMO and RENAMO had been involved in the perpetration of serious abuses and crimes, neither won the civil war, and their interpretations of the origins of the war were strikingly different, there was a tacit consensus that it was better to "leave the past alone" (Hayner 2001, p. 183). Priority was given to forward-looking approaches focusing on politico-legal reforms and investment in the country's socioeconomic development. The few opinions expressed by urban civil society leaders suggested that it was too difficult to conduct fair trials or to establish an effective truth commission because the civil war had affected the entire country, had involved so many categories of national and international perpetrators, and the crimes were too numerous to count. Revisiting the past might have triggered new cycles of vengeful violence at the community level. It was also believed that local cultural beliefs and practices could offer legitimate and peaceful means to heal the wounds and divisions caused by the war. Thus, the government opted for nonjudicial methods like official commemorations and reparations, whereas survivors developed their own justice processes to settle accounts for wartime crimes on the basis of their own cultural beliefs and practices.

Commemoration

In 2002, ten years after the end of the civil war, the FRELIMO government acknowledged October 4, the date when the General Peace Agreement was signed, as an official public holiday to commemorate peace and reconciliation (through Law 12/2002 of 30 April

2002). The law did not mention the suffering of the victims of the civil war, but this gesture was politically meaningful as it acknowledged the significance of the war and paved the way for the legal recognition of reparation to benefit a certain category of civil war survivors.

Reparations

The new Mozambican Constitution of 16 November 2004 stated that "the State secures special protection for those that became handicapped during the armed conflict that terminated with the signature of the General Peace Agreement in 1992, as well as for the orphans and other direct relatives" (Article 16.1). The basic law did not specify how exactly state institutions would grant this right or war survivors benefit from it. This has proved problematic, the more so given that no specific reparations law has been passed to date.

Law 2/1995 created the parliamentary standing Commission of Petitions by virtue of Article 80 of the 1990 Constitution and Article 79 of the 2004 Constitution, which reads that "every citizen has the right to present petitions and complaints to the competent authority to demand the reestablishment of his violated rights or in defense of the general interest." According to Law 2/1996, which regulates the right to present petitions and complaints to competent authorities, the Commission of Petitions accepts petitions submitted by any Mozambican whose rights were violated by state authorities or private institutions. The law does not mention the right for reparations for civil war victims, but in the few cases in which rulings were made, state institutions were ordered to grant reparations for losses incurred during the civil war.

The commission is formed of fifteen deputies (ten of them representing the FRELIMO and five the RENAMO-Electoral Union Coalition). The eligibility criteria for petitioning is to have experienced injustices as a result of state or non-state administrative acts or a failure of the state or non-state agents to act according to the legally stipulated administrative procedures. The Commission does not offer reparations but can recommend that state or private institutions responsible for human rights violations repair the damages incurred by Mozambican citizens. According to Law 2/1996, the failure to act according to the rulings or recommendations of the Commission of Petitions is considered a crime of disobedience punishable by the courts.

Since its creation in 1996, the Commission of Petitions has received around 1,000 complaints mostly concerning work-related violations or injustices perpetrated by state officials or private sector managers. Only very few cases were related to losses incurred as a result of the civil war. In 2003, four individuals demanded reparations for the trucks they had ceded, through an agreement, to the Mozambican National Defense Forces during the civil war. The trucks were burned and destroyed during military ambush, but the owners were never compensated by the state for the loss. Petitions were submitted to the Commission of Petitions and the Defense Ministry was summoned to provide clarification on the cases. The Commission concluded that the Ministry had failed to fulfill its obligations as stated in the wartime agreement and should therefore repair these wartime damages. The Defense Minister promised to pay the reparation of the trucks. This case illustrates transitional justice through reparation, but the limited amount of reparations for wartime losses was given in the absence of a Law on Reparations. In its ruling, the Commission was less concerned with deciding the appropriate level of war damages than with recognizing that the state had failed to fulfill its contractual obligations with these four citizens.

Community-Driven Transitional Justice

The most systematic and well-documented community-driven transitional justice processes have taken place in rural central Mozambique. In the Gorongosa region, residents claimed that the spirits of the soldiers who died in the war (*gamba*) broke the prevailing silence and compelled survivors to settle accounts with past crimes as a precondition for pacifying and reconciling the community. The perceived interventions of the *gamba* spirits reaffirmed the local ethic of reciprocity, which holds that conflicts stemming from serious injuries leading to death continue unless redressed via legitimate community-level institutions such as traditional healers and the traditional courts. As impunity profoundly disturbs community life, the living and the spirits must seek resolution. Because the cultural identity of the Gorongosa people is communitarian (not individualistic), responsibility and guilt for serious violations are also collective. As such, the *gamba* is understood to strike the family of the perpetrators. *Paza* healers, who are specialists in unveiling secret facts, and traditional (community) courts settle the conflicts triggered by the *gamba* spirits. The *paza* healers and traditional courts are both old local institutions that have existed since precolonial times.

Prevalent in rural areas, the community courts apply local cultural norms and state laws. Until the end of the civil war, these courts adjudicated minor cases concerning family and community issues or nonpublic crimes, but since 1992 they have also heard some cases involving serious abuses and crimes committed during the civil war. The 1992 Amnesty Law prohibits state and community courts from adjudicating war crimes, so when community court judges hear cases related to wartime crimes, they usually do not encourage an active resolution of the case. Thus, the judges safeguard the interests of the central government by observing the amnesty law and dissuading the plaintiffs' quest for justice. The judges recommend reconciliation between the parties without seriously investigating the civil war events – in other words, reconciliation without comprehensive truth telling. The use of the amnesty law by community courts has deterred war survivors from approaching these courts, and explains the very small number of cases brought before community courts to date. Yet when wartime violations involve the presence of *gamba* spirits, judges launch hearings because these unsolved cases can create severe family and social conflicts and instability. The *gamba* spirits take primacy over the amnesty law and compel judges to adjudicate wartime conflicts by allowing comprehensive hearings and conducting serious investigations to fully disclose wartime crimes; in essence, community court judges have chosen to disregard the law and hear the cases.

According to Law 4/1992 on Community Courts, the courts can only hand down reparations in the form of financial compensation, material goods, or social work, not prison sentences. The courts can compel the accused to appear in court. Failure on the part of the accused to act accordingly results in the case's referral to the state courts, which can then issue orders of imprisonment. Judges of community courts do not refer conflicts involving *gamba* spirits to state courts because the former have no culturally trained judges able to correctly handle such complex cases. These cases are solved only at the community level. Although community courts are established throughout the country, they have been involved in the adjudication of serious wartime crimes almost exclusively in central Mozambique. These investigations and the public unveiling of wartime crimes in community courts are incrementally restorative for the families directly involved and for the community at large.

In 2001–2008, ten cases involving twenty-five alleged perpetrators (living and dead) were presented to community courts in Gorongosa. The cases related to serious wartime abuses and crimes: false denunciations to belligerent armies resulting in severe physical and psychological damage, rapes and forced marriages, illegal imprisonments in non-state prisons, torture, and assassinations. The alleged perpetrators collaborated with the community court judges in order to reach a resolution, although such resolution takes place outside state institutions. If the alleged perpetrator is dead, the living kin members assume responsibility to resolve the conflict. These resolutions break the postwar silence and impunity and facilitate local-level individual and collective truth telling and social reconciliation. The resolutions receive no media attention because they take place in remote locations of the former war zones and, as such, the media and urban elites are not aware that such struggles against war-related impunity take place.

Trials presented to community courts follow a traditional model of procedural and restorative justice. Kin and community members participate in the proceedings, and the audience is sometimes invited to intervene to provide further insight into disputes. Sometimes judges enlist the support of a *gamba* or a *paza* healer to assess the accusation and determine culpability. But the judges, not the healer, hand down the verdict based on the hearing and according to the solidity of the incriminating evidence. Regardless of how serious the violation, the final resolution always includes financial compensation, material goods, or community service. The winning party can opt for one of these three types of reparations.

Conclusion

The Mozambican government has done little to come to terms with the legacies of its civil war besides instituting a day of commemoration and launching an essentially nonfunctioning legal initiative for reparations. However, in the central regions of the country, local communities, through community courts and *paza* healers, have, in ten cases, been able to mete out justice, punish perpetrators, and grant victims reparations for their sufferings.

In central Mozambique, the local ethic of reciprocity has prevented survivors from forgetting serious wartime disputes. These community-driven efforts to achieve resolution result from the political and legal appropriation of some state laws and a desire for local autonomy from the central government. Some wartime conflicts were resolved by a combination of institutions and agents, with the collaboration of alleged perpetrators, survivors, and *gamba* spirits. Resolution, brought about by community courts or traditional healers, obeys the traditional, local principles of procedural and restorative justice. These processes reflect a struggle against impunity that links transitional justice and local identities and traditions.

Victor Igreja

Cross-references: Accountability Mechanisms; Amnesty; Hybrid Courts; Reparations; Traditional justice.

Further Readings

Hayner, Priscilla. 2001. *Unspeakable Truths: Confronting State Terror and Atrocity*. New York, Routledge.

Igreja, Victor. 2010. Traditional Courts and the Struggle against State Impunity for Civil Wartime Offences in Mozambique. *Journal of African Law*, 54(1): 1–33.

———. 2009. The Politics of Peace, Justice and Healing in Post-war Mozambique. In *Peace versus Justice? The Dilemma of Transitional Justice in Africa*. Eds. Chandra Sriram and Suren Pillay. KwaZulu-Natal: University of Kwa-Zulu Natal Press.

———. 2009. Justice and Reconciliation in the Aftermath of the Civil War in Gorongosa, Mozambique Central. In *Building a Future on Peace and Justice: Studies on Transitional Justice, Peace and Development. The Nuremberg Declaration on Peace and Justice*. Eds. Kai Ambos, Judith Large and Marieke Wierda. Berlin: Springer.

———. 2008. Memories as Weapons: The Politics of Peace and Silence in Post-Civil War Mozambique. *Journal of Southern African Studies*, 34(3): 539–556.

Igreja, Victor and Beatrice Dias-Lambranca. 2008. Restorative Justice and the Role of *Magamba* Spirits in Post-Civil War in Mozambique. In *Traditional Justice and Reconciliation after Violent Conflict: Learning from African Experiences*. Eds. Luc Huyse and Mark Salter. Stockholm: International IDEA.

Namibia

The Republic of Namibia had a tenuous and conflictual colonial past, first under Germany rule, then under apartheid South Africa. Since achieving its independence in 1990, the country has faced intermittent calls to deal comprehensively with its egregious past, which includes the Nama and Herero massacres of 1904–1907 by the Germans and the disappearance of thousands of others during South Africa's occupational rule (1915–1989). The calls for investigations have not left out the liberation movement, which is alleged to have instigated the deaths of Namibians accused of spying for South Africa. Successive governments have repeatedly spurned appeals to systematically look into these past abuses. While some in the Namibian government maintain that investigating the past could threaten the country's stability, many analysts believe that the real reason why the government is reluctant to deal with the past is the fear that such a move would expose the complicity of prominent post-independence government officials in the human rights abuses, especially those perpetrated during the liberation war. While the Constitution of 1990 provides for redress of social, economic, and educational imbalances arising from past discriminatory laws and practices, and appeals for national reconciliation, the country has yet to fully come to terms with its colonial past.

The Repressive Past

Namibia's history of brutal human rights abuses can be traced to the onset of German colonization in 1884. The Germans brought Namibia (then known as German South-West Africa) under their control by entering into Protection Agreements with indigenous communities, especially the Nama and Herero. In return, they were given access to the land of the indigenous communities. Over time, however, the German settlers engaged in arbitrary seizures and started to threaten the traditional ways of life of the indigenous communities. As a result, the Herero and the Nama took up arms against the German settlers. The military conflict that ensued ended up in the massacre by the Germans of about 10,000 Nama (half the population) and 65,000 Hereros (about 80 percent of the population). Many others were imprisoned or driven out of their land into the Kalahari Desert, where they died of mass starvation. Demands for reparations for these violations remain alive in Namibia today.

South Africa, which occupied Namibia in 1915 and administered it as a League of Nations mandate territory from 1919, changed the colony's name to South West Africa and administered it as its fifth province, with Namibia's white minority being represented in the whites-only Parliament of South Africa. The South African government appointed administrators who enjoyed extensive powers in the colony. During this period, Namibia witnessed some of the most atrocious human rights abuses carried out by the South African National Defense Force and its notorious counterinsurgency paramilitary unit called Koevoet (Afrikaans for crowbar), known for torturing civilians to extract information about the activities of the liberation movement, the South West Africa People's Organization (SWAPO), and its military wing, the People's Liberation Army of Namibia (PLAN). Koevoet was largely composed of local Namibian fighters commanded by South African officers. In 1978, the South African army and Koevoet committed many atrocities, including the raid on a SWAPO camp at Cassinga in southern Angola, in which more than 600 people died, and other attacks on SWAPO facilities in and around Chetequera, southern Angola, in which more than 300 Namibians died and hundreds of others were captured. Many other atrocities committed by the South African army and Koevoet have not been comprehensively documented.

During the liberation struggle, SWAPO and PLAN were also accused of human rights abuses and leading a reign of terror against their own members and innocent civilians. The fact that SWAPO was frequently betrayed by local spies and informers (*askaris*) working for the South African regime led to a sense of mistrust exacerbated by ethic alignments and differences over strategies. Some SWAPO leaders often responded overzealously to any suspicions in order to destroy perceived spies within their ranks. Allegedly thousands of people suspected by SWAPO were detained and tortured in camps in Zambia and Angola after the mid-1960s, escalating through the mid-1980s. Such incidents included the Kongwa Crisis that occurred in the 1960s at the Kongwa camp in Tanzania and involved the incarceration of SWAPO cadres who dared to question the SWAPO leadership; and the Shipanga Crisis in the mid-1970s (named after the SWAPO leader Andreas Shipanga), which involved the arrest and transfer from Zambia to Dar es Salaam, Tanzania, of the SWAPO "dissidents" who attempted to create alternative SWAPO leadership after accusing the movement of corruption and unresponsiveness. Their arrest and transfer was carried out by the Zambian army at the behest of SWAPO. Most of them ended up languishing or dying in jail. There was also the SWAPO Spy-Drama of 1983–1985, which included the detention and torture of hundreds of SWAPO members in Angolan prison camps. These episodes have been the focus of recent calls for investigation.

Transitional Justice

Independent Namibian governments, constituted mainly of SWAPO leaders, have done very little to reckon with the past. Lustration was effectively blocked, and a blanket amnesty prevented court trials. However, the government did document names of some of the people who disappeared during the liberation struggle in an official report.

Amnesty and Lack of Lustration

Article 141 of the 1990 Constitution allowed those holding public office on the date of independence to retain their positions in the name of "national reconciliation," thus blocking any lustration attempts (see entry on Lustration). Thus, many supporters of the apartheid regime retained their positions in the post-independence government. This measure allowed elite reproduction, rather than elite replacement, and, from a criminal justice viewpoint, impunity on the part of the former perpetrators, who were not brought to justice.

Many victims and their relatives believe that the government, by allowing perpetrators to escape accountability, has neglected their needs. Civil society groups such as Breaking the Wall of Silence (BWS), the National Society for Human Rights (NSHR), the Legal Assistance Centre (LAC), the Forum of the Future, Citizens for an Accountable and Transparent Society, the Women's Lobby and the Peace Center, and the Council of Churches of Namibia have promoted accountability for past abuses and have provide support to the victims.

Government and Civil Society Truth-Telling Initiatives

After assuming office in 1990, independent Namibia's first President Sam Nujoma, who had been the head of SWAPO and Commander-in-Chief of PLAN during the liberation struggle, declared his commitment to reconciliation as opposed to the pursuit of justice through the courts. The idea of public hearings into past human rights abuses, however, slowly became the subject of open discussions. In 1990, for instance, opposition leader Moses Katjioungua filed a motion in parliament seeking to establish a Judicial Inquiry Commission to probe the question of detainees in SWAPO camps. The motion was opposed by most legislators representing the ruling SWAPO. Then, legislator Vekuii Rukoro (representing the Namibia National Front, NNF) asked the government to invite the International Committee of the Red Cross (ICRC) to look into the issue of those declared missing, given the Committee's previous work and support programs to SWAPO fighters and civilian activists detained by apartheid South Africa. The Namibian parliament passed that proposal in June 1991. The ICRC's final report *Missing Namibians*, released in June 1993, listed 1,700 names of missing and deceased people. The ICRC acknowledged that its report was not comprehensive, because it received no information from SWAPO on what happened within its command structure, and was based only on information received from the governments of South Africa, Namibia, Angola, Zambia, and Botswana. After the report's release, the Namibian government declared that national reconciliation had been achieved, while parliament refused to discuss the report.

The issue of past human rights abuses became the focus of public discussion with the publication in 1994 of *Namibische Passion* (*Namibia: The Wall of Silence*), a book authored by German Reverend Siegfried Groth. The book included accounts of SWAPO abuses based on testimonies of former fighters. The Namibian government reacted strongly to the book's assertions. President Nujoma called it "false history," while other SWAPO leaders questioned the patriotism and loyalty of the book's supporters and labeled them "unpatriotic" "foreign remnants of fascism" who were endangering national reconciliation. To counter the book, the government released *Their Blood Waters Our Freedom*, a title referring to the Namibians who died in the liberation struggle, sacrificing their lives for the sake of independence. The document listed about 8,000 people who died in exile while at the hands of SWAPO and referred to them as "heroes." Former detainees and the National Society for Human Rights (NSHR) maintained that the document had many errors, including what they called falsifications and failure to list many other names of those missing.

Namibia: The Wall of Silence inspired a group of former detainees to establish the Breaking the Wall of Silence (BWS) movement, whose aim was to petition the government and the ruling SWAPO to facilitate discussions on the fate of those who disappeared and assist the survivors, especially those falsely accused of being spies or traitors. Until 2010, the BWS was unable to meet with government officials to discuss the issue of former detainees. Calls for systematic and impartial inquiry into Namibia's past human rights abuses have failed to materialize. While the SWAPO governments have repeatedly asserted that reconciliation has been achieved in Namibia, many Namibians disagree.

Reparations

Demands for reparations have two focal points: the gross human rights violations perpetrated by the Germans against the Herero and Namas people at the beginning of the twentieth century, and the culpability of SWAPO. While the South African Defense Forces were also involved in human rights abuses in Namibia, there have been few demands for reparations directed at them or at South Africa.

Regarding the first focal point, when the German Chancellor Helmut Kohl visited Namibia in September 1995, some 300 Herero tribal members presented a petition demanding symbolic and financial reparations for facing "genocide" at the hands of the German colonizers during the 1904–1907 war. This demand went unanswered. With regard to the second focal point on the culpability of some of the SWAPO leadership, civil society organizations such as the BWS, the NSHR, and the LAC continued to ask for accountability and reparations, but successive SWAPO governments refused to establish a comprehensive program to look into claims of human rights violations within SWAPO ranks and to offer commensurate reparations, fearing that such an initiative would draw attention to SWAPO's culpability. The government, instead, selectively offered nominal compensation only to the war veterans by building houses for some of them and honoring their participation in the liberation struggle. It also passed the War Veterans Subvention Act 16 of 1999 that established the War Veterans Trust Fund and Administration Board to grant subventions to war veterans and dependants of the deceased. The Act was repealed in 2006 with the establishment of the Ministry of Veterans Affairs that was tasked with administering the affairs of the veterans and their dependants. Despite the establishment of this ministry, war veterans have continued to complain about the government's disregard of their demands for compensation and threatened to grab farms, especially those owned by government ministers. Civil society groups have called the government's measures political gimmicks, not genuine reparations.

Refusal to Cooperate with the South African Truth and Reconciliation Commission

In 1997, the South African Truth and Reconciliation Commission (TRC; see separate entry) sought to conduct some of its hearing inside Namibia in regard to abuses committed by the South African army. The Namibian government rejected the request, arguing that Namibia would not emulate the South African example and that the issue of past atrocities in Namibia was a closed wound that the Namibian people would not wish to reopen. However, the real problem for SWAPO was seemingly the dilemma of exposing itself to accusations of human rights abuse.

Excavations of Graves

In 2005, construction workers working on a new sewage-processing plant at Eenhana, close to a former South African military base in Northern Namibia, discovered mass graves suspected to be those of SWAPO fighters killed in April 1989, toward the end of South Africa's occupation of Namibia. Some argued that the existence of these graves was public knowledge. The police were called in and shortly thereafter the Namibian President Hifikepunye Pohamba visited the site and led a tribute to those buried at Eenhana. The graves brought to the fore the question of those who disappeared during the war. Former President Sam Nujoma, the leader of SWAPO at the time when the killings are suspected to have happened, laid responsibility for the mass graves on the South African apartheid regime. In South Africa, General Constand Viljoen, former head of the South African Defense Forces, denied responsibility on the part of the Defense Forces, while General Jannie Geldenhuys, the chief of staff of the South African Defense Forces from 1985 to 1990, promised to help Namibia unravel the truth if he was asked to do so by the South African government. This never happened. In 2008, the Namibian government built a Memorial Shrine at Eenhana in honor those who sacrificed their lives during the liberation struggle.

Reconciliation Attempts

Several government initiatives fit into the reparation and reconciliation agenda, although they were not pursued in an organized and comprehensive manner. These include government initiatives aimed at reintegrating soldiers, providing financial support for war veterans and war orphans, and honoring and commemorating the liberation struggle. As few of them have been directed at victims, it is debatable whether these measures constitute genuine reconciliation efforts. The government has also built houses for war veterans in various parts of the country. The liberation struggle and those who fought for it were honored by erecting memorials and declaring some national holidays, such as Independence Day on March 21, Heroes Day on August 26 to commemorate the Namibian War of Independence, and Cassinga Day on May 4 to remember the South African airborne attack on a SWAPO refugee camp and military base in the Angolan town of Cassinga in 1978. Some of these initiatives have been met with skepticism by human rights organizations that consider them to be politically expedient but not a genuine attempt to mend a fractured past.

Conclusion

Although colonial Germany and South Africa committed untold human rights abuses against Namibians, the question of the detainees and the missing has remained a thorny issue in independent Namibia. The question reflects the conflict between SWAPO's fear of implicating its leadership in human rights violations against innocent Namibians (resulting from efforts to protect the liberation struggle from infiltration by South African agents) and the victims' search for justice. The challenge is to reconcile these competing demands. By resisting calls to comprehensively investigate past crimes, including those committed by the Germans and the South African apartheid regime, the Namibian government has conveniently relegated its own dismal human rights record to the background. While the feeling that Namibia has not yet fully come to terms its past continues to linger inside Namibia, the likelihood of establishing any comprehensive transitional mechanism is, with time, increasingly becoming remote.

Emmanuel Kisiangani

Cross-references: Amnesty; Conspiracy of Silence; Genocide; Lustration; Reintegration of Former Combatants; Reparations; Truth and Reconciliation Commission of South Africa.

Further Readings

Breaking the Wall of Silence Movement. 1997. *Report to the Namibian People: Historical Account of the SWAPO Spy Drama*. Windhoek: BWS.
Christo, Lombard. 2001. The Detainee Issue: An Unresolved Test Case for SWAPO, the Churches and Civil Society. In *Contemporary Namibia. The First Landmarks of a Post-apartheid Society*. Eds. Ingolf Diener and Olivier Graeffe. Windhoek: Gamsberg Macmillan, pp. 161–184.
House of Lords. 1916. German Atrocities and Breaches of the Rules of War in Africa. In *The Sessional Papers of the House of Lords*, vols. 5–6. London: H.M. Stationery Office.
Groth, Siegfried. 1995. *Namibische Passion* [Namibia: The Wall of Silence]. Wuppertal: Peter Hammer Verlag.
International Committee of the Red Cross. 1993. *Missing Namibians: I.C.R.C. Final Report*. Geneva: ICRC.
Maletsky Christof. 2005. Nujoma Lays the Blame at Thatcher's Door. *The Namibian*, November 25.
Oloka-Onyango, Joe. n.d. *The Status of Human Rights Organizations in Sub-Saharan Africa: Namibia*. University of Minnesota, Human Rights Library. Available at: http://www1.umn.edu/humanrts/africa/namibia.htm (accessed September 9, 2010).
Saul, John and Leys Colin, eds. 1995. *Namibia's Liberation Struggle: The Two-Edged Sword*. Athens: Ohio University Press, pp. 40–65.
South West Africa People's Organization. 1996. *Their Blood Waters Our Freedom*. Windhoek: South West Africa People's Organization.

Nepal

The peace process that started in 2006 in Nepal saw a number of commitments to transitional justice, but in the early stages there have been poor institutional and legal developments and limited implementation of these commitments. Despite significant evidence in a number of cases, no members of the security forces or of the Maoists (that is, the Unified Communist Party of Nepal, CPN-M) have been prosecuted to date. Victims or their families have not received compensation. There have not been proper investigations and criminal justice proceedings. Since 2008, transitional justice issues have been secondary concerns as political discourse has focused on the Constituent Assembly elections, which transitioned Nepal from a monarchy to a parliamentary republic, gave an overwhelming victory to the Maoists, and ended the protracted civil war.

The Repressive Past

Contemporary unrest in Nepal began in 1962 when the Panchayat governance system, literally meaning assembly of five wise and respected elders chosen and accepted by the village community, suspended the constitution and banned all parties, leading to the formation of the dissident Jana Andolan (People's Movement) of 1980. In 1990, after months of nationwide strikes, King Birendra allowed a constitution providing for popular sovereignty, multiparty democracy, and basic human rights. Nepal subsequently had twelve unstable elected governments.

Although February 13, 1996 is considered the beginning of the Jana Yuddha (People's War), the insurgency grew from the introduction of democracy in 1990. Governmental inadequacy resulted in corruption and an increasing gap between the dominant elite in Kathmandu and the dependent rural majority outside of the capital. Structural inequality reinforced ethnic and regional cleavages, predisposing people to armed struggle. Many young, disempowered Nepali people approved of the Maoists' agenda: the end of the feudal monarchy, the nationalization of state's resources, and the redistribution of wealth and land. The Maoists gained strength and began by recruiting young people from the remote regions of Nepal.

By 1995, the police increasingly resorted to arbitrary arrests, torture, rape, and extrajudicial killings. Violence escalated and led to an armed insurgency in favor of establishing a republic. The insurgency was supported by various communist formations and the reform-oriented, centrist political formation, the Nepali Congress, formed in exile in India in 1946 with the objective of establishing a constitutional democracy. The regular Nepalese police were reinforced with the paramilitary Armed Police Force. The Royal Nepalese Army was deployed to combat the rebels. These security forces were given additional powers to arrest and detain suspects on preventive detention orders under the Terrorist and Disruptive Activities (Control and Punishment) Ordinance of 2001. The Royal Nepalese Army's involvement did not control the insurgency but it increased the war's lethality for civilians.

In 2001, when most of the Royal Family was assassinated by Crown Prince Dipendra, Prince Gyanendra, who had served as king from 1950 to 1951, was named king. He ended Nepal's brief experiment with democracy and converted the constitutional monarchy into a dictatorship. The Nepalese parliament was dissolved and King Gyanendra assumed all executive powers, including those as supreme commander over the police and armed forces. The brutality of the conflict on both sides escalated and many civilians were caught in the middle, while the People's Liberation Army (PLA), the armed wing of the Maoists, gained control of an estimated 75 percent of the countryside. The ten-year-long internal conflict resulted in the deaths of more than 15,000 people, many of them civilians, and displaced more than 200,000. In 2003–2004, Nepal had the highest number of new cases of disappearances reported to the United Nations. These included thousands of temporary enforced disappearances and abductions, of which 1,000 became permanent. Victims included Maoist guerrillas, supporters, sympathizers, and other marginalized rural people.

In February 2005, a state of emergency was declared and the Royal Nepalese Army took control of all state institutions. Severe restrictions on civil liberties were imposed, including the preventive detentions of thousands of journalists, politicians, and human rights activists. Nepal was isolated by censoring the press, restricting communication, and controlling travel.

As opposition to the king's rule increased, the CPN-M and the Seven Party Alliance (SPA), a coalition seeking an end to autocratic rule in the country, formulated the 12-Point Understanding. The CPN-M and the SPA agreed to establish democracy and end autocratic monarchy; to form an interim government for holding constituent assembly elections; to respect human rights and press freedom; and to investigate past incidents of human rights abuses. Concerted protest against the king's regime culminated in April 2006 with the restoration of parliament. The SPA and CPN-M continued to hold talks that ultimately led to a cease-fire. On November 21, 2006, the Comprehensive Peace Agreement officially ended the insurgency. But the king's regime continued to suppress political and civil rights, including by strictly censoring and restricting the freedom of expression and information, movement, and assembly. In January 2007 the House of Representatives promulgated the Interim Constitution. The interim government, which included the CPN-M, was established in April 2007. Nepal abolished its 240-year-old monarchy in December 2007 and is now the Federal Democratic Republic of Nepal.

Transitional Justice

The commitments made in the Comprehensive Peace Agreement included the establishment of several transitional justice mechanisms. The Agreement called for the following two bodies to address abuses: (1) a Truth and Reconciliation Commission (TRC) to be established in order "to probe into those involved in serious violation of human rights and crime against humanity in course of the armed conflict for creating an atmosphere for reconciliation in the society" (Article 5.2.5); and (2) a National Peace and Rehabilitation Commission "for the normalization of the difficult situation that arise as a result of the armed conflict, maintain peace in the society and run relief and rehabilitation activities for the victims of conflict and those displaced" (Article 5.2.4).

The Comprehensive Peace Agreement contained no details on the mandate of these bodies or guidance on their formation. Three years after the signing of the Agreement, the TRC and the Peace and Rehabilitation Commission have not been formed yet. Additionally, the Agreement stated "both sides agree to make public within 60 days of the signing of the agreement the correct and full names and addresses of the people who 'disappeared' or were killed during the conflict and inform the family members about it" (Article 5.2.3). In July 2007, the government announced the formation of a Commission on Disappearances.

Draft Bill of the Truth and Reconciliation Commission

In July 2007, the Peace and Reconstruction Ministry released the Draft Truth and Reconciliation Commission Act, which allowed the formation of an independent and impartial commission to investigate and make public the facts concerning gross violations of human rights and crimes against humanity committed by both the government and the Maoists between February 13, 1996 and November 21, 2007. The Commission may exercise the same powers as conferred to courts in accordance with existing laws for acquiring information or testimonies, examining witnesses and evidence, and carrying out inspections (Section 16). It is empowered to foster reconciliation between the victim and any individual found responsible by the Commission (Section 23). The Commission may ask the perpetrator to make an apology to the victim for past offenses or recommend government action against the perpetrator.

According to the bill, the Commission will include up to seven members appointed on the recommendation of a committee constituted with consensus of the political parties represented in parliament (Section 4). This raised concerns about the transparency and independence of the Commission. The bill also empowered the Commission to recommend amnesty even for "gross violation of human rights" or "crimes against humanity," if these acts were carried out with the objective of fulfilling the perpetrator's duties, if they had a political motivation, if the perpetrator made an application indicating regret, or if victims and perpetrators agree to a reconciliation process. It is expected that the Maoists and government authorities will be given amnesty on the grounds that both parties were fulfilling public and political duties. The draft states that amnesty will not be provided to any person involved in inhuman and cruel murder, torture, or rape. But the vagueness the terms "inhuman or cruel" allow a wide margin of appreciation for the commission.

The Office of United Nations High Commissioner for Human Rights in Nepal and other international organizations criticized the draft for failing to reflect the 2005 United Nations Basic Principles and Guidelines on the Right to a Remedy and Reparation for Victims of Gross Violations of International Human Rights Law and Serious Violations of International Humanitarian Law. Following extensive criticism, the Peace and Reconstruction Ministry conducted three regional consultations on the TRC draft bill between December 2007 and February 2008. As of the time of this writing, the bill is yet to be passed and the TRC is not yet set up.

Judicial Interventions in Cases of Enforced Disappearances and the High Level Commission of Inquiry on Disappeared Persons

As noted earlier, the United Nations Working Group on Enforced or Involuntary Disappearances reported that in 2003 and 2004, Nepal recorded the highest number of new cases of enforced disappearances in the world. During the conflict and the peace process, families of the disappeared submitted habeas corpus applications. Most of these were immediately dismissed following difficulty in providing significant evidence or denials by the alleged perpetrators.

In August 2006, the Supreme Court established a three-member Detainee Investigation Team to investigate the disappearance of four detainees. The Team recommended criminal charges against perpetrators and compensations to the families of the victims, and asked the government to create new legislation criminalizing abductions and enforced disappearances as well as an investigative commission on disappearances. In November 2008, the government released the Enforced Disappearances (Charge and Punishment) Ordinance, which the Council of Ministers approved shortly afterward. But the bill was found to be deficient by victim groups and human rights organizations. Concerns were expressed over a number of provisions in the bill: the definitions of disappearances were not in line with the International Convention for the Protection of All Persons from Enforced Disappearance; victims were not entitled to receive reparations as a matter of right; the definition of victims did not include dependents; the maximum penalty of five years of imprisonment was too lenient; the formation of the Commission was not transparent and inclusive; the Commission's powers were unclear; and immunity could be enjoyed by persons cooperating with the investigation. In April 2009, the government submitted another bill to parliament to substitute the criticized Enforced Disappearances Ordinance.

On June 1, 2007, the Supreme Court ruled on eighty-nine habeas corpus petitions stating that the government had failed to undertake any effort to address the issue of disappearances. The Court ordered the government to provide compensation to the families of the victims, to form a commission of inquiry on allegations of enforced disappearances, and to formulate a specific anti-disappearance law. These were to comply with international human standards, namely the United Nations International Convention on the Protection of All Persons from Enforced Disappearances and the Criteria for Commissions on Enforced Disappearances.

The government responded by forming a High Level Probe Commission on Disappeared Persons. Local and international organizations again criticized the government for not complying with the Supreme Court and international standards. Nepal's previous negative experiences with inquiry commissions caused people to question the value of this new commission. In 1990, the Commission of Inquiry to Locate the Persons Disappeared during the Panchayat Period had been formed to investigate allegations of human rights violations during the autocracy of 1961–1990 and to identify the final place of detention of the disappeared. The Commission submitted its report in 1991 identifying thirty-five persons disappeared by the state. It recommended action against police and officials. These recommendations were never implemented.

Disarmament, Demobilization, and Reintegration of Ex-Combatants

An agreement reached in June 2007 by the Seven-Party Alliance called for disarmament, demobilization, and reintegration of the 19,000 former Maoist soldiers. A special committee was to be established to supervise and coordinate this process. Two years after the agreement, this special committee has not begun its functions. The committee is expected to face difficulties because of differing views on whether or not the former Maoist combatants should be integrated into the National Army. A UN Mission in Nepal (UNMIN) was established in 2007 to monitor the management of weapons and armed personnel of both the Maoist and government forces and to consolidate cantonment sites.

The question of who controls the army remains a complicated one. The army was historically controlled by the king, who is now deposed. The president of the federal republic is now the commander-in-chief of the army, but he will exercise his powers only under the interim constitution. In May 2009, Nepal fell again into political turmoil after the government's second-largest party pulled out of the ruling coalition in protest for the sacking of the country's army chief who resisted integrating Maoist guerillas into the Nepalese Army. Prime Minister Pushpa Kamal Dahal (Prachanda)'s move to sack the army chief was opposed by President Ram Baran Yadav. On May 4, 2009, Prachanda announced his resignation. Three weeks later, Madhav Kumar Nepal, the secretary general of the Unified Marxist-Leninist Party, became the prime minister. On June 30, 2010, he resigned, after months of pressures from the Maoist who demanded his ouster. In July 2010, the Maoists reached out to other parties to form a coalition government.

Conclusion

Key issues of transitional justice in post-conflict Nepal include the state of impunity, as nobody has been prosecuted yet for the crimes committed during the conflict, the security vacuum, and redress for victims. The legal framework concerning the prosecution of violators and redress for victims remains inadequate. The legal process is disrupted by corruption and political pressure. The transitional justice process and mechanisms have not been transparent or participatory, failed to comply with international standards, and were weakened by political developments, including increased ethnic and regional instability and the recent resignation of the prime minister.

The Nepalese peace process, centered on the integration of the country's two armies and the drafting of a new constitution, remains fragile after the breakdown of trust following the 2008 election of the Constituent Assembly. As of this writing, the new constitution has not been written, a draft bill on the establishment of the Commission on Disappearances had not been passed by parliament, and the Bill on the Truth and Reconciliation Commission has not been finalized yet.

Irene Pietropaoli

Cross-references: Amnesty; Commission of Inquiry to Locate the Persons Disappeared during the Panchayat Period; Compensation Packages; Nepal; Disappeared; Reintegration of Ex-Combatants; Truth Commission.

Future Readings

Aguirre, Daniel and Irene Pietropaoli. 2008. Gender, Transitional Justice and Development: The Case of Nepal. *Oxford Journal on Transitional Justice and Development*, 2(3): 1–22.

Amnesty International. 2007. *Nepal: Reconciliation does not mean impunity: A Memorandum on the Truth and Reconciliation Commission Bill*. Available at: http://www.amnesty.org/en/library/asset/ASA31/006/2007/en/e2023c77-d373-11dd-a329-2f46302a8cc6/asa310062007en.html (accessed July 7, 2010).

Cochran-Budhathoki, Karon and Scott Worden. 2007. *Transitional Justice in Nepal: A Look at the International Experience of Truth Commissions*. Washington, DC: United States Institute of Peace. Available at: http://www.usip.org/files/resources/transitional_justice_nepal.pdf (accessed July 7, 2010).

Comprehensive Peace Agreement Concluded Between the Government of Nepal and the Communist Party of Nepal (Maoist). 2006. Available at: http://www.usip.org/resources/peace-agreements-nepal (accessed July 7, 2010).

Dahal, Dev Raj. 2005. *Nepal: Supporting Peace Processes through a Systemic Approach*. Nepal: Berghof Foundation for Peace Support.

Fullard, Madeleine. 2009. *Disappearances in Nepal*. New York: International Center of Transitional Justice. Available at: http://www.ictj.org/static/Publications/ICTJ_NPL_Disappearances_pb2008.pdf (accessed July 14, 2010).

International Center of Transitional Justice and Advocacy Forum. 2008. *Nepali Voices: Perception of Truth, Justice, Reconciliation, Reparations and the Transition in Nepal*. Available at: http://www.ictj.org/images/content/8/3/830.pdf (accessed July 7, 2010).

Pasipanodya, Tafadzwa. 2008. A Deeper Justice. Economic and Social Justice as Transitional Justice in Nepal. *Oxford Journal on Transitional Justice and Development*, 2(3): 378–397.

Netherlands

The reconstruction of democracy and rule of law in the Netherlands after liberation from Nazi German oppression in 1945 was extensively prepared by the government in its London exile. Transitional justice was mainly conducted by specially created, not existing, institutions. Although moral in wording and harsh on collaborators, many procedures took into account the demands of social, economic, and administrative reconstruction.

The Repressive Past

The Nazi occupation of the Netherlands (1940–1945) was atypical. The German administration was civilian, not military, in nature, because Hitler considered the Dutch to be a Germanic "brother people," although only a small minority sympathized with National Socialism. Anton Mussert's National Socialist Movement (Nationaal-Socialistische Beweging, NSB) had 80,000 members during the occupation, out of a population of 9 million. It gained considerable power in the local government, but it never became a real partner of the German occupier in national or international policy making. Hitler appointed the Austrian Arthur Seyss-Inquart as Reichskommissar, chief administrator of the occupied Netherlands. Except for Queen Wilhelmina and her cabinet, who fled to London when the invasion began in May 1940, all government personnel kept their posts and worked under the occupier.

During the first year of the occupation (May 1940–April 1941), the German regime was mild and seemed to comply with international law. This convinced most civil servants, including judges, to retain their posts. In doing so, they accepted the first questionable regulations, such as reporting the number of their Jewish grandparents in the "Aryan declaration," which they had to provide in the autumn of 1940. As German persecution of the Jews, Nazification, and economic exploitation of the country became more apparent, leaving office became increasingly difficult or even prohibited. Such a step was also problematic given the Dutch government's 1937 instructions to civil servants to retain their posts as long as possible without actively supporting the enemy's policies. Most Dutch officials found themselves trapped in their offices. Should they stay and risk being involved in the oppressor's crimes, or resign and risk persecution or poverty? Moreover, many considered a takeover of their position by Dutch Nazis the larger evil.

Only 1 percent of all Dutch judges and mayors resigned out of principled objections to Nazi policies. The judiciary offered advice to the occupation government on legislative matters, and on several occasions magistrates filed official protests with the German occupiers, but this was never made public. The German personnel policy focused on the local, more than the national, administration. By 1943, 9 percent of the judiciary had been replaced by Nazi sympathizers, and more than 25 percent of mayors had been replaced by NSB members, most of them lacking essential qualifications.

Notwithstanding widespread rejection of both the German occupation and the rise of National Socialism, during 1940–1942, the judiciary, the civil service, and the population for the most part behaved in a way that was later termed "accommodation": the large grey area between resistance and active collaboration. The dilemma of leaving or remaining in office posed itself more forcefully in 1943–1945, when repression and recession took their toll.

To control and exploit the occupied Netherlands, the occupier made use of various German police organizations, the Dutch section of Hitler's party, the Nationalsozialistische Deutsche Arbeiterpartei, and the Dutch bureaucracy and police. The Dutch police assisted in rounding up Jews for deportation to the transit camps. Special courts, presided over by NSB members, were created to try political offenses such as defamations and assaults between Nazis and their adversaries, while the Weerbaarheidsafdeling (WA), the paramilitary branch of the NSB, patrolled the streets.

In reaction to Nazi terror, major strikes occurred in February 1941, against a violent roundup of Jews in the capital; in April–May 1943, against large-scale forced labor in Germany; and in September 1944, when a national railway strike, ordered by the government in exile, sought to hinder German troops and aid the liberation of the Netherlands. The German authorities reacted to these strikes by accelerating oppression; the 1944 railway strike contributed to the famine the following winter. After the 1943 strike, resistance groups organized assistance to people in hiding (Jews or people evading forced labor), tried to destroy municipal registers, shot some cruel Nazis, and published many illegal pamphlets and newspapers. During the occupation, some 2,800 Resistance members were killed in action or after being captured, or were tried or deported.

As in other occupied territories, Jews were robbed of their possessions and deprived of their rights and status as legal subjects. The percentage of Jews killed by the Nazis sets the Netherlands apart. More than 70 percent (100,000 of 140,000 persons) were killed, more than in any other West European country, including Germany and Austria. This is explained by the substantial manpower employed in the process, the strong grip of the Schutzstaffel (the SS) on the preparation and execution of the measures, the geographical problems facing escape across the borders, the forced cooperation of the Jewish leadership, and the accommodating attitude of the Dutch bureaucracy and police.

Transitional Justice

In their London exile, Queen Wilhelmina and her government planned the rigorous removal of all collaborationists, especially NSB members, from Dutch public affairs. After the liberation of the southern provinces in September 1944 and of the rest of the country in May 1945, the former Resistance groups, who supported radical measures, strongly influenced the procedures locally. This contributed to chaos. Months later, the government took full control of transitional justice and shifted focus from retribution to social, economic, and administrative reconstruction. Most transitional justice procedures were concluded by 1955.

Purges

In London, the exiled Dutch government decided to purge Nazis (NSB party members) and civil servants who had accommodated the occupation regime. The 1944 Purge Act (Zuiveringsbesluit) E 14 set up the means to eventually purge these two categories, mentioning that the latter "could not be expected to cooperate faithfully in the reconstruction of the fatherland" after the war (Article 3). Resistance groups demanded purges according to absolute norms of right (having actively resisted the occupier) and wrong (having collaborated with or accommodated the occupier). Upon liberation, the temporary Military Administration of the liberated Netherlands undertook provisional purge measures, aided by local purge commissions that included representatives of the Resistance.

Initially, many different purge commissions and authorities were involved in procedures that were chaotic and not transparent to the public. There were complaints about excessive and arbitrary suspensions and uncertainty as to the outcome of procedures. Additionally, the two categories explicitly mentioned in the Purge Act turned out to be too broad, and the need arose for sanctions other than dismissal to be imposed. Therefore, a new Purge Act F 132 was adopted in 1945 to provide additional sanctions: demotion, transfer, and official reprimand.

In practice, not the extended list of purged and available sanctions provided by the new law but the pragmatic criterion of postwar "trustworthiness" was used to effect the purge. Trustworthiness was interpreted differently across regions. Purges mainly aimed to restore trust in public administration. Civil servants' trustworthiness was determined in reference to the 1937 governmental instructions, which obliged them to remain in office as long as possible. The purge officials had to determine when job retention benefitted the occupier more than the occupied.

The Central Organ for Purging the Civil Service (Centraal Orgaan op de Zuivering van het Overheidspersoneel, COZO), created in April 1945 by the government, was unable to provide unity, transparency, and legal certainty to the purge. This disappointed and frustrated the government, the COZO, the former Resistance, the general public, and those under scrutiny, and prompted the Minister of Interior to decentralize and delegate purge powers to new provincial purge committees in October 1945. He also made sure that the former Resistance lost its influence on purge procedures. Lawyers were added to the many purge bodies, and procedures conformed more to rule-of-law principles.

After this decentralization, the government focused on a swift and orderly conclusion of the purges. A problem was the lack of complaints by members of the public, which were needed to initiate individual purge procedures. After the most serious cases were dealt with, interest in purges waned, as people wanted to get on with their lives and rebuild the economy. After the Secretary-General for Economic Affairs H. M. Hirschfeld (1940–1946) was honorably discharged at his own request, many felt that superiors got off lightly, while accommodating officials in the lower ranks were blamed instead. Hirschfeld had worked closely with the Germans, but received public acknowledgment for both mitigating some of their measures and serving the interests of the people by maintaining a fair distribution of food staples. His colleague, the Secretary-General for the Interior, was not so lucky: his cooperation in the Nazification of the public administration produced less positive results. Because of his "weakening influence on the spirit of resistance" and resulting loss of public confidence, he was discharged honorably, before he was ready to leave the post.

More than half of all mayors were purged, not all of them NSB members. In the lower echelons of the public administration, 30,000 cases resulted in 17,000 dismissals and 6,000 other disciplinary measures such as demotion or non-eligibility for promotion.

The purge of the Dutch Supreme Court (Hoge Raad) posed specific problems. The Court had collectively signed the "Aryan declaration" and accepted the dismissal of its Jewish president and the creation of political criminal courts. In 1942, it had ruled that, given the circumstances of the occupation, Dutch judges could not examine the occupier's ordinances for compatibility with international law. This decision, labeled by one lawyer as "the judgment of total surrender," was disappointing for the Resistance. Because the Supreme Court tried to save the Dutch judiciary from Nazi infiltration by remaining in office, the justices chose not to risk dismissal by protesting publicly against any of the occupier's measures. This cost the Court and the entire judiciary their credibility as conveyors of justice.

In September 1944, upon the liberation of the southern provinces, the exiled government suspended all prewar appointees in the Supreme Court, thus marking the beginning of a long and devastating conflict between the justices, who had been appointed for life, and the government that insisted that the justices should voluntarily resign. Instead of doing so, the prewar justices pointed out the unconstitutionality of their suspension and questioned the ability of the ministers, who spent the war in London, to realistically assess the difficulties of working under the occupier. The dispute, played out in pamphlets and newspapers, was solved in November 1946 by the appointment of a new Court president who helped restore confidence in the judiciary. Meanwhile, the prosecution of suspected collaborators with the enemy had been entrusted to Special Courts and tribunals (see discussion later).

As difficult and delicate as it was, the purge acquired an undeserved image of chaos and unfairness. Judged from the rigid perspective of the Resistance, it failed to apply the "absolute norms" of moral right and wrong mentioned previously. From a pragmatic viewpoint, however, it restored confidence in public administration, although the Dutch authorities had neither the capacity nor the willingness to purge every last tainted bureaucrat.

Prosecutions

During and after liberation, fewer revenge killings took place than in Belgium or France. A well-known example of postwar popular retribution was shaving the heads of women who had been romantically involved with Germans. In addition, 165,000 people were prosecuted on suspicion of collaboration and/or National Socialist sympathy. More than 120,000 of them were interned in makeshift detention camps. Arrests were brutal, initially detainees were systematically maltreated, and life in the camps was often difficult. In the summer of 1945, administrative chaos fueled pessimism that all necessary court procedures would not be concluded in the foreseeable future.

Because there were more detainees than the prison system could accommodate, the conditional release of those accused of less serious charges became unavoidable, on condition that they had behaved well and stopped advocating National Socialism. From 1945 to 1950, 90,000 political prisoners were released, and a special institution, the Foundation for the Return of Political Offenders (Stichting Terugkeer Politieke Delinquenten, STPD), was set up for their reintegration in society. Although the issue remained controversial and the disappointed public grew increasingly indifferent, the government reasoned that conditional release was inevitable.

Out of 450,000 files, 165,000 cases were investigated and 65,000 persons were convicted. The prosecutions were conducted rapidly and the guilty were punished severely. A Special Jurisdiction dealt with these cases, for several reasons. First, the judiciary had lost much of the public's confidence and was deemed unfit to judge suspected collaborators. Nevertheless, many individual judges were still trustworthy, so more than half of the Special Courts judges could be recruited from the regular courts. Second, the new institutions allowed for a different composition of the courts. Three civilian and two military judges were appointed to each Special Court. In the Special Tribunals, for the less serious cases, lay judges were introduced. Third, the caseload was still high, and regular courts had much on their plate already dealing with nonpolitical crimes.

The judges appointed to the Special Courts and the Special Court of Cassation, the only appeal instance for cases related to wartime crimes and collaboration, were selected from among the most patriotic, anti-Nazi lawyers in the country. For example, the only three judges who had resigned in protest against the occupier's policy were appointed as president of the Special Court of Cassation and president and vice-president of The Hague Special Court. The Special Tribunals dealt with persons who had acted against the interests of the Dutch people. Most of the accused were NSB members or opportunistic non-resisters, who took advantage of the situation, mostly economically. The presiding judges of the Special Tribunals were lawyers, who were aided by lay assessor judges.

Two new offenses were created for the jurisdiction of the Special Courts: aiding and abetting persecution by the enemy, and using powers given by the enemy to cause financial loss to somebody else. For existing offenses connected to aiding the enemy, the maximum penalties stated in the Criminal Code were raised, and the death penalty was reintroduced for offenses punishable with fifteen years jail time. The government declared non-applicable Article 1 of the Dutch Criminal Code, which included the ban on retroactivity, without consulting parliament. Parliament did not challenge the decision.

Death sentences were handed down in 152 cases and carried out in 40 of those. These numbers are much lower than in Belgium and France and in line with Norway and Denmark. Even before the country's liberation, the government in exile decided that the NSB leader Mussert had to be executed for supporting the Nazi occupation and betraying the Dutch people.

After the conditional release of many political prisoners accused of aiding the enemy or taking undue advantage of the occupation, a pardon policy for those already condemned was developed based on both pragmatic and principled motives. On the one hand, the government wished to reform the prison system and to end procedures regarding political prisoners. On the other hand, (Christian) charity, compensation for maltreatment in detention camps and the return to democracy and rule of law demanded leniency and quick reintegration of these prisoners accused of collaboration. In May 1959, only forty-four political convicts remained in prison. By 1964, only the infamous "Breda Four" were still incarcerated, in the Breda prison: Franz Fischer, Ferdinand aus der Fünten, and Willy Lages, organizers of the deportation of Jews from Holland; and Joseph Kotälla, a sadistic warden at the Amersfoort hostage camp. The death sentences of these four Germans were converted to life imprisonment. As they became symbols of Nazi oppression, repeated proposals for their release by consecutive Ministers of Justice raised strong opposition inside and outside of parliament. Fischer and aus der Fünten were released as old men in 1989, and they died the same year.

Of all purges and prosecutions, those involving members of the trade and industry sector were probably most restricted by the demands of the economic reconstruction of the country. Some important industrialists were not prosecuted because of their supposed indispensability for national economic recovery, although they had produced army supplies for the enemy. They had been licensed to trade with the enemy by the Dutch Secretary-General for Economic Affairs and the government attorney, who advised the government in legal proceedings.

Reparations

A main concern for the postwar Dutch authorities was the country's socioeconomic reconstruction. After the war, many Dutch citizens, including the 300,000 forced laborers, camp survivors, and prisoners of war who returned from Germany, lacked basic necessities. Reparation included care for those officially labeled victims of war. Forced laborers, Jews, and Resistance fighters received financial aid to ensure their subsistence. Their numbers increased from 2,600 in 1954 to 5,200 in 1976. Invalids also received aid in proportion to the degree of invalidity.

Soldiers and civil servants who had worked in the Dutch East Indies also asked the Dutch government to pay them overdue salaries, which had not been paid during the Japanese occupation of the Dutch Indies. The Dutch government denied responsibility, claiming that, according to the principle of territoriality, the Dutch Indies – and later the Republic of Indonesia – was responsible for covering the backpay, in accordance with the international law on state succession. This was a bitter disappointment for the soldiers and civil servants, who received no backpay.

Resistance members disabled by the war and the family of Resistance fighters killed during the war could apply for special pensions. The family of a resistance fighter could receive almost the equivalent of his last salary. By 1970, 6,000–7,000 were entitled to such pensions. In 1971, the burden of proof was reversed: applicants no longer had to prove that their disability was a direct consequence of their Resistance activities. As a result, the number of recipients rose to 9,900 in 1981. The payments enabled the beneficiaries to keep the lifestyle they had before the injury or death of the Resistance fighter in question. Similar pensions were granted after 1986 to Resistance members who fought in the Dutch Indies under the Japanese occupation.

Property Restitution and Compensation

In 1941–1942, several German spoliation organizations were created in the Netherlands. Jews, Gypsies, communists, Jehovah's Witnesses, members of secret societies, Jewish companies, and non-Jewish associations and foundations lost their property (dwellings, factories, plants, and other assets) to the Germans, who sold some of it to others. Jews were forced to hand over their assets to the German bank Lippmann & Rosenthal, located in Amsterdam. Upon their return from the camps or from hiding, many Jews found out that their houses had been sold to others and were occupied by the new owners. This is why the restitution of Jewish property dragged on for years.

After the war, some real estate was returned to its initial owners. The Dutch government also offered compensation for property requisitioned by the spoliation organizations. For real estate, the injured parties could file a request with the Restitution Council, the governmental agency dealing with property restitution in the Netherlands. The Council could annul or change legal relations created or modified during the occupation, and propose an amicable settlement in a formal decision. Unsatisfied parties could present the case to the Council's adjudication department, which decided in first and final instance the appeal. In most cases, the wartime buyer was presumed not to be bona fide. If the buyer could not prove otherwise, the property was returned to the initial owner, while the buyer could submit a claim against one of the spoliation organizations, which still possessed many assets in the Netherlands at the end of the war. Those who had bought property from the organization had to return it in exchange for the money they paid for the property. The organization then returned the property to the initial owner.

The Restitution Council's adjudication process was marred by problems. The judges had unlimited discretionary powers, and they could decide cases according to their own sense of fairness and reasonableness, which varied significantly across cases and judges.

In doing so, the judges sometimes placed the demands of economic reconstruction above the demands of corrective justice. In such cases, the initial owner had to share in the loss of the party who had knowingly bought the stolen property from the Nazis.

Conclusion

After World War II, the perspective of the Resistance dominated discussions and publications about the war and transitional justice. Since the 1980s, the dilemmas of the officials and citizens who were neither Resistance heroes nor Nazi sympathizers, but felt forced to accommodate the German occupation in order to survive it, have been increasingly appreciated. While immediately after the war unpatriotic citizens were severely punished, afterward the desire to promote the country's democratic and economic reconstruction directed government policy toward leniency and closure.

Derk Venema

Cross references: Court Trials for Redress; Property Restitution; Purges; Reparations.

Further Readings

Mason, Henry. 1952. *The Purge of Dutch Quislings. Emergency Justice in the Netherlands.* The Hague: Nijhoff.
Meihuizen, Joggli. 2003. *Noodzakelijk kwaad. De bestraffing van economische collaboratie in Nederland na de Tweede Wereldoorlog* [Necessary Evil. Punishment of Economic Collaboration in the Netherlands after World War II]. Amsterdam: Boom.
Romijn, Peter. 2000. "Restoration of Confidence": The Purge of Local Government in the Netherlands As a Problem of Post-War Reconstruction. In: *The Politics of Retribution in Europe. World War II and Its Aftermath.* Eds. István Deák, Jan T. Gross and Tony Judt. Princeton: Princeton University Press.
———. 2002. *Snel, streng en rechtvaardig. De afrekening met 'foute' Nederlanders* [Swift, Strict, and Just. Settling Accounts with Dutch Collaborationists]. No place: Olympus.
Veraart, Wouter. 2005. *Ontrechting en rechtsherstel in Nederland en Frankrijk in de jaren van bezetting en wederopbouw* [Deprivation and Restitution of Property Rights during the Years of Occupation and Post-War Reconstruction in the Netherlands and France]. PhD Dissertation, Erasmus University Rotterdam, November 10. Available at: http://publishing.eur.nl/ir/repub/asset/7046/Veraart_dissertatie.pdf (accessed October 24, 2010).

New Zealand

New Zealand differs from other countries that engaged in transitional justice because, in this case, "transition" refers to a long, well-established, and continuing process that enables the state to redefine itself and its institutions to take into account the values and significance of its indigenous population. The mechanisms outlined in this entry have traditionally been labeled "transitional justice" processes, but the discourse of transitional justice has featured relatively little in the processes attendant to this transition. Yet these processes, undertaken since the 1990s, provide models of socioeconomic and political change for states struggling with contested identities. The change undertaken in New Zealand allows the state to address the legacy of past violations against the Maori.

Historical Background

Contemporary New Zealand is a model state in terms of adherence to human rights values. It has a well-established legal system that pays heed to human rights issues, is a stable democracy with a well-ensconced rule of law, and has free and fair, if not always completely effective, institutions. Yet the foundation of the state was based on a repressive past that included a contract undertaken by the incoming European settlers, referred to in New Zealand as the *parekha*, and the indigenous population, the Maori. Early historical accounts demonstrate the relative nature of the term "indigenous," given that the Maori themselves were settlers on the two islands constituting New Zealand through migration from the Pacific Islands. The Maori association with New Zealand began in the fourteenth century, whereas *parekha* migration only began in the nineteenth century. Unlike the experience in Australia, when the *parekha* first arrived on New Zealand's shores, they were met with a significantly better organized tribal structure, which made the possibility of conquest difficult, and helped shape their early impression of the Maori.

The relevant historical backdrop to a discussion of transitional justice in this case contains several periods: (1) pre-settlement society (pre-1769); (2) the *parekha* settlement process (1800–1900); (3) the Treaty of Waitangi (1840); (4) the politics of retraction of parity (1840–1900); (5) the modern quest for social equality (1970–present); and (6) the issue of immigration, which continues to change the contemporary demographics of the state. To analyze the transitional justice tools used in New Zealand, focus must be placed on the Maori and the attempts to use reparative measures to address their disempowerment.

New Zealand's pre-settlement history is dominated by legends: one of these narrates the discovery of the islands around 925 AD by Maori explorer Kupe who, after returning to Hawaiki (Tahiti), the Maori ancestral home, instructed others on its location. A group of Maori may have subsequently been blown off course in a storm, thus arriving and settling on what was identified as Tiritiri o te Moana. Many Maori trace their descent to fleets of canoes from around the middle of the fourteenth century. The history of these groups has been traced by some anthropologists to Austronesians who arrived from Asia, by others to groups that sailed on rafts from South America.

Maori societies were internally well organized, with clear social hierarchies under often despotic rulers, and a strong element of the "sacred" in their spiritual beliefs. Unlike in Australia, evidence of well-established precolonial communities made any colonial declaration of *terra nullius* implausible. As a result, New Zealand's history of indigenous peoples is significantly different from its neighbor's. The Maori were warriors experienced in strategic warfare, so any settler plans for subjugating them through open warfare were deemed unrealistic. Thus, New Zealand was colonized differently from other British dominions in that the greatest proportion of land was acquired through purchase rather than outright conquest.

It was not until Captain Cook came across the islands in 1769, drawing up the first maps of the territory, that European settlement became a possibility. Cook described the Maori as "a brave, warlike people, with sentiments void of treachery" (Sinclair 1959, p. 32). As whaling and trading expeditions mounted from Sydney Harbor grew, settlement became ever more probable. Health problems never encountered before began to affect the Maori, whose social fabric was being eroded through the introduction of alcohol, prostitution, and venereal diseases. This led to a demand for *utu* (revenge) within the Maori. In addition, the availability of weapons from traders meant that society was increasingly armed and engaged in internecine intertribal warfare, which, while not new, wreaked higher levels of devastation.

In seeking to determine the desired type of colonial intervention, an initial plan to empower the traders and residents against the native population was rejected as useless against an indigenous population that could rise up easily in defiance. Instead, opinion mobilized behind the proposal of William Hobson (a sea captain, who subsequently negotiated on behalf of the Crown), who recommended the signing of treaties with the Maori for the acquisition of certain pockets of territory, similar to the "factories" set up by the British East India Company in India. While this led to New Zealand's de facto annexation, the British Crown did not exercise effective control outside the settlements, or factories. Significant philosophical arguments occurred from 1840s to 1860s between "organized colonizers" and "humanitarians" over the direction of British policy in New Zealand. The debate culminated in a decision that, while parts of New Zealand annexed by Hobson would become dependencies of New South Wales, indigenous populations would be dealt with fairly, and land would be acquired with a Crown grant. The drafting and signing of the Treaty of Waitangi in 1840, ostensibly a contract between the Crown and the Maori, suggested that the humanitarians had won, although subsequent events suggest that this victory was not as clear-cut as first appeared.

Despite the vaunted ambitions of partnership between Maori and *parekha*, the experience at the beginning of the nineteenth century was tilted toward domination of the Maori by the settlers, with law serving as a handmaiden of dispossession. The first "democratic" Constitution of 1852 excluded Maori on the basis that franchise was given to individual (not collective) landowners. While the colonist state was being consolidated, the Maori were organizing on the basis of nationalism (*kotahitanga*) – a shared vision to eliminate colonization. The election in 1858 of a Maori King, the Waikato chief, Te Wherowhero, under the title of Potatau 1, with trappings of sovereignty (a flag, Council of State, code of laws, magistrate and police force, and a land surveyor), highlighted the competition for land that was unfolding. The rise in tensions resulted in an intensive war between Maoris and the settlers in 1854–1864, which continued as a low-intensity struggle until the late 1880s.

The need for colonies to become self-reliant prompted a blatant violation of the Treaty of Waitangi through land confiscations, with nearly 3 million acres of Maori land requisitioned in Waikato, the East Coast, and Taranaki. The Maori Land Court Act of 1865 attempted to redress the legal balance, but resulted in legal subterfuge, separating the Maori from their lands. While the ostensible function of the court was to convert customary Maori title to freehold title, in its first decade of operation the court named a restricted number of holders in the title deeds in contravention of conventional Maori custom of collective ownership, rendering significant numbers of Maori landless. Meanwhile, parliament passed legislation concerning land and Maori were easily duped by opportunists who dispossessed them in return for pitiful remuneration.

Fears grew that the Maori would be wiped out in New Zealand through land dispossession and disease contracted from exposure to Europeans. These dissipated by dawn of the twentieth century, when Maori population figures began to recover after touching a nadir of 42,000 in 1896, a significant drop from the estimated 250,000 Maori on the two islands in the mid-1700s. War between the Maori and settlers provided cause for the passage of the Suppression of Rebellion Act of 1863, under which the Crown confiscated further parcels of land.

Concerned over the state of health, diminishing population, and land dispossession, the Maori united to form the Young Maori Party in the 1890s, in a bid to focus on measures to improve the conditions of their communities. In 1900, Mauri Pomare, a Maori, was appointed Medical Officer of Health to the Maoris and, together with others, began the job of providing medical assistance and health education. While these measures were productive, the loss of land following the Treaty of Waitangi was considerably more difficult to overcome. An aggravating factor then, which remains relevant today, was the urban-rural divide, with significant numbers of Maoris living in rural communities, while most Europeans lived in cities and towns. As a result, the Maori found it difficult to access services that were readily available in cities.

Transitional Justice

The Treaty of Waitangi of 1840 significantly impacted on the aspirations of indigenous peoples globally. It represents a definitive moment of New Zealand history and reflected how the Maoris were perceived at the time of settlement; it was also a source of rights. The Treaty was signed by William Hobson, Consul and Lieutenant-Governor, on behalf of the Crown, and a number of Maori chiefs. The document consists of a preamble and three short articles. While the treaty was progressive for its time, problems arose concerning its interpretation and the significant discrepancies between the English- and Maori-language versions. The English text significantly reduces the benefits to the Maori, in comparison with the formulations in the Maori version, which was the version to which the vast majority of the chiefs agreed.

Through the treaty, the Crown gained rights, whereas the Maori chiefdom lost significantly. In addition, when the misinterpretation of the treaty and its subsequent violations are taken into account, the Crown respected few of the promises undertaken. In the aftermath of World War II, discussions did take place aiming at "final" settlements with the Taranaki, the Ngai Tahu, the Tainui, and the Whakatohea tribes. These resulted in payments in perpetuity or payments of fixed sums over a number of years, although it was not always acknowledged as to whether this was compensation for confiscated land or damages for injury. In any case, the payments remained nominal and the act authorizing them was repealed in 1955. The discussion then lay dormant until the passage of the Treaty of Waitangi Act of 1975. By this stage, Maori holdings accounted for only 3.1 million acres (about 5 percent of the available land), almost all individually owned. A further 67,000 acres was held in "native reserves," subject to the control of government-appointed trustees, usually non-Maori.

At the same time, Maori supported by liberal segments in society pushed for greater recognition of New Zealand's heritage in 1973, when February 6 was first celebrated as Waitangi Day, although there was little to celebrate. By 1975, the Maori mobilized under the banner of "Not One Acre More of Maori Land" under the charismatic leadership of Dame Whina Cooper, a Maori, and marched on Wellington, New Zealand's capital. This protest instigated the formulation of the Treaty of Waitangi Act and the creation of a Tribunal to adjudicate on disputes concerning the original Treaty of Waitangi of 1840.

The Waitangi Tribunal

The Waitangi Tribunal (see separate entry) was slow to get started, with the relative paucity of claims filed before it until 1985 attributed to: (1) its narrow mandate, which restricted the historical time period concerning which it could accept claims; (2) the overtly legalistic proceedings, alien to the Maori; and (3) the fact that the Tribunal could only make nonbinding recommendations to the government. The appointment of Maori Edward Taihakurei Durie to chair the Tribunal was a key turning point in Waitangi history. It resulted in major changes to Tribunal operations, greater confidence in the institution, and the extension of its mandate to cover violations post-1840. The work of the Tribunal on the Motunui-Waitara claim in 1983 (concerning ownership over fishing reefs more than 50 kilometers in length off the Taranaki coast) was significant in establishing the credentials of the institution.

Under the amended Treaty of Waitangi Act of 1985, claims were invited challenging historic acquisitions of property through confiscations, expropriations, title grants, and Crown and private purchases, intertwining contemporary claims with conceptual claims to rivers, lakes, minerals, and geothermal resources. In keeping with the extended mandate of the Tribunal, more staff was appointed and the Tribunal bench increased to seven, four of whom were required to be Maori. This requirement was rescinded in 1988, when the Act underwent further modification, and the panel was increased to sixteen without ethnic quotas.

Although the Treaty has been the subject of significant debate over its legal significance, political implications, and philosophical leanings, only in the last few decades has a concerted effort been undertaken to undo some of the dramatic historical violations perpetrated against the Maori. Significantly, in 1985, the extension of the Waitangi Tribunal's mandate was accompanied by an official apology and a concrete plan toward reconciliation based on parity of rights between *parekha* and Maori, and settlement of all major tribal claims by 2000. The failure to meet that deadline has seen an extension of the mandate until 2010, with all claims expected to be resolved by 2020. The process has involved successes as well as failures and has been beset with difficulties generated by seeking "national" solutions – that is, centralized solutions for communities that remain essentially decentralized. While the notion of restitution is better developed in New Zealand than elsewhere, mainly because of a sympathetic government and a population that has engaged in significant soul-searching, the greater visibility of the Maori has enabled them to be successful in advancing particular claims, and even then, more centralized tribes have been significantly more successful than others. Much of this relates to the organization of Maori society at the time of the arrival of the settlers, in *hapus* (clans) and *whanuas* (extended families).

The question of compensation has remained open in terms of how it was measured and dispensed. There is no binding precedent for proceedings before the Tribunal with settlements negotiated directly between the tribes and the government. Controversy also flared when the government announced its intention to set aside a fiscal cap of NZ$1 billion (equivalent to US$726 million) for restitution. The restitution process is well under way and is generally well received by the Maori.

Much needs to be highlighted in the relative success of claims for restitution, reparation, and reconciliation, as can be seen in: (1) the significant presence of the Maori in New Zealand's demographics; (2) the relatively high percentage of urbanized Maori with access to law and quasi-legal processes such as the Waitangi Tribunal; (3) the prevalence of high rates of intermarriage between the Maori and the *parekha*; and (4) the relatively low rate of competition from other minorities within the country, which has allowed the development of a bicultural society.

The construction of an overtly bicultural state is a measure of success in the context of human rights in New Zealand. The rise of the Maori to social prominence has been a key factor in addressing past violations against the community. This has been helped by high-level political participation. For instance, there are currently 21 Maori members of parliament (of a 120 member House) representing a range of different political parties. However, socioeconomic indicators suggest that considerable work remains to be done. In addition, there are several outstanding claims before the Tribunal, and it is difficult to imagine how competing claims will be resolved. The persistence of focus on the Maori has also been accompanied by relative neglect of Pacific Islanders who, despite sharing several characteristics with the Maori, have not benefited from any of these measures. The arrangement arrived at with the Maori has not been made to apply to Pacific Islanders, despite the fact that some have lived in New Zealand for a similar length of time.

Conclusion

New Zealand's attempt to engage with its past violations against the Maori has arisen out of a shared belief among both its indigenous and settled inhabitants in the need for such a process. This attempt has taken place against the backdrop of a genuine reorientation of the state's ethos and values and a reappraisal of its historical foundations. These discussions have not been formally framed in terms of transitional justice, but the processes used, involving both compensation and restitution, suggest that this is a model that could be followed in many other states where indigenous rights have been violated in the past. While states like Canada, Australia, and the United States have encountered similar issues vis-à-vis indigenous rights, New Zealand has gone the farthest in seeking to provide substantive remedies for such violations.

Joshua Castellino

Cross-references: Restitution of Property; Waitangi Tribunal.

Further Readings

Castellino J. and D. Keane. 2009. *Minority Rights in the Pacific: A Comparative Legal Analysis*. Oxford: Oxford University Press.
Concluding Observations of the United Nations Committee for the Elimination of All Forms of Racial Discrimination, New Zealand, UN. Doc. CERD/C/NZL/CO/17 (August 15, 2007).
Durie, M. H. 1998. *Te Mana Kawanatanga: The Politics of Maori Self-Determination*. Auckland: Oxford University Press.
Sinclair, K. 1959. *A History of New Zealand*. Harmondsworth: Penguin Books.
Upson-Hooper, K. 1998. Slaying the Leviathan: Critical Jurisprudence and the Treaty of Waitangi. *Victoria University of Wellington Law Review*, 28(4): 683–717.
Waldron, W. 2003. Indigeneity? First Peoples and Last Occupancy. *New Zealand Journal of Public International Law*, 1(1): 56–82.

Nigeria

On the heels of Nigeria's transition to democracy in 1999, the Human Rights Violations Investigations Commission (the Oputa Panel, so called after the name of its chairman) was established as the cardinal transitional justice mechanism in the post-authoritarian period. The Oputa Panel submitted its report in June 2003. However, the report remains officially unpublished and unimplemented, even though it has been posted on the Internet by a group of civil society organizations in the country. The Federal Government of Nigeria (FGN) premises its position not to publish the report on a Supreme Court decision on a challenge of the "coercive" powers of the Oputa Panel to summon witnesses brought by some ex-military rulers of the country. Nigeria also employed lustration and trials as transitional justice measures to secure the new democratic order.

In dumping the Oputa Panel's Report, with its wide-ranging and far-reaching recommendations for accountability and institutional reforms, the Nigerian state set the stage for real and potential conflicts and gross violations of human rights in the country both by public and private actors. Since 1999, the country has witnessed several ethnic and intercommunal conflicts resulting in the loss of hundreds of lives and millions of dollars in property. This has led to the view in certain quarters that not only has the transition to democracy failed to deliver on justice and restoration of the rule of law, but also that impunity and state-sponsored violence have remained unchecked, if not increased, in the country.

The Repressive Past

On January 15, 1966, Nigeria's military took over power from elected civilian leaders in a bloody coup. Another coup followed six months later. A crop of leading political officeholders, including the prime minister, were murdered in the putsches. The events that followed the latter coup led to a bloody thirty-month-long civil war from 1967 to 1970 in which hundreds of thousands lost their lives. Property worth millions of dollars was also destroyed in the war, which left thousands maimed for life. From 1966 to 1999, the country was subjected to nearly thirty years of authoritarian rule (interjected by a short spell of democratic governance from 1979 to 1984) under seven military regimes. The military ruled by draconian decrees and edicts. Many of these limited the jurisdiction of the courts. With the military repeatedly imposing emergency rule, gross violations of human rights were prevalent.

Between 1966 and 1993, more than 200 military officers and civilians were brought before military tribunals on charges related to at least 7 instances of actual or alleged coup plots, tried without regard to due process, convicted, and sentenced to death. Although the military sometimes directed its guns at its own, it was the civilian population that bore the brunt of military repression. There was widespread deployment of lethal force by security agents and the police against civilians: for example, in the 1990s, protests against unpopular economic policies were met with the shooting and killing of hundreds of demonstrators.

Special Military Tribunals (SMTs) were established to try a number of civil offenses, including armed robbery, drug trafficking, corruption in public office, and "economic sabotage." SMTs were almost invariably chaired by serving senior military officers and composed mainly of members of the military and security agencies as well as a few civilians. They commonly imposed the death penalty and the convicted were in some instances summarily executed, in breach of their constitutional right of appeal. Others were sentenced to long terms of imprisonment.

Cases of public execution in defiance of due process included that of Ogoni Rights activist and renowned author Kenule Saro-Wiwa and some other members of the Movement for the Survival of the Ogoni People (MOSOP) referred to as the "Ogoni nine." The military rulers institutionalized abuse of office, corruption, a vicious cycle of lawlessness, violence, and impunity in the Nigerian polity. The General Sani Abacha regime

(November 1993–June 1998) was especially noted for its ruthlessness to political opposition and the struggle for democracy in the country.

Transitional Justice

So strong was the current of opposition to continued violations of human rights that the first steps toward transitional justice – the prosecution of a handful of notorious military and security operatives of the penultimate military regime – were commenced by Abacha's successor, General Abdusalam Abubakar. But this was a half-hearted attempt, no doubt conditioned by the reality of the precarious balance of power in the short life of that "transitional regime" itself. Abubakar was mostly interested in handing over the reins of power to an elected civilian regime. He was well aware of the local and international opposition to continued military rule following General Ibrahim Babangida's infamous 1993 annulment of the most credible electoral process to date. Moreover, the minions of General Abubakar's predecessors remained in the corridors of power and could attempt to seize the reins of government if the opportunity presented itself.

Lustration and Trials

Between July 1998 and May 1999, there was a largely symbolic lustration of about 200 "political" military officers from active service. These were officers that had held political "postings" (appointments) as governors or administrators of the various states, cabinet ministers, and chairmen of important state agencies, public corporations, and similar government institutions. Most of them had been corrupt and accumulated fabulous wealth well beyond their legitimate earnings. The experience had made holding political office, rather than military service for which they were engaged, very attractive and an incentive for coup plotting.

In the almost three decades of military authoritarian rule, discipline and cohesion of the armed forces had become greatly weakened. Junior officers who had benefited from political postings became incorrigible in view of their enhanced financial positions in an increasingly materialistic society. It was rightly felt that to develop and sustain professionalism of the armed forces, it was necessary to rid the ranks of "political officers." Ridding the armed forces of this class was a very important measure to facilitate a sustainable democratic culture in the country.

Further, about fifteen notorious members of the Abacha regime that ruled from November 1994 to June 1998, who were generally believed to be arrowheads of state-sponsored killings and violence, were arraigned for various serious offenses ranging from murder and kidnapping to arson. Some of those arrested and charged included a former chief of army staff, the chief security officer of the former head of state (Abacha), his chief police detail, his son Mohammed, his former chief security adviser, and a former military administrator of one of the states in the country.

While some of the trials became moribund because of the absence of political will to proceed, many others have (except in one instance) not been concluded largely because of the exploitation of a very weak criminal procedure process that remains unreformed since the colonial era. Thus, more than ten years on, the trials have not been concluded. Rather, they have moved back and forth through all levels of the court system and remain in progress.

The Truth-Telling Process

The truth-telling process remains the notable transitional justice mechanism adopted in the post-authoritarian/military era in Nigeria. The Obasanjo administration garnered positive public acclaim when it set up the Oputa Panel (see separate entry), and its work was well received. At the submission of its work, President Obasanjo commended the Oputa Panel, noting that the public hearings had the strong potential to serve as a deterrent to human rights violations.

Notwithstanding its popularity, at least a section of the Nigerian public seemed to have viewed the Oputa Panel as more of a juridical forum than an unencumbered avenue for investigating the past. This is reflected in the fact that at the public hearings, many petitioners, respondents, and witnesses were represented by some of the leading legal practitioners in the country. Even those who took serious exception to participating in the public hearings (sections of the elite who felt threatened by the truth) ensured appearance by legal proxy. The composition of the Oputa Panel largely of lawyers may have contributed to this juridicalization of the truth-telling process in Nigeria.

The very nature of a truth commission, with its focus on establishing the truth about the past as a measure of accountability, commonly attracts challenges of various types to its operations. However, in the case of the truth-telling process in Nigeria, there were some avoidable problems thrown in its way from its inception. As stated earlier, the seven-member panel was headed by Chukwudifu Oputa, a retired and respected Justice of the Supreme Court of Nigeria. This from the outset gave the panel much credibility among a highly skeptical populace as to the true intentions of the new government. However, the composition of the panel was strongly challenged for being unrepresentative of the country's diversity. Some segments of the country, specifically the Muslims (North and South), felt alienated by the constitution of the membership. For example, Rev. Matthew Kukah, a Catholic priest and a minority Christian from the North, is viewed as a vociferous anti-Muslim sociopolitical commentator and opinion leader. Oputa himself is a Catholic from the South East, and four of the other five members were Christians. The secretary, though not regarded as a member, was also a Christian. Only one member was confirmed to be a Muslim. In a country where more than half the population is Muslim, and religion is a sensitive and divisive issue, that was problematic.

Voicing the feelings of the northern Muslim elite, Mohammed Haruna, a seasoned journalist, media, and public affairs commentator, faulted the lopsided composition of the Oputa Panel and dismissed it as a witch hunt. Moreover, considering the size of the country, the scope of the mandate, and the heterogeneous nature of its population, a seven-member panel was rather inadequate. It was not sufficient to effectively cover the diversity in the country. It is important to recall in this regard that the Oputa Panel, following pre-commencement deliberations with civil society groups, specifically requested an increase in the number of its commissioners, but this was not implemented. The Nigerian government did not pay any serious heed to the concerns expressed about the composition of the Oputa Panel. The reasons for the government's attitude remain unclear, but it may not be unconnected with the authoritarian hangover of the president, which was to permeate all facets of his eight-year tenure.

Further, the Oputa Panel has been established without adequate preparations or public consultations. This, with the benefit of hindsight, is ill-informed at best, if not outright suspect. By comparative standards, the Nigerian truth commission was a modest undertaking, yet the Oputa Panel remained inactive for the better part of a year after it was inaugurated, as it was incapacitated by the paucity of funds. The government had reportedly made no budgetary provisions for it despite its being a campaign issue. Some viewed this as a deliberate attempt to utilize the Oputa Panel to the political advantage of the regime that established it. Indeed, the Oputa Panel was only able to commence operations after a take-off grant of US$400,000 was made to it by the Ford Foundation.

Equally worthy of mention are the shaky legal foundations on which the Oputa Panel was established. The Tribunals of Inquiry Act was a colonial legacy. Principally designed for specialized inquiries, it fell well short of the more extensive remit of a truth commission in a post-military transitional society like Nigeria at the end of the twentieth century. The work of the Oputa Panel was affected by the fact that it was not established pursuant to a tailor-made law by the post-authoritarian parliament. The lesson to be learned is not to proceed with the delicate process of truth seeking without specific "made-to-fit" legislation. Such legislation is required to clearly spell out the powers and limits of the process.

Another challenge the truth-telling process faced was the rather feeble international support for its work. While it attracted some international attention in its initial stages, this did not translate into positive advantage for the Panel's work, nor was it sustained during its most crucial stages. For example, the non-implementation of the final report and recommendations, including reparations for victims, has hardly attracted international censure. Although now a matter for conjecture, it is quite plausible that international attention, monitoring, and support for the truth-seeking process in Nigeria may well have positively affected the outcomes of the truth-telling process. For example, international focus on the work of the Oputa Panel could have turned the management of the truth-telling process into a litmus test for the government that established it. As it turns out, however, the transition moment is now irretrievably lost.

The failure of implementation of the laudable report ostensibly in compliance with a Supreme Court judgment continues to haunt the Nigerian polity in its bid to chart a path for peace, justice, and democracy. There is, moreover, no unanimity on the effect of the Supreme Court judgment on enforceability of the recommendations. Although some agree that the decision may have rendered nugatory aspects of the recommendations that related to the plaintiffs, they contend that the Supreme Court judgment was no excuse for the refusal to implement the Oputa Panel's recommendations. Some insist the Supreme Court in fact endorsed the Panel and that its creation was in any case valid under international conventions to which the country is party. Thus, they argue, the government ought to implement the recommendations. The latter view would appear to be strengthened by the failure of the government to offer an explanation on the specific aspects of the judgment, which prohibited it from publishing and implementing the recommendations. The failure of the regime that initiated it, as well as the continued silence of the successor government on the matter, has been telling.

The government's refusal to publish and implement the report and recommendations of the Oputa Panel remains widely condemned. In all events, the fallout of the decision continues to plague/cast a shadow on the sociopolitical and economic life of the country. The non-release of the report has been viewed as one of the cardinal reasons for the continued agitation by some segments of the population on a number of issues. A notable consequence of the non-implementation of the Oputa Panel's recommendations on redressing decades of injustice and deprivation in the country is the persisting and ubiquitous (albeit low-level) conflict, violence, and criminality in the oil- and gas-rich Niger Delta area of the country. This has had far-reaching impact on peace, security, and development in Nigeria's post-military authoritarian period.

The failure to conscientiously implement transitional justice has also been cited as one of the country's attempts at political reform that was abandoned midstream. Many groups and individuals have made repeated requests for the release and or implementation of the Oputa Report. The calls for positive government action have, however, been consistently ignored. In the aftermath of the non-implementation of the Oputa Panel Report, there has been an upsurge in violent property crimes and intercommunal and ethnic conflicts in the country. Hopes for a new dawn in the wake of the transition have gone largely unfulfilled.

Conclusion

There has been a failure of transitional justice implementation in the post-authoritarian/military era in Nigeria. Even the symbolic trials commenced in the wake of the political transition have been largely moribund for political and technical reasons. The lustration measures have at best produced a crop of very powerful ex-military officers who have emerged as key political players in the transition to civil governance with largely ill-gotten wealth secured from years of authoritarian rule. The lustration process was only directed at disengaging this crop of officers from active military service and nothing else. Because they were not barred from seeking elective office, they have emerged as a strong force on the political front. Benefiting from their deep pockets, they are now in key elective positions or have sponsored candidates for elections to protect their interests.

Worse still, the major mechanism for obtaining accountability and justice for victims of impunity – the truth-telling process – has been frustrated by a combination of dynamics, most prominent of which is the deficiency of sincerity on the part of the initiating regime. As a process, the truth-telling mechanism did a commendable job of seeking to establish the truth about the course of executive and legislative governance in the pre-transition period. It assisted the bid to legitimize the post-authoritarian civilian administration, but the value of its well received work remains questionable.

Civil governance is seriously challenged, if not jeopardized, by the growing incidence of militia violence and sabotage of oil and gas facilities in the country. Rivers, one of the states in the country's oil-producing areas hardest-hit by violence, set up its own truth commission in 2008. The report of this commission (recently submitted) has predictably generated interest. It remains to be seen if the state government will implement it. A myriad of conflicts that have since ensued to challenge institutional reform, good government, and development in the country have provided ample evidence of the danger inherent in neglecting to address the impunity that was the defining feature and legacy of the authoritarian period.

Hakeem O. Yusuf

Cross-references: Human Rights Violations Investigations Commission, Oputa Panel; Truth Commission.

Further Readings

Aka, Philip C. 2003. Nigeria since May 1999: Understanding the Paradox of Civil Rule and Human Rights Violations under President Obasanjo. *San Diego International Law Journal*, 4: 209–276.

Falana, Femi. 2004. When Will Leaders Pay for their Iniquities? *This* Day, December 20.

Oputa Panel Report, May 2004. Available at: http://www.dawodu.com/oputa1.htm (accessed September 17, 2009).

Osaghae, Egosa E. 1998. *Crippled Giant: Nigeria since Independence*. London: Hurst and Co.

Yusuf, Hakeem O. 2008. Oil on Troubled Waters-Multinational Corporations and Realising Human Rights in the Developing World: A Nigerian Case Study. *African Human Rights Law Journal*, 8: 79–108.

———. 2007. Travails of Truth: Achieving Justice for Victims of Impunity in Nigeria. *International Journal of Transitional Justice*, 1 (2): 268–284.

———. 2007. The Judiciary and Constitutionalism in Transitions: A Critique. *Global Jurist*, 7 (3): 1–49.

Northern Ireland

The Northern Ireland's transition is especially complex: (1) it involves two sovereign countries (the United Kingdom and the Republic of Ireland); (2) a new democratic consociational form of government was created in Northern Ireland within a state (the United Kingdom) that was already a democracy overall; and (3) in parallel came a shift from violent political conflict to (relative) peace in which the main non-state entity remained armed until seven years after the peace agreement. The transition came after a stalemated conflict that left a legacy of serious human rights violations involving state and non-state actors. This complexity and the dynamics of stalemate explain why the peace process adopted, initially at least, a "piecemeal" approach to dealing with the past.

The Repressive Past

The roots of the Northern Ireland conflict lay in the seventeenth-century Plantation of Ulster (Ireland's most northerly province), where Scottish and English settlers achieved dominance over or displaced the native Irish. In the early twentieth century, Ireland, led by the nationalists, sought independence, but in Ulster there was resistance from those who wished to preserve the union with Britain ("unionists"). The upshot was the creation of Northern Ireland in 1921 as a self-governing devolved region within the United Kingdom. The new entity had a two-thirds unionist majority, while nationalists, who sought unification with Ireland, comprised one-third of the population. While the Northern Ireland conflict is frequently described in religious terms (Catholic: nationalist and republican versus Protestant: unionist and loyalist), it is more accurate to see it as ethno-national, with religion as one component in ethno-national identity.

After 1921, Northern Ireland partly resembled a formal democracy: there were regular elections to parliament; the devolved government was selected from among legislators; and a British-style judiciary existed. Yet the Unionist party was continually in power; the judiciary was extremely quiescent; unionists gerrymandered electoral boundaries, and wealthy voters (generally unionist) were allowed multiple votes in local elections; the paramilitary police reserve (B Specials) was intimidating; repressive legislation was regularly invoked; and there was discrimination in jobs and the allocation of public housing.

In the late 1960s, a Northern Ireland Civil Rights Association was formed and soon achieved a significant degree of mass mobilization. Once it embarked on street protests, security forces repressed the movement. Rioting became intercommunal, pitting nationalists against loyalists. In a situation of intimidation and violence, populations shifted, with many nationalists driven from their homes in Belfast and unionists from theirs in Derry/Londonderry.

Following extreme pressure on the local Royal Ulster Constabulary (RUC) and B Specials, the British Army was deployed on the streets in August 1969. Initially welcomed in nationalist areas as protectors, relations soon declined because of abrasive military strategies and increased activity by the non-state [Provisional] Irish Republican Army (IRA). Armed non-state entities also emerged or consolidated out of loyalist mass mobilization. The Ulster Defense Association (UDA) and the Ulster Volunteer Force (UVF) indiscriminately attacked nationalist civilians, seeking to justify these as reprisals for IRA violence. Attacks were organized by these groups alone and in collusion with security force elements.

The violent conflict included three phases. In 1968, the conflict's eruption was followed by militarization, with the British Army holding supremacy in counterinsurgency. Internment without trial was introduced in 1971 and abandoned in 1975.

The second phase of "criminalization, normalization and Ulsterization" ran from 1977 to 1982. "Ulsterization" signified an increasing counterinsurgency role for local security forces (the RUC and the Ulster Defense Regiment). "Normalization" referred to processing those suspected of involvement in political violence through special juryless "Diplock courts" (established in 1973) on the basis of confessions obtained in one of three interrogation centers. "Criminalization" indicated that newly convicted non-state entity prisoners were treated as ordinary criminals (and no longer enjoyed "special category" status).

The third phase (1982–1994) saw media censorship and initiatives aimed at maximizing convictions in the Diplock system. These initiatives included the abrogation of the right to silence and the use of "supergrasses" – former terrorists, the prosecution claimed – who gave evidence against their erstwhile accomplices. The Diplock courts, but not the appeal courts, accepted such evidence as a basis for conviction. Few new initiatives came after 1990, as a behind-the-scenes peace process led to the 1994 non-state entity cease-fires.

There is no definitive database of conflict deaths, with agreement on victim status and of agency responsible. The CAIN database lists 3,526 conflict deaths between 1969 and 2001 out of a population of 1.6 million. *Lost Lives* lists 3,665 deaths for the 1966–2001 period. Details of the killings attributed to the main actors, including responsibility for civilian deaths, are as follows: CAIN attributes 1,709 deaths to the IRA, of whom 512 (30 percent) are listed as "civilian," but *Lost Lives* attributes 1,778 deaths, of whom 642 (36 percent) are "civilian"; CAIN attributes 668 deaths to the main loyalist UVF and UDA/UFF, of which 87 percent are "civilian," whereas *Lost Lives* lists 957 deaths and no breakdown regarding "civilians"; CAIN attributes 297 to the regular British Army, of whom 150 (51 percent) are listed as "civilian," but *Lost Lives* attributes 301 deaths, of which 158 (52 percent) are "civilian." Total state security force numbers varied from 33,000 to 44,000, giving a ratio of security force members to head of population of 36–48: 1.

Transition and Transitional Justice

The 1998 peace deal, the Belfast/Good Friday Agreement, was negotiated by the British and Irish governments and most of the elected parties in Northern Ireland (including Sinn Féin that, with the IRA, formed the Republican Movement). It stipulated a consociational regional government for Northern Ireland. This, coupled with an agreed formulation on Irish self-determination and the building of institutional links with the Republic of Ireland, largely remedied the democratic deficits experienced by nationalists. Unionist concerns were addressed when the Republic of Ireland renounced its claim to jurisdiction over Northern Ireland as of right, and by provision for new institutions binding both parts of Ireland and all regions of the United Kingdom closer together.

The conflict wound down on the state and non-state sides. The Agreement addressed institutional reforms of the security apparatus without reference to an impugned past. The British Army first withdrew from the streets, then reduced its numbers to that of a garrison force. The Agreement stipulated the creation of a commission to make recommendations on policing. Following the resulting Patten Commission Report, the RUC was renamed the Police Service of Northern Ireland (PSNI) and underwent change interpreted as modernizing reform (by RUC supporters) and as an attempt at more fundamental transformation (by RUC critics). The Agreement said little about the past and contained no institutional blueprint for dealing with it. Yet for reasons discussed later, the past refused to go away.

Alleged State Abuses

The main areas of concern regarding security forces have been the use of lethal force and alleged threats against lawyers; conduct in the interrogation room; and alleged brutal treatment of the civilian population in nationalist areas. The lethal force concerns break down into allegations of: unlawful killings in public-order situations (such as the Bloody Sunday killing of thirteen protesters by paratroopers at a 1972 march); the operation of a "shoot to kill" policy in which IRA suspects were shot when they could have been arrested; and allegations of security forces' collusion in UDA and UVF killings (including the deaths of prominent defense lawyers who worked in the Diplock courts).

Interrogation practices included the "torture lite" techniques from the early 1970s (hooding, wall-standing, sleep deprivation, food deprivation, and use of "white noise") and the less subtle methods described in *Donnelly v. UK* (beatings, forced administration of drugs). There has also been renewed focus on allegations of physical and psychological abuse in the interrogation centers in the late 1970s and 1980s.

The Bloody Sunday Inquiry

The British government established the Bloody Sunday/Saville Inquiry (see separate entry) in 1998 to investigate the events of the Bloody Sunday. Comprising both British and international judges, the tribunal heard in 2000–2005 oral evidence from 921 civilian and military witnesses, and received 2,500 written statements. The proceedings have been controversial. While its terms of reference leave scope for investigation into the wider context of the Blood Sunday events, in practice the tribunal restricted its cross-examination to the immediate context. The Inquiry's Report, published in June 2010, deemed all deaths unjustified, laid responsibility on members of the Parachute Regiment, and thus made a definitive finding of fact. However, the Report ignored international human rights law and possible international humanitarian dimensions of the killings, and exonerated those at the governmental level whose decisions affected the deployment of the paratroopers.

The "Collusion Inquiries"

In 2002, Justice Peter Cory was asked to examine six controversial deaths involving alleged security force collusion (the Republic of Ireland engaged in a parallel process). The Inquiries Act of 2005 enhanced the protection of intelligence interests (with a corresponding blunting of truth-finding capacity). A crucial issue for these inquiries is whether collusion allegations can be effectively investigated through the atomized approach entailed by a multiplicity of individual inquiries, with each being held with little reference to the other, or whether it might be better to explore patterns of alleged wrongdoing across a range of cases.

The first to report was the Billy Wright Inquiry, which investigated the shooting dead in prison of an anti-peace process loyalist by a republican prisoner (non-IRA). The Report refused to adopt the definition of collusion utilized by the Police Ombudsman and Judge Cory. Using a narrower definition, it found that Wright's death was not a result of collusion. Rather, it placed the blame on inadequacies in the Prison Service, a move that deflected criticism from the intelligence failures and destroyed documents uncovered by the Inquiry.

Police Ombudsman

The Police Ombudsman office was created under the Police (Northern Ireland) Acts of 1998–2003. In contrast to previous police complaints mechanisms, the new Ombudsman operated with its own team of investigators and could investigate the actions of individuals within, and the practices of, the police service. A change in the Ombudsman's mandate in 2001 facilitated extensive retrospection. The first appointee, Nuala O'Loan, used her powers to investigate and publicly report on cases spanning the entire conflict, and thus effectively employed the Office as a transitional justice vehicle. In 2007, O'Loan left office and was replaced by Al Hutchinson, who showed less enthusiasm for pursuing investigations into older allegations.

The Historical Enquiries Team (HET)

The HET was established by the PSNI Chief Constable in 2005, as a "free-standing" PSNI unit answerable to the Chief. It must examine all 3,268 conflict-related deaths within Northern Ireland between 1968 and 1998 to ensure that investigative and evidential opportunities are exploited. Where viable opportunities emerge, a case is submitted to the Public Prosecution Service for consideration. In most instances, it is envisaged that prosecution will not ensue. HET seeks to achieve "closure" for family members of the deceased by providing them with a Review Summary Report (RSR) giving them information about the circumstances of death. HET, envisaged to exist for six years, conducts examinations chronologically, beginning from 1968. While the HET has provided families with information about their relative's death and gained approval from some local nongovernmental organizations, former RUC officers act as gatekeepers of the flow of intelligence into HET. This raises issues concerning possible suppression of evidence and the former officers' level of impartiality and independence on the issue of responsibility for deaths.

The Commission for Victims and Survivors

In 1997, the British Secretary of State for Northern Ireland tasked Sir Kenneth Bloomfield, a former civil servant, to begin an examination of victims' issues. His recommendations, which said little about security force killings, focused on deaths caused by non-state entities and suggested the establishment of a Commission. In 2008, new legislation created the Commission for Victims and Survivors. Following some controversy, four commissioners were appointed to maximize cross-community standing. Of these, one had suffered family loss at the hands of the IRA and another at the hands of the British Army and of loyalists.

The Commission monitors service provision and provides a consultation forum for victims and survivors. This service orientation is evident in the statutory definition of victim, which included those injured in the conflict, those providing care for such people, and those left bereaved by the conflict, but not the most important category of the conflict's victims (the dead), apparently because of controversy around creating hierarchies of victims. As this definition was also adopted in the most recent initiative on dealing with the past, the Eames-Bradley Report (see discussion later), the debate on its adequacy is certain to resurface.

Initiatives Affecting State and Non-State Entities: Bottom-Up Truth Recovery

There have been several initiatives on dealing with the past and reflecting bottom-up, non-state perspectives. Among these is "Healing Through Remembering" (initially supported by the Community Relations Council), focused on commemoration and analysis.

The most successful bottom-up initiative with a demonstrable capacity for truth recovery has been the Ardoyne Commemoration Project (ACP), which focused on all ninety-nine conflict-related deaths in one nationalist district of Belfast. The project was run by local people with assistance from academics who developed the research methodology. Using participatory action techniques, a picture was built up of the context of the fatalities, determining agency responsibility, and elucidating how death came about (mostly at the hands of loyalist paramilitaries and the British Army). Nine deaths were attributed to the IRA. As yet, no comparable project has emerged from within loyalist communities.

Alleged Non-State Abuses

The issues that have dominated analysis of armed non-state entities in the transition include initiatives springing from within the movements, obligations externally imposed, and unaddressed or unresolved issues. Apologies, with layers of conditionality, have emerged both from the IRA and from loyalist non-state entities.

There have also been initiatives on strategies for dealing with the past that have come chiefly from prisoner groups associated with non-state entities, or from joint initiatives by such groups and human rights organizations. These outputs point to sharp communal divisions as to whether it is necessary or desirable to have retrospective exploration (with further divisions on what constitutes the past). Loyalists appear to feel that dealing with the past offers little political gain (in view of collusion allegations), whereas republicans see the process as opening political opportunities.

As regards externally imposed obligations, the two main issues have been locating the bodies of the disappeared (ten to twenty people shot and secretly buried by republicans, mostly IRA) and weapons decommissioning. Because of increased pressure from victims' groups for the location of the bodies of the disappeared, an Independent Commission for the Location of Victims' Remains was established following a UK-Ireland treaty. The legislation provided a partial amnesty whereby any evidence obtained from located bodies was inadmissible in criminal proceedings, as was information regarding locations of graves. Seven bodies were located to date.

A similar legal template was adopted in relation to non-state entity weapons decommissioning with the enactment of legislation establishing the Independent International Commission on Decommissioning. Inspection and sealing of arms dumps intensified after the 9/11 attacks. The IRA destroyed the last of its weaponry in September 2005. Other non-state entities followed, with several completing in February 2010, just before the legislation granting partial amnesty was due to expire.

That amnesty made material obtained from decommissioned weapons inadmissible in criminal proceedings and provided immunity from prosecution for a range of firearms and explosive offenses in respect of anything done in accordance with a decommissioning scheme. The Agreement made no provisions for general amnesty, but it stipulated that prisoners convicted of politically motivated offenses, whose organizations were on cease-fire, were to be released within two years. Legislation gave the task of deciding on eligibility for release to a Sentence Review Commission.

Among unresolved issues affecting non-state entities that emerged during the transition are the question of security force collusion in paramilitary killings, the paramilitary ill-treatment of suspected informers prior to their execution, and the issue of responsibility for ill-treatment raised in relation to paramilitary "punishment" attacks on those accused of "antisocial" activities (for example, burglary). There has also been a focus on patterns of killings by the IRA in border areas. Reverse claims and counterclaims have been made about the large population displacements that figured early in the conflict.

The Eames-Bradley Report: A Holistic Alternative?

Despite the plethora of initiatives during the transition, pressure for something more than the piecemeal approach grew. Paradoxically, the partial success of the piecemeal model created a dynamic whereby the uncovering of particular facts generated demands for follow-up investigations in new areas, creating a cycle of positive reinforcement. Northern Ireland has vibrant nongovernmental organizations, skilled in maximizing opportunities for human rights advocacy. The key imperative driving the need for examining the past was the effect of litigation under the European Convention on Human Rights (ECHR) with respect to the right to life (Art. 2). This established that the state had failed in its procedural obligations under Art. 2 in several cases in which the deceased had died in shoot-to-kill incidents, or in which security force collusion with loyalist non-state entities was alleged.

Reflecting these imperatives, in 2007, the British Secretary of State for Northern Ireland announced the formation of the Consultative Group on the Past with a mandate to "consult across the community on how Northern Ireland society can best approach the legacy of the events of the past 40 years; [and to] make recommendations... on any steps that might be taken to support Northern Ireland society in building a shared future that is not overshadowed by the events of the past" (Report of the Consultative Group on the Past, p. 44). The group was jointly chaired by Robin Eames (former Protestant Archbishop) and Dennis Bradley (a former Catholic priest involved in policing changes). Following public meetings, a report was published in January 2009.

The Report recommended a Legacy Commission (a limited truth commission) presided over by an International Commissioner and two other commissioners. The mandate for the proposed Commission, to be discharged within five years, was described in terms of four strands, of which (2)–(4) appear focused on deaths arising from the conflict: (1) A Commission to address such issues as tackling sectarianism to "help society towards a shared future," and with the Commission for Victims and Survivors for Northern Ireland to establish a Reconciliation Forum. (2) A new Review and Investigation Unit to conduct individual police investigation of "historical cases." If sufficient evidence is obtained, the case is to go to Director of Public Prosecutions; if evidence insufficient, the case is to be referred to (3) or (4). (3) A new Information Recovery Unit to provide individual victims' families with details of circumstances that resulted in victims' deaths. (4) A Thematic Examination Unit to examine "linked or thematic cases emerging from the conflict" rather than focus on individual cases as under (2) and (3). These mechanisms' heavy focus on conflict-related deaths reflected the Group's findings that "the issue of alleged collusion has not been properly dealt with" up to this point (p. 124). The Group's reference to an examination under strand 4 of a "particular area of paramilitary activity" is assumed to refer to IRA attacks in border areas.

The group recommended that families of all of those killed in the conflict receive a "recognition payment" of £12,000, criticized for equating "dead terrorists" with members of the security forces killed in the conflict. The British government unilaterally rejected the recommendation. A public consultation followed, but the British government's inconclusive response left open the question whether any of the Report would be implemented. The unilateral manner in which payments were rejected raised the question of whether the government could be trusted to oversee a truth process centrally concerned with the actions of its agents. The Report rules amnesty out for the moment, but hints that it might be desirable in five years. Non-state entities suggested that they would contribute little to the truth process the report envisaged. This led to suggestions that it might be necessary to incentivize participation by "trading amnesty for truth" by providing a conditional amnesty on the South African model.

Conclusion

Northern Ireland is a site of contest between the "piecemeal" and the "holistic" models for dealing with the past. The piecemeal approach was successful in providing a means to deal with discrete chunks of the past in a way that permitted the peace process to move ahead. Over time, the model became unsatisfactory. Its successes have pointed to lacunae in relation to other areas, generating a dynamic of incrementally increasing demand. This dynamic reflects the problems experienced by the liberal democratic state in recognizing its systematic failures. While the piecemeal approach may have appeared to offer the hope of labeling failings as the actions of "bad apples" rather than as having been institutionalized, its failures have now been highlighted. A holistic model, like that suggested in the Eames-Bradley Report, offers the tantalizing prospect of addressing state and non-state abuses, but for the state it risks further highlighting systematic failures, and could entail the challenge of crafting a conditional amnesty compatible with international law.

Colm Campbell

Cross-references: Amnesty; Bloody Sunday Inquiry; Courts for Redress; Truth Commission.

Further Readings

Bell, C. 2003. Dealing with the Past in Northern Ireland. *Fordham International Law Journal*, 26(4): 1095–1147.
CAIN Web Service. *Conflict and Politics in Northern Ireland (1968 to the Present)*. University of Ulster. Available at: http://cain.ulster.ac.uk/ (accessed November 16, 2010).
Campbell, C. and C. Turner. 2008. Utopia and the Doubters: Truth, Transition and the Law. *Legal Studies*, 28(3): 374–395.
Consultative Group on the Past. 2009. *Report of the Consultative Group on the Past*. Belfast.
Donnelly v. UK, Application 5577, 5583/73, Decision of the Commission, 5 April 1973.
Lundy, P. 2009. Can the Past Be Policed? Lessons from the Historical Enquiries Team Northern Ireland. *Law and Social Challenges*, 11 (Spring/Summer): 109–171.
McEvoy, K. 2007. Beyond Legalism: Towards and Thicker Understanding of Transitional Justice. *Journal of Law and Society*, 34(4): 411–440.
McKittrick, D., Seamus Kelters, Brian Feeney, and Chris Thornton. 2001. *Lost Lives: The Stories of the Men, Women and Children Who Died as a Result of the Northern Ireland Troubles*. Edinburgh: Mainstream Publishing.

Pakistan

Despite its troubled history and recent attempts to liberalize the regime, Pakistan has failed to implement transitional justice. Since its independence in 1947, Pakistan has been plagued by serious human rights problems, including mistreatment of religious and ethnic minorities and discrimination against women. These problems have worsened as Islamic extremists pursued their ideological agenda. Attempts by civil society organizations and political parties loosely grouped around the small urban middle class to institute transitional justice have made only fitful progress in certain areas.

The Repressive Past

Pakistan was conceived as a state where Indian Muslims could escape religious persecution and discrimination in predominantly Hindu India. Its founder, Muhammad Ali Jinnah, envisioned the country as a secular state with equal rights for its Muslim and non-Muslim citizens. This vision unraveled almost from inception. The 1947 partition of British India into the newly created states of India and Pakistan was bloody, as Sikhs and Hindus in India attacked their Muslim neighbors and drove them into Pakistan, and Muslims in Pakistan turned on the Sikh and Hindu minorities. Between 500,000 and 1 million persons were killed in the sectarian bloodletting in Punjab and Bengal. Jinnah's early death in 1948 removed the last barrier to the widespread discrimination against religious and ethnic minorities that has continued to the present day.

Civilian rule ended with a military coup that installed Army Commander Ayub Khan in power in 1958. The army has played a dominant role in Pakistan ever since. Pakistan was established as a multiethnic state with two wings, East Pakistan (formerly East Bengal) and West Pakistan, separated by 1,000 miles of Indian territory. East Pakistan was overwhelmingly Bengali, a highly homogenous ethnic group with its own distinct language and culture, but divided religiously between Muslims and Hindus. Although inhabited by various ethnic groups sharing no common language, West Pakistan was dominated by the Punjabis, who represented 44 percent of the total population of 34 million.

Bengalis felt marginalized in Pakistan almost from the beginning. Their sense of inferiority was confirmed in 1948 when Jinnah rejected their demand for a dual-language state and declared Urdu, the lingua franca of West Pakistan, the sole national language. In 1970, Bengali grievances led to a revolt brutally repressed by the Punjabi-dominated Pakistani army. Up to 500,000 Bengalis were murdered in army-conducted anti-Bengali and anti-Hindu purges in East Pakistan, and hundreds of thousands of Bengali women were raped by Pakistani soldiers. The bloody crackdown ended when Indian and Bengali forces defeated the Pakistan army and East Pakistan emerged as the new country of Bangladesh in 1971 (see entry on Bangladesh).

After East Pakistan seceded to form Bangladesh, the remaining provinces faced their own ethnic tensions, caused largely by suspicion, cultural prejudices, and competition for resources and government revenues. Pakistan's most important ethnic groups were the Punjabis and the Seraikis of the Punjab province (accounting for 44 percent and 11 percent of the population, respectively), the Pashtuns of the Northwest Frontier province (15 percent), the Sindhis of the Sindh province (14 percent), and the Muhajirs and Baluchis of Baluchistan (8 percent and 4 percent, respectively). The Baluchis, Pashtuns, Muhajirs (immigrants from India and their descendants), and other ethnic groups chafed under the dominance of the Punjabis, who controlled the military and police forces and used extended periods of military rule to increase their power. In the 1970s, Baluch grievances broke out in a rebellion brutally suppressed by the Pakistani military. A Baluch separatist insurgency reemerged with a series of killings of non-Baluch in Baluchistan in 2006. The province, located in Western Pakistan and bordering on Iran in the west and India in the south, remains tense and wracked by violence.

Since independence, the dominant Muslims have engaged in widespread discrimination against the Sikhs, Hindus, and Christians, which together account for less than 5 percent of the population. Minorities are largely frozen out of employment and business and are victims of periodic attacks by Muslim organized gangs, which include destruction of property, physical violence, and sexual abuse of minority women. The Pakistani police often fail to provide protection to minority communities, and those guilty of attacks are seldom arrested or prosecuted.

The second-class status for religious minorities was codified and legitimated during the rule of General Zia ul Haq (1979–1989), who abandoned Jinnah's concept of a secular Pakistan and adopted a program of Islamization of Pakistan, introducing the Hudood

Ordinance in 1979. The law, which introduced the Islamic Sharia law, including punishments for extramarital sex and alcohol consumption, was condemned as a setback for women, as hundreds of rape victims were incarcerated for adultery. Under Haq, religious minorities were barred from obtaining high rank in the military and civil service, and discrimination and persecution increased.

As Islam became more dominant under the patronage of the Pakistani political and military elite, tension increased between Islamic sects. Pakistan is home to the second-largest Shia community in the world (estimated at 10–30 percent of the country's Muslim population). When militant Sunni Muslim groups launched bloody attacks on Shia mosques and communities, Shia extremists responded with similar attacks against the Sunnis. In 1974, Pakistan declared the small Ahmadiya community to be non-Muslim. Ahmadiyas regard their sect's founder, Mirza Ghulam Ahmad, as a prophet. This is considered apostasy by many Muslims, who regard the Prophet Muhammad as the "seal of the Prophets." The Prevention of Anti-Islamic Activities Act of 1984 deprived Ahmadiyas of their status as an Islamic sect. As a result, life became increasingly difficult for Ahmadiyas and many were forced to flee Pakistan.

Pakistan has a dysfunctional public education system, which has been increasingly supplemented by thousands of madrassas, or Islamic religious schools, funded from abroad (largely Saudi Arabia). Primarily Sunni, many madrassas have inculcated an extreme version of Islam based on Wahhabism, which preaches that religious minorities, including Shias and Ahmadiyas, should be driven out of the country in order to "purify" Pakistan of their influence. The rising Islamist sentiment has led to calls for radical restrictions on the activities of women and numerous attacks on women not sufficiently compliant. Under the Hadood Ordinances, the testimony of Muslim women does not have the same weight in court cases as that of men. Married Pakistani women who are victims of rape can be imprisoned for adultery, and males can be convicted of rape only if male witnesses provide eyewitness testimony.

Pakistan suffers from a dual and contradictory system of governance, with the secular educated urban middle class confronting traditional elites consisting of feudal landlords, the Islamic religious establishment, and their supporting political parties. The urban middle class and its supporters would like to see more effective and less corrupt governance and ruling institutions that begin to address the needs of the people. They are also calling for Pakistan to guarantee civil rights to all of its citizens, regardless of their religious and ethnic affiliation or gender. Traditional feudal elites have overlapped with the military, with much of the officer corps belonging to this social class. Their principal concern has been to perpetuate their hold on power. They view the educated middle class as a threat to their political monopoly. The elites, including the army, have patronized Islamist political parties and organizations to manipulate public opinion, thus increasing the legitimacy of these parties' discriminatory agenda.

Pakistani elites have failed to provide functional governance, basic social services, or a functional judiciary system. Islamist organizations have moved to fill this vacuum, administering parallel education and justice systems and social service organizations that often provide more effective services to the poor masses than the nonfunctional or totally corrupt institutions of the Pakistani state. This vacuum has thus contributed to Pakistan's "Talibanization," as a frustrated population comes to embrace Islamist institutions and ideologies also present in neighboring Afghanistan. As Talibanization spreads, the position of religious minorities and women continues to deteriorate, with growing restrictions on female participation in education, the economy, and public life.

Until the recent economic downturn, Pakistan's small urban middle class was growing in numbers and political and economic power. This group embraces a more modernist and secular outlook critical of Pakistan's long history of discrimination and abuse and has pressed for Pakistani integration into the international mainstream. The middle class has tried to counter Islamization, make inroads into dominance by feudal elites, and introduce more effective and less corrupt social and governing institutions by supporting secular political parties such as the Pakistan People's Party (PPP) and a plethora of social service organizations such as nongovernmental and feminist organizations. Recently, the urban middle class has also found allies within the military and the judiciary (see later discussion).

Transitional Justice

The Pakistani governmental and social institutions have largely failed to address the repressive past, both because the country has been rocked by political instability and because the political class and the general public have shown little interest in coming to terms with the human rights violations that permeate daily life. Some judicial reforms have been introduced, the observance of human rights has been strengthened, and the PPP government has attempted to move away from a strictly Muslim and Punjabi agenda that previously discriminated against women and religious and ethnic minorities. Pakistani reformers have attempted to revise the Pakistani national narrative by opening a serious examination of past abuses in the media and education system along with corrective action. However, it is too early to say whether these limited transitional justice efforts will take hold or survive over the longer term.

Reform of the Judiciary

The partnership between the middle class on the one hand and the military and the judiciary on the other hand became most effective in 2007, when it rallied behind Chief Justice of the Supreme Court Iftikhar Muhammad Chaudhry. His family migrated to Baluchistan from India, and he has long been associated with the PPP. Shortly after being appointed by President Pervez Musharraf, Chaudhry reversed years of judicial complacence, began to hear public litigation cases involving human rights violations, publicly opposed military dictatorship, and called for the rule of law. He also declared President Musharraf's declaration of emergency and the suspension of civil rights to be illegal. In the Hasba bill case, Chaudhry ruled that the Pakistani police did not have the legal power to enforce observance of Islamic practices and values on the Pakistani people. Under Chaudhury's leadership, the judiciary gained new credence with the Pakistanis, who began to view it as a means of addressing past abuses. Between June 2005 and March 2007, 30,000 additional cases, many dealing with the power of the military and perceived human rights abuses, were filed with the Supreme Court. This led Musharraf to view Chaudhry's judicial activism as a threat to the military's hold on power.

On March 9, 2007, Musharraf fired Chaudhry, who indicated opposition to Musharraf's proposal to change the constitution to allow him to renew his presidential mandate.

The Supreme Court ruled that Chaudhry's dismissal was illegal and ordered his reinstatement. On November 3, Musharraf declared emergency rule and again dismissed the Chief Justice. This was the first time that the Pakistani judiciary did not meekly comply with directives from the Pakistani military. Musharraf concluded that his appointment of Chaudhry was a mistake and hoped to dismiss him and replace him with a more compliant Chief Justice.

This move energized the nation's lawyers, who mobilized in Chaudhry's defense and enlisted mass support. On June 13, 2008, the Lawyers Guild formed a 1.5-kilometer motorcade bringing 100,000 persons to Islamabad to press for Chaudhry's reinstatement. In August, President Musharraf resigned and was replaced by Asif Ali Zardari, the widower of the slain former Prime Minister Benazir Bhutto. At the time of her assassination, Bhutto headed a powerful political dynasty started by her father Zulfikar Ali Bhutto, the founder of the PPP. The Bhutto family has had an uneasy relationship with the Pakistani military ever since Zia ul Haq deposed Zulfikar in a 1977 military coup and executed him in 1979. Although the Bhutto family belongs to Baluchistan's feudal elite, the PPP has espoused secular and liberal values with varying degrees of success and come into conflict with the Muslim religious establishment. On March 21, Zardari reinstated Chaudhry as Chief Justice, thus demonstrating that the middle classes could organize a mass movement that could have some success in the struggle against the abuse of political power and for the due process of law.

Young lawyers displayed political clout during their agitation in support of Chief Justice Chaudhry, but the judiciary remained weak, ineffective, and corrupt, and favored the wealthy. In April 2010, the country attempted to address these systemic problems by amending its constitution to remove the power of the president and prime minister to directly make judicial appointments, replacing that power with a two-tier nomination system whereby a judicial commission will propose nominees and a special parliamentary committee will confirm them. This reform was needed as, in the absence of an effective judicial system, many Pakistanis have turned to *jirgas* (tribal councils), village elders, or landlords to solve personal and property disputes and even criminal cases. These alternatives have often blocked transitional justice because they have a vested interest in maintaining the traditional economic and social systems and opposing social change.

Several trends have also strengthened Islamist forces at the expense of transitional justice. The worldwide economic downturn of the late 2000s was devastating to the Pakistani economy, and particularly to the urban middle class, which is tied into the global economy and the world trading and financial systems. Economic hardship has undermined the reform movements that galvanized around Chief Justice Chaudhry in 2007 and 2008.

Reforms of the Military

Despite the many setbacks to the equality of women in Pakistan, the military has moved to provide employment opportunities. In 2003, the Pakistani Air Force accepted women cadets and began training women as pilots. The first graduated in 2007. The army has opened the National Guard (a civil defense unit) to women, and there are moves afoot to recruit women for combat positions within the army and navy. Despite these efforts, the Musharraf government failed to amend or repeal the elements of Sharia law introduced under Haq. Women still do not enjoy equal protection under the law and remain victims of domestic and spousal abuse, as well as wholesale discrimination in education, the workplace, and in regards to personal property rights.

Increased Mass Media Pluralization

The mass movement led by the nation's lawyers was aided by the proliferation of independent mass media in Pakistan. In 2000, there were only three state-run television stations in the country, but by 2008, there were more than fifty privately owned channels, including twenty news channels and wide public access to international media. This wide variety of media has broadened access to more reliable information and antigovernment views. Likewise, Pakistan's print media were very outspoken in their criticism of the Musharraf regime. While there has been increasing pressure on Pakistani media outlets to take a conservative Islamic approach, liberal news sources can openly espouse transitional justice, social change, and progressive views on social and religious issues with little censorship or harassment.

Since 2008, the move for transitional justice has suffered setbacks. Pakistan became increasingly unstable as the civil war raging in Afghanistan spilled over and Islamic extremist groups opened a campaign of antigovernment violence. Although restrictions placed on the media during the 2007 emergency declaration were largely lifted one year later, after the demise of the Musharraf regime, the media has retreated from its earlier activist stance and adopted a more jingoistic and sensationalistic point of view. This became evident after the November 2008 terrorist attacks in Mumbai. During the attacks, terrorists landed by boat from Pakistan and indiscriminately murdered Indians and non-Indians in the city of Mumbai. Most international media determined that the attacks were conceived and directed by terrorist groups based in Pakistan and were aimed at increasing Indian/Pakistan animosity. In response to the widespread allegations, most Pakistani media took a strong anti-India stance.

Women and Politics

Pakistani women in educated urban circles have found increased opportunities for education, employment, and political empowerment, but this is in stark contrast to the position of women generally. The reserved seats for women in political institutions (33 percent at the local level and 17 percent at the national and provincial level) are largely ignored. Instead, women are excluded from positions of leadership or power and usually can gain prominence only through kinship links to powerful males.

Violent Setbacks to Transitional Justice

As noted earlier, the war in neighboring Afghanistan has also come to Pakistan with a vengeance. The Pakistani army is locked in a bitter struggle with Pakistani Taliban elements in the tribal areas on the western border. In response, Islamist groups have unleashed a wave of terror within Pakistan, setting off a string of bombing attacks in major urban areas that have killed hundreds, including high-ranking military personnel. The military campaigns characterized by often indiscriminate bombing and shelling have displaced hundreds of thousands of Pakistani civilians, devastated homes, and killed civilians. In addition, the Pakistani army has been accused of murdering civilians in revenge for terrorist attacks.

The deteriorating Pakistani security situation following the army's offensive operations against Pakistani Taliban in Swat in 2009 has been accompanied by an increase in lawlessness and criminality, with criminals often masquerading as Islamists. The Pakistani Taliban, a nexus of often unconnected Islamist and criminal groups, have engaged in brutality and violence and have spread fear in areas they control. The growing sense of desperation has strengthened the hand of the military and caused a turn toward traditional Islamic values. Pakistani society feels beleaguered from within and without and unsure of the future. At the same time, there is a growing sense of anger directed against the United States in particular and the West in general, with many in Pakistan seeing the United States and India allied against the Pakistani state and determined to impose foreign values (like equal status for women and religious minorities and a more secular approach to governance). This upsurge in nationalism has dulled calls for reform and replaced them with calls for Islamic unity.

Pakistan's religious minorities are finding few sympathetic voices in such an environment, and those once interested in supporting reform are under increasing pressure to remain silent. This latest trend has only reinforced Pakistan's inability to come to grips with earlier atrocities such as the mass killing that accompanied the partition of British India and the establishment of Pakistan, Pakistan's violent suppression of Baluchi insurgencies, and its attempted suppression of the Bangladesh independence movement.

Faced with political instability and repeated military coups almost since its founding, Pakistan has yet to establish a sense of stability and security that would enable it to seriously address transitional justice. Its religious and ethnic minorities have faced repeated and often violent repression and denial of basic civil liberties. While the government has acknowledged abuses and apologized for them, these efforts have been sporadic and uncoordinated. In some cases, especially those that receive extensive media coverage, the government has paid monetary reparations to those who lost property or family members or experienced injury or humiliation, but these efforts have not been widespread, systematic, or long term. Pakistan's military and its feudal elites have refused to accept responsibility for these abuses, preferring to call for "Muslim unity" and Pakistani patriotism in the face of foreign threats from India, the United States, and Israel.

Conclusion

There is a need for transitional justice in Pakistan. The country's history is replete with bloody chapters that have yet to be addressed. The Islamic republic, founded to provide a homeland for Indian Muslims, has failed to provide a safe and secure home for its own religious minorities. Political manipulation of Islam has led to greater extremism, less tolerance, and more violence. Islamist extremists increasingly preach hatred not only against religious minorities, but against sects within Islam that they deem to be insufficiently "pure." This has led to calls for religious cleansing. Likewise, ethnic minorities, especially in Baluchistan, have yet to see their grievances addressed. A nascent movement to provide transitional justice coalesced around the growing urban middle class. This movement scored some initial successes but was unable to influence the powerful forces wracking the country. Instead, extremist ideologies, often justified by references to Islam, have been used to fill the vacuum. This has encouraged the formation of extremist groups with growing influence.

Jon P. Dorschner

Cross-references: Causes of Failure of Transitional Justice; Conflict (Ongoing) and Transitional Justice; Media and Transitional Justice; Reforms of Military, Police, Secret Police; Reparations.

Further Readings

Khan, Yasmin, ed. 2008. *The Great Partition – The Making of India and Pakistan*. New Haven: Yale University Press.
Mezzera, Marco and Safiya Aftab. 2009. Country Case Study: Pakistan. *Initiative for Peacebuilding*. Available at: http://www.initiativeforpeacebuilding.eu/ (accessed June 30, 2010).
Ott, Mack. 2010. *Nation Building – The World's Unfinished Business*, unpublished manuscript.

Panama

Panama's repressive past and approach to transitional justice mirror that of many other Latin American countries: the country experienced decades of military rule (1968–1989) that abruptly gave way to democracy as the Cold War ended, and immediately began to engage its past through a wide range of mechanisms. Yet, unlike its neighbors, Panama's democratic transition was the result of foreign intervention – the 1989 U.S. invasion – a factor that has severely complicated its approach to transitional justice. Panama has to confront two types of past abuses – those committed under military rule, and those committed during the invasion – and it has not always been free to make its transitional justice decisions without international influence. Panama is therefore still actively debating issues of transitional justice at the time of this writing.

The Repressive Past

The military dominated Panamanian politics in the twentieth century. In 1904, the government created the National Police, which began to grow in strength in the 1930s and the 1940s, particularly under the leadership of General José Remón. In 1952, when Remón became president, he reorganized the National Police along military lines into the National Guard. In the two decades that followed, the National Guard increasingly intervened in politics, finally overthrowing President Arnulfo Arias in a coup in 1968, just eleven days after he had taken office. After the coup, a power struggle ensued within the National Guard, and one of the coup leaders, Lieutenant Colonel Omar Torrijos, emerged as the dominant leader in 1969. He then ruled the state as a dictator from 1969 to 1981, when he died in a mysterious plane crash. While Torrijos had a strong constituency in the country – attributed to his charismatic leadership style, socialist-leaning domestic programs, and nationalist foreign policy initiatives – repression was widespread and particularly directed against guerrillas loyal to the ousted Arias.

After the death of Torrijos, General Manuel Antonio Noriega, the former Chief of Military Intelligence, took over the leadership of the country. Noriega further consolidated the dictatorship by reorganizing the National Guard into the Panamanian Defense

Forces under his command. In doing so, he created special commando units that aided him in thwarting several coup attempts and in terrorizing the population to prevent any domestic opposition from forming. Under Noriega's rule, the population lived in fear of the Defense Forces: the regime held thousands of political prisoners and more than 100 individuals were killed or disappeared.

Even though Noriega was a key Cold War ally, the United States was gradually growing tired of his corruption and involvement in the illegal drug trade. In the 1989 Panamanian presidential elections, the United States gave US$10 million to the opposition candidate, Guillermo Endara, who represented a coalition of opposition parties. Endara appeared to be victorious in the election, but Noriega annulled the results and maintained power. In response, in December 1989, the United States launched operation Just Cause, the military invasion of Panama. Within days, the country was occupied, the Defense Forces were eliminated as a fighting force, and Noriega was captured and whisked away to Miami to stand trial for drug trafficking, racketeering, and money laundering.

The number of casualties Panama sustained during the occupation remains disputed. The United States has prevented any serious investigations into abuses committed by its forces during the invasion, and estimates of civilian deaths range from the Pentagon's official figure of just 516 to 2,500–3,500 by the United Nations and other international and Panamanian organizations. More than 15,000 civilians were internally displaced, many as a result of the heavy bombing of the El Chorrillo neighborhood of Panama City. The U.S. military provided temporary accommodations for around 3,000 refugees at the Albrook air base, but the others were left to fend for themselves. Following the initial invasion and destruction of the Defense Forces, massive rioting and looting occurred throughout the country. Estimates for economic damages caused by the invasion have been as high as US$2 billion. In the end, Panama emerged in 1990 as a tenuous democracy with poor internal security and a long history of human rights abuses stemming from decades of military rule.

Transitional Justice

Panama's approach to transitional justice since 1990 has been comprehensive. The government has enacted a wide range of mechanisms, including amnesties, a truth commission, trials, and security sector reforms. Yet the process has been incomplete. The country remains divided in its views on the former military regime, and consequently transitional justice efforts face stiff resistance, reforms are not implemented fully, and policies are often reversed when new politicians, with different political leanings, come to power.

Reforms of the Military and the Security Sector

Just days following the invasion, the United States installed Endara, the apparent winner of the 1989 elections, as President of Panama. During Endara's term (December 1989– September 1994), one of his policy priorities was to reform the security sector. After twenty years of military repression, the public was in favor of abolishing the military completely. Immediately after taking office, Endara disbanded the 3,500 Defense Forces troops in combat units, most of whom entered civilian life. Other significant moves followed, including demilitarizing the Air Force (which became the unarmed National

Air Service) and Navy (which became the Coast Guard), and transferring specific units, such as the presidential security detail, to separate ministries. In February 1990, the government formally terminated the Defense Forces and created the new Public Force. By summer 1990, there were only 11,000 total troops in the Public Force, down from 18,000 in the Defense Forces before the transition. A 1994 constitutional amendment prohibited the creation of a standing military force.

Controversy over this process was intense. In creating the Public Force, the government was forced to use many former members of the Defense Forces, citing a lack of sufficiently trained individuals to staff the new police force, the need to show to former members of the Defense Forces that there was a place for them in society, and fears that they might transform into guerrilla units and contest the government. The government also contended that, while the new leaders of the Public Force were members of the Defense Forces, they were largely junior officers who were not high enough in the Defense Forces to have been enmeshed in corruption and human rights violations. Still, public opinion was overwhelmingly against the process, with 75 percent of Panamanians objecting to how the Public Force was created. The election of President Ernesto Perez Balladares in 1994 further complicated matters. Balladares was a long-time member of the Democratic Revolutionary Party (PRD), the political arm of Torrijos, Noriega, and the Defense Forces. After taking office, Ballardes proceeded to appoint many of the worst-known Defense Force human rights abusers as key government advisers, ministers, and ambassadors.

Prosecutions

While security sector reform dominated the headlines immediately after the transition, criminal proceedings in domestic courts also began against former members of the Defense Forces for human rights violations committed during the military rule (1968–1989). These trials, which continued throughout the 1990s, were successful in convicting hundreds of individuals for murder, torture, and other crimes committed during military rule. Most notably, Noriega was convicted of murder in 1993 and sentenced in absentia to twenty years in prison.

Yet the results were mixed. The number of convictions was low compared to the hundreds of total cases initiated. Political bias led to many cases being thwarted in the investigation stage by police or dismissed by sympathetic judges, and juries acquitted several individuals, leading, at times, to massive street protests. Furthermore, while the conviction of Noriega was a moral victory for Panama, he remained in U.S. custody, where he had been sentenced to forty years in prison in 1992 for drug trafficking, racketeering, and money laundering. In 1999, the United States refused an official Panamanian extradition request, and even after Noriega's release in 2007 (his sentence was reduced to seventeen years based on good behavior), he was not sent back to Panama. Instead, the United States honored an extradition request from France, and Noriega is currently serving a seven-year prison sentence in France for money laundering. France has promised to extradite Noriega to Panama after his sentence is over (2017), at which point Noriega will be eighty-three years old.

Because of the setbacks in achieving accountability domestically, victims have been forced to reach outside of Panama. Most notable and emblematic of these endeavors is the case of Heliodoro Portugal. In 1970, Portugal was a political activist who was picked up by Torrijos' soldiers, imprisoned at a military base, and later killed. When new evidence surfaced in the early 2000s, his daughter, Patricia, was able to pressure the government to deal with the case. Yet only one man went to trial in the case, former army officer Ricardo Garibaldo, who ran a prison camp at the time of Portugal's death. The charges were dismissed, and Garibaldo died of a heart attack before an appeal could be heard. Left with no options domestically, Portugal took her father's case to the Inter-American Court of Human Rights, which in 2008 ruled against Panama, declaring the government responsible for Portugal's death and ordering it to publicly recognize its guilt, provide his family monetary compensation for its suffering, and honor him by naming a public park or street after him. During his presidency (2004–2009), Martín Torrijos, son of the former dictator, refused to comply with the court's ruling.

Amnesties

A final impediment to criminal prosecutions in Panama has been the use of amnesties. Although President Endara made a point of distancing himself from Noriega's regime, near the end of his term, in June 1994, he pardoned 578 former officials accused of crimes under Noriega. The pardon included many high-ranking officials, including the former General Chief of Staff of the armed forces Colonel Roberto Diaz Herrera. Shortly thereafter, within days of taking office in September 1994, President Ballardes pardoned 222 of Noriega's associates, who had been prosecuted since the democratic transition in 1989. These amnesties and pardons prevented further prosecutions and reversed many of the gains human rights advocates had made in the early 1990s.

Truth Commission

The election of President Mireya Moscoso, widow of former President Arias, in 1999 led to a shift in Panama's approach to transitional justice. Shortly afterward, the remains of four human skeletons were discovered on the grounds of a former military base, and pressure mounted for investigations into the abuses committed under military rule. On January 18, 2001, Moscosco created the Truth Commission of Panama (see separate entry) via Executive Decree 2. Its mandate was to establish a clear picture of the human rights violations committed under military rule and collect information to aid in identifying victims and determining their whereabouts. The Commission began its work in January 2001, operated for fifteen months, and issued its Final Report (Informe Final de la Comisión de la Verdad de Panamá) on April 17, 2002. The public report provided information on 110 individuals disappeared by the government from 1968 to 1989, along with a series of recommendations to the government, including the payment of financial reparations to victims identified in the report, further excavations of suspected gravesites, the improvement of human rights education and training, prosecutions for the perpetrators identified in the report, and the creation of a permanent follow-up human rights commission.

Despite the positive step forward for human rights, the Truth Commission faced significant political and logistical barriers. The PRD mounted a strong protest, accusing the Commission of selective justice by ignoring abuses committed before 1968 and those committed by the United States during the invasion. At times, Commissioners were the target of threats. The Commission was underfunded and struggled with the government for the necessary resources to conduct it work. In addition, Torrijos' victory in the 2004 presidential elections further hindered the Truth Commission's effectiveness. During his campaign, Torrijos purchased several full-page advertisements in Panamanian newspapers to discredit the Truth Commission and its findings. After taking power, he took no action to implement any of the Commission's recommendations.

Reparations

Thus far, transitional justice has focused on human rights violations committed by the Noriega and Torrijos' military regimes. Uniquely, one mechanism has focused on crimes committed by the United States during the invasion. In the years following the invasion, the United States paid US$6,500 each to families who lost their homes and were displaced during the conflict. The money was provided to build a new house or apartment in select areas in and around Panama City. In total, the United States paid US$42 million for the reconstruction of houses, infrastructure, and businesses destroyed in the attack and subsequent looting. In addition, the Endara government requested US$2 billion in U.S. aid to repair the economy generally. The U.S. Congress refused to approve the full amount, but granted US$420 million to Panama to be used for balance-of-payments support, public investment, job creation, private sector reactivation, judicial reform, and police services. Finally, the Panamanian government pursued symbolic reparations. On the first anniversary of the U.S. invasion, President Endara declared the day a "national day of reflection," and Panamanians marched in protest of the United States.

Conclusion

Overall, since its transition in 1989, Panama has embarked on a comprehensive approach to transitional justice. In dealing with crimes committed by past military regimes and those committed in the context of the U.S. invasion, Panama has pursued trials, enacted amnesties, created a truth commission, implemented security sector reform, and received international reparations. Yet the effectiveness of these efforts remains in question. Because of the changing political climate in the country, many efforts were not completely implemented or reversed. The process of recovering from past violence in Panama thus remains a work in progress.

Andrew G. Reiter

Cross-references: Truth Commission of Panama.

Further Readings

Fishel, John. 2000. The Institutional Reconversion of the Panamanian Defense Forces. In *Post-Invasion Panama: The Challenges of Democratization in the New World Order*. Ed. Orlando J. Perez. Lanham, MD: Lexington Books, pp. 11–28.

Reichstein, Matthew. 2008. The Extradition of General Manuel Noriega: An Application of International Humanitarian Law to Answer the Question, "If So, Where Should He Go?' *Emory International Law Review*, 22(2): 857–889.

Truth Commission of Panama. 2002. *Informe Final de la Comisión de la Verdad de Panamá* [Final Report of the Panama Truth Commission]. Available at: http://www.defensoriadelpueblo.gob.pa/sub.php?spid=4535 (accessed December 5, 2010).

Papua New Guinea

Papua New Guinea is the most ethnically diverse state in the world, with between 5,000 and 7,000 separate groups in a population of slightly more than 5 million, and around 840 languages spoken, estimated to represent a quarter of the world's stock. Despite this extreme ethnic and linguistic fragmentation, Papua New Guinea has enjoyed an unbroken, stable multiparty democracy since gaining independence from Australia in 1975. It is one of the developing world's only multiparty consolidated democracies, but it ranks low in terms of development, and almost 70 percent of the population is illiterate. Lying at the meeting point of Southeast Asia, Australia, and Oceania, its territorial borders derived from a decolonization process that ignored existing ethnic and linguistic schisms, and in the absence of an anticolonial struggle, the nascent state was left with little sense of common identity. Hence, the national motto is "unity through diversity," an apt summation of the central government's task since independence. Two conflicts have threatened to undermine the development of stable political institutions, in Irian Jaya (Papua), on the territory of Indonesia, and in Bougainville, 1,000 miles to the northeast of the capital, Port Moresby. Violence and crime through urban gangs and tribal fighting are often cited as this state's greatest problem, although levels do not exceed those found in many other states.

The Repressive Past

Irian Jaya

The conflict in Irian Jaya, or Papua, does not directly concern Papua New Guinea, given that the region forms part of Indonesia. In this sense, Irian Jaya is a part of Southeast Asia and is not within the grouping known as the Pacific Island Countries. Still, the Papuans of Indonesia are culturally and religiously aligned with Papua New Guinea, forming part of the traditional geographical grouping of Melanesia. Furthermore, some 40,000 people in West Sepik (Sandaun) and Western (Fly), the two border provinces of Papua New Guinea, qualify under the Papua New Guinea-Indonesia border agreement of 1979 as having customary rights to move back and forth across the border.

The Free Papua Organization (Organisasi Papua Merdeka, OPM) first appeared in the mid-1960s and became a popular revolt by the mid-1970s. The flow of refugees into Papua New Guinea, reaching a crisis-level of 10,000 in 1984–1985, gave the state a means of involving itself in the resolution of the conflict. However, Papua New Guinea remained careful not to provide overt support for the "West Papuan" independence movement and confined its role to protests against Indonesian incursions and human rights violations, as well as humanitarian assistance for the displaced.

The OPM has since renounced all violence and committed itself to the peaceful achievement of its aims. A controversial policy of transmigration promoted by the Indonesian state has diluted the dominance of indigenous Melanesian Papuans, and contemporary accounts are of a regional population almost half of which is comprised of migrant settlers, many from Java. In Papua New Guinea, remaining refugees are concentrated in the area of East Awin, under the protection of the United Nations High Commissioner for Refugees.

Bougainville

The North Solomons Province (referred to prior to 1975 as the District of Bougainville and still known simply as Bougainville), comprises some 170,000 people who form nineteen major language groups, with many other dialects spoken. Although geographically and anthropologically part of the Solomon Islands, Bougainville is politically part of Papua New Guinea. The remotest province of Papua New Guinea, Bougainville is comprised of two islands, Buka and Bougainville, and several islets and atolls. The conflict in Bougainville began in 1988 and formally ended in October 1997, with the signing of the Burnham Truce between representatives of the national government of Papua New Guinea, the Bougainville Transitional Government, the government-backed paramilitary Resistance Forces, the Bougainville Interim Government, and the Bougainville Revolutionary Army. The conflict between PNG government security forces and Bougainville resistance groups caused widespread death, trauma, and destruction and contributed to a crisis of government in Papua New Guinea. By the mid-1990s, up to a third of the population of Bougainville was displaced and living in official government-run "care centers" and many more in unofficial "bush camps." The numbers killed are contested, although they certainly numbered in the thousands, representing the most significant conflict in the Pacific Island Countries since World War II.

According to Amnesty International, human rights violations by government security forces (Papua New Guinea Defense Forces) included unlawful killings and disappearances of civilians, arbitrary arrest and unlawful detention, torture or ill-treatment, forced labor in care centers, and rape and sexual harassment of women. There was a general failure on the part of the state to investigate human rights violations. The Bougainville Revolutionary Army perpetrated killings of noncombatants and captured soldiers, as well as hostage taking.

The initial cause was widespread resentment of the gold and copper mine at Panguna in central Bougainville, which consistently violated customary rights of indigenous Bougainville landowners. The development of the copper and gold mine at Panguna began in 1964, with the arrival of a party of prospectors on behalf of the Australian branch of Rio Tinto Zinc in London. The villagers opposed the mining project, with continuing opposition expressed at every occasion before village tribunals. In 1966, the Australian Minister for Territories Charles Barnes came to Kieta to tell the people that there would be no direct benefit for landowners, but "the development would be for the benefit of Papua New Guinea as a whole." It was a massive enterprise, bigger than any mine in Australia, with some 10,000 workers. Almost all artisans were foreign and two-thirds of the laborers were from other parts of Papua New Guinea, exacerbating secessionist sympathies. The Australian government had discouraged a referendum on separation at the time of the colonial handover, and gave full support to Papua New Guinea as it applied to the United Nations for termination of the mandate and membership as a unified sovereign state. Australian enthusiasm for the Panguna mine was in some way based on a desire to find sources of internal revenue for the new state, reducing dependence on Australian aid. Hence, the Australian government ignored local objections and warnings that Bougainville was a particularly inappropriate location for such a large-scale enterprise.

Popular discontent about the mine was aggravated by the heavy-handed response to protests by police and the Papua New Guinea Defense Forces. However, separatism had long been evident in Bougainville, at least since the 1960s, as a result of remoteness, historical grievances against Australian colonialism, cultural and linguistic diversity, perceived ethnic differences from mainland Papua New Guinea, and links to the neighboring Solomon Islands. Bougainville attempted secession just prior to Papua New Guinea's independence in 1975, with a 1976 settlement emphasizing a process of decentralization. In 1988, the conflict erupted around the Panguna mine, leading to the declaration of a state of emergency the following year. This was met with armed resistance, with disaffected groups consolidating around the Bougainville Revolutionary Army under the leadership of Francis Ona, and a civil war against the state began. Failed cease-fire agreements led to the unilateral proclamation of the island as a republic in 1990, which was rejected by the Papua New Guinea government and not recognized by any other sovereign state.

Bougainville contains many regional and subregional groupings, and there was no unitary source or theater of the 1988–1997 conflict. For example, the Siwai region of southwest Bougainville saw a vicious subregional war largely driven by internal issues. Commentators have noted that it may be more accurate to describe the Bougainville crisis as a series of conflicts rather than a single independence movement, with Bougainvilleans identifying themselves along subregional ethnic or linguistic lines, often divided on questions of independence or autonomy. However, the principal conflict was between the separatists, as represented by the Bougainville Revolutionary Army, and the Papua New Guinea state, as represented by the Papua New Guinea Defense Forces.

Transitional Justice

Irian Jaya

Since 2001, a special autonomy law has given the region an increase in provincial revenues, encouraging economic growth. The eventual establishment of a Papuan People's Assembly in 2004, after a series of delays, has seen representation of Papuan social and cultural rights at the regional level. The Papuan People's Assembly is considered crucial to realizing autonomy in the region, and it provides for a cultural representation of Papuans. Its powers are largely influential rather than authoritative, and although it can approve or make suggestions on candidates for governor or vice-governor of the region, as well as comment on draft provincial bills relating to the protection of the rights of Papuans, there have been few results beyond the level of persuasion. As a result, there is apparent dissatisfaction with the Papuan People's Assembly, as many of its proposals and recommendations are ignored and its powers remain limited to expressions of Papuan interest that cannot be enforced. The overall effect of the special autonomy law after ten years is similarly being questioned. In 2005, the law was symbolically returned to the central government following mass demonstrations. Independence is implicitly demanded in light of insufficient implementation of special autonomy.

The idea of a Melanesian Union has been circulating at least since 1958, when John Kerr, then Governor-General of Australia, proposed uniting the Australian-controlled territory of New Guinea and the Dutch territory of Papua (then called West New Guinea) during negotiations between the Australian and Dutch colonial governments. Support for the move would have been forthcoming from all except Indonesia, but the idea was rendered inoperable by the ensuing support of Australia and the United States for an anticommunist Indonesian state. In the 1980s, the Melanesian Solidarity Group for Justice and Dignity (MelSol) emerged in the University of Papua New Guinea in Port Moresby, advocating unification of the Papuan peoples in Papua New Guinea and Irian Jaya. Nevertheless, Papuans on both sides of the border are relatively unenthusiastic about the idea, and successive Papua New Guinean governments have consistently stayed resolutely silent on the possibility of uniting with the region, even during the more intense years of the conflict with its ensuing refugee flows. Similarly, Papuan supporters are keen on proposed independence rather than unification with Papua New Guinea. It is perceived that separation would first be required if unification were to subsequently take place, with the latter unnecessary to the political goals of the separatists.

Indonesia insists that Papua is a domestic issue, although the involvement of international civil society actors through documentation of human rights abuses has, to a certain extent, led to the internationalization of the pro-independence Papuan movement. This movement is involved in constant lobbying of the United Nations to list the region as a non-self-governing country. International lobby groups such as West Papua Action, based in Dublin, Ireland, have questioned the validity of the Act of Free Choice of 1969, which subordinated the region to Indonesian rule in a highly manipulated referendum. In 1996, the organization successfully involved the Irish government's committee on foreign affairs, which expressed its deep concern at "the inadequacy of the 1969 Act of 'Free' Choice as a genuine expression of self-determination on the part of the people of West Papua", and called on the Irish government to "request the United Nations to investigate and act on the allegations of human rights abuses and on the question of the validity of the 1969 Act of 'Free' Choice." Saltford (2003) comprehensively documented the UN involvement in the "betrayal" of Papua. Yet Indonesia's growing democratization and the apparent refusal of Papua New Guinea or any other state to offer support to the independence movement mean that the self-determination on the part of the people of West Papua is unlikely to be realized in the near future.

Human rights protection, at present focused on the right to development and the appropriation of indigenous land for forestry, mining, or construction projects, has become a negotiable issue with Jakarta, as long as it remains removed from political aspirations of independence. Hence, the international support for Papua has shifted largely to prevention of human rights abuses, promotion of good governance, and channeling of development aid. Papua New Guinea has not been active in raising awareness of human rights abuses or assisting development, and has forfeited any claims to interest in the region beyond repatriation of refugees. Grassroots sympathy with the movement is, however, widespread, aided by an established community of Papuan political exiles in Papua New Guinea.

Bougainville

An unarmed Truce Monitoring Group commanded by the New Zealand Defense Force and aided by Australia, Fiji, and Vanuatu oversaw the initial implementation of the truce, before command shifted to Australia under a Peace Monitoring Group in 1998. Crucially, the Peace Monitoring Group was also unarmed. According to an Australian account of peace monitoring in Bougainville, there were many separate peace initiatives at different times during the ten-year conflict, reflecting the complexity of the island's situation as a result of its extreme diversity. Australia financially underwrote the cost of the peace mission, including a pledge of AUS$100 million for reconstruction over five years, from 1997 to 2002. Some of that funding involved restoration of law and order.

The central political impact of the Bougainville crisis is its potent symbolism of the essential weakness of the Papua New Guinean state, with the potential for other provinces to follow. Thus in 1994, the New Guinea Islands leaders threatened to secede if the national government continued recentralization through reform of the provincial government law. The threat was ultimately not carried out, but the leaders went as far as drafting a constitution and designing a flag, citing the Bougainville precedent. Thus, the Papua New Guinea government's concern was that any concessions made to Bougainville would lead to similar demands in other provinces. Furthermore, the principle of eminent domain, whereby the benefits of mining are accrued by the state and distributed throughout, has been replaced by a culture of compensation of landowners. In the wake of the Bougainville conflict, there has been a shift from paying resource rents to the state to paying resource rents to indigenous landowners in the immediate vicinity of the operation. Such changes mark the retreat of the state before local interests. The benefits of this can be limited even to the minority of locals who receive them.

The Solomon Islands played an important role in facilitating early dialogue between the disputants, although its government was often criticized by Papua New Guinea as being overly sympathetic to the Bougainville cause. Australia's involvement was treated with suspicion because of its political and historical links to the Papua New Guinea government and the Australian ownership of the Panguna mine. Hence, New Zealand acted as a neutral intermediary in the initial peace process stage. The comprehensive Bougainville Peace Agreement of August 2001 took more than thirteen years to materialize, with some forty-six major agreements negotiated, and it will take at least a decade more to conclusively determine its success. According to the Agreement, the people of Bougainville will freely decide the matter of secession from Papua New Guinea via a referendum on independence to be held within fifteen years (and not less than ten years) of the 2005 election of the Bougainville Autonomous Government. It also provides amnesty and pardon for those involved in the conflict.

Therefore, the future of Bougainville will be decided by its people, in a referendum for independence. A national newspaper editorial remarked that Papua New Guinea is an observer in a transition it has no power, short of military intervention, to control. It can only hope that Bougainville will opt to remain with Papua New Guinea. However, a steady movement toward eventual independence is no longer considered to represent a significant threat to Papua New Guinean sovereignty in its other provinces and regions, given the history of Bougainville and its strong geographic and cultural identity, in particular its shared heritage with the Solomon Islands.

For Bougainville, the population as a whole needs to be included in the recovery process, incorporating strategies for empowerment and capacity building that are adaptive of ethnic and linguistic diversity. If Bougainville becomes a constitutional republic, the task of a future constituent assembly would involve the delineation of the role of customary or traditional indigenous law. The Papua New Guinea constitution already includes some interesting provisions relating to the role of the courts in sourcing the underlying customary law, and Bougainville will need to consider its own fractious relationship between common and customary law, particularly in the area of dispute mediation and landownership. Furthermore, it is not known how effective a potential future state would be at preventing internal conflicts, given the schisms experienced during the secessionist war.

The United Nations Observer Mission to Bougainville (UNOMB) formally closed its activities in June 2005 with the formation of the autonomous government, completing the political role of the United Nations. The success of the Bougainville peace process was attributed by the then UN Secretary-General to consistent and cooperative efforts of the Papua New Guinea government and the Bougainville parties to the peace agreements, and the strong support of the neighboring states and donor countries. The mission was considered in the Secretary-General's final report as an example of how a small UN team can work efficiently and effectively.

Conclusion

Papua New Guinea has been the focus of much anthropological attention, but domestic researchers are increasingly involved in charting a national identity that does not conform to Western studies. Upon independence, there were many predictions that the state of Papua New Guinea would not succeed, and indeed it is reported that Australia and Indonesia at one stage negotiated a contingency plan for governing the country should it collapse. Yet Papua New Guinea has not collapsed, and its achievement thus far in overseeing an extraordinary mixture of peoples needs to be recognized. The secessionist conflict in Bougainville has had a strong effect on the confidence of the Papua New Guinea government to hold together the greatest array of ethnic and linguistic groups gathered within the borders of any state in the world. Irian Jaya to the west indirectly concerns the Papua New Guinea government, and its strict policy of noninterference is somewhat at odds with popular sympathy for the Papuan cause. Securing stronger enforcement of law and order is regularly posited as being central to the future stability of the state, although this is true of many developing states, and Papua New Guinea may not suffer disproportionately in this regard. Papua New Guinea's constitutional and political mechanisms deserve greater attention, and the peace process in Bougainville, largely studied only from an Australian perspective, should be of interest to all parties involved in resolving smaller-scale regional conflicts or disputes throughout the world. Furthermore, the constitutional arrangements for marrying indigenous customary law and common law provide an interesting model for research on the coexistence of imposed and indigenous legal systems.

David P. Keane

Further Reading

Bowd, Reuben. 2009. *Simple Solutions to Complex Matters: Identifying Fundamental Principles of Alternative Dispute Resolution in the Multinational Effort to Broker a Resolution to the Bougainville 'Crisis'*. Canberra: Strategic and Defense Studies Centre, Australian National University.
Claxton, Karl. 1998. *Bougainville 1988–1998: Five Searches for Security in the North Solomons Province of PNG*. Canberra: Strategic and Defense Studies Centre, Australian National University.
Saltford, John. 2003. *The UN and the Indonesian Takeover of West Papua, 1962–1969: The Anatomy of Betrayal*. London: Routledge.
Waiko, John. 1993. *A Short History of Papua New Guinea*. Oxford: Oxford University Press.
Wehner, Monica and Donald Denoon. 2001. *Without a Gun: Australians' Experiences Monitoring Peace in Bougainville, 1997–2001*. Canberra: Pandanus Books.

Paraguay

After the overthrow of dictator Alfredo Stroessner Matiauda's regime in 1989, the first two transitional governments considered the prosecution and punishment of the perpetrators of human rights violations a priority. As a result, the transitional justice regime of the first few years after the overthrow was characterized by the use of criminal justice in its classic form as the means to discover, investigate, and eventually punish human rights related crimes committed during the Stroessner regime.

After this initial period, subsequent governments implemented mechanisms to allow for reparations to the victims of the overthrown regime and to satisfy demands for disclosure regarding the diverse circumstances of the repression perpetrated during its duration. However, no new procedures were implemented to facilitate the public need for a measure of overall truth and reconciliation, leaving only the existing, ordinary rules of criminal procedure as a means to this end.

The Repressive Past

General Alfredo Stroessner governed Paraguay from August 15, 1954 until February 2, 1989. During this period, Stroessner established an authoritarian regime intended to perpetuate itself in power. To do so, he relied on the support of members of the ruling Colorado Party (Asociación Nacional Republicana, Partido Colorado) and the armed forces, a union that lasted for nearly thirty-five years.

From the beginning, repression was a tool for the maintenance and protection of the regime, through which members of the opposition were neutralized and the population subjugated. The regime sought to eliminate any potential risk that might threaten the continuity of the government. In this context, the regime's priority was to prevent the organization of opposition groups with common interests and problems.

After the initial purges in the main ranks of the armed forces, police, and Colorado Party, Stroessner formed and directed a repressive machine that was mainly composed of personnel from these institutions. This apparatus had a centralized, institutional, obedient, and vertical chain of command supported by a vast and varied intelligence and counterintelligence system with an extensive network of undercover informants.

Unlike other countries with a repressive past, no clandestine police or military structures were created in Paraguay that were different from, or parallel to, the official and public ones. Rather, these institutions themselves were directly responsible for the repression.

The government tried to repress public debate through programs of censorship, regulation, and control of events in public spaces, causing those in the opposition to meet privately or not at all. The only accepted public gatherings were official ones, such as the official party meetings, trade union meetings, cultural meetings and events, as well as national celebrations. The regime prohibited the operations of some political parties and opposition political associations; others were allowed to act, but only to a very limited extent. Moreover, the government prohibited some trade unions, social organizations, and media outlets outright.

The regime used repression as a tool of governance throughout the years of its existence, with varying periods of increased intensity focused on specific groups and individuals. The regime considered the members of armed resistance movements and those people suspected of supporting them as a major threat. These people were often the victims of forced disappearance and extrajudicial executions. Those who participated in political, social, or cultural opposition were often the victims of unlawful detentions, illegal deprivation of liberty, and torture. Some were even killed during torture sessions. This group included members of peasant, indigenous, and religious organizations, leadership and members of trade unions, media personnel, and nonaligned military men.

Some of the worst human rights violations occurred in the mid-1970s within the framework of Operation Condor (Operación Condor), a political repression campaign involving assassinations and intelligence operations implemented by the governments of the Southern Cone of South America. Actions were often coordinated among those repressive regimes. This made monitoring of and reporting on Paraguayan citizens living abroad, the exchange of political prisoners, and other coordinated measures possible. It is believed that during Operation Condor, a significant number of Paraguayan citizens disappeared abroad and some foreign citizens disappeared while living in Paraguay.

Official reports estimate that under the Stroessner regime, 19,862 people were arbitrarily detained, 18,772 were tortured, 59 were extrajudicially executed, 336 were victims of forced disappearance, and 3,470 were forced into exile. Many of these victims were actually victims of multiple repressive measures.

These reports also enumerate a wide range of other abuses, including sexual violence, principally against indigenous children and women; property confiscation; violations of freedoms of the press, expression, and association; denial of the rights to information, privacy, defense in court, and equal protection under the law; and denial of the right to take part in public affairs.

The Stroessner regime came to an end with the coup d'état of February 2–3, 1989, and a faction of the Armed Forces led by General Andrés Rodriguez, a former ally of Stroessner, took over.

Transitional Justice

After the fall of the Stroessner regime, some of the principal perpetrators of repression were prosecuted and sentenced. Later, the state made efforts to grant compensation to the victims of human rights violations that occurred between 1954 and 1989. In recent years, efforts have been oriented toward revealing the truth behind the repression of the Stroessner years through the creation of a Truth and Justice Commission (Comisión de Verdad y Justicia).

Prosecutions

Because the Paraguayan Congress never passed any amnesty legislation, there were no obstacles to the prosecution of the perpetrators of human rights violations. The criminal justice system thus convicted and sentenced a few middle- and high-ranking military and police officials. Some of the sentences were up to twenty-five years in prison, the highest sentence permitted under the Paraguayan legal system. Among the most high-profile persons convicted were Pastor Milciades Coronel, Chief of the Investigation Department of the National Police, and General Francisco Alcibiades Brítez Borges, Chief of Police of Asunción, the country's capital. Both were important figures in promoting government repression.

However, Alfredo Stroessner, the dictator, was never prosecuted. The Brazilian government granted him political asylum, and he died on August 16, 2006. His Interior Minister, Sabino Augusto Montanaro, was granted political asylum in Honduras. He lived there until May 2009, when he suddenly returned, apparently for private reasons, to Paraguay. Montanaro is now eighty-six years old, with reported health problems. At present, several medical examinations are under way to determine Montanaro's capability to face pending criminal prosecutions. The fact that Stroessner was never punished and that Montanaro has avoided prosecution until now shows the limited scope of the proceedings against those considered primarily responsible for the injustices that occurred.

The number of prosecutions for human rights violations initiated after the overthrow of the dictatorship is not high, considering the volume and magnitude of what happened and that the regime lasted for almost thirty-five years. By 1989, when initiatives to investigate and prosecute these crimes (in particular forced disappearances and extralegal executions) came into existence, most of the evidence had disappeared, making proof of the allegations nearly impossible.

The prosecutions that were initiated lasted an excessive amount of time. The criminal justice system rendered its first verdict in 1999, ten years after the overthrow of the dictatorship. Between May 2006 and March 2008, the Truth and Justice Commission submitted ten criminal complaints to the criminal justice system, principally regarding cases of torture and forced disappearance of persons. These criminal complaints are now being processed by the Attorney General's Office.

Reparation

In March 1996, the Paraguayan Congress passed Law 838 on Compensations to Victims of Human Rights Violations Perpetrated during the 1954–1989 Dictatorship, establishing a legal framework that offered the possibility of some compensation for victims of the dictatorship. Organizations of victims drafted the bill and presented it to the Paraguayan Congress in 1992. Despite support for the bill from many members of the lower house, it was shelved for more than three years. Finally, after considerable modification, the bill was passed.

The president at the time, Juan Carlos Wasmosy, vetoed the bill, alleging that the Paraguayan state was not liable for the crimes committed by former state officials, but rather that these officials were solely liable for their acts during the dictatorship. Despite this, the Congress overrode the presidential veto. The government then filed a request for judicial review of the constitutionality of the law, and the Supreme Court, as a provisional remedy, suspended the law. Two years later, in 1998, the Supreme Court rejected the request for judicial review.

When the law finally took effect, an additional problem occurred, in that the Ombudsman (Defensor del Pueblo), the head of the institution that was to be in charge of the analysis and decision about the claims of compensation, had not yet been appointed. The lack of a political consensus delayed this appointment until the end of 2001.

By 2003, around 260 victims had been declared beneficiaries of compensation resolutions. However, the government took legal action against the resolutions granting compensation in order to avoid payment. The Executive Branch policy was changed by President Nicanor Duarte Frutos when he took office in 2003. The president ordered the voluntary dismissal of the pending legal actions and the payments finally began the following year.

Law 838 established a system of monetary compensation that requires beneficiaries to be a victim themselves or a direct relative of a victim of at least one of the following abuses: forced disappearance, summary or extrajudicial execution, torture with severe and manifest physical and mental consequences, or deprivation of liberty for more than one year without an order from a competent authority, or as a consequence of prosecutions or sentences in which the Laws 294 of 1955 on the Defense of the Democracy and 209 of 1970 on the Defense of Public Peace and Citizens' Freedoms were applied.

The amount of monetary compensation was to be in relation to the nature of the abuse suffered by the victim, and it was to be paid in the local currency, Guarani. The accumulation of claims, and consequently the accumulation of amounts of monetary compensation, was not allowed. In other words, a person subjected to multiple abuses in a single situation could only claim compensation for one type of abuse (for example, unlawful deprivation of liberty or torture, but not both).

The amount of the compensation was fixed in minimum daily legal wages – a unit representing the amount of money established by law as the remuneration of a worker for a day of work. For cases of forced disappearance of persons and summary or extrajudicial executions, the amount established by the law is the equivalent of 3,000 daily wages (US$32,000); for cases of torture, the amount is up to the equivalent of 2,500 daily wages (US$27,000); for cases of unlawful deprivation of liberty, the amount is up to the equivalent of 1,500 daily wages (US$16,300), and a minimum of the equivalent of 500 daily wages (US$5,500). (The U.S. dollar amounts noted here were calculated taking into consideration the current legal daily wage and the current exchange rate.)

Law 838 originally set a deadline of thirty months from its promulgation for the submission of claims. This deadline was extended for another thirty-six months in 2002 and for additional twenty-four months in 2004. In 2006, the deadline for submission of claims was abolished altogether.

The beneficiaries started to receive actual compensation in 2004, eight years after the promulgation of Law 838 and fifteen years after the overthrow of the dictatorship. The extensive process and slow pace of implementing the law, as well as the complexity of the required proceedings, generated considerable public dissatisfaction. Furthermore, some victims criticized the compensation system, the meager amounts granted, and the lack of nonfinancial reparations. Despite these complaints and criticisms, the majority of victims and their families took advantage of the financial reparations.

Law 838 also entitled the National Congress to award medals and diplomas as a form of official apology on behalf of the Paraguayan State to the victims of the dictatorship. However, there are no records of any awards having been granted to date.

File Access

On December 22, 1992, during a judicial proceeding, a criminal judge discovered an important number of documents from the archives of Stroessner's Police, specifically documents belonging to the Police Investigations Department. Two days later, similar documents were seized under the authority of another criminal judge from the National Office of Technical Affairs (Dirección Nacional de Asuntos Técnicos), a police department. These documents mainly recorded human rights violations that had taken place during the dictatorship. They are known together as the Archives of Terror. The documents consist of detainees' registries and lists, confidential reports, reports of surveillance of political parties, student groups, and trade unions, immigration control records, phone tap records, reports of the surveillance of citizens' residences, and photographs.

On March 26, 1993, the Supreme Court, with the purpose of preserving these documents, set up the Documentation and Archives Center for the Defense of Human Rights (Centro de Documentación y Archivo para la defensa de los Derechos Humanos) in the Supreme Court building. In 1993, documents were added to the archives from police station No. 3 in Asunción and the Office of the Governor of the Caaguazú department. Between 2001 and 2002, documents from the central police headquarters and several police stations in Asunción were also added. Since its establishment, the Documentation Center has been open to the general public for research and file access, yet only victims have access to the full files.

Since the discovery of the Archives of Terror, civil organizations promoted the establishment of a Museum of Memory, Dictatorship and Human Rights (Museo de la Memoria, Dictadura y Derechos Humanos). The museum opened in 2002 and is currently located in the building of the former National Office of Technical Affairs. This was a Police Department office established in 1956 and was one of the principal sites of the acts of repression. The museum was created to increase public awareness of the abuses perpetrated during the dictatorship through the exhibition of documentary evidence about specific actions taken against detained persons, as well as tools of torture and photographs of disappeared people.

Congress declared that 2003 was to be the Year of Historic Memory. In that year, numerous seminars and presentations took place in several institutions with the purpose of stimulating the younger generation to research subjects related to the repression during the dictatorship and to review the Archives of Terror and other evidence of repression.

Truth and Justice Commission

In 2003, the Congress created the Truth and Justice Commission. The establishment of the Commission was principally an initiative of human rights organizations and the victims of the dictatorship. The Inter-American Commission on Humans Rights had also recommended its establishment.

The Memory Roundtable and the Archive of Repression, a conglomerate of civil society organizations established in October 2002, drafted the bill that later became the law that established the Commission. The government appointed the commission members on July 2, 2004, but it took until February 2005 to develop the infrastructure and elements necessary to begin its mandated activities. It was composed of one representative of the government, one representative of Congress, four representatives proposed by the Commissions of Victims of the Dictatorship (composed of direct victims and family members), and three representatives proposed by other civil organizations. Commission members were required to be Paraguayan citizens with recognized high ethical standards, a certain prestige and legitimacy in society, and identifiable with the defense of democracy and democratic institutions.

The Commission was not established as a body with the authority to conduct criminal or civil proceedings. Rather, it was assigned the principal task of discovering and disclosing violations of human rights committed by state officials and those who collaborated with them between May 1954 and October 2003, the period encompassing the dictatorship and the first fourteen years of transition. In addition, the TJC was authorized to preserve the testimony of victims, try to determine the whereabouts and present condition of those people affected by the violations, identify those who carried out the acts of repression, preserve evidence of human rights violations, provide evidence to the judicial system in order to facilitate the prosecution of further perpetrators of human rights violations, contribute to the official discovery of the truth about the repression, and establish the political and moral liability of the state. Given the lengthy list of authorized activities, it is important to note that the priority objectives of the Commission can best be summarized as revealing the truth about the repression and human rights violations and seeking the investigation and punishment of those responsible by authorized state bodies.

To attain its objectives, the Commission had the authority to interview all persons who had relevant facts about the time period and actions under investigation, to visit all necessary places, to gather materials, data, and all necessary evidence, to hold public hearings, to undertake the necessary security measures to protect victims and witnesses, and to establish all necessary mechanisms to ensure societal participation. The law that established the Commission required public agencies to collaborate with it in its investigations and to provide pertinent documents and information. The law also authorized the Commission to issue summons for civil servants or any other person to appear before it, and to request judicial assistance in order to force the appearance of those summoned in cases of repeated and unjustified refusal to appear.

In meeting its obligations, the Commission interviewed more than 2,000 people, analyzed their testimony, and reviewed information from numerous archives. The results of its investigation are contained in the final report, *Do Not Let This Happen Again* (Anive Haguã Oikó in Guarani, Paraguay's second official language). The report constitutes an unparalleled contribution to the acknowledgment of the recent past in Paraguay because it contains information about the context in which the authoritarian regime emerged in Paraguay and the extent to which other such regimes in the region influenced the Paraguayan regime, information about the political and social characteristics of the Stroessner regime, precise data about the circumstances of repression in Paraguay, and the number of victims of illegal deprivation of liberty, torture, forced disappearance, extrajudicial executions, and exile that were attributed to the repressive apparatus of the dictatorship.

The report represents an important advance in the clarification of the truth about many grave violations of human rights that occurred between 1954 and 1989. However, as the commission itself admits, there is still more work to be done. In the education field, the Commission has promoted the teaching of a course dealing with "Authoritarianism in the Recent History of Paraguay" in schools. Another important activity of the Commission has been the work to establish a genetic database of blood samples from relatives of forced disappearance victims in order to facilitate identification in the event of future discoveries of clandestine graves. The Commission also participated in providing psychological assistance to victims and witnesses, and in drafting medical and psychiatric reports with the purpose of supporting compensation claims of victims processed by the Ombudsman's Office.

The Commission concluded its mandate in August 2008 and delivered a portion of its report to national authorities at an official event. On this occasion, President Fernando Lugo apologized to victims on behalf of the Paraguayan state for the violations of human rights that occurred under previous periods of dictatorship.

Conclusion

Transitional justice in Paraguay has positive and negative aspects. The criminal justice system has punished some high- and mid-level officials of the repressive apparatus, but those who were principally responsible, as well as an undetermined number of lower-ranking officials, have never been prosecuted. Many victims took advantage of monetary compensation, but the compensation system was neither adequate nor easy to access. As a consequence, neither the criminal justice system nor the compensation system met their overall objectives.

The work of the Truth and Justice Commission, on the other hand, did meet important objectives and represents an unparalleled advance in the acknowledgment of human rights violations that occurred in Paraguay. While much remains to be done, finding ways to adequately demonstrate the important findings already made should be a priority.

Since the regime change, the absence of the real political will of the Paraguayan state to cooperate financially and politically with the implemented mechanisms was seen as a fundamental flaw of transitional justice. While not a complete explanation, this lack of political will was associated with the fact that the first five transition governments belonged to the same political party that was the foundation of the Stroessner regime. In August 2008, a representative of that political party lost the presidential election and was democratically replaced, creating increased hope that a new government unconnected to the past will lead the way to a fuller understanding of that past and to the development of institutions that will prevent its repetition.

Kai Ambos and César Alfonso, with the assistance of Roberto Úbeda

Cross-references: Access to Secret Files; Court Trials for Redress; Paraguay Nunca Mas; Reparations; Truth Commission.

Further Readings

Alfonso, César. 2009. Informe sobre Paraguay [Paraquay Report]. In *Justicia de Transición. Con Informes de América Latina, Alemania, Italia y España* [Transitional Justice. Reports from Latin America, Germany, Italy and Spain]. Eds. Kai Ambos, Ezequiel Malarino and Gisela Elsner. Montevideo/Bogotá: Konrad Adenauer Stiftung/Temis, pp. 345–355.

Coordinadora de Derechos Humanos Paraguay [Paraguayan Human Rights Coordination] 2006. *Informe Sombra al Pacto Internacional de Derechos Civiles y Políticos* [Shadow Report on the International Covenant on Civil and Political Rights]. Asunción: Ed. Litocolor, pp. 69–75.

Gauto, Dionisio and García, Nelson. 2005. Derecho a la Reparación rehabilitación e indemnización: Avances, estancamientos y deudas [Rights to Reparation, Rehabilitation and Compensation: Advances, Stagnations and Debts]. In *Derechos Humanos en Paraguay* [Human Rights in Paraguay]. Asunción: Ed. Litocolor, pp. 149–157.

Hittenberger, Birgit. 2007. *Das Archivo del Terror in der Vergangenheitsaufarbeitung in Paraguay* [The Archive of Terror in past rebuilding of Paraguay]. Norderstedt: Ed. Grin.

Peru

Since the 1970s, Peru has experienced a transition to democracy, a brutal civil war, renewed authoritarianism, and ultimately a return to relative peace and stronger democracy. Since 2000, Peru has embarked on a dramatic process of transitional justice that has favored prosecutions of insurgents, human rights abusers within the armed forces, and even a former president. Though not without serious flaws, transitional justice has progressed faster than in neighboring countries, and with greater emphasis on prosecution than reconciliation.

The Repressive Past

In 1980, Peru returned to the democratic fold after twelve years of military rule. At the same time, the Shining Path, a brutal Maoist insurgency, launched a campaign of terrorism upon the country. Its strongholds were in the highland regions largely populated by impoverished indigenous peasants, but they ultimately operated in every district of the country and engaged in car bombings and other attacks in the capital, Lima. The Shining Path funded itself through extortion and, to varying extents over the years, through alliances with drug traffickers. (Peru is one of the major producers of coca, the basic element used to produce cocaine.) The MRTA, a smaller communist guerrilla movement, also became active in the early 1980s. Unlike most of the Latin American insurgencies of the latter half of the twentieth century, these groups were fighting against a democratically elected government rather than authoritarian ones.

For the first two years of this insurgency, the newly elected government of President Fernando Belaunde Terry (1980–1985) made little effort to combat the Shining Path. Belaunde, who had previously been elected to the presidency in 1963 and then removed from power by a military coup in 1968, hesitated to empower the armed forces to launch a full-scale counterinsurgency operation. Meanwhile, the Shining Path took advantage of the weakness of the central government throughout the Andean region of the country, where the marginalized population of Quechua-speaking Indians had weak ties to a national identity and government based in mainly Spanish-speaking, mestizo, coastal Lima. The rebels gained support from some of these communities by exercising an effective, if brutal, form of justice through popular trials that often ended in the execution of local criminals and capitalists. The Shining Path claimed to fight on behalf of the poor and the indigenous. However, according to public opinion polls, only a minority of Peruvians – and only a minority of the poor or the indigenous – ever expressed support for the movement. Indeed, given the government's failure to offer them protection from the rebels, thousands of peasants joined *rondas campesinas*, self-organized patrol groups aimed at defending the local population from cattle rustlers, rebels, and other security threats.

After its initial tepid response, by 1982, the Peruvian state began to take the Shining Path seriously and dispatched troops into conflict zones. Peruvian human rights groups organized themselves and collected evidence of shocking brutality on the part of the armed forces. Most districts of the country were ultimately placed under a state of emergency, which gave the armed forces direct control over local government and shielded them from the scrutiny of the press in their counterinsurgency operations. The armed forces and rebels alike engaged in massacres of civilians. Among the bloodiest of these were the 1983 massacre of sixty-nine peasants by the Shining Path in Lucanamarca, and a comparable 1985 massacre by the armed forces in Accomarca.

Between 61,000 and 78,000 people died over the next two decades as a result of the conflict, and many more were displaced, falsely imprisoned, coerced into cooperating with one side or another, or tortured. Rather than replacing the *rondas campesinas*, the armed forces supplied them with arms and treated them as allies in the struggle against the Shining Path. While many members of both the armed forces and the *rondas campesinas* fought valiantly against the rebels, all sides in the civil conflict committed grievous human rights abuses.

After both the centrist government of President Belaunde (1980–1985) and the center-left government of President Alan Garcia (1986–1990) failed to restore peace and economic prosperity to Peru, the public turned to a populist but largely unknown figure in the 1990 elections. President Alberto Fujimori quickly escalated the counterinsurgency effort and called upon Congress to approve draconian antiterrorist legislation to make prosecuting suspected terrorists faster and easier, to grant new powers to the armed forces and intelligence agencies, and to weaken civil liberties protections. In 1992, Fujimori – with the backing of the armed forces – launched a "self-coup," in which he summarily dismissed Congress, the courts, and most other political functionaries he could not directly control. This allowed Fujimori to rule by decree for nine months, preside over the writing of a new constitution, and ultimately to remain in power until 2000.

Despite Fujimori's authoritarianism, he enjoyed considerable public support, in large part because the public credited him with defeating the insurgents. By decree, Fujimori enacted laws establishing military tribunals in which suspected terrorists would be tried by anonymous, hooded judges. (This would protect the identity of the judges, who might otherwise be targeted for intimidation or assassination by the Shining Path.) Between 95 percent and 97 percent of the cases tried by the new military tribunals resulted in conviction, so virtually all of the thousands of suspects rounded up by police and military personnel landed in prison, regardless of whether proof of their participation in terrorist activity existed. Then, in September 1992, Abimael Guzman, the leader of the Shining Path, was captured by police in Lima. The movement soon fell apart, and most of its leaders were captured in the following years. Even though the Shining Path continues to operate in Peru and stages occasional terrorist attacks, its numbers have dwindled to a few hundred and the "war on terrorism" was considered concluded by 2000.

Despite the diminution of the power and size of the Shining Path, government forces continued to engage in human rights abuses throughout the 1990s. Most notorious were the crimes committed by the Colina Group, a paramilitary force of army intelligence officers who carried out disappearances and murders such as the 1991 Barrios Altos massacre, in which seventeen people were gunned down in a Lima neighborhood, and 1992 Cantuta University killings, in which nine students and a professor were abducted from the campus after it was placed under military control and were later found dead. Fujimori carefully cultivated the armed forces, his key allies throughout his decade in power. When members of Congress attempted to investigate the Cantuta University cases, the president sided with the Army, whose commander sent tanks through the streets to force Congress to back down. Fujimori and his allies in Congress shielded the armed forces from prosecution for these and other human rights abuses by passing a 1995 amnesty law that overturned human rights convictions for military officers and placed a blanket immunity over all military and police officials for any crimes allegedly committed since 1980. When the validity of this amnesty was challenged before the Inter-American Court of Human Rights, Fujimori removed Peru from the Court's membership and jurisdiction. In the final months of Fujimori's administration, he attempted but failed to negotiate a new amnesty law to cover both military and civilian officials from prosecution for a wide range of crimes, including drug trafficking and human rights abuses.

After winning an unconstitutional third term as president in the fraudulent elections of 2000, Fujimori was assailed by revelations of massive corruption that had been leaked to the press. By the end of the year, Fujimori had fled to Japan and faxed a letter of resignation to the Peruvian Congress. The sudden tumult of regime collapse created a window of opportunity for advocates of transitional justice to translate much of their agenda into national policy.

Transitional Justice

After Fujimori's sudden resignation, the presidency fell to Valentín Paniagua, who had recently been made president of Congress. His interim administration of eight months marked a major turning point for Peru and the beginning of the transitional justice process. During this period, the Supreme Court revoked the 1995 amnesty laws, and Paniagua oversaw the reversal of much of Fujimori's antiterrorist legislation. Paniagua fired numerous holdovers from the Fujimori administration, launched prosecutions against members of the armed forces and government implicated in corruption and human rights abuses, and restored Peru's membership in the Inter-American Court of Human Rights. It was therefore during this interim administration and those of Paniagua's successors, Alejandro Toledo (2001–2006) and Alan Garcia (2006–2011), that the transitional justice process unfolded. The Peruvian human rights community, organized into a powerful coalition under an umbrella nongovernmental organization called the Human Rights National Coordinator, was able to influence questions of transitional justice in part because of a major surge in the legitimacy and respect these groups enjoyed in 2001, when many of the complaints they had been making about Fujimori's authoritarianism over the previous decade were proven justified.

Truth

In the 1990s, there was little consensus about the need for transitional justice in Peru. Because many members of the Shining Path had been captured, prosecuted, and imprisoned, much of the public felt it was best to leave the past behind. The armed forces and *rondas campesinas* had, in the eyes of many, protected the country from savage terrorists and should not now be scrutinized for potential abuses. When human rights organizations called for investigations of military abuses, they were accused of sympathy with the terrorists by members of the armed forces, critics within the press, and Fujimori. When human rights advocates pointed out that tens of thousands of Peruvians had been sent to prison under antiterrorism legislation that violated basic standards of due process, they were again lambasted as in league with the Shining Path. However, in 2000 and 2001, bald evidence of military corruption precipitated a shift in public attitudes toward the armed forces. Revelations that high-ranking military officers had participated in narcotics trafficking, illegal arms sales, and self-enrichment persuaded the public that full investigations of the armed forces were warranted. This clear support for corruption investigations also strengthened the case for human rights investigations. In addition to the armed forces, individuals from virtually every key governmental or social institution – including the press, courts, Congress, and intelligence agencies – were unmasked as corrupt cronies and henchmen of Fujimori. Videos and testimony detailing the extent to which these institutions had been surreptitiously subverted by the administration enthralled the public in the years to come and created a hunger for truth and accountability that had been absent only a year or two before.

The human rights nongovernmental organizations clustered together under the auspices of the Human Rights National Coordinator also perceived Paniagua and Toledo as key allies in transitional justice. Upon accepting the interim presidency, Paniagua vowed not to run for office in the 2001 elections, which he was responsible for overseeing. This granted his administration an aura of impartiality that allowed him to take bold measures to expose uncomfortable truths. Toledo began his presidency with a patina of credibility too, as he had spearheaded public protests against Fujimori in 2000. He was also the first indigenous, Quechua-speaking president in Peru's history, and so was expected to prioritize redressing the grave wrongs done to that population during the conflict.

Throughout the civil conflict, human rights nongovernmental organizations had amassed evidence of the crimes committed by all sides, but because they were barred from many regions of conflict, and because they themselves were often the target of assassination by both the state and the rebels, they struggled to gain an accurate picture of the scale of atrocities. Indeed, before the Peruvian Truth and Reconciliation Commission released its final report in 2003, most Peruvian human rights organizations grossly underestimated the death toll of the conflict. In short, a massive amount of misinformation existed about the nature of human rights abuses committed since 1980, and the information that was available was widely doubted and only partial. A key demand of human rights organizations, then, was to establish the truth about the recent past. The body tasked with this mission was the Peruvian Truth and Reconciliation Commission (see entry on Truth and Reconciliation Commission [Peru]). According to the commission, 54 percent of the deaths and the majority of human rights abuses and crimes investigated were carried out by the Shining Path. Another 1.5 percent of the deaths were attributed to the MRTA, and 44.5 percent were attributed to agents of the state. The vast majority of victims were poor, Quechua-speaking, indigenous individuals residing in rural regions of the country.

Apology

In November 2003, three months after receiving the final report of the Truth and Reconciliation Commission, President Toledo publicly apologized on behalf of the state to all those who suffered violence, terror, and abuse between 1980 and 2000. He restated the key findings of the Truth and Reconciliation Commission and promised to take immediate steps to implement sweeping reforms recommended by the commission to ensure improvements in security and the socioeconomic status of the communities most directly affected by the violence. He also promised to reform state institutions to prevent future abuses of citizens' rights.

Reform

Peru has reduced the size of its armed forces and removed hundreds – perhaps thousands – of individuals implicated in human rights abuses from its ranks. The Minister of Defense is now generally civilian. Members of the armed forces are exposed to human rights training and have not engaged in any pattern of gross violations since 2001. Police forces have been largely demilitarized, and the courts have taken measures to restrict military powers during states of emergency and to limit military court jurisdiction. The court system itself remains badly in need of reform to improve efficiency, reduce corruption, and gain autonomy from political influence.

Reparations

One of the key recommendations of the Truth and Reconciliation Commission was to implement a comprehensive reparations program to benefit victims. In 2005, the Congress passed reparations legislation, but it was not until 2008 that a registry of victims was initiated to determine systematically who qualified for reparations. By the end of the year, approximately 10,000 individuals and more than 3,500 communities were listed on the general victims' registry. A separate registry identified internally displaced people, but was not integrated into the general registry. In 2007 and 2008, the government spent several million dollars in social programs identified as part of the reparations programs, including mental health programs. However, communities, rather than individuals, were the recipients of these reparations programs. Furthermore, much of the money budgeted for reparations went unspent because of problems approving and coordinating projects, and that which was spent generally took the form of poverty eradication and general social programs, without a clear reparatory motive. In general, the implementation of reparations has been slow, disorganized, and unsatisfactory in the eyes of the victims who expected to receive them.

Prosecutions

Unlike many truth commissions, the Peruvian one directly called for prosecutions in the cases of human rights abuses it detailed. With the release of its final report, the Commission also forwarded forty-four cases to the Public Prosecutor's Office for investigation and trial.

Members of the Shining Path were most responsible for deaths and human rights violations, but most of its leaders were already in prison. The controversial question was whether their convictions were legitimate, given that most of them were handed down by Fujimori's specially created military tribunals. In January 2003, just months before the release of the Truth Commission's report, Peru's courts overturned the conviction of Abimael Guzman and ruled the bulk of the Fujimori-era antiterrorism legislation unconstitutional. This decision concurred with a 2001 Inter-American Court of Human Rights decision and entitled those convicted under the legislation to retrials in civilian courts. Despite intense public disapproval and fear that thousands of terrorists would now be released from prison, the courts ultimately retried hundreds of cases and released hundreds of prisoners who had been convicted without sufficient evidence. (Thanks to the work of Peruvian human rights groups, hundreds of innocent prisoners convicted under antiterrorism laws had been released during the Fujimori and Paniagua administrations as well.) The new trials, though not popular, established the extent to which the Peruvian state was willing to go to restore its democratic credentials. All major figures in the Shining Path were ultimately reconvicted by civilian courts. Retrials continued after 2009.

Prosecuting members of the armed forces implicated in human rights abuses has proven more difficult. Most so accused before 2001 never saw trial, and those who did were tried in military courts rather than civilian ones. Despite a 2004 decision by Peru's highest civilian court ruling that military courts had no jurisdiction over human rights cases and could not guarantee due process, military courts continued to investigate and prosecute alleged human rights violators. Nevertheless, by the end of 2005, criminal indictments had been issued for 368 individuals in cases forwarded to civilian courts by the truth commission. Almost all of these indicted were current or former members of the armed forces. By 2009, many more cases had been initiated against members of the armed forces, and some individuals accused of human rights abuses who had fled Peru were being extradited back to face trial. Although a handful of cases have resulted in convictions, the slow pace of Peruvian courts means that many more remain unresolved. Those who have sought justice for human rights violations in the courts have routinely received anonymous death threats. Hundreds of human rights cases have not made it to the courts at all, often because of a lack of evidence. Each year, more bodies are exhumed and identified.

After fleeing Peru in late 2000, Fujimori took refuge in Japan, whose officials granted him citizenship based on his Japanese parentage. Japan refused to extradite Fujimori to Peru to face prosecution for corruption, abuse of authority, and human rights violations. The former president occasionally boasted that he would return to Peru to seek reelection, yet it came as something of a surprise when he attempted to make good on this promise. In November 2005, Fujimori flew to Chile, from whence he hoped to launch his candidacy for the 2006 presidential elections in Peru. He was instead promptly taken into custody by Chilean authorities and ultimately extradited to Peru in September 2007. In December, his prosecution for human rights violations began. The trial covered three cases, the most notorious being the Barrios Altos and Cantuta University killings carried out by the Colina Group. The charges against Fujimori alleged that this death squad connected to Army Intelligence Service acted under the president's orders when perpetrating dozens of murders in these cases. In April 2009, a three-judge panel of the Supreme Court convicted Fujimori of murder, aggravated kidnapping, battery, and crimes against humanity. His sentence of twenty-five years in prison for these crimes will be added to his sentences for other convictions related to corruption.

It should be noted that both the frontrunners in the 2006 presidential elections have been investigated for human rights violations. Ollanta Humala is a former Lieutenant Colonel in the Peruvian Army; two months after losing the presidential election, he was indicted on charges that he was a party to torture, disappearance, and murder on a military base in 1992. He lost to Alan Garcia, who also served as president from 1986 to 1990. Two months after winning the 2006 election, the public prosecutor dropped a case against Garcia for allegedly orchestrating extrajudicial killings of Shining Path prisoners after a riot at El Fronton prison in 1986. A 2000 decision by the Inter-American Court of Human Rights held the state responsible for these extrajudicial killings and called for Garcia's prosecution. Human rights abuses were widespread during Garcia's first term, and his commitment to transitional justice is widely doubted.

Conclusion

A decade has not yet passed since Peru embarked on its process of transitional justice. The country has opted for a fairly holistic approach, including a truth commission, prosecutions, reparations, and reforms. Today, the courts are at the center of efforts to establish accountability, a task they will grapple with for many years to come. The public's willingness to vote for individuals implicated in human rights abuses and the general absence of concerted efforts at reconciliation, reparation, and social justice for the indigenous population indicate that transitional justice in Peru remains a work in progress.

Rebecca K. Root

Cross-references: Accountability Mechanisms; Amnesty; Apology; Court Trials for Redress; Reforms of Military, Police, and Secret Police; Reparations; Truth Commission; Truth and Reconciliation Commission (Peru).

Further Readings

Comisión de la Verdad y Reconciliación (Peru). 2004. *Informe Final* [Final Report]. 9 volumes. Lima: Universidad Nacional Mayor San Marcos and Pontificia Universidad Católica del Perú.
Gamarra, Ronald. 2009. A Leader Takes Flight: The Indictment of Alberto Fujimori. In *Prosecuting Heads of State*. Eds. Ellen Lutz and Caitlin Reiger. New York: Cambridge University Press.
Gorriti, Gustavo. 1999. *The Shining Path: A History of the Millenarian War in Peru*. Chapel Hill: University of North Carolina Press.
Laplante, Lisa and Kimberly Theidon. 2007. Truth with Consequences: Justice and Reparations in Post-Truth Commission Peru. *Human Rights Quarterly*, 29: 228–250.
Root, Rebecca. 2009. Through the Window of Opportunity: The Transitional Justice Network in Peru. *Human Rights Quarterly*, 31: 452–473.
Youngers, Coletta. 2003. *Violencia Política y Sociedad Civil en el Perú: Historia de la Coordinadora Nacional de Derechos Humanos* [Political Violence and Civil Society in Peru: History of the National Coordinator of Human Rights]. Lima: Instituto de Estudios Peruanos.

Philippines

Filipino society remains divided into the rich and the poor. The poor are organized in civil society groups, but corruption, violence, and human rights abuses characterize everyday life. Although measures aimed at transitional justice through prosecution of perpetrators of human rights violations, reparations to victims, truth seeking regarding past crimes and the fate of the disappeared, and institutional reforms of the army, police, and secret police have been implemented since 1986, their results were limited by opposition from the army, police, and members of the political elite. The establishment of a truth commission under President Benigno Aquino in 2010 represents a new effort to right past wrongs, but the commission will have to deal with the de facto impunity of members of the army and the police.

The Repressive Past

As part of the Spanish East Indies, in the sixteenth century, the rural, indigenous Filipino population was organized in *encomiendas*, a system in which a member of the indigenous elite (a *principalia*) or a Spanish colonist controlled a number of laborers obliged to pay tax to the Spanish crown and provide labor and surplus production to their overlords. The system brought communally held land and resources under elite control and created a large class of dispossessed indigenous people. As a result of public criticism from the Catholic Church, by the late seventeenth century, the *encomiendas* was replaced by *repartiemento de labor* (temporary forced labor) and the *haciendas* (agricultural enterprises in which laborers were paid for their services). By the nineteenth century, many *haciendas* were controlled by landed families of mixed Filipino and Chinese origin or Filipino *principalia* families. Having access to education, these families entered local government. As central government exerted only limited control over rural territories, these families became major power brokers in Filipino politics, a fact that turned the Philippines into a "cacique democracy" controlled by elite, not popular, interests.

In 1896, the Katipunan independence movement engaged in armed revolt, without being able to defeat the Spanish colonial government. The outbreak of the Spanish-American War in April 1898 gave the struggle much needed momentum. By that summer, the revolutionaries controlled most of the Philippines, except the capital, Manila. The revolutionaries declared the Philippines independent on June 12, but the United States negotiated a separate peace with Spain and annexed the islands. In the ensuing Philippine-American War (1899–1902), the Filipino forces were defeated in open battle but successful in guerrilla warfare. In response, the Americans targeted the guerillas' civilian support. This led to displacements, mass incarceration in detention camps, and killings of villagers, the most notorious being the 1901 U.S. retaliation after the Balangiga massacre in Samar Province (which resulted in 2,000 to 3,000 dead).

The 1902 Philippine Bill established both American sovereignty and Filipino political rights, extended the U.S. Bill of Rights to include the Filipinos, appointed two resident Filipino commissioners to the U.S. Congress, and created an elected Philippine bicameral parliament. However, it left the society relatively unchanged, as the elite provided the elected Assembly members, and supported independence to satisfy its interests, not to further social change. Land reform, desired by the rural population, was publicly supported by the U.S. representatives in the Philippines but frustrated by the Filipino elite and the U.S. government. For example, in 1903, the Filipino government purchased from the Pope 165,000 hectares of friar lands intended to be credited for the agrarian reform, but U.S. authorities vetoed this course of action and sold the land to wealthy elite families at market price, far beyond the reach of common farmers.

The 1916 Philippine Autonomy Act established that independence for the Philippines was the United States' goal as well, and would be granted once "stable government" was achieved. By 1929, Philippines' independence gained support from the U.S. sugar and tobacco producers, farmers, and labor organizations fearing competition from Filipino production and immigrants. Following the 1934 Philippine Independence Act, the Philippines and the United States created the Philippine Commonwealth, which had its own constitution (enacted in 1935) and Supreme Court. The Philippines was to gain independence after a ten-year transition period during which the United States maintained a military presence on the island, imposed a graduate tax on Philippine products exported to the U.S. market, and reclassified Filipinos as aliens under American immigration laws.

World War II strongly impacted this schedule. Japanese forces defeated the combined Philippine-American forces in winter 1941–1942 and set up a puppet regime rooted in the Filipino elite. A popular, mainly rural guerrilla movement resisting the Japanese and aiming for independence continued armed fighting. The guerilla groups allowed peasants and tenants to occupy land and oust landlords, and prevented the Japanese from entering these territories. By the end of World War II, large sections of Filipino territory were under guerrilla control. Groups like the People's Army against the Japanese

(Hukbong Bayan Laban sa mga Hapon, or the HUKs) opposed the U.S.-supported elite who favored a return to prewar clientelism and landlordism. Although many legislators had collaborated with the Japanese, under U.S. pressure, Filipino President Sergio Osmena allowed them to maintain their posts after the end of the war. As such, the prewar elite survived the war.

The first presidential election of April 1946 was followed by Philippine independence in July. The election was won by Manuel Roxas, a candidate linked to the established families and political clans. He strongly opposed the influence of the HUKs and others who asked for land reform. Although opposed by nationalists and land reformists, the 1946 Bell Trade Act ensured far-reaching U.S. control over the Filipino economy and natural resources in exchange for rebuilding funds and allowing the United States continued usage of the military bases in the Philippines. The Filipino government and its American advisors deemed the HUKs and the left-wing National Peasant Union (Pambansang Kaisahan ng mga Magbubukid) a communist threat and kept them from entering parliament. In the countryside, landlords who had fled during the war returned to demand rent, and employed armed forces and police support against resisting peasants. Many peasants were World War II veterans who had retained their weapons.

As their demands for reform were ignored and legal attempts at gaining government influence blocked, in 1946, the HUKs took up arms against the government, changed their name to People's Liberation Army (Hukbong Mapagpalaya ng Bayan), and capitalized on rural resistance. Government reactions varied from violent, indiscriminate counterterrorism measures to reconciliation attempts. While the army and the paramilitaries burned villages and killed real and suspected HUK fighters and sympathizers, the government created a new Agrarian Commission, which concluded that the division of harvests between tenants and landowners in Central Luzon (the heartland of rice cultivation and the HUK rebellion) exploited the tenants. The amended 1933 Rice Tenancy Act allowed for a 70–30 division in favor of the tenants, while authorizing a similar division favoring the landlord (Wurfel 1954). In 1948, the HUKs were declared an illegal organization when they gained support from the Philippines Communist Party (Partido Komunista ng Pilipinas or the PKP), a Comintern organization not well known among the rural population. By 1950, the PKP described the HUKs as their military arm. This prominent communist threat, which was close to the Korean War theater in a friendly state that housed American army bases, brought U.S. forces to assist the Philippines government in fighting the HUKs and the PKP. By 1954, the HUKs and the PKP were defeated and the former guerrilla member Ramon Magsaysay was appointed Defense Secretary. As the fighting progressed, both sides terrorized the rural population through killing, rape, theft, robbery, and kidnapping. HUK fighters and PKP members and sympathizers were arrested, killed, and incarcerated for such crimes, while government and militia soldiers were usually not persecuted.

With more than 40,000 dead, wounded, or missing, the fighting showed the effect of rural discontent. After becoming president in 1953, Magsaysay addressed this problem through resettlement and agrarian reform. Demobilized surrendered HUK fighters and landless farmers were resettled to less populated areas. Magsaysay inspired the 1955 Land Reform Act, which aimed at improving the tenants' situation, but lost its power after elite congressmen added more than 200 amendments that exempted large estates from reform.

Thus, a large poor social segment was dominated by influential landholding families who controlled government and blocked reform. Violence by private militias and crime was rife because of the easy availability of arms, and patronage networks were as important in gaining political power as elections. Candidates used their ties to local bosses to obtain votes and, once elected to the legislature, rewarded these contacts and ignored the voters. Popular demands for an end to patronage, corruption, and crime and for greater democracy and government protection lacked wide support.

In 1965, Ferdinand Marcos became president. Initially he was quite popular as he stimulated government reform and national development and deployed the army to combat criminal gangs. But his government resorted to violence, intimidation, and vote buying to ensure reelection in 1969. Marcos became unpopular after he installed supporters and cronies in key political and business positions to consolidate his grasp on power and resources. As disappointment over his lack of reform grew, opposition consolidated. In 1970, the PKP-affiliated Patriotic Youth (Kabataang Makabayan) rallied against government corruption and Marcos's presidency, while the underground Communist Party of the Philippines (Partido Komunista ng Pilipinas, CPP) organized major protests and demonstrations. Urban anti-regime demonstrations increased in frequency and bloodshed, and in 1969, the CCP established the New People's Army (Bagong Hukbong Bayan, NPA), which engaged in a "protracted people's war."

In the southern Philippines, the Muslims harbored strong anti-regime sentiments as consecutive governments had neglected the area and discriminated against them. In the Jabidah Massacre of 1968, the Filipino army killed between 14 and 200 Muslim army recruits. A single recruit, Jibin Arula, survived, but his report did not convince the government to indict the culprits. Public pressure brought the government to start court martial proceedings, but the case led to no convictions. The massacre and ensuing government reaction gave rise to the Moro National Liberation Front (MNLF) guerilla movement, which sought independence for the Muslim areas in southern Philippines.

In August 1972, Marcos used a grenade attack at an opposition party's political rally in Manila as a pretext to suspend the writ of habeas corpus. Pointing to the threat of communist and Muslim insurgents, Marcos put the Philippines under martial rule that September. The new 1973 Constitution (and its amendments of 1976, 1980, 1981, and 1984) gave the president near-autonomous executive power. Under martial law, peaceful opposition was very difficult. The communist guerrillas became the rallying point for anti-Marcos sentiment. The army killed, harassed, raped, and intimidated those suspected of participating in or aiding the guerrillas, destroyed and stole property, forcibly resettled entire villages, set up business ventures while ignoring local claims to lands and forests, and closely cooperated with the landed elite, clearing villagers from lands on request. After being more disciplined than the regular army, the NPA troops proceeded to torture and kill civilian opponents. Refugees from the countryside moved to the cities and swelled the ranks of the urban poor. To control the cities, the regime used intimidation, abduction, torture, and the extrajudicial killing of opponents, a practice known as "salvaging," because the bodies sometimes ended up in isolated salvage or junk yards. Estimates of the number of victims under the 1965–1986 Marcos regime include 3,000–5,000 murdered, 35,000 tortured, and 70,000–120,000 detained extrajudicially. Aside from the communist guerrillas, a small group of human rights lawyers known as the Free Legal Assistance Group, founded by Jose Diokno, publicly opposed the regime. After 1977, the regime acknowledged that human rights crimes took place, freed political prisoners, and introduced limited human rights reforms, a transformation facilitated by transnational advocacy (Jetschke 2011, 89–129). Even afterward, government forces committed human rights violations, and the regime defended such actions as necessary and in the state's interest.

After constitutional amendments in 1980 and 1981 cemented his position as head of state, Marcos lifted martial law. In 1983, the public assassination of Benigno Aquino, a popular opponent of the regime, discredited the regime nationally and internationally. In the 1986 elections, Benigno's widow, Corazon Aquino, challenged Marcos. When the rigged results indicated a victory for Marcos, army soldiers rebelled. The soldiers gained the support of Aquino and the Catholic Church, and millions flocked to the soldiers' camp. As a result, Marcos fled the Philippines for the United States.

The country faced numerous problems. Marcos's cronies and the elite were still in powerful positions, communist and Muslim guerrillas were fighting the state, the powerful army and the police were compromised by the "salvaging" of opponents, the government was tainted by corruption and nepotism, while the rural population was dissatisfied with its limited access to land and political influence. Aquino had to reform the country, mete out justice, and bring all parties together. In 1987, a new constitution limited presidential powers, reestablished the bicameral legislature, guaranteed an independent judiciary, and launched economic policies. Article XIII of the Constitution tasked congress with reducing social, political, and economic inequalities. Article 3.15 reinstated the writ of habeas corpus, except for rebels and invaders. Articles 4–8 stipulated agrarian reform and land redistribution.

Human rights violations continued to occur. The NPA and MNLF fought on, and some 200 private militias were organized to support the army and the police to fight the insurgents and often to allow local bosses to take physical control of an area and prevent land reform. The Mendiola Massacre of 1987, in which thirteen to nineteen farmers were killed after government forces dispersed a demonstration demanding agrarian reforms, stained Aquino's presidency. By 1992, more than 800 salvagings, 1,000 summary executions, and 20,000 arrests and illegal detentions by police, army, and militias had been reported to human rights organizations (Jetschke 2011, 173).

At the same time, civil society organizations became stronger. The impact of vigilantism in local politics decreased steadily after the 1960s as the National Citizens' Movement for Free Elections (NAMFREL) and church originations monitored activities at polling stations (Linantud 1998). The implementation of the 1988 Comprehensive Agrarian Reform Law (CARP) saw small landholders and peasants assert their legal rights through local initiatives, national nongovernmental organizations, and peasant organizations (Franco 2008). Nongovernmental organizations have played a strong role in indigenous land claims. Following Article IX.12 of the Constitution, a National Commission on Indigenous Peoples was created to protect and promote the well-being of indigenous groups following the 1997 Indigenous Peoples Right Act, which recognized ancestral lands and domains for which indigenous individuals and groups could obtain certificated titles. The application of the Act is closely monitored by nongovernmental organizations that assist and support indigenous groups in lodging claims with the state (Hirtz 2003) and critically monitor conflicts between rights protected by the Act but endangered by other legislation such as the 1995 Mining Code.

Reacting to armed opposition has remained a major problem for the government. In the south, the government and the MNLF reached a settlement that included the establishment of the Autonomous Region of Muslim Mindanao (ARMM) in 1996, but the Moro Islamic Liberation Front (MILF), an offshoot of the MNLF that rejected the settlement, has fought on. The MILF became associated with international terrorism after Abu Sayyaf, an Islamic terrorist group associated with Al-Qaeda, kidnapped tourists from Malaysian resorts in Borneo in 2000 and 2001 and members of the Indonesian terrorist organization Jemaah Islamiyah found refuge among the MILF (Rodell 2005). Under Presidents Joseph Estrada (1998–2001) and Gloria Macapagal-Arroyo (2001–2010), the Philippines army, with U.S. support, fought against the MILF with all-out violence, hurting civilians. Attention for human rights abuses and repairs of past wrongs stood low on the government's agenda. The NPA was reclassified as a terrorist organization. The Arroyo government pointed to strong links between the insurgents and human rights groups acting as a front for the NPA (Jetschke 2011, 253), as well as between insurgents and journalists, some of whom were murdered or disappeared, allegedly by government actors. In 2006, the government tempered its accusations after Amnesty International condemned the human rights violations and the crackdown on the activity of nongovernmental organizations (Amnesty International 2006).

Transitional Justice

The country has adopted a Presidential Commission on Human Rights, court trials, and the Truth Commission as transitional justice methods, but none have been efficient.

The Presidential Commission on Human Rights

In 1986, President Aquino established the Presidential Committee on Human Rights to investigate individual complaints of human rights abuses committed by or on the order of government officials. The seven-member Committee was chaired by human rights lawyer Jose Diokno. From the beginning, the Committee's work has been limited by lack of resources and active opposition from the military and bureaucracy. In 1987, all the Commissioners resigned to protest the killing of peaceful demonstrators by military forces in the Mendiola Massacre. The Committee never produced a report and was succeeded by the National Commission on Human Rights, created on the basis of the 1987 constitution. The Commission, which consists of four members and a chairperson, investigates all forms of human rights violations committed in the Philippines. From 2007 to the time of this writing, Loretta Ann P. Rosales has been its chair. Because it had too many cases and few resources, the Commission was quickly overwhelmed. In 1991, while hearing the *Cariño v. The Commission on Human Rights* case, the Supreme Court established that the Commission had investigative powers only to the extent that it could provide advice or recommendations to a court of law, without having adjudicative powers itself.

Court Trials

In 1983, twenty-two illegally detained and tortured individuals filed a claim against their military torturers in the *Aberca et al. v. Ver et al.* court case. The case went through all court levels before reaching the Supreme Court in 2005, where, at the time of this writing, it still sits. Other individual cases remain open at the time of this writing, including a 1986 class suit for damages filed by more than 10,000 victims of human rights abuses against the estate of Ferdinand Marcos (*Hilao v. Estate of Ferdinand Marcos*).

The Philippines Truth Commission of 2010

On July 30, 2010, a month after being sworn in, President Benigno Aquino created the Philippine Truth Commission of 2010 through Executive Order 1 to investigate allegations of corruption and human rights violations under the administration of President Gloria Macapagal-Arroyo (2001–2010). Within months, however, the Supreme Court declared the Executive Order unconstitutional on the grounds that such an investigation would violate equal protection of the law because members of an administration would be singled out and accused of corruption, whereas members of other past and present administrations would not be, although they could be equally guilty. The Court stressed that the Executive Order could also serve as a tool for "vindictiveness and selective retribution" (Vehicle of Vengeance 2011).

Conclusion

Despite a past riddled with human rights abuses, the Philippines has engaged in only a few transitional justice programs that have been largely ineffective in satisfying victims and publicly identifying perpetrators. Given the political clout of military and police officers tainted by past involvement in human rights, the culture of impunity continues.

Larens Bakker

Cross-references: Court Trials for Redress; Truth Commission.

Further Readings

Amnesty International. 2006. *Amnesty International Report 2006 – Philippines*. New York: Amnesty International.
Aquino, Benigno. 2010. *Executive Order 1*, July 30. Available at: http://www.gov.ph/2010/07/30/executive-order-no-1/ (accessed October 3, 2011).
Carranza, Ruben. 2011. *From Marcos to Another Aquino. Impunity, Accountability and Transitional Justice in the Philippines*. Makaty City: EPJUST, NMM Monograph Series No. 2.
Franco, Jennifer. 2008. Making Land Rights Accessible: Social Movements and Political-Legal Innovation in the Rural Philippines. *Journal of Development Studies*, 44 (7): 991–1022.
Hirtz, Frank. 2003. It Takes Modern Means to Be Traditional: On Recognizing Indigenous Cultural Communities in the Philippines. *Development and Change*, 34(5): 887–914.
Jetschke, Anja. 2011. *Human Rights and State Security. Indonesia and the Philippines*. Philadelphia: University of Pennsylvania Press.
Linantud, John. 1998. Whither Guns, Goons and Gold? The Decline of Factional Violence in the Philipines. *Contemporary Southeast Asia*, 20(3): 298–318.
Rodell, Paul. 2005. The Philippines and the Challenge of International Terrorism. In *Terrorism and Violence in Southeast Asia. Transnational Challenges to States and Regional Stability*. Ed. Paul Smith. Armonk: M.E. Sharpe, pp. 122–141.
Vehicle of Vengeance. 2011. *Journal Online*, July 27. Available at: http://www.journal.com.ph/index.php/news/editorial/10145-vehicle-of-vengeance (accessed October 3, 2011).
Wurfel, David. 1954. The Philippine Rice Share Tenancy Act. *Pacific Affairs*, 27(1): 41–50.

Poland

As other postcommunist countries that transitioned to democracy through round-table talks, Poland delayed the implementation of transitional justice. The prolonged round-table negotiations gave communists ample opportunity to destroy evidence of their wrongdoing, including secret police files. After 1989, few investigations into communist crimes reached trial stage, and those that did rarely resulted in sentences. Victim compensation programs have been limited, and rehabilitation was frequently used in lieu of trials. Lustration did not start in earnest until 1998. It was followed by the creation of the Institute of National Remembrance, an archive storing and granting victims access to their files. The Institute has spearheaded memorialization and educational campaigns, including the rewriting of history textbooks and the opening of the Museum of the Warsaw Uprising in 2006. A vast property restitution program was implemented in 1993. Overall, politicians are more committed to transitional justice than citizens, whose interest in holding autocrats accountable for past human rights violations has steadily declined.

The Repressive Past

Communism was not Poland's first experience with authoritarianism since it gained independence in 1918. The first dictator was Jozef Pilsudski, who led a legion of Polish fighters within the Austrian Army in the fight for Poland's independence. He emerged as the nation's hero during the Polish-Soviet war of 1920. By 1926, the fragmented parliament of independent Poland produced sixteen cabinets. Frustrated with this inefficient democracy, in May 1926, Pilsudzki staged a coup d'état and became the prime minister. Under his Sanation regime, which sought the moral healing of the Polish body politic, constitutional amendments curtailed the role of parliament in favor of the office of the president, nominated by Pilsudski. Pilsudski's regime persecuted and imprisoned political opponents (including communists and Polish and Ukrainian nationalists) in the Bereza Kartuska concentration camp and the Brest Fortress, where 7,000 political prisoners perished. The communist and postcommunist governments did not include reckoning with abuses of the Sanation regime as part of their transitional justice program.

The Nazi occupation of Poland, which commenced with Warsaw's surrender on September 28, 1939, was responsible for imprisonment combined with forced labor (which affected 1.5 million people), genocide of 3 million Polish Jews, and the killing of 1.8 million non-Jewish Polish civilians. While Germany occupied the western and central parts of Poland, in September 1939, the Soviet Union invaded eastern Poland. The number of Stalinist victims in Poland is estimated at 1.8 million, including 150,000 death casualties. These included the 21,000 Polish officers killed by the Soviet secret police, the NKVD, in the Katyn Forest (see entry on Commission to Counter Attempts to Falsify History at the Expense of Russian Interests). Hundreds of thousands were displaced and/or had their land and property expropriated.

The Yalta Peace Conference of 1945 assigned Poland to the Soviet sphere of influence. The Soviets were welcomed by one segment of the antifascist resistance (the Polish Committee of National Liberation, PKWN, the self-proclaimed government of Soviet-liberated Poland), but despised by another (the Home Army, Armia Krajowa, the military wing of the Polish government in exile that regarded the Soviet aggressor-turned-liberator as Poland's enemy and the PKWN as traitors). Civil war broke out between the two groups before World War II was over. The communists won, but were unpopular. They appeased hundreds of thousands of displaced Poles by redistributing land, a process begun with the PKWN-issued Decree on Land Reform of 6 September 1944. The Decree redistributed large estates to landless and smallholding farmers and expropriated the land of Polish citizens forcefully detained in the Soviet Union after Poland's invasion of September 17, 1939, and of Germans living in western Poland, who were forcefully repatriated to Germany in 1946. Of the 9.3 million hectares confiscated as a result, 6 million were redistributed. By 1949, 5 million families moved to western Poland, where they received land taken over from the Germans. After taking control of Poland in 1945, to boost their popularity, the communists did not return land expropriated by the Nazis to its rightful owners. Instead, they added it to the pool of assets redistributed to landless peasants.

The most violent period of communist rule lasted until the death of Joseph Stalin in 1953. During this time, the Polish communist regime led by President Boleslaw Bierut prosecuted Home Army soldiers, Sanation regime supporters, and anyone raising Bierut's suspicion. Stalinist rule in Poland included show trials of communists who challenged the official line (like Wladyslaw Gomulka and Marian Spychalski), often resulting in the death penalty, and culminated in the quashing of a workers' protest in Poznan, when communist authorities opened fire on workers. Until 1989, violent crackdowns on anticommunist protests preceded turnovers in power followed by brief "thaws."

As the regime matured, violent crackdowns on dissident protests became fewer; the regime moved toward clandestine methods of harassing the opposition. The government's shield and sword was the secret police, the Bureau for Public Security (Urzad Bezpieczenstwa), later renamed the Security Service (Sluzba Bezpieczenstwa, SB). The SB employed 15,000–25,000 people every year from 1975 to 1989 and infiltrated dissident groups with thousands of informants who, after 1989, became lustration targets. The SB faced its greatest challenge with the emergence of Solidarity, a trade union independent from the communist regime. Its membership reached close to 10 million at the height of its popularity, when strike activity forced the communist government to negotiate with Solidarity leaders. Solidarity's legalization in 1980 was the result of negotiations between the Polish communist government and the civil society. The "thaw" lasted eighteen months. On December 13, 1981, Wojciech Jaruzelski, leader of the ruling Polish United Workers' Party, proclaimed martial law and appointed the Military Council of National Salvation (Wojskowa Rada Ocalenia Narodowego, WRON) as his cabinet. The Council delegalized Solidarity and other civil society associations, monitored phone conversations, introduced curfew hours, banned strike activity, and authorized riot police units to use firearms against protesting workers. A riot police unit sent to pacify the Wujek coal miners in December 1981 shot dead nine and injured twenty-one coal miners (see later discussion).

Afterward, 9,862 Solidarity leaders were arrested. As a result of the interviews and interrogations with the detained leaders, the SB recruited more than 1,500 new informers. This wide infiltration of Solidarity improved the surveillance of the underground opposition throughout the 1980s. Six years after martial law was suspended in 1983, round-table negotiations held by the communist and Solidarity leaders in the presence of Catholic Church representatives resulted in the first elections in which non-communist candidates were allowed to run. After the 1989 elections, Jaruzelski, who became Poland's first post-1989 president as a result of the round-table arrangements, asked Solidarity leader Tadeusz Mazowiecki to form the cabinet. It was the first government in the Soviet bloc led by a dissident leader. Because the new cabinet relied on the support of some members of the former Communist Party and its satellite parties, Mazowiecki sacrificed transitional justice for the sake of effecting economic and political reforms.

Transitional Justice

During the twentieth century, Poland experienced three repressive regimes, but nearly all transitional justice measures have been directed against the communist regime. The Polish postcommunist transitional justice program included lustration, file access, rehabilitation and compensation for victims, and property restitution. Trials for human rights violations have been few. Memorialization and rewriting of history books have taken place under the auspices of the Institute for National Remembrance (see separate entry).

Lustration

The first attempts to pass a lustration law were stalled by the Mazowiecki government as part of his "thick line" policy, which separated the communist past from the democratic present without holding former communists accountable for human rights violations. Six different lustration bills were submitted to parliament, but work on them came to a halt in 1993. After the communist successor parties, Democratic Left Alliance (Sojusz Lewicy Demokratycznej, SLD) and Polish People's Party (Polskie Stronnictwo Ludowe, PSL), won the 1993 elections, lustration and transitional justice were put on a back burner.

Seeking to prevent an electoral loss in the 1997 elections at the hands of the Solidarity opposition, on April 11, 1997, the ruling SLD-PSL coalition passed a very mild lustration law. The Law on the Conditions of Holding Certain Public Positions required candidates for public office to declare before elections whether they had worked for or consciously collaborated with the SB. Instead of banning from office candidates who declared collaboration, the *Official Gazette* published the declaration and voters could withdraw their support from the candidates. All statements denying collaboration were transferred to a state prosecutor, who used the SB secret archives to assess their accuracy. If the prosecutor found evidence that the declaration was false, the public official was tried before the Lustration Court (see separate entry). Successive amendments enhanced the law's effectiveness, range, and scope, without renouncing the confession-based mechanism. They also replaced the Lustration Court with the Warsaw Court of Appeal, although the task of verifying lustration declarations rested with the state prosecutor from the Institute of National Remembrance.

In 2006, lustration was extended to include top governmental officials chosen in national and local elections, cabinet members, leaders of the judiciary, top officials in the state health care and social welfare systems, editors-in-chief of the public media, administrators and faculty of public and private universities, high school headmasters, managers of the national postal service, and CEOs of companies where the state was the main shareholder. They were dismissed or demoted if they lied about being officers and informers of the SB and police units placed under SB command (such as the riot police), faculty and administrators of police academies, members of the border guard patrol, military intelligence and counterintelligence officers, and employees of the communist Agency for Religious Beliefs or of the Censorship offices. By 2007, more than 23,000 persons had been investigated. After the lustration law was expanded, the relationship between the State Prosecutor for Public Interest and the Institute of National Remembrance deteriorated. The State Prosecutor's Office directed to the Institute 137 questions concerning 3,425 persons, but the Institute's responses covered only 776 persons. The Office drew attention to fifty-nine declarations submitted by public officials holding highest national office (secretaries of state, vice-ministers, regional governors), of which the Institute never responded to fourteen.

According to information provided to the author in September 2011, the verification process was still ongoing and as of that date, out of 290,857 declarations (2,560 confirming collaborations), the examination of 19,005 had begun. Out of those, 15,639 have been completed as follows: (1) in 15,380 cases, the declarations have been determined truthful and not raising suspicion; (2) in 207 cases, lustration has been initiated; and (3) 41 cases were instances of auto-lustration, meaning the lustrati was not under obligation to subject himself to verification, but chose to do so to clear his name, because it had been tarnished by the media or because his political party asked him to do so. The lustration bureau of the IPN has reached 100 final decisions in the cases raising suspicion: 47 declarations were found to be lustration lies and 26 to be truthful declarations disagreeing with the prosecutor's recommendations; in 25 auto-lustration cases, the lustration bureau agreed with the prosecutors that the declaration was truthful, and in 2 cases to be lustration lies. Three cases were dismissed by the bureau as not warranting an investigation.

Access to Secret Files

Simultaneously with lustration, the issue of establishing a publicly accessible archive of SB files was addressed. Since 2001, the Institute has granted victims access to their files produced by the Nazi and communist security services between 1939 and 1989. The Institute records, collects, stores, processes, secures, makes available, and publishes SB documents produced between July 22, 1944 and July 31, 1990, and documents of the security authorities of the Third Reich and the Soviet Union related to Nazi crimes, communist crimes, and other war crimes or crimes against humanity perpetrated against Polish nationals or Polish citizens of other nationalities between September 1, 1939 and July 31, 1990. The Institute documents politically motivated reprisals instigated or ordered by members of the judiciary and law enforcement agencies, and the actions of the SB. It manages archival records from the Department of National Security and the Ministries of Interior, Defense, and Justice. The most sensitive archival files relate to SB collaborators. Special provisions protect the privacy of people mentioned in the files.

Trials and Rehabilitation

The reproduction of communist judges and prosecutors made the punishing of communist perpetrators difficult. To break up this network, in 1998, parliament allowed communist-era judges to face disciplinary courts, whose decisions could terminate their careers. In 1998, the Council of Judges investigated the pension privileges of fifty-one Stalinist-era judges and annulled those of thirteen retired judges and four deceased judges. In 2000, the Council investigated another nineteen cases and dismissed nine of them, annulling pension privileges of thirty-nine persons. By December 2001, it further annulled the pension privileges of two retired judges and one deceased judge. Trials dealing with communist crimes have also concerned the forced suppression of the 1970 strikes in Gdansk and the martial law period.

In 1990, the minister of justice reopened the trial of twelve defendants (including Ministers of Defense and Interior, and ten Politburo members) who in 1970 authorized the use of firearms at the Gdansk shipyard, which killed 44 protesting workers and injured 200. Proceedings against Wojciech Jaruzelski, then Minister of Defense, were discontinued, but reopened following an Appellate Court decision. His case was merged with that of three other codefendants, who were too ill to gather all four defendants in court to read the charges. The trial against the perpetrators of the 1970 shootings lasted four years because of the defendants' poor health and the abundant documentation (90 volumes of 200 pages each) that the prosecution presented in court.

A case that lasted four years, but in which charges were dropped for lack of evidence, prosecuted those following orders to open fire on the striking coal miners in Wujek. Adjudicating under the martial law, on January 20, 1982, the Military Prosecutor acquitted the riot policemen responsible for the death of the coal miners, finding that the policemen had acted in self-defense and used weapons pursuant to regulations. Nineteen days later, the Silesian Military Court sentenced four strike leaders to prison sentences of up to four years. In 1991, the case was reopened. Twenty-four persons, including Kiszczak, were indicted for authorizing the use of firearms against workers. On the first day the court was in session, in March 1993, Kiszczak submitted a doctor's note stating that he was too ill to stand trial. The case was moved to Warsaw, so that the ill Kiszczak could attend the hearings. Those who had followed orders remained to stand trial in Katowice. In November 1997, eleven riot policemen were acquitted, and the cases of the remaining eleven were dismissed for lack of evidence. The judges could not determine who had fired the fatal shots and who fired shots into the air to keep the coal miners at bay. In 1998, the Katowice Appeals Court invalidated the decision on procedural grounds and sent the case back for reconsideration. The original panel of judges excused itself from deciding the case, citing personal reasons. In 1999, the public defenders of the riot policemen resigned from the case, citing their anticommunist dissident past as justification.

October 1999 marked the initiation of the second Wujek trial, which lasted through 2001. After hearing 300 witnesses, the court acquitted all defendants in October 2002. The verdict was a direct result of the presiding judge's refusal to admit as evidence the Tatra Mountaineers' Report, prepared by three Solidarity members who, while working undercover as trainers at an antiterrorist boot camp, recorded conversations among the riot police troops who perpetrated the Wujek massacre. All copies of the report were considered lost, until one of them surfaced in 2007. The report included some policemen's admission of responsibility for shooting coal miners. The court was concerned that the Mountaineers report was tampered with because it had been missing for such a long time.

The trial of those who gave the order to shoot in the Wujek massacre – the masterminds of the martial law – encountered similar stumbling blocks. In 2008, the Institute of National Remembrance brought a case against nine WRON members. Jaruzelski, Kiszczak, and Stanislaw Kania were accused of "participating in a criminal military organization, appointed with the aim of committing crimes" (Dz.U. z 1998 r. Nr 155, poz. 1016). Jaruzelski faced additional charges for pressuring the communist parliament to retroactively pass decrees he had already used to arrest thousands of Solidarity leaders. Kania and Kiszczak were also accused of conspiring to implement another martial law in 1989. These three defendants were too old and sick to stand trial. Their average age was eighty-two and, according to doctor's notes, they could sit in court only three to four hours a day. At the same time, because Polish courts applied strict rule-of-law standards in regard to evidence quality, it was frequently impossible to attribute individual responsibility to those who had given the orders to shoot.

Property Restitution and Re-privatization

Property restitution programs had to first decide whether to compensate property lost by Polish citizens within Poland's post-1945 borders or also that within its pre-1945 borders. In 1991, the minister of privatization proposed a limited program that substituted in-kind restitution with partial monetary compensation. In 1990, there were 70,000 claims for property restitution throughout Poland, of which 4,500 were for buildings in Warsaw. That number doubled within a year. The estimated value of disputed property was 12.5–15 billion zlotys (US$5–6 billion).

After 1993, the SLD offered 80,000 former owners bonds for purchasing shares in privatized companies instead of their original property, but former owners set up the Polish Union of Property Owners and demanded in-kind restitution. Pointing out that such restitution would bankrupt the state, the government proposed to use 5 percent of the profits derived from selling stocks of privatized companies to compensate owners for their property loss. When in 1996 Parliament approved the Bill on Commercialization and Privatization to compensate former owners of properties illegally seized by the communists, the Polish Union of Property Owners lodged a protest with the European Council over delays in compensating them and threatened to ask the Brussels-based World Union of Real Estate Owners to file a protest with the United Nations. The Polish Parliament specified the categories of citizens and property eligible for restitution in 1999, when the government and the opposition proposed different bills.

The government's bill would have benefited 90,000 Polish citizens whose property was confiscated in Polish territories lost to the Soviet Union after World War II. Those seeking compensation for property lost between 1944 and 1962 could get 50 percent worth of their claims, either as part of the property in question or in reprivatization bonds. The law estimated that Poland could face 170,000 claims from 2.5 million people, totaling US$27–32 billion (half of Poland's annual budget). The state treasury committed to earmark 15 percent of revenues from privatization to satisfy restitution claims. The Polish Union of Property Owners demanded that the bill include confiscations carried out between 1939 and 1962. The opposition's bills were more limited. A special parliamentary committee appointed to accord these bills limited the government's proposal by compensating only Polish citizens residing in Poland for property seized after 1945 by communist authorities, and compelling descendants of former owners to pay an inheritance tax upon being compensated for land and buildings confiscated by the communist regime.

In March 2001, parliament adopted the Reprivatization Law. Descendants of former property owners accounted for 80 percent of all property restitution claimants in Poland. By 2005, only 110,000 restitution claims had been recognized as valid (34 percent of those who lost property during the communist period could not document it). After President Alekxander Kwasniewski vetoed the Reprivatization Law in 2001, no other law provided for property restitution. Thus, no restitution law was implemented in Poland. A restitution program meeting the demands of international organizations would bankrupt the state, but the amount of compensation that Poland could afford to award to the victims of expropriations was deemed insufficient from the viewpoint of influential international groups, the World Jewish Congress, and other diaspora organizations.

Rehabilitation of Former Political Prisoners

Numerous former political prisoners were rehabilitated after 1989. Most rehabilitation acts extend to victims of Stalinism, deal with a specific freedom fighter, and are passed via acts of either house of the legislature by an overwhelming majority of votes. The financial consequences to these resolutions are miniscule.

Memorialization

Memorialization in the form of naming city streets, squares, and other landmarks after anticommunist heroes has been widespread. In 2006, the Museum of the Warsaw Uprising opened in Warsaw. The Museum, which is the first of its kind, contains interactive exhibits attracting more than 40,000 visitors each year. The memorialization campaign of the Institute for National Remembrance is intertwined with its educational initiatives. Conducted by its Bureau of Education, memorialization consists of academic research and publications for broader audiences aimed at enhancing the awareness of Polish citizens of the country's recent history. Each month, the Institute carries out up to 100 educational initiatives for the broader public.

Rewriting History Textbooks

In Poland, rewriting history textbooks has unfolded rather slowly. It was only in 2010 that the Institute endorsed the first official contemporary history textbook, titled *From Independence to Independence*, which was distributed to high school teachers for free. The Institute President Janusz Kurtyka wanted the textbook to focus on topics key to the Polish collective memory and discuss the factors contributing to and impeding Polish independence. The textbook was prepared by young historians interested in the problems of postcommunist Poland and sensitive to the importance of honoring the heroes who fought against totalitarianism. Kurtyka also wanted the authors to critically assess certain historical periods of history.

Conclusion

Poland's by far most extensive transitional justice mechanism has been lustration, but other transitional justice mechanisms have been implemented, with limited results. More than two decades after 1989, the Polish people seem increasingly disinterested in coming to terms with the communist past.

Monika Nalepa

Cross-references: Access to Secret Files; Commission to Counter Attempts to Falsify History at the Expense of Russian Interests.

Further Readings

Bertchi, C. 1994. Lustration and the Transition to Democracy: The Cases of Poland and Bulgaria. *East European Quarterly*, 28(4): 435–437.

David, R. 2003. Lustration Laws in Action: The Motives and Evaluation of Lustration Policy in the Czech Republic and Poland (1989–2001). *Law and Social Inquiry*, 28: 387–439.

Dz.U. z 1998 r. Nr 155, poz. 1016.

Kersten, K. 1991. *The Establishment of Communist Rule in Poland, 1943–1948*. Berkeley: University of California Press.

Korbonski, S. 1978. *The Polish Underground State: A Guide to the Underground, 1939–1945*. New York: East European Monographs.

Osiatynski, W. 2007. Poland Makes Witch Hunting Easier. *The New York Times*, January 22. Available at: http://www.nytimes.com/2007/01/22/opinion/22osiatynski.html?_r=1&oref=slogin (accessed December 8, 2010).

Staniszkis, J. and J. T. Gross. 1984. *Poland's Self-Limiting Revolution*. Princeton: Princeton University Press.

Portugal

The Portuguese military coup of April 25, 1974 launched the beginning of the "third wave" of democratic transitions in Southern Europe. The coup was led by middle-rank military, in the midst of a three-front colonial war in Angola, Mozambique, and Guinea-Bissau. Consequently, this was a transition without negotiations or pacts between the dictatorial elite and opposition forces, meaning the floor was open for accountability and punishment. The coup's nonhierarchical nature accentuated both the real and the symbolic break with the past. The military did not immediately abandon political power, but became institutionalized (through the Movimento das Forças Armadas, MFA), and transformed itself into the dominant force behind the provisional governments.

The nature of the Portuguese transition to democracy and the consequent state crises of 1975 created a window of opportunity in which the reaction to the past was much stronger in Portugal than in other South European countries. The transition's powerful dynamic strongly shaped the consolidation of democracy.

The Repressive Past

Portugal's right-wing dictatorship lasted from 1926, when a military coup d'état overthrew the First Republic, until April 25, 1974. There were two different political regimes during this long period of authoritarianism. The Military Dictatorship of 1926–1933 gave way to the civilian authoritarian regime of Prime Minister António de Oliveira Salazar, a conservative Catholic politician and university professor who remained Portugal's dictator until he was incapacitated in 1968. He was replaced by one of his disciples, the ultraconservative law professor Marcello Caetano. After a brief period of "liberalization," in 1974, both Caetano and his regime were overthrown in the so-called Carnation Revolution by the military coup that set Portugal on the path to democracy.

Under the Salazar dictatorship, political repression was effected by the political police, the Vigilance and State Defense Police (Polícia de Vigilância e Defesa do Estado, PVDE), created in 1933 through the unification of police forces inherited from the Military Dictatorship. Despite two name changes, Salazar's political police maintained a constant presence and was not abolished until the restoration of democracy in 1974. While formally under the control of the Interior Ministry, its independence increased, dominating the investigation and presentation of cases to the courts for political crimes. The PVDE, which had its own prisons, became the backbone of the repressive system, arresting, torturing, and occasionally murdering opponents of the regime. The political police's operations in the colonies escalated between 1961 and 1974, with the outbreak of the anticolonial wars in Angola, Guinea-Bissau, and Mozambique.

Some characteristics of the political repression remained constant throughout the New State of 1933–1974. First, after the 1930s, political repression affected both pro-democratic dissidents and organized clandestine groups, especially the communists. Second, the legal and illegal political activism of the opposition was strongly correlated with the repression applied by the dictatorial regime. Third, the use of military courts characterized many civilian dictatorships, but in Salazar's New State it was another facet of the military presence within the authoritarian political system – a legacy of its origins in the Military Dictatorship of 1926–1933. Lastly, army officers controlled the press censor, the political police leadership, and the militia, the Portuguese Legion (Legião Portuguesa, LP), an anticomunist paramilitary body, which had its own information service.

The dictatorship also had legal instruments to remove all civil servants who opposed the government, and these purges were repeated, particularly in the wake of legal and clandestine demonstrations. After 1931, a declaration of repudiation of communism and of other "subversive" activities became mandatory for those taking a civil service position.

With the end of World War II, the New State underwent institutional changes, bringing limited pluralism. Opposition forces were allowed to operate legally during election campaigns, during which media censorship was less intrusive. The military courts were abolished and replaced by Plenary Courts (Tribunais Plenários, TP) – courts for political crimes, composed entirely of civilian judges. These courts remained in existence until 1974. In 1945, the regime established the exceptional application of habeas corpus, but the political police's authority strengthened as they were the only ones allowed to handle political prisoners and to invoke "security measures" in order to prolong imprisonment. The Commission on the Black Book of Fascism, created in 1977 to collect information on the use of repression by the regime, estimated that the real number of victims exceeded the 30,000 individuals officially acknowledged to have been imprisoned during the 1940s. After 1945, political repression was increasingly judicialized, opponents were rarely murdered (although the Portuguese political police killed opposition leader General Humberto Delgado in Spain in 1965), but the political police could still prolong prison terms limitlessly.

Transitional Justice

The transition and subsequent democratic consolidation evolved in stages, each corresponding to a different phase of transitional justice initiatives and counter-initiatives.

The revolutionary period (1974–1975) comprised the downfall of the regime. During this complex transition phase, the Portuguese society was deeply divided. This period was characterized by a clear break with the past, facilitated by the political radicalization of the Portuguese society. Disagreements within the military concerning the nature of decolonization, the implementation of agrarian reform, and the nationalization of large economic units fuelled the crises. Many measures adopted during this period were based on "revolutionary legitimacy" and thus stood outside the normal legal procedures. The judiciary, therefore, had a minor role. This was a period of legal and "wild" administrative purges, calls for punishment, long preventive detention of political police officers and some collaborators, and controversy over the political police archives and their alleged appropriation by left-wing parties immediately after the coup.

The first laws promulgated by the new authorities legitimized the dismissal of the president, the cabinet ministers, and the leaders of the National Party, which had dominated the Portuguese New State. In April 1974, the new military leaders sent President Américo Tomás and Prime Minister Marcelo Caetano into exile. Caetano, who refused to return to Portugal, died in Brazil in 1980. Other political leaders were dismissed.

In the first days of the transition, the military issued an amnesty for political crimes, thus liberating all political prisoners, even those accused of violent crimes like the execution of political police informers. At the same time, the military authorized the return of the political exiles.

The most widespread measures adopted in this period were the purges (or vetting) directed against collaborators with the political police, the state apparatus (bureaucrats, professors, the military, police forces, etc.), other regime organizations and institutions, and the private sector. Civil society involvement was intensive, particularly through the actions of trade unions, small political groups and parties of left-wing and extreme-left persuasion, and workers' commissions (*comissões de trabalhadores*). The actions undertaken by grassroots political organizations, the growing challenge posed by the extreme left during the crisis, and the left's influence within the military led to the "Hot Summer" of 1975, when Portugal was close to a civil war. Although seen as an attempt by the Portuguese Communist Party to impose a new dictatorship with Soviet support, this was a situation of imminent (and occasionally effective) conflict produced by the growing challenge posed by the extreme left, and the emergence of an antirevolutionary and anticommunist movement in the north of the country.

The political police was dismantled and many of its officers were arrested days after the coup. This was a popular demand voiced on the day of the coup, when people surrounded the political police headquarters. Some political police officers were kept in preventive detention for twenty months, and many were not released until February 1976.

The military created the Commission for the Abolishment of the Political Police/the Portuguese Legion and the Portuguese Youth (Comissão de Extinção da PIDE/DGS e LP) in June 1974. Its role was to prepare criminal proceedings for trial, even before the retroactive law had been issued, and to cooperate with other purge institutions. During this initial transition, the lack of both coordination and adequate legislation and the urgency of other political and economic matters led to the postponement of the trials. In the end, the top leaders were punished with light sentences.

In the so-called PIDE hunt, members of the political police who had not fled the country were arrested and then had to wait two years in protective custody for their trial. In the end, those who appeared before the military tribunals received only light sentences (normally the time they already served). Those who had good military active service reports from the colonial war period received especially benevolent treatment. Despite public demonstrations and criticism, the sentences served as notice that judicial legality and the rule of law had been reestablished following the excesses of the turbulent 1974–1975 period.

Lustration/Purges

The army was the first institution to be purged, and it was here that the break with the past was clearest. The New State's old elite was forced to retire. Immediately after the coup, the MFA handed to the National Salvation Junta (Junta da Salvação Nacional, JSN) chief representative the names of the sixty generals who had pledged allegiance to the authoritarian regime. The JSN placed them on the reserve. Special military commissions administrated the purges, and the first provisional governments approved their work. Incompetence became the official criterion for removal, as it became impossible to sustain political criteria such as "collaboration with the old regime," given that the entire army had collaborated with the New State during the colonial war.

Two months after the coup, the Inter-Ministerial Purge and Reclassification Commission (Comissão Inter-Ministerial de Saneamento e Reclassificação) was created. Responsible directly to the Council of Ministers, the commission coordinated the purge commissions in the ministries. Purges lacked direction and had no consistency. The concept of collaborator was enlarged as the transition became dominated by left-wing revolutionary strategies. Where strong trade union and worker commission pressure was exerted, as in the Ministries of Labor and Education, forced removals were more frequent. According to the inter-ministerial commission, the decisions of the ministerial commissions were very uneven, depending on the party to which the minister belonged and the degree of trade union and social movement pressure. The purges were carried out by the MFA, the Portuguese Communist Party (PCP), and other small but influential extreme-left parties.

The first legislation (Decree-law 277/74, 25 June) stated that civil servants could be purged for three reasons: undemocratic behavior in the course of duty after the coup; inability to adapt to the new democratic regime; and incompetence. Punishment ranged from transfer to another post to dismissal. The government decided that maximum penalties should be applied first to the dictatorships' governmental elite members; political police collaborators; leading members of either the MP, the Portuguese Legion, or the National Party; and the heads of the dictatorship's censorship board. A second law (Decree-law 123/75, 11 March) adopted in 1975 determined that purges could be administered based on individual political behavior under the authoritarian regime. Most affected were the Ministries of Labor and Education. Legal purge proceedings against professors, teachers, and educators were based on two criteria: holding high-level posts under the dictatorship and collaborating with the political police by denouncing students and opposition professors. As in the Ministry of Labor, secret collaborators were the most sought after, and purges affected low-ranking ministry officials who gave information to the PIDE-DGS. Least affected was the Ministry of Justice because its ministers promoted very few purges.

In the first two years of transition, the economic elite was also hard-hit by nationalization, state intervention, and the flight of industrialists and entrepreneurs from the country. The "wild" purges were concentrated in the large enterprises in the industrial area around Lisbon and in the banking and insurance sectors. The frequent calls of the workers' commissions for purges fueled emigration. Purges were carried out in businesses independently of the unions, whose control was shared by the Communist Party and the extreme-left parties. The workers' commissions implemented most "wild" purges, which the Communist Party often did not control. The wave of nationalization purges and forced retirements of the pre-constitutional period profoundly affected the entrepreneurial sector.

Democratic Consolidation and the "Politics of the Past"

The second phase of democratization lasted from December 1975 to the democratic consolidation of 1982. The Hot Summer ended on November 25, 1975, when the country held its first free elections in more than five decades. In these elections, the Communist Party was defeated by the moderate forces inside and outside of the MFA supported by the Socialist Party and the Social Democratic Party, which unexpectedly occupied a center-right position on the political spectrum. Those elections marked the beginning of democratic institutionalization, although that process remained under the tutelage of the Council of Revolution until 1982.

With democratic consolidation, the right-wing parties sought to criminalize the radical elites of 1975, while the moderate left denounced both authoritarianism and the excesses of 1975. The end of the transition marked the end of retroactive justice and the reintegration of many of the condemned. After democratic legitimacy was established, the political police officers were tried in military courts, after having spent several months in preventive detention. Although the military were still important players in the democratic game, the measures adopted during this period became more consistent with the rule of law.

Despite the outburst of violence by some radical groups, political reconciliation dominated the late 1970s, shaping the government's response to the legacy of the dictatorship. The official discourse of the first two constitutional governments led by the Socialist Prime Minister Mário Soares and by the first democratically elected President Ramalho Eanes (in 1978, Soares was succeeded by Nobre da Costa as prime minister) favored reconciliation and pacification. Between 1976 and the early 1980s, steps were taken to reintegrate the victims of the wild purges. Under pressure from right-wing and center-right parties, purges ceased and were reevaluated as excesses of the early transition period. New legislation was passed and measures were adopted to reverse the severe effects of the wild purges carried out in the economy. The purge commissions in the ministries ceased to operate in 1976, and the Council of the Revolution, which took up their role, reinforced legal mechanisms to support rehabilitation.

The Commission for the Assessment of Purge Appeals and Re-classifications (Comissão de Análise de Recursos de Saneamentos e de Reclassificação), created in February 1976, was composed of legally qualified military officials and civilians with no links to the previous regime. According to a report into its activities, the commission believed that "it is necessary to repair the damage that was done during the 1974–75 period, when many of the purges were 'merely arbitrary'" (CARSP, Relatório de Actividades 1976–1977–1978, 1). Most of those purged had their punishment altered to compulsory retirement. The remainder received a payment in lieu of lost earnings and restoration of their seniority for the purpose of calculating retirement pension entitlements. In cases where trade union or student resistance to the reintegration was particularly vociferous, those who were to be reintegrated were simply transferred to other institutions, or remained at home until emotions calmed down before returning to their posts.

The abolition of punitive legislation affecting the dictatorial elite and the process of democratic consolidation encouraged some leading figures of the old regime to return to Portugal from their imposed exile. The last president of the New State, Américo Tomás, who maintained "political silence" until his death, returned in 1980, as did some former ministers.

Encouraged by the favorable context, purge victims organized into the Movement for the Reintegration of the Wrongly Dismissed (Movimento Pró-reintegração dos Despedidos Sem Justa Causa). With the abolition of the Council of the Revolution, many outstanding appeals were transferred to administrative courts, while the Commission for the Abolishment of the Political Police became little more than a document archive accountable to parliament.

As the punitive measures ceased, some symbolic ones were initiated. A state body that came closer to the classical truth commission was the Commission for the Black Book on Fascism, created in April 1977. This government agency, established to denounce the abuses of the authoritarian regime, was responsible to the presidency of the Council of Ministers and was composed of socialist and left-republican intellectuals and politicians. Using the dictatorship's archives as a source of information, the Commission published twenty-two volumes of primary documentation denouncing the regime's repression, treatment of political prisoners, censorship, and the collaboration between economic groups and the political police.

Another legacy of the dictatorship dealt with in this period was the vast documentation of the political and repressive institutions. Salazar's archives were kept at the Presidency of the Council of Ministers when the dictator died in 1970. This archive, which had been meticulously maintained by Salazar, gives a unique account of forty years of Portuguese political history. Given the nature of the collapse of the dictatorial regime, the military also took possession of these archives, together with the political police archives. During the transition, accusations regarding the disappearance of documents pitted the center-right and the socialists against the communists and the military. Parliamentary debates concerning the future of the archive were often heated and passionate, with some parties calling for the destruction of the documents. Important public debates about the archives began in the 1990s, when they were opened to the public. Their incorporation into the national archives and consequent limited release to the public was a controversial victory for historians and left-wing parties against some proposal to destroy them. Files may be freely consulted only if the person they refer to has been dead for at least fifty years. Otherwise, access is granted only with the permission of that person or his/her descendants. Most documents, expunged of names, are open for consultation.

The symbols of the dictatorial regime did not require great attention. Given that Salazar did not establish a dictatorship set upon his charismatic image, the problem of what to do with the symbols of the regime and the image of the dictator was not pressing in Portugal. The only public statue of Salazar, built in his hometown after his death in 1970, was bombed twice, being partially destroyed in the first attack and irreversibly damaged in the second (in 1978). A few streets and other public places were renamed after famous opposition figures – republicans, communists, and socialists alike – while Salazar's name was removed from all public monuments, squares, and the bridge over the Tagus River, renamed the 25 April Bridge (Ponte 25 de Abril).

After 1982, no measures, episodes, or claims indicated a feeling of injustice or impunity toward the wrongdoers and collaborators of the Portuguese dictatorial regime or any widespread movement in terms of symbolic and memorial acts. By 1985, on the eve of Portugal's accession to the European Economic Community, the legacy of the regime and the transition was no longer felt. No right-wing party represented the old elite or acted as a carrier of authoritarian values inherited from Salazarism. The new democratic institutions drew on the legacy of political opposition to the dictatorship.

Parliament debated the rehabilitation of victims. The Movimento Não Apaguem a Memória (NAM), a nongovernmental organization, was created to preserve the memory of the resistance of the victims of the dictatorship. A great effort was made to exclude from political parties people associated with the New State and to find leaders with democratic credentials. Occasional claims for acknowledgment and preservation of memory of the New State's victims meet only with indifference and lack of support.

The only important measure related to the legacy of the dictatorship is the constitutional clause prohibiting parties with a "fascist ideology" (Article 46). This provision was retained after subsequent constitutional revisions, and in the 1990s – despite criticism regarding its usefulness – it was used against a group of the extreme right.

Conclusion

Almost immediately after 1974, Portugal eliminated the institutional legacies of the authoritarian regime and replaced important elites. The regime's most important political institutions were dissolved, and the "authoritarian enclaves" that had survived the transition of the 1970s and the 1980s were eliminated. The dissolution of the more repressive institutions (the PIDE and the Portuguese Legion) was accompanied by purges and the partial criminalization of their members. This was possible as a result of the interweaving of the MFA into the state structures and its emergence as an authority regulating conflicts. Ultimately, the transition has become a much more divisive issue in contemporary Portuguese society than the history of the dictatorship itself.

António Costa Pinto

Cross-references: Court Trials for Redress; File Access; Lustration; Political Police; Purges; Repression.

Further Readings

Madeira, João and Irene Pimentel. 2007. *Vítimas de Salazar. Estado Novo e Violência Política* [Victims of Salazar. The New State and Political Violence]. Lisbon: Esfera dos Livros.

Pinto, António Costa. 2006. Authoritarian Legacies, Transitional Justice and State Crisis in Portugal's Democratization. *Democratization*, 13(2): 173–204.

———. 2008. Political Purges and State Crisis in Portugal's Transition to Democracy. *Journal of Contemporary History*, 43(2): 305–332.

Raimundo, Filipa. 2007. *The Double Face of Heroes. Transitional Justice and the Political Police (PIDE/DGS) in Portugal's Democratization (1974–6)*. MA Dissertation. Institute of Social Sciences, University of Lisbon.

Rosas, Fernando, I. Pimentel, J. Madeira, I. Farinha, and M. Rezola. 2009. *Tribunais Políticos. Tribunais Militares Especiais e Tribunais Plenários durante a Ditadura e o Estado Novo* [Political Courts. Military Courts during the Dictatorship and the New State]. Lisbon: Temas e Debates.

Romania

Romania's violent exit from communism, its faltering transition to liberal democracy, and the persistence in power of parts of the former party apparatus all contribute to the state's evident reluctance to confront its communist past. President Traian Basescu was the first Romanian head of state to officially condemn the abuses of the former communist regime in 2006 after receiving the report of an official investigation commission. Yet, each of the steps taken since 1989 in terms of transitional justice has been taken reluctantly, after long delay and with disputed political legitimacy.

The Repressive Past

Communist power arrived in Romania alongside the west-bound Soviet army in the summer of 1944. Before the war, the left in Romania was profoundly weak thanks to the agrarian nature of society and the antinationalist policies of the Communist Party. In 1940, a pro-Nazi National Legionary State was set up under the direction of army officer Ion Antonescu. The Antonescu regime survived until it was overthrown by a coup in August 1944 as the Axis powers retreated before the Red Army. This combination of weak political roots for the domestic left and the Soviets' need to replace the power structures of a hostile state meant that, when it came, the communist takeover was brutal and absolute.

Antonescu was arrested, tried, and executed in 1946. King Michael, who had led the coup that overthrew Antonescu, was exiled by the communist regime, which had gained full power within six months of the coup. Hundreds of opposition party members were arrested in the spring of 1945 after the Communist Party had secured control of key ministries in the government and of the internal security forces. After rigged elections delivered an overwhelming victory to the communist-dominated government bloc in November 1946, arrests and intimidation of regime opponents began afresh. Prominent opposition leaders were imprisoned and opposition parties were either dissolved or forcibly merged into the governing party – it is calculated that almost 2,000 noncommunist party members and members of the pre-communist political elite lost their lives in the late 1940s. Following the communist takeover at the center, the imposition of the new ruling doctrine in other areas followed, including religion, the judicial system, education, and the nationalization of property. In the early years of communist rule, scores of priests were arrested and some 80,000 peasants were arrested for resisting collectivization of agriculture.

Through the 1950s, the state security police – the Securitate – pursued opponents of the regime. Many were imprisoned (Sighet in the north of the country becoming one of the most notorious for housing political prisoners). Some were executed and tens of thousands were forced to labor on the Danube–Black Sea Canal, which came to be known as the Death Canal thanks to the brutality of the work regime. Romania also followed the pattern of other communist states in the early 1950s of purging the party leadership through show trials. A number of senior party members were executed and others were imprisoned.

Romania's communist era is best known internationally for the eccentric dictatorship of Nicolae Ceausescu. Ceausescu came to power in 1965 and at first gave the impression of taking a liberalizing route – condemning Securitate abuses under his predecessor and the Warsaw Pact invasion of Czechoslovakia in 1968. It was a false dawn, however, as these early signs of liberalization proved merely to be maneuvers aimed at consolidation of Ceausescu's hold on power. By the mid-1970s, Ceausescu embarked on a project to create a personalized dictatorship that relied on the assimilation of the symbols of nationalism, on nepotism, and on the notorious program of "systematization." Systematization involved the destruction of villages and the forced concentration of their populations in new, more easily controlled locations. It was followed by the destruction of a large part of Bucharest city center to make way for a new government quarter, the centerpiece of which was the enormous House of the People, still the second-largest building in the world (after the Pentagon). Public displays of opposition to the regime were rare and when they did occur – as happened in the mining areas of the Jiu Valley in 1977 and among industrial workers in Brasov ten years later – protests were met with harsh repression by the forces of the state.

Growing international condemnation of the regime's human rights record eventually led Ceausescu to cut his ties with Western governments and with Western finance. During the 1980s this resulted in extreme economic hardship for the Romanian population as goods were diverted for export and food and other supplies were rationed to ever-reducing levels. At the same time, Ceausescu demanded the expansion of the Romanian population into a super-race. Abortion was banned in 1966 (leading to the death of 10,000 Romanian women from failed "backstreet" operations, according to some estimates), taxes were introduced to penalize the childless, and thousands of unwanted children were taken into state care.

Transitional Justice

Ceausescu was toppled in December 1989 after a short but bloody uprising that swept away the leading figures of the communist regime. In their place appeared a new governing structure – the National Salvation Front – that claimed its legitimacy from the streets and the barricades. Romania in the communist era had been marked by a lack of domestic dissent and of organized opposition structures, which meant that home-based dissident elites had not formed to provide an alternative power structure. Instead the National Salvation Front quickly came to be dominated by second-rank communist apparatchiks who went on to govern until 1996. This undoubtedly contributed to the reluctance on the part of government to pursue measures aimed at redressing the abuses of the former communist regime. The disputed nature of the December 1989 revolution also became an important dimension of how transitional justice was approached.

The "Events of December"

Summary justice was meted out to Nicolae Ceausescu, and his wife Elena, on Christmas Day 1989. A hastily convened ad hoc military court tried and executed them for genocide, use of arms against the population, the destruction of buildings, and the undermining of the national economy. Immediately thereafter, the National Salvation Front outlawed the death penalty. All three of the Ceausescu's children were arrested following the revolution, although the eldest, Valentin, was not charged with any crimes.

The events of December 1989 became a hotly contested topic as the National Salvation Front consolidated its hold on power and fears grew that the Front was serving as a screen for continued communist rule. The number of deaths, and the identities of those responsible for shooting antigovernment protesters during the revolution, are still disputed (initial reports claimed tens of thousands had died in cities like Bucharest, Cluj, and Timisoara, but later estimates were around 1,000). The new government blamed Securitate units loyal to Ceausescu for the shootings, and claims that foreign mercenaries were somehow involved quickly gained currency. As the Front consolidated its hold on power, opponents of the new regime also began to question whether the revolution was genuinely a spontaneous popular uprising or orchestrated as part of a preplanned coup.

A Senatorial Commission was set up to investigate the revolution, but views about what took place had rapidly formed along party lines, and when the Commission concluded in September 1996, its official report was accompanied by a "minority" report from opposition members who disputed the official findings. Emil Constantinescu, the center-right candidate for the presidency in the November 1996 elections, had claimed as a candidate that it was necessary to establish the real truth about the revolution, but when he came to power, no further official enquiries were launched.

Restitution of Property

The opposition to the National Salvation Front (and to the Social Democratic Party that evolved from the Front) was dominated by reactivated "historic" parties from the prewar era. As such, the opposition's agenda was heavily influenced by the concerns of its aging leadership elite, high among which was the restitution of confiscated property. Large estates had been expropriated under Law 187 of 1945 and the program was expanded in 1949. Estimates of the number of domestic properties that were confiscated from 1950 onward vary between 240,000 and 640,000. Hundreds of church properties were also confiscated – an issue that took on an ethnic slant, because the denominations most affected were those of the Hungarian community. A further dimension to the issue was added by the question of restoring property to the Royal Family, including assorted castles that became more familiar to Romanians as state-run tourist attractions.

The left-led governments between 1990 and 1996 showed great reluctance to restore property to pre-nationalization owners. Legislation in 1990 and 1992 allowed tenants of nationalized property to buy their apartments at discounted rates. The 1992 legislation in particular provoked an outcry from opposition politicians who accused the government of favoring communist bureaucrats and secret police officers who had dislodged the previous owners from their homes.

Victory for the center-right in the 1996 elections brought with it less satisfaction for the demands of restitution campaigners than they hoped. The new government did not amend 1995 legislation that severely limited the cases where property could be directly returned to its previous owners (as opposed to their being compensated for the loss of the property). The coalition government also experienced major problems reaching agreement over the size of larger landholdings that could be restored (including valuable state-run forestry holdings, for example).

After being returned to power in the 2000 elections, the Social Democrats introduced new legislation (Law 10/2001) that took steps toward "natural" restitution (the return of property to its pre-nationalization owners) and set out the terms for compensation, but it still fell short of the demands of campaigners. The law had been introduced thanks to pressure from the European Union (EU) as Romania upped its bid for accession. After its introduction, attention shifted to the slow pace with which compensation claims were resolved, leading to a growing number of cases being taken to the European Court of Human Rights.

The Opening of Political Police Files

Romanian internal security forces, the Securitate, are reported to have been one of the largest such forces, per capita, in communist Europe. Its network of informers was vast. Its array of targets was similarly substantial: the security service itself claimed there were 100,000 informers, but campaigners for the release of Securitate files estimate the figure to be much higher. Pressure to expose those among the Securitate's network of informers who remained active in public life and to allow Romanian citizens to view their files was driven by the Association of Former Political Prisoners. In 1993, one of the founding members of the Association, Constantin "Ticu" Dumitrescu, proposed a draft law in the Senate. It aimed at giving citizens access to their own files and making public files of those engaged in public life, but was defeated by the left-dominated parliament. Dumitrescu tried again after the center-right's election victory in 1996, and the result was surprising. The law progressed slowly through parliament and was subject to a series of major amendments, the most controversial of which were "national security" restrictions on access to certain personal files, the politicization of appointments to the Council responsible for overseeing the release of the files, and the retention of the files under the control of the reformed security services. Senior members of Dumitrescu's own party, the National Peasant Party, orchestrated attempts to block the legislation, leading to speculation that they themselves had been Securitate informers. The much-amended legislation was finally passed by parliament in October 1999 and came into effect in early December as Law 187/1999 on Access to One's Own File and Unmasking Securitate as a Political Police.

The legislation set up a National Council for the Study of Securitate Archives (Consiliul National pentru Studierea Arhivelor Securitatii, CNSAS) which was responsible for vetting the records of candidates for public office and managing the release of files to individuals. The politicization of the Council – with parties being entitled to appoint members in proportion to their parliamentary strength – robbed it of legitimacy and led to constant partisan infighting among the members. The Council was criticized for the slow speed with which it processed applications. Its methods of investigation also attracted criticism, with one member admitting that the Council did no more than check if someone existed on the card index of files and if they did not appear they were declared clean (see entry on National Council for the Study of Securitate Archives).

Lustration

An issue closely linked to the status of the Securitate files was the role of communist officials in public life after the fall of Ceausescu. The anticommunist movement in Romania adopted the Timisoara Declaration as their manifesto – the Declaration was published in March 1990 in the city seen as the cradle of the 1989 revolution. Its Point 8 was key, demanding that Communist Party activists and Securitate officers be banned from standing for elected office for the first three legislatures.

No legislation banning communist officials from public office has been passed in Romania and, as has been noted, the National Salvation Front, its successor the Social Democrat Party, and also the far-right Greater Romania Party have each provided a political berth for members of the former regime apparatus (so too, to a lesser extent, have some other parties). There were no banning provisions in the version of the Dumitrescu law that was passed by parliament. Instead it was hoped that candidates exposed as collaborators with the communist regime would be shamed by their records and voluntarily withdraw. Except in a handful of cases (mainly affecting the center-right parties), this did not happen.

The failure of lustration to win widespread popular support in Romania may in part be attributable to the National Salvation Front's success in personalizing the sins of the communist regime to Ceausescu and his family. It no doubt also owed much to the size of the Communist Party itself. There were 4 million members of the party at its height – almost one-third of the country's adult population – and Social Democrat politicians were quick to remind their opponents (and the population) that most families would thus potentially be affected by legislation targeted at Communist Party members.

After the center-right won elections again in 2004, there was renewed hope in some quarters that lustration would return to the agenda. A number of proposals were put forward that failed to receive backing from the political parties that dominated parliament. A law that would have introduced limited lustration measures was promoted by the government but it fell afoul of the Constitutional Court.

Commissions of Investigation

Aside from the parliamentary investigation of the events of December 1989 (referred to previously), two significant investigation commissions have been instigated by the Romanian presidency. The first was the International Commission on the Holocaust in Romania (commonly known as the Wiesel Commission) and the second was the Commission on the Communist Dictatorship (commonly known as the Tismaneanu Commission) (see the entries on International Presidential Commission on Studying the Holocaust in Romania and Presidential Commission for the Study of the Communist Dictatorship in Romania).

The Wiesel Commission was set up by Social Democrat president Ion Iliescu to investigate the effects of the Holocaust in Romania and to make recommendations for improving public knowledge about Holocaust-related crimes in the country. The Commission was chaired by the Romanian-born Nobel Peace Prize winner Elie Wiesel.

The National Legionary State had instituted anti-Semitic legislation that resulted in the confiscation of property, the banning of Jews from a wide range of professions, the banning of mixed marriages, and internment. A series of pogroms resulted in deaths and the destruction of property. Deportation of Jews and Roma to Nazi concentration camps began in 1942. An estimated 100,000–175,000 were deported, with the Antonescu regime being responsible for the death of 280,000 to 380,000 Jews and Roma. A fund to provide financial compensation for victims of the Antonescu regime had been established in 2000 and limited restitution of compensated property was also agreed.

Yet the crimes of the Antonescu regime were little known in Romania thanks to the policy of the communist regime that maintained that the Holocaust did not take place in Romania. Indeed, the Commission itself was set up by Iliescu after his own statement to this effect resulted in widespread international condemnation. The Wiesel Commission reported in 2004 and made various recommendations about public education in relation to the Holocaust. Romania held its first-ever Holocaust Memorial Day in October of the same year.

Romania is one of the few European countries to implement a truth commission to investigate its communist past. The Tismaneanu Commission was set up in the spring of 2006 and was asked to report before the end of the year so that President Traian Basescu could receive its findings (and issue a formal condemnation of the communist regime) before Romania joined the EU on January 1, 2007.

The Commission pursued an academic approach to the subject and did not hold public reconciliation hearings in the style of the South African Truth and Reconciliation Commission (see separate entry). Its composition was questioned by some and its findings were criticized as inaccurate in places because two commission members were unveiled as former Securitate agents, and the report had to be amended before its publication by the Bucharest-based Humanitas press. Yet it met its deadline for reporting and remains an important element in Romania's attempt to come to terms with its communist past.

Court Trials

In 1988, the Ceausescu regime introduced a wide-ranging amnesty law that hampered postcommunist attempts to prosecute the perpetrators of communist-era repression. A further restriction was placed on prosecutions by the statute of limitations contained within the Penal Code of 1968, which meant that, for example, only murders committed after 1975 and tortures committed after 1982 could be pursued. As a result, very few members of the communist elite or their agents have been tried for acts of repression (members of the Ceausescu family being notable among the exceptions).

A large number of prosecutions were brought relating to the events of December 1989. These prosecutions have been characterized as show trials and have been criticized for focusing only on members of the Securitate (the army enjoying a form of popular immunity thanks to the perception that they fought on the side of antigovernment protesters during the revolution). Other criticisms have been made of the trial procedures, and a number of the defendants received presidential pardons after they were convicted. Following the elections of a center-right government in 1996, the scope of the trials was widened to include more army officers and some cases were reopened.

Memory and Learning

The final element of transitional justice in Romania considered here relates to processes of learning and the reshaping of public memory. In one sense these almost subliminal measures to deal with the past are among the least noticed. Yet at the same time they can prove powerful and enduring in their effects.

In common with other former communist countries, Romania quickly made efforts to erase public symbols of the outgoing regime. Statues were promptly removed and street names changed. Romania's national day was also moved to December 1, the date of the proclamation of a union between Transylvania and the other Romanian provinces in 1918. New high school history textbooks have been introduced that give a more balanced account of Romania's fascist and communist pasts.

The opening of Securitate files has given rise to a growing number of studies of the regime's record and the publication of details of victims – these studies represent a form of individual, not state-sponsored, justice. In 2005, the government also set up the Institute for the Investigation of Communist Crimes in Romania (see entry on the Institute for the Investigation of Communist Crimes and the Memory of the Romanian Exile). This body has, like so many of Romania's transitional justice measures, become something of a political football.

Several research institutes have been founded to examine the history of the Jewish community in Romania. And in 2005, the government set up the National Institute for the Study of the Holocaust in Romania.

Conclusion

Romania has experienced a troubled path toward transitional justice. The persistence in power of elements of the former communist regime has meant that each step toward redress has been met with political resistance. Direct redress, the restitution of confiscated property, the banning of communist officials from public office, and the opening of secret police files were all resisted strongly up to 1996, and the record since then has been rather disappointing. Starting in 2000, the EU accession process and then the election of a new center-right government in 2004 each gave fresh impetus to less direct forms of redress in the form of commissions of investigation. Two decades after the fall of Ceausescu and with a new political elite in charge, there seems little prospect now that the more radical measures called for by campaigners in the 1990s will ever be introduced.

Ed Maxfield

Cross-references: Amnesty; Court Trials for Redress; Decommunization; Institute for the Investigation of Communist Crimes in Romania; International Presidential Commission for Studying the Holocaust in Romania; National Council for the Study of Securitate Archives; Presidential Commission for the Study of the Communist Dictatorship in Romania.

Further Readings

Deletant, Dennis. 1999. *Romania under Communist Rule*. Iasi: The Center for Romanian Studies.
Grosescu, Raluca and Raluca Ursachi. 2009. *Justitia Penala de Tranzitie din Romania Postcomunista*. Bucharest: Polirom.
Siani-Davies, Peter. 2007. *The Romanian Revolution of December 1989*. New York: Cornell University Press.
Stan, Lavinia. 2009. *Transitional Justice in Eastern Europe and the Former Soviet Union: Reckoning with the Communist Past*. London: Routledge.

Russia

Two decades after the collapse of the Soviet Union, Stalin's popularity soared in nationwide polls, as many Russians recalled the country's former prestige and their previous sense of security. This nostalgia was part symptom and part consequence of the fact that Russia made no substantial attempt to come to terms with the legacy of seven decades of state-sponsored repression. As a result, the significance of the past and the past itself remained open to negotiation, and former victims, or their surviving children, experienced what they perceived as the injustice of witnessing the official invalidation of their history.

The Repressive Past

During the Soviet terror, particularly in the 1930s, millions of ordinary citizens, well-known political actors, and party loyalists were arrested for "counterrevolutionary activities" and dispatched to barely habitable regions in the north and far east of the Soviet Union to mine nickel, chop wood, excavate gold, or build railways leading nowhere, but mostly just to waste away through hard labor and hunger under abhorrent conditions.

Already under Lenin, repression and the use of forced labor were considered an acceptable means of preserving the state's power. In 1918, he legalized a decree sanctioning the existence of work camps, and by the early 1920s, sixty-five concentration camps existed, including the first Correctional Labor Camps in the Solovetsky Island monasteries in the far north.

At the end of the 1920s, compulsory grain requisitioning was introduced, and peasants were forced to join collectives. This was accompanied by de-kulakization, a campaign to eliminate rich peasants (kulaks) as a class. In 1929, the northern regions were colonized with prisoners because the existing prisons could no longer accommodate their numbers. Tens of thousands of peasants, engineers, and scientists were dispatched to these remote areas. By 1930, the Chief Administration of Corrective Labor Camps and Colonies (Glavnoye Upravleniye Ispravytel'no-Trudovykh Lagerey i Koloniy, GULAG) system of labor camps had fully come into being. The state's draconian agricultural policies resulted in a massive famine in 1932–1933 during which more than 5 million victims perished.

By 1934, violence and terror had become an integral part of Soviet life, as Leningrad Party Secretary Sergey Kirov was assassinated. This political murder was used as a pretext to arrest thousands and execute hundreds of citizens for complicity in the alleged conspiracy that lay behind it. It ushered in an era of purges that would eventually claim millions. The years 1936–1938 witnessed the show trials of the leaders of the revolution. Confessions, obtained under torture and scripted, were considered the best evidence of an individual's guilt. Almost all of the defendants were shot. Tens of thousands of others were sentenced without trials, taken to killing fields on the outskirts of Moscow or Leningrad, executed, and thrown into mass graves. Those who were not immediately executed were sentenced to anywhere between eight and twenty-five years of hard labor. The ranks of Gulag prisoners swelled.

The war did not prove a deterrent to internal terror. In 1940, offenses such as arriving at work twenty-one minutes late were criminally punishable. During this time, political repression was also carried out along national lines. From 1942 to 1945 entire national groups suspected of collaboration with the Germans were deported to the far reaches of the empire to fend for themselves in inhospitable places. After the war, terror struck returning prisoners of war, who had survived Nazi concentration camps only to be sent to the Soviet Gulag with ten- to twenty-five-year sentences on charges of spying or treason. In 1949, a new wave of arrests sent many returning prisoners into "eternal exile" – prison without walls. Various other campaigns led to thousands of arrests, incarcerations, and executions. Apparently a massive purge of Jews was also being prepared, but Stalin's death on March 5, 1953 prevented it.

The demise of the dictator marked the end of mass terror and mass victimization. The post-Stalin leadership immediately declared an amnesty that released more than 1 million prisoners from the camps. The majority of political prisoners languished for another three years, until Nikita Khrushchev's Secret Speech in 1956. In this report to a closed session of the Twentieth Party Congress, Khrushchev focused on Stalin's crimes against the party elite rather than the principal victims of the terror, who were ordinary citizens. Nevertheless, the disclosures led to the liberation of a great majority of surviving prisoners and exiles in the second half of the 1950s.

The scope of the Stalinist terror and the question of how many victims were repressed in what period and under which article of the Soviet Criminal Code have been the subject of heated debate before and since the opening of official archives. The range of estimates is wide because the victims include those who were incarcerated in labor camps, starved by the 1932–1933 famine, subjected to de-kulakization, deported, and killed outright. Moreover, a review of the cases not included in these categories would double the number of political prisoners calculated in the Gulag statistics. The accuracy of the figures is further confounded by the fact that the statistics include re-arrests and moribund victims who were sometimes released only so that their death would take place outside the camp. Deaths from terror are estimated to range from a few million to more than 20 million. There is relative consensus that from 1930 to 1956, some 17–18 million individuals were sentenced to detention in prisons, colonies, and camps.

Transitional Justice

Aside from symbolic reparations, the post-Soviet governments have implemented none of the known and/or institutionalized transitional justice mechanisms. Not one henchman was tried, nor one truth commission instigated, not one official monument to the victims of Stalinism was erected, victim compensation was limited, as were official acknowledgment of past injustices and archival access, and the record in the history textbooks was a political narrative.

Prisoner Releases and Other De-Stalinization Measures

In the period between Stalin's death and Khrushchev's Secret Speech, tens of thousands of prisoner releases took place. Some of these returnees applied for "rehabilitation" – judicial exoneration – but the process was slow and tedious. For many, this status remained unattainable for decades to come, and when rehabilitation was granted, it was usually in the spirit of a conditional pardon.

After Khrushchev's Secret Speech, releases began on a massive scale. Well more than 5 million victims returned to Soviet society in the 1950s. While officials from Khrushchev on down denounced the Stalinist repression, the system of governance did not renounce repression, and arrests on political articles continued. This dualism hampered the rehabilitation process. Nevertheless, despite the ambivalent attitude toward returnees, the Gulag was talked about, written about, and dramatized on stage. Stalin's body was removed from the Lenin Mausoleum and placed along the Kremlin wall, and a proposal to build a monument to victims of the terror was discussed.

The politics of de-Stalinization were abandoned when Khrushchev was ousted in 1964, and under Brezhnev a process of re-Stalinization was instituted. A Stalin bust was placed outside the Lenin mausoleum, the Gulag became a tabooed theme, and returnees became silent witnesses. They were to remain in that vulnerable status until the second half of the 1980s, when Mikhail Gorbachev ushered in the second period of de-Stalinization with his glasnost and perestroika policies.

In a speech on the seventieth anniversary of the October Revolution, Gorbachev broke decades of official silence when he declared that thousands of party members and other Soviet citizens had been repressed under Stalin. This was a gross understatement, but it was the first public admission of state terror since Khrushchev. It allowed researchers, survivors, and family members of victims to investigate and discover the real numbers. Returnees reemerged with their stories of repression and expressed demands for rehabilitation, restitution, privileges, information on the fate of lost loved ones, apologies, official acknowledgment of their plight, and, in some cases, revenge.

Memorial

Already in the summer of 1987, an eleven-person group called the Historical Enlightenment Society Memorial was bringing the Stalinist past back onto the public agenda. They campaigned on the streets of Moscow in support of the creation of a monument to victims of Stalinist repression. Within a year they had gathered thousands of signatures and counted prominent figures among their ranks. By 1988, Memorial had expanded its goals to encompass the establishment of a research center in Moscow with an archive containing information on victims of Stalinism, a museum, and a reception room to assist former victims. They searched for and found mass graves from the Stalin era containing tens of thousands of victims, lobbied for official recognition of these sites, and in 1990, Memorial placed a monument to the victims of totalitarianism in the center of Moscow, right across from the Lubyanka, the notorious secret service headquarters.

In subsequent years, Memorial accumulated an immense archive of documents and memoirs attesting to the repression, and it gained international recognition, including Nobel Prize nominations, as the key watchdog organization for human rights abuses in Russia. The organization's research center published numerous scholarly works on the causes and consequences of Stalinism. Perhaps more immediately relevant to the surviving families, Memorial published lists of names of those who were executed, and created a museum at a former labor camp site in Perm. Today, its Moscow headquarters houses a modest museum, while the St. Petersburg Memorial has created a virtual, Web-based museum, where visitors can view artifacts, art, and objects of life in the Gulag.

Since its inception, Memorial has been dogged by official resistance. The massive evidence they have gathered on the systematic repression that came to characterize Soviet governance and their demands for a full official assessment of the Soviet past unsettle the foundations on which the present state is resting.

Rehabilitation

In his 1987 Revolution Day Speech, Gorbachev announced that an eight-member commission had been set up to by the Politburo of the Central Committee of the

Communist Party of the Soviet Union to study the repression that took place during the 1930s, the 1940s, and the early 1950s. This commission, chaired by Mikhail Solomentsev and including the architect of perestroika Aleksandr Iakovlev, continued the process begun under Khrushchev. As a result of the commission's investigations, between 1987 and 1989, some 840,000 individuals, including prominent figures such as the Bolshevik leaders Nikolai Bukharin, Lev Kamenev, and Grigori Zinoviev, were rehabilitated.

After the Soviet Union collapsed in 1991, the Yeltsin administration immediately began its attempts to rectify past injustices, passing a law that established a Rehabilitation Commission to oversee the implementation of the law on rehabilitation. The Commission also had to consult the Russian archives of the civil and military tribunals, the Procuracy, the secret services, and the Interior Ministry in order to obtain supporting documents for the petitioners. Archival access has proceeded in fits and starts, and remains problematic to date. The rehabilitation law paved the way for survivors, who had missed the window of opportunity for exoneration during the Khrushchev and Gorbachev eras, to apply for this status. If granted, they could receive 75 rubles (US$2.50) for each month spent in detention, up to a maximum sum of 10,000 rubles, half-priced medication, free dentures, one free train ride per year, and a state-subsidized burial. The Commission, under the chairmanship of Aleksandr Iakovlev, included historians and former prisoners of the Stalinist and dissident eras.

Between 1992 and 1997, 4 million applications for rehabilitation were filed. Some former prisoners refused to apply because they wanted nothing to do with the system that had incarcerated them, and they did not want to think of themselves as criminals, which was implied by the label of rehabilitation. Many described an unofficial attitude similar to the conditional pardon of the Soviet era, as they struggled to obtain paltry compensation and meager privileges.

The victims' descendants were also heirs to the problems of rehabilitation. Only in 1996 was legislation passed that enabled the children of "enemies of the people," many of whom had spent their childhood in orphanages, to claim the status of victim, rather than merely "aggrieved." Victim status rendered them eligible for rehabilitation. However limited the privileges attendant to this status were, they were better than nothing, and the restoration of property and compensation were dependent on rehabilitation. A few hundred thousand of these survivors applied for and received rehabilitation. By 2009, 4.5 million victims of political repression were rehabilitated and a few hundred thousand cases were still pending.

Rehabilitation was an unproven path for coming to terms with the past, but expedient for the Russian government because it addressed the victims and the crimes without acknowledging culpability or admitting *who* or *what* was to blame.

The Trial Issue

Soviet Russia did not condemn its own system of governance for many reasons. Among them is the fact that people would have been judging themselves. But what about post-Soviet Russia? In 1992, an opportunity presented itself. At that time, a hearing was held to determine the constitutionality of a ban on the Communist Party. It attracted old communists defending the system and new democrats representing the victims of that same system. To the regret of human rights activists, who hoped for nothing short of a

Nuremberg trial of the Communist Party, this legal forum did not venture beyond the issue at hand.

Many former victims were incensed by the fact that there was never even a moral condemnation of the Communist Party. They believed that Russia would benefit from a "Nuremberg Trial without blood." They maintained that those found guilty of these crimes against humanity could receive the maximum penalty and then be pardoned. Survivors point out that identifying the victims is only one step in dealing with the repression. A further step would require identifying their oppressors, still mostly unnamed. Discussion on the terror remains limited to the crimes and the victims, and not the perpetrators or culpability. In the absence of institutionalized transitional justice mechanisms, Stalinism and its victims occupy a lacuna in the nation's image of itself.

Commemoration

The commemoration of victims is one of the key elements of any transition from a past repressive regime to democratization. Consequently, in a society committed to this goal, former holidays honoring the former regime can no longer be commemorated. In post-Soviet Russia, November 7, the "Day of the Revolution," created a problem because it had always been a day off from work as well as a day set aside for glorifying the October Revolution and the leaders who were recognized as standard-bearers. On November 7, 1987, as noted earlier, Gorbachev made a speech that opened the door a crack for those who wanted to investigate the real numbers of victims. Ten years later, on November 7, 1997 – the eightieth anniversary of the revolution – Yeltsin proposed that this day become the "Day of Agreement and Reconciliation."

Yeltsin's proposal never got off the ground and was abolished by Vladimir Putin in 2005. The Revolution Day holiday, in its turn, was canceled in early 2005 and replaced by a holiday on November 4 that marked Russia's 1612 victory over Polish invaders. In the midst of these changing and shifting symbols and meanings, 26 percent of the Russians polled on the ninetieth anniversary of what was formerly Revolution Day thought that the Revolution provided the impetus for the country's social and economic development. Even so, continued official commemoration of that day could have been politically delicate. So, too, was the "Day of Reconciliation," because it was discordant with the state's goal of deemphasizing the repression of the Soviet past. The new November 4 "Day of National Unity" holiday offered a solution with a new message of a strong nation, unified against external threats.

On October 30, 2007, the Day of Victims of Political Repression, and the seventieth anniversary of the year that mass reprisals and executions began in the Soviet Union, Putin took a symbolic step toward commemorating victims. On this occasion, the Russian leader undertook the first top official visit to the Butovo artillery range, an area in the south of Moscow where an estimated 20,765 citizens were executed between August 1937 and October 1938 alone. This killing field was in operation from 1930 until after Stalin's death in 1953.

Many former victims considered the official gesture too token. Gathering on that same day at the monument to victims of totalitarianism, survivors railed against the fact that they still lived a miserable existence. They maintained that their status was scarcely officially recognized and that they had little or no help from state benefits. The crowd was made up of the children of victims of Stalinist repression, now in their seventies and eighties. The Moscow monument, a stone from the Solovetsky Islands, the first labor camp under Lenin, was erected by a victims' organization (Memorial) – not the state. To date, there is not a single official commemorative plaque in Moscow to victims of Stalinism.

One of the fundamental components of dealing with an onerous past is the official and public recognition of each individual who suffered. On this occasion, Memorial read aloud lists of thousands of victims' names. In their effort to restore names and call attention to this part of Soviet history in this symbolic year, the organization also released a compact disk containing the names of 2,614,978 victims of state terror. They hoped that society and the government would devote the same kind of attention to recalling and recording the remaining names of terror victims as they did to those who fell in the Great Patriotic War (the Russian name for the 1941–1945 war against Nazi Germany). They also hoped for condolences, apologies, and calling a crime a crime. That is very unlikely, largely because of apathy, the preferred narrative, and the fact that such acts would require a state admission of culpability. That is not the national memory promoted by the post-Soviet Russian government. For the time being, and for some time to come, remembrance has been delegated to nongovernmental organizations as the terror is increasingly relegated to the recesses of official memory.

National Memory: Textbooks and Official History

The triumph of expedient national history over actual national history is demonstrated by the sanitized version of the Stalinist past approved for history teaching in Russian high schools. In a 2007 televised meeting with social studies teachers, Putin argued that Russia should not be made to feel guilty about the Great Purge of 1937, because a lot of countries had "problematic pages" in their past. This meeting was partially to promote a new textbook covering Russian history from 1945 to 2006. The contents were not unlike Soviet-era textbooks, with guidelines directing teachers how to place Stalin and Brezhnev in a favorable light and Gorbachev and Yeltsin in an unfavorable light. Shortly after the meeting, the Duma (Russian parliament) passed a new law authorizing the Ministry of Education to recommend which textbooks should be published and used in schools.

In consequence, educational materials were hewn to reflect which way the political winds were blowing. In 2008, in an effort to promote patriotism among younger people, a new teachers' manual entitled *The History of Russia 1900–1945* was approved for use in schools. Herein teachers were instructed on how to address the period of Stalinist repressions. They were told to explain that Stalin's actions were "rational" governance in a concrete historical situation. The text also acclaims his consistent efforts to reshape the country into an industrialized state. Given that the scope of the repression does not fit into this conceptualization, the manual suggests working the numbers by, for example, excluding some categories of victims, and counting only those sentenced to death or executed. The additional millions who languished and then died from disease and forced labor in the Gulag were not included in these figures.

The Shadow of Stalin

In a 2005 nationwide survey, 32 percent of those polled credited Stalin's leadership with the victorious outcome of the Great Patriotic War, and believed that this overshadowed whatever defects he might have had and any mistakes he may have made. A later survey found that 40 percent of respondents viewed Stalin as one of the three most "eminent" figures of all times.

A fundamental reason why this discussion could rise again and again is because all of the official attempts to reckon with the Stalinist past were inconsistent – an inconsistency borne of ambivalence. What people choose to remember about the past is always a selection of events, regularly informed by and tailored to present needs. These needs include the need for a national identity and the need for a national history, however mythologized. The popularity of Putin (an ex-KGB colonel) has partially been attributed to people's nostalgic yearning for the Soviet past, complete with its symbols, emblems, and anthems. Chief among these resurrected symbols is Stalin himself, whose role in history has been fashioned to fit a mythologized narrative, as evidenced in the new textbooks.

In 2009, leading and following this trend, the state undertook the management of the historical narrative with the establishment by presidential decree of a "Commission to Counter Attempts to Falsify History to the Detriment of Russian Federation Interests." The commission was made up of state and public officials and historians, who were charged with looking at accounts of past events for misrepresented or manipulated facts that cast Russia in a negative light. Memorial activists expressed concern about achieving truth by the resolution of a state commission.

Two decades after the collapse of the Soviet Union, the work of historians and civil society actors who challenged the official narrative of present or past events had become more marginalized. In open societies, such challenges tend to be a core value. In closed societies, the remnants of which Russia is far from shedding, challenging the official history or story by scholarly or civil means has proven ineffective because that narrative may be defending a core value of non-accountability.

Conclusion

Since Stalin's death, the view of the Stalinist past has been adjusted to fit the needs of some individuals and of the nation. Efforts to bring the Soviet repression into the arena of public discourse were not officially encouraged. In the Soviet era, there was a fairly consistent recognition that a fuller history of the repression could undermine the legitimacy of the regime, and in the post-Soviet era, the past was promoted as a rallying point for patriotism and national pride.

With no established transitional justice mechanisms in place, it is not clear whether and how a confrontation with the facts of what happened can change public and official perceptions. Nor is it clear how much ability or willingness there is to undergo the wrenching process of judgment. The full integration of the history, causes, scope, and consequences of Soviet repression into the official narrative may be politically insurmountable in the short term. It would require a fundamental shift from a system of governance that devalues human rights toward a democratic ethos that prioritizes them. Russia has no historical democratic traditions for balancing individual rights with collective responsibilities. For now, there are at least two competing narratives. Both contain elements of truth but address different issues, endorse different priorities, and interpret events differently. If these narratives can shift from dueling to dialoguing, Russia will begin to come to terms with the Soviet past.

Nanci Adler

Cross-references: Court Trials for Redress; International Historical-Enlightenment and Human Rights Society Memorial; Political Police; Rehabilitation.

Further Readings

Adler, Nanci. 2005. The Future of the Soviet Past Remains Unpredictable: The Resurrection of Stalinist Symbols Amidst the Exhumation of Mass Graves. *Europe-Asia Studies*, 57(8): 1093–1119.
———. 2004. *The Gulag Survivor: Beyond the Soviet System*. New Brunswick: Transaction.
Applebaum, Anne. 2003. *Gulag: A History*. New York: Doubleday.
Golovkova, L. A., ed. 2004. *Butovskii Poligon* [Butovo Poligon]. Moscow: Izdatel'stvo ALSO.
Iakovlev, A., Artizov, A., Kosakovkiy, A., Naumov, V., and Shevchuk, I., eds. 2000, 2003, 2004. *Reabilitatsiia: Kak eto bylo, t. I; t. II; t. III*. [Rehabilitation: How It Was, volumes I–III]. Moscow: Mezhdunarodnyi Fond Demokratiia.

Rwanda

Rwanda has faced enormous transitional justice challenges, principally the need to address egregious crimes committed by hundreds of thousands of everyday Rwandans during the 1994 genocide. The focus of the Rwandan experience has been the mass prosecution of genocide suspects through three tiers of judicial institutions: the United Nations International Criminal Tribunal for Rwanda (ICTR), the Rwandan national courts, and the *gacaca* jurisdictions, which operate at the community level. Few countries have pursued post-atrocity accountability as determinedly or systematically as Rwanda.

The Repressive Past

Between April and July 1994, Rwanda experienced one of the most devastating waves of mass killing in modern history. In around 100 days, approximately 800,000 Tutsi (who constituted 11 percent of the overall population of Rwanda, which stood at around 8 million in 1994, while Hutu constituted nearly 84 percent) were murdered along with their perceived Hutu and Twa sympathizers, and hundreds of thousands more were exiled to neighboring countries. Today, Rwanda's ethnic makeup is roughly the same as in 1994, as large numbers of Hutu and Tutsi have returned from the diaspora. What distinguishes the Rwandan genocide from other cases of mass murder in the twentieth century is the use of low-technology weaponry, the mass involvement of the Hutu population in the crimes, the social and cultural similarities of the perpetrators and victims, and the astonishing speed of the killings. The majority of murders were carried out brutally with basic instruments such as machetes, spears, and spiked clubs and often near victims' homes.

Rwanda has a lengthy history of Hutu-Tutsi antagonism, but there are few recorded instances of violent conflict before the late 1950s. Before colonialism, "Hutu" and "Tutsi" were effectively socioeconomic labels, signifying a near-feudal class system of Tutsi aristocrats and Hutu peasants. The categories were permeable, however, and individuals could move between them if their status altered in terms of wealth and prestige. In 1919, Belgium gained control of Rwanda under a League of Nations mandate and initially favored the Tutsi economically, socially, and politically. The most significant contribution by the Belgians to the widening social, cultural, and economic divide between Hutu and Tutsi was the introduction of ethnic identity cards in 1933. The Belgians issued an identity card to every Rwandan man and woman, which indicated whether he or she was a Hutu, Tutsi, or Twa. Numerous factors determined an individual's ethnic categorization, including his or her ownership of cattle. Individuals with ten or more heads of cattle were classified as Tutsi, along with their offspring; those with fewer than ten were classified as Hutu. After 1933, people received their ethnic classification according to their father's line. This system continued throughout the twentieth century until it was abolished after the genocide. It was often on the basis of identity cards that Hutu killers identified Tutsi whom they massacred in 1994.

For more than twenty years, Belgian colonial policy in Rwanda reinforced perceptions of Tutsi superiority and Hutu subjugation. After World War II, however, the Belgian colonial administration in Rwanda was placed under a UN trusteeship, which – in the era of growing African nationalism – was designed to move the country toward independence. The Belgians recognized that the Hutu majority would inevitably dominate the nation socially and politically during any transition toward democratic government. To ensure a smooth transfer of power, the colonial administrators gradually began to shift allegiances to the Hutu, offering them jobs in the civil service and promoting them to other positions of influence. The result was a growing sense of Hutu empowerment.

As Hutu gained control of the primary levers of power in Rwandan society, the years immediately preceding independence in 1962 and the rest of the 1960s were characterized by mass violence between Hutu and Tutsi. In 1959, the newly formed Hutu political party, the Parti du Mouvement de l'Emancipation des Bahutu (PARMEHUTU), mounted a successful revolt against the Tutsi chieftancy. Beginning in 1959 and continuing into the early 1960s, PARMEHUTU characterized all Tutsi as lapdogs of the colonial powers and oppressors of Hutu, and incited mass killings of Tutsi. After independence, violent crackdowns by Hutu leaders on those viewed as subversives created a culture of fear and stymied open debate and criticism of the government. In turn, government impunity became the rule as few Rwandans were willing to confront the violent and near-absolute authority of the Hutu leadership. In the political realm, the new Hutu hierarchy, led by the first elected Rwandan president, Grégoire Kayibanda, built on the country's existing, highly centralized administrative structure, establishing the pattern for Rwandan bureaucracies over the next four decades.

Events in the early 1990s are important for understanding the genocide. On October 1, 1990, the Rwandan Patriotic Front (RPF), comprising many descendants of Tutsi refugees who fled Hutu violence after 1959, invaded Rwanda from Uganda. Government forces repelled the RPF and a guerrilla war broke out in the northeast of the country. Events both within and outside of Rwanda exacerbated ethnic tensions during this period. The assassination on October 21, 1993 of Burundian President Melchior Ndadaye, a Hutu, by members of the Tutsi-led army led to mass killings of Burundian Hutu and the exodus of thousands of refugees to Rwanda, sparking fears among Rwandan Hutu that the violence would spill across the border. Many Hutu politicians – aided by extremist media sources such as the Hutu newspaper *Kangura* and the country's largest radio station *Radio-Télévision Libre des Mille Collines* (RTLM) – used the violence in Burundi as justification to call for greater suppression of Tutsi in Rwanda. Meanwhile, Rwandan President Juvénal Habyarimana, supported by the French government, was training Hutu youth militias called *interahamwe* – Kinyarwanda for "those who stand together" or "those who fight together" – in order to attack Tutsi.

On the night of April 6, 1994, President Habyarimana and Burundian President Cyprien Ntaryamira were returning from regional talks in Tanzania. At around 8:30 P.M., as their plane neared Kayibanda Airport in Kigali, two missiles fired from near the airport's perimeter struck the aircraft, which crashed into the garden of the presidential palace, killing everyone onboard. Within an hour of the crash, government roadblocks were set up across Kigali and troops and *interahamwe* began stopping vehicles and checking identity papers. Killings began at the roadblocks and Presidential Guards and militiamen went house to house, killing Tutsi and Hutu accused of collaborating with Tutsi.

The killing spree spread rapidly beyond Kigali into towns and villages across Rwanda. In the following weeks, government leaders fanned out from the capital to incite the entire Hutu population to murder Tutsi, backed by messages of hate on RTLM. By most estimates, around 250,000 Tutsi were killed in the first two weeks of the genocide. The killing, torture, and rape of Tutsi were far from spontaneous or indiscriminate and not, as the government tried to tell foreign diplomats and the international media both at the time and after the genocide, merely a proportional military response to the RPF invasion. The violence was the result of long-term planning and systematic implementation by the Hutu regime. One source of evidence of the planning behind the government's campaign of violence was the extent to which the orchestrators of the genocide targeted key Tutsi and Hutu moderate political leaders in the immediate aftermath of Habyarimana's death. Their aim was to wipe out any semblance of political opposition before launching wider attacks against Tutsi.

Transitional Justice

After the 1994 genocide, the United Nations was quick to propose international prosecutions as a response to mass crimes in Rwanda and – against the wishes of the Rwandan government – established the International Criminal Tribunal for Rwanda (ICTR) to prosecute the orchestrators of the genocide (see entry on International Criminal Tribunal for Rwanda). The Rwandan government argued that, along with internal problems with the ICTR such as its location outside of Rwanda and its lack of a provision for the death penalty, it would also fail to address the culpability of many everyday Rwandans in the genocide and the need for truth, healing, and reconciliation at the community level. Several years of debate led to the bolstering of the Rwandan national courts to enable them to handle genocide cases and ultimately to the establishment of the *gacaca* jurisdictions. The following sections deal with each of these institutions in turn.

International Criminal Tribunal for Rwanda

On November 8, 1994, the UN Security Council authorized the establishment of the ICTR to prosecute the primary orchestrators and most serious perpetrators of the genocide. Modeled partly on the International Criminal Tribunal for the former Yugoslavia (ICTY; see separate entry) and based in Arusha, Tanzania, the ICTR was intended to help end impunity in Rwanda by prosecuting the leaders of the genocide, while leaving lower-level perpetrators to the Rwandan national courts (see entry on Court Trials for Redress). The ICTR began formal proceedings in November 1995 and commenced its first trial in January 1997. By August 2009, the ICTR had completed forty-five cases, leading to thirty-eight convictions. Several of the ICTR's decisions established major international criminal law precedents regarding the definition of crimes (especially genocide, rape as a tool of genocide, and incitement to genocide) and the culpability of perpetrators (including on the basis of joint criminal enterprise, which allows for the prosecution of individuals for crimes committed by others, provided it can be shown that all of the individuals concerned had a common criminal purpose).

The ICTR has faced severe criticism for the time and finances it has expended in the prosecution of a relatively small number of cases. The Tribunal has also faced significant political challenges. In December 2000, relations between the ICTR and the Rwandan government soured when Prosecutor Carla del Ponte announced that she had opened investigations into crimes allegedly committed during and after the genocide by the RPF, which today constitutes the ruling party in Rwanda. In 2002, del Ponte complained that since the announcement of investigations into RPF crimes, the Rwandan government had deliberately impeded the progress of the ICTR, for example by banning the travel of Tribunal witnesses from Rwanda to hearings in Arusha. Bad blood between the government and the ICTR continued to hamper the Tribunal's progress, until the appointment in 2003 of a new Prosecutor, Hassan Bubacar Jallow, a move that appears to have improved relations between the two bodies and subsequently increased the efficacy of the ICTR.

In mid-August 2004, Jallow reviewed the government's proposal that some of the individuals convicted by the ICTR should serve their sentences in Rwanda. The ICTR had initially opposed this move because of Rwanda's use of the death penalty. In 2007, Rwanda removed the death penalty from national legislation, prompting the ICTR to commence proceedings to transfer several suspects from Arusha to the Rwandan national courts. So far, none of these suspects has been transferred after the ICTR's appeals chamber blocked the move, upholding the statement by defense lawyers that their clients would not receive a fair trial in Rwanda because of perceived executive interference in the judiciary and the unwillingness of defense witnesses to testify in Rwandan courts.

Rwandan National Courts

In 1996, with the assistance of the UN, foreign governments, and human rights groups, including Avocats Sans Frontières and the Danish Centre for Human Rights, the Rwandan government began a massive overhaul of the national judiciary. This involved training new judges and lawyers and establishing new courts across the country to begin dealing with the immense backlog of approximately 130,000 genocide suspects detained in prisons across Rwanda. Major reforms were necessary as the national judiciary had been almost entirely destroyed during the genocide, with most judges and lawyers killed or having fled the country and the legal infrastructure decimated. Furthermore, the national court system suffered from a lengthy history of corruption and repression. Before the genocide, the courts were highly politicized and invariably a tool of an authoritarian executive. These factors necessitated the post-genocide vetting and training of judicial personnel, although Rwanda did not employ any form of official vetting or lustration law.

In an attempt to speed the prosecution of genocide cases in the national courts, the government passed the Organic Law of August 1996 (Loi Organique No. 8196 du 30/8/96 sur l'Organisation des Poursuites des Infractions Constitutives du Crime de Genocide ou de Crimes contre l'Humanité, Commises à Partir de 1er Octobre 1990), which divided genocide suspects into four categories depending on the severity of their crimes – broadly, orchestration of the genocide; torture, murder, or injury with intent to kill; injury without intent to murder; and property crimes – and established a plea-bargaining scheme that offered decreased sentences in exchange for suspects' confessions. The Chief Prosecutor of the Supreme Court launched genocide investigations in each of Rwanda's ten districts. He established judicial panels comprising lay magistrates who received four months' judicial training, while 320 judicial police inspectors compiled dossiers on the genocide prison population.

The national courts were initially slow in hearing the cases of genocide suspects. By 2000, the courts had heard only 2,500 genocide cases, less than 3 percent of the genocide backlog. Of those cases, around 400 accused were acquitted and 300 received the death penalty. Plea-bargaining in these cases was extremely rare, with fewer than 20 percent of defendants pleading guilty. It was clear that, at this rate, the vast majority of genocide cases would never be heard. This realization precipitated the creation of the *gacaca* jurisdictions, which were expected to deliver justice more efficiently, while also pursuing more subtle social goals such as reconciliation by encouraging direct community participation in genocide prosecutions. *Gacaca* was not intended to replace the national courts in the hearing of genocide cases, but rather to relieve the immense pressure on the national system by addressing the vast numbers of low-level suspects, while leaving more senior accused to the national courts and the ICTR. Over time, the division of labor with the ICTR became a significant challenge to the national courts, with the two institutions often clashing over their right to jurisdiction over particular genocide cases.

Gacaca *Jurisdictions*

In response to the social, political, economic, and legal problems created by the overcrowded prisons, the Rwandan government in 2001 instituted the *gacaca* jurisdictions to try lower-level genocide suspects (initially those in the third and fourth categories of crimes, as outlined previously), most of whom had been imprisoned for more than a decade. *Gacaca* – which has become the centerpiece of Rwanda's post-genocide transitional justice process – comprises around 9,000 community-based courts, each overseen by locally elected judges who receive several weeks of legal training before undertaking the task of hearing and judging genocide cases. Broadly speaking, the purpose of *gacaca* is twofold: (1) to decrease the prison population by processing the massive backlog of genocide cases more rapidly than is possible in the Rwandan national judiciary or the ICTR; and (2) to deal with a range of community-based problems arising from the genocide, such as those related to truth, healing, and reconciliation.

The pilot phase of *gacaca* commenced in 2002, followed by the extension of *gacaca* across Rwanda. For the first three years of operation, *gacaca* gathered basic information from the community regarding the events of the genocide, including lists of victims and suspects. In March 2005, *gacaca* entered its most crucial phase, as it began judging and sentencing the first wave of genocide suspects, many of whom, as a result of their conviction at *gacaca*, have now been sentenced to new prison terms. *Gacaca* hearings normally take place in an open space outdoors, and the role of the community is to provide eyewitness testimony, debate the content of others' evidence, and assist the judges in determining the guilt or innocence of suspects. Sentences for those convicted by *gacaca* range from community service for low-level offenses through to life imprisonment in more serious cases. *Gacaca* continues to judge and sentence genocide suspects imprisoned since 1994 and has in recent years identified many new suspects who were not rounded up during the initial incarceration process but are now expected to face justice at *gacaca*. After modifications to the Gacaca Law in 2008, *gacaca* began hearing cases in the highest category of genocide crimes, including the orchestrators and planners of the genocide and individuals accused of committing rape and other acts of sexual violence. This reform was again an attempt to lighten the load on the national courts, which were laboring under the weight of around 10,000 high-level genocide cases.

Gacaca has successfully prosecuted approximately 400,000 genocide suspects, an indication of the vast number of new suspects identified as gacaca has progressed, in addition to the number of suspects imprisoned directly after the genocide. Having succeeded in assembling thousands of communities face to face to debate genocide events, *gacaca* has also gathered an impressive record of information on how the genocide occurred at the local level, based on documentation of evidence provided by local communities. Furthermore, *gacaca* has promoted reconciliation in many communities by facilitating face-to-face dialogue between survivors and perpetrators during *gacaca* hearings, which has allowed direct dealing with the legacies of the genocide.

Meanwhile, the *gacaca* process has faced two principal challenges. First, the end of the information-gathering phase suffered from very low turnouts of the population in many *gacaca* jurisdictions, which greatly hampered the judicial process, particularly given *gacaca*'s reliance on active popular participation during hearings. Many Rwandans found the *gacaca* process overly time-consuming, with hearings often requiring a full day per week. This entailed a major social and economic burden especially in subsistence farming communities. Moreover, many Rwandans found *gacaca* hearings and their constant recounting of genocide events highly traumatizing, while others avoided *gacaca* for fear of prosecution. At the beginning of the *gacaca* trial phase (which in many communities started in 2005 and 2006), many Hutu fled Rwanda for fear of indictment. In Burundi, the United Nations High Commissioner for Refugees granted refugee status to approximately 2,000 Rwandans who cited the threat of unlawful prosecution through *gacaca* as the primary cause of their departure, although it appears that many of these individuals were simply avoiding facing justice for their alleged crimes and such statements reflected little of the substance of *gacaca*.

Second, as the trial phase of *gacaca* has progressed, many genocide survivors have grown disillusioned with the system because of the perceived lenient sentences handed down to many convicted *génocidaires*. *Gacaca*'s plea-bargaining scheme has encouraged tens of thousands of genocide suspects to confess to their crimes and in return decreased their prison sentences and in many cases commuted their sentences to community service, which they often perform in state-run camps far from the locations where they committed their crimes. Many survivors consider this inadequate punishment for crimes as serious as genocide. Furthermore, corruption of some *gacaca* judges and intimidation of witnesses in some communities have hampered the justice process. *Gacaca* has therefore forfeited some of its popular legitimacy, especially among genocide survivors, who the government claims represent one of the primary constituencies of the process.

Conclusion

Fifteen years after the genocide, Rwanda's transitional justice process has produced highly variable results. The ICTR has successfully prosecuted many of the most senior planners of the genocide; however, it is questionable whether this has had a substantial long-term impact in terms of peace, stability, and ending impunity in Rwanda. The national courts have consistently struggled to handle the immense backlog of the most serious genocide cases, but nevertheless they have gradually increased productivity. Over time, the community-level *gacaca* hearings have become the major forum for post-genocide justice and reconciliation, with almost every Rwandan adult having attended hearings and many participating directly in the process. Many communities have displayed the marked impact of *gacaca* in terms of greater understanding of the events of the genocide and improved community relations, especially among Hutu and Tutsi. However, all three levels of justice institutions have struggled to deal effectively and consistently with a history as deeply divided as Rwanda's and an event as destructive as the genocide.

Phil Clark

Cross-references: Burundi; Community Justice versus Transitional Justice; Congo, Democratic Republic; Court Trials for Redress; Gacaca Courts; Genocide; International Criminal Tribunal for Rwanda; International Criminal Tribunal for the Former Yugoslavia; International Tribunals; Reconciliation; Uganda.

Further Readings

Clark, P. and Z. D. Kaufman, eds. 2009. *After Genocide: Transitional Justice, Post-Conflict Reconstruction and Reconciliation in Rwanda and Beyond*. New York: Columbia University Press.
Drumbl, M. 2000. Punishment, Postgenocide: From Guilt to Shame to Civis in Rwanda. *New York University Law Review*, 75 (5): 1221–1326.
Kamatali, Jean-Marie. 2003. The Challenge of Linking International Criminal Justice and National Reconciliation: the Case of the ICTR. *Leiden Journal of International Law*, 16 (1): 115–133.
Morris, M. 1997. The Trials of Concurrent Jurisdiction: The Case of Rwanda, *Duke Journal of Comparative and International Law*, 7 (2): 349–372.
Peskin, V. 2008. *International Justice in Rwanda and the Balkans: Virtual Trials and the Struggle for State Cooperation*. Cambridge: Cambridge University Press.

Serbia

Serbia's transitional justice record is mixed. The challenges the country has faced have been enormous: Serbia's recent past was plagued by the wars initiated and mass atrocities committed by the regime of Slobodan Milošević, who ruled the country from 1989 to 2000. The regime and its criminal practices were supported by the majority of the Serbian population. Dealing with such a past requires a combination of transitional justice methods and mechanisms addressing the legal, political, and moral legacies of the crimes. With much hesitation, and under significant pressure from the international community, Serbia adopted limited transitional justice after the regime change of 2000. So far the results have been disappointing because of lack of political support and a widespread culture of denial. Called to address the atrocities of the Yugoslav wars of the

1990s, Serbia gave almost no attention to the crimes of the communist regime, which ruled the country from 1945 to 1990.

The Repressive Past

Transitional justice in Serbia has been shaped by wars, mass atrocities, and the dissolution of the Socialist Federal Republic of Yugoslavia, which was followed by a prolonged process of the establishment of the successor states. With ethnic Slovenians forming 90 percent of its population, Slovenia was first to secede from the federation, after a short armed conflict in June 1991. Croatia's population was 12 percent ethnic Serb, giving Serb-controlled rump Yugoslavia a pretext for fighting hard, for four years, against Croatia's bid for independence; Serbia's ultimate goal, however, was the territorial expansion necessary for the creation of a Greater Serbia. In 1992, Macedonia and Bosnia-Herzegovina declared independence. As Yugoslavia's most ethnically diverse region, Bosnia-Herzegovina was home to significant Serbian (31 percent) and Croatian (17 percent) ethnic minorities. By the time the tenuous Dayton Peace Accord was achieved in 1995, Bosnia-Herzegovina had been partitioned into three different regions, each governed by the Bosnian, Serbian, or Croat groups. In 2006, Montenegro gained independence without an armed conflict, having quit the confederal union with Serbia created in 2003. Finally, in March 2008, the former autonomous Serbian province of Kosovo became the seventh independent state formed on the territory of Yugoslavia. In 1999–2007, Kosovo was placed under United Nations (UN) control pursuant to Security Council Resolution 1244. In all these conflicts, the Serbian state was involved in human rights violations committed on the territory of Serbia and other successor republics.

The establishment of independent Croatia, Bosnia-Herzegovina, and Kosovo involved wars that produced a vast number of casualties, material destruction, and serious human rights abuses, including rape, torture, imprisonment, and the forced expulsion of entire ethnic groups (known as ethnic cleansing). The three wars – in Croatia (1991–1995), Bosnia and Herzegovina (1992–1995), and Kosovo (1998–1999) – were initiated by the Serbian regime of Milošević under the pretext of protecting the Serbian minority living in these regions. The majority of the atrocities were committed by this regime, its paramilitary units, and its puppet regimes in the occupied parts of Croatia and Bosnia. Importantly, the regime enjoyed the backing of the majority of the Serbian population, who endorsed nationalism under the guise of the protection of Serbian national interests.

Unlike other postcommunist states, Serbia underwent two regime changes: in 1991 from communism to the Milošević regime, and in 2000 to democracy (albeit one that has illiberal tendencies). Despite the adoption of the new constitution and the first multiparty elections of 1991, Milošević's Serbia functioned as a façade democracy. The loyalty of the citizens was achieved through ideological manipulation and the threat of force. The constitutional system, with its institutions, rules, and procedures, was reduced to an authoritarian tool used arbitrarily. Human rights were routinely violated, but the repression was selectively focused on non-Serbs and those ethnic Serbs who opposed the official nationalist ideology and participated in antiwar activities. In the 1990s, one-third of Serbia's population consisted of national minorities (Albanians, Hungarians, Bosniaks, Croats, Slovaks, Romanians, Ukrainians, Roma), who were exposed to different forms of discrimination. The regime oppressed the Albanians (both in Kosovo and in southern

Serbia). Bosniaks in the Sandžak region were threatened, robbed, abducted, and killed by the Army of Bosnian Serbs, who were freely passing the border between Bosnia and Serbia. As a result, 80,000 Bosniaks emigrated from Serbia. Croats were also forced to leave their homes. In 1993, the entire Croatian population of the Hrtkovci village, amounting to some 10,000 people, was expelled by Serbian Radical Party militants. The minority rights to education and information in mother tongue were substantially reduced. The Serbs also saw their independent media, university autonomy, and liberal nongovernmental organizations encroached upon.

The regime change of 2000, as a result of the elections organized that year, created the promise of a break with the structural and normative patterns of the previous communist and nationalist authoritarian rules: one-party rule, official ideology, command economy, and denial of human rights under communism, and extreme nationalism, war, mass crimes, and widespread corruption under the Milošević regime. The situation immediately after the ousting of Milošević was extraordinarily complex. Beside "standard" economic, legal, and political challenges posed by the legacies of the old regime – overcoming ideological domination, lawlessness, disrespect for human rights, and command economy to acquire observance of human rights, political pluralism, the rule of law, free market economy, and an independent civil society – the transition process acquired a new dimension, because the recent past was marked by mass atrocities. Many Serbs questioned whether the new, democratic Serbia needed to reckon with the crimes of the Milošević regime.

Transitional Justice

So far, Serbia's democratic transition has been unsuccessful because of poor choices and incomplete implementation of institutional reforms. Democratic institutions and values remain victims of the Serb citizens' and elites' refusal to acknowledge the wrongs of the Milošević regime in the name of Serbian national interest. Prime Minister Zoran Đinđić, a courageous liberal reformer who became the head of the government in 2001, was an exception, but even he considered that institutional reforms in state administration and the economy should take precedence over transitional justice. He made brave but isolated moves in dealing with the past, most importantly by handing Milošević to the Hague Tribunal in March 2001. He was assassinated in March 2003 by war criminals who saw him as a threat. His assassin, Zvezdan Jovanovic, was sentenced for forty years in prison. Jovanovic was a member of the paramilitary Red Berets unit, responsible for war crimes in Bosnia. After 2000, the unit was integrated into the Serbian police forces. This paved the way for a forgive-and-forget strategy based on the institutional and normative continuity with the old, nationalist regime. This policy resulted in public acceptance of the culture of denial through which people subscribe to a distorted representation of the past. As public opinion polls show, many Serbs claim that they do not know about the atrocities, that atrocities did not happen, that what happened was not criminal, and that the Serbian nation was a victim. In a 2004 poll exploring attitudes toward the Yugoslav wars, only 50 percent of respondents claimed to have heard that Sarajevo had been under siege for more than three years, and of these only 40 percent believed the siege happened and only 16 percent agreed that those events involved war crimes; 71 percent heard about the discovery of mass graves of Albanian civilians killed in 1998–1999, and of these 31 percent believed it to be true and 25 percent agreed that it was a war crime (Bandović 2005, 336).

Since 2000, there have been strong incentives for pursuing transitional justice. Serbia has been under pressure from the international community to cooperate with the International Criminal Tribunal for the Former Yugoslavia (ICTY; see separate entry). Successive post-2000 governments have pledged to aid Serbia's integration into the European Union (EU), but the Union made accession conditional on the arrest of prominent war criminals, most notably the Commander in Chief of the Army of the Bosnian Serbs Ratko Mladić, widely believed to be hiding in Serbia. The Interim Trade Agreement signed by the EU and Serbia in April 2008 will come into operation once Serbia proves its full cooperation with the ICTY. Although the 2008 arrest of the wartime political leader of Bosnian Serbs Radovan Karadžić is encouraging, the EU insisted that the Agreement remain on hold as long as Mladić is not captured. In December 2009, however, the EU agreed to unblock the Agreement, having acknowledged the report of the ICTY Chief Prosecutor Serge Brammertz to the UN Security Council, which stated that Serbia made "constant progress" in its efforts to cooperate with the Court. Serbian liberal civic organizations are committed to opposing the denial, silence, and forced forgetting, and to fighting impunity and forgetting. The clash between the dominant policy of denial, on the one hand, and the combined pressure coming from the international community and the liberal nongovernmental organizations, on the other hand, has produced a checkered landscape of transitional justice in Serbia.

Truth and Reconciliation Commission

The Truth and Reconciliation Commission of Yugoslavia (Komisija za istinu i pomirenje) was established in 2001. It ceased to exist in 2003, more than a year before its three-year mandate expired, without fulfilling any of its tasks. The Commission was established by presidential decree, amid a fierce ideological struggle among reformists and conservatives in the coalition that ousted Milošević. It was widely seen as an attempt by the conservatives to conciliate with the international community, which insisted on Serbia confronting its recent wrongs. The Commission was poorly designed, both in its mandate and competencies. Its search for causal explanations in a wider historical perspective, combined with the lack of subpoena powers and governmental and social support, paralyzed the Commission's activity. The Commission failed to achieve its goal also because of its ambiguous attitude to the Serbian crimes. The Commission's documents and attempted activities suggest that its implicit goal was to diminish Serbian responsibility for the atrocities of the 1990s.

International Criminal Tribunal for the Former Yugoslavia (ICTY)

The ICTY is an ad hoc court established by the UN Security Council Resolution 827 of May 1993, which included the Statute of the ITCY. The Statute defined the Court's jurisdiction, organization, and the rules of procedure. The Court is mandated to deal with the war crimes committed after 1991 on the territory of the former Yugoslavia. Located in The Hague, it was the first war crimes court established by the UN since the Nuremberg and Tokyo tribunals (see entries on Nuremberg Trial and International Military Tribunal for the Far East).

The ICTY is generally regarded as the most important institution in fighting impunity in the former Yugoslavia. While its contribution to transitional justice deserves praise, the

Tribunal's practice has faced significant problems. The ICTY does not have its own law-enforcement agency, but instead must rely on the assistance of domestic and international police forces (in Bosnia and Kosovo) in capturing indicted war criminals and obtaining data and evidence. Serbia has been widely criticized for its refusal to fully cooperate with the ICTY, although it formally endorsed its duty to assist the Tribunal by the Law on the Cooperation with the Hague Tribunal (2003). The most important problems include the regime's reluctance to capture defendants, provide ICTY investigators access to the sites of atrocities, secure availability and protection of witnesses, and supply the prosecutor with official documentation related to the crimes.

Although in November 2009 only two suspected Serbian war criminals indicted by the Tribunal remained at large (Mladić and Goran Hadžić, former president of the so-called Republic of Serbian Krajina, located in Croatia), other problems persisted. Victim and witness protection remained inadequate, if not absent. The ICTY officials complained that the Serbian Defense and Interior Ministries withheld requested documents. The "completion strategy" laid down by the UN Security Council Resolutions 1503/2003 and 1534/2004, which originally required the Tribunal to finish all proceedings by 2010 (the deadline was subsequently extended to 2012), provided yet another incentive for evading the duty to assist the ICTY.

Since the assassination of Premier Đinđić, successive Serbian governments have cooperated only under direct pressure from the international community. After 2003, most state institutions and parliamentary parties have continued to manipulate nationalist sentiments, working with nationalist cultural elites to reinforce the claim that the ICTY's very existence and activity provide evidence of an anti-Serbian bias resulting from the widespread anti-Serbian sentiment of the international community.

This distrust and obstruction was especially evident until the 2008 general elections, which replaced the coalition government led by the nationalist Democratic Party of Serbia with one led by the liberal Democratic Party. Starting in 2004, the government treated the Hague defendants as heroes, as reflected by the Law 35 on the Rights of Defendants in Custody of the International Criminal Tribunal, and the Rights of Members of Their Families. Beside guaranteeing paid legal aid to the accused, the Act offered to remunerate their salaries and grant their families different forms of the financial support. Given such official positions, it is unsurprising that most of the Serbian public views the work of the Tribunal with distrust and open hostility. According to a December 2009 public opinion survey, 72 percent of respondents held a negative attitude to the Tribunal because it was partial, anti-Serbian, illegal, or under the influence of the United States. Further, 55 percent believed that Radovan Karadžić was not guilty, whereas 64 percent believed that Ratko Mladić should not have been arrested and sent to The Hague (Franovic 2009).

Domestic Trials

The ICTY completion strategy anticipates that the closure of the Hague proceedings will be followed by an increasing role of domestic trials, and calls for strengthening the capacity of domestic courts to deal with war crimes. In 2003, the Serbian parliament passed the Law 67 on the Organization and Jurisdiction of Government Authorities in Prosecuting War Crimes Perpetrators, which set up three special institutions for handling war crimes: the Office of the War Crimes Prosecutor of the Republic of Serbia (OWCP), the War Crimes Chamber of the District Court in Belgrade (WCC), and the War Crimes Investigation Service of the Serbian police (WCIS).

The work of the OWCP and the WCC has been hampered by political obstacles coming both from the government and the radical nationalist opposition parties, the lack of investigative support from the unreformed police, frequent intimidation of witnesses by former perpetrators and members of the public, and the lack of resources (these institutions lack both qualified staff and adequate financing). The few first-instance trials completed by late 2009 were obstructed by the Supreme Court of Serbia. In the landmark *Ovčara* case, the WCC in 2005 sentenced fourteen defendants to 231 years in prison combined. Ovčara is the location in Croatia where the Yugoslav army and Serbian paramilitary forces executed 200 Croatian civilians in November 1991. However, in December 2006, the Serbian Supreme Court reversed the judgment and ordered a retrial on the grounds of "incomplete fact-finding" and a "wrong application of law." Retrial before the WCC was completed in March 2009, with fourteen defendants sentenced to 193 years in prison combined.

The position of these institutions improved after the 2008 elections. Still, while the new government is less ambiguous in its commitment to prosecute war crimes, it has failed to strengthen the authority of the Prosecutor and the WCC. In particular, it made no effort to change these institutions' negative public perception. Nationalist political parties and intellectuals continue to present these bodies as imposed from the outside with the aim to prosecute Serbian "true patriots."

Against all odds, the Prosecutor and the Chamber have demonstrated independence from the Serbian government and general public, and the capacity to apply legal expertise to the cases presented before them. By establishing strong ties to their counterparts in Bosnia-Herzegovina, Croatia, and Montenegro, they have increased their capacity to oppose denial and impunity in the region. By November 2009, six first-instance trials were completed and another eight trials involving fifty-one defendants were before the court or in the pretrial phase. While investigations and trials remain limited to low-level suspects and there are still problems in protecting witnesses, the recent record of domestic trials deserves a positive evaluation.

Lustration

Following Đinđić's assassination, the small Civic Alliance party initiated a lustration law to vet the state apparatus of those individuals who held important positions under the Milošević regime, especially in the army and police. In June 2003, the Serbian parliament passed the Law 58 on Accountability for Human Rights Violations. This lustration law was never applied, because MPs from the nationalist parties prevented the election of the commission that, according to the law, was to assess involvement in human rights violations. The law targeted all human rights violations committed by officeholders when acting in their official capacity after March 1976 (when the International Covenant of Civil and Political Rights came into force). The following officeholders or candidates were to be screened: members of parliament, president of the Republic, head and members of government, officials in local governments, judges, university rectors and faculty deans, National Bank governor, taxation authorities, and heads of the most important police and army departments. The nationalist representatives believed that the removal of the tainted officials was no longer an option because "it is too late for lustration." Since 2008, the centrist Democratic Party has ruled together with Milošević's Socialist Party of Serbia (SPS), which has close ties to the old repressive apparatus that perpetrated the war crimes during the 1990s. By proclaiming an "end of confrontations" for the sake of a joint effort toward Serbia's EU accession, the Declaration of Reconciliation signed by the two political formations called for closing the books, thus effectively exonerating SPS agents of responsibility for their past crimes.

Rehabilitation of the Victims of the Communist Regime

The communist regime in Yugoslavia committed many crimes, especially in the early postwar years. Only after the fall of Milošević it became possible to raise publicly the question of responsibility for such crimes. In 2006, Serbian parliament passed the Law 33 on Rehabilitation. The right to rehabilitation is guaranteed to all persons who were in legal or extralegal manner, for political or ideological reasons, deprived of life, liberty, or other rights from April 6, 1941 (the date of the beginning of World War II in Yugoslavia) until the date of the Law's coming to force. Rehabilitation process takes place before the district court, on the initiative of any interested individual or legal person. By December 2009, approximately 800 persons have been rehabilitated.

Reparations

A program of reparations for victims of human rights abuses and war crimes requires the successor regime to publicly acknowledge and assume responsibility for the physical, material, psychological, and moral suffering of victims, and to undertake measures for the restitution of status and property, compensation for different types of harm, and legal, moral, and psychological rehabilitation.

Given its culture of denial, however, Serbia remains unresponsive to the victims of atrocities committed by the Milošević's regime in Bosnia-Herzegovina, Croatia, and Kosovo. Serbian political elites have refused to acknowledge the harm done to non-Serbs. Demands for acknowledgment and reparations are rejected as unfounded or one-sided. In June 2005 and March 2007, the Serbian parliament refused to adopt a declaration submitted by liberal nongovernmental organizations that asked it to condemn the mass crimes committed by the Bosnian Serb army against Bosnian Muslims in Srebrenica in July 1995. The ruling Democratic Party of Serbia and the nationalist opposition Socialist Party and Serbian Radical Party jointly maintained that focusing on the Srebrenica massacre would distort the picture of recent atrocities by suggesting the Serbs had the main responsibility for the crimes committed during the Yugoslav wars.

The Role of the Civil Society

During the wars, several civic organizations committed to peace and human rights were formed in Serbia. Since the regime change of 2000, these organizations have focused on the issues of transitional justice so often neglected by the state. They combat the dominant cultural and political attitudes of impunity, lies about recent events, and indifference to the victims. The most prominent are the Humanitarian Law Center in Belgrade, the Belgrade Center for Human Rights, the Women in Black, the Center for Peace and

Democracy Development, the Helsinki Committee for Human Rights in Serbia, and the Committee of Lawyers for Human Rights. These organizations have gathered substantial data about atrocities, including a list of the killed and missing persons in different war areas, databases of human rights violations, witness statements, oral history interviews, photographs, video documentation, media archives, and the ICTY trial transcripts. Their work has narrowed the scope for literal denial of atrocities (claims that atrocities did not happen), although interpretative denial (claims that the many killings perpetrated by the Serbian units constituted a legitimate strategy to "defend national interests") persists.

As many victims and perpetrators reside in different post-Yugoslav states, truth-seeking institutions and practices need a regional dimension. Because of the difficult relations that persist among governments in the region, such initiatives have arrived from nongovernmental organizations. In 2008, three organizations – the Humanitarian Law Center, the Research and Documentation Center (Bosnia and Herzegovina), and Documenta (Croatia) – formed a regional coalition aimed at fighting impunity and the forced suppression of memories. They are gathering a comprehensive database of all victims of Yugoslav wars and work on the establishment of a new regional truth commission.

Conclusion

More than ten years after the Yugoslav wars, Serbia is still confronted with the unresolved legacies of its criminal past. The policy of silence and denial has proven unsuccessful. Crime-related questions – the cooperation with the ICTY, controversies over domestic trials, tensions in relations with other ex-Yugoslav states, and aggressive nationalist ideology – continue to dominate political and cultural agenda in Serbia. While authorities and nationalist cultural elites have demonstrated little willingness to confront past wrongs, hope is provided by the readiness of domestic courts to hear cases of war crimes and the perseverance of liberal nongovernmental organizations in dealing with these legacies.

Nenad Dimitrijević

Cross-references: Court Trials for Redress; International Criminal Tribunal for the Former Yugoslavia; International Military Tribunal for the Far East; International versus Domestic Norms and Actors; Nuremberg Trial; Truth and Reconciliation Commission, Yugoslavia.

Further Readings

Bandović, I., ed. 2005. *The Activity of ICTY and National War Crimes Judiciary*. Belgrade: Belgrade Centre for Human Rights.

Dimitrijević, Nenad. 2008. Serbia after the Criminal Past: What Went Wrong and What Should Be Done. *International Journal of Transitional Justice*, 1(1): 5–23.

Franovic, Lidija. 2009. Vecina gradana Srbije protiv izruzenja Mladica Hagu. E-Novine, August 8. Available at: http://www.e-novine.com/mobile/drustvo/33006-Veina-graana-Srbije-protiv-izruenja-Mladia-Hagu.html (accessed December 22, 2009).

Freeman, Mark. 2004. Serbia and Montenegro: Selected Developments in Transitional Justice. *International Center for Transitional Justice Case Study Series*. Available at: http://www.ictj.org/images/content/1/1/117.pdf (accessed October 15, 2009).

Ivanišević, Bogdan. 2007. Against the Current – War Crimes Prosecutions in Serbia (2007). *International Center for Transitional Justice Prosecutions Case Studies Series*. Available at: http://www.ictj.org/images/content/7/8/780.pdf (accessed October 15, 2009).

Ljudska prava u Jugoslaviji, Izveštaj za 1998 [Human Rights in Yugoslavia, 1998 Report]. Belgrade: Belgrade Centre for Human Rights.

Orentlicher, Diane. 2008. *Shrinking the Space for Denial: The Impact of the ICTY in Serbia*. Belgrade: Center for Transitional Processes.

Sierra Leone

Sierra Leone has pursued multiple avenues of transitional justice. It is one of the rare cases where both a truth commission and a tribunal were employed, and in 2009 it began implementing a reparations program. Transitional justice mechanisms enjoy widespread support across the general population, although many question the political will of the postwar governments to carry out the truth commission's recommendations.

The Repressive Past

In March 1991, the Revolutionary United Front (RUF) invaded Sierra Leone from Liberia, touching off a horrific eleven-year civil war. The RUF, led by Foday Sankoh, drew its members from the large numbers of uneducated and unemployed Sierra Leonean youth, but garnered almost no popular support because its chief tactic was to terrorize civilians. The army of the Sierra Leone government was ill-disciplined and poorly paid, and its lawless conduct led citizens to call them sobels – soldiers by day and rebels by night. Unable to rely on the army, the Sierra Leone government increasingly turned to the Civil Defense Forces (CDF), a tribally based militia. An army-led coup in May 1997 overthrew the democratically elected government of Ahmed Tejan Kabbah; the junta, the Armed Forces Revolutionary Council (AFRC), invited the RUF into the government. This triggered an intervention on behalf of Kabbah by a Nigerian-led peacekeeping force authorized by the Economic Community of West African States.

In January 1999, AFRC/RUF forces entered Freetown, the capital of Sierra Leone. The three weeks the rebels controlled the capital marked the war's most intensive period of human rights violations. International pressure built for a negotiated solution. On July 7, 1999, the Sierra Leone government and RUF signed the Lome Accord, which provided for an immediate cease-fire; the disarmament, demobilization, and reintegration of combatants; the creation of a UN peacekeeping force; and a power-sharing arrangement. However, the RUF refused to sign an agreement unless it contained a full amnesty. Article IX granted "an absolute and free pardon" to Sankoh specifically and to "all combatants and collaborators" for "anything done by them in pursuit of their objectives" up to July 7 (Peace Agreement between the Government of Sierra Leone and the Revolutionary United Front of Sierra Leone 1999). At the last moment, the UN representative penciled in a reservation – the UN did not recognize that the amnesty extended to international crimes. Lome also provided for the establishment of a truth and reconciliation commission.

The RUF's repeated breaches of the Lome Accord brought renewed fighting, and in May 2000 it began attacking UN forces as well. In June, the Sierra Leone government wrote to the Security Council requesting the establishment of a criminal tribunal to prosecute the RUF. UN Resolution 1315 authorized a court for Sierra Leone in August. UN forces, reinforced by hundreds of British troops, brought an end to the fighting by mid-2001; the Sierra Leone government officially declared the war over in January 2002.

The conduct of the war was marked by appalling brutality against civilians by all factions, although the RUF and the AFRC committed the vast majority of the abuses. An estimated 60,000 people were killed and 2 million people were displaced, nearly half of the population. Arson, a frequent tactic of the rebels, left 51,000 people homeless and destroyed a large swath of Freetown in January 1999. The AFRC/RUF forces looted and pillaged at will.

The use of child soldiers, most of them abducted, was widespread; nearly 75 percent of boys and 81 percent of girls who served with the RUF reported being forcibly abducted. Perhaps as many as half of the RUF's combatants were between eight and fourteen years old. To prevent escapes, the RUF cut or branded the letters "RUF" into the child's body and enforced draconian punishments on those caught running away. Children were given drugs and alcohol to facilitate the killing and abuses. Victims themselves, many child soldiers also perpetrated vicious crimes. Nearly 7,000 children went through the disarmament, demobilization, and reintegration process at the war's end.

An estimated 250,000 women and girls were raped and forced into sexual slavery, or experienced other crimes of sexual violence. Rebels engaged in "forced marriages"; as a "bush wife," a woman was forced into an exclusive relationship in which she was expected to cook, clean, submit sexually to her fighter-"husband," and raise their children.

One of the most gruesome aspects of the war in Sierra Leone was the use of purposeful amputation. Of the at least 4,000 victims, only about a quarter survived. The vast majority of amputations were at the wrist or above the elbow, but rebels also cut off people's fingers, ears, legs, lips, and noses. Sometimes both hands would be amputated. The choice of victims was random, although about 75 percent were men, and the cutters were frequently children.

Transitional Justice

By the time the war was over, Sierra Leone had two transitional mechanisms in place – a truth commission and a criminal tribunal. Although this was not intended, the Truth and Reconciliation Commission (TRC) of Sierra Leone and the Special Court for Sierra Leone operated simultaneously for several years. Both gave special attention to two vulnerable groups – children and women – and both were hybrid institutions with high levels of international involvement at all stages. The United Nations played a particularly critical role in these efforts, not only supplying funding and expertise, but maintaining peace and stability through its peacekeeping presence from 1999 to 2005. With 17,500 troops, the United Nations Mission in Sierra Leone (UNAMSIL) was the world's largest peacekeeping force. UN efforts are currently coordinated through the Peace-building Commission, which made Sierra Leone one of its first countries of focus in 2006. In early 2009, Sierra Leone began a long-awaited reparations program.

Truth Commission

In the run-up to the Lome negotiations, local civil society groups strongly advocated for a truth commission, which was included in Article XXVI. The TRC's mission was to investigate and report on the causes of the war; provide an impartial historical record of human rights abuses and violations since 1991; address impunity; provide a forum for both the victims and the perpetrators of human rights violations to relate their experiences; help restore the victims' human dignity; facilitate healing and reconciliation; and make recommendations to prevent a repetition of the abuses. Special attention was to be paid to the victims of sexual violence and to the experiences of children. In December 2000, after broad consultations with Sierra Leonean society, the UN Office of the High Commissioner for Human Rights (OHCHR) produced a draft statute. The breakdown of the Lome Accord forced a lengthy delay in commencing the TRC process. Nonetheless, beginning in 2001, local and international nongovernmental organizations carried out sensitization activities to raise awareness of the TRC, including radio campaigns, public skits, and distributing posters and other informational materials.

The TRC was inaugurated in July 2002. Methodist Bishop Joseph Humper led the commission; he was joined by three other Sierra Leonean commissioners – Laura Marcus-Jones, John Kamara, and Sylvanus Torto – and three international commissioners – Yasmin Louise Sooka (South Africa), Ajaaratou Satang Jow (The Gambia), and William Schabas (Ireland). The TRC had a three-month preparatory period (July–October) and one year in which to complete its work, with the possibility of a six-month extension. It had broad investigatory powers, and its recommendations were binding on the Sierra Leone government. The public embraced the TRC process; a poll in the fall of 2002 found that three-quarters of Sierra Leoneans believed the TRC was necessary, and 58 percent were willing to testify.

Beginning in December 2002, the commission gathered more than 8,000 statements, and local nongovernmental organization the Campaign for Good Governance collected another 1,500. From April to August 2003, the commission conducted ninety public hearings, spending one week in each of Sierra Leone's twelve provinces, and heard testimony from 350 individuals. It held provincial and national reconciliation ceremonies, which sometimes included perpetrators publicly apologizing for their misdeeds and then receiving forgiveness from tribal elders. Attendance was high, and Radio UNAMSIL carried the hearings live. The TRC delivered its widely anticipated report in October 2004.

The TRC's institutional performance suffered from management difficulties, funding shortfalls, and delays. The interim secretariat appointed to set up the commission's operations during the preparatory phase failed to get a permanent staff in place by October, when statement taking was to commence. The United Nations stepped in to oversee the hiring process, but it was January 2003 before the commission was fully staffed. Statement taking was delayed, the schedule of public hearings was cut back, and research started late. Mismanagement contributed to the commission's funding woes by discouraging donors. The Sierra Leone government was too poor to pay for the commission, and OHCHR struggled to attract funding. The TRC's eventual cost of about US$5 million was half of its original budget. Delays plagued the TRC at every step, from its establishment to the distribution of its report, which was not completed until fourteen months after the end of public hearings. Because of printing problems, it was not publicly available in Sierra Leone until August 2005, although it had been posted on the Internet.

The TRC-Special Court relationship was generally cordial. However, the two clashed over the question of whether CDF leader Sam Hinga Norman, who was in the Special Court's custody awaiting trial, could publicly testify to the commission as a perpetrator.

The Special Court trial chamber ruled against his appearance, arguing it would compromise his right to a fair trial by violating the presumption of innocence. Despite early concerns that ex-combatants would not testify to the TRC for fear of prosecution, a significant percentage of statements came from perpetrators.

The TRC's report ran nearly 2,000 pages. Child-friendly, senior secondary (grades 10–12), and video versions were also developed. The report stated that the war's central cause had been "endemic greed, corruption and nepotism" that had reduced most people to poverty and made the state largely irrelevant to their daily lives. It warned that the conditions that caused the war persisted, and lamented that public officials showed no sense of urgency in meeting the country's challenges. The commission issued extensive recommendations. Among its most critical recommendations, the TRC called for the creation of a Human Rights Commission, the repeal of discriminatory laws against women, passage of a Child's Rights Act, a reparations program, and the creation of a TRC Follow-Up Committee.

The government responded in its June 2005 White Paper. Civil society groups and human rights advocates sharply criticized the response as vague, noncommittal, and failing to seriously engage with the recommendations. The Sierra Leone government made no specific commitments for implementing the TRC's recommendations. Parliament was slow to enact legislation meant to address TRC imperatives, and a Follow-Up Committee had not been created by the end of 2009.

Although Parliament passed implementing legislation for the National Human Rights Commission in August 2004, the five commissioners were not sworn in until December 2006. Chaired by Jamesina King, it issued its first report in August 2008. However, it faces serious funding issues. In October 2006, a new citizenship act was passed, which permits citizenship to be conferred directly through the mother. In June 2007, parliament passed three more bills connected to the rights of women: the Domestic Violence Act, the Devolution of Estates Act, and the Registration of Customary Marriage and Divorce Act. Together, the three acts criminalized domestic violence; outlawed wife inheritance; required customary marriages and divorces to be registered; gave women the right to acquire and dispose of property in their own right; provided that if a man died without a will, his wife and children would get the majority of the estate; required the consent of both parties for marriage; and stated that dowries do not have to be returned in the event of separation or divorce.

The Child's Rights Act followed in September 2007. It created a National Commission for Children, repealed the Corporal Punishment Act, and provided for rights compatible with those expressed in the Convention on the Rights of the Child and its Optional Protocol. An Anti-Corruption Act was passed in 2008, establishing an independent Anti-Corruption Commission, with the power to prevent, investigate, prosecute, and punish corruption by public officials. The Commission ordered all senior public officials to declare their assets by January 31, 2009; President Ernest Bai Koroma went first as a model for others. A reparations program began in 2009.

The TRC largely fulfilled its mandate. Nearly all Sierra Leoneans were aware of its existence and most understood its purpose and supported its work. Given the high level of public interest, holding additional hearings in the provinces could have been justified if the time and money had been available. The commission's ambitious report provided a trenchant analysis of the causes of the war, an exhaustive examination of the abuses committed, and extensive recommendations. Its long-term contributions to social reconciliation have, however, been undermined by the snail's pace at which the Sierra Leone government is implementing its recommendations.

Reparations

During the TRC's public hearings, witnesses made it clear that they wanted reparations. They frequently pointed to the disarmament, demobilization, and reintegration process, through which ex-combatants received cash, in-kind support, and skills training. Given their desperate conditions, victims likewise wanted immediate help, preferably in cash. The TRC report called on the National Commission for Social Action (NaCSA) to coordinate a reparations program focused on amputees and war wounded, victims of sexual violence, children, and war widows. It recommended free healthcare, therapy, and prosthetic devices for amputees; free prosthetic devices and therapy as well as medical support for other war wounded; free health care, including fistula surgery, for victims of sexual violence; and free education up to senior secondary level and support for the removal of scars left by branding for children. Skills training would be provided for amputees, war wounded, victims of sexual violence, and war widows. Amputees, war wounded, and victims of sexual violence who experienced a 50 percent reduction in earning capacity would receive monthly pensions. The TRC made clear it considered reparations to be the primary responsibility of the government. In its White Paper, the Sierra Leonean government promised to "use its best endeavors" to put a program into place, "taking into consideration the resources available." Civil society groups decried this weak commitment.

NaCSA's directorate for reparations finally opened in September 2008 and launched a reparations program in January 2009. However, of its US$14 million budget for 2009–2010, NaCSA had less than US$3.5 million available to it, US$3 million of which came from the UN Peace-building Fund. Given its limited funding and a potential pool of 100,000 eligible people, NaCSA decided to focus on the provision of housing to amputees and other war wounded, even though this had not been one of the TRC's recommendations. Of the 960 amputees and severely war-wounded people registered nationally, 460 still needed housing, at the cost of US$6,500 per unit. Other components of the program such as skills training and monthly pensions will be delayed until more funds are available.

The TRC report pointedly observed that reparations are essential to healing and reconciliation, and that without them, victims would view the TRC process as incomplete. Yet eight years after the war's end, the government has made little progress toward compensating the victims. War-affected groups, especially the amputees, are angry at the government's neglect of their needs.

Court Trials

The Special Court began operation in mid-2002. It is a mixed international-local, or hybrid, court. Authorized by the Security Council at the request of the Sierra Leone government, the United Nations and the government share responsibility for making key appointments, notably of the judges. The Special Court has two three-judge trial chambers and a five-judge appeals chamber. Funding is provided by voluntary contributions from interested states. The statute includes both international and local crimes.

More than 50 percent of the staff is local, although most top positions have been held by internationals. The court is located in Freetown. Through its innovative structure, the court's architects hoped to make international criminal prosecutions quicker, less expensive, and more relevant and legitimate to the victimized community. The court has had mixed success in meeting these institutional goals. Its multi-defendant trials have not moved more quickly than similar proceedings at the Yugoslav and Rwanda tribunals. Voluntary funding has failed; the Special Court has faced constant funding pressure despite its modest cost. Its greatest success has come in its connections to the local community. It enjoys strong grassroots support thanks to an innovative outreach program that is widely considered to be the model for future outreach efforts. Leading court officials routinely make public appearances to discuss the court's activities; the court works closely with civil society groups on a range of justice and rule of law issues; video summaries of the trials are screened in every province; and weekly radio summaries are broadcast.

The Special Court's mandate is to try those who bear the greatest responsibility for crimes committed in Sierra Leone after November 1996. Many Sierra Leoneans, forced to see the individuals who perpetrated serious crimes against them walking freely on the streets, have expressed frustration at the court's narrow focus on the architects of the violence. The Special Court has prosecuted the leaders of all the main factions for crimes against humanity, war crimes, and other violations of international humanitarian law, including former Liberian president Charles Taylor. Determined to confront the shocking abuse of vulnerable groups in the war, it pioneered the prosecution of forced marriage and the recruitment/use of child soldiers. It also successfully prosecuted the first charges of intentionally attacking the UN peacekeeping forces.

Four trials have opened since June 2004, with the AFRC, CDF, and RUF cases completed. The AFRC defendants – Alex Tamba Brima, Brima Bazzy Kamara, and Santigie Borbor Kanu – were sentenced to between forty-five and fifty years for crimes including murder, rape, pillage, mutilations, and the recruitment/use of child soldiers. The CDF trial provoked controversy, because many Sierra Leoneans, including trial judge Bankole Thompson, believed the CDF had fought to preserve democracy and protect the country from a barbarous enemy. Nonetheless, the trial chamber ruled that the prosecution had proven that Moinina Fofana and Allieu Kondewa committed war crimes, although it cited just cause as a mitigating factor in handing down relatively light sentences. On appeal, both men were also found guilty of crimes against humanity for murder and inhumane acts. The Appeals Chamber rejected just cause as a mitigating factor and raised the sentences to fifteen years for Fofana and twenty years for Kondewa.

The RUF trial closed in October 2009, when the Appeals Chamber upheld the trial judgment. Issa Sesay and Morris Kallon were sentenced to fifty-two and forty years, respectively, for crimes including murder, mutilations, forced marriage, the recruitment/use of child soldiers, and murdering UN peacekeepers. Augustine Gbao received a twenty-five-year sentence for similar charges, although he was found not guilty of the recruitment/use of child soldiers.

The Taylor trial is the Special Court's highest profile prosecution. His June 2003 indictment represented the first time a sitting head of state in Africa was indicted for international crimes. The court alleges that as the patron of the RUF, Taylor bears responsibility for crimes committed in Sierra Leone, including murder, rape, and the recruitment/use of child soldiers. Because Sierra Leoneans almost universally blame

Taylor for the calamity of the war, his prosecution is central to ensuring the court's relevance to the local population. Concerns about regional stability forced the Special Court to move some of its operations from Freetown to The Hague, where it is trying Taylor. The trial opened in January 2008, and when the defense opened its case in July 2009, Taylor took the stand in his own defense.

The two prime purposes of criminal prosecutions in Sierra Leone are to establish a credible system of justice and accountability and to end impunity. The Special Court's trials have been fair, credible, and to international standards. The court has identified and held accountable the individuals responsible for ordering and supervising some of the war's worst abuses. By those benchmarks, the Special Court has been a success.

Conclusion

The Special Court and TRC have gone a long way toward fulfilling key transitional justice objectives. Together, they have constructed a detailed, impartial narrative of the abuses committed during the war and assigned responsibility for those violations; addressed impunity at the highest levels, especially by bringing Taylor to trial; combated harmful social attitudes toward victims of sexual violence; and given victims the opportunity to tell their stories. Sierra Leone has not slipped back into civil war. But the Special Court and TRC can only go so far in securing peace and reconciliation. As the TRC warned, the conditions that sparked the conflict in 1991 have not been seriously addressed. State capacity is poor, corruption is rampant, and desperate poverty is endemic. Despite strong economic growth, youth unemployment is extraordinarily high. Deeply discriminatory practices toward women and children continue to have social sanction. The March 2009 violence between supporters of the two main political parties was an ominous reminder of how fragile Sierra Leone's stability is. If the contributions of the Special Court and TRC are to be consolidated, Sierra Leone's government and elite need to demonstrate the political will to effect meaningful change.

Beth K. Dougherty

Cross-references: Amnesty; Child Soldiers and Transitional Justice; Court Trials for Redress; Reparations; Sierra Leone Truth and Reconciliation Commission; Special Court for Sierra Leone; Truth Commissions.

Further Readings

Amnesty International. 2007. *Getting Reparations Right for Survivors of Sexual Violence*. New York: Amnesty International.

Howarth, Kathryn. 2008. The Special Court for Sierra Leone – Fair Trials and Justice for the Accused and Victims. *International Criminal Law Review*, 8: 399–422.

Peace Agreement between the Government of Sierra Leone and the Revolutionary United Front of Sierra Leone. June 3, 1999. Available at: http://www.sierra-leone.org/lomeaccord.html (accessed October 20, 2009).

Schabas, William. 2003. The Relationship between Truth Commissions and International Courts: The Case of Sierra Leone. *Human Rights Quarterly*, 25: 1035–1066.

Sierra Leone Government. 2005. *White Paper on the Report of the Truth and Reconciliation Commission*. June. Available at http://www.mnadvocates.org/sites/608a3887-dd53-4796-8904-997a0131ca54/uploads/White_paper.pdf (accessed November 12, 2009).

Special Court for Sierra Leone. Official Web site. Available at: http://www.sc-sl.org (accessed November 7, 2009).

Witness to Truth: Report of the Sierra Leone Truth and Reconciliation Commission. 2004. Available at: http://trcsierraleone.org (accessed November 7, 2009).

Slovak Republic

During the first fifteen years after the 1989 "Velvet Revolution," Slovakia's approach to transitional justice made it an outlier among formerly communist countries. More than most, it seemed disposed toward forgiving and forgetting the injustices of the preceding period. Still, since late 2004, Slovakia's citizens have engaged in a substantive societal conversation about their past.

The Repressive Past

The Czechoslovak Socialist Republic's (1948–1989) early years were brutal, with the state security service – *Štátna bezpečnost*,' or ŠtB – terrorizing the population into submission to the communist regime, which overthrew a shaky postwar democracy. The Communist Party directed this terror as it attempted to secure control of every aspect of societal life, abolishing the distinction between public and private and directing governmental activity from the local to the national levels. The Stalinist-era show trials were among the bloodiest in the region, continuing even after Stalin died. De-Stalinization did not begin in earnest until the early 1960s. Thereafter, pressure for reform built and the Prague Spring began in 1968, a period of significant liberalization. This was crushed that August by a "fraternal" Warsaw Pact invasion. The resulting regime instituted "Normalization," a process intended to retrench the Party's power and undermine opposition. The Party purged its reformers and instituted repressive policies, using the ŠtB to accomplish these purposes.

As was common in Eastern Europe, Czechoslovakia's secret police had one officer per 1,200 to 1,700 people; with a population of 15 million, it generally had 9,000 regular employees. While numbers fluctuated over time, it also had around 30,000 people in its network of informers – people whose primary employment was not with the ŠtB, but who agreed for one reason or another (sometimes positive incentives, such as travel or children's education, sometimes blackmail) to inform on others to the secret police.

During the regime's early years, it targeted members of pre-communist-era political parties, nationalists, churches, former "representatives" of the capitalist system, and people involved in espionage and sabotage. During its last decades, it monitored society for "internal threats" (notably, these activities were not carried out by the army, which was outward-looking) in the spheres of the mass media, education, industry, ideology and culture, agriculture, health care, transport, services and trade, science and research, and other areas. It particularly targeted Charter 77, which posed a strong challenge to the regime's rule, based in part on the human rights documents the state itself had signed.

Although imprecise, available figures give a sense of the ŠtB's impact on the lives of Czechoslovak citizens. Between 1948 and 1989, at least 250,000 people received sentences for political reasons, nearly half in absentia. Of those, 22,000 were sentenced to forced labor and 243 were executed. Somewhere between 3,000 and 8,000 people died in the brutal conditions of prisons, labor camps, and uranium mines (mostly during the 1950s), and more than 600 people were killed crossing the border. Approximately 7,000 people were imprisoned in psychiatric institutions. The ŠtB also monitored mail, checking tens of millions of packages per year. In addition, it sought to draw citizens into its network of informers, either through incentives or through blackmail. More broadly, as the Czech human rights community Charter 77 extensively documented, the regime consistently violated the freedoms of the press, expression, association, religion, and the rights to education, information, privacy, defense in court, equal protection under the law, to take part in public affairs, to establish trade unions, to humane treatment for prisoners, and to leave the country.

Transitional Justice

After the November 1989 Velvet Revolution toppled the communist regime, the Czech and Slovak Federative Republic (as the state was renamed) quickly instituted restitution, rehabilitation, and lustration laws, and prosecuted some former officials. From 1993 onward, following Slovakia's Velvet Divorce from the Czech Republic, the country continued with a much milder approach to transitional justice, with its main efforts focused on truth revelation through file access.

Restitution and Rehabilitation

Less than six months after the Revolution, in April 1990, the newly democratic Czechoslovak Federal Assembly passed the Law on Judicial Rehabilitation (119/1990), which allowed citizens who had been tried and imprisoned for political reasons by the communist state to request that the state nullify the verdict against them and compensate them financially. Special judges were charged with adjudicating the claims. The following year brought the Law on Extrajudicial Rehabilitation (229/1991), which returned to previous owners property confiscated by the communist government. It also provided monetary compensation and rehabilitation for persons who had not been convicted of political crimes but had been persecuted for democratic activities or membership in a particular social class or a property-owning or religious group. The redress covered such violations as unjust imprisonment in labor camps, expulsion from schools, and termination of employment. The purposes of the laws were both reparation for past harms and, with regard to property restitution, the privatization of the almost entirely state-owned economic sector. Support for this approach to restitution was particularly strong on the right, which was influential in the Czech Republic.

Lustration

The following autumn, the state pioneered a transitional justice method – lustration. Responding to "wild screenings" and political scandals based on the secret lists of informants and agents in the ŠtB files, the Federal Assembly passed the Lustration Law (451/1991), the first in postcommunist Europe. The resulting law applied to those who, between February 25, 1948 (the communist takeover) and November 17, 1989 (the beginning of the Velvet Revolution), fell into the following categories: Communist Party officials from the district level up; employees of the State Security, including not only full-time ŠtB officers but also those who collaborated with them part time by signing secret agreements to inform on others; People's Militia members; political officers in the Corps of National Security; members of purge committees in 1948 or after August 21, 1968 (the Soviet invasion); students at KGB schools for more than three months; and owners of ŠtB "conspiration apartments." For five years, these people could not be employed in most elected or appointed positions in the federal and republican levels of government (although, importantly, it did not include the position of Member of Parliament), rank above colonel in the army, management positions in state-owned enterprises and joint stock companies, the official press agency, top positions in Czechoslovak, Czech, and Slovak radio and television, top academic positions, and the Supreme Court, judgeships, and prosecutorial posts. Employees and applicants for employment would have to be certified by the Ministry of the Interior or be dismissed, demoted, or rejected for employment. Citizens eighteen years and older could ask to have their files reviewed, but could not see them personally. Political parties, publishers, and radio and television producers could have an employee who shapes the intellectual content of communication media screened if that staff member consented, and the results could not be publicized unless the person agreed. Anyone could prompt the investigation of a senior official for a deposit of 1,000 crowns (approximately US$35), which they would lose if the official's record was clean. The law was set to expire on December 31, 1996.

The law's passage was preceded by an intense debate, including between former dissidents. Federal Deputy Premier Pavel Rychetský, a Czech Charter 77 signatory, oversaw the bill's drafting, and Deputy Václav Benda, also a former Czech dissident and one of the Charter's most famous signatories, introduced it to parliament and became its most vigorous defender. Other prominent former dissidents, including President Václav Havel, Czech Prime Minister Petr Pithart, Federal Minister of Foreign Affairs Jiří Dienstbier, and Petr Uhl, were highly critical. According to Roman David, the law's defenders argued that it was necessary to change personnel, to protect national security and public safety against the influence of networks of former elites and the potential for blackmail of new elites, to bring a small measure of justice, to protect the rights of those screened through a legally regulated process, and to reveal the truth. The bill's opponents argued that it violated human rights (often comparing it to McCarthyism), that it was legalized vengeance, and that it used the principle of collective guilt.

Notably, when the law came up for a vote, every deputy from the Movement for a Democratic Slovakia (HZDS) voted against it. The party was founded in March 1991 by then-prime minister of the Slovak half of the federation (and Minister of the Interior from January to June 1990), Vladimír Mečiar, as he and a group of supporters broke away from the Slovak umbrella party Public Against Violence amid growing allegations that he was abusing his office. Shortly thereafter, the Slovak National Council dismissed him and his entire cabinet. The Slovak Defense and Security Committee's resulting investigation found that not only was there evidence that Mečiar had been an ŠtB collaborator (although the pages in the register containing his name had disappeared), but also that he had abused both the offices of Interior Minister and Prime Minister, and particularly his access to the ŠtB files, in order to protect himself and his friends and to harm his rivals.

The attempt to remove Mečiar from power boosted his popularity, and the HZDS, which was full of former communists and state enterprise managers and had a left-leaning nationalist-populist orientation, emerged as the most powerful Slovak party in the June 1992 elections. On the Czech side, the victor was Václav Klaus's center-Right Civic Democratic Party (ODS), every one of whose deputies had voted *for* the lustration law. Thereafter, the HZDS and the ODS led the negotiations over the state's future, which soon deadlocked. Among the demands the HZDS declared not negotiable was the revocation of the lustration law, which met no sympathy on the Czech side. Within months, Czech and Slovak leaders decided that their differences were irreconcilable and at midnight on January 1, 1993, the Velvet Divorce produced two new states.

While there had been some lustration in Slovakia under the common state, the law had not produced thorough screening. After the new state's founding, it was essentially ignored, except for a January 1994 constitutional challenge by the Mečiar government on the grounds that it violated international human rights treaties. The Court rejected this, but the state did not apply the law, which expired in 1996.

The key reason for Slovakia's choice not to pursue this transitional justice strategy was the lack of political will. Given the makeup of the HZDS, as well as that of the formerly Communist Party of the Democratic Left (SDL'), lustration would have been a disaster for them. Moreover, because under communism Slovakia had not had a strong dissident movement, it had fewer counterelites available for leadership in the new democracy than other Central European countries. This was partly because the last twenty years of communism in Slovakia were less repressive than in the Czech lands, and the regime was less illegitimate. In turn, it was easier for Slovak elites associated with the former regime to return to the political stage in the new democracy, and because they regained power quickly, they were able to undermine the legal framework designed to screen them out of the political sphere, mostly by ignoring it. Moreover, while Slovaks did express support for lustration, they also elected a leader who, according to the law's criteria, should have been excluded from positions of leadership.

Prosecutions and Criminality

The one piece of transitional justice legislation passed during the Mečiar governments (1992–1998) is the Law on the Immorality and Illegality of the Communist Regime (125/1996), which declared that the Communist Party "did not prevent its members from committing crimes." The law produced no repercussions for these crimes.

Three years later, under the more liberal governance of Mikuláš Dzurinda (1998–2006), former dissident and Minister of Justice Ján Čarnogurský set up the Department for the Documentation of Crimes Committed by the Communist Regime. It primarily provided legal advice to people seeking restitution or rehabilitation after having been incarcerated or persecuted by the communist regime. Čarnogurský had originally sought to found an Office for the Documentation of the Crimes of Communism similar to the one in the Czech Republic, but found little support, and the new Department had only two members, including himself.

While the new state thus formally recognized that serious crimes occurred under the previous regime, almost nothing has been done to punish those who committed them. The only successful prosecution to date was of General Alojz Lorenc, head of the ŠtB at the time of the Velvet Revolution. He was tried in 1992 for abuse of power, in particular for using illegal methods against dissidents, and was sentenced to four years' imprisonment, but as the federal state split, he escaped to his native Slovakia. A case was opened against him there in 1995 and he was charged in 2000. In late 2001, he was tried in a Bratislava military court and convicted of similar but fewer crimes than in his original trial, and was given a suspended fifteen-month sentence. By then a successful businessman, he emphasized that he felt no guilt for his actions. Charges have also been brought against former high Czechoslovak official Vasil Bil'ak for treason (for signing the letter that invited the Warsaw Pact to invade Czechoslovakia in 1968), but a regional court returned the case to the prosecutor (a decision upheld by the Supreme Court). In late 2007, prosecutors described the investigation as being in a preliminary stage; Bil'ak was then ninety years old.

With one trial, then, criminal justice cannot be considered a substantive element of Slovaks' response to the past, and it has accomplished neither justice via the punishment of those responsible for serious injustices nor a strong historical record of the previous regime's crimes. The reasons for this are several. Prosecuting crimes committed by the former Czechoslovak regime is difficult. The passage of time has damaged many cases, as often the victims are no longer alive, there are few to no witnesses, and original materials have been destroyed. Many of the accused were originally policemen, prosecutors, judges, and high political officials who had professional knowledge of how to destroy evidence. Many crimes were committed in buildings owned by the state police, when victims were in investigative custody, detention, or prison, minimizing the number of witnesses and making it more likely that the crimes would never be exposed. Officials falsified the cause of death on medical records, and people pled guilty under unacceptable conditions, still giving the appearance of being convicted according to the law. Finally, many files were destroyed during the Velvet Revolution, and thereafter, the new Slovak Intelligence Service (SIS) was often unwilling to provide access to the classified documents relevant to potential prosecutions.

That said, facing these challenges, the Czechs have prosecuted far more individuals from the same former regime than the Slovaks; further factors must be at work to explain the extremely low Slovak prosecution rates, and these can be found at both the elite and societal levels. On the former, the lack of elite turnover hampers the pursuit of criminal justice, as elites who had strong connections with the communist state are unlikely to take a prosecutorial attitude toward it thereafter. The lack of lustration also reflects a perspective on the past that is less condemnatory than in some countries, and this would also likely produce a weaker drive for criminal justice among elites. On the societal level, there was a lack of upward pressure for criminal justice. Even though the majority of people were not members of the Communist Party, almost everyone had someone close to them who was connected to it, and people had been forced to participate in the regime's sham elections. Many argue that these factors can impede the development of grassroots or civil society pressure for prosecutions and the establishment of a historical record of past wrongs.

File Access

Despite an apparent lack of broad societal interest in transitional justice, and in the ŠtB legacy more specifically, in the autumn of 2001, former dissidents Ján Langoš and Ján Čarnogurský brought the issue to the parliamentary agenda, each offering a bill that would open the secret police archives to the citizenry. Langoš's was more expansive and included not only the communist period, but also the archives from the Slovak state during World War II, which had existed under Hitler's tutelage.

Langoš's bill passed in the summer of 2002. The law set up an Institute for National Memory (Ústav pamäti národa, or ÚPN) where people can access the files, and which was also tasked with investigating and publicizing the darker aspects of the state's fascist and communist past. Act No. 553/2002, known as the "Law on the Nation's Memory," states its rationale and purposes in its preamble, which include "the duty to prosecute crimes against peace, humanity and war crimes," "the duty of our state to achieve satisfaction for those were damaged by the state, which violated human rights and its own laws," "the duty of our state to disclose the activity of repressive authorities," and "to express our conviction that those who do not know their past, are condemned to repeat it, and that no unlawful act on behalf of the state against its citizens may be protected by secrecy and may not be forgotten."

Toward these ends, under Langoš's leadership, the ÚPN set up over the course of 2003 in a Bratislava court building and began accepting applications to view the files. One serious complication was the SIS's unwillingness to hand over the files, despite the legal requirement, which stalled the ÚPN's progress in making them publicly available. Finally, in late 2004, the ÚPN undertook its first dramatic disclosure: on November 16, the day before the fifteenth anniversary of the Velvet Revolution, it published the ŠtB registers, which included the names of both those targeted for surveillance and those employed by the secret police (including part-time informers), from Eastern Slovakia online. It subsequently published them from all areas of the country.

This sparked public interest and prompted much media discussion, as the names of prominent politicians, clergy members, sports stars, university officials, and others were revealed in the registers. An intense debate developed over whether such people should step down from public office, and opinion polls showed strong public support for their resignation. The media also published detailed background information on the methods and motivations of the ŠtB, and society confronted many difficult questions raised by the information in the files. Unfortunately, the ÚPN project was dealt a harsh blow when Langoš was killed in a car crash in June 2006, and its many foes in government took the opportunity to try to undermine its future. It nevertheless eventually gained new leadership and has continued its activities.

On the question of effectiveness, the ÚPN offers a mixed picture. It has done little to ensure the prosecution of past crimes, but its truth revelation role has been strong, prompting societal engagement with the legacies of Slovak history's darker elements where there had previously been very little. In doing so, its work has mitigated the sense of impunity fostered by the failure of other transitional justice mechanisms.

Conclusion

Nearly twenty years after the Velvet Revolution, Slovakia's experience with accountability mechanisms offers a mixed picture. On the one hand, lustration and criminal justice have been almost entirely ineffective, allowing former elites to escape punishment for human rights abuses and, especially in the 1990s, to undermine the development of liberal democracy. On the other, the case shows that even under inhospitable circumstances, it is possible to use the dissemination of information about the past on the Internet to prompt substantive engagement with the central, thorny questions of what people associated with the former regime are accountable *for*, and what the implications of such accountability *should* be. This, in itself, is a form of justice.

Nadya Nedelsky

Cross-references: Access to Secret Files; Court Trials for Redress; Czech Republic; Institute for National Memory; Lustration; Office for the Documentation and the Investigation of Crimes of Communism; Property Restitution; Reforms of Military, Police, Secret Police; Rehabilitation of Political Prisoners; Reparations.

Further Readings

David, Roman. 2003. Lustration Laws in Action: The Motives and Evaluation of Lustration Policy in the Czech Republic and Poland (1989–2001). *Law and Social Inquiry*, 28: 387–439.
Lesná, L'uba. 2007. Eighteen Years after the Revolution, No Justice. *The Slovak Spectator*, November 19. Available at: http://www.spectator.sk/articles/view/29874/2/ (accessed February 9, 2009).
Nedelsky, Nadya. 2009. Czechoslovakia, and the Czech and Slovak Republics. In *Transitional Justice in Eastern Europe and the Former Soviet Union: Reckoning with the Communist Past*. Ed. Lavinia Stan. New York: Routledge.
———. 2004. Divergent Responses to a Common Past: Transitional Justice in the Czech Republic and Slovakia. *Theory and Society*, 33: 65–115.
Williams, Kieran. 2001. The StB in Czechoslovakia, 1945–89. In *Security Intelligence Services in New Democracies: The Czech Republic, Slovakia and Romania*. Eds. Kieran Williams and Dennis Deletant. New York: Palgrave.

Slovenia

In the decades following the demise of communist rule and the dissolution of socialist Yugoslavia, very few transitional justice measures have been implemented in Slovenia. Furthermore, the dearth of such measures has been matched by a lack of sustained societal interest in enacting transitional justice initiatives. Although there have been flashes of heated public activity and sporadic political action in the realm of transitional justice, a forgive-and-forget approach predominates, with a common understanding that Slovenia has achieved a consolidated democracy without recourse to transitional justice.

The Repressive Past

The first communist secret service in Slovenia was the Slovenian partisan-headed Varnostna Obveščevalna Služba (1941–1944). By 1944, this service was supplanted by the all-Yugoslav Department for the Protection of the People, known as the Organizacija za Zaščito Naroda (OZNA), which was succeeded in 1946 by the centralized State Security Directorate, Uprava Državne Bezbednosti (UDBa).

The Federal People's Republic of Yugoslavia was established in 1945 by Marshal Josip Broz Tito, who used the UDBa to brutally persecute suspected and actual Nazi collaborators in 1946–1947. The number of collaborators executed by the UDBa is estimated to be in the tens of thousands, and those held in concentration camps to be in the hundreds of thousands. The most infamous Slovenian massacres that the UDBa participated in include those at Kočevski Rog, Škofija Loca (Crngrob), Teharje, and Ljubljana (Šentvid). In 1948, the UDBa focused on persecuting Cominformists – high-ranking officials who, in the aftermath of the Tito-Stalin split, were suspected of sympathizing with the Soviets. An estimated 50,000 Yugoslav citizens were investigated by the UDBa, and thousands were interned in prison camps at Goli Otok in Croatia, Stara Gradiska in Bosnia-Herzegovina, and Sremska Mitrovica in Vojvodina.

Economic challenges and ideological shifts resulted in an easing of secret police repression by the early 1950s, which made the UDBa one of the least repressive secret services in the communist world. A number of factors in the mid-1960s worked to further weaken the power of the secret police, including the formalization of Worker's Self-Management, decentralization of power to the republics, and the 1966 dismissal of Vice President Aleksander Ranković, who controlled the UDBa. That same year, the UDBa was renamed the Služba Državne Varnosti (SDV), a service that was weakened by decentralization and by the increasing influence of the Yugoslav People's Army (the Jugoslovenska narodna armija, JNA) and of the Military Counterintelligence Service (the Kontraobvešajna Služba, KOS). KOS participated in the post-1966 purge of the SDV in Slovenia and increasingly found itself charged with protecting the state from internal and external enemies.

By the 1970s, Croatian nationalism and attendant émigré and dissident movements were the primary focus of the secret services. Slovenian, Kosovar (Albanian), Montenegrin, and Serbian émigré organizations in Western states were also monitored and infiltrated, and, in a number of cases, leaders of these organizations were assassinated. By the 1980s, with Tito dead (in 1980) and the federation unraveling, the SDV increasingly became a de facto tool of the Slovenian republic-level leadership. By the mid- to late 1980s, the SDV in Slovenia monitored fewer than 1,000 people for anti-regime sympathies. The SDV was officially prohibited from acting against those in positions of power in Slovenia by virtue of a 1985 Slovenian decree, precisely at the moment when Slovenian authorities were challenging federal authorities by increasing political and economic liberalization. Where the SDV did not act, the KOS and JNA did.

On March 25, 1988, the Defense Council of Yugoslavia (Svet Obroženih Sil of the SFRJ) declared liberalization in Slovenia to be antirevolutionary. Reprints of the meeting's minutes came into the hands of journalist Janez Janša, who was later arrested and tried with three others in relation to possessing (although not publishing) this secret information. These actions inspired what is known as the Slovenian Spring, where civil society movements influenced the establishment of an independent and democratic Slovenia.

Transitional Justice

On June 25, 1991, Slovenia declared its independence, endured a short ten-day war, and swiftly consolidated a stable liberal democracy, all with only a few transitional justice measures. While there were initiatives regarding privatization and property restitution for those dispossessed of their property during the communist regime, there were no initiatives to redress injustices perpetrated by the secret police, nor were there provisions for lustration. Given the lack of lustration laws, there were little grounds to pursue court trials. Trials did not figure prominently in Slovenia's transition; rather, lustration was a topic that inhabited the realms of political maneuvering and public debate. Even in cases of the most flagrant of crimes, such as the massacres of Nazi collaborators at the end of World War II, in which mass gravesites of more than 100,000 people have been found and officially documented by the Slovenian government, not one of the surviving perpetrators of these massacres has been brought to trial.

Restitution

Of the transitional justice measures undertaken in postcommunist Slovenia, most notable is the 1991 Law on Denationalization, which legislates the restitution of property nationalized and confiscated in Slovenia after World War II. The law stipulates the restitution of property to those who apply for its return and whose property was nationalized between 1945 and 1963.

Restitution proceeded fitfully in the first half of the 1990s and was effectively suspended in the second half of the 1990s. However, at the dawn of the 2000s, half of claims were resolved and by 2003 almost all restitution claims had been resolved primarily through restitution in kind. The resolution of claims was bolstered by European Union (EU) pressure to ensure the government was enacting its own laws as well as liberalizing the property market and affording a greater role for foreign property owners. While property restitution was not mandated by the EU, carrying out Slovenian law was a requirement for Slovenia's accession to the EU in 2004.

Much of the controversy over restitution centered on the single largest claimant in Slovenia: the Roman Catholic Church. A complicating factor was that much of what the Church claimed had for decades been used and occupied by others. Another element was the controversy over restitution of feudal lands as well as restitution of lands in national parks, particularly in Triglav National Park. This was coupled with the contention that the 1991 law was hasty and not clear enough to allow for swift restitution.

Issues such as size limits on property for restitution, the category of land in question, citizenship of beneficiaries, and proof of no previous compensation were not delineated in the 1991 law. This lack of clarity led to a number of political and legal stumbling blocks such as the 1992 law that only allowed for the restitution of properties of less than 200 acres, a law that was annulled by the Constitutional Court in 1993. There was such a lack of clarity in the Denationalization Law that the Slovenian parliament effectively suspended it from 1995 until 1998. However with the election of a new government and the desire to fulfill requirements of EU accession, property restitution proceeded swiftly.

Property restitution in Slovenia was a process that was kick-started with a hastily drafted law in 1991, stalled until 1995, frozen until 2000, and swiftly concluded by 2004. Resolution of property in the Slovenian case has meant that most property was returned to their rightful owners. However, what allowed for successful restitution was the spirit of compromise that allowed difficult cases to be resolved by either restitution in kind or by financial compensation buoyed by commitment to the rule of law.

Commissions of Inquiry

At independence in 1991, genuine debate and inquiry into the role of partisans and collaborators in World War II Slovenia arose, with special concern for objectively assessing the extent of postwar reprisals. This was exemplified by the 1992–1996 Parliamentary Commission for the Investigation of Post-War Mass-Murders, Dubious Trials and Other Irregularities (also known as the Jože Pučnik Comission for the name of its chair). More than a decade since the Commission concluded its work, the reports are yet to be made public. With these material and historical transitional justice issues accounted for, there was little public outcry for further measures, largely because the level of oppression and secret police injustices were less onerous in Slovenia than in other communist states.

In 2005, the Slovenian government established a related commission, the Commission to Resolve Questions of Concealed Graves, a respected body that documents existing mass graves and seeks out new gravesites of Nazi collaborators massacred as World War II came to an end. In the last several years, the commission has unearthed and registered more than 2,000 new gravesites, with more than 100,000 victims. Even with the undisputed evidence of massacres, the general public has refrained from demanding legal remedies. This is not to say these and other crimes perpetrated by the communist authorities have gone undisclosed. Rather, transitional justice in Slovenia has come to mean widespread public acknowledgment and condemnation of these crimes with the explicit absence of requirements of legal retribution.

In the postcommunist decades, there has been a great wave of popular and scholarly works on the injustices of the past, with people enjoying the freedom to express a diverse and controversial range of standpoints. As part of this explosion of public dialogue, memorialization both in print and practice has become the norm. News organizations regularly discuss transitional justice issues while memorials to victims of the communist regime as well as the Ten Day War of Independence are scattered throughout the country. Ceremonies commemorating the mass graves of Nazi collaborators killed by Tito's partisans at the close of World War II, such as the annual ceremony at Kočevski Rog, are among the most dramatic expressions of these new freedoms.

Lustration

Slovenia established a liberal democratic order with the help of communist officials whose tolerance of civil society movements during the waning years of the communist regime ensured that lustration was not a primary political consideration in the postcommunist era. Even at the onset of transition, lustration was not treated as a requirement to ensure the rule of law.

For the most part, Slovenia's center-right parties (also known as the Spring Parties because of their rise during the Slovenian Spring) have been proponents of lustration and public access to secret police files, while the center-left parties, many of them comprised of former communist-era elites, have generally argued against these transitional justice measures. Calls for lustration have periodically arisen, but have been dismissed as attempts to create political scandal to enhance political power rather than bolster the rule of law. The most notable attempts at establishing a lustration law in postcommunist Slovenia include the UDBa Amendment, the Resolution on the Illegality of the Communist Totalitarian regime, and the Bill on the Suppression of Consequences Inflicted by the Communist Totalitarian Regime (also known as the Lustration Bill).

The UDBa Amendment (Udbovski Amandma) to the parliamentary election law of 1992 was proposed as a means of ensuring that secret service collaborators would be prevented from running for a seat in the Slovenian National Assembly. The amendment would have required those running for election to sign a declaration regarding former collaboration with the SDV and/or foreign intelligence services. But in the year when it was proposed, the amendment did not receive the two-thirds voting threshold in parliament required to make it law. Those answering in the affirmative would have been prohibited from running for election and holding a seat.

In 1997, the Spring Parties spearheaded another failed attempt at lustration legislation, this time with the Resolution on the Illegality of the Communist Totalitarian Regime and the Bill on the Suppression of Consequences Inflicted by the Communist Totalitarian Regime (the Lustration Bill). Reaching the floor of parliament after the 1997 presidential elections, the Resolution called for prosecution and redress through lustration that would affect government officials, mayors, lawyers, and journalists, and included a proposed Lustration Court. The second bill was a general indictment of the communist regime and did not prescribe any action against those who perpetrated crimes in the name of that regime. Both the Resolution and the Bill failed to pass, and no subsequent attempts at lustration legislation or measures to officially denounce the communist regime were made. This was perhaps a result of the concomitant difficulty in ensuring access to accurate and comprehensive secret police files that could prove individual culpability in the crimes of the communist regime.

Secret Police File Access

Lustration requires access to reliable secret police files. In the Slovenian case, access was complicated by two main factors: post-1990 privacy laws and the disappearance of the majority of secret police files.

The Personal Data Protection Act, enacted in 1990, legislates that an individual must provide written consent to access personal data, and that no one other than the individual on whom the file was compiled can access a given file. Numerous articles in the Criminal Code also address privacy concerns. Short of self-indictment, there is no legal means for the public to know of secret police collaboration or of the extent of an individual's involvement in the crimes of the communist regime. Even in cases where the files of prominent Slovenians have unofficially been made public, the reliability of the files is dubious, largely because of the recognition that the majority of Slovenia's secret service archives had disappeared by the time of independence.

Initially stored in Belgrade from 1986 to 1989, the vast majority of Slovenia's secret police and police files were transported to the Slovenian National Archives in the Gotenica Bunker, under the Central Active File of the Slovenian Ministry of Interior, the Republiškega Sekretariata za Notranje Zadeve Socialistične Republike Slovenije (RSNZ). The 1 million files were coded and included information on the reasons for investigation of victims, the activities of common criminals, and the recruitment of agents and collaborators. However, before any postcommunist evaluation of the files could occur in 1990, the center-right governing coalition announced that the majority of the archives had mysteriously disappeared. The contention was that communist elites, on the eve of democratic transition, destroyed the files before they could be incriminated. Why and how the files disappeared remains unresolved. Some 3,000 secret police files on Slovenes remain.

While the disappearance of the files remains a mystery, in 2003, abbreviated records of the approximately 1 million files resurfaced on the Internet. In April 2003, UDBa.net (http://www.UDBa.net) made its online debut, causing a short-lived firestorm of controversy. The Web site listed the names of everyone who had a secret police and police file, but did not contain the actual file. File codes, names of parents, dates of birth, citizenship information, employment history, and criminal record information of individuals were included on the UDBa.net list. Whereas the vast majority of the files were connected to regular police investigations, 100,000 files were listed as secret police files. Bereft of the content of the files, readers were left to speculate as to who was a secret police informant, collaborator, agent, or victim.

A number of prominent Slovenians, including politicians, were listed as having secret police files, with no way to verify why their files existed. Some have claimed that the file codes for the categories of informant, collaborator agent, and victim are easily identifiable, but no one has come forward to conclusively and systematically establish who was in which category. Authenticity of the UDBa.net listings was never confirmed by the government, although independent experts vouched for their authenticity. Claims of authenticity were further bolstered when it was revealed that Slovenia's Honorary Consul for Australia and New Zealand, Dušan Lajovic, created UDBa.net with microfilm copies of original paper files. A supporter of lustration, Lajovic claimed to have been in possession of the documents as early as 1991. While the authenticity of the files was quickly confirmed, several government investigations failed to establish how Lajovic came to possess these files and the strongest government action against Lajovic was simply his dismissal as Honorary Consul. Fearing that the information might compromise Slovenia's chances at EU accession, he chose 2003 to release the information, only to have the site swiftly blocked by the Slovenian government. Given the lack of conclusive evidence as to who was an agent or collaborator, the UDBa.net affair failed to arouse sustained public interest in lustration. Even more telling was that even after the UDBa.net affair, relatively few Slovenians sought access to their own files.

The UDBa.net controversy highlighted a prominent transitional justice divide in Slovenia. Some argue that individuals in current positions of political power who committed politically motivated crimes in the past should be held accountable, in order to strengthen the rule of law and provide a measure of justice. Others argue that the privacy rights of all individuals – including prominent political leaders – enshrined in postcommunist law should take precedence, in order to ensure the continued rule of law. The latter reasoning has predominated in postcommunist Slovenia, where no calls for lustration have been successful and access to reliable and complete secret service files is virtually nonexistent.

Conclusion

In postcommunist Slovenia, property restitution of communist-era nationalized and confiscated property was swift, and an informed dialogue on partisan and collaborationist crimes emerged. However, the failure to deal with communist-era secret police transgressions, the curtailment of public access to communist-era secret service files, and the absence of lustration legislation resulted in an absence of comprehensive transitional justice measures.

Each attempt at lustration legislation has resulted in failure, and there is no way to conclusively ensure that public figures who violated human rights during the communist era are not in positions of power today. This is partly because lustration and secret service transgressions are becoming progressively less of a public or political concern. There are ever fewer victims of communist-era abuse of power who have a personal stake in calling for redress, truth, and justice. Also, for the majority of Slovenians, there is an understanding that communist-era secret police abuses in their country were not as pervasive as in other states, and that their communist-era elite, while perhaps engaging in abuses of power during the communist regime, were the very same people largely responsible for liberal democratic transformations. While scandals concerning transitional justice periodically arise, there is little sustained support for comprehensive transitional justice measures.

Tamara Kotar

Cross-references: Access to Secret Files; Lustration; Property Restitution.

Further Readings

Brejc, M. 1994. *Vmestni čas: varnostno informativna služba in nastanjane nove slvoenske države 1990–1993* [Intermediate Term: The Security Information Service and the Establishment of the New Slovenian State]. Ljubljana: Mladinska knjiga.
Kotar, Tamara. 2009. Slovenia. In *Transitional Justice in Eastern Europe and the Former Soviet Union: Reckoning with the Communist Past.* Ed. Lavinia Stan. London: Routledge, pp. 200–220.
Lajovic, D. S. 2003. *Med svobodo in rdečo zvezdo* [Between Freedom and the Red Star]. Ljubljana: Nova obzorja.
Parliamentary Commission for the Investigation of Post-War Mass-Murders, Dubious Trials and other Irregularities. 2003. Porocilo o Raziskovanju povojnihsodnih procesov [Report on the Research on Post War Trials]. *Nova Revija*, Ljubljana, January–March, pp. 16–55.
Republic of Slovenia. 1991. Zakon o denacionalizaciji [Law on Denationalization]. *Uradni List*, no. 12.
Republic of Slovenia. 1993. Komisijo za nadzor nad delom varnostnih in obveščevalnih služb [Commission to Oversee Intelligence and Security Services]. *Uradni list*, no. 12.
Republic of Slovenia. n.d. Komisija Vlade Republike Slovenije za Reševanje Vprašanj Prikritih Grobišč [Commission of the Republic of Slovenia to Resolve the Questions of Concealed Graves]. Available at: http://www.mddsz.gov.si/si/delovna_podrocja/vojni_invalidi_veterani_in_zrtve_vojnega_nasilja/vojna_grobisca/komisija_vlade_rs_za_resevanje_vprasanj_prikritih_grobisc/ (accessed January 31, 2010).
Seliškar, Z. 1970. *Zgodovina organov za notranje zadeve v Socialisticni Republiki Sloveniji* [History of the Organs of the Interior Ministry in the Socialist Republic of Slovenia]. Ljubljana: Mladinska knjiga.
Tomasevich, J. 2001. *War and Revolution in Yugoslavia 1941–1945: Occupation and Collaboration.* Stanford: Stanford University Press.
UDBa.net Web site, once available at: http://www.UDBa.net.

South Africa

Since the beginning of its colonial history, South Africa has been plagued by issues of racism and discrimination. First the Dutch East India Company, then British colonialists, and finally successive white governments instituted divide-and-rule policies in order to subordinate the black – African, Indian, and Colored (or people of mixed race) – population. By the 1960s, armed liberation movements were conducting guerilla attacks against institutions they perceived to be representative of the oppressive white apartheid government. Then, in 1994, after negotiations between the liberation movements and the government, South Africa held its first democratic election. This election and the employment of numerous transitional justice mechanisms averted the outbreak of a full-blown civil war. Although sometimes referred to as a political miracle, the transition from armed struggle to democracy was the result of years of conflict and suffering and a carefully honed transitionary peace process. Central to the process was the Truth and Reconciliation Commission (TRC; see separate entry), designed to expose and acknowledge past violations of human rights and explore ways of establishing social cohesion and coexistence between former enemies. Since the 1994 election, political violence has been minimal and, in large measure, blacks and whites have sought to live in peaceful coexistence.

The Repressive Past

The earliest black African settlements in what later became known as South Africa date back to 270 C.E. By 600 C.E., Iron Age communities had spread to other parts of the country. Moreover, those known to be South Africa's "first people," the Khoikhoi had, in turn, already settled in the southern parts of the country from the beginning of the Common Era.

The beginning of the colonial period began to unfold with the arrival of Portuguese navigators Bartholomew Dias and later Vasco da Gama, in what is today Mossel Bay and St. Helena Bay in 1488 and 1497, respectively. The arrival of the Dutch East India Company in 1652 set the scene of the racial and territorial conflict that was to come. South Africa was controlled for almost 150 years by the Dutch. The first British occupation of the Cape occurred in 1795. After temporarily handing the territory back to the Dutch, they again occupied the Cape in 1806. This British takeover resulted in the migration of several emerging Boer communities, who were essentially of Dutch origin and the ancestors of the today's Afrikaner community, into the Eastern Cape and the northern parts of the country. The discovery of minerals in the Boer republics established in the Free State and Transvaal areas led to the Anglo-Boer War in 1899–1901. The British victory in this war led to the establishment of the Union of South Africa in 1910.

At the top of the social hierarchy during this period were the white settlers and at the bottom were indigenous people and slaves. By the early eighteenth century, the number of slaves of Asian descent in South Africa exceeded the white settler population. These racially defined hierarchies were intensified during British colonial era through war and land appropriation, which resulted in the forced labor of large sections of the black population in the mines.

With the declaration of Union in 1910, the newly elected government introduced additional laws to further curtail the rights of the black majority. These laws included the Mines and Works Act of 1911, which restricted black people to menial work, the Native Land Act of 1913, which set aside 10 percent of the arable land in South Africa for the black population, and the intensification of the pass legislation (first initiated by the postwar colonial government in 1905) that required black Africans to carry an identity document (the infamous pass) and thereby regulated their movements.

In 1948, the National Party, in coalition with the Afrikaner Party – which opposed the governing United Party under General Jan Smuts – came to power, introducing apartheid rule in a more decisive and ideological manner. Among the most infamous legislation passed to further apartheid were the Group Areas Act of 1950 and the Bantu Education Act of 1953. Apartheid not only excluded blacks from the voters' roll but ensured that they resided in segregated areas and were subjected to inferior education, with contact between races reduced to a minimal servant-master relationship. During the 1960s and 1970s, forced removals and resettlements took place as the government moved black populations into designated areas, many of which were incorporated into independent homelands or Bantustans.

The black population was by no means passive in its acceptance of its oppression. The African National Congress (ANC), founded in 1912, and other worker groups were at the center of this resistance. These included the Communist Party of South Africa (CPSA), renamed the South African Communist Party (SACP) in 1953, and the Pan Africanist Congress (PAC), which broke away from the ANC in 1959. In June 1955, the Congress of the People campaign was launched as an alliance of all the anti-apartheid forces. It was composed of the ANC, the South African Indian Congress, the South African Coloured People's Congress, the South African Congress of Democrats, and the South African Congress of Trade Unions (SACTU), and eventually resulted in the formation of a nonracial united front known as the Congress Alliance. In June 1955, this Congress adopted the Freedom Charter, which aimed to form a nonracial democratic state. In 1959, the dissident PAC led nationwide demonstrations against the pass laws, which resulted in the Sharpeville massacre, with police killing sixty-nine protesters. In response to continued protests and strikes, the government banned the ANC and the PAC and declared a state of emergency. (The CPSA had already been forced to dissolve in 1950 as a result of the Suppression of Communism Act). Many ANC, PAC, and CPSA/SAPC leaders and activists were arrested and tried under the General Law Amendment (Sabotage Act) of 1962 and related legislation. These events contributed to the formation by the ANC of Umkhonto we Sizwe (Spear of the Nation, MK) and by the PAC of Poqo as military wings of the struggle. Armed resistance remained part of the opposition for the remainder of white rule, with attacks evolving from isolated bombings of power stations to a concerted military underground resistance strategy.

In response to such resistance, the white government reacted with increased repression and tough police measures. There were several declarations of states of emergency and violent police reprisals against peaceful marches, including the killing of protesting school children in Soweto in 1976. The protests spread across the country, resulting in 1,000 direct killings within the next six months and an intensification of security force action against any form of resistance. Several leading activists died in custody, including Black Conscious leader Steve Biko. By the mid-1980s, the social order was collapsing. Black resistance movements stepped up their opposition, international outrage was mounting against white oppressive rule, and the government was employing increasingly harsh measures to prevent the outbreak of a civil war.

As the conflict intensified, secret meetings were held between government leaders and Nelson Mandela (the ANC's most prominent leader who became its president on his release from prison) and, on July 5, 1989, a meeting took place between President P. W. Botha and Mandela. At the same time, meetings were held between high-level government and ANC officials in exile. These included the Mells Park talks in England in October 1987 and February 1988, which served as a stepping-stone to an initial meeting in October 1989 in Switzerland between delegations of the ANC and the National Intelligence Service of the apartheid state. On February 2, 1990, the newly elected president F. W. De Klerk lifted the ban on the ANC and other dissident political parties. One week later, Mandela was released from prison. After extended negotiations, a political settlement was reached, leading to a democratic election in 1994.

One of the pressing concerns in these negotiations was what mechanisms would be used by the new government to address the gross violations of human rights committed during the years leading up to the transition. A related concern was how the newly democratic South Africa was to redress the grievances of the victims of such abuses.

Transitional Justice

The South African transition gave new life to the international transitional justice debate initiated in Latin American countries and elsewhere in earlier years. The country was in dire need of mechanisms to assist the transition from its oppressive past to a new democratic future. These included a decision by parliament to pass the TRC Act, which empowered the TRC to grant amnesty to perpetrators. Such grants of amnesty were dependent on specific criteria. Those who were denied amnesty or refused to apply for amnesty were subject to criminal trials. In brief, the legislation governing the TRC required a process designed to investigate human rights abuses perpetrated on both sides of the country's political divide.

The ANC Truth Commissions

The ANC conducted its own internal investigations into allegations of abuse by its followers, particularly in ANC camps outside of South Africa (see entries on Commission of Enquiry into Certain Allegations of Cruelty and Human Rights Abuses against ANC Prisoners and Detainees by ANC Members and Commission of Enquiry into Complaints by Former African National Congress Prisoners and Detainees). These violations were primarily against ANC members accused of collaborating with South African security forces. Investigations showed that prisoners were beaten and tortured because of their alleged collaboration with the South African security forces. In some situations, enemies of the ANC were murdered and/or assassinated. The ANC investigations (including the Stuart Commission in 1984, the Skweyiya Commission in 1992, and the Motsuenyane Commission in 1993) emerged largely as a result of mounting pressure from within the ANC and in response to allegations and concerns expressed in the international community about violations of human rights in its camps. They contributed to the creation of a milieu of accountability and transparency within the ANC and South Africa more generally. Moreover, because of their timing, these enquiries showed to the population that the ANC was ready to account for its violations of human rights in contrast to the government that continued to deny abuses by its security forces. In so doing, the ANC emerged as the first liberation movement in the world to acknowledge the need to act on human rights abuses committed by its own members in dealing with the past.

The Truth and Reconciliation Commission

At the time of the negotiated settlement in South Africa, the three general options for dealing with the past were the pursuit of alleged perpetrators through criminal justice, blanket amnesty for all perpetrators, and a policy of amnesia or forgetfulness – a willingness to simply ignore the past. Many human rights organizations in South Africa, and the world as whole, insisted that it was the moral and legal duty of the incoming regime to prosecute those responsible for human rights violations. This would have allowed for the exposure of the crimes of apartheid and the punishment of those who had committed gross human rights violations. However, this option was not feasible. Nuremberg-style trials (see separate entry) could only have been conducted in a situation where victor's justice prevailed. In South Africa, the white regime was still in control of the army and critical state institutions. Indeed, many of those who would have been prosecuted were the very people who were needed to ensure that a violence-free election could occur and the new constitution could be implemented. If apartheid leaders and generals in the army and police force were to have faced prosecution and the possibility of extended jail sentences, it is unlikely that they would have surrendered power.

A second option considered was that of blanket amnesty (as occurred in Argentina and Chile; see separate entries). The government hoped for this option, arguing that it was best for South Africa to "wipe the slate clean" and enact a definitive break from the past. Unlike the Latin American transitions, however, in South Africa the demands for justice prevailed.

In brief, both the option of Nuremberg-style trials and a blanket amnesty were impossible. Moreover, victims of apartheid were simply unable and unwilling to forget the past. Something needed to be done to address the crimes. It was decided in the "post-amble" to the interim constitution that amnesty of some form would have to be granted. This resulted in the formation of the TRC. It was not mandated to pursue retributive justice; rather, conditional amnesties would be granted to perpetrators of gross human rights violations where it was judged that their crimes were political in motivation, proportional to that political goal, and when a perpetrator fully disclosed these events in public hearings before the TRC's amnesty committee.

The process was focused on truth telling (see entry on Truth [Truth Seeking and Truth Telling]). The TRC was designed to uncover as much truth about the history of oppression and struggle in South Africa as possible (in the period between 1960, which marked the beginning of the armed struggle, and 1994, when the first democratic elections happened). It was hoped that this would provide victims with vital information and acknowledgment as to what happened to their loved ones. To obtain amnesty, perpetrators of human rights abuses would be forced to acknowledge publicly what they had done. One of the TRC's primary aims was to prevent anyone from denying the crimes that had been committed or claiming that they had no knowledge of them. This was an attempt to enable everyone to face up to the crimes of the past, whether committed by themselves or in their name.

Those who first envisaged the TRC and later oversaw its conduct hoped that public acknowledgment of the past would allow the country to begin to bind together and thereby break the cycles of violence. It was hoped that a single inclusive history could be created for South Africans as a whole, black and white, and that such a history would foster reconciliation between previously divided communities. Thus, the TRC, as well as being the only process that both sides accepted for dealing with the past, was also envisioned as a mechanism that could begin to foster a sense of national identity across previous racial divides.

Criminal Prosecutions

In conjunction with the TRC, there was also provision made for criminal trials for those who failed to apply to the TRC or were denied amnesty by it. Amnesty was essentially the "carrot" of the TRC process, whereas the possibility of criminal prosecution was the "stick" intended to persuade perpetrators to apply for amnesty. Two of the most notable trials conducted were those of Magnus Malan, the former Minister of Defense, and Dr. Wouter Basson, an apartheid chemical weapons expert who was alleged to have developed chemical agents for use against enemies of the state. Both trials cost the South African state vast sums of money and both failed to achieve convictions as the state was unable to prove its case beyond all reasonable doubt. Thus, fears concerning the pursuit of retributive justice through the courts were validated to some degree. Moreover, given the specific nature of any court charges, the extent and breadth of the truth disclosed through the sole use of trials, as opposed to their combined use with the TRC, would have been limited.

However, most high-profile perpetrators on both sides failed to apply for amnesty and were not criminally charged. Such a failure to prosecute was the result of an apparent lack of political will on the part of the government because of a fear that trials would initiate a process that the TRC was supposed to close. Moreover, those trials that did occur resulted in restrained judgments. For example, a mere suspended court sentence was imposed on the former president, P. W. Botha, for failing to cooperate with the TRC. Thus, there was a lack of accountability at the highest level of command as many perpetrators neither faced the TRC nor were prosecuted. However, some perpetrators of human rights violations lower down the chain of command were convicted and imprisoned. Among others, these included a leader of an apartheid hit squad, Eugene de Kock, and noted perpetrator of human rights abuses, Ferdie Barnard, a member of the Civil Cooperation Bureau that was a secret unit, reporting directly to the Minister of Defense, General Magnus Malan.

The prosecution saga in South Africa remains both contested and unresolved. The government has taken initiatives to lay this matter to rest. These include suspended sentences for the former Minister of Police Adrian Volk and several police officers in exchange for limited disclosure of information in in-camera hearings. Despite opposition to the nonpublic disclosure associated with these cases and the failure to hear evidence from victims, several moves have, during the past two years, again been made by the government to pardon apartheid-era offenders.

Restitution and Reparations

In the concluding section of its Final Report, the TRC provided a list of recommendations to the government of South Africa and to the society more generally. Most of these addressed issues of restitution, reparations, and development. The failure to properly implement many of these recommendations is commonly regarded as among the most poignant failures of the government concerning the work of the TRC. The government, for example, took five years to respond to the TRC recommendation to grant reparations, and then made a one-off payment to each TRC-listed victim of a mere R30,000 (some US$4,500). Community reparations, intended to bolster community development, have, in most instances, not received the kind of priority attention that the TRC sought to initiate. This failure, despite a majority government being elected, is attributable to the government's prioritizing of alternative developments, a lack of capacity by the civil service to deliver on these projects, and, arguably, a residual sense of resentment toward the TRC in government circles because of its finding against the ANC.

Conclusion

The TRC was never going to be more than a cautious beginning exploration of the possibilities of reconciliation. It should arguably have reached deeper into the nation's memory by holding a sharper and more penetrating mirror before the nation, persuading it to reflect with a more rigorous, penetrating gaze on the origins of what gave rise to the gross human rights violations it highlighted. Maybe it was too soon for this to happen. This is precisely why the conversation on the past needs to continue.

The South African TRC did not succeed in depolarizing the South African nation. Not all former perpetrators chose to use the TRC as an opportunity to deal fully with their past. Senior politicians and generals in the security forces refused to take responsibility for the deeds of their foot soldiers. Most beneficiaries of apartheid have refused to acknowledge the privileges they carry with them into the present. The full extent of the apartheid infrastructure has not been acknowledged or wholly faced by most white people; neither has the new government adequately succeeded in changing the economic dimensions of these structures. Moreover, state institutions have not been able to transform themselves adequately, and insufficient attention has been given to the roots and the nature of racism. The redress of poverty and human insecurity remains a major challenge facing South Africa. Without making any dire prediction of a popular revolutionary upsurge in the short to medium term, this entrenched inequality can only result in new forms of struggle. The social and political discontent surrounding the election of Jacob Zuma as ANC president in 2008 (in the wake of the forced resignation of President Thabo Mbeki) and as president of South Africa in 2009, and the increasing joblessness and sense of economic alienation felt by South African society, is an indication of this beginning to happen.

Generative conversation in post-conflict situations needs necessarily to result in new horizons of thought and action, and to make conflict prevention central to its program of socioeconomic and political reconstruction and transformation. It is here that transitional justice processes – which include accountability, a broad sense of conflict resolution, an attempt to redress the fundamental causes on the conflict through conflict transformation mechanisms, and socioeconomic development – need to promote ongoing transformation.

The case of transitional justice mechanisms in South Africa is a complicated one. On the one hand, South Africa has made the transition from oppression to the democracy. Clearly the institution of the TRC, as a result of the negotiated settlement, contributed significantly to this process. On the other hand, the response of the government and society to the findings and recommendations of the TRC – not least regarding prosecutions and reparations – have cast a shadow over the South African transition.

Charles Villa-Vicencio and Ilan Cooper

Cross-references: Argentina; Chile; Court Trials for Redress; Nuremberg Trials; Property Restitution; Rehabilitation of Political Prisoners; Reparations; Truth and

Reconciliation Commission, South Africa; Truth Commissions; Truth (Truth Seeking and Truth Telling).

Further Readings

Alexander, Neville. 2002. *An Ordinary Country: Issues in the Transition from Apartheid to Democracy in South Africa*. Pietermaritzburg, South Africa: University of Natal Press.
Asmal, Kader, Louise Asmal, and Ronald Roberts. 1996. *Reconciliation through Truth: A Reckoning of Apartheid's Criminal Governance*. Cape Town: David Philip.
Boraine, Alex. 2000. *A Country Unmasked: Inside South Africa's Truth and Reconciliation Commission*. Oxford: Oxford University Press.
Foster, Don, Paul Haupt, and Maresa De Beer. 2005. *The Theater of Violence: Narratives of Protagonists in the South African Conflict*. Oxford: James Currey.
Villa-Vicencio, Charles. 2009. *Walk With Us and Listen: Building Sustainable Reconciliation in Africa*. Washington, DC: Georgetown University Press.
Villa-Vicencio, Charles and Wilhelm Verwoerd. 2000. *Looking Back, Reaching Forward: Reflections on the Truth and Reconciliation of South Africa*. Cape Town: University of Cape Town Press.

South Korea

The modern history of South Korea was tainted by Japanese colonialism, internal unrest, the Korean War, and four repressive military and authoritarian regimes, which produced many civilian victims. Since democratizing in 1987, South Korea has launched criminal prosecutions, truth commissions, and reparation programs. Remarkable progress in this area was made under Presidents Dae-Jung Kim (1998–2003) and Moo-Hyun Roh (2003–2008). However, since the inauguration of President Myung-Bak Lee, who opposes transitional justice, relevant laws and institutions have been reexamined.

The Repressive Past

Recent South Korean history was marked by Japanese colonialism (1910–1945), the U.S. military occupation (1945–1948), the war with the communist North Korea (1950–1953), the dictatorship of Syng-Man Rhee (1948–1960), and the military and authoritarian regimes of Chung-Hee Park (1961–1979), Doo-Hwan Chun (1980–1988), and Tae-Woo Roh (1988–1993). South Korea experienced three political transitions from the past abusive regimes to democracy (1945, 1960, and 1987) and one from war or internal conflicts to peace (1953).

The repressive Japanese colonial rule, marked by political repression and economic exploitation, ended when the Japanese emperor surrendered to the Allied forces in 1945 (see entry on Japan). Korean suffering under Japanese colonialism had been exacerbated during and after World War I and World War II. In 1919, a nationwide independence movement led to 7,500 South Koreans being killed, 16,000 wounded, and 47,000 arrested. Koreans suffered the most after the outbreak of the second Sino-Japanese War in 1937, when their country became a reservoir of manpower and resources for the Japanese military and industry, and thousands of Korean women were forced to work as sex slaves, known as "comfort women," for the Japanese military. Some 140,000 men and women were victims of forced labor (60,000 in the military and 80,000 in industry) during World War II.

After the liberation of 1945, the situation did not improve for several years. Until 1950, Korea faced political turmoil and armed strife between the U.S. occupation forces and leftist Korean political groups. In 1948, two important events occurred: the Jeju events (see entry on the National Committee for the Investigation of the Truth about the Jeju April 3 Events) and the Yeosu-Suncheon military revolt. Both started as armed uprisings initiated by communist groups and ended with the mass killings of civilians by communist insurgents, the police, and the military. Approximately 15,000 civilians were killed, mostly by the military, police, and paramilitary groups in Jeju, and some 2,000 were killed in Yeosu-Suncheon, mostly by the military.

The Korean War (1950–1953), which pitted communist North Korea against capitalist South Korea (backed by the U.S. military), left 643,744 combat deaths and injuries and marked the height of civilian massacres in Korean history. During the war, the nationwide systemic killings of civilians were committed by all parties to the conflict. For example, 700 villagers in Geochang were murdered by the South Korean 9th Regiment in 1951 and 400 refugees were killed in Nogeun-ri by the U.S. 7th Cavalry Regiment in 1950. Strikingly, massacres occurred in both combat and noncombat areas. Massacres of civilians suspected of being communist supporters or being related to communists occurred nationwide immediately after the outbreak of the war. Under President Rhee, the military and the police killed at least 300,000 without due process.

After the war, the Rhee dictatorship lasted for seven more years, engaging in anticommunist policy, suppressing civil and political rights, censoring opposition, and regarding any criticism of the regime as a breach of the National Security Act. Political opponents like Bong-Am Cho (representing the Progress Party) were severely punished, even condemned to death. Communists were purged from the police, the military, the Congress, and the public administration, and many lost their lives. In 1960, Rhee's dictatorship was overturned by student-led demonstrations prompted by electoral fraud and the murder of a student protestor by the police.

Democracy lasted for only a year. People's discontent grew as they experienced economic decline as a result of political instability. After staging a military coup in May 1961, General Chung-Hee Park pursued anticommunism, sought export-based economic growth, and suppressed basic human rights. Like Rhee, Park silenced his opponents, maintained low wages for workers, prevented labor unionization, and terrorized citizens to make them submit to authoritarian rule. Prominent political opponents like Jong-Gil Choi and Joon-Ha Jang were mysteriously found dead in 1973 and 1975, respectively, while Dae-Jung Kim was kidnapped by the secret service and almost drowned in the Pacific Ocean in 1973. In 1971, opposition grew when Park amended the constitution. The dictator was assassinated by one of his subordinates in 1979.

The brief moment of democratization known as the Seoul Spring was followed by another military coup, staged by Generals Doo-Hwan Chun and Tae-Woo Roh in December 1979. The generals became presidents in 1980–1988 (Chun) and 1988–1993 (Roh), pursuing anticommunist, development-oriented, and authoritarian policies. During their rule, the level of repression and surveillance equaled that of the Park regime. The most important resistance to military rule occurred in 1980 in Gwangju and was mainly triggered by the martial law of May 17, 1980. Brutally suppressed by the military, the protests left 5,060 victims (including 154 dead, 70 missing, and 3,028 injured, as well as 1,628 arrests, tortures, and detentions). The victims were mostly civilian, mainly students and youth who opposed military dictatorship.

In 1987, Chun amended the constitution to obstruct the formation of an opposition party. The constitutional amendments and the death of a university student as a result of drowning-in-the-tub torture united South Korean civil society against Chun. Students, politicians, and ordinary citizens participated in the demonstrations. As a result of public pressure, Tae-Woo Roh, Chun's proclaimed successor, agreed to organize direct presidential elections on June 29, 1987, when Roh was elected president because the opposition divided its support between Young-Sam Kim and Dae-Jung Kim. (Chun did not run for reelection.)

Transitional Justice

Since 1948, three types of transitional justice measures were adopted in South Korea: criminal prosecutions, truth commissions and investigatory committees, and reparation, the second being the most frequently employed choice.

Truth Commissions

The Special Committee and Court for the Punishment
of Pro-Japanese Collaborators

Shortly after the Republic of Korea was established in 1948, Special Act 3/1948 created the Special Committee and Court for the Punishment of the Pro-Japanese Collaborators, designed to investigate and punish collaborators with the Japanese colonial rule. Sang-Deok Kim, a respected leader of the national independence movement, headed the ten-member Committee, which had its own enforcement unit and ten regional offices. The Special Court was composed of sixteen judges who had the authority to sentence former collaborators to death for crimes of treason or murder. Within four months, the Committee arrested 305 suspected collaborators and named 1,000 others it planned to further investigate. Subsequently, the Court investigated 682 cases, indicted 221, and convicted 14 collaborators.

However, the Committee and Court were doomed to fail because they lacked the support of the government, which included members of the colonial-era elite who had retained their positions under the protection of the U.S. military government. President Rhee was the Committee's most vocal opponent, refusing to remove identified former collaborators from high positions in his administration. With his protection, former collaborators vehemently accused the Committee and Court members of being communists who threatened national unity by evaluating the past. The Committee and Court members were constantly under the threat of assassination, and in 1949 the police raided their offices. The activities of the Committee and Court gradually withered because of strong resistance from powerful former collaborators, reflecting the fact that finding the truth about the past was an ideologically controversial political issue. The Special Act was annulled in 1951.

The Special Committees for the Investigation of Pro-Japanese Collaborators
and of Forced Labor under the Japanese Rule

Because of the failure of this first attempt to investigate and punish them, the issue of the pro-Japanese collaborators reemerged when the Special Act 7203/2004 was enacted.

In 2005, the Special Committee for the Investigation of Pro-Japanese Collaborators was established. The eleven-member Committee, headed by history professor Dae-Gyeong Seong, had the same mandate as its predecessor but was much less powerful because its objective was limited to investigating and identifying former collaborators. In 2010, the new Committee published its final report, consisting of 25 volumes of 21,000 pages in total and naming 1,005 collaborators.

In addition, the Special Committee for the Investigation of Forced Labor under the Japanese Rule was created by Special Act 7174/2004. The eleven-member Committee headed by economics professor Gi-Ho Jeon has investigated the issue of forced labor under the Japanese colonial rule. At the time of this writing, that Committee has already received 142,527 applications and is still working.

The National Committee for the Investigation of the Truth about the Jeju April 3 Events

Because the Jeju massacres started as communist uprisings, addressing civilian massacres related to these events were extremely difficult under anticommunist regimes where the dead and missing were believed to be either communist guerillas or their supporters. Victims and their families had to remain silent because, for more than fifty years, any actions to address civilian deaths were deemed illegal according to the National Security Act. Special Act 6117/2000 established the National Committee for the Investigation of the Truth about the Jeju April 3 Events (see separate entry), which is still working at the time of this writing, screening victims and carrying out commemoration projects. In 2003, the Committee released its final report with the names of 15,093 victims, and President Roh made two official apologies to the victims in 2003 and 2006. Most textbooks have departed from previous characterization of the events as a communist rebellion and moved toward a more balanced description of the armed uprising and civilian sacrifices. In addition, small monetary subsidies were selectively granted since 2003 to the victims and their family members who suffered economic hardship and physical and mental illness as a result of the events.

The Special Committee for the Investigation of Geochang Events

After his inauguration as the first civilian president in 1993, Young-Sam Kim, whose main support base was the Gyeongsang province, promised to investigate and make reparations to the victims of the Geochang massacres and other similar cases in the province during the Korean War (1950–1953). The Special Act 5148/1996 on Recovering the Honor of Victims of the Geochang Event and Others was enacted in 1996, and the Special Committee for the Investigation of Geochang Events started investigations in 1997. It acknowledged the responsibility of the military and identified 548 victims and 785 family members. Although the Special Act addressed massacres that had occurred in other parts of the country, the Committee investigated only the Geochang massacre. Except for a few commemoration projects, no further actions were taken beyond this investigation to redress those crimes. Lawsuits brought by the victims' families against the government for monetary compensation ended without success in 2008.

The Congressional Committee for the Investigation of Civilian Deaths

The second attempt to investigate the civilian deaths during the Korean War occurred immediately after Rhee's resignation in 1960. The Congress created the Committee for the Investigation of Civilian Deaths, composed of nine lawmakers and headed by Congressman Cheon Choi. The Committee was to conduct preliminary fact finding on the civilian mass murders by the South Korean military and police during the war in order to draft further legislation on redressing those crimes and compensating victims. Although the victims and their families had high expectations, the investigations were abandoned after only two weeks. The resulting 7,000 pages of stenographic records and the victims' applications were deposited with the congressional archives. The Committee's failure to fulfill its mandate is partly attributable to the timing of its creation. Although Rhee had stepped down, the National Assembly still included many perpetrators directly or indirectly responsible for the massacres. Lawmakers established the Committee as a result of public pressure, but some committee members and the chair were reluctant to unearth a past in which they themselves had been involved. For example, Choi was the police director of the most heavily affected area (Jeju, Gyeongsang) during the war.

The Congressional Committee on Gwangju

After 1987, two kinds of human rights abuses under the military and authoritarian regimes drew national attention: the massive deaths and injuries of protestors in Gwangju in 1980, and the systematic deaths and disappearance of opposition leaders and activists (1961–1988). After President Chun stepped down in 1988, a nationwide focus was given to the 1980 Gwangju massacre, for which Chun and the incumbent Tae-Woo Roh bore responsibility. Lawmakers established the Congressional Committee on Gwangju and held public hearings by summoning seventy relevant persons, including Chun. It was the first time in Korean history when the former president was brought into public hearing and questioned. However, the Committee lacked support from the Roh regime and the power to force reluctant perpetrators to testify in public.

The Presidential Truth Commission on Suspicious Deaths and the Presidential Truth Commission on Military Suspicious Deaths

The deaths and disappearances of students, activists, and politicians under the military and authoritarian regimes (1961–1993) received attention under President Dae-Jung Kim (1998–2003), who was nearly drowned in the Pacific Ocean by Korean Central Intelligence Agency (KCIA) agents in 1973. Special Act 6170/2000 created the Presidential Truth Commission on Suspicious Deaths (see separate entry) to identify the causes of deaths suspected to have been carried out directly and indirectly by government agents during the 1961–1993 period. The Committee investigated 85 individual cases and published 2 reports totaling 6 volumes of more than 4,300 pages. On its recommendation, the Presidential Truth Commission on Military Suspicious Deaths was created in 2006. Until 2010, it further investigated the suspicious death cases that occurred in the military.

The Truth and Reconciliation Commission

The third attempt to investigate civilian deaths during the Korean War came only in 2000. After the coup led by General Chung-Hee Park in 1961, the transitional justice movement was suppressed. In addition, the military police systematically destroyed any evidence of massacres, including monuments and mass graves. It thus took almost forty years to reorganize the movement. In 2000, victims and families created the National Association of the Bereaved Families of the Korean War. Its dedicated activism, and the support of President Moo-Hyun Roh, led to the adoption of the Framework Act 7542/2005 on Clearing up the Past Events for Truth and Reconciliation and the creation of the Truth and Reconciliation Commission (TRC; see separate entry). At the time of this writing, the TRC has received 8,175 individual applications concerning civilian massacres during the war and confirmed state responsibility for 76 percent of cases.

Criminal Prosecutions

The Military Tribunal against Perpetrators of Geochang Massacre

The first attempt to prosecute the civilian massacres committed during the Korean War came after the South Korean army murdered 700 villagers in Geochang in 1951. Immediately following the massacre, an ad hoc Investigation Committee, composed of lawmakers and government ministers, was created by Congress. After the investigation, the committee transferred the case to the standing military tribunal. Three army officers were convicted for murder and destruction of evidence, but they were pardoned by President Rhee during the war (1951–1953) and even held high positions in his administration. Families of victims could not collect the remains of the dead and were constantly under surveillance and threat. Because of the Geochang case, victims of other much more severe massacres nationwide remained silent under the Rhee regime. The perpetrators of these other crimes were never forced to assume responsibility.

Court Proceedings against Dictators and Their Subordinates

Demands for truth and justice constantly increased during the first civilian government of President Young-Sam Kim (1993–1998), when human rights lawyers and activists filed several criminal lawsuits against Chun, Roh, and their subordinates. After intensive investigation, the Seoul District Prosecutor's Office acknowledged the crimes of general murder in the course of suppressing Gwangju protestors in 1980, but decided not to prosecute the case on the grounds that the coup of 1979 and the violent suppression of protestors was not subject to legal jurisdiction because these measures were "highly political behavior beyond the legal judgment" (Jeong 1995). After the public and the political elites denounced the decision, Congress, with President Kim's support, approved Special Act 5029/1995, which removed the statute of limitations and provided the grounds for prosecution. Chun and Roh were arrested, tried, and sentenced to death and imprisonment, respectively, but later pardoned by President Dae-Jung Kim as a widely supported gesture of reconciliation.

Reparation and Restoration Programs

Reparations to Gwangju Victims

In response to growing national attention, Congress adopted Act 4266/1990 for Compensating the Victims of the Gwangju Democracy Movement, the first law to grant governmental reparations to victims of state violence. By 1998, individual reparations worth 210 billion Won (US$175 million) had been made to 4,537 victims (247 deaths, 64 missing, 2,865 injuries, and 1,361 arrests or indictments).

Reparations and Restoration for the Victims of Pro-Democracy Movement

Act 6123/2000 on Reparations and Restoration for the Victims of the Pro-Democracy Movement granted individual reparation and restoration for the victims of suspicious deaths and other governmental abuses under the military and authoritarian regimes (1961–1993). At the time of this writing, 13,408 individual applications were under examination by the reparation committee.

Conclusion

Examinations of past events that have deeply scarred and divided a society are always difficult, the more so when those events are more than fifty years old and consecutive military and authoritarian regimes have systematically concealed the truth and intentionally destroyed the evidence. This explains the impressive number of transitional justice measures adopted by South Korea after 1987. Overall, these measures resulted in presidential apologies, the establishment of memorial parks and museums, the revision of official documents and history textbooks, and the creation of permanent research or memorial foundations. Victims and their families could clear their names of the false accusation of being communists or communist sympathizers. However, too many initiatives were launched under Presidents Dae-Jung Kim and Moo-Hyun Roh (2000–2008). Both opponents and supporters of transitional justice have questioned whether all these measures could be effectively carried out with limited budgetary means without causing public transitional justice fatigue or severe backlash by the opponents. These concerns turned out to be valid when President Myung-Bak Lee criticized the committees and proposed downsizing their budget by merging various committees and rejecting the committees' requests for renewal.

Hunjoon Kim

Cross-reference: Japan; National Committee for the Investigation of the Truth about the Jeju April 3 Events; Presidential Truth Commission on Suspicious Deaths; Truth and Reconciliation Commission, Republic of Korea.

Further Readings

Han, In Sup. 2005. Kwangju and Beyond: Coping with Past State Atrocities in South Korea. *Human Rights Quarterly*, 27: 998–1045.
Han, Sung-Joo. 1974. *The Failure of Democracy in South Korea*. Berkeley: University of California Press.
Hayes, William A. 2005. Do Springs of Democracy Lead to Falls of Justice? State-Civil Contests for Political Accountability in South Korea. *Journal of Human Rights*, 4: 251–265.
Jeong, Woong-Ki. 1995. The Prosecution Exempted All Related to the Gwangju Event from Indictment. *The Chosun Ilbo*, July 19.
Kim, Sunhyuk. 2000. *Politics of Democratization in Korea*. Pittsburgh: University of Pittsburgh Press.
Truth and Reconciliation Commission of South Korea. 2008. *Truth and Reconciliation are Steps for the Future*. Available at: http://www.jinsil.go.kr/English/index.asp (accessed January 3, 2010).

Spain

After the death of dictator General Francisco Franco in 1975, Spain implemented a transitional justice program based on consensus and strictly limited to providing reparations for victims and removing the symbols of the dictatorship, with no role for criminal justice. Transitional justice involved a general amnesty simultaneously covering persons condemned by, and officials of, the Franco regime. The unprecedented character of amnesty, the strong consensus among political parties on democratization, the lack of criminal justice, the ad hoc implementation of reparatory justice, and the removal of symbols are known collectively as the "Spanish model," built around the forgive-and-forget principle. After 2000, the model has been challenged. Nongovernmental organizations' efforts in the field of exhumations and pressure from left-wing parties led to the condemnation of the Franco regime in 2002 and the adoption of the Law 52/2007 Recognizing and Expanding the Rights and Establishing Measures in Favor of Those Who Suffered Prosecution or Violence during the Civil War and the Dictatorship (known as the Law on Historical Memory). However, despite growing demands, the Spanish model has remained consistently averse to any kind of measure related to justice for perpetrators.

The Repressive Past

Between 1936 and 1939, Spain was ravaged by a bloody civil war in which the nationalist forces, supported by Fascist Italy and Nazi Germany, fought the republican forces, aided by the Soviet Union. After winning the war, which left between 190,000 and 500,000 people dead, General Franco and his Fascist supporters instituted a forty-year-long dictatorship whose specific nature was described by Juan Linz as authoritarian. Initially, Franco's Spain had a totalitarian character, but after the fall of the Nazi and Fascist regimes and in response to increased international criticism, it became an authoritarian regime in which anticommunism and Catholicism (elevated to the status of official state religion) complemented a semideveloped organicist view of society and state that equated the two to living organisms with specific functions similar to the functions organs have in human bodies. Its anticommunism helped the regime survive and win international support: in 1955, the United States sponsored Spain's accession to the United Nations, despite Western Europe's critical view of the regime. (In 1964, Western European states did not accept Spain as an associate member of the European Economic Community because of its lack of democracy and disrespect for human rights.)

Patterns of violence and repression reflected this evolution: the most extensive and arbitrary violence occurred during the civil war and the years immediately following it (up to 1942). Franco's forces considered any person who fought against them guilty of the crime of military rebellion. Penalties ranged from the death sentence to internment in concentration camps (the last of which was closed in 1962) or forced enrollment in disciplinary battalions. Conscripts fulfilling their military obligations in the anti-Franco republican army were enrolled in Disciplinary Battalions of Working Soldiers, which were in fact forced labor units known for their very tough discipline. Political parties that did not support Franco's cause were banned, civil servants who opposed Franco were purged, and properties were confiscated from those who opposed Franco.

In 1939, repression was entrusted to special nonmilitary authorities. The Law for the Purge of Public Employees allowed for the removal of public servants for political reasons, and the Law on Political Responsibilities became a key repression tool by defining as crimes a large number of deeds, including having supported a political party of the Republic coalition government. The Law for the Repression of the Freemasonry and Communism of 1940 created the Special Court for the Repression of Freemasonry and Communism). After 1940, the dictatorship tried members of the republican forces in the *General Case Instructed by the Prosecutor on Criminal Acts Committed throughout the National Territory during the Red Domination of Spain*. These trials also investigated noncriminal actions such as involvement in the political activities of governmental authorities, security and armed forces, and left-wing parties from 1931 to 1939. Investigations and prosecutions lasted until the early 1960s and included the publication in 1943 of the book *La dominación roja en España: Causa Genera [The Red Domination in Spain: General Cause]*. The resulting sentences included confiscation of property, fines, removal from public posts, and prison terms of twenty to thirty years for top officials and twelve to twenty years for lower-ranking members of administration, political parties, and the army or mere supporters of the Republic. The Law of State Security of 1941 and the revised Criminal Code of 1940 included a long list of crimes against the nation's reputation, security, and unity, apart from crimes such as sedition, rebellion, and illegal political activities.

In the 1960s, repression sought to prevent potential popular mobilization against the regime's anticommunist ideological foundations. In 1963, a new Court for Public Order assumed the functions formerly assigned to the Special Court for the Repression of Freemasonry and Communism, and the Criminal Code criminalized strikes and unauthorized associations and meetings. All political and union-related crime cases previously heard by the military or Special Court were turned over to the Court for Public Order and its police arm, the Political Social Brigade of the Police, which were the regime's main repressive instruments in its later years. In 1969, Franco approved Decree-Law 10 Prescribing All Crimes Committed before April 1, 1939, which amounted to an amnesty. Repression lasted even after his death in 1975, into the first stages of democratization.

Transitional Justice

In post-Franco Spain, transitional justice consisted mainly of compensation and reparations for victims, offered by the national government. Local authorities tackled symbolic measures (mainly the removal of symbols of the dictatorship and their replacement with symbols of the new democracy), but they lacked a coherent framework, and as such, some regions did more than others in this regard. As a result of the 2006 government report, *Inter-ministerial Commission General Report for the Study of the Situation of Victims of Civil War and Francoism*, Law 52/2007 sought to address calls for transitional justice by providing a comprehensive approach to the issue and proposing new measures, but it only led to calls for a renewed effort to come to terms with the past more vigorously.

Exhumation and Identification of Victims

Under Franco, 140,000 people were disappeared (*desaparecidos*) or killed, and their remains were not identified. Because the post-Franco authorities made no effort to open common graves, nongovernmental organizations became the driving force for the recovery of the remains and the identification of victims. Between 2000 and 2008, the Association for the Recovery of Historical Memory (Asociación para la Recuperación de la Memoria Histórica, ARMH) recovered the bodies and remains of 400 people from some 200 common graves. Exhumations were complicated by the lack of clear protocols for opening the graves and inspecting their contents, and the lack of cooperation on the part of the local authorities competent in exhumation. Moreover, the 2007 law failed to recognize "identification and/or location" of remains as the victims' right or the government's duty, making instead the central authorities' responsibility to exhume and identify victims complementary to private and regional actions. In April 2009, the Senate rejected amendments to the 2007 law that obliged central authorities to locate and identify victims.

Local governments' actions have depended on their ideological position. Regional governments that did act included those of the Basque Country, Catalonia, Galicia, and Andalucia. In the Basque Country, an Inter-departmental Commission was created in 2002 to facilitate the identification and location of persons executed during the civil war, and one year later, the Human Rights Department of the Basque Country signed a collaboration agreement with the Aranzadi Science Society (Sociedad de Ciencias Aranzadi) to open local common graves and identify the remains. By 2003, the Basque government had reviewed 490 applications from individuals and associations. Nine graveyards were opened in the region. The total count in the Basque Country is 8,560 disappeared or dead between 1936 and 1939, of which 2,352 were prisoners who had been shot.

So far, the Catalan government has developed the most comprehensive approach to dealing with these issues. In June 2004, it supported the drafting of an exhumation protocol, and in 2007 it approved a four-year program to raise awareness about ex-prisoners, disappeared persons, and common graves, to coordinate and assist the exhumation of common graves, and to map sites with the remains of disappeared persons. In June 2009, the Catalan parliament passed a law obliging the regional government to locate and exhume and/or dignify of the mass graveyards including the remains of both republican and nationalist disappeared persons on Catalan territory. Overall, the Catalan government has identified 3,113 disappeared persons and has mapped 179 mass graveyards. Catalonia has also been active in the field of identification of victims.

The Galician government sponsored the academic project Victims, Names, Voices, which seeks to count the victims, disclose their fate, and record their testimony. In 2003, the Andalucian government created a Technical Committee for the identification of the victims and their exhumation. Best known were efforts to recover the remains of poet Federico García Lorca, which rendered no conclusive results.

Justice for Victims: Restitution, Rehabilitation, and Reparations

Justice for victims, both material and symbolic, has been the most robust component of the Spanish transitional justice.

Public servants purged by the Franco regime were allowed to return to their posts in 1976, followed by local civil servants one year later. In 1986, military personnel repressed by Franco were rehabilitated and allowed to rejoin the army.

As the *Informe general* recognized, nothing was done to annul Francoist sentences (*Informe general* 2006: 30). Moreover, by 2008, the Supreme Court had rejected forty-two applications for reviewing such sentences (Gil 2009). As there was legal continuity with the Franco regime, the Supreme Court Military Chamber rejected the reassessment of Francoist military trials on the grounds that they were carried according to the law in force at the time. Law 52/2007 did not annul the decisions of those trials, but declared as illegitimate all sentences of special or ordinary courts that repressed political or ideological conducts. In 2001, the Congress of Deputies rehabilitated *guerrilleros*, the isolated guerrilla groups that after the civil war fought against Franco, by purging from their records the terms *bandoleros* (bandits) and *malhechores* (malefactors).

In 1996, the Spanish Parliament granted Spanish nationality to members of the International Brigades (foreigners who fought in the Spanish civil war in support of the Republic). Law 52/2007 extended this benefit to descendants of exiled persons who escaped Franco's repression after the civil war. Some 500,000 individuals from Argentina, Uruguay, Cuba, Chile, Venezuela, Mexico, and France could become Spanish nationals this way. Applications were accepted from December 28, 2008 to December 28, 2010. By May 2009, 39,134 applications had been submitted, 10,010 persons obtained Spanish nationality, and 13,696 applications were pending final approval.

Spanish transitional justice has emphasized economic compensations. The emphasis is much stronger on pensions than on indemnities. A total of 574,000 applications asked for both indemnities and pensions (*Informe General 2006*, 57) which up to 2005 amounted to a total sum of 16,356 million Euros. Of these, 391 million Euros covered indemnities and 15.965 million Euros covered pensions. In January 2006, the *Informe general* counted 95,943 beneficiaries and mentioned that in 1991, these persons absorbed 26 percent of the total cost of pensions in Spain (*Informe general 2006*, 57).

Restitution of assets and property has targeted political parties, trade or labor unions, and, less often, public institutions (such as the Catalan government during the civil war). Individuals have not received their property back other than official and personal documents confiscated by the Franco regime.

Prosecutions, Criminality, and Purges

The only attempt to deliver criminal justice was represented by the proceedings Judge Baltasar Garzón initiated in 2008 at the National Audience, a first-instance court hearing cases of terrorism, drug trafficking, and crimes against humanity. For him, the absence of investigation of crimes meant impunity for perpetrators, and "opening up the judicial proceeding was a form of institutional rehabilitation in front of the silence that has not only granted extinction of criminal responsibility but also impunity" (Auto Diligencias Previas 2008, 56). He argued that the decision to kill and disappear people was consciously planned and executed and therefore a crime against humanity. As perpetrators violated the Constitution of 1931 and the legal order of that time, the National Audience was the applicable jurisdiction. To address the problem of retroactivity (see entry on Ex Post Facto Issues), Garzón argued that the crime of forced disappearance was a permanent one equivalent to illegal detention in the framework of crimes against humanity. Forced disappearances were used to impede the identification of victims of Francoist forces and the eventual pursuit of justice by victims' relatives. On the eventual coverage of the crimes by the 1977 amnesty law, the judge argued that the crime persisted because the victims were never found, and as such amnesty cannot be applied. Moreover, in his view, Law 46/1977 on Amnesty did not cover genocide, crimes against humanity, and war crimes committed outside combat. The judge also proposed the creation of a Group of Experts and a Group of Judicial Police to research disappearances, and mandated the exhumation of nineteen common graves, including that in which García Lorca is presumed to be.

These proceedings met strong opposition from various quarters, including the prosecutor, who challenged the judge's competence on the matter. (In the Spanish legal system, the instructing magistrate [*juez instructor*] technically constructs the case but does not conduct the trial. The prosecutor, who represents the state, demands a certain qualification for the crime and, eventually, a certain sentence and penalty. Hence, he/she may disagree with the instructing magistrate.) In response to the prosecutor's appeal, the Penal Chamber ruled that the judge was not competent to hear the case and ordered the halt of all exhumations ordered by Garzón. Three magistrates opposed this ruling as, in their view, it may open the door for foreign or international jurisdictions to consider themselves competent to hear similar cases. The fact that these crimes are recognized by international law and the lack of action from national courts could justify external courts' involvement.

File Access

Access to files of Francoist repression from 1936 onward has not been a central issue in Spain's reckoning with the past. Rather, complaints have related to the dispersion, lack of regulation of relevant archives, and lack of a general overall regulation of archives in Spain. There was, however, a long-standing political debate around the transfer of official documents that Franco confiscated in Catalonia after the war to the current Catalan authorities. Finally, Law 21/2005 on the Restitution to the Catalonian Government of Documents in the General Archive of the Spanish Civil War and the Creation of the Documentary Center on Historical Memory permitted the transfer of these official documents to the Catalan government and transformed the General Archive of the Civil War (which kept all kind of documents related to Francoist repression) into the Documentary Centre for Historical Memory and General Archive of the Civil War. It became an independent archive located in Salamanca and accessible to all citizens.

Symbolic Measures

The Franco regime created numerous symbols (including statues, street names, and coins and bank bills) that permeated everyday life in Spain. Transitional justice would have required the removal of these symbols, but in practice the country chose to leave these symbols untouched. Until the 2007 Law, there was no unitary policy of removing these symbols. Scattered initiatives at the national, regional, and local levels targeted specific symbols and, as a result, the Francoist symbols have slowly disappeared, while some continued to coexist with democratic and historic symbols. In many localities, street names glorified the Franco regime, the civil war, and the military/political leaders of the winning side.

Removal of different symbols varied in speed and intensity. The national flag with Franco's coat of arms, coins, and stamps featuring Franco, and other authoritarian symbols were withdrawn by the early 1980s, but the changing of street names with references to Franco, his political and military elite, and authoritarian regime was much slower. At the time of this writing, many streets in different Spanish cities still retain those names. As the Franco regime was highly personalized, his statues dominated other types of monuments during his rule. Numerous monuments were dedicated to the leaders of the regime, its generals, and leaders of the fascist party (the Falange). Removal of these statues proceeded slowly. The last statue of Franco was removed only in 2009. Some of the removed statues have been stored in military barracks.

The most important Francoist monument is the Valley of the Fallen, located near Madrid, which includes an enormous basilica and monument. Another Francoist monument, the Arch of Victory in Madrid, is dedicated to those who fell for God and Spain. It has attracted much less attention than any other monument, despite its size and conspicuous location at the northwest entry of the capital.

Education and Awareness

Spain's reckoning with the past has largely neglected education. The Spanish authorities have adopted no clear policy on teaching history, although there were notorious shortcomings in factual knowledge. The Royal Decree 1467/2007 Establishing the Structure of the Baccalaureat that regulated the history of Spain curriculum in secondary schools asked students to examine the factors that contributed to the start of the civil war. This implicit neutral position seems inconsistent with a critical review of the dictatorship. For grades 12 and 16, the view of the period in geography and history is presented as economic history, and most textbooks do not refer to the darker side of the Francoist regime, such as the repression mechanism and its victims.

Conclusion

Spain presents a model of partial transitional justice in which criminal justice has been conspicuously absent initially, whereas later efforts sought to provide victims with restitution, rehabilitation, and reparations. In this respect, the model has moved from the traditional forgive-and-forget approach to a new one in which forgetting has been replaced with numerous measures that nevertheless carefully avoid criminal justice.

Carlos Closa

Cross-references: Ex Post Facto Issues.

Further Readings

Auto Diligencias Previas Proc. *Abreviado 399 /2006 V Juzgado Central de Instrucción Nº 005*. Madrid: Audiencia Nacional, October 16, 2008.

Aguilar, Paloma. 2008. *Políticas de la memoria y memorias de la política: el caso español en perspectiva comparada* [Politics of Memory and Memory of Politics: The Spanish Case in Comparative Perspective]. Madrid: Alianza editorial.

De Andrés. Jesús. 2006. *Los símbolos y la memoria del Franquismo* [The Symbols and Memory of Francoism]. Madrid: Fundacion Alternativa. Available at: http://www.falternativas.org/estudios-de-progreso/documentos/documentos-de-trabajo/los-simbolos-y-la-memoria-del-franquismo (accessed July 29, 2010).

Gálvez, Sergio. 2006. El proceso de recuperación de la "memoria histórica." *International Journal of Iberian Studies*, 19(1): 25–51.

Gil, Alicia. 2009. *La justicia de transición en España: de la amnistía a la memoria histórica* [Transitional Justice in Spain: From Amnesty to Historical Memory]. Madrid: Atelier Libros Jurídicos.

Informe General de la Comision interministerial para el estudio de la situación de las víctimas de la Guerra Civil y del Franquismo [Inter-ministerial Commission General Report for the Study of the situation of victims of Civil War and Francoism]. July 28, 2006. Available at: http://www1.mpr.es/uploads/media/pdf/6/informegeneral2_1232475655.pdf (accessed August 11, 2010).

La Causa General. *La dominación roja en España.* Available at: http://www.causageneral.net/ (accessed August 10, 2010).

Linz, Juan. 2000. *Totalitarian and Authoritarian Regimes.* Boulder: Linne Ryenner.

Todos los Nombres. n.d. Official Web site. Available at: http://www.todoslosnombres.org/ (accessed July 29, 2010).

Sri Lanka

Despite decades of political violence entailing widespread human rights violations, there has been little political commitment to engage in transitional justice initiatives in Sri Lanka. Past attempts have focused primarily on commissions of inquiry into disappearance, an abuse that constituted a central feature of the state's counterinsurgency strategy and wider rule. While the findings and recommendations of such commissions provide some basis on which to engage in transitional justice discourse, political commitment to either act on them or encourage public debate about the aspiration of "never again" has been largely absent. Given their narrow mandates, limited powers, and reliance on those in power to realize their recommendations, commissions of inquiry have increasingly been viewed with skepticism by many Sri Lankans.

The Repressive Past

Since the 1970s, tens of thousands of persons have disappeared in Sri Lanka, primarily at the hands of government security forces. Disappearances have largely taken place in two primary contexts: an armed insurgency by the ethnic Sinhalese nationalist Janatha Vimukthi Peramuna (JVP) from 1987 to 1990 in the south, and the two-decade-long separatist conflict with the ethnic Tamil nationalist Liberation Tigers of Tamil Eelam (LTTE) in the north and east. While presidential commissions established in the 1990s found that more than 20,000 persons had disappeared, a number of local human rights groups believe that the actual figure may have been up to two or three times higher.

The first cases of disappearance were reported in 1971 in the context of an armed JVP insurgency in which thousands of Sinhalese youth disappeared following arrest. The insurgency was met by the United Front government with the imposition of emergency regulations and deployment of security forces. While allegations were reported in the north throughout the 1970s, disappearance reemerged as a key counterinsurgency strategy in late 1984 in the context of the escalating LTTE separatist armed struggle. Hundreds of young ethnic Tamil men suspected of supporting or sympathizing with the LTTE were forcibly removed from their homes or arrested and disappeared, often in retaliation for LTTE attacks on ethnic Sinhalese civilians.

The number of reports of disappearances rose considerably from mid-1987, particularly in the southern and central provinces, leading up to the 1988–1990 "time of terror," considered the most violent period in Sri Lankan history. Thousands of persons were disappeared or extrajudicially executed, primarily by government security forces, in the context of a second armed insurgency by the JVP in the south during this period. While Sinhalese male youth suspected of belonging to or supporting the JVP were primarily targeted for disappearance, the insurgency was used as a guise under which the ruling party was able to disappear supporters of the main opposition party and other alleged opponents to its rule. The annihilation of the JVP coincided with the collapse of a fourteen-month cease-fire agreement and resumption of hostilities with the LTTE in June 1990. With the outbreak of the second Eelam War, security force personnel was transferred to the north and east, where they effectively implemented the same counterinsurgency tactics against the LTTE, of which disappearance was a salient feature. Within months, scores of disappearances and extrajudicial killing were reported.

The involvement of security force personnel in disappearance was facilitated by Emergency Regulations, which granted the military sweeping powers along with broad impunity from prosecution. The Emergency Regulations removed basic constitutional safeguards while providing the security forces extraordinary powers of arrest and detention with fewer checks and balances on their actions. Several provisions contained within them created a legal framework conducive to disappearance, including provision for arrest without a warrant, indefinite detention based on vaguely defined charges, and no requirement to publish lists of authorized places of detention. Moreover, security force personnel were granted the power to dispose of dead bodies without public notification or post mortem examination, a provision that countered any opportunity to conduct investigations into custodial deaths. The Prevention of Terrorism Act (PTA) of 1979 also gave the police extraordinary powers to arrest without a warrant on mere suspicion and to detain persons for extended periods. Under the PTA, confessions extracted under torture or threat were permissible as evidence, in contravention of the Sri Lankan Constitution. The PTA was used as complementary law to that of the Emergency Regulations from its enactment. Such legislation, which became a central feature of governance at the expense of addressing the underlying political and socioeconomic grievances behind the violence, virtually replaced normal law for almost two decades.

Four presidential commissions of inquiry established to investigate disappearances from 1988 to 1994 found that the state, at the highest level, made possible the arrest or abduction and disappearance of persons without accountability. Statistics reveal that security force personnel (including the police and army as well as civilian home guards) were responsible for at least 67 percent of the 7,238 disappearances inquired into by the Presidential Commission of Inquiry into the Involuntary Removal or Disappearance of Persons in the Western, Southern and Sabaragamuwa Provinces (southern zonal commission) in which the identity of the perpetrator was noted by complainants. The involvement of politicians of the ruling United National Party (UNP) government was highlighted by complainants before the commissions, making recommendations concerning institutional reform all the more important. The commissions found, moreover, that all sides to the respective conflicts, including the JVP, LTTE, and a number of armed pro- and antigovernment militant groups, including death squads as well as private individuals, were responsible for serious human rights abuses such as disappearance, torture, and extrajudicial killings.

In the south, the majority of victims of disappearance and extrajudicial killings were young, ethnic Sinhalese rural male youths. In most cases, individuals disappeared following arrest or abduction from public locations, including bus stops, at any time of the day. The southern zonal commission found that of 8,739 complaints of disappearances before it, the majority of the disappeared were low-income earners (including cultivators, laborers, and traders) and 63 percent were aged between fifteen and twenty-nine years. However, the commission noted that persons from all walks of life were disappeared, including students, journalists, lawyers, teachers, Buddhist monks, trade unionists, and public servants.

As the JVP primarily directed its violence toward agents of the state, the state in turn targeted the JVP and its supporters, as well as the main opposition and other political parties. However, as the security forces took the view that the JVP sought out youth with leadership potential for recruitment, the responding counterinsurgency focused on the elimination of youth with perceived leadership qualities. In practice, however, all forms of dissent were equated with subversion. Indeed, persons acting on behalf of the disappeared, including family members and lawyers, were themselves threatened, abused, and, in many cases, disappeared. Operating with impunity under what was effectively a proxy command structure driven by narrow political interests, the security forces engaged in the repression rather than protection of the population, thereby creating an atmosphere of extreme uncertainty and fear. The resulting chaos provided an opportunity for existing social cleavages and political rivalries to come to the fore, leading to the involvement of a wide range of actors in the violence, including private groups and individuals, for political or personal gain. Within such a context, disappearance provided the perfect means to eliminate opponents without revelation of the truth, the identity of the perpetrators, or their motives. For this reason, a key transitional justice challenge for Sri Lanka is that of revealing, acknowledging, and addressing the involvement of all actors in the violence.

In the north and east, most victims were young ethnic Tamil male youths disappeared following arrest during cordon-and-search operations conducted by the security forces (including the army, navy, Special Task Force, and police). Scores were also reportedly disappeared in broad daylight from refugee camps and other places of shelter, including schools and churches, as well as from military checkpoints or their homes. For its part, the LTTE utilized abduction and killings as a means to control the Tamil community while deliberately targeting Sinhalese villagers to provoke the security forces. State-sponsored retaliation was therefore directed at Tamil civilians, a tactic that inadvertently strengthened support for the LTTE cause. The Presidential Commission of Inquiry into the Involuntary Removal or Disappearance of Persons in the Northern and Eastern Provinces (northern and eastern zonal commission) established that most of those disappeared were younger than thirty years of age and low-income earners. Many were targeted on the basis of their ethnicity and age alone.

Transitional Justice

The People's Alliance won power in 1994 after seventeen years of UNP rule on a reformist platform to establish commissions of inquiry into the disappearances of the late 1980s, achieve a political solution to the conflict with the LTTE, and end the culture of impunity. In November 1994, President Kumaratunga established three geographically focused commissions responsible to inquire into disappearances, thereby raising expectations among families of the disappeared and other survivors of political violence that the perpetrators would be promptly brought to account. Given Kumaratunga's willingness to identify herself with the families of the disappeared after her own husband's political assassination in 1988, many Sri Lankans held the view that a new era of justice and human rights had begun.

The three presidential commissions of inquiry were responsible for investigating allegations of disappearance from January 1, 1988 to 1994. However, with 10,136 outstanding complaints before them at the expiration of their mandate in May 1997, a fourth and final Presidential Commission of Inquiry into Involuntary Removal and Disappearance of Certain Persons (All Island) was established in April 1998 to complete investigation of the outstanding complaints. The all-island commission delivered its final report to the president in May 2000.

The commissions investigated, through testimony taking, whether persons were involuntarily removed or disappeared from their places of residence and to ascertain their present whereabouts. The commissions had the power to inquire into and report on complaints and allegations of disappearance at the hands of agents of the state, paramilitary groups acting in collaboration with them, subversives, including insurgency groups, and unknown persons. They were tasked with establishing the identity of the perpetrators, identifying legal proceedings that should be taken against them, and recommending preventive and other measures, including compensation for the families of the disappeared.

All four commissions found evidence of a widespread practice of disappearance, extrajudicial killings, and other forms of political violence undertaken primarily by state officials as well as by the insurgent JVP and LTTE movements and other pro- and antigovernment armed groups. However, few of the commissions' numerous and far-reaching recommendations were realized, and it was not long before complaints of disappearances and extrajudicial executions were reported under the watch of the People's Alliance, albeit on a considerably smaller scale.

During their tenure, the three initial commissions received a combined total of 27,526 complaints, verifying disappearance in 16,742 cases. The commissions were the first significant nationwide effort on the part of any Sri Lankan government to address state-sponsored political violence. The commissions' reports provide an overview of the nature and circumstances of the disappearances and the perpetrators. They offer a vivid account of personal and collective trauma, providing insight into the environment of terror, suspicion, and fear created as a result of widespread violations and the climate of impunity that prevailed. The need to recover the truth and expose the perpetrators in a context in which there had been a systematic effort on the part those involved to deceive and to conceal their actions or complicity was highlighted by the commissions themselves. To this intent, the four commissions' reports comprise an important official political and historical record of state-sponsored violence and its ramifications.

The commissions' recommendations are extensive and far-reaching. Indeed, the sheer range, scope, and number of recommendations reflect the complexity of the phenomenon of disappearance. The recommendations highlight preventive mechanisms including prosecutorial action as well as legal and administrative reform. They also seek to address the impact of disappearance on the families of the victims in relation to matters such as property, employment, inheritance, and social alienation.

A substantial number of recommendations focus on establishing mechanisms to facilitate expeditious prosecutorial action and reform of the security forces. Particular attention was given to ensuring that officials with chain-of-command responsibility were criminally liable, eliminating private armies sponsored by politicians, and reforming the Emergency

Regulations, including those that permitted the disposal of bodies without inquiry or inquest. The commissions recommended the immediate closure of secret and unauthorized places of detention and public access to information on all places of detention. Both the southern zonal commission and all-island commission recommended that a special committee be established under the auspices of the National Human Rights Commission to record evidence concerning perpetrators and recommend amnesty for those who confessed their participation in violations and provided full evidence of accompanying circumstances.

In light of the discrimination faced by many families of the disappeared on the basis of a political opinion imputed to them, the fact that many victims were family breadwinners, and the importance of compensating families for the state's failure to prevent the violence, recommendations sought to reestablish the relationship between families of the disappeared, the wider community, and the state. Concerned that future grievances held by children of affected families could be ignited in the form of another insurgency, the commissions emphasized restitution. Recommendations in this regard encompassed the principle of collective responsibility on the part of the Sri Lankan society as a whole to assist and support victims' families. They included a special tax to provide income support to affected families, the provision of vocational training and guaranteed employment for relatives of the disappeared, as well as a policy of positive discrimination toward relatives of the disappeared in relation to state employment.

Criticisms of the commissions have focused on their limited mandate and the lack of authority afforded to them to act on their own findings and recommendations. However, the commissions' impact was clearly undermined by an entrenched political culture with a preference for military solutions to substantially political problems. In terms of the operations of the commissions, the government's reliance on the security forces to fight the LTTE ensured that state officials had little incentive to cooperate or comply with commission proceedings. Security force personnel was able to simply deny all knowledge and involvement in disappearances and related abuses and resist efforts on the part of the commissions to obtain police and military records.

The People's Alliance government was slow and selective in responding to the commissions' recommendations while rarely publicly commenting on their findings. Initially, recommendations such as the payment of compensation and the provision of living assistance to families of the disappeared were acted on. From 1995 to 2003, compensation was provided to the families of 17,740 disappeared persons, including government employees. However, recommendations regarding equity in payment regardless of the political affiliation of the victim were not adhered to, as various departments and local authorities refused to pay compensation to the relatives of alleged terrorists and subversives disappeared during the violence. Many observers were also critical of the discrepancies in compensation based on the professional standing of the victims, as relatives of disappeared public servants received three times the amount awarded to relatives of other missing persons. Compensation effectively became, therefore, an additional source of grievance, further widening social cleavages among and between affected families and their communities rather than serving as reparations. However, such initiatives effectively came to a halt in 2006 when the National Human Rights Commission stopped disappearance investigations, stating that because its findings could result in recommendations to award state compensation, it required special government directions to continue.

Perhaps the most serious failure of the People's Alliance administration, however, concerned prosecutions and restoration of the rule of law. As the act of disappearance is not a criminal offense under Sri Lankan law, prosecutors were reliant on punishable offenses under the Penal Code, including that of abduction with intent to murder, wrongful confinement, torture, rape, and murder. While provisions of the Evidence Ordinance of Sri Lanka were not applicable to commission proceedings, thereby enabling the commissioners to come to findings based on the balance of probability, they provided lists of suspected perpetrators to the president with the intention that legal proceedings be initiated. As separate criminal proceedings were required under general law, however, the commissions had no power or influence over the extent to which the information they provided was used for this purpose.

The commissions identified perpetrators in relation to 3,861 cases of disappearance, leading to investigations in relation to 1,560 security force personnel, of whom 597 were indicted. Over the ten years from 1998 to 2007, however, only twenty-seven military, police, and civil administrative officials were convicted of abduction and wrongful confinement. Others have been subject to disciplinary action. None of the senior officials identified by the commissions were prosecuted; in fact, in a few instances, some were promoted. Recommendations to hold officers with command responsibility criminally liable for disappearances perpetrated under their command were not realized. Conversely, recommendations that no defense of due obedience to orders from superiors be entertained were similarly overlooked.

Furthermore, questions were raised about the legitimacy of the Disappearance Investigation Unit (DIU) established within the police department in 1997 to investigate disappearances, given that it was in effect partly responsible to probe its own department. Despite commitments on the part of President Kumaratunga in 1994 that the culprits would be punished, disappearance-focused investigation and prosecutorial mechanisms were established not at the inception of the commissions' mandate to complement their work, but rather upon the commissions' recommendations years later. For complainants before the commissions, therefore, there were no guarantees of concrete prosecutorial action, legal reform, or indeed of their own personal safety. They were expected to provide testimony in a context in which the state machinery that provided for the disappearance of their relatives remained untouched. Many such families failed to appear before the commissions for fear of their own safety, particularly where those responsible remained in positions of power. Some observers maintain, moreover, that despite a lack of political leadership and transparency with regard to prosecutorial action, any remaining momentum to hold those responsible to account was quashed when the UNP was returned to power in 2001.

The reluctance of the People's Alliance and successive governments thereafter to implement the commissions' recommendations directed at restricting the powers of state agents and holding them to account has ensured that the machinery that provided for the widespread practice of disappearance remained largely intact. The policies of the People's Alliance against the arbitrary use of state violence, at least in the early stages of its rule, were directed at addressing the abuses of the previous regime. Failure to address the structural sources of violence including grievances over land, education, employment, and political access ensured that the threat of another period of political violence remained ever present. Indeed, many observers noted that the power of political violence was merely transferred from one entity to another in the form of the new government.

As an official national account of state-sponsored political violence and its consequences, the commissions' reports had the potential to provide the foundation for national discourse on the aspiration of "never again." However, the conflict with the LTTE and consequent human rights violations, lack of political will to utilize the commissions' reports as the basis of a reformist agenda, and lack of publicity and public debate on the commissions' findings ensured that the opportunity was lost. Moreover, prohibitions on public access to commission hearings, which could otherwise have provided an opportunity to forge a common identity based on shared experience and enabled the wider community to locate themselves in the process, served instead to limit public ownership of the process.

Conclusion

The reports of the presidential commissions of inquiry into disappearance provide a historical memory of an era of political violence in Sri Lanka. While establishing the disappearance of more than 20,000 people, however, key recommendations of the commissions, including the need to dismantle the institutionalization of violence, reestablish the rule of law, and address impunity, have not been realized. Moreover, despite international and domestic pressure, the emergency legislation that is widely recognized as the basis for disappearance was not brought into line with international human rights standards regarding due process of law and the treatment of detainees. The institutionalization of political violence in which disappearance became a salient feature remained therefore largely unaddressed.

Jane Thomson

Cross-references: Accountability Mechanisms; Commissions of Inquiry into the Involuntary Removal or Disappearance of Persons; Compensation Packages; Conflict (Ongoing) and Transitional Justice; Court Trials for Redress; Presidential Commission of Inquiry into Involuntary Removal and Disappearance of Certain Persons (All Island).

Further Readings

Amnesty International. 2009. *Twenty Years of Make-Believe. Sri Lanka's Commissions of Inquiry*. ASA 37/005/2009.

Presidential Commission of Inquiry into the Involuntary Removal or Disappearance of Persons in the Central, North Western, North Central and Uva Provinces. 1997. *Final Report of the Commission of Inquiry into the Involuntary Removal or Disappearance of Persons in the Central, North Western, North Central and Uva Provinces*. Part I. Sessional Paper No. VI. Colombo: Department of Government Printing.

Presidential Commission of Inquiry into the Involuntary Removal or Disappearance of Persons in the Northern and Eastern Provinces. 1997. *Final Report of the Commission of Inquiry into Involuntary Removal or Disappearance of Persons in the Northern and Eastern Provinces*. Sessional Paper No. VII. Colombo: Department of Government Printing.

Presidential Commission of Inquiry into the Involuntary Removal or Disappearance of Persons in the Western, Southern and Sabaragamuwa Provinces. 1997. *Final Report of the Commission of Inquiry into Involuntary Removal or Disappearance of Persons in the Western, Southern and Sabaragamuwa Provinces*. Sessional Paper No. V. Colombo: Department of Government Printing.

Taiwan

Since the lifting of martial law in 1987, state institutions and private organizations have repeatedly attempted to address the atrocities committed during the Japanese colonial period (1895–1945) and the Kuomintang government (1945–1987). Taiwan's international status is disputed and domestically challenged by those supporting unification with the People's Republic of China and those favoring an independent Taiwanese state. The political polarization has prevented a united attempt to address past atrocities. Moreover, the current rapprochement with China undertaken under President Ma Ying-jeou of the ruling Chinese Nationalist Party (Kuomintang) has seriously undermined Taiwan's democratic development and reversed almost all previous transitional justice efforts.

The Repressive Past

In April 1895, the Treaty of Shimonoseki brought an end to the Sino-Japanese War, which had erupted a year earlier. According to the treaty, China ceded Taiwan to Japan (see a separate entry on Japan). Under the Japanese, the Taiwanese endured harsh cultural and political policies. Native languages were banned and businesses were required to hire only applicants proficient in Japanese. Death sentences were carried out for minor offenses. During the first decade of Japanese rule, more than 5,000 Taiwanese were executed. A surveillance network (*baojia*) was set up in 1898 to detect opposition members. Each ten households formed an administrative unit (*jia*). A *bao* (consisting of ten *jia*) was administered by Japanese officials who reported suspicious behavior to the police. A crime committed by one family member led to the punishment of all families of that *jia*. Aboriginal tribes suffered most under Japanese rule. Approximately 1.5 percent of the 3 million inhabitants of Taiwan (registered by the census of 1905) were aboriginal. The Japanese established a special government agency for "barbarian" affairs, which committed several massacres of aborigines. Those who survived the atrocities were subject to forced labor on plantations.

Starting in the early 1920s, the Japanese government enforced assimilation policies that considered Taiwan an extension of Japan and required that the Taiwanese be educated to understand their role and responsibilities as Japanese subjects. As a consequence, the Taiwanese were given more political and social rights. Many Taiwanese were elected or appointed to local councils. The educational system was gradually liberalized and finally desegregated in 1941. Taiwanese students were also allowed to pursue university studies in Japan.

With the start of the Second Sino-Japanese War in 1937, the Japanese intensified the promotion on the island of the philosophy of the Japanese spirit (*yamato damashii*), which held that all the Taiwanese people were subjects of the Japanese emperor, in preparation for the forced conscription of the Taiwanese into the Imperial Japanese Army and Navy. Some Taiwanese soldiers were recruited to fight in mainland China against the troops of Chiang Kai-shek and Mao Tse-tung. Others remained in Taiwan and worked as prison guards in fourteen camps where 4,350 Allied prisoners of war were interned from 1942 to 1945. Prisoners were under constant threat of death and subject to torture, forced labor, malnutrition, and severe beatings. One-fourth of the inmates were killed, many after digging their own graves. Some 800 Taiwanese women were forced to work as comfort women (see separate entry) for the Japanese army during World War II.

At the end of the war, the United States, as the principal occupying power of Japanese territory, authorized the Chinese President Chiang Kai-shek to administer Taiwan. At the time, the Chinese Kuomintang government promoted Han nationalism with the aim of establishing a Han nation, consisting of one state, one people, and one language. As part of this attempt, the Kuomintang government sought to assimilate the native population of Taiwan through social control and education. The Han nation-building process severely affected the native population. Regulations forbade the use of Japanese, aboriginal, and Sinitic languages other than Mandarin. Ethnic origin and the ability to speak Mandarin allowed one to qualify for public and political positions and became instruments of social control. The Kuomintang government purged state institutions of the Taiwanese, and within a few years the Mainlanders held most key positions in government and state-run industries. In official government documents, the purges were justified with the claim that the "primitive prostitute culture" of the "local population" lacked the ability to govern the island.

Social and political injustices caused by the Han-nationalists' dogma of racial superiority and widespread bureaucratic inefficiency led to public protests and culminated in a massacre of February 28, 1947 (known as the 2–28 Massacre), in which Chiang Kai-shek's troops brutally killed thousands of Taiwanese civilians. Two years later, the Han nationalists lost the civil war on the Chinese mainland and retreated to Taiwan. Martial law was imposed from 1949 to 1987.

The defeat on the mainland and Mao Zedong's subsequent proclamation of the People's Republic of China as the de facto and de jure successor state of the Kuomintang's Republic of China caused a crisis of legitimacy for the Chiang Kai-shek regime. On the international stage, the United States assisted Chiang Kai-shek in maintaining that the Kuomintang government was the sole legitimate government of China. Domestically, this position, while untenable from a juridical point of view, was kept alive by promoting Han nationalism and persecuting opponents. At the end of the 1980s, socioeconomic consequences of rapid economic growth, such as a growing middle class and labor disputes, and pressure from the international community, especially from members of the U.S. Congress and organizations such as Amnesty International, forced the Kuomintang regime to initiate political reforms. Martial law was lifted in 1987. Subsequent constitutional amendments paved the way for democratization.

During the authoritarian period (1945–1987), several laws restricted political rights and civil liberties. The National General Mobilization Law, promulgated on March 29, 1942, authorized the government to restrict freedom of speech, publication, writing, correspondence, assembly, and association. Articles 100 and 101 of the Criminal Code of 1935 (also known as the Sedition Law, promulgated on January 1, 1935) were the most feared pieces of legislation because they prohibited committing and planning acts that endangered the state. Given that any opposition to the Kuomintang regime could be interpreted as a threat to the state, the law provided a legal basis to persecute political opponents. Political rights and civil liberties were further restricted in 1949 with the proclamation of the martial law. It gave the military the right to prohibit religious activities and strikes by traders, students, and workers and allowed military courts to try offenses against the internal and external security of the state and other offenses punishable under the Criminal Code, such as sedition.

The military, the police, and a Kuomintang network of informers protected the authoritarian state. The most feared state agency was the Taiwan Garrison Command (TGC), a secret security body founded in 1945 under the Ministry of Defense. The Garrison Command was responsible for suppressing activities viewed as promoting communism, democracy, and Taiwan's independence. The Kuomintang also used informers to persecute political opponents at home and abroad. Once blacklisted, opposition figures and their families were systematically harassed by Garrison Command officers and/or disappeared overnight.

Several detention centers and military prisons operated between 1949 and 1987. The largest were the Chingmei Detention Centre and the Ankeng Military Prison situated in northern Taipei County. Two other major facilities were located on Green Island. First, the New Life Correction Centre, which operated from 1951 to 1965, housed up to 3,000 political prisoners. The Green Island Reform and Re-education Prison (Oasis Villa), opened in 1972, became the home of Taiwan's prisoners of conscience until 1987. Between 1965 and 1972, most political prisoners were held at the Taiyuan Prison in Taitung County. Prison conditions were inhumane. Prisoners of conscience were subject to forced labor and systematic torture. They were reportedly tied up and beaten, had pepper-water and gasoline forced through their noses, received electric shocks, and had their teeth removed without anesthetics and their fingernails plucked out.

The total number of victims of the Kuomintang terror is unknown, because many executions were extrajudicial and not recorded. According to declassified information, most extrajudicial executions were carried out in the 1950s, when 130,000 people went missing. Torture and (extrajudicial) executions were widespread and systematic until the late 1970s. Reports by the Ministry of Justice, parliamentary interpellation, and other government sources suggest that 30,000 political trials involving more than 200,000 individuals were held in military courts. About 20 percent of the accused were sentenced to death or punished with lifelong imprisonment. Some 60 percent received prison terms between one and fifteen years. Others had to undergo reformatory education.

Transitional Justice

Since martial law was lifted in 1987, there have been several different approaches to dealing with the crimes of the Kuomintang regime. The first attempt to address the past occurred between 1988 and 2000 under the presidency of Lee Teng-hui, a native of Taiwan who succeeded Chiang Ching-kuo after his death in 1988. Lee had a close relationship with the former dictator, whom he considered his political mentor.

Compensation and Apology (1988–2000)

The immediate post-martial-law years saw several large-scale protests demanding political and social reforms. Although human rights activists and victims of the Kuomintang atrocities called for transitional justice, in 1988, President Lee started his term in office with a press conference merely stating that the people of Taiwan should look forward and forget the past. Lee's long career in the repressive regime and his close friendship with his predecessor prompted his refusal to address the past. Political realities, however, forced Lee to rethink his transitional justice policies. Unlike his predecessors, Lee was neither a Mainlander nor a staunch supporter of Chinese nationalism. Senior party leaders aware of his support for Taiwanese nationalism repeatedly attempted to oust him from the party leadership and the presidency. As his conflict with the conservative wing of the

Kuomintang intensified, Lee saw in public support the key to his political survival, and thus presented himself as a statesman who listened to the people. Consequently, Lee readjusted his transitional justice policies to neither neglect public opinion nor endanger his political career. During his presidency (1988–2000), he pursued a policy of apology and compensation without investigating the role of the Kuomintang government in the atrocities.

In 1990, the government set up a committee of historians (officially named the Executive Yuan 2–28 Incident Committee, after the executive branch of the Taiwanese government, known as the Executive Yuan) to conduct research on the causes and scope of 2–28 Massacre. Its final report was published in 1992. Three years later, President Lee publicly apologized for the massacre and declared February 28 a national holiday. That same year, the 2–28 Memorial Foundation was established to provide monetary compensation to the victims of the massacre. Applications were accepted until 2006. The Foundation analyzed more than 2,000 cases. In about 30 percent of the cases, the victims were killed in the massacre. About 10,000 victims or heirs received monetary compensation totaling US$218 million. Individual compensations were proportional to the victim's suffering and limited to US$180,000. In 1998, pressure by victims' organizations and the Democratic Progressive Party (DPP), Taiwan's largest opposition party, led to the creation of the Foundation for Compensating Improper Verdicts on Sedition and Communist Espionage Cases during the Martial Law Period, which compensated victims of the White Terror (1949–1987) and their heirs. Again, individual compensations depended on the victim's suffering and were limited to US$180,000. Four categories of injustices were recognized: death sentences, imprisonment, reformatory education, and property confiscation. The Foundation accepted applications until December 16, 2010, and provided monetary compensation to more than 7,000 applicants.

Apart from the crimes committed during Kuomintang rule, there was pressure from supporters of Chinese nationalism and women's groups to investigate the human rights abuses during the Japanese occupation of Taiwan (1895–1945). In 1992, the Taiwanese Comfort Women Investigative Committee was established by different government agencies, the Academia Sinica (Taiwan's National Academy of Sciences), and the Taipei Women's Rescue Foundation. The committee was tasked with identifying former comfort women who were still alive and gathering historical information about the comfort women system in Taiwan. In total, fifty-six former comfort women were found. Since July 1995, the government has offered a monthly subsidy to them on humanitarian grounds. In 1997, a parliamentary resolution urged the government to demand that Japan apologize and compensate the former comfort women. The Taiwanese government increased the monthly subsidy from US$200 to US$500, but refrained from pressuring Japan for political and ideological reasons (see later discussion).

In 2001, nine former comfort women filed a lawsuit against the Japanese government demanding an official apology and 10 million yen (US$95,000) each in damages. The case was dismissed by the Japanese Supreme Court in 2005, on grounds that all wartime compensation issues had been settled by international and bilateral treaties.

Identifying the Perpetrators (2000–2008)

In 2000, President Lee's policy of apology and compensation was abrogated by his successor, Chen Shui-bian, who believed that all previous government policies failed to address the question of who was responsible for past crimes. Chen Shui-bian was the first Taiwanese president who was not a Kuomintang member. During the martial law era, the Kuomintang persecuted Chen for his opposition activity. As a former human rights lawyer, Chen supported the improvement of Taiwanese democracy. His transitional justice initiatives and other measures designed to improve human rights standards encountered institutional and political obstacles. According to the constitution, for example, the president is the head of state but not the chief executive with veto powers. He thus lacks the means to push through legislation when his party does not enjoy a majority of parliament seats. During Chen's mandate (2000–2008), the Kuomintang and its supporters controlled parliament and transitional justice became tied to national identity. As the key perpetrators of Kuomintang atrocities were Chinese nationalists, demands for transitional justice have come mostly from supporters of Taiwanese nationalism, while resistance to it has come from Chinese nationalists. President Chen's calls for transitional justice have thus been interpreted as racial persecution. During the 2004 presidential election, the Kuomintang compared President Chen with Adolf Hitler in official campaign advertisements and asked the people to end Chen's dictatorship.

Rewriting History Textbooks

Although the Taiwanese were subject to human rights abuses during the Japanese colonial period, they still support Japan. Some of the most important Taiwanese nationalist leaders hold degrees from Japanese universities and are well connected with right-wing politicians there.

The almost deifying attitude of Taiwanese nationalists toward Imperial Japan and Japanese right-wing intellectuals like writer Kobayashi Yoshinori, who denies the existence of the Nanjing Massacre and other crimes committed by the Japanese in the 1930s and 1940s, makes it difficult for ideologically polarized Taiwan to pursue transitional justice. The polarization is reflected in almost any discourse on transitional justice, including the debate on the content of school textbooks. Taiwanese nationalists support detailed descriptions of Kuomintang atrocities in textbooks, whereas Chinese nationalists complain that Japanese war crimes are not properly addressed. The textbook controversy has prevented any significant changes in the content of high school textbooks. Textbooks list the gross human rights violations committed by the Kuomintang and the Japanese military as historical facts without discussing the severity of the crimes or raising the question of responsibility; there are victims but no perpetrators in most textbooks.

Memorialization

Supporters of President Chen's transitional justice efforts attacked the Kuomintang for refusing to accept responsibility for the 2–28 Massacre and the White Terror. The KMT does not deny that the 2–28 Massacre took place, but refuses to acknowledge its active role in it. In official statements, party leaders claimed that the massacre was caused by language barriers and corrupt local government officials. Thus, the Kuomintang and Chiang Kai-shek cannot be held responsible for killing thousands of civilians. Kuomintang officials have either kept silent or have justified the human rights abuses of the White Terror by claiming that they were lawful and necessary to protect Taiwan from communist infiltration. They further note that the Kuomintang under Chiang Kai-shek and his son turned Taiwan into an economic miracle. The former dictators should therefore be considered heroic leaders who deserve a special place in world history. The state should protect places commemorating their political, social, and economic achievements. Any attempt to close, remove, or rename those historic sites amounts to an act of treason.

The Taiwanese nationalists disagree with the Kuomintang interpretations of these two tragic historical events and the positive appraisal of the Chiang family. In their view, Chiang Kai-shek and his son were brutal dictators who do not deserve heroic status in a modern democratic state. During Chen's presidency, dozens of statues were thus removed, the former dictators' mausoleums closed, and public places renamed.

The 2–28 Memorial Foundation Truth Division

President Chen was determined to challenge the Kuomintang's interpretation of the 2–28 Massacre and asked the 2–28 Memorial Foundation in 2001 to set up a special division, the Truth Division, to investigate the KMT's role in the massacre. In 2004, the Truth Division began to research the question of legal and political responsibility for the massacre.

The final report, released in February 2006, concluded that Chiang Kai-shek was the prime culprit of the 2–28 Massacre. The findings of the committee of historians and jurists proved helpful in the new Democratic Progressive Party government's attempt to gain more public support for its transitional justice policies. As a consequence, two important public places were renamed. In 2006, Taiwan's main international airport was renamed the Taoyuan International Airport, after the name of the locality where the airport is situated. A year later, the Chiang Kai-shek Memorial Hall in Taipei became the National Taiwan Democracy Memorial Hall.

The Kuomintang and its supporters, who controlled the parliamentary majority, could not accept the final report and responded by freezing the budget of the foundation during a parliamentary budget screening session. In 2006, John Chiang, a grandson of Chiang Kai-Shek and high-ranking Kuomintang member, sued the foundation and the historians who had authored the report for libel and demanded US$150 million in compensation. Libel is a criminal offense in Taiwan. The Taipei District Public Prosecutors Office, however, argued that the report was a public judgment of historical events and refrained from indicting the historians.

Return of Property Illegally Confiscated by the Kuomintang

Since the Committee released its report, there has been growing support for legislation demanding that the Kuomintang return property it had obtained illegally or by improper means during the White Terror. Lacking a parliamentary majority, the government decided to hold a referendum on the return of the "stolen assets" in January 2008.

The Kuomintang urged the people of Taiwan to boycott the referendum on the return of Kuomintang property to the state. Consequently, only 26 percent of the voters cast ballots in the January 2008 referendum, well below the required 50 percent of eligible voters needed to validate the result of the referendum. About 91 percent of those who cast votes supported the passing of legislation that would return the Kuomintang assets.

Since the return of the Kuomintang to power in 2008, the topic has not been discussed again.

Chinese Historical Revisionism (2008–present)

In May 2008, President Chen was succeeded by Ma Ying-jeou (representing the Kuomintang). An outspoken supporter of Chinese nationalism, Ma is known for his ambivalent view of democratic institutions and transitional justice. Ma won 58 percent of the vote, although only 20 percent of the population is made up of Mainlanders or their descendants; the results reflected widespread protest voting rather than popular support for Chinese nationalism. Soon after his inauguration, most of the previous government's transitional justice policies were reversed without public consultations. The former dictators' mausoleums were reopened. The National Taiwan Democracy Memorial Hall was renamed the Chiang Kai-shek Memorial. Museums and other places commemorating the Kuomintang atrocities were "sanitized," in the sense that important exhibits illustrating the reign of terror were removed from the Taipei 2–28 Memorial Museum and two important memorial parks were built on the grounds of the former Chingmei detention center and the Green Island Oasis Villa. Moreover, the Kuomintang government has tried to repurpose commemorative sites, such as the Taiwan Human Rights Chingmei Cultural Park, by renaming and turning them into cultural centers with art performances that no longer commemorate the victims.

Conclusion

Since 1987, transitional justice in Taiwan proceeded in three main stages. First, between 1988 and 2000, President Lee Teng-hui of the Chinese Nationalist Party promoted a policy of compensation and apology. Second, from 2000 to 2008, his successor, Chen Shui-bian of the opposition Democratic Progressive Party, made transitional justice a priority. His transitional justice policies aimed to remove the historical legacies of the Kuomintang dictatorship by distinguishing the party from the state, to investigate the responsibility for past atrocities, to make people aware of the wrongfulness of the atrocities, and to establish legal and institutional mechanisms preventing the reoccurrence of political persecution. Third, since 2008, President Ma Ying-jeou (Kuomintang) and his government have reversed almost all previously adopted transitional justice policies. President Ma's rapprochement with communist China and his unification policies are likely to minimize future transitional justice initiatives.

Christian Schafferer

Cross-references: Japan.

Further Readings

Lee, Yan-hsian, Yang Chen-long, and Chang Yan-hsian, eds. 2006. *Ererba shijian zeren guishu yanjiu baogao* [Report on the Responsibility for the 2–28 Massacre]. Chonghe: 2–28 Memorial Foundation.
Wu, Nai-teh. 2005. Transition without Justice, or Justice without History: Transitional Justice in Taiwan. *Taiwan Journal of Democracy*, 1(1): 77–102.
———. 2004. Huiyi jiangjingguo, huainian jiangjingguo [Reformer or Dictator? Reassessing the Role of Chiang Ching-guo in the Democratic Transition]. *Proceedings of the Seventh Conference of the National Archives Taipei*, 7: 467–502.

Turkey

Turkey is slowly coming to terms with its past, although transitional justice is rarely applied, and then only at the initiative of victims' groups and nongovernmental or international organizations. Before the dismantling of the Ottoman Empire in 1915, the government sought the deliberate and systematic destruction of minorities. In the decade before and after the establishment of the Republic of Turkey in 1923, more than 1 million people were killed, disappeared, imprisoned, tortured, or expelled from Turkey and Turkish-controlled territories. Most victims belonged to ethnic or other non-Muslim minorities, including Armenians, Greeks, and Kurds, accounting for one-fifth of the country's population. Even though many of these atrocities and war crimes occurred before 1923, serious investigations and criminal prosecutions of those responsible for them have not been concluded to date.

At the center of transitional justice claims in Turkey is "the Kurdish issue" – that is, the Kurds' separatist claims to an independent Kurdish state and the violent conflict that led to thousands of Kurds being disappeared or killed since the 1980s. Pogroms against the Kurds date back to the early days of the Turkish Republic. Other issues are Turkey's relationship with Greece, the imposed division of Cyprus into Greek and Turkish sectors after the Turkish military invasion in 1974, and the island's possible reunification. Although the Armenian genocide has been important in Turkey's foreign relations and its negotiations with the European Union (EU), it is not a transitional justice priority for the Turkish government and society. Above all these issues stand the military coups against the Turkish governments of 1960, 1971, 1980, and the attempt in 1997, which the country must address first.

Since 1963, Turkey's bid to join the European Community/EU has underpinned its political will to democratize. Its earlier membership in the Council of Europe and the European Court of Human Rights, the United Nations, and NATO has also exposed Turkey to criticism and pressure for constitutional and military reforms. Recently, victims' groups, the United States, Turkey's EU allies, and neighbors (Armenia, Greek-Cyprus, and Greece) have asked for more accountability from the Turkish government and military, which carry part of the legacy of past human rights abuses. Inside Turkey, attempts to reckon with the past have frequently risen since 2004, when negotiations for EU membership started.

Turkish transitional justice mainly deals with the significant political role of the military, although it is not directly responsible for the pre-1923 massacres, pogroms, and genocide. Attempts to acknowledge or denounce these crimes can be prosecuted under the Penal Code and military laws that hold Turkey's territorial integrity as the main priority. Since 2005, Article 301 of the Penal Code punishes those who contest the Turkish nation and thus challenge Turkish "pride" and nationalism. Articles 125 and 131, restricting freedom of expression by recognizing offenses against dignity, intimidate citizens who query the role of the military or ask it to take responsibility for past atrocities.

Several civil society groups and nongovernmental organizations have asked the Turkish government to acknowledge the atrocities, come to terms with the past, and rehabilitate victims and those discriminated against and excluded. They aim to bring perpetrators to justice, establish history, truth, or reconciliation commissions, and adopt other measures. Since 2002, their success has largely depended on the Justice and Development Party (Adalet ve Kalkınma Partisi, AKP) government (Santana, 2008). Although the secret police and the army have undergone modest reforms and, since 2010, can face trial for the crimes they perpetrated during the coup of 1980, a culture of impunity still dominates.

The Armenian, Greek-Cypriot, and Greek governments and Kurdish victim organizations have denounced Turkey's nontransparent judiciary and lack of political will to acknowledge past wrongdoings and to take responsibility for them. Additional pressure comes from the United Nations, the EU, the NATO, the Parliamentary Assembly of the Council of Europe, the European Court of Human Rights, and France, Sweden, Germany, and the United States, where many Armenians and Kurds live. They call on the Turkish government to become more active in transitional justice, reconciliation, and peace stabilization in the region. Turkey will meet these expectations only if its political elites respect the rule of law and name perpetrators, and if the government fosters trust in democratic institutions by combating impunity and allowing open public debates about the past (Amnesty International 2007).

The Repressive Past

Turkey became a republic with the Treaty of Lausanne (1923), after decades of internal and external wars through which the Ottoman Empire's rulers unsuccessfully tried to preserve the empire. Turkey was allied with Germany and Austria-Hungary in World War I, but remained neutral in World War II. The empire's collapse and the subsequent wars fueled Turkish nationalism, seeking to keep what was left of the country's territory and integrity. By the time the republic was established, Turkey had lost 85 percent of the former empire's territory. Many Turks had been victims of persecution, expulsion, and human rights abuses in Greece, Bulgaria (see separate entry), Syria, and other countries. Before and after 1923, the military sought to retain as much territory as possible, even by employing ethnic cleansing, atrocities, and war crimes. In 1949–1950, Turkey embraced a multiparty system and formal democratic reforms meant to break with the politics of the Ottoman Sultanate, but could not stop radical nationalism.

Turkey must address five major past events: (1) the Armenian genocide (1915–1918), (2) the expulsion and pogroms of the Greek minority during the Greek-Turkish war of 1919–1922 and in 1955, (3) the military invasion of Northern Cyprus in 1974, (4) the post-1978 persecution and massacres of the Kurdish minority (internationally considered as a low-intensity war), and (5) the military coups of 1960, 1971, 1980, and 1997. The ongoing suppression and censorship of its own citizens, torture, and other human rights crimes have also hampered transitional justice.

The Armenian Genocide (1915–1918)

The Armenian genocide resulted from the Tehcir "Deportation" Law of 1915, which sought to regulate the "settlements" of Armenians and to relocate them to the Syrian desert, then part of the Ottoman Empire, where most of them died. According to the law, those deported were not to be harmed and their property was to be returned to them after World War I. The Tehcir Law was abolished in 1916, but the massacres and deportations continued, reparations were never envisaged, and the property was never returned to its lawful owners. Approximately 1 million people perished between 1915 and 1923 as a result of starvation, murder, and ill-treatment. Later, the massacres were named the Armenian Genocide (Phillips 2005).

Turkey affirmed its obligation to reckon with war crimes during the martial trials of 1919–1920, which accused the generals and representatives of the last Ottoman Sultan Mehmet VI of alleged involvement in the massacres and deportations of hundreds of thousands of Armenians and Greeks during and shortly after World War I. Two years after the Republic of Armenia was established in 1918, the country was incorporated into the Soviet Union. Thus, until 1990, Armenian leaders and survivors of the massacres could not raise legal or political claims against Turkey, because it was a NATO ally and because war crimes were committed by Russian and Ottoman troops alike during World War I. As the martial trials were never completed, it remained an open question whether and to what extent the Turkish military and government should assume responsibility for the war crimes committed by their Ottoman predecessors.

The Expulsion and Pogroms of Greeks (1919–1922 and 1955)

Greece started its quest for independence from the Ottoman Empire in 1830. Both sides committed atrocities, ethnic cleansings, and war crimes during the Greek-Turkish War of 1919–1922, in which Ottoman troops tried to reclaim parts of its territory and power. The war divided Turkey's multiethnic society through discrimination, pogroms, and expropriation. By 1923, more than 1.5 million Greeks had fled the empire and more than 500,000 Turks had fled Greece based on an official resettlement agreement between the two countries. Neither country acknowledged responsibility for crimes committed during deportations and resettlements. In 1932, Greeks were expelled from more than thirty different professions. When in 1955 violent outbreaks between Greek and Turks emerged in Cyprus (then under British protectorate), acts of revenge occurred on the Turkish mainland. Thousands of Greeks were killed or had their property expropriated, and other Greeks left the country without receiving justice or compensation. Pogroms against the Greek minority in Turkey continued until the 1960s.

The Invasion of Northern Cyprus (1974)

The Turkish invasion of Northern Cyprus in 1974 and the island's subsequent division still strain bilateral relations between Greece and Turkey. In 1974, Greek and Turkish Cypriots on both sides of the island were expelled and their property was expropriated by their counterparts. Both the Greek and the Turkish side used severe violence in the attempt to eliminate the other ethnic group from the island. At the time of this writing, an estimated 200,000 people are still displaced and thousands others have been disappeared since 1974. Those responsible for these crimes can to be found on both sides. Many displaced people lost their property and houses during Turkey's invasion and subsequent expulsions, leading to restitution claims. The need to reckon with these past crimes was slowly acknowledged as Greece, Cyprus, and Turkey sought EU membership (International Crisis Group, 2009).

The Persecution of the Kurds

Turkish policy and warfare against Kurds of Eastern Anatolia stem from the desire to preserve the country's integrity in the face of separatist calls from rebel armed groups like the Kurdistan Workers Party (Partiya Karkerên Kurdistan, PKK) that began their terror resistance in 1984. The Kurds have asked for secession in response to the persecution, discrimination, and human rights abuses they endured for decades at the hands of the Turkish authorities. Since 1984, the Turkish army has increased its presence in the region. Allegations of disappearances, ill-treatment, torture, arbitrary imprisonment, killings, bombing of Kurdish villages, severe repression, and deprivation of citizenship rights in the Kurdish enclave remain unaddressed. More than 6,000 deaths of Kurds have been reported, and thousands of Kurds have been displaced or have fled the country since the mid-1980s.

The Military Coups

The 1960, 1971, and 1980 military coups, in which the Turkish military deposed elected governments, increased fear of political instability and led to a culture of impunity, given that no military officials were ever convicted for their crimes. Another coup organized in 1997 failed. The coups, which came in response to governmental reforms that hurt the interests of the military elite, aimed to restrengthen the military's political control over the country.

Transitional Justice

Debates on Turkey's need to come to terms with its past started in 1991, when Armenia proclaimed its independence from the Soviet Union and Turkey undertook sweeping reforms of its Constitution and Penal Code in hopes of accession to the EU. However, Turkey has not settled disputes with Armenia over the Armenian Genocide and with Greece over Cyprus. The Turkish government claims that Turkish Cyprus is an independent state over which Turkey has no influence. In reality, Northern Cyprus is a Turkish protectorate that depends economically and politically on Turkey. Nationalist groups, Islamic parties, and the Turkish political elites and military leadership, all opposed to each other, have hampered transitional justice by protecting their own members and sympathizers.

Armenian Victims

Turkey never officially recognized the pre-1918 Ottoman pogroms, massacres, and expulsion of Armenians as genocide. Turkey's first President Kemal Atatürk (1923–1938) denounced the Ottomans' ill-treatment of the Armenians, but undertook no legal or political measures to address those injustices. The Treaty of Lausanne was the first to give rights to Turkey's non-Muslim minorities, including Christian Armenians. In 1949–1950, however, the Turkish political-military elite launched additional democratic reforms giving the military greater political influence. The Armenian "issue," as it is called in Turkey, remains unaddressed and attempts to publicly discuss the crimes are denounced. Writers, intellectuals, survivors, and members of the Armenian Church in Turkey who have raised the issue suffered repression or prosecution.

In 2005, on the occasion of the ninetieth anniversary of the start of the Armenian Genocide, the Turkish authorities criticized condemnations of the genocide by the European Parliament and the U.S. Senate. When Nobel Prize–winning Turkish writer Orhan Pamuk publicly addressed Turkey's refusal to acknowledge the genocide, he was indicted for crimes against the Turkish nation. Investigation of Pamuk came to a halt only after international protests. That same year, Bilgi University in Istanbul held a conference on "Ottoman Armenians during the Decline of the Empire: Issues of Scientific Responsibility and Democracy," which received international, but no local, coverage. Nevertheless, it raised the Armenian "issue." In 2007, 100,000 people demonstrated on the streets after the murder of the Armenian-Turkish journalist Hrant Dink by extremists in Istanbul, and claimed that "We are all Armenians." The Turkish intellectual elite and significant parts of the civil society suggested that they would no longer accept censorship and prosecution when talking about the massacres of World War I. By December 2008, 30,000 Turks signed an online letter addressed to Armenians and apologizing for the massacres of 1915–1918. Slowly, books on those events – usually referred to as massacres, not genocide – have entered Turkish bookshops, but most of them are in foreign languages and thus accessible only to the small foreign-language-trained elite. Since 2005, every year in April – the month in which the Armenian Genocide is commemorated – civil society groups launch candlelight ceremonies to commemorate the massacres. These commemorations take place in Ankara and other major cities without any repercussions. Despite recent meetings between Turkish and Armenian officials, relations between the two countries remain strained.

The Turkish-Armenian Reconciliation Commission (TARC) worked from 2001 to 2004. Created by nongovernmental organizations, financed by the United States, and composed of civil society representatives interested in exploring cooperative activities between Turks and Armenians, the Commission met in Geneva and Moscow. It aimed to bring Turks and Armenians together at the table and facilitate discussions. After commissioning a third-party report discussing whether the actions of the Ottoman Empire amounted to genocide, the Commission discontinued its work. The report was never officially published.

Greek Victims

A Greek-Turkish Reconciliation Initiative was launched in 1986, and discontinued shortly thereafter. Although the initiative was meant to address the pogroms and expropriations perpetrated against the Greeks during the early years of the Turkish republic, it mainly dealt with Cyprus, seen as reflective of Turkish-Greek resentment. Rapprochement in 1999 revealed that EU accession talks for Turkey had to be linked to a solution for the division of Cyprus in 1974. Thus, transitional justice claims cannot be separated from the Greek-Turkish-Cyprus triangle and the EU accession debate. As long as Greece and Turkey act as Cyprus's kin states, the pre-1974 pogroms and deportations and the war crimes of 1974 in Cyprus are common to all three countries. The EU is the strongest potential catalyst for Greek-Turkish reconciliation, given that Greece and Turkey seem disinclined to foster reconciliation on their own initiative. Greece has supported Turkey's EU accession in the hope of addressing transitional justice through international channels.

Cyprus

The European Court of Human Rights and the EU have both put pressure on Greece and Turkey to foster transitional justice measures, including reparations for those who had to leave their property on either side of today's divided Cyprus. The European

Court has ruled several times on property claims by Greek Cypriots against Turkey, and the EU has called on all sides to seek reconciliation. Since 2006 and on the initiative of Turkey, the Turkish-Cypriot Immovable Property Commission set up by the Turkish government has examined claims for restitution, compensation, and exchange of property and dwellings lodged by Greek and Turkish Cypriots in Northern Cyprus. By early 2011, 974 applications had been lodged with the Commission, 151 of them being concluded through friendly settlements and 7 through formal hearing. Other property restitution cases launched by Greek Cypriots were lodged with the European Court. The Court repeatedly ruled or revised decisions of property restitutions against both the Greek Cypriot and Northern Turkish Cypriot sides.

Kurdish Victims

Transitional justice related to the injustices perpetrated against Kurds is demanded mainly by Turkish intellectuals, the Turkish diaspora, nongovernmental organizations like the independent Turkish Human Rights Association (İnsan Haklari Derneği, IHD), and victims' groups such as the Association for Solidarity and Support of Relatives of Disappeared People (Yakınlarını Kaybeden Ailelerle Yardımlaşma ve Dayanışma Derneği, YAKAY-Der) and the Kurdish Mothers of Peace (also called crying or Saturday mothers, representing those who disappeared during the 1980s and the 1990s). Since the mid-1990s, these organizations have met regularly, launched petitions, and initiated trials and peaceful protests. By 2011, the IHD and the YAKAY-Der had filed with the Turkish courts more than 1,500 cases related to disappearances and other human rights violations perpetrated against Kurds. Because of lack of jurisdiction derived from the constitutional prohibition to investigate and prosecute the actions of the military, including those directed against the Kurdish minority, most of these cases have been rejected or dismissed. These groups also held meetings, street demonstrations, and conferences like the one on Transitional Justice and Enforced Disappearances organized in 2009 in Istanbul. They asked the Turkish government to stop harassing Kurdish human rights defenders, and continue exhumation and identification of the bodies found in mass graves in Kurdish provinces in Eastern Anatolia. More than 80 mass graves with between 10 and 170 dead bodies in each have been found so far. According to these groups, the government should also create a centralized database of genetic information of disappeared persons and prosecute army, police, and secret police officers involved in the disappearances.

The Military Coups

None of the leaders of the military coups of 1960, 1971, 1980, and 1997 was ever convicted for the crimes against civilians or other minorities. Article 15 of the 1982 Constitution made it impossible to examine the constitutionality of the laws and decrees passed by the military administration after 1980. As after each coup the military reinstated the constitution and allowed elections, it claimed to uphold law and order (Oktem, Kerslake and Robins, 2010), thus reinforcing the unwritten amnesty that military leaders have enjoyed and intensifying the culture of impunity. In response to domestic and international pressure, in 1982, 2001, 2002, 2008, and 2010, Turkey undertook constitutional and legislative reforms recognizing minority rights and religious freedom and paving the way for trials against perpetrators. A 2010 referendum on the constitution abolished the protection from prosecution for the leaders of the 1980 coup, who can be tried under the Civil Penal Code. While justified as necessary for preparing the country for admission into the EU, the constitutional changes have allowed the AKP government to strengthen its position relative to the military and opposition.

Since 2008, the Ergenekon court trials, named after a mystic Anatolian mountain region, were launched. They indicted hundreds of suspects, including the military leaders of the 1980 coup, for crimes against the state. The trials are expected to uncover many past crimes and human rights violations conducted in the name of national security. Some see the trials as the beginning of sustained transitional justice that will strengthen Turkish democracy. Others believe they are politically motivated and detrimental to the rule of law. For them, the ruling AKP initiated the trials in an effort to discredit its political opposition, including the military. Thus, rather than redress the past, seek truth and justice, and reinforce the rule of law, the trials may divide Turkish society. Turkish journalists Ertuğrul Mavioğlu and Ahmet Şık, who in 2010 wrote a strongly controversial book about the Ergenekon case, titled *Kırk Katır Kırk Satır* [Between a Rock and a Hard Place], also faced indictment because they denied that these trials would help Turkey face its past.

Conclusion

Civil society and victims' groups, the Turkish diaspora, the Greek and Armenian governments, and international actors are the main promoters of transitional justice measures in Turkey. The main obstacle to comprehensive transitional justice that would include truth commissions, trials, reparations, legal reforms, and the revising of de facto amnesties and the culture of impunity is Turkey's traditional military elite. While the army and police leaders are responsible for most of past atrocities, crimes, and human rights abuses, they cannot be held accountable. No court cases have been launched against military and police leaders responsible for disappearances, murders, or torture. The government must assume more responsibility for promoting transitional justice by amending the legislation, creating history or truth commissions, fostering open dialogue, and envisaging public apologies. Penal Code reforms, constitutional amendments, a change of policy toward Armenia, Greece, and Cyprus, and willingness to allow Kurdish and other victims' organizations to protest and peacefully claim their rights are slowly paving the way for future transitional justice measures. These reforms could open ways for more civic and victim engagement, fair trials, and commemoration policies leading to reconciliation. The EU accession talks, started in 2004, have been important in this regard, as the EU made it a prerequisite for Turkey to adopt key political and legal reforms that could facilitate transitional justice.

Anja Mihr

Cross-references: Amnesty; Bulgaria; Military Justice; Property Restitution; Reparations.

Further Readings

Amnesty International. 2007. *Turkey. The Entrenched Culture of Impunity Must End*. London. AI index: EUR 44/008/2007.

International Crisis Group. 2009. *Cyprus: Reunification or Partition?* Europe Report no. 201. Brussels, September 30.
Mavioğlu, Ertuğrul and Ahmet Şık. 2010. *Kırk Katır Kırk Satır* [Between a Rock and a Hard Place], 2 vols. Istanbul: İthaki Yayınları.
Oktem, Kerem, Celia J. Kerslake, and Philip Robins, eds. 2010. *Turkey's Engagement with Modernity, Conflict and Change in the Twentieth Century*. New York: Palgrave Macmillan.
Phillips, David. 2005. *Unsilencing the Past: Track Two Diplomacy and Turkish-Armenian Reconciliation*. Oxford: Berhang Books.
Santana, Nil S. 2008. Transformation of the Turkish Military and the Path to Democracy. *Armed Forces & Security*, 34(3): 357–388.

Uganda

Uganda has utilized a significant number of transitional justice practices ostensibly to deal with its history of human rights abuses since the country gained its independence in 1962. Yet it is unclear that Uganda has adopted transitional justice in any real way. Rather, the country has been and continues to be governed by rebel leaders who show no real signs of embracing democracy or justice – *or* transition. Uganda continues to ignore its repressive past and to allow abuses to continue unabated in parts of the country.

The Repressive Past

In 1894, the central region of Uganda was formally declared a protectorate of the British Empire, which continued to colonize other regions of what is now Uganda until 1933. Before that time, a series of indigenous kingdoms and chieftaincies had controlled the territory. The British allied themselves with one kingdom, Buganda, and as a result of this colonial policy, many of the other kingdoms deeply resented Buganda. Added to this mix were Muslim traders from the east African coast and Christian missionaries. All of this meant that Uganda was the scene of significant ethnic and sectarian conflict throughout the early twentieth century.

In March 1961, internal autonomy was granted to Uganda. Complete sovereignty was granted on October 9, 1962, when Ugandans elected a National Assembly and drafted a semi-federal constitution. The independent country's first prime minister was Milton Obote, who held office from 1962 to 1971. Obote's term in power was characterized by significant numbers of riots and armed attacks. Many of these violent protests were carried out in protest against Obote's consolidation of power. Other uprisings came from within the Ugandan military.

Idi Amin served as Obote's army commander. In 1971, Amin overthrew Obote, suspended the constitution, and ruled under a provisional government structure, a position in which he remained until 1979. Amin earned himself the nickname "the butcher" as he and the military and paramilitary mechanisms of the state carried out a systematic campaign of murder and torture against anyone he saw as standing in his way throughout his eight years in power. He targeted those suspected of having supported Obote. In 1972, Amin expelled more than 70,000 ethnic Asians living in Uganda and confiscated their property. No exact figures of the number of people who were killed under Amin exist, although conservative estimates place the figure at between 300,000 and 500,000. In April 1979, Amin was defeated by a coalition of forces, including Obote and Yoweri Museveni, who became the country's president in 1986. As a result, Amin fled into exile in Libya. Interim governments were appointed in 1979 and 1980.

In 1980, after rigged elections, Obote returned to power. Obote and his forces then retaliated against those he saw as having supported Amin, especially targeting an area called the Luweero Triangle, north of the capital, Kampala. As part of this campaign, paramilitary forces under the direction of Obote raped, tortured, looted, and destroyed property. Conservative estimates place the number of those killed during this period at approximately 300,000 to 500,000. Obote remained in power until July 1985, when he was overthrown by a faction of the Ugandan military. For the next six months, a military council governed the country, until it, too, was overthrown.

Museveni and the National Resistance Movement (NRM, formerly the National Resistance Army) seized power in January 1986. Museveni had spent decades fighting against the regimes of Amin and Obote, as well as the transitional regimes that controlled the country between 1985 and 1986. Yet his ascension to power did little to assuage his competitors. Between 1986 and 2011, Museveni faced more than twenty-seven armed insurgencies. At the time of this writing, Museveni remains in power as the country's president, after a number of questionable election outcomes.

One of the longest-lasting and most brutal rebellions that occurred under Museveni's rule was the conflict in northern Uganda, conducted in large part by a disaffected and disgruntled group that wanted Museveni out of power. Led by Joseph Kony, the Lord's Resistance Army (LRA) waged a brutal campaign of violence on the people of northern Uganda beginning in 1986. It is estimated that between 30,000 and 45,000 children were abducted by the LRA, turned into child soldiers (see separate entry), and forced to commit the most heinous of acts, often against their own families. At the height of the conflict in 2004, as many as 1.8 million people were estimated to have been internally displaced within the region and living in protected camps for the internally displaced, a figure that represented more than 80 percent of the region's population. This conflict resulted in extreme poverty, dislocation, and trauma throughout the region, while those in the south of the country remained unaffected and largely unaware of what had taken place in the north.

Transitional Justice

Uganda had early experience with mechanisms of transitional justice. Prominent transitional justice authors including Hayner (2000) cite Uganda's Amin Commission as the first truth commission to have been appointed (see entry on Commission of Inquiry into Disappearances of People in Uganda since the 25th of January, 1971 from 1st July 1974 to 2nd January, 1975). Since that time, the country has employed a number of other mechanisms to deal with the many acts of violence that have been perpetrated since 1962. Yet these mechanisms have been implemented on an ad hoc basis, with little attention to a cohesive plan or coordinated attempt to bring about a planned result. Instead, these practices were largely adopted for reasons of political expediency, and not out of any genuine concern for confronting the past.

Commission of Inquiry into Disappearances of People in Uganda since the 25th of January, 1971 from 1st July 1974 to 2nd January, 1975 (Amin Commission)

In 1974, at the urging of the international community, which had begun to hear reports of the abuses Amin and his forces were perpetrating, Amin appointed the Commission of Inquiry into Disappearances of People in Uganda since the 25th of January 1971 from 1st July, 1974 to 2nd January, 1975. The Commission was to establish who had been disappeared, who was still missing, and who was responsible. Effectively, Amin set up a sham inquiry to look into charges of abuse that emanated from within his own regime. As such, he simply prevented the Commission from considering anything that would implicate him or his supporters. He clearly had no intention of abiding by the Commission's recommendations. The Commission's work was kept a secret, and its findings were never publicly disseminated, in large measure because of chaotic interference from Amin. Its commissioners were discriminated against, forced into exile, or themselves disappeared.

Commission of Inquiry into Violations of Human Rights

In 1986, not long after he seized power, Museveni appointed the Commission of Inquiry into Violations of Human Rights (see separate entry) as part of his Ten-Point Programme designed to demonstrate to the international community that he was doing as it wished. The Programme also included democracy, security, national unity, and independence, among other goals. This Commission was mandated to inquire into "the causes and circumstances" of all mass murders, arbitrary arrests, abuses committed by law enforcement agents and the state security agencies, and discrimination that had taken place between the time of independence in 1962 and January 1986, when Museveni and the NRM assumed power; it was also to suggest ways of preventing such abuses from recurring. The Commission was additionally expected to determine the role of various state institutions in both perpetrating and hiding gross human rights violations. As many as 608 witnesses testified before the Commission. The Final Report of the Commission, which is 720 pages in length, was not released until more than eight years later, in 1994, and was never publicly disseminated. The Commission was severely hampered by a willful lack of support from Museveni and the Ugandan government in regard to funding, permanent office space, and general issues of capacity, as well as the lack of cooperation of other government organizations such as the Criminal Investigations Division and the Directorate of Public Prosecutions. Its vast mandate, too, took a toll on what the Commission was able to accomplish. In the end, few are aware that the Commission ever existed, and those who are can scarcely point to its having had any effect.

The Amnesty Act (2000)

In November 1999, parliament passed an Amnesty Act, which was enacted in January 2000. The Act provides for amnesty to be granted to anyone engaged in war or armed rebellion against the government of Uganda from the time that Museveni seized power in January 1986, whether through actual participation in combat, collaboration with rebel forces, or the provision of assistance to rebel movements. The amnesty was intended by its creators as a means of ending the conflict in Northern Uganda, and in particular to deal with those children who had been abducted into service as child soldiers with the LRA.

The amnesty was further expanded to apply to anyone who had participated in one of the other rebellions waged against Museveni. This expansion was an attempt by Museveni and the NRM to detract attention from the conflict in the north and thereby minimize their responsibility for it. Significant questions were later raised as to potential interaction between the amnesty and the future prosecution of Joseph Kony and other LRA leaders by the International Criminal Court, although at the time of this writing, Kony and his deputies have not yet been arrested. The amnesties were slow to be granted, and by 2008 only slightly more than 22,000 former combatants had received amnesty. Slower still were the rehabilitation packages that were to have accompanied the amnesty certificates.

International Criminal Court

After significant pressure from the Office of the Prosecutor (OTP) of the International Criminal Court (ICC; see separate entry), in December 2003, Museveni formally requested that the ICC investigate the actions of the LRA in northern Uganda. The referral of the situation in northern Uganda was significant in that it was the first to be taken up by the Court. It is clear that Museveni hoped that, by complying with the wishes of the OTP, he would avoid any implication in the events that had taken place in the region. The ICC subsequently opened an investigation, and the Chief Prosecutor issued arrest warrants for Kony and four other senior members of the LRA. The five warrants outlined atrocities committed by each of the men, including more than 2,200 killings and 3,200 abductions in more than 820 attacks. Kony, for example, was charged with twelve counts of crimes against humanity and twenty-one counts of war crimes, including rape, murder, enslavement, sexual enslavement, and forced enlistment of children. Yet at the time of this writing, none of the warrants had been executed, and Kony and his LRA forces remained at large. The government of Uganda went back and forth on whether to support the ICC, and in 2010 the ICC Act was passed, which would allow Uganda to try Kony and the others in the national War Crimes Division of the High Court if the Pre-Trial Chamber if the ICC allows. At the time of this writing, this had not yet been determined.

Conclusion

Overall, the practices employed in Uganda to deal with the serious abuses that have taken place since 1962 have been unsuccessful. Rather than addressing a particular issue with any kind of coordinated plan, the four mechanisms discussed earlier represent an awkward series of attempts by successive regimes to cover up their own actions. Uganda's "transition," if it had started at all, certainly has stalled.

Joanna R. Quinn

Cross-references: Amnesty; Causes of Failure of Transitional Justice; Conflict (Ongoing) and Transitional Justice; Commission of Inquiry into Disappearances of People in Uganda since the 25th of January 1971 from 1st July, 1974 to 2nd January, 1975; Commission of Inquiry into Violations of Human Rights; International Criminal Court; Truth Commissions.

Further Readings

Hansen, Hölger Bernt and Michael Twaddle, eds. 1991. *Changing Uganda: The Dilemmas of Structural Adjustment and Revolutionary Change*. London: James Currey.
Hayner, Priscilla. 2000. *Unspeakable Truths: Confronting State Terror and Atrocity*. London: Routledge.
Ofcansky, Thomas P. 1996. *Uganda: Tarnished Pearl of Africa*. Boulder: Westview.

Quinn, Joanna. 2010. *The Politics of Acknowledgement*. Vancouver: UBC Press.
———. 2004. Constraints: The Un-Doing of the Ugandan Truth Commission. *Human Rights Quarterly*, 26(2): 401–427.
Twaddle, Michael and Hölger Bernt Hansen, eds. 1998. *Developing Uganda*. Athens: Ohio State University Press.

Ukraine

Since proclaiming independence from the Soviet Union in 1991, Ukraine has been divided over the communist past. This is partly because Eastern Ukraine was Soviet for seventy years (1922–1991), whereas the Soviet Union annexed Western Ukraine, historically part of Poland, only in 1939. Given that the Ukrainian regions suffered differently at the hands of the Soviet regime, they have different narratives about its crimes. The politically unstable post-Soviet Ukraine has focused on symbolic commemoration of the victims of Soviet repression, as a result of pressure from some politicians, the victims, their relatives, and social activists. It did not punish perpetrators, identify secret agents, or condemn communist crimes, given the unwillingness of the communist political police, the Committee for State Security (Komitet Gosudarstvennoy Bezopasnosti or KGB), and its successors to share the secret archives with the Ukrainians and the unwillingness of the Ukrainian elites to reveal their connections with the communist regime.

The Repressive Past

Millions of Ukrainians suffered greatly from Soviet terror. Some resisted the imposition of Soviet rule in 1918–1922 and forced collectivization of agriculture in the 1930s and the 1950s, suffered from the Great Famine of 1932–1933 (the Holodomor, in Ukrainian "death by hunger") and Great Terror of 1937–1938, opposed Western Ukraine's annexation in 1939, fought against the Red Army in World War II, or were labeled as traitors by the Soviet authorities because they simply survived the Nazi occupation. Some were starved to death or executed, while others died in Soviet prisons or served years of hard labor outside Ukraine. By the late 1930s, rich peasants (*kulaks*), capitalists, big landowners, nobility, and white-collar professionals (*intelligentsia*) were eliminated through arrests, executions, and man-made famine. The total number of victims in the Soviet Union could exceed 18 million, several million of whom were from Ukraine. Three to ten million died in the Holodomor. During the Great Terror, 300,000 people were arrested in Ukraine. In 1937, 122,000 persons were executed. As of January 1, 1953, Ukrainians were second only to Russians among adult "special deportees," comprising one-fifth of the total 2.8 million deportees in the Soviet Union. More than 450,000 ethnic Germans, several hundred thousand Romanians and Poles from Ukraine, and 200,000 Crimean Tatars were deported. About four out of ten deportees died from diseases and malnutrition.

A well-developed secret police network of informers, agents, and prison guards helped implement mass killings, man-made famine, and purges. Under the rule of Josef Stalin (1922–1953), the Ukrainian Soviet leaders showed loyalty to the regime by asking the Kremlin to designate people for imprisonment, exile, and execution. Until November 1938, troikas (three-person panels of high-ranking police officers, procurators, and

Communist Party officials) handled up to 1,500 cases a day and sentenced "enemies of the people." Sentences were not subject to appeal, and those condemned to death were executed immediately after the sentence was pronounced. Many troika members were themselves imprisoned or executed in later purges, which continued until Stalin's death in 1953.

Transitional Justice in Soviet Ukraine

Weeks after Stalin's death, the Central Committee of the Communist Party of Soviet Union (CPSU) condemned the "unlawful activities" of the KGB in fabricating a criminal case against doctors who allegedly conspired to murder Stalin. Nikita Khrushchev, the First Secretary of the Communist Party of Soviet Ukraine (1938–1949), became Stalin's successor in 1953. He pushed for the KGB's subordination to the party by asking government inquiry commissions to uncover the KGB's illegal activities. In May 1954, the Soviet government created regional rehabilitation commissions made up of party functionaries and procurators in each Soviet republic. The commissions, which discussed sentences of all Stalinist troikas, courts, and military tribunals, released thousands of people from exile and labor camps in the 1950s and early 1960s. From July 1954 to March 1956, the Ukrainian rehabilitation commissions reviewed 81,921 cases regarding 130,464 persons sentenced for "counterrevolutionary crimes" and repealed (or lowered) sentences in 36,166 cases (for 52,445 persons).

Khrushchev denounced Stalinist repression in a secret speech at the Twentieth Congress of the CPSU in 1956. He focused on crimes perpetrated against party functionaries in 1935–1940, without acknowledging the suffering of ordinary citizens, who formed the bulk of the victims, or the deportation of Crimean Tatars, who unsuccessfully lobbied for permission to return to Crimea. From 1953 to 1961, 290,967 persons were rehabilitated in Ukraine.

Khruschev's ouster from office in 1964 largely ended rehabilitation and de-Stalinization. In 1967, the Soviet government rehabilitated the Crimean Tatars, but did not resettle or compensate them for suffering, death, or confiscated property. Until 1991, it evicted, deported, and imprisoned the Tatars who returned to Crimea. The government monitored the population, prosecuted "subversive elements" like the Ukrainian Helsinki Group but not Stalinist human rights violators, confiscated property, and rewrote history books to eliminate Stalin's glorification.

To reform the Communist Party and build socialism "with a human face," Soviet President Mikhail Gorbachev denounced Stalin in November 1987. His *glasnost* (openness) allowed Soviet citizens to learn about the communist past and Stalinist repression. Many Ukrainian political prisoners were pardoned, released from prisons, and allowed to run for political office, while the Soviet Parliament condemned mass deportations of ethnic groups, including the Crimean Tatars. The party leaders in Ukraine publicly condemned the Holodomor, ordered the publication of archival materials about it, and created rehabilitation commissions attached to the regional Communist Party committees and involving employees of Procuratura, a law-enforcement agency that filed rehabilitation claims with the commissions. In 1989, the commissions were transferred to the Supreme Council of Ukraine and the regional and city councils, their membership was expanded to include legislators and civil society actors, and their mandate was extended to protect the rights of rehabilitated persons and to erect monuments to and rebury victims of Stalinist terror. By April 1989, 400 legislators and 20 nongovernmental organizations participated in the work of the commissions. Grassroots organizations like Memorial (see entry on International Historical-Enlightenment and Human Rights Society Memorial) and the Ukrainian Society of Political Prisoners and Repressed collected documents about victims of Stalinism. The commissions quickly became overloaded. In 1988–1989, they processed claims of 15,610 victims, including 9,051 persons rehabilitated via court decisions, while accumulating a backlog of 240,000 claims related to judicial and 90,000 claims related to extrajudicial repression. Ukraine was the first Soviet republic to launch rehabilitation, through Law 962-XII/1991 on Rehabilitation of Victims of Political Repressions in Ukraine, which rehabilitated victims of Soviet repression (1917–1991) and compensated the victims.

Government officials' unwillingness to uncover the past delayed the recognition of some Stalinist crimes. Fewer persons were rehabilitated in Western Ukraine, which had the largest share of filed rehabilitation claims and the strongest anti-Soviet sentiment in Ukraine. The Supreme Court of Soviet Ukraine repeatedly refused to handle the rehabilitation claims of deportees and those sentenced by Stalinist military tribunals. In 1987–1988, a special government task force uncovered a mass grave in the forest of Bykivnya, near Kyiv, Ukraine's capital, and announced that 6,329 victims of Nazism were buried there. In 1989, another task force determined that the 6,783 persons buried in this mass grave were victims of Stalinism. In 2009, the government converted the mass grave into a memorial park supervised by the Institute of National Memory.

While Memorial educated the public about Stalinist repression and the impact of Soviet rule on Ukrainians, Gorbachev repeatedly demanded from his subordinates increased numbers of rehabilitated victims of Stalin's purges, in order to show that the anti-Stalin rhetoric led to reform of the Communist Party and the Soviet Union to a better future. The leaders of Soviet Ukraine faced pressures from above and below. They grudgingly supported these truth-telling efforts that questioned their rule, the Communist Party, and its secret police. This controlled truth telling quickly went out of control in 1991, when the Soviet Union collapsed.

Transitional Justice in Postcommunist Ukraine

The independent Ukraine rehabilitated, compensated, and commemorated victims of Stalinism, reformed the secret police, declassified secret archives, recognized the Holodomor as genocide, and created the Institute of National Memory.

Rehabilitation and Compensation of Victims of Stalin's Purges

After 1991, the rehabilitation commissions quickened their processing of requests. Their work depended on the cooperation of different governmental agencies with different understandings about how to handle the requests and award rehabilitation and compensation. In 1993, parliament clarified the rehabilitation procedure to ensure uniformity across rehabilitation commissions and courts, which reviewed complaints against the commissions. By 2001, commissions had reviewed 307,450 cases, rehabilitated 248,710 persons, and denied rehabilitation to 117,243 others. Despite pressure from victims and their families, parliament did not extend rehabilitation to the victims' children born in the labor camps or exile, rehabilitate persons deported because of their ethnicity, or compensate victims for moral harm. In 2002, the Constitutional Court ruled that parliament's failure to include moral harm compensation for victims was constitutional, although the preamble of Law 962-XII stated that parliament "strives to provide feasible at this time compensation for material and moral damage caused by illegal repression, rehabilitated and their families." Compensation was limited to seventy-five minimum monthly salaries (US$1,000 in 1999), paid over five years. In 1996, survivors of prisons and labor camps had US$5 added to their monthly pensions, while victims of exile and deportation received half that amount.

The Communist Party Ban

After Ukraine declared its independence, parliament leaders blamed the Communist Party of Ukraine (CPU) for complicity in the failed coup d'état against the Soviet President Gorbachev, which threatened Ukraine's independence because the country would have remained a Soviet republic if the coup had succeeded. In 1991, Parliament froze the CPU's bank accounts, ordered police to seal and guard its property, and banned the party. The ban transferred the party's enormous financial resources and infrastructure to the Ukrainian government.

In 1993, the new Communist Party was formed. The party unsuccessfully campaigned to repeal the CPU ban and claim the CPU's valuable property. In 1997, 139 communist legislators asked the Constitutional Court to lift the ban, both because parliament had impinged on the prerogative of the judiciary, which had exclusive power to ban parties, and because the ban violated the freedom of association of party members. In 2001, the Court declared the ban unconstitutional, but stated that the new party was not the CPU's legal successor and could not claim the CPU property (Trochev 2003). In May 2002, the new party merged with the old CPU (reconstituted in 2001).

Reforms of the Secret Police

In 1991, parliament abolished the KGB, established the Security Service of Ukraine (SBU), appointed former KGB agent Yevhen Marchuk as its head, and set up a commission to screen all former KGB officers who wished to work in the SBU for loyalty to independent Ukraine. The commission, composed of legislators of all stripes, included dissidents persecuted by the Soviet regime and KGB bosses who supervised their criminal prosecution. Within months, it rejected a third of high-ranking KGB officers, who retired on their own, went to Russia, or left for more lucrative positions in the private sector, but retained the KGB chiefs in most regional SBU offices and kept other KGB officers and its network of informers intact. The KGB officers composed the core of the SBU, while the KGB veterans enjoyed generous pensions. By mid-2009, at least one-fifth of Marchuk's subordinates had worked in the KGB. No KGB official responsible for terror was brought to account. By 2009, several lustration proposals modeled after the Czech or Polish programs were introduced in parliament, but none got off the ground.

Access to Secret Archives

Under Marchuk's watch, much of the KGB archives remained under SBU control. Some archives were trucked from Kyiv to Moscow in 1991. Files that could compromise the

SBU chiefs and the new ruling elite were destroyed by the KGB staff before it became the SBU. The SBU has claimed that it does not know the extent to which secret archives were destroyed or removed from Ukraine. While in the 1990s Moscow cooperated with the SBU on declassifying some archives, this cooperation stopped with the appointment of Vladimir Putin, a former KGB colonel, as Russia's president.

The SBU kept the Ukrainian KGB archives related to Stalinist terror and authorized very limited file access for victims and their relatives, rehabilitation commissions, and scholars, subject to broad restrictions in the name of the national interest and other persons' reputation. Law 962-XII/1991 allowed victims and their relatives to access files that contained no information that presented other persons in a negative light, while Law 3814-XII/1993 on National Archival Fund and Archival Institutions imposed a seventy-five-year ban on the release of confidential files of individual citizens. Until 2003, the SBU archive received about 1,000 access requests per year.

To shield his agency from accusations of being a KGB successor, Marchuk promoted the publication of declassified documents about Stalin's purges and bios of the victims of Stalinist repression in Ukraine. In 1994, he launched the journal *From the Archives of VUChK-GPU-NKVD-KGB* to publish previously secret materials about Stalin's rule. The SBU also funded and prepared films and books about the victims of Stalin's regime.

Acting on President Viktor Yushchenko's order and his Edict 37/2009 on Declassifying and Publishing Materials Related to the Ukrainian Liberation Movement, Political Repressions and Holodomors, the SBU declassified some 800,000 files about Stalinist purges and opened information halls to the public in fourteen cities, where citizens can freely photocopy declassified files stored in digital format. It pledged to declassify all materials from 1917 to 1991 and estimated that anyone would have access to 1,000 volumes of declassified files by late 2010.

Declassifying files about post-1953 persecution proceeds at a slower pace. In mid-2010, only 2 percent of classified KGB materials about that period remained in the SBU archives, as the others had been destroyed or transferred to Moscow. The SBU leaders warned that access will not result in criminal charges against KGB agents or the publication of the files, and that the "truth that Ukraine's people needed to know has already been revealed to them" (Kabachiy 2010). As such, few Ukrainians have accessed their KGB secret files.

Recognizing the Holodomor as Genocide

President Leonid Kravchuk (1991–1994) used the term "genocide" in his 1993 Edict on Measures in Connection with the 60th Anniversary of the Holodomor, ordered the Foreign Ministry to request that the Holodomor be placed on the UNESCO calendar, and publicly admitted that the Holodomor was a "planned genocide against our own people" (Kas'ianov 2010). In 2002–2003, parliament asked the United Nations to recognize the Holodomor as genocide and issued an Appeal to Ukrainians declaring the Holodomor as genocide that must be condemned by the Ukrainian society and the international community. The term "Holodomor" gained wide acceptance in Ukraine, and in 2003, three in four Ukrainians had heard of that historical episode (Finkel 2010). President Yushchenko (2005–2010) tirelessly lobbied to recognize the Holodomor as genocide against Ukrainians and a humanitarian catastrophe of the twentieth century, on par with the Holocaust.

Law 376-V/2006 on the Holodomor of 1932–1933 in Ukraine declared it a "genocide of the Ukrainian people" (Article 1) and made its public denial "an affront to the memory of the millions of victims of the Holodomor" (Article 2), without criminalizing it. In 2009, Yushchenko convinced the SBU to launch a criminal case against 136 deceased perpetrators of the Holodomor, including Stalin. The SBU declassified some materials, assembled evidence against Stalin and his operatives in Ukraine, charged seven top communist officials, insisted that the case had no legal consequences for Russia as successor to the Soviet Union, and sent a 330-volume case to the court in 2009. In January 2010, the Kyiv Appellate Court heard the case, recognized that Stalin and six others planned and committed genocide against 3,941,000 persons, but closed the case because the defendants were deceased. Yushchenko hoped the case would help him win the 2009 presidential elections, but Kravchuk and presidential candidate Viktor Yanukovych criticized it as an unjust retroactive application of criminal law. After winning the elections, President Yanukovych blamed Yushchenko's policy for dividing Ukraine and insisted that the Holodomor had targeted not only Ukrainians but also other ethnic groups. In 2010, 20 percent of Ukrainians approved and 40 percent disapproved of Yanukovych's policy of halting attempts at achieving recognition of the Holodomor as genocide.

Commemoration

Throughout the 1990s, commemoration of victims of Stalinism depended on the grassroots initiatives of holding vigils and public meetings, organizing exhibitions in museums, and erecting monuments. Since 1993, May 18 has marked the anniversary of mass deportations from Crimea as the Day of Memory of Victims of the Deportation of Crimean Tatars. In 1998, the last Saturday of November became the Day of Remembrance of the Victims of the Holodomor, later renamed as the Day of Remembrance of the Victims of the Holodomor and Political Repressions. That year, President Kuchma ordered the construction of a national museum-monument to Holodomor victims in downtown Kyiv, whose construction started in 2004. Yushchenko made the commemoration of all communist-era victims a personal priority. In 2007, he declared the third Sunday in January as the Day of Remembrance of Victims of Political Repressions, and funded the construction of monuments and museums, education programs, media campaigns, and the publication of archival research. Law 376-V/2006 on the Holodomor called for the construction of a national museum-monument to the victims, officially opened in 2009.

Commemoration of the past also involves the controversial glorification of the Organization of Ukrainian Nationalists (OUN-B) and its military wing, the Ukrainian Insurgent Army (UPA), which were outlawed by the Soviet Union for fighting for an independent Ukraine and against the Red Army during and after World War II (Wanner 1998; Marples 2007). Both organizations are respected as freedom fighters in Western Ukraine and despised as Nazi collaborators in Eastern Ukraine. In the late 1990s, the first museums about the OUN-B and the UPA opened in Western Ukraine. In 2003, exhibition "Not to Be Forgotten: The Chronicle of Communist Inquisition, 1917–1991," organized by Memorial, listed the OUN-B and UPA as victims of Stalin. The exhibition became a full-fledged Museum of Soviet Occupation in 2007. In 2009, the National Memorial Museum of Victims of the Occupation Regimes was opened in a renovated former prison in Lviv.

In 2007 and 2010, respectively, President Yushchenko posthumously proclaimed Roman Shukhevych, the UPA commander during the 1940s, and Stepan Bandera, the OUN-B leader and a Ukrainian nationalist, as Heroes of Ukraine. Yushchenko then asked Parliament to recognize the UPA members as war veterans or victims of Stalin's terror, as some municipalities in Western Ukraine had already done. Parliament and local governments in Eastern Ukraine refused to comply with the request. In 2009, only 14 percent of Ukrainians viewed these organizations positively. President Yanukovych promised to deprive Shukhevych and Bandera of their titles.

The Ukrainian Institute of National Memory

Law 376-V/2006 on the Holodomor created the Institute of National Memory, modeled after the Polish Institute of National Remembrance (see separate entry), as a central government agency for restoring and preserving the national memory of the Ukrainian people. Its task of uncovering the truth about those who fought for Ukrainian statehood during Soviet rule is controversial because some defenders of independent Ukraine (OUN-B and UPA) sided with Nazi Germany during World War II. The Institute has forty-five employees and relies on the goodwill of the state and the SBU archives to assemble its own archives. It published the nineteen-volume *National Book of Memory* of victims of the Holodomor, including the names of 882,500 victims of death by starvation from 13,000 villages.

The Institute has faced chronic problems of funding, personnel, and cooperation from the SBU. In 2010, President Yanukovych replaced the Institute's leadership and turned its agenda away from condemnation toward a less critical reconciliation with the Soviet past. Historian Valeriy Soldatenko, the Institute's new Director and a Communist Party member, has blamed Yushchenko for honoring Bandera and Shukhevych, and denied that the Holodomor was genocide of the Ukrainian people.

Conclusion

Ukraine shows the difficulty of reconciling with the past in politically fragmented countries. The Ukrainian leaders who tried to promote transitional justice achieved only symbolic recognition of the victims of Soviet oppression, because of the unwillingness of the KGB and its successors to open the secret archives, and the unwillingness of Ukrainian elites to reveal their connections with the Soviet secret police. Ukrainians remain split on the issue, and many of them do not see the process of evaluating the communist regime as a priority as it touches on the highly contested issues of national and civic identity and the foundation of the Ukrainian state.

Alexei Trochev

Cross-references: Court Trials for Redress; Genocide; Institute for National Remembrance, Poland; International Historical-Enlightenment and Human Rights Society Memorial; Rehabilitation of Political Prisoners.

Further Readings

Finkel, Evgeny. 2010. In Search of Lost Genocide: Historical Policy and International Politics in Post-1989 Eastern Europe. *Global Society*, 24(1): 51–70.

Kabachiy, Roman. 2010. Ukraine's Stolen Memory. *OpenDemocracy.net*, May 5. AAvailable at: http://www.opendemocracy.net/print/54081 (accessed November 5, 2010).

Kas'ianov, Georgii. 2010. The Holodomor and the Building of a Nation. *Russian Politics and Law*, 48(5): 25–47.

Marples, David. 2007. *Heroes and Villains: Creating National History in Contemporary Ukraine*. Budapest: Central European University Press.

National Book of Memory of Victims of the 1932–1933 Holodomor in Ukraine [Knyha pam'yati zhertv Holodomoru 1932–1933 rokiv v Ukrayini]. Kyiv: Ukrainian Institute of National Memory, 2008. Available at: http://www.memory.gov.ua/ua/publication/content/1522.htm (accessed November 5, 2010).

Rehabilitated by History [Reabilitovani istoriyeyu]. Available at: http://www.reabit.org.ua (accessed November 5, 2010).

Trochev, Alexei. 2003. Ukraine: Constitutional Court Invalidates the 1991 Ban on the Communist Party. *International Journal of Constitutional Law*, 1(3): 534–540.

Wanner, Catherine. 1998. *Burden of Dreams: History and Identity in Post-Soviet Ukraine*. University Park: Pennsylvania State University.

Uruguay

Uruguay experienced dictatorship between 1973 and 1985, during which the state security forces committed large-scale human rights abuses, including torture, disappearance, and political assassinations. This repression was the military's response to the threat posed by the armed guerrilla movement, the *pamaros*, who were pursuing a Marxist political agenda in the context of regional radical leftist movements started in Brazil, Argentina, and Chile. Although the question of accountability for those abuses was at the forefront of the politics of transition to democracy, officially Uruguay embraced impunity and a forgive-and-forget approach through amnesty laws. A distinctive feature of political transition in Uruguay has been the use of legal measures to legitimize actions that are either unconstitutional or against international law. When parliamentary and legal channels to pursue accountability have been blocked, nongovernmental organizations have played an important role in promoting "truth politics," and families have demanded accountability concerning the disappeared. In short, transitional justice has been a contested issue from the 1980s onward.

The Repressive Past

The military dictatorship that took control of Uruguay in 1973 was the culmination of a "slow coup" that began in 1968 with the declaration of a state of emergency by the government of Jorge Pacheco Areco, representing the Colorado Party, historically the most elected party in the history of Uruguay, with almost uninterrupted dominance during the twentieth century. The state of emergency was instituted in an effort to confront the growing armed insurgency of the Tupamaros, an urban guerilla organization drawing support from the National Liberation Movement (Movimiento de Liberación Nacional) and trade unions in poverty-stricken rural areas. The 1968 state of emergency was a shock for Uruguayans, who had long-established democratic traditions and claimed to be the first welfare state internationally under the inspired leadership of José Batlle y Ordóñez in 1903. At the height of the insurgency in 1970 and 1971, the Tupamaros promoted radical change through staging armed action and dramatic gestures, including the release of approximately 100 prisoners and the kidnapping and public interrogation of prominent citizens in Tupamaros-controlled Cárcel del Pueblo (People's Prison) for their alleged crimes against the Uruguayan people.

The Tupamaros were defeated by the end of 1973 by a military counteroffensive and Death Squad (Escuadron de la Muerte) composed of police officers who were granted extensive repressive powers to eliminate the Tupamaro armed insurrection. Even after the Tupamaros's defeat, the military dictatorship continued to expand its hold on the government. Between 1973 and 1985, the dictatorship imprisoned more than 55,000 people out of a total population of around 3 million and conducted extensive interrogation of ordinary Uruguayans. The majority of prisoners were convicted in military courts, and the rest were detained without trial. It is widely claimed that nearly all prisoners were routinely tortured (Mallinder 2009; Skaar 2007; BaWeschler 1998). While disappearance was also used as a means of repression, it was on a very limited scale in comparison with Argentina. Around 164 Uruguayans disappeared – 32 in Uruguay and 132 in Argentina – in contrast to 30,000 persons who disappeared in Argentina.

The disappearance of Uruguayans in Argentina points to another feature of dictatorship and repression in the Southern Cone countries: the coordination of military repression under Operation Condor, the repressive campaign officially implemented in 1975 by the Southern Cone governments of South America in the hope of eradicating socialist and communist influence and opposition to the participating right-wing governments. In the name of national security, Chile, Argentina, Uruguay, Bolivia, Paraguay, and Brazil shared intelligence, seized suspects, assassinated each other's subversives, and conducted cross-border raids. This meant that fugitives from one regime could not find refuge in a neighboring state. These militaries cooperated by using criminal methods to eliminate subversion. The extent of the cooperation in Operation Condor has become apparent through the release of official archives in Uruguay, the discovery of a comprehensive archive in the Paraguayan capital Asunción, and criminal investigations in Argentina, Uruguay, and Spain. Examples of Uruguayan-Argentine cooperation under Operation Condor are the assassination of two Uruguayan parliamentarians, Zelmar Michelini and Héctor Gutiérrez Ruiz, in Buenos Aires in 1976 and the forced disappearance of the Argentine citizen Maria la Madrid Gelman in Buenos Aires in 1976 and her transfer to Uruguay, where Uruguayan security forces abducted her newborn child, Macarena Gelman, and suppressed the identity. Macarena was only identified living in Uruguay in 2000.

The dictatorship's domination of a small compact society meant that there was almost no organized opposition. The entire population was classified according to their security status. Every civil servant, including teachers at primary, secondary, and tertiary levels, were obliged to sign a "democratic faith" pledge, a document that affirmed that the signatory abided by the regime's rules. Citizens who signed were classified category A; those who refused to sign were classified category B, suspected of being potential subversives; and those classified as category C were regarded as enemies of the state and were already in jail, actively being pursued, or in exile. No other country in Latin America was able to exert this degree of control over its population. This military domination of society in part explains the military regime's overconfidence when, in 1980, it initiated a plebiscite to permanently entrench its power above parliament through constitutional reform. The plebiscite was defeated and began the military's slow retreat back to the barracks.

During the dictatorship, human rights advocacy was limited. It really only emerged after 1981, when the military had begun to negotiate their withdrawal from power. Established in 1981, the Peace and Justice Service (Servicio Paz y Justicia, SERPAJ; see separate entry) was the most important such human rights advocacy group, but it was declared illegal from 1981 (when it was founded) until 1983. Afterward there were no legal defense organizations, and the professional lawyers association Colegio de Abogados (College of Lawyers) refused this role. The main groups that emerged were Movimiento de Madres y Familiares de Procesados por la Justicia Militar (Movement of the Mothers and Family Sentenced by Military Justice), constituted in 1982 by relatives of political prisoners who denounced prison conditions and sentences; Madres y Familiares de Desaparecidos en Uruguay (Mothers and Family of the Disappeared in Uruguay), organized in 1983 by the families of the disappeared, who denounced disappearances and demanded the return of the disappeared alive; and Servicio Ecumenico de Reintegración (Ecumenical Service for Reintegration, SER), set up in 1984 as an ecumenical church organization that addressed the needs of ex-prisoners and assisted in their reintegration in society. SERPAJ played an important role in supporting these organizations.

While opposition was suppressed at home, the Uruguayan exile community was active in denouncing the military government's human rights abuses to the United Nations Human Rights Committee, the Organization of American States, and the International Committee of the Red Cross. They also sought support from international nongovernmental organizations such as Amnesty International and the International Commission of Jurists.

Transitional Justice

In Uruguay, transitional justice measures to promote truth, justice, and reconciliation were blocked by an amnesty law negotiated between the military and political elite to allow the military to withdraw on their terms. The amnesty law, Law 15848 on the Expiry of the Punitive Claims of the State (Ley de Caducidad de la Pretensión Punitiva del Estado) of 22 December 1986, commonly referred to as the Expiry Law, shielded the police and the military from prosecution and absolved the state from prosecuting human rights abuses by quarantining them in the past. There was also no strong sense of collective responsibility for the victims of repression whose needs tended to be privatized or medicalized. Uruguay's transitional justice profile was distinctive because the Expiry Law was ratified by popular vote in 1989, the state promoted partially restorative justice through a negotiated agreement of the political class that included nearly all the political parties, and an activist human rights organization took responsibility for conducting a limited unofficial truth commission and published a *Nunca Mas* report to document the scale and character of human rights abuses under the dictatorship. The Uruguayan case also highlights the fact that transitional justice is often a long-term process and accountability may be delayed rather than completely avoided.

The Expiry Law was the eventual product of a controlled reopening of electoral politics. Just as the dictatorship arrived as a "slow coup," so too the return to democracy involved the military's "slow retreat" to the barracks. As noted earlier, this retreat was unintentionally triggered by none other than the military in November 1980, when they lost a plebiscite designed to consolidate their power through constitutional reform. The electorate voted against the plebiscite by 56.1 percent, a result that in turn led the military to begin negotiations with selected political leaders to withdraw from government on the military's terms. These negotiations culminated in the August 1984 Naval Club Agreement, which established November 11, 1984 as the date for new democratic elections.

The new democratic government of President Julio Maria Sanguinetti, which was sworn in on March 1, 1985, had no mandate for truth and justice and only a limited restorative justice agenda. The demands for truth recovery came second to the demands for the release and compensation of the political prisoners, the aspect of the repression that had directly affected so many Uruguayan families. Under the Law of National Pacification of 1985 (Ley de Pacificación Nacional), all political prisoners were pardoned and released if their political crimes were committed after January 1, 1962, except those who had committed "crimes of blood" – that is, crimes inflicting serious injury or death. Police and military officers responsible for cruel or inhuman treatment and for the detainment of people who disappeared were explicitly excluded from this amnesty. Public servants dismissed under military rule and imprisoned or forced into exile had their jobs restored under the Law for the Reintegration of the Exonerated (Ley de Reposición de Destituiduos). In total, approximately 10,500 public employees had their jobs returned and 6,000 pension benefits were granted. These legislative initiatives promoted a practical reconciliation between the opponents and the supporters of the dictatorship within the state political and administrative institutions. The measures were restorative and sought to rehabilitate the democratic state by reconciling the political parties and civil servants. In addition, in 1985, the government created a National Commission for Repatriation (Comisión Nacional de Repatriación) to encourage and support the return of all exiles to Uruguay as a form of reconciliation.

The return of democratic politics allowed opponents of the Naval Club Agreement to challenge it through their capacity to initiate parliamentary investigations into human rights abuses. In April 1985, a parliamentary initiative established two investigative commissions to provide information to the courts on the disappeared and the 1976 assassinations of the Uruguayan legislators Michelini and Gutiérrez Ruiz (noted previously). Some military officers were so outraged by these parliamentary investigations that they challenged the senators to a then-outlawed duel. Both commissions found evidence against the military, but the government did not follow up with legal prosecutions.

The initiative to launch 734 individual investigations into human rights abuses in the courts in December 1986 precipitated a confrontation with the military, which refused to cooperate. The Sanguinetti government responded by introducing the Expiry Law and thereby enacting a total amnesty for the police and the military. In response, the deputies created the National Pro-Referendum Commission (Comisión Nacional Pro-Referendum) to campaign for a referendum on the Expiry Law based on Article 79 of the 1967 Constitution, which allowed for a referendum if the signatures of 25 percent of the total number of electors from the previous election were collected in support within one year of a law's promulgation. While the deputies succeeded in forcing the referendum, they failed to overturn the law, achieving only 47 percent in support of its repeal. President Sanguinetti's assessment of the outcome was that "Amnesty was the price to pay for democracy" (Barahona de Brito 1997, 151).

In response to the Sanguinetti government's failure to initiate prosecutions, the SERPAJ launched its own popular truth commission, described as "bottom-up truth recovery." Based on a representative survey sample of 311 ex-political prisoners, the SERPAJ produced an "unofficial" *Nunca Mas – Violación a los Derechos Humanos (1972–1985)* [Never Again – Human Rights Violations 1972–1985] report in March 1989. The systematic and violent nature of the repression and intimidation was revealed in the fact that almost every political prisoner reported been tortured. The SERPAJ saw itself as outside the state, representing the victims betrayed by the political class in the transition to democracy.

Opposition to the Expiry Law continued through the activities of human rights advocacy organizations, victims groups, and family members. Their efforts have included petitioning the president to investigate individual cases of disappearance, documenting past human rights abuses, memorializing the disappeared (every year, on May 28, a march is organized in Montevideo, the country's capital), petitioning the Inter-American Human Rights Commission on cases of human rights abuse and accountability, and providing medical and counseling support to the families of the disappeared and former political prisoners.

The national barrier to legal remedy created by the Expiry Law prompted victims groups and human rights advocates to launch international legal actions to pressure the Uruguayan government to initiate prosecutions. In 1989, the Institute for Legal and Social Studies of Uruguay (Instituto de Estudios Legales y Sociales del Uruguay, IELSUR), a legal defense human rights organization, took eight cases related to disappearance to the Inter-American Commission of Human Rights (IACHR), which ruled against the validity of Uruguay's amnesty laws. In 1992, the IACHR, in a decision on the Expiry Law, ordered Uruguay to pay reparations.

Human rights organizations have also used the civil courts to seek compensation as well as to try to force the government to launch investigations into disappearances. The IELSUR has pursued cases under civil law – that is, cases that fell outside the parameters of the Expiry Law – for pecuniary reparation for the suffering caused by the state or its agents. Individuals have also petitioned the president to meet his obligations under Article 4 of the Expiry Law, which calls on the head of state to investigate the fate of the disappeared. In response to a civil court decision in Montevideo in 2000, the new President Jorge Batlle Ibáñez, who won the presidential elections that year, established the Commission for Peace (Comisión para la Paz), charged with investigating human right abuses perpetrated during the dictatorship (1973–1985). The Commission was allowed to investigate the fate of the disappeared – the where, when, how, and why the atrocities or human rights infringements were committed – but not to look into who had committed them.

Human rights victims' organizations have also continued to demand criminal prosecutions. Mothers and Family of Uruguayans Detained and Disappeared (Madres y Familiares de Uruguayos Detenidos Desaparecidos) has been active in documenting the fate of the disappeared and tracing missing children. They collaborate with similar organizations in Latin America under the umbrella of the Latin American Federation of Associations of the Families of the Detained and Disappeared (Federación Latinoamericana de Asociaciones de Familiares de Detenidos-Desaparecidos, FEDEFAM). One strategy they have adopted to attract other legal jurisdictions to prosecute cases of disappearance has been to gather evidence of Uruguayan and Argentine disappeared people of Spanish and Italian background and thereby have Spanish and Italian courts prosecute those who committed human rights violations against citizens of these two European countries. Professional associations were another arena to challenge impunity.

The Medical Federation of the Interior (Féderación Médica del Interior, FEMI) expelled those members they found had collaborated in the torture of prisoners.

The objective of the Expiry Law may have been to quarantine the past, but it did not. The Expiry Law has gradually been eroded by actions of parliament, the judiciary, and human rights activists. Since 2006, significant compensation was awarded to former political prisoners, ratification of the law on forced disappearance allowed the prosecution of former military leaders, in individual cases judges have declared the Expiry Law unconstitutional, the Supreme Court has declared the Expiry Law unconstitutional in case relating to the death in 1974 of Nibia Sabalsagaray in a military establishment, and the movement to have the Expiry Law annulled continued. However, contradicting this gradual erosion of amnesty was the recent defeat of the plebiscite (October 2009) to annul the Expiry Law, at a time when a left-wing coalition government, the Broad Front (Frente Amplio), was once again voted into power and the former Tupamaro guerilla, José Mujica, was elected President. This apparently contradictory outcome does not mean the Expiry Law will not continue to be subverted by activist judiciary or that it might not be overturned through legislation. The solution of erasing the past from public discussion highlights a very private legacy of repression in Uruguay in which national reconciliation remains inhibited by privatized memories of repression.

Conclusion

A quarter-century after the end of the dictatorship, the transitional justice issues of justice, reconciliation, and compensation remain on the national political agenda. The Uruguayan case of impunity suggests that the transition to democracy is shaped by the circumstances under which re-democratization occurs and the extent to which reconciliation is at the forefront of the political agenda. The distinctive character of transitional justice in Uruguay rested on the way it was conducted in the political arena – the business of the democratic state was rehabilitated through reinstating all political parties using parliament as an arena to initiate investigations and publicly test the public's position on amnesty through plebiscite. Human rights organizations have also remained important in maintaining public debate and pursuing alternative legal channels internationally as a means to challenge impunity.

Michael Humphrey and Estela Valverde

Cross-references: Accountability; Argentina; Peace and Justice Service of Uruguay; Reconciliation.

Further Readings

Barahona de Brito, A. 1997. *Human Rights and Democratization in Latin America*. Oxford: Oxford University Press.

Instituto de Estudios Legales y Sociales del Uruguay. Official Web site. Available at: http://www.ielsur.org (accessed December 13, 2009).

Loveman, L. 1998. High Risk Collective Action: Defending Human Rights in Chile, Uruguay and Argentina. *The American Journal of Sociology*, 104(2): 9–33.

Madres y Familiaries de Detenidos / Desaparacidos. Official Web site. Available at: http://www.serpaj.org.uy/familiares (accessed December 13, 2009).

Mallinder, L. 2009. Uruguay's Evolving Experience of Amnesty and Civil Society's Response. Working Paper 4, March. In *Beyond Legalism: Amnesties, Transition and Conflict Transformation*,

Queen's University Belfast. Available at: http://ulster.academia.edu/LouiseMallinder/Papers/92679/Uruguay's-Evolving-Experience-of-Amnesty-and-Civil-Society's-Response (accessed August 14, 2009).

Peace and Justice Service (Servicio Paz y Justicia). Official Web site. Available at: http://www.serpaj.org.uy (accessed December 13, 2009).

Skaar, E. 2007. Legal Development and Human Rights in Uruguay: 1985–2002. *Human Rights Review*, 8: 52–70.

Weschler, L. 1998. *A Miracle, a Universe: Settling Accounts with Torturers*. Chicago: University of Chicago Press.

Venezuela

Until recently, Venezuela rarely received media attention, but since the election in 1998 of Hugo Chávez Frías as president, the country has been under close scrutiny by the international community. The election saw the rewriting of the Venezuelan Constitution, which marked the establishment of the Fifth Republic in 1999 and a sharp break with the institutions and practices of the Fourth Republic (1958–1998), when most significant human rights violations took place. Although important to the Chávez government, which has restructured key formerly repressive and corrupt institutions (like the state security and the judiciary), transitional justice has been stalled by various Fifth Republic institutions and complicated by both the opposition's former control of key governmental and judicial institutions and the government's new centralization and re-politicization of the bureaucracy and the judiciary. The deep-rooted political changes, and the limited transitional justice effected to date, must be understood in the context of the major restructuring of state and political institutions effected by the Fifth Republic.

The Repressive Past

As a result of the popular uprising of January 1958, the dictatorship of Marcos Pérez Jiménez, which had ruled the country since 1952 with the backing of the United States, came to an end. Afterward, Venezuela was considered a democracy because it avoided the military dictatorships that gripped other Latin American countries from the late 1960s to the mid-1990s. But at the same time subtle and more targeted repression was directed against dissidents denouncing political corruption, poorly considered economic policies, and Venezuela's ties to the United States. The most notable periods of repression were the 1960s, the 1980s, and the early 1990s.

After the 1959 Cuban revolution, Venezuela, like other Latin American countries, faced increased left-wing insurgency. While small in numbers, these guerrillas engaged in acts of kidnapping and attacked military and police headquarters. In response, governments used the actions by the guerillas to justify measures against all dissidents using both peaceful and violent methods, suspended constitutional guarantees, and sent the army into many poor neighborhoods, which resulted in widespread fighting, death, and destruction. By the late 1960s, most leftist guerrillas – which never numbered more than a few hundred members in total – were destroyed or internally disbanded, with numerous ex-rebels openly entering the political arena.

The guerrillas abandoned armed struggle in favor of electoral politics, but state repression continued. Community activists and workers were constant targets, especially for the

General Sector Direction of Intelligence and Prevention Services (Dirección General Sectorial de los Servicios de Inteligencia y Prevención, DISIP), which tortured suspects. Cuban-born Venezuelan Luis Posada Carriles, a notorious anti-Castro militant, was DISIP chief of operations in the early 1970s. On October 6, 1976, a Cuban civilian airliner exploded in mid-flight, killing seventy-three passengers. Accused of masterminding the crime, Posada Carriles was arrested, only to be found not guilty by a Venezuelan military court. After this court decision was overturned and the retrial commenced, he escaped from Venezuela avoiding justice. He currently resides in the United States, although the Venezuelan authorities requested his extradition.

By the late 1980s, as widespread popular discontent against the government's economic policies grew, the DISIP expanded its activities. When the government of President Carlos Andrés Pérez signed a structural adjustment economic reform program with the International Monetary Fund (without the consent of Congress), the economic impact of the sharp price increase in gas and transport prices provoked protests and looting in the capital on February 27, 1989. The violence that quickly spread throughout the country, and the subsequent state repression, became known as the Caracazo. With the pretext of restoring order, the military was sent into the shantytowns, where it shot civilians. According to government reports, 277 people were killed and 1,009 were wounded, but these figures were considered too low. Bart Jones (2007), citing medical personnel, concluded that 1,000–1,500 people may have been killed. Credible Venezuelan human rights organizations identified by name 399 people killed during the Caracazo.

The Caracazo produced the largest number of human rights violations in Venezuelan modern history. As a result of the violence and rising discontent throughout the country, state repression increased after February 1989. According to Amnesty International reports drafted in 1993 and 1996, the Venezuelan governments of the 1980s and the 1990s used violence to quell dissident activists in Caracas' shantytowns through arrest, torture, and in some cases murder by security forces. Although student leaders and trade unionists were targeted, most victims came from the poorest segments of the Venezuelan society.

According to the Venezuelan Human Rights Action and Education Program (Programa Venezolano de Educación-Acción en Derechos Humanos, PROVEA), 105 cases of torture were documented from October 1992 to September 1993. Another human rights organization, the Support Network for Justice and Peace (Red de Apoyo por la Justicia y la Paz), reported ninety incidents of torture in March–May 1993, and all major human rights organizations asserted that the number of cases documented remained low because of the victims' unwillingness to come forward for fear of retribution. Amnesty International also noted that torture persisted in the country because the courts failed to investigate reports of abuse and indict those responsible. Very few offenders were prosecuted and even fewer were convicted, partly because of the lack of independence of the Institute of Forensic Medicine, whose doctors examined cases of torture.

While different Venezuelan state authorities were involved in persecuting political opponents, the country's police forces were responsible for the most serious human rights abuses against people it perceived to have committed a crime. This was possible because there was no centralized police body; rather, every district or municipality had its own force.

Finally, Venezuela's prison system has long witnessed frequent serious human rights violations. Poor funding for prison administration and infrastructure and lack of well-trained staff members, along with high levels of corruption, have been endemic. These problems were exacerbated by overcrowding and poor living conditions for prisoners. According to experts, the annual number of deaths in prison reached 600 in 1992. A key contributing factor was that during the 1990s, prison riots were accompanied by excessive violence. For example, during one riot at the Barcelona prison, two groups of inmates fought each other with sticks and guns for control of the institution. Six inmates were killed and twenty wounded, and a police report noted that the bodies of the dead inmates were found decapitated. In another case, on January 4, 1994, a riot at the Sabaneta prison in Maracaibo left 104 prisoners dead and 80 wounded. As a result, Sabaneta became known as "the prison of death."

During the 1980s and 1990s, state repression was accompanied by high rates of street crime, unemployment, and sharply increasing poverty rates as government revenues from taxes on oil profits declined and more state assets were privatized. For example, between 1987 and 1994, the prices of essential foods, household items, transport, and electricity increased by 50–100 percent, real wages fell by 20–50 percent, while per capita spending on social programs like health and education declined by almost 50 percent. As a result of these policies Venezuela's leading political parties – Democratic Action (Acción Democrática, AD) and Committee of the Independent Electoral Political Organization (Comité de Organización Política Electoral Independiente, COPEI) – became unpopular. After the 1958 Punto Fijo agreement, which marked the regime change from dictatorship to democracy, these parties had monopolized the state and private sectors and stalled the development of a nonpoliticized state bureaucracy, at the exclusion of the political left. Corruption and the crossover of government officials to the private sector once their terms in office expired were common, as was the multiplication of well-paid positions in the state oil company Petróleos de Venezuela S.A. (PDVSA), an important Venezuelan economic actor.

Two failed military coup d'états occurred in 1992. The February coup was led by a group of lieutenant colonels, including Hugo Chávez, who had organized clandestinely since the early 1980s as the Revolutionary Bolivarian Movement (Movimiento Bolivariano Revolucionario 200, MBR-200). Named after the nineteenth-century Venezuelan independence leader Simón Bolívar, the organization opposed the economic policies of Venezuelan governments, the widespread political corruption, and the country's close ties to the Unites States. While the February coup saw 14 dead soldiers, another 50 injured, and 80 civilians hurt in the fighting, the more violent November coup resulted in 174 dead soldiers and civilians. After spending two years in prison, Chávez and his fellow coup plotters were pardoned by President Rafael Caldera, who won the 1994 elections after leaving COPEI to form the National Convergence (Convergencia Nacional) party. The election marked the end of the thirty-five-year-long rule of the Democratic Action and COPEI. After reorganizing the MBR-200 as the Fifth Republican Movement (Movimiento Quinta Republica, MVR) and forming a broad left-wing coalition, Chávez won the 1998 presidential election.

Soon after taking office, Chávez clashed with the opposition, constituted by traditionally powerful and established political players with strong ties to the private sector, because he refused to give them key government positions. (In many Latin American countries, ministries often include members of opposition political parties if the ruling party feels the need to make special concessions to traditional economic and political elites to remain in office.) His government redrafted the constitution to make the state responsible for meeting the citizens' economic needs and promoting general prosperity.

Transitional Justice

Venezuela has embraced a limited number of transitional justice methods, including court trials, reforms of the police and secret police, compensations for victims, and official acknowledgment of past wrongdoing. These measures were complemented by the condemnation of the Caracazo human rights violations by the Inter-American Commission on Human Rights. Most efforts to come to terms with the past have tried to redress the human rights violations perpetrated during the Caracazo.

International Condemnation and Official Acknowledgment

In 1998, the Inter-American Commission on Human Rights condemned the actions of the government of Carlos Andrés Pérez (1989–1993), the first Venezuelan president forced to resign by the Supreme Court after having misappropriated 250 million bolívares (some US$110,000). The Commission referred the case to the Inter-American Court of Human Rights, which in 1999 concluded that one decade earlier the Venezuelan state had committed serious human rights violations that included extrajudicial killings. The Chávez administration did not contest the court's decision and accepted the state's responsibility for its crimes.

An internal investigation launched after the 1989 massacre was stalled until the Chávez administration took office in 1999. Even afterward, it proceeded slowly, as parts of the bureaucracy and the judiciary opposed the central government's move to hold accountable those responsible for past human rights abuses. It was not until 2004–2005, when the government purged these bureaucracies, held by AD and COPEI members or supporters, and replaced them with Chavistas or government sympathizers, that some progress was made in transitional justice. For example, in July 2005, the Venezuelan state accepted responsibility for the disappearance of three people after police and military forces were mobilized in the wake of heavy floods in 1999. The DISIP is believed to have disappeared two of the victims. In the past, such actions by the DISIP would have merited little enquiry from state authorities.

Court Trials

In 2006, the Attorney General's Office reopened the case of the murder of nine political activists in the Yaracuy state by the DISIP in May 1986. Charges were brought against nearly thirty DISIP officers, with ten arrest warrants filed. The Attorney General's Office has made less progress in relation to the massacre in the eastern state of Anzoategui of twenty-three political activists of the armed guerilla Americo Silva Front. The massacre was conducted by state security forces in October 1982. As of this writing, it is expected that charges will soon be made against some suspects. According to the Attorney General's Office, 756 people were murdered or disappeared by state security forces during the 1960s, 1970s, and 1980s. A special parliamentary commission investigates these crimes, along with the Body of Scientific, Penal and Criminal Investigations (Cuerpo de Investigaciones Científicas, Penales y Criminalísticas, CICPC) experts.

On October 1, 2009, in a cemetery in Caracas, the Attorney General's Office exhumed the remains of 125 bodies believed to be victims of the Caracazo. Afterward, the Office filed a request with Interpol for the arrest of the former Venezuelan President Carlos Andrés Pérez, presumed to be living either in the United States or in the Dominican Republic. Charges were also brought against two military officers and Defense Minister Italo del Valle Alliegro. No arrests have been made to date.

Overall, transitional justice through court trials has been slow and by no means conclusive, mainly because of the opposition of the judiciary, the armed forces, and the police to Chavez's rule and to investigating their own past actions. This was most evident when in April 2002, a military coup briefly ousted President Chávez. Despite evidence to the contrary, in August of that year, the Supreme Court ruled by a slim margin that the incident was not a coup d'état, but rather a "power vacuum." In May 2004, after the government appointed new judges and prosecutors, the Supreme Court's Constitutional Chamber overturned the decision and ruled that Chavez's recusal as president was unconstitutional and the military officers responsible for the coup should stand trial. When the judiciary was criticized for being pro-Chávez instead of impartial, the government defended the new appointments as a response to the previous judges' lack of impartiality.

Some pro-Chavez members of the judiciary have been physically attacked. On November 18, 2004, the leading state prosecutor Danilo Anderson was assassinated shortly before he was due to indict 400 people for their involvement in the coup. At the time of this writing, eight anti-Chavez politicians and businesspeople were sentenced for their role in the coup, while ten police officers were charged with the deaths of three demonstrators. Six of the officers were sentenced to thirty years in prison combined. The total death toll during the coup was in the dozens, mostly supporters of Chávez. Finally, while the judiciary is moving forward in holding accountable those responsible for the coup, most high-level military participants, including Pedro Carmona, the self-appointed president during April 11–13, 2002, have not stood trial, having fled to Colombia or the United States.

Reforms of the Police and the Secret Police

While the Chávez government has recently promoted army officers and judges supportive of its political agenda, reform of the state security, the police, and the prison system, as well as adequate training of their personnel regarding human rights, has been slow. In 2006, the Chávez administration conducted a nationwide consultation with local police forces and community organizations. Two years later, in April 2008, the National Assembly adopted Organic Law of the Police Service and the National Police, which outlined a new model of law enforcement based on the consultation process, and prohibited the police from carrying live ammunition at protests and strikes. In 2009, a national Police Academy offering courses in human rights was created to train Venezuela's new centralized police force.

Finally, with regard to prison reform, the country's current prison population of 20,000 has decreased substantially from the all-time peak of 31,400 in 1992. Conditions in Venezuela's 32 prisons remain poor, with 415 inmates killed in 2007 as a result of prison violence. According to the government, nine new prisons with modern facilities will soon open, and during recent years inmates have benefited from the government's new literacy and education programs.

Compensations and Victim Redress

Along with these developments and some small monetary compensation paid to the victims of the Caracazo in the form of pensions by the governmental Committee of Families of the Victims of February–March 1989 (COFAVIC), transitional justice has been slow. Civil society organizations such as Support Network for Justice and Peace and Faith and Happiness (Fe y Alegría) have had a tense relationship with the COFAVIC. For example, the Chávez government has sought to try past human rights violations in national courts, not through the establishment of an independent tribunal with international observers. Also, the COFAVIC leaders were criticized for allegedly embezzling a portion of the Caracazo victims' payments since 1989. While the government did not adopt all recommendations proposed by Venezuelan human rights organizations, cooperation between them has improved. In 2009, the Support Network for Justice and Peace treated forty cases of torture and other abuses by state security forces, roughly the same number as in 2008.

Conclusion

In Venezuela, obstacles to transitional justice have been numerous and the process of achieving it is by no means concluded. On the one hand, the Chávez government has made great strides to end the repressive and exclusionary practices of the state institutions of the Fourth Republic. Investigations regarding the Caracazo and other past state crimes, as well as police and prison reform, are moving forward, albeit slowly at times. On the other hand, after 2006, Venezuela under the Chávez government has witnessed a greater concentration of power in the executive, a reversal of the 1999 Constitution, and re-politicization of state institutions. The country has been polarized, its people either passionately supporting the government or wanting to see its end, with some even considering a violent overthrow preferable to a continuation of Chavez's rule. Almost every facet of the current government's policies has become a contentious point of debate. The government has not renewed some of the opposition's television and radio licenses, justifying this by pointing to their support for the 2002 coup or their noncompliance with the new media code's clause on "social responsibility." These developments might not support transitional justice or the establishment of an independent and nonpoliticized bureaucracy and judiciary.

Rodrigo Acuña and Estela Valverde

Cross-references: Court Trials for Redress; Reforms of Military, Police, Secret Police.

Further Readings

Fernández Blanco, P., M. Guillén, and J. Suggett. 2009. *Human Rights and Police Reform in Venezuela: A Venezuelan Perspective*. April 3. Available at: http://www.venezuelanalysis.com/analysis/4349 (accessed October 8, 2009).

Hellinger, D. C. 1991. *Venezuela: Tarnished Democracy*. Boulder: Westview Press.

International Crisis Group. 2009. *Venezuela: Accelerating the Bolivarian Revolution*. November 5. Bogotá/Brussels. Available at: http://www.crisisgroup.org/home/index.cfm?id=6376&l=1 (accessed November 10, 2009).

Jones, Bart. 2007. *¡Hugo! The Hugo Chávez Story: From Mud Hut to Perpetual Revolution*. Hanover: Steerforth Press.

Rosen, F. 2007. Breaking with the Past: A 40th Anniversary Interview with Margarita López Maya. *NACLA Report on the Americas*, 40 (3): 4–8.
U.S. Department of State. 1993. *Venezuela Human Rights Practices* 1993. Washington, DC. Available at: http://dosfan.lib.uic.edu/ERC/democracy/1993_hrp_report/93hrp_report_ara/Venezuela.html (accessed June 23, 2009).
Wagner, S. and G. Wilpert. 2005. *Venezuela's Intelligence Service to Be Restructured.* June 17. Available at: http://www.venezuelanalysis.com/print/1198 (accessed June 25, 2009).
Wilpert, G. 2009. *Smoke and Mirrors: An Analysis of Human Rights Watch's Report on Venezuela.* October 17. Available at: http://www.venezuelanalysis.com/analysis/3882 (accessed June 25, 2009).

Vietnam

After the end of the First Indochina War (1954), communist-dominated Vietnam underwent a series of economic, but not political, reforms. A market economy was introduced, but the Communist Party has retained its control over the country. In the absence of regime change, very little transitional justice has taken place to date.

The Repressive Past

From 1946 to 1954, Vietnam was the scene of the First Indochina War. French colonial troops and, after 1949, South Vietnam army troops fought against the Viet Minh, a communist independence movement formed in 1941 by Vietnamese refugees in Southern China to fight the invading Japanese. When in September 1945 the Viet Minh under Ho Chi Minh declared the Democratic Republic independent, nationalist opposition in the South formed the competing State of Vietnam, the precursor of the Republic of Vietnam. Representatives of the two Vietnamese states met at the 1954 Geneva Conference, where it was decided that Vietnam would gain independence from France and each party would retreat to its respective side of the 16th parallel north and prepare elections to unify the country. Large groups of refugees moved between the two states: approximately 1 million Catholics fled to the South fearing persecution by the communists, and 150,000 socialists, communists, and their sympathizers moved to the North. All hostilities were to cease, but neither party kept to the agreement. The United States armed the unstable South Vietnamese regime for fear of a communist election victory that would facilitate the spread of communism worldwide, while the North reactivated Viet Minh groups in the South. The result was the Vietnam War, in which South Vietnamese and Western forces under U.S. leadership fought against the Vietnamese communist forces supported by the Soviet Union and China.

In 1969, in response to protests at home and abroad demanding an end to the war, the United States began withdrawing its troops and training and supplying the South Vietnamese army for combat operations. In the war, which ended in 1975 when the North Vietnamese army captured the South Vietnamese capital of Saigon, many noncombatant civilians were displaced, tortured, and killed by soldiers on both sides in fighting on the ground, air bombardments, and napalm attacks. Infamous examples include the March 1968 My Lai massacre (in which an American infantry company killed, raped, and beat up to 504 unarmed villagers, mostly women, children, and elderly people) and the January 1968 Hue massacre (in which the North Vietnamese killed 2,000 to 6,000 civilians and soldiers in South Vietnam). The press initially presented the My Lai massacre as a victory, but in 1969, a former soldier and a photographer revealed the true extent of the killings. When in January 1968 the National Liberation Front (Viet Cong), an originally South Vietnamese pro-independence group of Viet Minh fighters, captured the city of Hue, they replaced the city government with a new administration that, using predrafted name lists, rounded up South Vietnamese soldiers, government and police officials, intellectuals, and business and Catholic leaders. When American and South Vietnamese troops reconquered the city, many of these individuals were tried by ad hoc courts consisting of communist cadres and officers for "crimes against the Vietnamese people" or for being "enemies of the revolution." Defendants were almost invariably found guilty and sentenced to death by immediate execution. Others were summarily executed without trial and buried in mass graves. According to eyewitness reports, communist troops carried out such purges in conquered areas throughout the country.

In 1976, the Republic of South Vietnam and the Democratic Republic of North Vietnam merged to become the Socialist Republic of Vietnam. The Communist Party of Vietnam (Đảng Cộng sản Việt Nam) has ruled the country along communist lines by nationalizing the means of production, imposing democratic centralism and socialist legality, and adopting a new constitution. The party-state has placed the interests of the nation and the socialist state before individual interests and rights. The 1980 Constitution guaranteed fundamental freedoms, if they did not violate state interests (Article 67). In practice, this has meant that public assembly is permitted only for state-sanctioned purposes, and religions and religious practices are tolerated if they comply with state goals. (Catholicism, for instance, has a French colonial background and is therefore subjected to state monitoring.) The press is censored and there is little space for civil society. Vietnam recognizes twenty-nine mass organizations (including the Communist Party, the army, and women's, workers', and youth groups) and special interest groups (religious groups and professionals) that together constitute the Vietnam Fatherland Front (Mặt Trận Tổ Quốc Việt Nam), an umbrella organization guarding national unity and supervising the activities of the government. The Front, which does not operate independently from the party-state, influences social and religious policies and endorses candidates for election to state or party posts.

Vietnam participated in two more wars. The 1978–1979 war with Cambodia to remove the Khmer Rouge from the border areas led in turn to a brief war with China in 1979. When the first war started, Cambodia and Vietnam were engaged in a dispute over border territories in the possession of Vietnam but claimed by Cambodia. Cambodian Khmer Rouge forces raided Vietnamese territory and massacred ethnic Vietnamese living inside Cambodia. In retaliation, the Vietnamese army invaded Cambodia in December 1978. After conquering the Cambodian capital of Phnom Penh in January 1979, the Vietnamese declared Cambodia a "people's republic" and installed a puppet regime loyal to them. Without fully defeating the Cambodian opposition forces, the Vietnamese army kept the country under military occupation. The ongoing fighting, rising numbers of refugees, and worsening living conditions raised international concerns over the fate of Cambodia. Between 1979 and 1988, several UN resolutions called on the Khmer Rouge and the Vietnamese to observe human rights and for all invading forces to withdraw. The Vietnamese troops withdrew in 1989, and Cambodia regained its independence in 1991.

The Chinese government backed the Khmer Rouge and used the poor treatment of ethnic Chinese in Vietnam (known as the Hoa) and Vietnam's occupation of the Spradley Islands (which China claimed) to attack Vietnam in February 1979. The Hoa formed sizeable communities throughout Vietnam. As they used Chinese language and writing, maintained their own schools and organizations, and lived and worked within their own communities, the Hoa were distinguishable from the Vietnamese. As China became increasingly powerful and politically active, the Vietnamese feared a "fifth column" bent on China's expansion. The Hoa were asked to register as Vietnamese citizens, renounce their Chinese nationality, and profess allegiance to Vietnam at a time when Vietnamese attitudes toward them became distrustful. Vietnam allowed many Hoa to cross the border into China. Riots and fights with border guards and soldiers led to deadly incidents when thousands assembled at the border to cross it. This and a major Vietnamese offensive in Cambodia led China to invade Vietnam. Within weeks, the Chinese army approached Hanoi, but then aborted the expedition. Both sides claimed victory as the Chinese withdrew, taking all movable valuables from Vietnam and destroying everything else in their path. The war displaced 300,000 Hoa from Vietnam and Cambodia to China and Thailand, while 400,000 reached other Southeast Asian countries as boat refugees in 1979 and 1980. In 1991, after the Cambodian war with Vietnam, relations between China and Vietnam were normalized and the position of the Hoa featured on the mutual agenda. Hong Kong became a major destination for all Vietnamese boat refugees by allowing them to land and assisting them in moving to other countries, notably the United States. After 1982, Hong Kong locked up new arrivals in camps and in 1989, as countries received fewer refugees, began distinguishing political from economic refugees, repatriating the latter to Vietnam and China.

After 1976, mass collectivization of farms and factories was implemented in the South, where farmers largely owned their lands, unlike farmers in the North, who were mostly tenants. The authorities claimed that collectivization aimed at increasing productivity, but Southern farmers saw it as a threat to their property rights. Supply shortages, bureaucratic leadership, and state investment negatively affected Vietnam's agriculture.

In the South, approximately 1 million people – former soldiers and civil servants of South Vietnam, teachers, intellectuals, community and religious leaders, ethnic minorities who sided with the French or the Americans, and ethnic Chinese – were sent to reeducation camps, developing "new economic zones," or jail after 1975. Two million other people fled the country by land or sea. In the reeducation camps, inmates underwent rehabilitation programs by writing self-criticisms, attending indoctrination sessions, and engaging in hard labor. Officially, the camps were not prisons, so no trial took place. Bureaucrats, not judges, decided whether one was required to spend time in the camp. Inmates could not leave voluntarily and endured harsh and violent treatment. Reeducation programs initially lasted for weeks, but in 1976 they were lengthened to up to three years, followed by release or court trial. Many inmates were released within months, but no mechanisms controlled the process and those detained for longer periods had no appeal. Since the 1980s, releases have been determined by bribes or political connections, not due legal process. The camps gained international notoriety in 1989, when the Vietnamese government allowed former South Vietnam military personnel to emigrate to the United States, where these former inmates talked publicly about their experiences. Families of former South Vietnam soldiers and officials remain discriminated against in housing, employment, and study opportunities.

In 1986, the Vietnamese government adopted reforms (Đổi mới, meaning renovation) to stimulate the economy through the development of private enterprises and free-market initiatives alongside communal and state enterprises. Foreign investment has been allowed, together with long-term land use rights and greater individual freedom of management in agriculture, but the means of production remain under government control. Doi Moi led to economic improvements, but also prompted the regime adopting authoritarian measures in response to popular criticism. As the business sector has developed, the party-state's corruption and cronyism have become evident. Entrepreneurs depend on state agents for permits and goodwill. Corruption is rampant among civil servants. State enterprises have links to individual government and party officials who provide contracts for kickbacks. Although several senior officials have been convicted for corruption since the 1990s, citizens have few means of defense against such abuse. After 1988, de-collectivization provided the poor rural classes with land rights, but large tracts of prime land have been appropriated by businesses, often with elite backing. The unregistered land used by local communities remains an issue. Legally this common land is state owned, but local farmers invoke custom or rights received from pre-communist regimes. Land Law 5/1993 does not recognize such rights. Tensions over land have led to public protests by local communities. Rural Vietnamese with land grievances often travel to regional centers or Hanoi to demonstrate outside city halls or even the National Assembly offices. These protests go largely unreported in the media.

Since the introduction of Doi Moi, political consciousness has risen, calls for a multiparty democracy have been voiced, and public protests and criticism of government policies have appeared. Sidel (2008) used the term "motorbike constitutionalism" to describe this phenomenon. Economic prosperity increased the number of bikes, congesting the streets of cities throughout the country. When the Hanoi city government tried to curb ownership of motorbikes, citizens invoked their constitutional right to own private property (stipulated in Article 58 of the 1992 Constitution).

The 1992 Constitution introduced the concept of the law-based state (*nhà nước pháp quyền*), which entails that law must regulate society. This provision did not curtail the power of the party, because law could be used to implement party policies, but it led to growing popular awareness that law, not the party or the government, should regulate state-society relations and that both citizens and government officials are subject to its rule. The nascent civil society nevertheless faces considerable difficulties. Article 50 the 1992 Constitution guarantees human rights, but Article 51 makes the rights of citizens inseparable from their obligations to state and society. State control remains rigid in most fields.

Vietnam allows no political parties aside from the Communist Party, but pro-democratic movements exist both inside and outside the country. The Government of Free Vietnam is a U.S. and Thailand organization based in South Vietnam that aims at overthrowing the communist regime by force, if necessary. The Vietnamese Reform Party (Việt Tân) and Bloc 8406 are peaceful organizations. Việt Tân, represented both inside and outside Vietnam, announced its existence in 2004, and was branded a terrorist organization in Vietnam. In 2006, Bloc 8406 published a manifest calling for reform and freedom that was signed by hundreds of Vietnamese. These organizations' leaders were jailed for belonging to a terrorist organization and abusing democratic freedoms (Articles 84 and 258 of the Penal Code). In April 2011, the Viet Tan activist and lawyer Cu Hu Hay Vu was jailed for "propagandizing against the government" (Article 88 Penal Code). As the Penal Code does not further define the elements of this crime, checking or opposing accusations is highly problematic. The article gives the judiciary the power to convict journalists, writers, activists, and others who openly criticize the government, thus effectively providing the government with control over the press. The printed press has increasingly allocated space for critical comments, perhaps because party officials have diverse interpretations of freedom of speech.

The position of the ethnic Chinese has improved markedly. Vietnam has needed the networks of the Hoa business community, which expanded as a result of the exodus of Hoa refugees to other Southeast Asian countries. Decree 501/1996 affirmed the rights and obligations of the Hoa, granted them the right to education and use of the Chinese language, revoked employment limitations placed on them in 1982, and gave them full access to the Vietnamese economy and society.

Transitional Justice

Transitional justice in Vietnam has been limited to a handful of court trials related to the Vietnam, Cambodia-Vietnam, and China-Vietnam wars. South Vietnamese farmers lost their land through abusive collectivization, but the 1988 de-collectivization gave at least some of them their land back. No property restitution has been adopted to date, and the recent reforms have not extended to the repressive agencies of the communist regime (the police, the army, and the secret political police). Thousands of South Vietnamese citizens were jailed or sent to reeducation camps, but none were rehabilitated or compensated for the harsh treatment they endured, and the Vietnamese communist regime delivered no official apology. The history textbooks present the point of view of the authorities exclusively, keeping silent on human rights violations and their many victims.

Court Trials for the Vietnam War

Both the South and North Vietnamese armies committed mass killings of civilians, but perpetrators were not brought to justice. The Vietnamese government has avoided trials for fear of endangering its relations with the United States, taking the view that the presence of the U.S. troops and the massacres carried out by them were illegal. Regarding the atrocities committed by its own troops, the Vietnamese government maintains that soldiers may have made mistakes, but engaged in no premeditated mass murders.

In 1970, twelve American soldiers and fourteen officers were charged with committing the My Lai massacre and suppressing information of its occurrence. The U.S. court martial that heard the case acquitted all of them except for the lieutenant in charge, William Calley, who received life imprisonment for premeditated murder. The sentence was then shortened to only four years in prison. My Lai was not the only massacre. The Vietnam War Crimes Working Group Files, a collection of Pentagon reports and documents detailing atrocities committed by U.S. forces in Vietnam, indicated 320 other substantiated and 500 unproven cases of war crimes. The 320 substantiated cases led to only 23 convictions. Other cases resulted in official reprimands, fines, or, in most cases, no sanction (Turse and Nelson, 2006).

Court Trials Related to the Cambodia-Vietnam and China-Vietnam Wars

Cambodian and international nongovernmental organizations have documented the crimes (theft, rape, and torture of prisoners) perpetrated by Vietnamese soldiers during the Cambodian-Vietnamese war, but the Cambodian government brought no cases to bear against Vietnam. The countries' steadily developing economic ties prevail over past war crimes. No court cases have related to the China-Vietnam war.

Conclusion

Continued economic growth is crucial to the future of the communist regime, because charismatic leadership and nationalism can no longer legitimize the party rule (Thayer 2009, 21). However, the party has faced allegations of endemic corruption. Its strong authoritarian stance makes a regime change unlikely, but many Vietnamese desire freedom and democracy, as the rural protests, the motorbike constitutionalism, and the vocal opposition of the Vietnamese diaspora show. Political freedoms are not inevitable, as the regime could choose to increase economic freedoms for private enterprise instead of engaging in political reform.

Laurens Bakker

Cross-references: Development and Transitional Justice.

Further Readings

Gainsborough, Martin. 2003. Corruption and the Politics of Economic Decentralization in Vietnam. *Journal of Contemporary Asia*, 33(1): 69–84.
Gillespie, John. 2006. Evolving Concepts of Human Rights in Vietnam. In *Human Rights in Asia. A Comparative Legal Study of Twelve Asian Jurisdictions, France and the USA*. Eds. Randall Peerenboom, Carole Petersen, and Albert Chen. London: Routledge.
Sidel, Mark. 2008. *Law and Society in Vietnam. The Transition from Socialism in Comparative Perspective*. Cambridge: Cambridge University Press.
Thayer, Carlyle. 2009. Vietnam and the Challenge of Political Civil Society. *Contemporary Southeast Asia*, 31(1): 1–27.
Turse, Nick and Deborah Nelson. 2006. Civilian Killings Went Unpunished. Declassified Papers Show U.S. Atrocities Went far Beyond My Lai. *LA Times*, August 6. Available at: http://www.latimes.com/news/printedition/asection/la-na-vietnam6aug06,0,92368.story?page=1 (accessed April 14, 2011).
Wells-Dang, Andrew. 2010. Political Space in Vietnam: A View from the 'Rice-Roots'. *The Pacific Review*, 23(1): 93–112.

Zimbabwe

Zimbabwe gained independence from British colonial rule, which perpetrated crimes against the black majority, in April 1980, after a protracted struggle against the white colonial settlers backed by Britain. The country then adopted a policy of reconciliation with its colonial past, predicated on the premise of "forgive and forget." However, independent Zimbabwe has gone through multiple transitions, and crimes were committed against different ethnic and political groups, including the Ndebele people during the 1980s, and, since the late 1990s, the political opposition to Mugabe's regime. These crimes needed to be redressed through various transitional justice methods, but it was only in 2008 that the government took meaningful steps in this regard.

The Repressive Past

Three decades after gaining its independence, Zimbabwe is still transitioning to democracy, as colonialism was followed by chronic political instability and a succession of repressive regimes. This prolonged transition has not deterred the local civil society, political elites, and the international community from discussing the need for transitional justice. The colonial repression (1888–1980), the Matabeleland atrocities (1984), and the repression against all forms of opposition (1998 to the present) have been particularly intense. During other times, repression was significantly lower.

During the colonial period, the black majority was oppressed, its arable land confiscated, and its basic rights (including the right to vote and run for public office) denied, as it was forced to work for the white minority as cheap labor. Repression and exploitation lasted for almost a century. Zimbabwe's colonization officially began in October 1888, when Charles Rudd and the Ndebele King Lobengula signed a mining agreement, and lasted until April 1980, when the country was liberated after a protracted armed struggle for independence. A new constitution was adopted, and power was handed over to the black majority after the Zimbabwe African National Unity (ZANU) won the elections. That year, ZANU leader Robert Mugabe became prime minister, and he remains at the helm of Zimbabwe's politics at the time of this writing. The colonial crimes are not contested, and colonialism was declared a crime by the UN Declaration on Granting Independence to Colonial Countries and Peoples of 14 December 1960. Those crimes included apartheid-style segregation, economic crimes (land confiscation and forced labor), and grave human rights abuses (torturing black political opponents and their white sympathizers, banning black opponents, violating the blacks' freedom of expression, movement, and association, and illegally arresting and detaining people). Violations were systematic and part of government policy. The perpetrators included government agents, the secret police, and the army, and the white minority acquiesced. Violations sharply increased after the colony's Prime Minister Ian Smith took power and unilaterally declared independence from Britain in 1965.

Instead of bringing democracy, independence was followed by a seven-year-long armed conflict between the government and the opposition. The prolonged demobilization and disarmament of the pro-independence armed units sustained the conflict both because most armed units hid weapons in view of continuing the struggle, and because South Africa supplied dissenting groups with arms with the goal of destabilizing the new Zimbabwean government. The opposition contested Mugabe's rule, believing that he had come to power illegitimately by relying on the Shona majority and playing ethnic groups against each other. To the opposition, Joshua Nkomo (a member of the Ndebele minority) was the nation's real Father. True, when Mugabe assumed the country's leadership, the new state faced severe challenges. Zimbabwe had a powerful but hostile neighbor in South Africa, was ethnically and politically divided and insecure, and the armed military wings of its main political parties, the Zimbabwe African Nationalist Liberation Army (ZANLA) of ZANU and the Zimbabwe People's Revolutionary Army (ZIPRA) of ZAPU, terrorized the population. By early 1982, Zimbabwe faced serious security problems, particularly in the ZIPRA-dominated Matebeleland region, where antigovernment dissidents killed civilians and destroyed property indiscriminately. The government responded with a massive security clampdown, resulting in two overlapping conflicts. The first pitted the dissidents against government military units such as the 4th and the 6th Brigades, the Paratroopers, the Central Intelligence Organization (CIO), and the Police Support Unit. The second, between the government and suspected ZAPU supporters, targeted mainly unarmed civilians in rural areas that traditionally supported ZAPU, and at times ZAPU urban supporters. The government's 5th Brigade, the CIO, the Police Internal Security and Intelligence unit (PISI), and the ZANU-PF Youth Brigades committed many human rights violations, compounding the plight of civilians who were once more caught in a conflict not of their own making.

During that period, the North Korean-trained 5th Brigade became Zimbabwe's most notorious army unit. Within weeks of being mobilized in January 1983 under the command of Colonel Perence Shiri, the Brigade was responsible for mass murders, beatings, and property burnings in Northern Matabeleland, where hundreds of thousands of ZAPU supporters lived. In six weeks, more than 2,000 civilians were killed, hundreds of homesteads were burned, and thousands of civilians were beaten. Most of the dead were killed in public executions, involving one to twelve victims at a time. The largest number of dead in a single incident took place in a village in Lupane, where sixty-two men and women were shot on the banks of the Cewale River on March 5, 1983. More than 20,000 civilians were raped, tortured, disappeared, detained, killed and buried in mass graves, and starved. The figure includes people whose property was destroyed or who lived in constant fear and were terrorized by the 5th Brigade. This repressive episode ended in 1987, when ZAPU capitulated and joined Mugabe's ZANU in a Unity Accord that effectively left Zimbabwe with one political party, the Zimbabwe African Nationalist Union Patriotic Front (ZANU PF). Mugabe retained the leadership of the new political formation.

Since 1987, only academics and university students have openly opposed the one-party rule. When Eastern Europe embraced multiparty democracy, the Zimbabwean political elite supported the model of "democratic centralism" in which politics would be contested within a single political party, not by multiple formations. In Zimbabwe, democratic centralism was predicated on the assumption that multiparty politics was ethnically divisive, because the independent state included ethnic groups that constituted majorities in neighboring countries. Its leaders believed that to foster cohesion and development, politics had to be contested within one political party that controlled all spheres of life, the army, the police, trade unions, business, academia, and even the student movement. This ultimately led to dictatorship.

Opposition has been suppressed by the infamous CIO, which acted as a political police, arresting, torturing, detaining, and even allegedly murdering perceived or real political opponents. It acted in secret, and the mystery of not knowing who was in the CIO, what powers it had, and what it did fostered fear in the society. This served the government well, as it led to a docile populace. Repression against the general population abated between 1989 and 1998, but continued against targeted opposition when university students were arrested, detained, and assaulted for demonstrating against the government and the one-party state, and opposition leader Patrick Kombayi was wounded and permanently disabled days before the 1990 general election. The CIO were said to be responsible for the shooting.

Skyrocketing food prices, food shortages, and the negative effects of the Economic Structural Adjustment Programme (ESAP) supported by the World Bank led to the Zimbabwean people rising up in 1998 against the regime and the formation of a stronger opposition, the Movement for Democratic Change (MDC), in 1999. The 1998 riots against the price increase of basic commodities were the most violent the country had experienced since independence. During riots, the violence of the ordinary citizens was shocking, but less so than the violence of the state's response, and the ensuing demonstrations and expressions of dissent. Eight deaths, uncounted injuries, and thousands of arrests during those three days showed that Zimbabwe had entered a new era of repressive politics.

After the MDC was formed, the Public Order and Security Act (POSA) was passed in 2002 and the Access to Information and Protection of Privacy Act (AIPPA) in 2003. The 2002 Act prohibited public demonstrations unsanctioned by the police. Thus, demonstrations conducted by opposition parties and civil society groups became illegal, leading to the arrest, torture, detention, and assault of hundreds of thousands of demonstrators and activists. The 2003 Act muzzled the media, leading to the arrest of outspoken journalists and the closure in 2003 by order of the Supreme Court of independent newspapers such as the *Daily News*, published in the capital, Harare. As a result, student demonstrators were routinely arrested, tortured, detained, and then released without being charged for dissent.

During elections, repression reached new heights. The violence escalated in 2000, after the MDC contested the general elections, and the people voted in a referendum against a government-sponsored draft constitution. Violence accompanied all subsequent general and presidential elections (organized in 2002, 2005, and 2008). Morgan Tsvangirayi, the MDC opposition leader, withdrew before the second round of the 2008 presidential election, citing widespread violence against his supporters. This led to the Global Peace Agreement of 21 July 2008, signed by Tsvangirayi and Arthur Mutambara of the MDC and President Robert Mugabe, leader of ZANU PF, and the formation of a contested government of national unity involving all these political parties. None of these elections can be regarded as free and fair.

In 2005, the government instituted Operation Murambatsvina (reject the filth), designed to clean the cities of squatters and illegal buildings, which the government saw as hubs of criminal activity. However, the civil society believed that the Operation was meant to disperse opposition supporters and thus prevent them from voting in the 2005 parliamentary elections, given that they were only registered to vote in the urban areas where they lived. As a result of the Operation, 2.4 million people were displaced and lost their homes and livelihood, children were taken out of school, and hundreds of people died from disease, assaults, lack of antiretroviral care for HIV/AIDS patients, or starvation. The United Nations condemned the Operation, and human rights organizations recorded these violations and called for transitional justice.

Transitional Justice

Transitional justice in Zimbabwe has had false starts because of the government's desire to cover up the truth about past crimes perpetrated by various regimes and political actors. Repressive institutions have not been reformed, repressive legislation has not been amended or annulled, and well-known human rights violators have not been purged. The instruments of repression have continued intact, although justice has been attempted. Commissions of inquiry were set up by the government, prosecutions were launched by both by civil society and the state, and a national healing, reconciliation, and integration agency was set up in July 2009. All the government's attempts aimed not to expose but rather to hide the truth.

Prosecutions

As noted earlier, opposition leader Patrick Kombayi was shot in 1990 in Gweru, allegedly by CIO members well known in the city. In 1992, the press reported that the Attorney General's office was bringing charges of attempted murder against these CIO members in the regional court in Bulawayo. The state Prosecutor apparently wanted to bring a strong case before anything was published by the press and the case was prejudiced as a result. But the case never saw the light of day and what became of it is not public knowledge. The state was unable to prosecute perpetrators (such as ZANU PF youth militias, CIO agents, and ZANU PF, the army, police, and opposition supporters) involved in the violence that accompanied all post-2000 elections because they were granted presidential amnesties before the cases were concluded. Despite the public officials' public claims of trying to expose the truth, it has continued to remain hidden.

By contrast, civil society organizations such as the Zimbabwe Human Rights NGO Forum and the Zimbabwe Lawyers for Human Rights (ZLHR) brought human rights perpetrators to court in civil suits. Most of the cases were concluded as out-of-court settlements and High Court rulings, as the Attorney General's office defended the defendants (mostly ZANU PF supporters and state agents belonging to the CIO, the army, and the police). The civil suits represented a victory for transitional justice, because the courts admitted that human rights violations had occurred against the victims. However, victims and their families received paltry compensation, further eroded by the extremely high inflation rates. The court exercise became a symbolic gesture, and the compensation was an insulting and insufficient reparation for the harm done. The ill-equipped Office of the Ombudsman, responsible for investigating violations by public offices, was unable to deal with any cases of human rights abuses.

The Chihambakwe Commission of Inquiry

During the Matabeleland atrocities in 1983, the government instituted a commission of inquiry, the Chihambakwe Commission, to investigate the abuses and to provide recommendations. The Commission submitted its final report, but the government did not make its findings and recommendations public. Thus, although the Commission was meant to expose the truth, it was ultimately hidden. After the 1987 Unity Accord, the 5th Brigade was reportedly disbanded and its soldiers were reintegrated into the army. Some reports claim that the former members of the 5th Brigade refuse to take orders from anyone other than their former commander, Mugabe.

The Organ on National Healing, Reconciliation and Integration

The Organ on National Healing, Reconciliation and Integration was created in 2009 under Article 7(c) of the Global Peace Agreement, which urged the new government to consider "the setting up of a mechanism to properly advise on what measures might be necessary and practicable to achieve national healing, cohesion and unity in respect of pre and post independence political conflicts." The Organ is set up to identify mechanisms to deal with the past and secure the future by consulting with the Zimbabwean public and finding out what transitional justice mechanisms the people want to pursue in order to achieve national healing, reconciliation, and cohesion. It is led by three co-chairpersons: Sekayi Holland (representing MDC Tsvangirayi), John Nkomo (ZANU PF), and Gibson Sibanda (MDC Mutambara). Holland is the Organ's Minister of State in the President's office. The Organ seems confused on its mandate. Holland admitted that it has no clear mandate and no enabling legislation other than the Agreement, which includes no further details.

The Organ is a temporary body, to be disbanded once transitional justice mechanisms are identified and established, and after it finds out how Zimbabweans want to deal with the past. The information was already obtained through the extensive research work of the civil society, which found that Zimbabweans want accountability for and the truth about past wrongs, including colonial wrongs and Mugabe-era crimes. The Organ continues its work by holding public meetings throughout Zimbabwe and getting people's views on transitional justice, but it is doubtful that it will accomplish its broad mandate of national healing, reconciliation, and integration.

Property Redistribution

The government's land redistribution program aimed to return to the black majority the land that had been forcefully taken away by the white minority settlers during colonial times. Slow land redistribution led to land resettlement and invasion. During the first ten years of independence, land could not be redistributed because the constitution allowed for no redistribution or radical land reform. In 1990, land reform was further delayed because of fear that it would impede negotiations for majority rule in South Africa after Nelson Mandela's release from prison (see entry on South Africa). The Secretary General of the Commonwealth Enyeka Anyaoku sought to dissuade the ZANU PF government from launching radical land reform before South Africa's transition was complete. It was believed that radical land reform in Zimbabwe would make the South African apartheid regime fear that South Africans could also demand land reform. Land invasions began in 1997, when people in the Svosve region invaded farms belonging to white commercial farmers. In June 1998, the police were sent to remove the Svosve invaders from the land, but in 2000, war veterans feeling entitled to land because they fought for the country's independence until 1980 took up land invasions. Again, Svosve was at the forefront of invasions. In their quest for land, war veterans started a "liberation" war (*chimurenga*), in which thirty white landowners were killed, other whites and their farm laborers were assaulted or tortured, and their land was taken away.

Twenty years after independence in 2000, land resettlement was painfully slow. The white commercial farmers were determined to keep the land, much to the chagrin of the majority blacks and the war veterans who saw land as the most important reason for the liberation war. Intellectuals, politicians, and commentators were divided on the land issue. While Professor Masiplua Sithole believed Zimbabwe needed to concentrate on industry, ZANU PF and the political opposition saw land as important and issues of economic justice as part of the transition to majority rule. ZANU PF campaigned for the 2000 elections under the slogan "the land is the economy and the economy is the land," which resonated with the rural populations and helped ZANU PF to a narrow win. The government responded by overtaking the program and instituting the fast track land resettlement scheme, which legalized abusive land invasions. The fact that land has been taken away from the white minority and returned to the black majority is seen as a fait accompli. There is no indication that there will be a review of the process.

Conclusion

Zimbabwe's reluctant and incomplete engagement with transitional justice accountability mechanisms shows a tendency toward hiding the truth and circumventing justice more than exposing the truth and moving forward. This trend has continued even after the inclusive government was formed in 2008. While civil society continues to expose the truth, the government is bent on keeping it hidden. Transitional justice may be achieved only after Mugabe and ZANU PF lose control over the country.

Pondai Bamu

Cross-references: Property Restitution; South Africa.

Further Readings

Bamu, Pondai. 2008. *Zimbabwe: Transitional Justice without Transition?* Oxford Transitional Justice Research, December 18. Available at: http://www.csls.ox.ac.uk/documents/Bamu_Zim_Final.pdf (accessed September 18, 2010).
Catholic Commission on Justice and Peace and Legal Resources Foundation. 1997. *Breaking the Silence, Building True Peace.* Harare: CCJP and LRF.
Du Plessis, Max and Jolyon Ford. 2009. Transitional Justice. A Future Truth Commission for Zimbabwe? *International and Comparative Law Quarterly*, 58: 73–117.
Eppel, Sheri and Brian Raftopoulos. 2008. *Political Crisis, Mediation and the Prospects for Transitional Justice in Zimbabwe.* Oxford Transitional Justice Research, December 18. Available at: http://www.csls.ox.ac.uk/documents/EppelandRaftopolous_Zim_Final.pdf (accessed September 18, 2010).
Kajumulo Tibaijuka, Anna. 2005. Report of the Fact-finding Mission to Zimbabwe to Assess the Scope and Impact of Operation Murambatsvina. Available at: http://www.un.org/News/dh/infocus/zimbabwe/zimbabwe_rpt.pdf (accessed September 18, 2010).
Miles-Blessing, Tendi. 2010. *Making History in Mugabe's Zimbabwe. Politics, Intellectuals and the Media.* Pieterlen: Peter Lang.

Index

abductions, 20, 23, 115, 211, 226, 246, 271–272, 298, 317, 319, 380, 466–467, 470, 489
abuses, 2, 20, 34, 68, 84, 92–95, 99–100, 104, 123, 126, 140, 147, 160, 175, 222, 224, 237, 262, 264, 300, 307, 309–310, 343, 346, 368, 398, 445, 504, 512
  financial, 9
  human rights, 3, 6, 13, 23, 29, 44, 48, 72, 81, 84, 95–97, 109, 113, 115, 120–121, 124–125, 130–131, 150, 168, 172, 188, 193, 198, 209–214, 217–218, 221, 225–226, 228, 236, 243, 262, 268, 278, 285, 295–296, 298, 301, 303, 311–315, 318, 349, 354, 361, 372–377, 382–383, 407, 419, 424, 428, 438, 448–450, 456, 466, 475–476, 479–480, 482, 485–486, 497, 499–501, 506, 515, 518
  past, 83, 261, 263, 265–266, 311, 349, 353
  sexual, 30, 83, 168, 347, 365
  spousal, 351
  state, 193, 303, 341, 458
accomplices, 164, 340
accountability, 1, 3, 21, 84, 158–159, 170, 172, 215, 217, 220–221, 236, 263–266, 269, 280, 305, 313–314, 336, 338, 355, 374, 391, 412, 432, 451, 466, 497, 499
  criminal, 5–6, 70, 220
  individual, 28, 220
  legal, 228
  mechanisms, 5, 438, 520
acknowledgement, 29–30, 38, 84, 104, 116, 213, 219, 299, 369–370, 397, 449
  official, 24, 303, 406–407, 506
  public, 324, 442, 449
  social, 137
administration, 10–11, 50, 145, 181, 240
  colonial, 142, 173, 413
  public, 49, 52, 182, 205, 253, 302, 324–325, 453
  state, 135, 420
agents, 99, 316
  full-time, 8, 274
  intelligence, 18, 40–42, 164–165, 189–190, 230, 275, 334, 403, 424, 434, 443, 493–494, 501, 518
  secret, 11, 68, 236, 275–276, 287, 289–290, 490
  state, 16, 70–72, 99, 128, 263, 295, 304, 374, 456, 467–468, 470, 512, 515

amnesty, 37, 50, 53, 81, 90, 94, 100–101, 103–104, 117, 146–147, 160, 179, 198, 213, 217, 220, 252, 283, 319, 362, 393, 484
  agreements, 83, 89
  blanket, 1, 312, 426, 448–449, 500
  conditional, 14, 89, 345–346, 448
  general, 18, 169, 194, 344, 459
  laws, 7, 14–15, 21–22, 39, 70–71, 73, 97–99, 122, 154, 158, 184, 225, 228–229, 241, 248, 307, 309, 365, 372–373, 403, 462, 488, 497, 499–500
  partial, 344
Annan, Kofi, 90, 264
apartheid, regime, 313, 315
apologies, 31, 214, 302, 319, 343, 374, 407, 410, 458, 474–475
  official, 256, 258, 260–261, 305, 332, 367, 455, 475, 478, 513
  public, 29, 90, 111, 160, 485
Arbour, Louise, 4
archives, 142, 247, 274, 367, 384, 406–407, 463
  army, 59
  memory, 25
  police, 73, 386–387, 393, 437, 443, 494
  secret, 73, 75, 77–78, 132, 189, 199, 276, 386–387, 437, 443, 490, 492–494, 496
  state, 72, 396, 498
atrocities, 33, 49, 61–62, 64, 70, 79, 84–85, 100, 113, 115, 129, 156, 170, 172, 220, 255–256, 259, 285, 312, 352, 374, 454–455, 472, 479, 501, 513, 518
  mass, 121, 125, 243, 418–420
  Nazi, 37–39, 200–201, 204, 209, 288
  Soviet, 42, 288
  war, 155
audiences, 310
authorities, 16, 35, 42, 104, 135, 139, 152, 165, 189, 195, 203, 225, 275, 298
  government, 17–18, 29, 460
  judicial, 18, 52, 121, 181
  local, 80, 460–461, 469
  military, 102–103
  public, 68, 103
  state, 111, 163, 308, 376, 504, 506
authority, 8, 187
  abuse, 198, 376

authority (*cont.*)
  legal, 121
  statutory, 30
Aylwin, Patricio, 101–102
awareness, 5, 32, 130, 146, 361, 390, 428, 461, 464, 512
  public, 270, 368

Bemba, Jean-Pierre, 93–94, 96, 98, 114
Bouteflika, Abdelaziz, 14–15
Brazil: Never Again Project, 72
bureaucracy, 150, 240, 242, 322–323, 382, 503, 505–506, 508

catharsis, 246
Ceausescu, Nicolae, 398–404
change, regime, 26, 41, 97, 129–130, 168, 370, 418–420, 424, 505, 509, 514
church
  Orthodox, 267, 482
  Roman Catholic, 57–58, 100, 102, 128, 155, 216–217, 219, 222, 249, 287–288, 377, 381, 385, 441
citizens, 12, 46–48, 71, 77, 95, 127–129, 133, 139, 163, 175, 184, 229, 251, 256, 258, 291, 294, 297–298, 365, 384, 389, 419, 479, 491, 512
  ordinary, 8, 38, 405–406, 454, 517
citizenship, 52, 131, 159, 278, 376, 441, 444, 482
  laws, 275–277, 279, 429
citizenry, 7, 437
cleansing, 283
  ethnic, 61–62, 65, 121–123, 191, 202, 243, 263, 267, 419, 480–481
  religious, 352
clergy, 201, 235, 438
Clinton, Bill, 129–130
collaborators, 46–47, 49–54, 57, 77–78, 103, 126–127, 130, 134, 162, 164–165, 169, 171, 181, 184, 203, 245, 250, 253–254, 274–275, 289, 293, 322, 325, 393, 397, 426, 439, 442, 454–455, 495
  secret, 74, 78, 136, 289–290, 387, 394, 435, 442–444
combatants, 62, 107, 109–111, 115, 118–119, 127, 156–157, 160, 188, 282, 284, 320, 426–427, 429, 489
commemorations, 5, 42, 91, 166, 199, 243, 278–279, 288, 291, 307, 310, 343, 409, 455, 483, 485, 490, 495
commissions, 21, 24, 53, 56–57, 64, 66–67, 72, 190, 206, 242, 264–265, 292, 296, 341, 350, 394–395, 465, 469–470, 479, 485, 487
  history, 87
  inquiry, 4, 41, 59, 65, 83, 162, 166, 263, 320, 398, 402, 441, 466–468, 471, 488, 491, 500, 517–518
  lustration, 289–290
  parliamentary, 22, 234, 290, 296, 441, 506
  purge, 323, 395
  rehabilitation, 491–492, 494
  truth, 25, 29, 41–43, 55, 57, 65–66, 82–83, 88, 99, 101–102, 111–112, 125, 142, 145, 153–158, 212, 216–218, 222–224, 227–228, 283, 298, 300, 305, 307, 336–338, 345, 354, 356–357, 368, 375–376, 383, 396, 403, 406, 421, 425–427, 448, 452, 454, 499–500
community, 28–29, 31, 82, 146, 224, 240, 266, 309, 317, 333, 345, 361, 373, 400, 404, 416, 446, 469, 471, 499, 513
  development, 85, 450,
  diaspora, 283
  ethnic, 65,
  international, 5–6, 16, 23, 54, 62, 66, 81, 84, 87, 97, 144, 146, 158, 170, 228, 267, 278, 282–283, 291, 296, 418, 421–422, 448, 473, 487–488, 494, 503, 515
  leaders, 65
  legal, 269–270
  level, 307, 309, 412, 414
  local, 431
  members, 283, 310
  political, 200
compensation, 17–19, 24, 29, 32, 36, 38, 58, 63, 71, 94, 108, 124–126, 129, 146, 162, 178, 196–197, 199, 201, 206–208, 231, 242, 245–246, 250, 258–259, 265, 271, 288, 295, 303, 314, 319, 327, 331–333, 362, 366, 386, 399–400, 408, 424, 460, 468, 475, 477–478, 484, 500–502, 518
  administrative, 42
  economic, 111, 462
  financial, 24, 38–39, 64–65, 70, 73, 132–133, 137, 141, 151, 153, 309–310, 402, 441
  material, 132–133, 253
  monetary, 24, 39, 85, 214, 356, 367, 370, 389, 434, 455, 475, 508
  moral, 253, 493
  packages, 18, 153, 256
  payments, 130, 163, 469
  symbolic, 72
complicity, 181, 185, 214, 240, 293, 311, 405, 468, 493
confession, 157, 289–290, 340, 405, 416, 466
conflict, 60, 79, 81–82, 114–117, 146, 150, 155, 186, 192, 196, 225, 247, 267–271, 280, 304–305, 315, 334, 341–342, 350, 357–360, 393, 412, 432, 465–466, 471, 479, 487, 516
  armed, 26, 72, 96, 106, 112, 120–122, 216–217, 220, 266, 271, 281, 301, 308, 318, 334, 338, 419, 515
  civil, 372, 374
  ethnic, 80, 209, 272, 486
  identity-based, 81
  internal, 2–3, 106, 168, 307, 363, 452
  international, 1
  mediation, 264
  military, 311
  ongoing, 106
  political, 106, 209, 339, 518
  prevention, 451
  property, 272
  racial, 201, 446
  resolution, 119, 451
  social, 309
  territorial, 446
  wartime, 309–310

Index

constitutions, 10, 12, 14, 30, 41, 45, 56–57, 89, 101–102, 114, 128, 139, 163–164, 168, 174–177, 182, 210–213, 223, 228–229, 267, 276, 294, 299, 306, 308, 311, 313, 317–318, 320–321, 330, 336, 350, 362, 372, 378, 380, 419, 449, 453, 462, 466, 476, 482, 484, 486, 500, 503, 505, 508, 510, 512, 515
constitutionality, 12, 29, 108, 158, 366, 408, 484
corruption, 12, 56, 82, 84, 119, 188, 198, 210–211, 224, 263, 272, 312, 317, 321, 334, 354–355, 372, 375–377, 380–381, 383, 415, 420, 429, 432, 503, 505, 512, 514
courts, 8, 10–11, 16, 21–24, 27–29, 38, 41, 52–54, 61–62, 65, 71, 90, 100, 102–103, 117, 123, 125, 135–136, 159, 164, 170, 172, 178, 180, 183–184, 198, 203–204, 206, 208, 217, 220–221, 224, 229, 250–251, 258–259, 264–265, 268, 270, 277, 285, 287, 290–291, 294, 298–300, 306–309, 313, 318, 330, 362, 365, 372, 374, 389, 392, 424, 426, 434, 438, 450, 462, 484, 491–492, 518
  ad hoc, 147–148, 399, 421, 510
  administrative, 396
  appeals, 22, 76, 176–177, 251–253, 340, 386, 388, 495
  assizes, 50, 251–252
  civil, 22, 53–54, 117, 183, 375–376, 501
  community, 309–310, 416
  constitutional, 12, 64, 77–78, 108, 112, 133, 135–136, 231, 233–235, 295, 299, 402, 441, 493
  criminal, 50, 228, 324
  disciplinary, 387
  domestic, 60, 160, 238, 355, 422, 425
  gacaca, 416–417
  hearings, 40, 73, 75
  hybrid, 90, 148–149, 264, 270
  international, 35, 216
  local, 60, 62–63, 67
  lustration, 386, 443
  military, 21–22, 51–54, 70, 72, 101, 117, 119, 203, 211, 244, 252, 257, 375–376, 380, 388, 392, 395, 399, 437, 473–474, 498, 504, 513
  national, 6, 62, 83, 97, 100, 115, 221, 257, 412, 414–418, 463, 508
  proceedings, 56, 145, 152, 165, 171, 190, 196, 305, 325, 380, 457
  special, 36, 211, 237, 265, 283, 285, 323, 325–326, 340–341, 427–429, 432, 454, 460
  supreme, 11, 36, 59, 71–73, 77, 90, 103–104, 123, 135, 139–140, 150, 152–153, 156, 158, 165, 170–171, 210, 224, 228, 246, 271, 295, 303, 319–320, 324–325, 334, 336–337, 349–350, 366, 368, 373, 376, 378, 382–383, 416, 423, 435, 437, 461, 475, 492, 502, 506–507, 517
  systems, 83, 126, 169, 270, 335, 415
  traditional, 309
  trials, 6, 46, 49–50, 87, 95, 132, 231, 238, 248, 250, 254, 256–257, 261, 275, 277, 298, 307, 312, 382, 403, 430, 440, 485, 506–507, 511, 513
crime, organized, 106, 151, 299
crimes, 3, 6, 15, 19–20, 22, 26, 30, 34–36, 50, 55–57, 59, 66–68, 71, 79, 82, 85, 87–88, 94, 96, 99–100, 103–104, 106–110, 115, 140, 172, 181, 183, 185, 232, 243, 264, 284–285, 295, 301, 303–304, 309, 321–322, 325, 355, 357–358, 364, 366, 372, 374, 380, 399, 408, 410, 415–416, 418, 436, 449, 455, 457, 459–460, 462, 474–476, 490, 498, 500, 504, 506, 510, 514–515, 517
  against humanity, 11, 14, 18, 24, 36, 38, 80, 83, 90–91, 96, 99, 108–110, 115–118, 142, 147–148, 164–166, 185, 196, 219, 233, 237, 246, 256, 259, 277, 283, 289–292, 294, 299–300, 318–319, 376, 379, 387, 409, 431, 462, 489
  against peace, 256
  collaboration, 54, 444
  communist, 42–43, 136–137, 188, 232, 273–275, 277, 287–288, 291–293, 384, 387, 406, 419, 436–440, 442–444, 490–492
  economic, 9–10, 198, 202, 283, 515
  ethnic, 269–270, 514
  imaginary, 40
  mass, 188–189, 193, 414, 420, 424
  Nazi, 33, 35, 37–39, 167, 203–204, 207–208, 246–248, 250–252, 254, 277, 287, 292, 387, 402
  perpetrators, 83, 108, 130
  political, 132–133, 162, 198, 237–238, 249, 392–393, 434, 500
  property, 338, 416
  serious, 57, 81, 83–84, 116–119, 121, 140, 142, 145, 147, 184, 213, 221, 241, 251–252, 263, 268, 277, 289, 291, 299, 306–307, 393, 412, 427, 431
  sexual, 107, 148, 259, 427
  terrorist, 17
  war, 1, 4, 6, 21, 36–39, 46–48, 53–54, 60, 62–64, 66, 80, 83–84, 91, 96, 108, 115–118, 121–123, 140, 142, 148, 233, 241, 245–247, 250, 252–260, 270, 284, 289, 291, 294–295, 297–300, 305–307, 309–310, 326, 387, 420–425, 431, 463, 476, 479–485, 513–514
culpability, 61, 165, 296, 310, 314, 408–410, 414–415, 443

damage, 28, 41, 70, 88, 103, 117, 235, 254, 257, 259, 288, 395
  material, 493
  moral, 493
  psychological, 141, 310
damages, 52, 87, 125, 129–130, 226, 308, 331, 382, 475
  economic, 354
  nonmaterial, 125
  physical, 24
  psychological, 24
  war, 125, 308–309
decision makers, 41
deficit, democratic, 341
de Klerk, F.W., 447
demobilization, 97, 106–112, 118, 156, 224, 276, 320, 426–427, 430, 515

democracy, 78, 19–20, 25, 56, 69–70, 93, 98, 100–101, 127, 135, 152, 180, 186, 191, 216, 227, 233, 262, 293, 304, 317–318, 321, 329, 337, 339, 353–354, 358, 368, 380, 384, 391–392, 431, 433, 436, 446, 451, 459–460, 474, 476, 485–486, 488, 503, 512, 514, 516
  cacique, 378
  constitutional, 317
  liberal, 26, 398, 438, 440
  market, 61
  parliamentary, 49
  return to, 21, 150, 181, 326, 499
  transition to, 107, 212, 333–334, 370, 383, 391, 419, 452, 497, 501–502, 505, 515
democratization, 122, 212–213, 258, 286, 292, 361, 395, 409, 453, 459–460, 473
  institutional, 105
denial, 156, 230, 259, 297, 319, 420–421, 423, 425
  culture, 418, 424
  justice, 117
  public, 495
  rights, 51, 352, 365, 420
detention, 20, 57, 91, 100, 116, 132–133, 139, 152, 169–171, 209–210, 221, 251, 262, 312, 317, 320, 359, 365, 393, 395, 408, 437, 453, 466, 517
  arbitrary, 58, 80, 168, 171, 237, 268, 301, 303–304
  centers, 20, 25, 57–58, 61, 91, 153, 194, 255, 301–302, 304, 325–326, 378, 406, 466, 469, 474, 478
  clandestine, 99, 227
  illegal, 22, 150, 228, 381, 462
  practices, 3
development, 4, 6, 61, 73, 85, 158–159, 179, 332, 338, 358, 361, 370, 380, 437–438, 450–451, 453, 472, 505, 511, 516
  community, 85, 450
  economic, 44, 210, 256, 258, 307, 409, 451
  ethnic, 266
  legal, 316
  political, 321
  right to, 361
  social, 232, 307, 451
  sustainable, 179
dictatorship, 55–56, 87, 100, 116, 126, 144, 232, 235–236, 292, 317, 353, 366–369, 391, 393–395, 397–399, 452–453, 459–460, 464, 476, 497, 502, 516
  civilian, 209, 392
  Kuomintang, 478
  legacy, 396–397
  military, 20–24, 67–73, 149–150, 153, 209, 249, 391, 453, 497–499, 503
  Nazi, 33, 204, 279
  Soviet, 273, 279
  Stalinist, 208
Dirty War, 15
disappearances, 2, 16, 22–23, 28, 68, 70, 72, 80, 99–101, 103, 105–107, 169, 211, 225–226, 229, 237, 271–272, 302, 311, 317, 359, 372, 376, 396, 443, 456, 463, 465–471, 482, 484–485, 497–498, 501, 506
  forced, 16–17, 20–21, 56–58, 60, 71, 151–152, 220, 226–227, 268, 300–301, 303–304, 317, 319–320, 365–367, 369, 462, 498, 502
  political, 129
disarmament, 97, 109, 115, 515
Disarmament, Demobilization and Reintegration, 109, 118, 320, 426–427, 430
disclosure, 56, 59–60, 78, 164, 283, 297–298, 364, 406, 438, 450
discrimination, 45, 95, 184, 201–202, 207, 253, 274, 339, 348–349, 351, 419, 469, 481–482, 488
  ethnic, 190
  positive, 469
  racial, 202, 254, 445
  religious, 346–347
  social, 45
  women, 346
dismissals, 63–64, 68, 134, 156, 176, 180–181, 196–197, 205–206, 240, 253, 324, 350, 367, 393–394, 440, 444
disqualification, 64
dissidents, 55, 129–130, 198, 223, 281, 290, 306, 312, 317, 388, 392, 435–437, 493, 503–504, 515–516
  activities, 74, 127, 287
  cultural, 294
  elites, 399
  groups, 287, 385
  movement, 9, 436, 440
  protests, 385
documentation, 4–5, 53, 59, 66, 72, 94, 100, 124, 185, 247, 288–289, 299, 361, 388, 396, 417, 422, 425
documents, 37, 40, 47, 59, 72–73, 88, 99, 177, 228, 238, 268–269, 274, 287, 299, 342, 367–368, 396, 433, 437, 442, 444, 473, 492, 513
  archival, 163, 189, 290, 396, 407
  declassified, 494
  official, 458, 463
  personal, 463
  police, 275, 278, 290, 387
  secret, 72, 78, 235, 275, 278, 290, 387
donors, 96–97, 262, 264, 283, 428
  foreign, 58, 285
  international, 93
  private, 58

education, 1–2, 28, 30–32, 85–86, 119, 127–128, 133, 204, 230, 278, 292, 249, 351, 356, 378, 398, 420, 433–434, 446, 464, 470, 473–475, 505, 513
  civic, 199
  health, 331
  legal, 269
  political, 199
  public, 403
  system, 11, 348–349
Eichmann, Adolf, 246–247
elite reproduction, 313
elites, 9–10, 49, 69, 79, 110, 124, 154, 181, 187–188, 193, 208, 223, 225, 234, 257, 294–295, 297, 307,

Index

317, 336, 378–381, 391, 394–397, 399–400, 403, 406, 432, 435–438, 442–443, 445, 454, 490, 494, 496
- civilian, 69
- change, 53
- cultural, 422, 425
- economic, 161, 394, 505
- feudal, 44, 348–350, 352
- indigenous, 377
- intellectual, 161, 483
- military, 161, 175, 348, 464, 482, 485, 499
- political, 7, 37–38, 43, 77, 80, 82, 136, 161, 188, 212, 307, 348, 377, 398, 404, 424, 457, 464, 480, 482, 499, 505, 515–516
- traditional, 155, 215, 348, 485
- urban, 87, 310

equality, 32, 182–183
- before the law, 24, 184
- social, 329
- women, 350

European Court of Human Rights, 38, 135, 166, 190, 233, 277, 401, 479, 480, 483

European Union, 5, 97, 108, 114, 122, 167, 191, 238, 270, 291, 295, 401, 421, 441, 479

evidence, 2, 9, 37, 41, 58, 62, 76–77, 83, 91, 107, 124, 136, 147, 150, 164, 170, 172, 204, 218, 229, 232, 238, 264, 290, 295, 304, 318–319, 329, 338, 343–345, 356, 366, 369, 375, 383, 386, 405, 417, 435, 437, 442, 444, 450, 469, 495
- access to, 171
- collection, 109, 220, 291, 501
- destruction, 456–458
- documentary, 368
- factual, 304
- forensic, 304
- incriminatory, 213, 310
- lack, 122, 165, 286, 303, 376, 388
- oral, 341
- physical, 100, 219
- submissions, 29

executions, 6, 88, 127, 130, 139, 187, 211, 226, 230, 236, 239, 251, 277, 294, 301, 344, 371, 406, 409, 490, 510
- extrajudicial, 99, 301, 303, 365–367, 369, 468, 474
- political, 105
- public, 2, 334, 516
- summary, 2, 68, 95, 151, 168, 181, 183, 221, 238, 262, 280, 367, 381

exhumations, 124, 216, 219, 221, 459–461, 463, 484

expulsions, 61, 68–69, 121, 202, 271, 419, 434, 480–482

Extraordinary Chambers in the Courts of Cambodia, 89–90

fairness, 327

files, 25, 59, 68, 100, 238, 325, 396, 435, 437–438, 444, 494
- access, 12–13, 41, 59–60, 72, 77, 79, 136, 189, 195–196, 235, 278, 297, 367–368, 386–387, 434, 437, 463, 493–494

criminal, 41
- investigation, 122, 253
- military, 60, 73
- opening, 234
- personal, 12
- police, 9, 11, 136, 196–197, 233, 249, 279, 289, 295, 297–298, 300, 384, 401, 404, 442–444
- secret, 9, 11, 13, 56, 60, 77, 79, 136, 189, 196–197, 231, 233, 249, 275, 279, 287, 289, 295, 297–300, 384, 404, 442–444, 494
- security, 131
- surveillance, 42–43, 274

forces, 238, 241, 260, 352, 379, 426, 447, 459–460, 509–510, 513
- armed, 20, 22, 25, 47, 56–57, 59, 69, 73, 93, 97, 100, 102, 117, 120–123, 127, 154, 157, 210, 218, 223, 225–226, 228–229, 249, 276, 301, 317, 335, 356, 364, 370–374, 376, 379, 460, 507
- colonial, 306
- irregular, 61
- military, 41, 64, 81, 90, 106, 144, 267–268, 347, 354–355, 382, 506
- occupation, 54, 114, 453
- opposition, 14, 144, 391–392, 510
- paramilitary, 267–268, 423, 487
- peacekeeping, 431
- police, 64, 81, 120–123, 127, 157, 268, 317, 347, 374, 391, 393, 420, 422, 504, 506–507
- rebel, 97, 280, 488
- repressive, 68
- secret, 8
- security, 14–18, 20, 24, 45, 68, 70, 84, 90, 151, 171, 190, 222, 225–227, 240–241, 262, 269, 316–317, 340–341, 345, 359, 398, 401, 448, 451, 465–469, 497–498, 504, 506, 508
- special, 16
- state, 97, 107, 114, 155

forgiveness, 25, 84, 89, 96, 116, 178, 219, 290, 428

Franco, Francisco, 459–464

Garzón, Baltasar, 23, 98, 462–463

genocide, 26, 29, 57, 59–62, 79–81, 83, 88, 90–91, 115–116, 122, 142, 148, 162, 165–166, 170–171, 193, 201–202, 218–221, 237–238, 243, 246–247, 270, 277, 286, 314, 384, 399, 462, 492, 494–496
- Armenia, 479–480, 482–483
- cultural, 27
- law, 13
- Nazi, 38, 292
- Rwanda, 113, 412–418
- Soviet, 40, 43, 287, 290–292

Gorbachev, Mikhail, 187, 274–275, 277–278, 287, 407–410, 491–493

governance, 82, 177, 179, 211, 240–241, 334, 348, 352, 364, 407, 410, 436, 466
- civil, 338
- good, 361
- system, 1, 317, 348, 406, 408, 411

graves, mass, 88, 101, 124, 219, 243, 293, 315, 405, 407, 420, 440, 442, 457, 461, 484, 492, 510, 516

guilt, 239, 246, 256, 309, 356, 417, 437
  collective, 81, 435
  criminal, 207
  individual, 207, 405
  personal, 29

habeas corpus, 68, 100, 171, 210, 319–320, 380–381, 392
healing, 44, 219, 414, 416, 428, 430
  moral, 384
  national, 517–519
  psychological, 60
  social, 60, 172
  victim, 280
hierarchy, 8, 35, 37, 413
history,
  curriculum, 92, 260
  oral, 425
  rewriting, 13, 39, 41, 78, 91, 278, 384, 386, 390, 458, 476, 491, 513
  textbooks, 39, 42, 92, 137, 185, 191, 235, 259–260, 384, 386, 390, 403, 406, 410, 449, 458, 476, 491, 513
  wars, 27, 255
holiday, national, 25, 252, 315, 475
Holocaust, 142, 185–186, 202, 204, 243, 247, 278, 288, 290–292, 402–404, 494
  education, 292
  memorials, 165
  perpetrators, 289
  remembrance, 247
  survivors, 246
  victims, 245
Hoxha, Enver, 8–9
Hussein, Saddam, 236–239, 242

identity, 15, 23, 27, 30, 40, 45, 69, 78, 199, 243, 246–247, 358, 372, 446–447, 468, 471, 498
  civic, 496
  conflicts, 81
  cultural, 309, 362
  ethnic, 45, 339
  historical, 166
  national, 179, 194, 339, 363, 371, 411, 413, 449, 476, 496
ideology, 2, 28, 45, 137, 191, 201–202, 201, 291, 397, 419, 420, 425, 433
impartiality, 82, 120, 157, 343, 374, 507
impunity, 1, 4, 15, 55, 70–71, 83–84, 93, 95–98, 101, 103, 108–109, 149–154, 160, 169, 172–173, 188, 210, 215, 218, 220–221, 224, 228, 258, 262, 265, 300, 306, 309–310, 313, 321, 334, 338, 377, 383, 397, 413–414, 418, 421, 423–425, 428, 432, 438, 462, 466–468, 480, 482, 497, 501–502
incarceration, 201, 312, 378, 405, 417
indemnification, 108, 185
indignity, national, 183–184
indoctrination, 127–128, 511
information, 12, 35, 41–42, 50, 53, 64, 72–73, 77, 88, 100–101, 104, 109, 111, 130, 136, 142, 152–153, 164, 191, 196, 214, 218–219, 227–229, 245, 249, 256, 274, 289, 304, 312–313, 318, 342, 344, 351, 356, 369, 394, 396, 407, 416–417, 438, 443–444, 449–450, 469–470, 474–475, 494, 500, 513, 519
  access, 235
  documentary, 189
  genetic, 484
  public, 297
  right to, 235, 365, 420, 434
  secret, 440
informers, 76, 99, 140, 194, 230, 235, 312, 344, 385–386, 401, 474
  KDS, 76–78
  KGB, 42
  network, 433–434, 473, 490, 493
  part-time, 8, 74, 274, 438
  passive, 274
  police, 233, 393
  secret, 74, 127, 136, 274
injustices, 30, 32, 80, 129, 162–163, 170, 179, 189, 231, 308, 338, 366, 397, 405–406, 408, 433, 437, 440, 475, 482, 484
  administrative, 210
  communist, 40, 133, 136, 442
  historical, 155
  material, 133
  Nazi, 38
  political, 473
  social, 473
innocence, 37, 83, 206, 417, 429
Institute of National Remembrance, 384, 386, 388, 496
institutions, 4, 16, 27, 51–52, 67, 82, 126, 138, 142, 146, 177, 179, 186–187, 191, 199, 201, 203, 227, 230, 276, 289, 291, 302, 308–309, 325, 328, 341, 364, 373, 393, 396, 423, 434
  academic, 78
  democratic, 3, 38, 182–183, 368, 397, 420, 478, 480
  judicial, 83, 148, 412, 418, 503
  monetary, 93
  national, 51, 265
  political, 61, 116, 193, 351, 358, 396, 500, 503
  public, 36, 43, 192, 254, 289, 462
  repressive, 4, 95, 249, 396, 503, 517
  scientific, 75
  security, 171
  state, 33, 38–39, 51, 62, 78, 82, 113, 162, 214, 228, 239, 289, 308, 310, 317, 322, 335, 348–349, 374, 419, 422, 449, 451, 472–473, 488, 508
  transitional justice, 78, 84, 147, 213, 236, 241, 425, 427
intellectuals, 40, 45, 65, 76, 125, 136, 167–168, 236, 247, 260, 301, 396, 423, 476, 482, 484, 510–511, 519
Inter-American Commission of Human Rights, 21, 69, 71, 108, 153, 159–160, 220, 226–227, 368, 501, 506
Inter-American Court of Human Rights, 58, 71, 73, 103, 151–152, 220, 226–227, 356, 372–373, 375, 506

Index

interest, public, 59–60, 172, 193, 196–197, 236, 258–259, 290, 297, 386, 429, 438, 444
International Criminal Court, 4, 94–96, 113, 117, 147, 165, 190, 262, 264, 284, 489
International Criminal Tribunal for Rwanda, 83, 147, 412, 414
International Criminal Tribunal for the Former Yugoslavia, 60, 122, 147, 268, 299, 421–422
International Military Tribunal for the Far East, 255–256, 421
internment, 27, 50, 52, 61, 141, 180, 204, 244, 262, 340, 402, 459

judgments, 22, 36, 91, 118–119, 130, 141, 145, 182–184, 198, 219, 239, 257–258, 270, 303, 324, 337, 411, 423, 431, 450, 457
  criminal, 132
  public, 477
junta, 20–23, 25, 167–172, 210, 394, 426
jurisdictions, 62, 90, 118, 146, 148, 183, 204, 211, 341, 372, 462, 484
  court, 54, 90–91, 97, 123, 159–160, 251, 265, 285, 326, 375–376, 412, 414, 416–417, 421
  international, 169, 463
  legal, 457, 501
  military, 229
  national, 143, 257
  temporal, 82
  universal, 4, 6, 103, 159, 220
justice, 1, 6–7, 9–10, 14, 16–18, 22, 24, 41, 47–48, 57, 60, 62, 65, 73, 76, 79, 81–85, 101–104, 109, 115, 122–123, 130–131, 134, 148, 150, 155–156, 158, 161, 163, 169, 176, 186, 207, 213, 220, 223, 227, 229, 236, 238, 255, 268, 284, 309, 316, 337, 381, 404, 417, 435, 445, 479, 481, 513, 519
  absence, 19
  calls, 18, 99, 105, 215
  corrective, 328
  criminal, 91–92, 112, 195, 198, 203, 214, 232, 235, 313, 316, 364–366, 370, 437–438, 448, 459, 462, 464
  demands, 17–18, 24, 102, 151, 200, 457
  denial, 117
  formal, 157
  international, 91
  lack, 24, 221
  late, 159–160
  local, 106
  measures, 154, 157
  mechanisms, 113, 190
  military, 117
  people's, 183
  political, 184
  programs, 28
  punitive, 254
  restorative, 145, 149, 169, 171–172, 178, 209, 213, 310, 499–500
  retributive, 449–450
  retroactive, 194, 199–200, 232, 235, 395
  retrospective, 166
  right to, 41, 73, 108
  social, 32, 177, 179, 377
  summary, 399
  symbolic, 47, 166, 275, 278, 461
  system, 82, 100, 119, 145, 148, 152, 269–270, 285, 348, 365–366, 432
  victor's, 1, 176, 179, 239, 449

Kaing Guek Eav, 91
KGB, 40, 74, 161, 164–165, 167, 187, 189–190, 273–275, 277–278, 287–290, 411, 435, 490–491, 493–494, 496
  agents, 41–42, 189, 275–276, 287, 289–290, 493–494
  collaborators, 289–290
  files, 42–43, 189, 276, 278–279, 493–494
  operatives, 289–290
Khmer Rouge, 86–92, 510
Kwasniewski, Alexander, 389

laws, 9–10, 109, 132, 222, 232, 253, 360, 378, 393, 415, 479, 495
  amnesty, 1, 21–23, 70–71, 73, 97–101, 103–104, 122, 154, 158, 184, 217, 225, 228–229, 241, 248, 307, 309, 372–373, 403, 462, 497, 499, 501
  citizenship, 275–277
  civil, 90, 269, 501
  clemency, 15, 18, 109
  compensation, 231
  constitutional, 10, 134, 180
  customary, 362–363
  discriminatory, 32, 311, 425
  domestic, 91, 104
  genocide, 10–13
  humanitarian, 62, 115–118, 122, 155, 268, 283, 431
  human rights, 103, 115, 118, 342
  international, 29, 37, 62, 83, 90, 103, 116–118, 122, 155, 166, 233, 264, 268, 270, 283–284, 322, 324, 327, 342, 346, 431, 463, 497
  lustration, 10–13, 79, 134–135, 189, 234–235, 275–276, 386, 415, 423, 434, 436, 440, 442
  martial, 138, 380–381, 385, 387–388, 453, 472–476
  penal, 51
  privacy, 443
  reconciliation, 19
  rehabilitation, 75, 133, 408, 424, 434
  reparations, 24, 207, 308
  restitution, 46, 75, 207, 295–296, 389
  rule, 12, 68, 70, 83, 101, 113, 123, 136, 168, 179, 191, 198, 232–235, 321, 324, 326, 329, 334, 349, 389, 394–395, 420, 431, 441–442, 444, 470–471, 480, 485
  statutory, 204
leadership, 83, 94, 115, 122, 126, 174–177, 187, 190, 195, 225, 312, 314, 323, 331, 349, 353, 360, 365, 400, 413, 436, 438, 440, 496–497, 509, 511, 514–515
  army, 211
  communist, 76
  military, 168, 210, 226, 482

leadership (*cont.*)
  party, 8, 44, 398, 474
  police, 392
  political, 179, 470
  positions, 53, 75, 283, 290, 351, 436
  Stalinist, 406, 410
  structure, 10
legality, 182, 268, 394, 510
legislation, 10–14, 27–28, 42, 47–48, 50–51, 53–54, 65–66, 68, 70, 72, 103, 117, 129, 139–140, 148, 163, 174, 178, 180–181, 184, 201, 241, 245, 249, 253–254, 263–265, 271, 288, 295–298, 319, 330, 337, 339, 343, 372–373, 393, 396, 401–403, 408, 429
  amnesty, 365
  emergency, 471
  lustration, 75, 124, 443–444
  nationalization, 127
  reparations, 375
  retroactive, 36, 232
legitimacy, 32, 51, 81–82, 85, 123, 125, 172, 348, 368, 373, 399, 401, 411, 470
  crisis, 473
  democratic, 395
  domestic, 239
  international, 108
  political, 398
  popular, 93, 213, 417
  revolutionary, 393
Lubanga Dyilo, Thomas, 117–118
lustration, 10, 12, 41–43, 76, 154, 161, 164, 169, 234, 238, 288–289, 292, 295–297, 312–313, 335, 384, 402, 442
  certificate, 135
  commission, 289–290
  court, 386, 443
  declarations, 386–387
  demands, 74
  laws, 10, 12–13, 75, 79, 124, 134–135, 189–190, 233, 275–276, 386, 415, 423, 434, 436, 440, 442–444
  process, 13, 205, 338
  program, 167

Marcos, Ferdinand, 380–382
market, 378, 511
  capitalism, 163
  democracy, 7, 61
  economy, 420, 509
  labor, 68
  property, 441
massacres, 2–3, 15–16, 18, 57, 61, 66, 80–81, 106, 111, 121, 144, 150, 158, 202, 209, 218, 224, 249, 252–253, 255, 259, 270, 272, 306, 311, 371–372, 378, 380–381, 388, 424, 439–442, 447, 453, 455–457, 472–473, 475–477, 479–483, 506, 509, 513
  sites, 16
Medgyessy, Peter, 234–235
media, 11, 16–17, 38, 91, 111, 150, 176, 183, 192, 198–199, 230, 258–259, 336, 349, 364–365, 433, 435, 438, 512, 517
  attention, 204, 310, 503
  campaign, 16, 495
  censorship, 340, 392
  circles, 184
  events, 197
  independent, 122, 351
  international, 351, 414, 420
  private, 78, 172
  public, 78, 135, 172, 386
mediation, conflict, 264
memorialization, 24, 42, 47, 60, 65, 84, 87, 99, 192, 214, 231, 235, 256, 261, 384, 386, 390, 442, 476
  initiatives, 102, 104
memory, 18, 21, 26, 43, 47, 85, 91–92, 108, 142, 161–162, 166, 180, 185, 256, 259, 304, 397
  archives, 25
  collective, 390
  historical, 471
  initiatives, 105
  national, 410, 451, 496
  park, 24–25
  popular, 142
  private, 243
  public, 111, 403
  wars, 307
Mengistu, Haile Mariam, 167
Milosevici, Slobodan, 267–269, 294, 297
Milutinovic, Milan, 268
minorities, 44, 332, 479, 484
  ethnic, 44, 61, 125, 166, 262, 346–347, 349, 352, 419, 511
  national, 419
  regional, 193
  religious, 44, 347–349, 352
monuments, 25, 43, 48, 85, 104, 160, 192, 235, 286, 396, 406–407, 409–410, 457, 464, 491, 495
Moreno Ocampo, Luis, 96
movements, social, 70, 394
Mugabe, Robert, 514–520
murders, 16–17, 45, 57, 62, 77, 90–92, 96, 111, 118, 139, 157, 159, 201, 213–214, 220–221, 224, 232, 241, 244, 252, 263, 298–299, 306, 335, 355, 372, 376, 403, 416, 431, 454, 457, 470, 480, 483, 485
  campaign, 486
  mass, 202, 412, 456, 488, 513, 516
  political, 20, 225, 405
  state, 13
museums, 25, 46–48, 88, 104, 138, 142, 167, 188, 192–193, 235, 243, 247, 292, 368, 384, 390, 407, 458, 478, 495

Najibullah, Mohammad, 1–2
Nakasone, Yasuhiro, 259
National Commission on the Disappearance of Persons, 20
nationalism, 144, 187–188, 249, 267, 294, 330, 352, 399, 413, 419–420, 440, 473–476, 478–480, 514
National Truth and Justice Commission, 223

Index

officers, 8, 12, 22–23, 39, 47, 54, 74, 103, 123, 152, 205, 210–211, 240, 252–253, 301, 312, 343, 384, 510, 513
  army, 50, 80, 117, 213, 220, 273, 276, 287, 356, 392, 398, 403, 457, 507
  military, 20, 23, 46, 156, 184, 211, 217, 226, 228, 296, 334–335, 338, 372–373, 383, 500, 507
  police, 20, 23, 63–64, 89, 139, 226, 383, 393, 395, 400, 450, 484, 490, 498, 507
  secret, 76, 78, 127, 194, 234, 335, 372, 386, 400–401, 435, 484, 493
officials, public, 12, 63, 78, 110, 112, 233, 234, 271, 296, 304, 387, 411, 429, 518
Operation Condor, 56, 71, 100, 365, 498
oppression, 13, 29, 321, 323, 326, 442, 447, 449, 451, 496
owners, 42, 48, 75, 78, 86, 127, 133, 163, 176, 202, 206–207, 231, 272, 277–278, 287–288, 308, 327–328, 389, 400, 434–435, 441, 480
ownership, 64, 81, 85, 127, 133, 215, 249, 272, 330, 332, 359, 362, 413, 471, 512

peace, 15, 18, 19, 32, 34, 61, 82, 108–109, 112, 115, 118, 145–146, 224, 256, 337–338, 418, 432
  accords, 62, 155–156, 280, 282, 285, 419
  agreements, 3, 89, 95, 121, 218, 280–282, 285, 307–308, 318, 339, 363, 518
  civil, 14, 185
  negotiations, 118, 217–218, 221, 306
  process, 63, 110, 118, 154, 158, 217–218, 227, 282, 284, 316, 319, 321, 339–340, 345, 362–363, 446
  social, 185
  sustainable, 6
  talks, 114, 281–282
  treaty, 257, 259
peacekeeping, 427
  force, 114, 282, 426–427, 431
pension, 23, 43, 101, 124, 132, 156–157, 185, 196, 206, 231, 239–240, 246, 327, 387, 430, 462, 493, 500, 508
perpetrators, 4, 13–14
persecutions, 34, 38, 50, 54, 72, 74, 94, 118, 133, 163, 181, 243, 247, 301, 322, 326, 348, 480–481, 494, 509
  communist, 199
  Nazi, 39, 207
  political, 58, 67, 69, 75, 207–208, 253–254, 478
  racial, 207–208, 253–254, 476
  religious, 127, 207–208, 346
Pinochet Ugarte, Augusto, 98–99, 101–103, 159
police, 6, 11, 16, 18, 25, 34, 84, 120, 123, 127, 139–140, 145, 151, 153, 157, 181, 185, 201, 249, 265, 268, 270, 276, 285, 315, 317, 339, 347, 364, 368, 372, 381, 447, 453, 506
  judicial, 416, 463
  military, 457
  political, 8, 161, 273, 287–288, 294–295, 297, 300, 391–394, 396, 401, 490, 513, 516
  secret, 8–9, 11, 33, 99, 102, 134–135, 187, 196, 201, 233, 273–274, 287, 294–295, 298, 300, 377, 384–385, 400, 404, 433, 437–438, 440, 442–445, 484, 492–493, 496, 506, 513, 515
  state, 11, 33, 398, 437
policies, 28–29, 32, 88–89, 102, 115, 122, 131, 140–142, 161, 170, 173, 180, 326, 354, 402, 405, 413, 425, 448, 453, 463, 472, 475, 478, 485–486, 510, 515
  assimilation, 27–28, 472
  domestic, 138
  economic, 25, 30, 93, 187, 294, 334, 381, 503–505
  ethnic cleansing, 61
  extermination, 34
  foreign, 130, 158, 249, 291, 353, 363
  internment, 52
  memorialization, 65
  prosecution, 122, 126, 162
  reconciliation, 26, 272, 514
  rehabilitation, 206
  reparations, 85
  repression, 54, 223, 433
  restitution, 163
  self-reliance, 8
  transitional justice, 32, 35, 69, 73, 137, 155, 200, 474–475, 477–478, 485
policy makers, 170, 193, 291
politics, 10–11, 46, 61, 69, 218, 225, 234, 240, 280, 286, 329, 353, 395, 480, 497, 499, 515–517
  communist, 2, 275
  democratic, 120, 500
  memory, 111, 199
  racial, 179
  truth, 497
  vindictiveness, 213
poverty, 1, 9, 28, 106, 155, 157, 215, 224, 256, 322, 375, 429, 432, 451, 487, 497, 505
prisons, 6, 18, 21, 45, 50, 74, 76, 88, 117, 128, 130, 141, 194, 299, 301, 312, 326, 392, 415, 434, 490, 495, 504–505
  camps, 8, 287, 356, 440, 511
  illegal, 20
  military, 102, 474
  secret, 301–302
prisoners, 22, 44, 68, 87, 92, 141, 151, 184–185, 198, 294, 340, 342, 344, 461, 474, 513
  political, 10, 23–24, 52, 69–70, 74, 104, 129, 132–133, 194–195, 249, 288, 291, 301–303, 325–326, 354, 365, 380, 384, 390, 392–393, 396, 398, 401, 405–406, 474, 491–492, 499–502
  war, 34, 202, 244, 255, 299, 327, 405, 472
privacy, 278, 365, 387, 434
  laws, 443, 517
  rights, 196, 234–235, 444
propaganda, 37, 51, 92, 99, 116, 140, 183, 204, 249, 278
property, 22–23, 35, 38, 46–48, 65, 95, 117, 125, 190, 205–207, 480
  confiscation, 74, 80, 127, 132, 134, 161, 162, 169, 180, 185, 231, 253, 365, 398, 402, 404, 434, 460, 475, 481, 486, 491
  destruction, 3, 61, 115, 118, 121, 131, 347, 380, 402, 487

property (*cont.*)
  restitution, 9, 13, 42, 46, 75, 130, 133–134, 137, 162–163, 167, 172, 201, 242, 254, 288, 292, 296, 304, 327, 386, 389, 400, 424, 434, 440–441, 444, 462, 477, 484, 513
  rights, 42, 197, 250, 271, 351, 429, 511–512
  titles, 127
prosecution, 4, 16, 21, 35, 37, 47, 50, 63, 67, 70, 76, 84, 99, 101–102, 110, 116–118, 131, 136, 147–148, 157–158, 203–204, 210, 220–221, 224, 238, 263, 265, 268, 270, 285, 325–326, 355–356, 370, 375–376, 403, 416, 436–437, 452, 460, 462, 470, 500, 517–518
  criminal, 28, 83, 121–122, 126, 169, 198, 201, 226, 232, 365–366, 431–432, 450–451, 454, 457, 479, 493, 501
  domestic, 228–229, 299–307
  international, 414
  judicial, 146
  retroactive, 36
punishment, 2, 21–22, 34, 36–37, 49–51, 53, 68–70, 108, 132, 135, 137, 140, 145, 171, 181–184, 198, 238–239, 250, 256, 284, 301, 344, 348, 364, 369, 391, 393–395, 417, 427, 437–438, 449, 454, 472
purges, 8–11, 46, 48–49, 52, 87, 124, 139–141, 168, 181–182, 187, 194, 201, 250, 253–254, 257, 261, 274, 294, 323–325, 347, 364, 392–394, 406, 410, 440, 462, 473, 490–492, 494, 510
  administrative, 184
  civic, 53–54
  judiciary, 184
  mass, 14
  political, 167
  wild, 394–395

rape, 15, 18, 61–62, 71, 84, 96, 115, 118, 151, 155, 175, 267–268, 280, 306, 310, 317, 319, 348, 359, 379, 414–415, 417, 419, 431, 470, 489, 513
recognition, 16, 22, 70, 72, 88–89, 238, 260, 267, 291–292, 331, 411, 443, 492, 495
  international, 407
  legal, 30, 308
  official, 24, 407
  public, 60, 410
  state, 17, 186
  symbolic, 166, 496
reconciliation, 3, 5, 29–30, 39, 65, 82, 146, 173, 184, 191, 226, 232, 238, 240–241, 259, 272, 307, 315, 332, 403, 449, 499–500, 518–519
  laws, 19
  national, 13, 18, 26, 82, 86–87, 212–213, 311, 313, 428, 502
  process, 28, 30–32, 46, 147, 176, 179, 319
  societal, 82, 236, 310
redress, 58, 79, 81, 133, 211, 213, 231, 258, 311, 321, 404, 434, 443, 445, 451, 485, 508
  judicial, 217, 295
  moral, 72
referendum, 10, 15, 30, 41, 143–144, 147, 182, 187, 228, 267, 288, 359, 361–362, 477, 485, 500, 517

regret, 29, 319
reintegration, 3, 97, 110, 118–119, 122, 191, 204, 253–254, 320, 325–326, 395, 426–427, 430, 499
religion, 7, 86, 182, 287, 336, 339, 398, 434, 459, 510
remedies, 132, 220, 226–227, 272, 305, 333, 366, 442, 501
remorse, 258, 283
reparations, 23–24, 42–43, 58–59, 64–65, 67, 82, 84–85, 91–92, 96, 101–102, 104–105, 108, 111–112, 118–119, 124–125, 140, 152, 154, 159–160, 170, 178, 185–186, 206–208, 213–214, 217–218, 241–242, 253, 257–258, 264, 271, 283, 295, 303–305, 308–310, 314–315, 319, 326–327, 357, 366, 375, 424, 429–430, 450–451, 457–458, 461
repression, 21–22, 40, 55, 58, 72, 99–100, 127, 132, 150, 155, 161–163, 173, 188, 191–192, 194, 201, 216, 237, 262, 294, 301, 322, 352, 364, 368–369, 399, 405, 440, 452, 460, 462, 482, 491–493, 498, 501–504, 515–517
  agencies, 68, 70
  methods, 151
  military, 334, 354
  political, 41–43, 71, 75, 227, 286–287, 291, 365, 391–392, 408
reprisals, 84, 139, 224, 233, 235, 237, 252, 293, 340, 387, 409, 441, 447
reproduction, elite, 313
responsibility, 15, 82, 98, 107, 111, 119, 122, 148, 159, 180, 185, 204–205, 217, 220, 241, 251, 259–261, 265, 269, 299, 307, 315, 327, 340, 388, 421, 424, 451, 455, 468, 470, 476–477, 481, 488
  communitarian, 309
  collective, 469, 499
  criminal, 60, 70, 84, 125, 462
  individual, 60, 125, 256, 296, 304, 389
  institutional, 104, 146
  legal, 258
  moral, 258
  social, 508
  state, 14, 17, 20, 70–72, 107, 153, 303–304, 457, 461, 506
restitution, 30, 65, 70–71, 112, 199, 206–207, 450, 461
  property, 9, 13, 42, 46–47, 64, 75, 130, 133–134, 163, 172, 197, 245–246, 253–254, 271, 277, 288, 295, 304, 327, 332, 384, 389, 400, 434, 441, 513
restoration, 47, 145–146, 181, 288, 292, 318, 334, 362, 392, 395, 408, 457–458, 470
retaliation, 80, 148, 378, 465, 467, 510
revenge, 13, 52, 122, 171, 181, 213, 244–245, 325, 329, 352, 407, 481
rights, 2, 27–28, 30, 38, 46, 68, 71, 83, 123, 125, 128, 196, 209, 234–235, 249, 267–268, 291, 295, 302, 308, 323, 332–333, 340, 360–361, 416, 424, 513, 515
  civil, 21, 36, 44, 51, 53, 56, 171, 183–184, 248, 250, 262, 348–349, 453
  minority, 63, 420, 484
  political, 21, 51, 53, 56, 68–69, 99, 101, 171, 183, 248, 250, 262, 267, 453, 472–473
  property, 42, 133, 197, 250, 271, 351, 511–512

self-determination, 31
   to appeal, 10, 183, 334
   to defense, 68
   to dignity, 37
   to files, 11–12
   to information, 42, 235, 365
   to justice, 41, 73, 108
   to life, 190, 304, 344
   to petition, 58
   to reparations, 108
   to return, 65
   to truth, 41, 67, 108, 216
   to vote, 40, 281, 515
Roman Catholic Church, 57–58, 102, 128, 155, 216–217, 219, 222, 249, 288, 377, 381, 385, 441
rule of law, 12, 68, 70, 83, 101, 113, 123, 136, 168, 179, 191, 198, 232–235, 321, 324, 326, 329, 334, 349, 389, 394–395, 420, 431, 441–442, 444, 470–471, 480, 485
rules of procedure, 421

screenings, 11, 41, 89, 233–235, 296, 434, 436, 455, 477
   political, 8
   psychological, 8
secrecy, 87, 298, 438
Shoah, 202, 243–244, 246–247
slavery, 222, 255, 258–259, 427
society, civil, 4–5, 9, 23, 59–61, 65–66, 68, 74, 81–84, 104–105, 122, 124–125, 160, 178, 201, 212, 215–216, 218, 263, 283, 285, 292, 307, 313–314, 333, 336, 346, 361, 368, 385, 393, 420, 424, 427, 430–431, 454, 483, 485, 510, 512, 515, 517–518
soldiers, child, 92, 115, 427, 431, 487–488
sovereignty, 27, 30, 32, 103, 207, 232, 317, 330, 362, 378, 486
Special Court for Sierra Leone, 265, 282, 284, 427
Stalinism, 8, 188, 390, 406–407, 409–410, 492, 495
sterilization, 34, 202, 207
Stroessner, Alfredo, 364–367, 369–370
subpoena, 298, 304, 421
suffering, 7, 64, 66, 88, 90, 146, 158, 162, 202, 205, 207, 256–259, 261, 292, 308, 310, 356, 424, 446, 452, 475, 491, 501
surveillance, 187, 194, 230, 287, 294, 368, 385, 438, 453, 457, 472
   mass, 40–41, 274
survivors, 15, 80, 82, 85, 92, 99, 102, 104, 111, 116, 159, 180–181, 206, 218–219, 243–246, 301, 303, 305, 307–310, 314, 327, 343, 345, 407–409, 417, 467, 481–482, 493

Taylor, Charles, 280–282, 284–285, 431–432
tenants, 42, 127, 133–134, 163, 378–400, 511
terror, 21, 41, 87, 99, 109, 151, 155, 161–162, 167–168, 187, 219, 223, 230, 237, 268, 273, 277, 287, 312, 351, 374, 405–407, 410, 433, 465, 468, 474–478, 490, 492–494, 496
   Nazi, 37–38, 323
   war on, 1, 3

terrorism, 17–18, 22, 24, 129, 142, 221, 241, 299, 371–372, 382, 462
terrorists, 15–17, 180, 216, 241, 340, 345, 351, 372–373, 375, 469
testimonials, 15–16, 96, 104, 129, 147, 152, 156, 159, 170, 172, 213, 218–219, 221, 227–228, 263, 284–285, 291, 302, 305, 313, 318, 348, 369, 373, 417, 428, 461, 468, 470
textbooks, 25, 39, 42, 92, 137, 191–192, 235, 259–260, 278, 384, 390, 403, 406, 410–411, 455, 458, 464, 476, 513
The Hague, 60, 96, 122–123, 258, 284–285, 326, 420–422, 432
torture, 2, 6, 16–17, 21–22, 56, 58, 61–62, 68–71, 80, 91, 99–100, 102, 105, 118, 121, 127, 142, 148, 151–153, 159, 168, 180, 210–211, 215, 220–221, 223–226, 237–238, 251, 262, 280, 284, 299–301, 306, 310, 317, 319, 355, 365–368, 380, 414–415, 466, 472, 474, 486, 504, 508, 513, 517
torturers, 69, 132, 252, 306, 382, 503
trauma, 80, 145, 172, 243, 359, 468, 487
trials, 4, 6, 17, 22, 25, 35–37, 41, 47, 50–54, 57, 62–63, 76–77, 84, 88, 90–91, 96, 103–104, 110, 116–118, 122–123, 157, 170–172, 178, 198, 203, 228–229, 238–239, 246–247, 250–254, 256–257, 268, 277, 284–285, 290–291, 298–300, 335, 355–356, 375–376, 382, 387–388, 403, 408, 422–423, 429–432, 437, 474, 485, 506–507, 513
   criminal, 59–60, 198, 204, 215, 269, 448–450
   kangaroo, 127
   political, 12
   show, 194, 203, 230, 236, 294, 385, 398, 403, 405, 433
   summary, 250
   truth, 23
trust, 4, 130, 321, 324, 480
   building, 3
truth, 13–14, 41, 59, 81, 99, 102, 214, 373
   historical, 82, 111, 161, 288, 292
   judicial, 111
   official, 105, 155
   recovery, 63, 65–67, 343, 500
   revelation, 82, 134, 146, 185, 295, 298, 365, 369, 434, 438, 467
   seeking, 5, 46, 84–85, 116, 125, 141, 268, 272, 304, 337, 377, 425, 485
   telling, 60, 121, 125, 156, 160, 172, 199, 226–227, 266, 305, 309–310, 313, 336–338, 449, 492
tyranny, 211, 223

vengeance, 52, 146, 196, 210, 213, 219, 351, 383, 435
vetting, 4–6, 41, 47, 62–64, 84, 110, 118–119, 124–125, 183, 195–197, 199, 231, 233, 235, 241, 257, 275–276, 279, 285, 296, 393, 401, 415
victimizers, 191, 279
violence, 15–17, 19, 44, 79–82, 99, 116, 120, 140, 146, 155, 216–217, 241, 267–268, 270, 301, 307, 317, 338, 340, 358, 380, 405, 413–414, 449, 467, 487, 504–505, 507, 517–518
   mass, 113

violence (*cont.*)
    political, 20–21, 55, 58, 74, 101–102, 155, 168, 263, 340, 446, 465, 467–468, 470–471
    sexual, 64, 80, 83–85, 111, 115, 258–259, 365, 417, 427–428, 430, 432
    state, 16, 21–22, 25, 213, 304, 334, 458–459, 470
    symbolic, 50, 52

Wiedergutmachung, 245, 247
women, 2, 16, 34, 40, 45, 50, 52, 61, 68, 80, 83–84, 106–107, 111, 130, 161, 164, 171, 211, 243, 258–260, 265, 270, 325, 345–352, 359, 365, 399, 427, 452, 509–510, 516
    comfort, 472, 475
wrongdoer, 10, 397

For EU product safety concerns, contact us at Calle de José Abascal, 56–1°,
28003 Madrid, Spain or eugpsr@cambridge.org.

www.ingramcontent.com/pod-product-compliance
Ingram Content Group UK Ltd.
Pitfield, Milton Keynes, MK11 3LW, UK
UKHW051652180426
11946UKWH00005B/122